|exploring|

Adobe InDesign CS6

|exploring|

Adobe InDesign CS6

Terry Rydberg

Australia • Brazil • Japan • Korea • Mexico • Singapore • Spain • United Kingdom • United States

Exploring Adobe InDesign CS6
Terry Rydberg

Vice President, Career & Computing: Dave Garza
Director of Learning Solutions: Sandy Clark
Senior Acquisitions Editor: Jim Gish
Managing Editor: Larry Main
Product Manager: Meaghan Tomaso
Editorial Assistant: Sarah Timm
Vice President, Marketing: Jennifer Baker
Marketing Director: Deborah Yarnell
Associate Marketing Manager: Erin DeAngelo
Senior Production Director: Wendy Troeger
Production Manager: Andrew Crouth
Senior Content Project Manager: Glenn Castle
Senior Art Director: Jack Pendleton
Technology Project Manager: Jim Gilbert
Media Editor: Debbie Bordeaux

Cover: © Biwa Studio/Getty Images

Library of Congress Control Number: 2012930443

ISBN-13: 978-1-1336-9328-4

ISBN-10: 1-1336-9328-8

Delmar
5 Maxwell Drive,
Clifton Park, NY 12065-2919
USA

Cengage Learning is a leading provider of customized learning solutions with office locations around the globe, including Singapore, the United Kingdom, Australia, Mexico, Brazil, and Japan. Locate your local office at: **international.cengage.com/region**

Cengage Learning products are represented in Canada by Nelson Education, Ltd.

To learn more about Delmar, visit **www.cengage.com/delmar**
Purchase any of our products at your local college store or at our preferred online store **www.cengagebrain.com**

Printed in Canada
1 2 3 4 5 6 7 16 15 14 13 12

contents

contents

CONTENTS

contents

preface

INTENDED AUDIENCE

This book is intended for designers who are serious about their craft. It is ideal for students who desire an approach to instruction that focuses on software proficiency. It is an excellent choice for instructors and industry trainers who have been looking for a comprehensive textbook that includes handouts, projects, syllabi, and resources. What differentiates *Exploring Adobe InDesign CS6* from a reference book, is that it focuses on those InDesign features that are used 90% of the time. This concentrated approach, and mastery of design and production techniques presented in the text, leave the designer well prepared for using InDesign effectively in production settings.

Typesetting is an art, and typography is emphasized throughout *Exploring Adobe InDesign CS6*. The power of Adobe InDesign, when combined with the knowledge of typography, will give designers the ability to create documents with visual impact.

HOW TO USE THIS BOOK

Before beginning this book, readers should already know computer basics such as launching programs, using a mouse, saving files, and printing.

Exploring Adobe InDesign CS6's in-chapter exercises are supplemented with an array of projects at the end of the each chapter available for download at *www.cengagebrain.com*. These supplemental projects will require a higher degree of independent problem solving and application. Access to a computer with *Exploring Adobe InDesign CS6* will be essential for completing the practice exercises.

Chapters should be read in order, from the beginning to the end. The skills presented in earlier chapters create the foundation necessary for completing exercises in the later chapters. Techniques are first introduced, and then applied in the context of industry-level projects. This project-based approach uses critical thinking, review, and practice to help designers achieve mastery.

textbook overview

The textbook is organized so that techniques and skills are added layer upon layer.

CHAPTER 1: *The InDesign Workspace* Introduces the basic tools and functions of the program. If you are already familiar with Photoshop and Illustrator, this chapter will be a great review.

CHAPTER 2: *Type, Tools, and Terms* Establishes a knowledge base essential for setting type. You will use the Character and Paragraph formatting options in the Control panel, modify attributes of type and text frames, and learn to distinguish between serif and sans serif typefaces.

CHAPTER 3: *The Fine Art of Setting Type* Teaches how to identify the anatomical parts of letters, read markup, format paragraphs, and use hyphens and dashes correctly.

CHAPTER 4: *Combining Type and Images* Shows how to create linked and multi-column text frames. You'll place, scale and crop images, use optical and manual kerning, and work with the coordinate and measurement systems for precise sizing and placement.

CHAPTER 5: *Tabs and Tables* You will learn to set tabular copy, create tables from "scratch" and from prepared text files, and then add table headers and footers.

CHAPTER 6: *Grids, Guides, and Aligning Objects* Increases your productivity by creating publication grids, aligning and distributing objects, and managing stacked objects.

CHAPTER 7: *Text Wrap, Layers, and Effects* Brings order to your documents through the power of layers and text wrap. Feathering, transparency, and live corner effects are also introduced.

CHAPTER 8: *Type Continuity: Applying Styles* Focuses on speed and efficiency in preparing text-heavy documents. You will learn how to use the Pages panel and Snippets, and to create character and paragraph styles in the construction of an actual newsletter.

CHAPTER 9: *Master Pages and Object Styles* Introduces object styles and covers page continuity through the use of master pages. You will learn how to setup automatic page numbering and create continuation and jump lines. You'll create an object library and also use the Pages panel to add and delete pages.

CHAPTER 10: *Identity Systems* Shows you how to create an identity package for a new business. You will focus on design, typographic, and production considerations, as you put together marketing materials.

CHAPTER 11: *Designing With Type* Introduces special type techniques, including: text on a path, creating outlines and gradient blends, using the Pathfinder tool, and using the Page tool for multi-page size documents.

CHAPTER 12: *Color Essentials* Differentiates between additive and subtractive color, spot and process color printing. Introduces all the features of the Swatches panel. Explains color separations and printing options. Introduces mixed inks and mixed ink groups.

CHAPTER 13: *Production Essentials* Explains these important production concepts: resolution, dpi, ppi, bitmap, and vector artwork. You will use the powerful Links panel, enhanced in InDesign CS6. You will learn the difference between actual and effective ppi and how to prepare your images for the correct resolution and size. Finally, prepress expert, James Wamser summarizes his best prepress tips.

CHAPTER 14: *Basic Graphic Elements* Explores InDesign's drawing functions. You will learn how to create basic shapes, use the Pen tool, and integrate drawn elements with text. This is a great introduction to Adobe Illustrator,® another member of Adobe Creative Suite 6.

features

The following are some of the salient features of *Exploring Adobe InDesign CS6*:

- *Covers Mac and Windows versions of the software.*
- *Learning goals are clearly stated at the beginning of each chapter.*
- *A visually-oriented introduction to basic design principles and the functions and tools of **Adobe InDesign CS6**, that meets the needs of both students and professionals.*
- *Exercises and projects utilize tools and techniques that a designer might encounter on the job.*
- ***In Review** sections are provided at the end of each chapter to reinforce understanding and retention of the material covered.*
- *Learning resources downloadable from **www.Cengagebrain.com** contain directions and all the necessary components for completing additional projects that correspond to each chapter's learning goals.*

EXPLORING INDESIGN CS6
Artwork & Resources

- Go to: http://www.cengagebrain.com
- Type: Rydberg
- Click Exploring InDesign CS6 in the list of search results.
- When the book's main page is displayed, click the Access button under Free Study Tools.
- To download files, select a chapter number and then click on the Artwork & Resources tab on the left navigation bar to download the files.

NEW! *in Exploring Adobe InDesign CS6*

- *Expanded chapter content describes new features in InDesign CS6.*
- *New projects have been designed to utilize the new software features.*
- *Designer profiles and best practices in **Moving Toward Mastery** sections.*
- *The **Getting Started** section at the beginning of Chapter 1, discusses software installation and best production practices.*
- *A complete list of the fonts included with **Adobe InDesign CS6.***
- *Exploring Adobe InDesign CS6 includes a **CourseMate**, which helps you make the grade!*

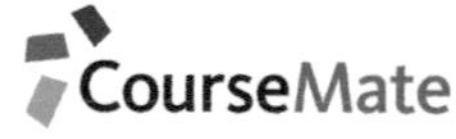

*This **CourseMate** includes:*

- *An interactive eBook, with highlighting, note taking and search capabilities.*
- *Interactive learning tools including chapter quizzes and flashcards.*
- *Instructional video lessons from **Total Training**, the leading provider of video instruction for Adobe software. These video lessons are tightly integrated with the book, chapter by chapter and include assessment.*
- *And more! Go to **login.cengagebrain.com** to access these resources.*

instructor resources

The Instructor Resources section, found on *Cengagebrain.com*, was developed to assist educators in planning and implementing their instructional programs. It includes detailed lesson plans for each chapter. The lesson plan summarizes the concepts, keyboard shortcuts, and project demonstrations covered in the classroom. Lesson plans are designed to be printed and saved in a three-ring binder. Also included, are finished InDesign documents for each project, that serve as instructor keys, a sample syllabus, a midterm, and a final written and lab exam. The complete Instructor Resources enhances consistency in instruction, among faculty members with diverse backgrounds and skill levels.

To access these resources go to: **http://login.cengage.com**. Once you login or create an account, search for the title under '**My Dashboard**' using the ISBN: **9781133693284**. Then select the instructor companion site resources and click '**Add to my Bookshelf**.'

how to use this text

The following features can be found throughout the book.

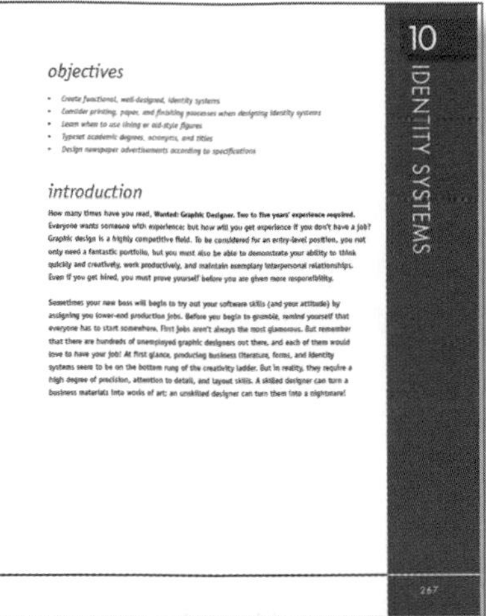
10
IDENTITY SYSTEMS
objectives
introduction

► CHAPTER OBJECTIVES

Chapter objectives describe the competencies that the reader should achieve.

DESSERTS MENU

► CHAPTER REVIEW AND PROJECTS

Review questions and supplemental projects assess learning and provide skills application.

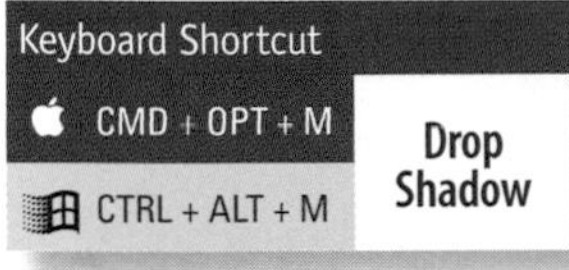
Keyboard Shortcut
CMD + OPT + M
CTRL + ALT + M
Drop Shadow

► KEYBOARD SHORTCUT CUES

Keyboard shortcuts are prominently displayed for ease of use.

► MOVING TOWARD MASTERY

type basics

WHAT IS A "FONT"?

*In the early days of printing, type was set by hand, letter by letter. A printer needed an actual piece of metal type for each letter and symbol in every size of any given typeface. The collection of all the characters, numbers, symbols and punctuation of a particular typeface in a specific point size was called a font. Our modern typefaces are not metal but digital, and you don't purchase a new font for each point size you plan to use. Today, the terms **font** and **typeface** are often used interchangeably, as in the case of this textbook.*

SERIF AND SANS SERIF FACES

***Serifs** are tiny finishing strokes on the end of the letter. Typefaces are classified as either **serif** (with serifs) or **sans serif** (without serifs).*

► GETTING STARTED

Located at the beginning of Chapter 1, this section provides the steps for customizing the application defaults that will be used throughout the book.

► DESIGN AND TYPOGRAPHY

Principles of design and typography are presented with corresponding chapter content. These basics will help the reader use type in a manner that is technically correct.

► MOVING TOWARD MASTERY
Use the chart below to identify each of the hidden characters in the text block shown underneath the portfolio.
Hard return ¶
Soft return
Spacebar
Tab »
End of story #
Your Portfolio
Don't underestimate the power of your portfolio. It must convince future employers that you can:
communicate visually
work within project specifications
understand and apply typographic principles
understand a design objective and articulate your creative rationale
create campaigns according to strategic marketing plans
Without a portfolio, you have no evidence to support the claims that are made in an interview!

► MOVING TOWARD MASTERY

Key concepts are grouped together for easy reference and review.

about the author

Terry Rydberg is a graphic design instructor at Waukesha County Technical College in Pewaukee, Wisconsin. In addition to twenty years in the classroom, she has extensive experience working as a designer and corporate trainer. *Exploring Adobe InDesign CS6* is her sixth book published with Delmar, Cengage Learning.

Her educational background includes undergraduate degrees in graphic design, printing and publishing, and adult education; and a masters degree in education. Her career parallels the industry's evolution from phototypesetting and paste-up, to digital production methods. Rydberg teaches advertising design, graphic design, typography, portfolio development, digital page layout, advanced digital page layout, and color theory. She is a regional InDesign trainer at colleges and conferences.

A committed educator, Rydberg has served as school board chair, graphics advisory board member, new instructor mentor, curriculum writer, and student advisor. In 2007, she received a *NISOD Excellence Award* from the National Institute for Staff & Organizational Development. She has also served as Chapter Rep for the Milwaukee InDesign User Group.

When she's not teaching, Terry and her husband, Mark, spend time at their farm in Minnesota where they raise chickens and enjoy their grandchildren.

acknowledgments

Others whose contributions to this book should be acknowledged are James Gish, Senior Acquisitions Editor; Meaghan Tomaso, Product Manager; Glenn Castle, Senior Content Project Manager; and Sarah L. Timm, Editorial Assistant. Their expertise, combined with Cengage's great marketing team, made this sixth edition a reality.

Deepest thanks to my colleagues and students who have shared a vision for this book:

- **John Shanley**, from Phoenix Creative Graphics, who patiently transformed awkward copy into elegant text, and made the directions clear and concise
- **David Espurvoa III** who provided whimsical illustrations
- Prepress expert **James Wamser** who generously shared his expertise
- **Jim Moran** and **Stephanie Carpenter** from the Hamilton Wood Type & Printing Museum, who allowed me to introduce readers to this phenomenal place
- Lettering artist, **Ian Brignell**, who is keeping alive the art of lettering, and **Catherine A. O'Toole**, Marketing Director, Brignell Lettering Design
- Finally, my gratitude to designers **Mélanie Lévesque, Andrea Peaslee, Erik P. Berg**; photographer **Billy Knight**; illustrators **Steve Miljat** and **Jeff Blackwell**; and the many other generous students who allowed their artwork and photography to be included in this book.

Many thanks to the instructors who are using this publication at the Harry V. Quadracci Printing and Graphics Center and at various colleges throughout the United States. Your suggestions and comments have been so helpful, and have been incorporated in *Exploring Adobe InDesign CS6*. Please let me know how the textbook is working in your class, and keep sending me great ideas!

With gratitude to my best friend, Shirley Tollefson.
You're a continual source of strength and encouragement!

questions and feedback

We welcome your questions and feedback. If you have suggestions that would be of benefit to others, please let us know and we will try to include them in the next edition.

To send your questions and/or feedback, contact the publisher at:

Delmar Learning
5 Maxwell Drive
Clifton Park, NY 12065-2919
Attn: Media Arts and Design Team
800-998-7498

Or the author at:

Harry V. Quadracci Printing and Graphics Center
Waukesha County Technical College
800 Main Street
Pewaukee, Wisconsin 53072
trydberg@mac.com

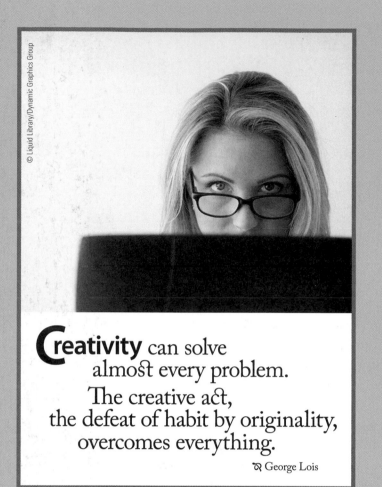

1

The InDesign Workspace

Creativity can solve
almost every problem.
The creative act,
the defeat of habit by originality,
overcomes everything.

℞ George Lois

objectives

- *Become familiar with the Adobe InDesign CS6 environment*
- *Understand how to use this textbook*
- *Use the Preferences options and settings*
- *Identify and use basic panels and tools*
- *Learn to use keyboard shortcuts*
- *Learn the concepts of frames, stroke, and fill*
- *Customize your workspace*
- *Save and print documents*

introduction

You are about to explore new horizons in digital page layout. This book will introduce you to Adobe® InDesign® CS6, today's standard in page layout software. For those of you who are already familiar with a page layout program, you will be delighted and impressed with InDesign's extraordinary capabilities and innovation.

After teaching and working with other major page layout programs for decades, I must admit I was a bit skeptical when I began working with InDesign. But in just a few weeks I was convinced that Adobe InDesign is the most creative, comprehensive, and intuitive page layout program on the market today. By the time you finish this book, I know you will agree. No other program in the graphics industry can compete with the astounding new features of InDesign.

Are you ready to begin mastering InDesign? We're going to begin with a *Getting Started* section found on the next four pages. This section will introduce you to best practices in production and provide tips for maximizing the features of your software. It will also help you understand how to best use this text. If you already have a basic knowledge of InDesign or are the type of person who never reads the directions, you may be tempted to skip this section. But understanding and following the instructions in this section are like checking your oil, tire pressure, and filling you car with gas before starting a road trip. And, what a trip this will be! If you hit a pot hole or run into a road block along the way, feel free to email me and I'll try to provide some roadside assistance (trydberg@mac.com). InDesign is a fantastic piece of software—and with practice and determination, you'll be cruisin' in no time at all!

getting started

▸ INSTALLING AND UNINSTALLING INDESIGN

Before you begin this book, you should be familiar with a computer keyboard and have a basic understanding of how to operate a mouse. You should know how to launch applications, make choices from menus, click with a mouse to select objects, and drag to highlight text. And you should already know how to load software.

When you install InDesign, make sure to write down or photocopy the activation code or serial number that came with your software and place it in safe keeping. This only takes a minute—and is much easier (and less frustrating) than trying to retrieve the information after it's lost.

*A single-user retail license activation supports two computers. For example, you can install the product on a desktop computer at work and on a laptop computer at home. If you want to install the software on a third computer, first deactivate InDesign on one of the other two computers. Choose **Help>Deactivate**.*

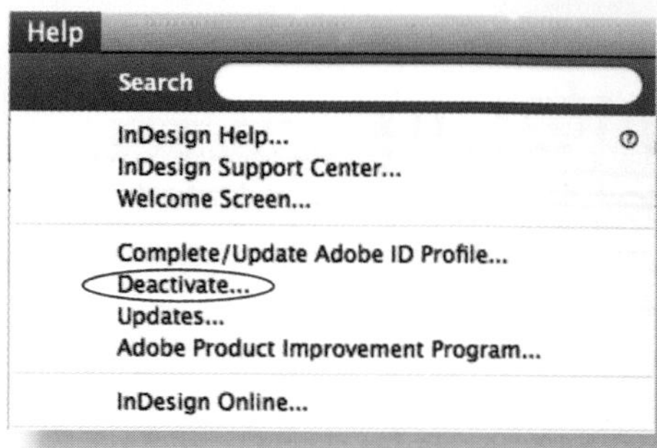

▸ FONTS

*The installation discs contain a variety of resources to help you make the most of your Adobe software. The **Goodies** folder contains bonus fonts that you will probably want to install. The complete list of typefaces bundled with InDesign can be found in the back of this book, just before the index.*

▸ ARTWORK AND RESOURCES

*As you work through this text, you will notice that there are exercises included in the narrative of the text, and more projects presented at the end of chapters. Completing these projects will move you toward mastery. To work on these projects, you will need to access text and images files from the **online companion resources**. You can access the online companion resources by following the directions in the box to the right. (These instructions are also repeated at the end of every chapter.) You will download a Zip file which corresponds to each chapter. This file expands to create folders containing the text and image files needed to complete all the tutorials. You'll also find a .pdf document with instructions for completing the end-of-chapter projects.*

EXPLORING INDESIGN CS6
Artwork & Resources

- Go to: http://www.cengagebrain.com
- Type: Rydberg
- Click Exploring InDesign CS6 in the list of search results.
- When the book's main page is displayed, click the Access button under Free Study Tools.
- To download files, select a chapter number and then click on the Artwork & Resources tab on the left navigation bar to download the files.

▸ MODIFY THE APPLICATION PREFERENCES

InDesign comes with a built-in set of defaults, called "preferences." Modifying some of these defaults will make your production much smoother. When you change defaults with InDesign launched, but with no document open, you are changing the ***application preferences.*** *Once they are changed, the changes will apply to all future documents.*

When you change preferences with a document open, the changes apply to the current document only. This is called changing the ***document preferences.***

▸ CHANGE THE APPLICATION PREFERENCES TO MATCH THOSE USED IN THIS TEXT.

1. Launch InDesign, but do not create a new document. You should see the *Menu*, the *Control* panel, and the *Toolbox*.

2. Press **Command+K** (Mac) or **Control+K** (Windows) to open the *Preferences* dialog.

3. Along the left side of the *Preferences* window, you will see a list of categories. Select each category and make the following changes:
   - *Type:* select **Apply Leading to Entire Paragraphs**
   - *Units & Increments>Ruler Units: Origin:* **Page,** *Horizontal:* **Inches,** *Vertical:* **Inches**
   - *Units & Increments>Keyboard Increments: Size/Leading:* **1 pt** *Baseline Shift:* **1 pt**

4. Accept changes and exit the dialog box.

5. Go to *File>Document Setup.* Deselect **Facing Pages.** Make sure the *Page Size* is set to **Letter.** Press **Return** (Mac) or **Enter** (Windows).

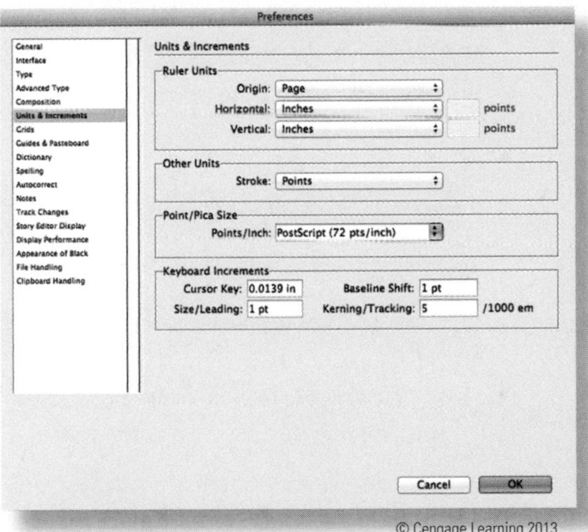

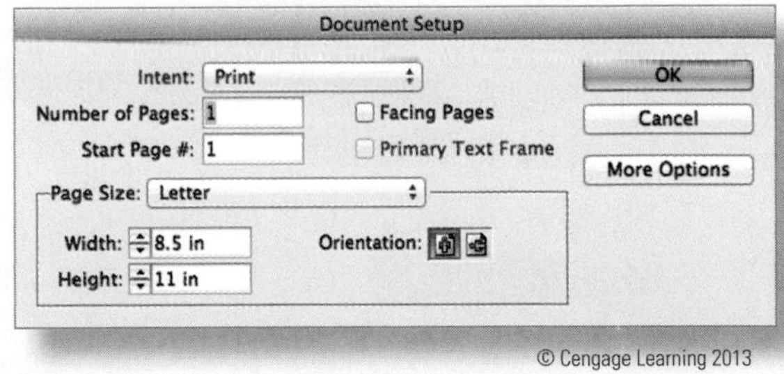

▸ BEST PRACTICES

1. ***Use keyboard shortcuts.*** *Throughout the book, you will be encouraged to use keyboard shortcuts whenever possible. Activating a keyboard shortcut, instead of selecting menus or opening panels, is a more efficient method of working. Keyboard shortcuts usually consist of a combination of modifier keys and letters or symbols. For Mac users, the modifier keys include* ***Shift, Control, Option****, and* ***Command****. Windows users use* ***Shift, Control*** *and* ***Alt****. Both platforms utilize function keys* ***F1–F12*** *found above the numbers on the keyboard. When a keyboard shortcut is listed as* ***Command+S****, this means: "Hold the Command key, press the S key, and release."* ***F5*** *means: "Press function key 5, and release." (When you're working on a laptop, you need to press the* ***fn*** *key with the number* ***5****) Throughout the text, important keyboard shortcuts will be displayed in color for easy reference. Try to memorize these shortcuts and use keyboard shortcuts whenever possible. Over the course of your professional career, the time you save using shortcuts will be significant.*

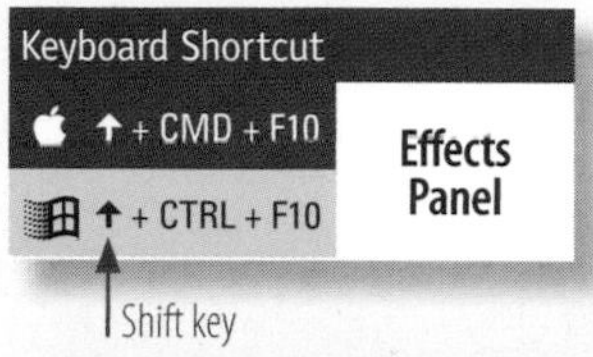

2. ***Open documents from a local hard drive.*** *When you store a document on a portable drive or a server, it is important to move the document to your local hard drive before opening it. Opening documents from storage media can cause damage.*
3. ***Do a Save As when your project is completed.*** *Each time you* ***Save*** *a document, InDesign adds more data to the document, but doesn't remove outdated data. When you choose* ***Save As****, InDesign completely rewrites the document, using only current information. This keeps your file size smaller and decreases the time required for printing or redrawing the image on the screen.*
4. ***Use the least number of text frames possible.*** *This keeps your document smaller and easier to maintain.*
5. ***Use context menus.*** *These are activated by holding the* ***Control*** *key and clicking (Mac), or clicking the right mouse button (Windows) when you have an object selected. This is a quick method of choosing commonly used commands.*
6. ***Use shortcut keys in dialog boxes.*** *Press* ***Return*** *(Mac) or* ***Enter*** *(Windows) instead of choosing OK. Press* ***Command+period*** *(Mac) or* ***Esc*** *(Mac and Windows) to exit a dialog box. In some dialog boxes, holding* ***Option*** *(Mac) or* ***Alt*** *(Windows) changes the Cancel button to a Reset button, allowing you to make changes without exiting the dialog box.*
7. ***Never remove the .indd file extension from any of your files.***
8. ***Use quality fonts.*** *InDesign works best with OpenType, Type 1 (PostScript), and TrueType fonts. Corrupt fonts can damage your document and crash your computer!*
9. ***Create folders to organize your projects.*** *Keep images used in the document organized inside the folder. Use the Package operation (introduced in Chapter 13).*

▸ DOCUMENT RECOVERY

InDesign has a built-in document recovery system that protects your files against unexpected power failures or computer crashes. Automatic recovery data exists in a temporary file that is separate from your InDesign document.

If you crash, here are the steps to recover your file.

- *Start your computer.*
- *Launch InDesign.*
- *InDesign will display any recovered documents. An asterisk will appear in front of the file name in the title bar of the document.*
- *Choose **File>Save As** and specify a new location and name for the file.*
- *If you had saved the document before crashing, and the recovered document is an older version that you don't want to keep, close the file without saving it.*
- *If InDesign can't open your document, it means it was permanently damaged during the crash.*

*This feature is designed for emergencies only. You should still save your documents often, and **make backups!***

▸ THIS IS A TEXTBOOK—PLEASE, DON'T SKIP THE PROJECTS!

This is a textbook, not an InDesign reference book. In addition to software techniques, you will learn design and typography concepts. You should work through the book in sequence. The skills presented in each chapter become the foundation for moving to the next level. As the projects get harder, the instructions become less detailed, forcing you to dig into your memory bank to apply the skills you learned in earlier chapters. The projects at the end of the chapter require you to apply newly-learned skills, while reviewing and reinforcing earlier techniques. I can guarantee that, if you systematically work through all the chapters and projects, you will gain mastery of the InDesign functions you will use 95% of the time.

Learning new software is like learning to play a musical instrument—you need to practice, practice, practice. The best way to learn software is to use it every day.

Finally, you should have fun learning InDesign! InDesign has brought much joy into my life. You might think it strange for a person to attribute such power to a piece of software. But by the time you finish this book, I think you'll understand what I mean!

the InDesign workspace

The InDesign workspace consists of the following items:

- *Document window*
- *Menu bar*
- *Application Frame and Application Bar*
- *Control panel*
- *Toolbox*
- *Panels*

VISUAL | 1–1 |

Look for this icon to launch Adobe® InDesign® CS6.

Launch InDesign by clicking the icon on the dock shown in Visual 1–1, or by double-clicking the icon in the *Applications* folder (Mac), or by selecting Adobe InDesign CS6 from the *Start* menu (Windows). When the program launches, you will be welcomed to InDesign by a screen that contains a host of options, including an overview of new features in InDesign CS6, tutorials, and learning resources (Visual 1–2). You can create new documents and open recent documents from this screen. You may want to place a check in the box in the lower left corner so that this screen will not appear when launching the program, but do this only after you have gone through the tutorial and overview opportunities.

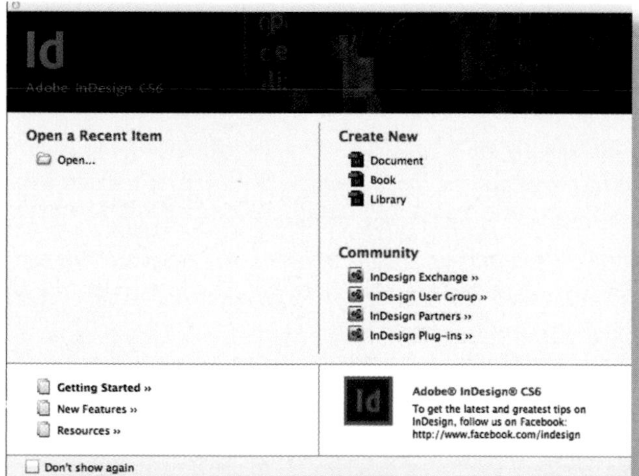

VISUAL | 1–2 |

This screen welcomes you to Adobe InDesign CS6.

▸ *Basic InDesign navigation*

We'll get started immediately by creating a sample document to introduce us to the document window and navigating through InDesign dialog boxes.

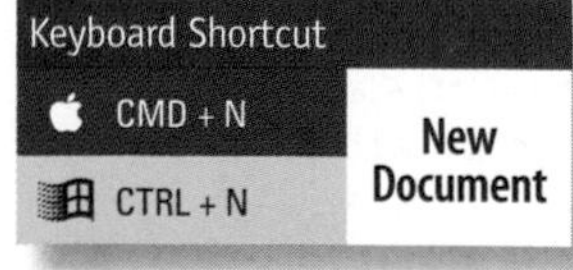

1. Press **Command+N** (Mac) or **Control+N** (Windows) to create a new document.
2. Press the *Tab* key to jump to the next field in the *New Document* dialog box (or any dialog box in InDesign). Press **Shift+Tab** to move backwards through the fields. Practice moving through each field in the *New Document* dialog box using these methods.

Pressing the *Tab* key is an excellent method of selecting any field. Another excellent method to select the field is by clicking on the name to the left of the field (Visual 1–3). Once you grow accustomed to selecting fields by clicking on the name to the left of the field, you'll wish all the software you use had that feature! (The most inefficient method of selecting a field is to place the cursor in the field and double-click or drag to highlight the area.) Once the content in a field is highlighted, type your new information over the old information. Don't re-select a field that is already highlighted!

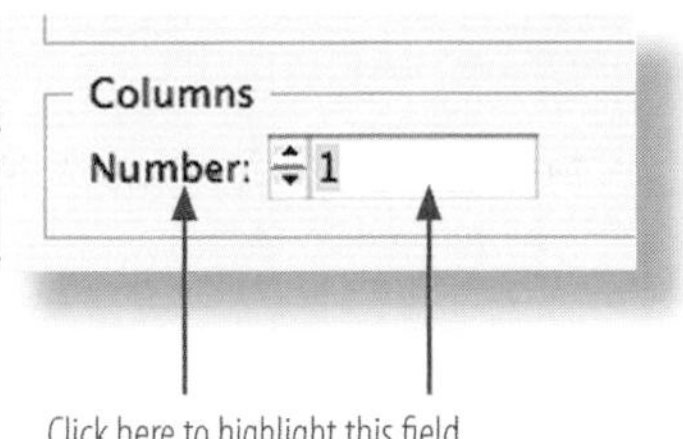

VISUAL | 1–3 |

Select a field by clicking on the name to the left of the field.

© Cengage Learning 2013

▸ *production tip*

Highlight a field by clicking on the icon to the left of the field. When a field is highlighted, enter your specifications—don't click and drag to rehighlight it.

3. Enter these values in the ***New Document*** dialog box: ***Intent:*** **Print**. ***Number of Pages:*** **1**. ***Page Size:*** **Letter** (8.5"× 11"). Be sure that the ***Facing Pages*** and ***Primary Text Frame*** options are not selected. ***Columns:*** **3**. ***Margins:*** **0.75"**. ***Orientation:*** **Portrait** (first icon). ***Portrait*** orientation means that the height of your document is greater than the width. ***Landscape*** orientation means that your document is wider than it is high (Visual 1–5).

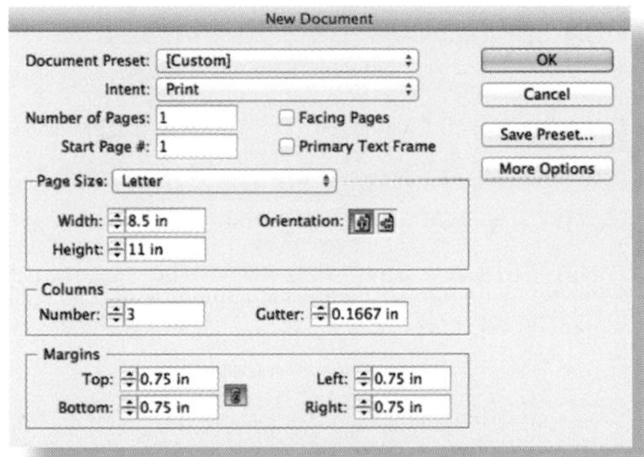

VISUAL | 1–4 |

The New Document dialog box.

© Cengage Learning 2013

VISUAL | 1–5 |

Portrait orientation means the height of your document is greater than the width.

© Liquid Library/Dynamic Graphics Group

In the middle of the *Margins* section is a link icon. This button appears on numerous InDesign panels. When the link is closed, the value you enter in one field is automatically transferred to the rest of the fields. If the link was closed when you entered the margin value, then 0.75" automatically appeared in the other three margin fields.

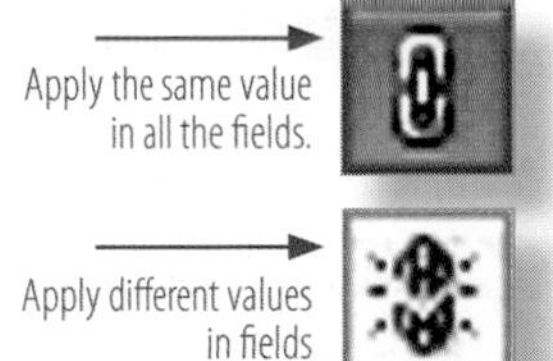

4. To accept changes and exit the dialog box, press **Return** (Mac) or **Enter** (Windows). It is not necessary to use your mouse to select OK. Similarly, you can press **Command+period** (Mac) or **Esc** (Mac and Windows) to exit the dialog box without accepting changes. We will continue working on our document, so keep it open.

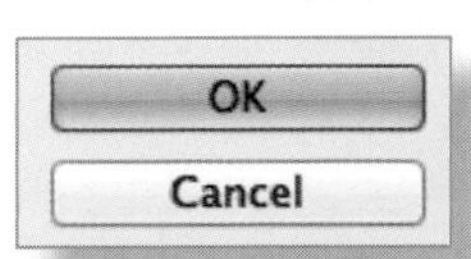

VISUAL | 1–6 |

Press Return (Mac) or Enter (Windows) instead of clicking OK. Press Command + period (Mac) or the Esc key (Mac and Windows) to activate the Cancel button.

© Cengage Learning 2013

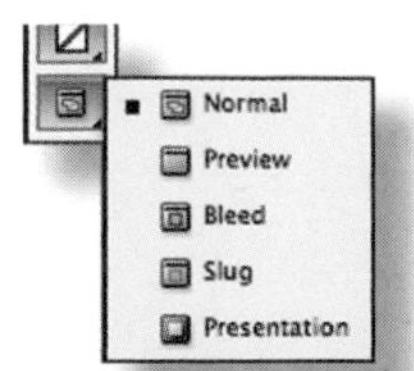

VISUAL | 1–7 |

Preview modes can be selected from the bottom of the Toolbox.

Five *view modes* can be found at the bottom of the *Toolbox* (Visual 1–7). You are viewing your document in *Normal* mode, the default viewing mode. When Normal is selected, you will see the document outlined in black, with magenta guides designating the 0.75" margin on all sides. Violet lines designate the column guides. Press W to switch to *Preview* mode. In this mode, all guides are hidden, and the *pasteboard* is changed to gray, the default preview background color. The pasteboard is the area surrounding the document, as shown in Visual 1–9. Press W again, and you return to Normal mode. *Bleed* and *Slug* view modes show areas created outside the document size. Bleeds and slugs will be introduced in Chapter 6.

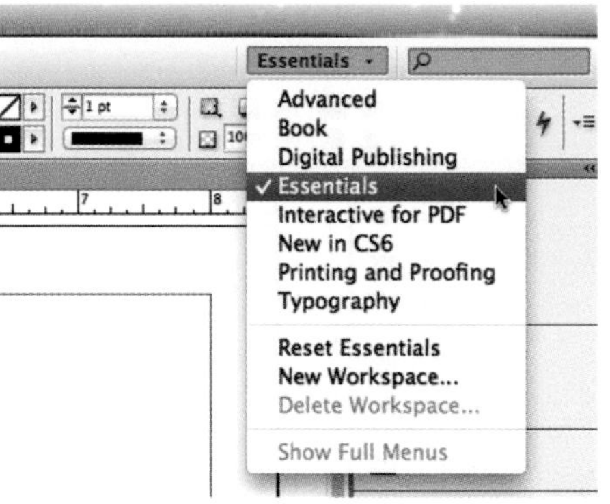

VISUAL | 1–8 |

Choose the Essentials workspace to make the layout of your document window match Visual 1–9.

You may see some differences as you compare your document window to the example shown in Visual 1–9. Let's make sure we're all looking at the same document workspace. Below the *Menu* is the *Application Bar.* On the far right end, is the *Workspace Switcher.* (Visual 1–8). Click on the *Workspace Switcher,* and you will notice that InDesign has several selections from which to choose. Notice that one of the menu options is *Reset Essentials.* As you're working on a document, you can quickly clean up your workspace by selecting the reset option. There's also a *New Workspace* menu option which allows you to save any customization you've made to the InDesign workspace. We'll cover that later in the chapter. For now, choose **Essentials**. When you release the mouse, your document window should look like Visual 1–9.

THE MENU BAR

The *Menu* bar stretches across the top of the document window and displays these categories: *InDesign* (Mac only), *File, Edit, Layout, Type, Object, Table, View, Window,* and *Help* (Visual 1–10). As you press and move your pointer across the *Menu* bar, you will see that underneath each category are menu items, most of which can be accessed by using keyboard shortcuts. Keyboard shortcuts are listed to the right of the menu items. This chart shows how to interpret the symbols listed with Mac keyboard shortcuts.

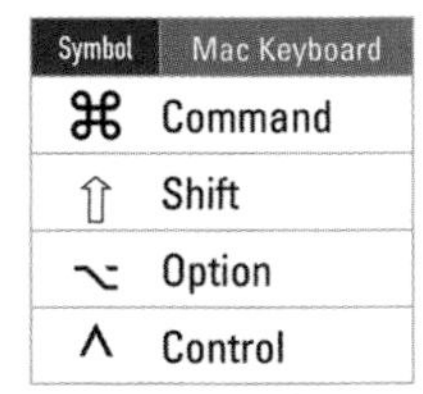

Symbol	Mac Keyboard
⌘	Command
⇧	Shift
⌥	Option
^	Control

Some menu items are followed by a triangle or ellipsis. When a triangle follows a menu item, it means that a submenu will open and more menu options will be displayed. An ellipsis means that a dialog box will open when the menu

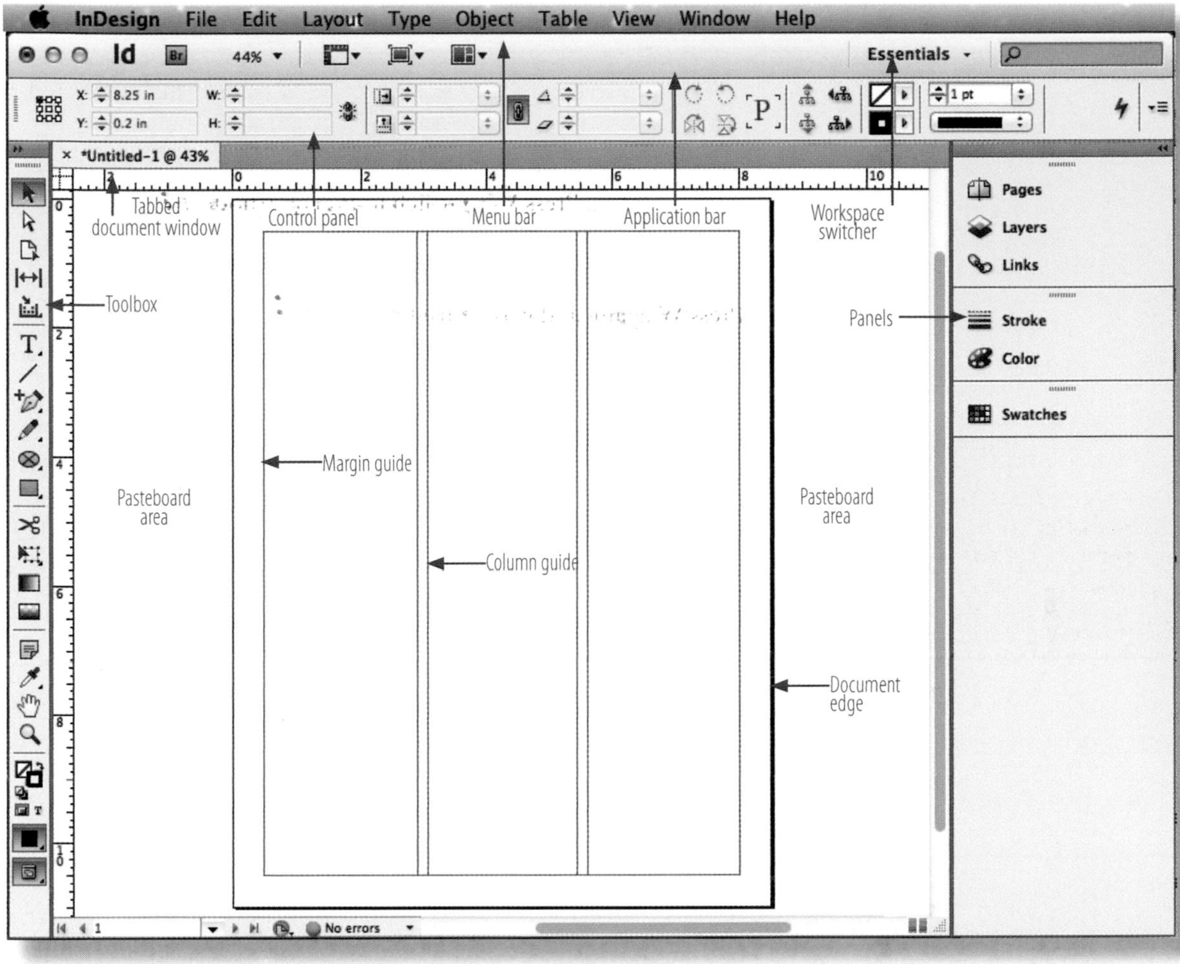

VISUAL | 1–9 | The document window shown in the Essentials workspace setting. © Cengage Learning 2013

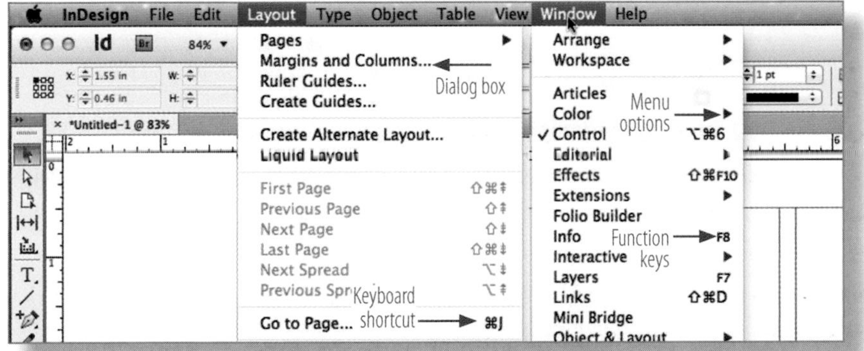

VISUAL | 1–10 |

The Menu bar runs across the top of the document window. Symbols to the right of menu items indicate keyboard shortcuts, sub menus and dialog boxes. © Cengage Learning 2013

item is selected (Visual 1–10). InDesign encourages you to customize your work environment to maximize productivity. As you work through this book you will be introduced to many of these InDesign features, and by the completion of the book you will have developed preferences for how you interact with your InDesign work environment. You'll also know how to integrate those preferences into your everyday use of InDesign.

VISUAL | 1–11 |

Features of the InDesign Toolbox.

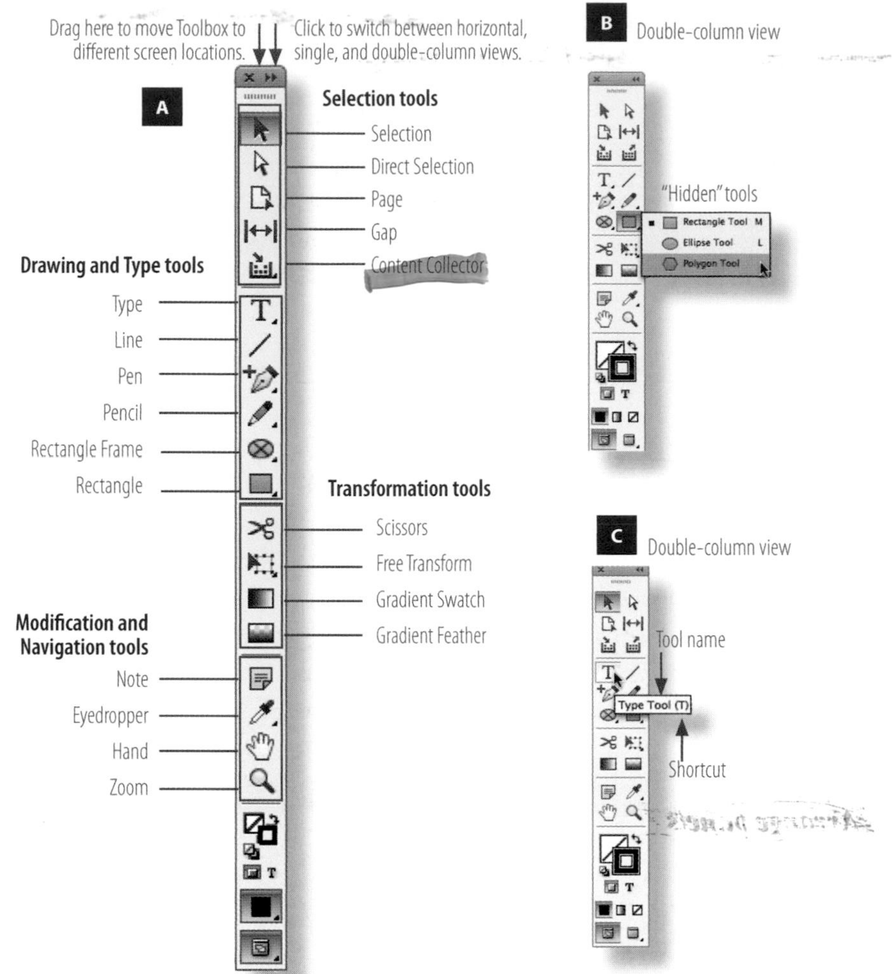

THE TOOLBOX

The *Toolbox, (*also called the *Tools panel)* is found on the left side of the document window. You can move the *Toolbox* to different areas of the document window by dragging the solid gray bar on the top of the panel (Visual 1–11A). Although you can't reposition the location of the tools inside the *Toolbox*, you can customize the overall layout of the *Toolbox*. If you click on the arrows in the upper right corner, you can toggle the display of the *Toolbox* between a horizontal row (if the panel is undocked), or single or double vertical columns (Visuals 1–11A and B). When you hover your pointer over a tool, you will see the tool name and keyboard shortcut (Visual 1–11C). Select a tool by clicking on it. When a tool is selected, its icon becomes highlighted. Notice that some tools have a triangle in the lower right corner. When you click on these tools and hold the mouse down for a second, you will see more choices "hidden" underneath (Visual 1–11B). These hidden tools are related to the main tool displayed in the *Toolbox*.

Tools are grouped according to function: *selection* tools, *drawing* and *type* tools, *transformation* tools, and *modification* and *navigation* tools.

Pressing the **Tab** key alternately hides and shows the *Tools* and other panels. Pressing **Shift+Tab** displays the *Tools* and *Control* panel, but hides the remaining panels. If the *Toolbox* becomes hidden on your document, go to the *Menu* bar, select **Window>Tools.** Or, select **Window>Workspace>Reset** (current Workspace). The *Toolbox* will return to its default location.

▸ *production tip*

If you accidently press the Tab key when you aren't typing, the Toolbox and other panels will disappear! Don't panic—simply press Tab again, and everything will reappear.

USING PANELS

InDesign uses panels to organize commands and are stored, or *docked,* on the right edge of the workspace. As you become more familiar with InDesign, you'll discover there are some panels you continually use. And there may be some panels you seldom use. InDesign has created preset workspaces intended to display panels that correspond with your particular workflow. InDesign allows you to customize the combination of panels to fit your preferences and the jobs you do. You can work in a panel while it is still grouped with other panels in vertical formation, or you can drag it out on the document area. Follow these steps to learn how to work with panels.

▸ *Arrange panels*

1. Choose each of the workspaces available in the ***workspace switcher*** pull down menu, found on the right end of the ***Application bar,*** above the ***Control*** panel (Visual 1–12). Notice that the panels on the right side of your InDesign window change according to the workspace you have selected. Panels are displayed in ***groups,*** in a vertical format on the right side of the InDesign window, in an area called the ***dock.*** Select the ***Advanced*** workspace, as you follow these steps.

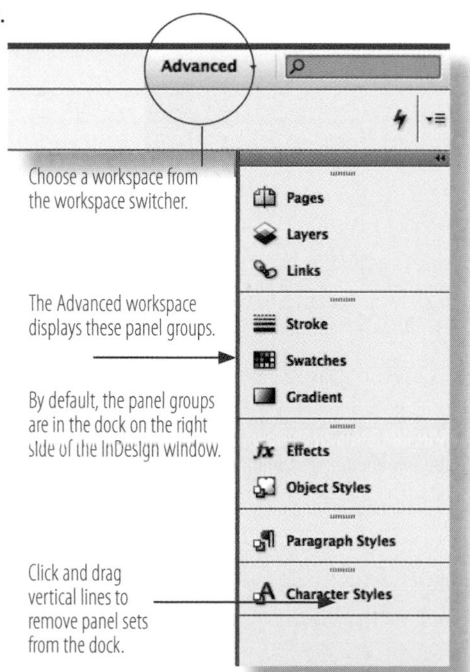
Advanced
Choose a workspace from the workspace switcher.
The Advanced workspace displays these panel groups.
By default, the panel groups are in the dock on the right side of the InDesign window.
Click and drag vertical lines to remove panel sets from the dock.
Pages
Layers
Links
Stroke
Swatches
Gradient
Effects
Object Styles
Paragraph Styles
Character Styles

VISUAL |1–12|

In this example, the Advanced workspace has been chosen from the workspace switcher on the Application bar. You can also choose a workspace from the Menu>Window> Workspace.

2. Click on a panel's name or icon and the panel window will open and close. Panels can also be opened with keyboard shortcuts. Press **F5** (function key 5) and the ***Swatches*** panel will open. Press **F5** again, and the panel will close.

3. Click on the grey bar on the top of the panel group and pull to the left. The entire panel group will be released from the dock. When the group is released, an "X" appears in the upper right corner (Windows). Click the *X*, and the panel group will close. You can make the panel group reappear by choosing ***Reset Advanced*** in the ***workspace switcher*** on the ***Application bar*** (Visual 1–13).

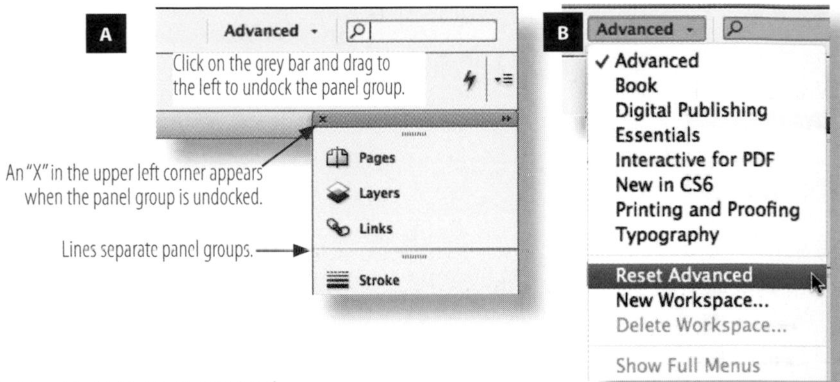

VISUAL |1–13|

Panels can be displayed in groups or as individual floating panels. Choose the Reset command to quickly revert your workspace back to its default state.

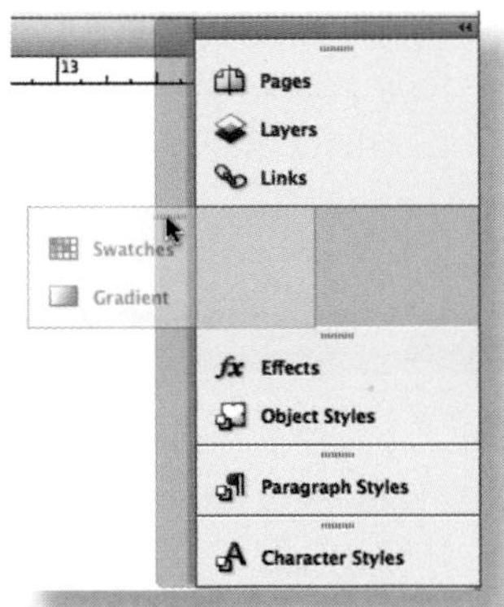

VISUAL |1–14|

Pull on the vertical lines to remove a panel set from the group.

4. Panel groups are broken down into ***sets***, which are separated by lines, as shown on the lower part of Visual 1–13A. These sets can be moved in and out of the dock by dragging on the short, vertical lines above each set. Click on the vertical lines and move each set from the dock (Visual 1–14). An "X" will appear in the upper right corner of each individual set. Click on the name of an individual panel and drag the panel to the left. You have just created a single, ***floating panel***.

VISUAL |1–15|

Panels can be resized so that the labels are hidden.

5. Panels can be made even smaller, so that the label is hidden, by clicking the left edge of the panel and dragging it toward the right. (Visual 1–15).

6. Choose ***Reset Advanced*** from the ***workspace switcher*** to reorganize your window. Pull the ***Swatches*** panel from the dock. Now, click on the double arrows in the upper right corner. This expands and collapses the panel window. Then, open the ***panel menu***. Panel menus display additional options, specific to each panel (Visual 1–16).

VISUAL |1–16|

Panels have additional features found in the menu options.

7. Panels can be stacked vertically on the document window. You can also dock the panels to the left edge of your screen. Select a panel. Click on the panel's name and drag it to the ***drop zone*** at the bottom of another panel. A blue bar appears as the panel enters the drop zone (Visual 1–17). Now, drag the panels into the dock on the left side of the screen. When you are finished, reset the *Advanced* workspace.

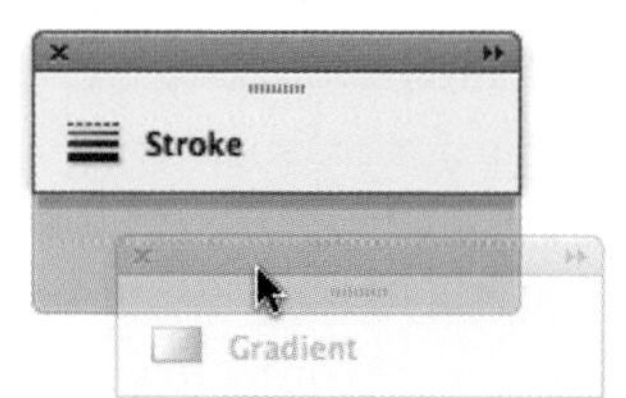

VISUAL | 1–17 |

A blue bar designates a "drop zone" when a panel is dragged into another panel set.

USING TOOLS

Set your *Toolbox* so that it is displayed in a single column, down the left side of your document window. The top tool (black arrow) is the *Selection* tool. Use it when you want to select, resize, or move an entire item (frame, line, text path, etc.). The second tool down, (white arrow) is the *Direct Selection* tool. Use it when you want to select just part of an item, the points on an item's path, the content inside the item, or to modify its shape. (If you are familiar with QuarkXPress, the *Selection* tool is similar to the Item tool and the *Direct Selection* tool is similar to the Content tool.)

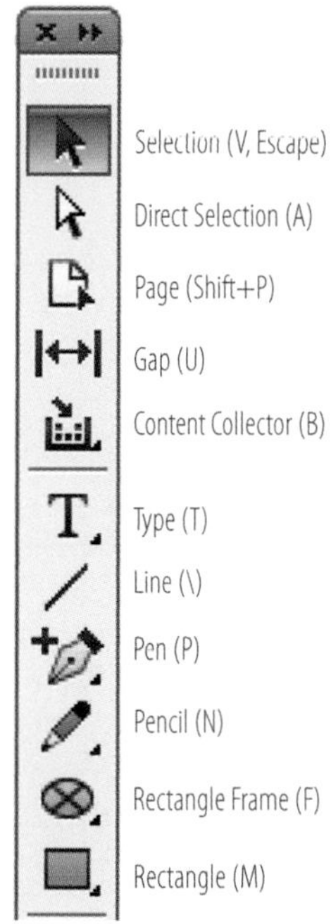

VISUAL | 1–18 |

When you hover over a tool with your mouse, the keyboard shortcut is shown next to the name of the tool.

Jump over the *Page, Gap,* and *Content Collector* tools and you will come to the *Type* tool. You will spend much of your time using the *Type* tool—typing, editing, or working with tables. Because you'll be using it so much, you'll learn to use keyboard shortcuts to switch from the *Type* tool to other tools without going over to the *Toolbox*. This will make you very efficient. Below the *Type* tool is the *Line* tool. Use this tool for drawing straight or diagonal lines.

Jump over the *Pen* and *Pencil* tools and you will find the *Rectangle Frame* tool. Notice the little arrow in the lower right corner. This means that other tools are "hidden" underneath the tool that is showing. We will use several of these tools as we continue working on the document created earlier.

▸ *Draw and resize a rectangle*

1. In the ***Toolbox***, click on the ***Rectangle*** tool. Your cursor will turn into little ***cross hairs*** with a dot in the middle. Go back to your document, click your mouse button somewhere on the left side of your document, and make a rectangle by dragging your mouse down and to the right. Release the mouse.

Let's take a look at the rectangle you have just drawn (Visual 1–19). The eight small hollow boxes at the corners and at each side of the rectangle are called *selection handles*. When the selection handles are visible, the item is considered *active*. Click somewhere else on your document. The selection handles disappear, meaning the item is *not active*. An item must be selected (active) in order to work with it. In addition to selection handles, shapes have *bounding boxes*. Bounding boxes indicate the outermost points of a shape, the "footprint." The bounding box for the rectangle you have just drawn is the same dimension as the rectangle. Look at the odd-looking shape in Visual 1–19. The rectangle that delineates its outer edges is the bounding box. A bounding box always has four straight sides, no matter what shape you have drawn. If the circle shown in the Visual 1–19 was activated with the *Selection* tool, the bounding box would be displayed as a square.

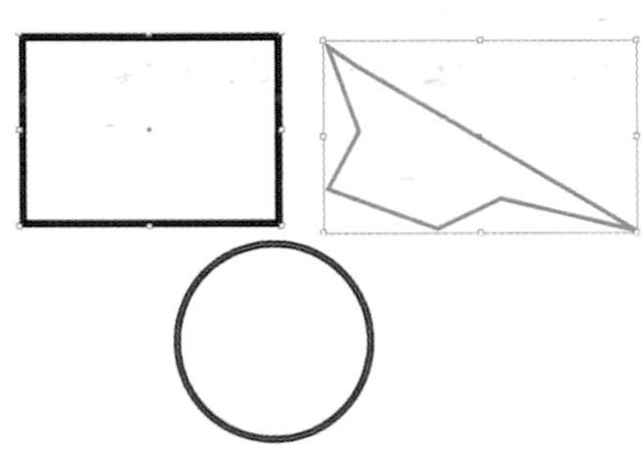

VISUAL | 1–19 |

Two of these three shapes are active. The circle is not active.

© Cengage Learning 2013

Default Selection tool cursor

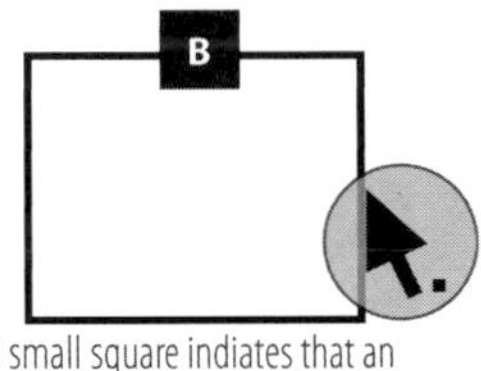

A small square indiates that an object is ready to be selected.

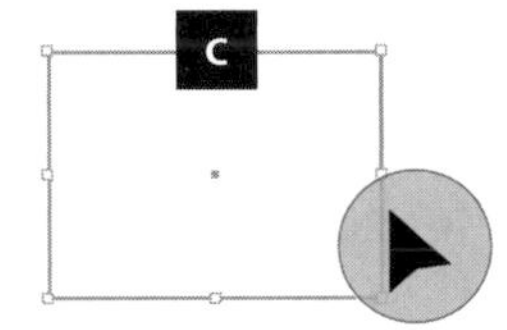

A "tail-less" cursor means that you can click and drag the selected object.

VISUAL | 1–20 |

The shape of the Selection tool cursor changes during use. Learn to recognize these icons.

© Cengage Learning 2013

2. Deselect the rectangle you drew earlier. Go back to the ***Toolbox*** and click on the ***Selection*** tool. Your cursor should now look like a ***black arrow*** (Visual 1–20A). Slowly move the ***Selection*** tool toward the edge of the rectangle (do not click the mouse button). When the arrow touches the edge, a small square appears next to the tail of the arrow (Visual 1–20B). This means you can now select the rectangle again. Click when the small box appears by the tail of the arrow and you will see your selection handles again. Your rectangle is now selected. Notice that when your rectangle is selected and you move your cursor over the edge of the rectangle (without clicking the button), the arrow icon loses its "tail" (Visual 1–20C).

3. With your rectangle selected, you can move the rectangle to a different place or change its size. To move it, click on the edge of the rectangle and drag it. Release the mouse button to "drop" the rectangle in the new location. To resize the rectangle, move the cursor over one of the selection handles. The icon turns into small opposing arrows, with a line in between (Visual 1–21). Drag the selection handles in, out, or diagonally to change the dimension of the rectangle. As it moves, the width and height will be displayed next to the arrow.

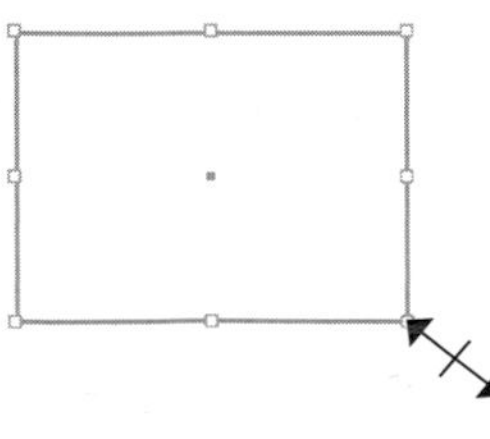

VISUAL | 1–21 |

When the Selection arrow is over a frame handle, it changes shape. The double-ended arrow means that you can drag the handle to change the dimensions of the object.

© Cengage Learning 2013

▸ *Use shortcuts to create and modify a rectangle*

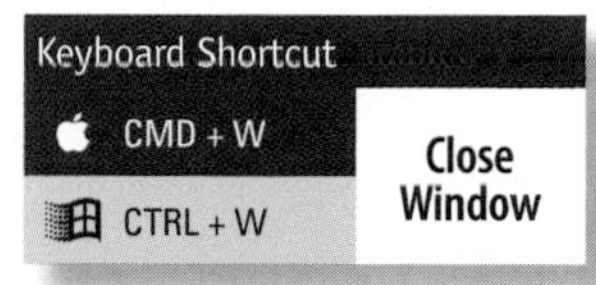

1. Close, but don't save the document you just made, by pressing **Command+W** (Mac) or **Control+W** (Windows). Use keyboard shortcuts to make a new document: **Command+N** (Mac) or **Control+N** (Windows). When the *New Document* dialog box opens, accept the document defaults, including **Letter** for page size, and **0.5"** for all margins. Choose the **Essentials** workspace.

2. Next, you will draw a rectangle, but instead of going over to the *Toolbox*, press the letter **M**. This will instantly select the *Rectangle* tool. Draw a rectangle and then press the letter **A**. You have now selected the *Direct Selection* tool. The *Direct Selection* tool differs from the *Selection* tool because you can modify just part of an object—one side, or one or more *anchor points*—instead of the whole item.

Default Direct Selection tool cursor

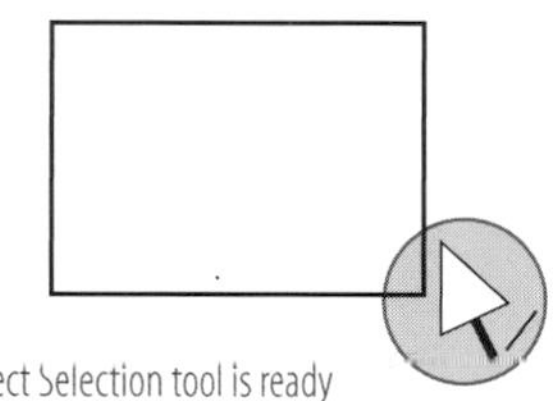
Direct Selection tool is ready to select the side of the frame

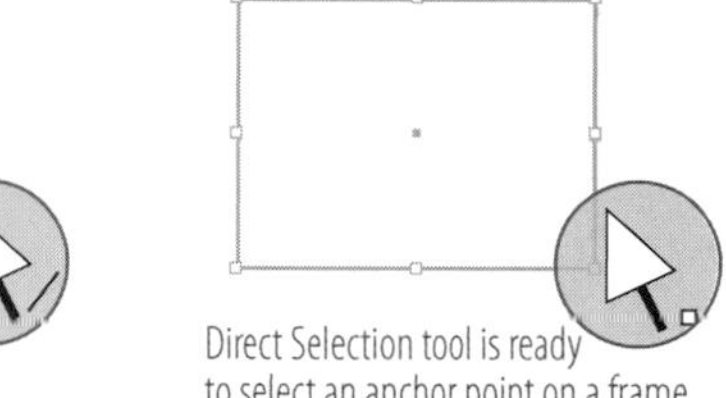
Direct Selection tool is ready to select an anchor point on a frame.

VISUAL | 1–22 |

The Direct Selection tool uses many of the same visual cues as the Selection tool, shown earlier.

3. Modify the shape of your rectangle using the *Direct Selection* tool by selecting and dragging the sides and anchor points. Your rectangle will quickly lose its rigid, 90-degree angles.

4. With your shape selected, bring the *Direct Selection* arrow slowly to the tiny box in the center of the object. Notice that the white arrow becomes a black arrow. Click and move the object around.

   Always deselect an object when you are finished working on it. You can deselect an object by clicking any blank area in the document, or by using the keyboard shortcut: **Shift+Command+A** (Mac) or **Shift+Control+A** (Windows).

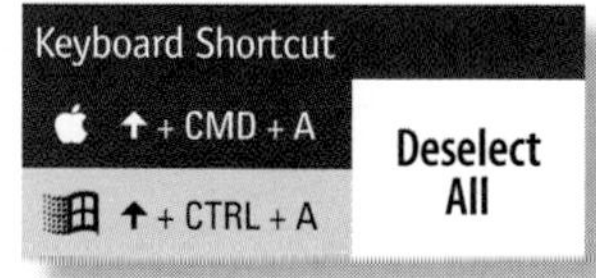

▸ *Place text into a frame*

You will appreciate your good typing and keyboard skills as you begin to spend more time working with text. In the next exercise, you will learn how to enter text and draw some basic shapes.

▸ *production tip*

Get into the habit of deselecting an object when you're finished working on it.

1. Close your document without saving it by pressing **Command+W** (Mac) or **Control+W** (Windows). Use the keyboard shortcut to make a new, one-page document that is **7"** wide and **6"** high (use the **0.5"** default margins).

2. Notice that your document is *landscape* format, because it is wider than it is high. Press **M** to select the *Rectangle* tool and draw a rectangle. Now press **T**. Your cursor

changes into a vertical bar with a small cross hair near the bottom and dotted lines around it (Visual 1–23). Click inside the rectangle and notice the blinking cursor in the upper left corner of the rectangle. Your rectangle has become a text frame, and the blinking cursor means you're ready to type.

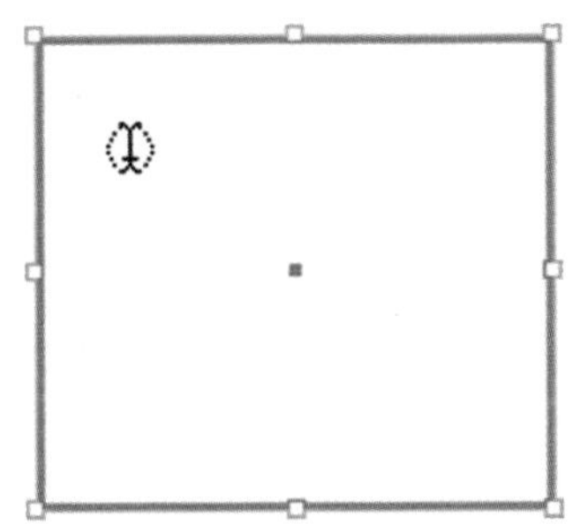

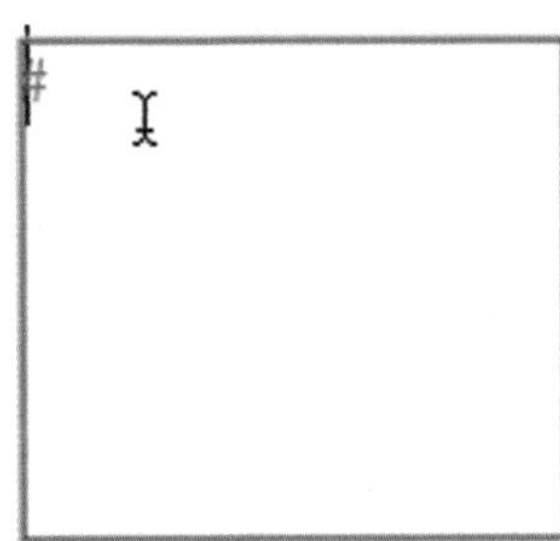

VISUAL |1–23|

Clicking on any shape with the Type tool will convert it to a text frame. When you see the blinking cursor, you are ready to type.

Keyboard Shortcut
CMD + A
CTRL + A
Select All

3. You can also create a text frame by dragging with the ***Type*** tool cursor. As you draw the frame, the width and height are displayed (Visual 1–24). When you release the mouse, you are ready to type. Type a sentence or two about yourself, your dog, or your weekend—anything you want. Highlight all the text with **Command+A** (Mac) or **Control+A** (Windows). There are other methods of selecting your text. For instance, you can drag and highlight text with your mouse, or choose ***Select All*** from the ***Edit*** menu, but those methods are slower. Keyboard shortcuts are always the way to go!

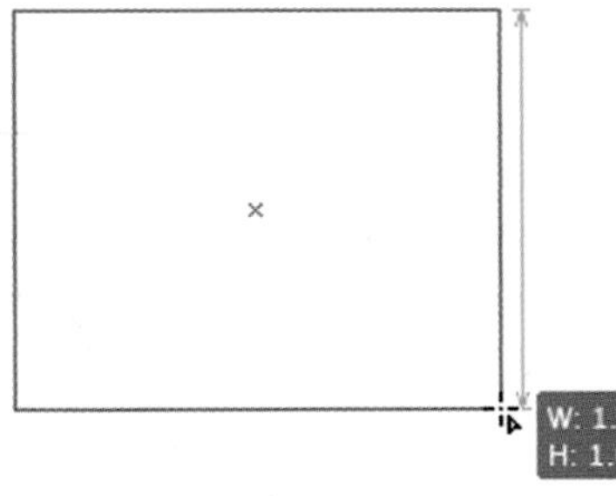

VISUAL |1–24|

It's most efficient to create a text frame by dragging the Type tool cursor. The width and height measurements are displayed as you draw.

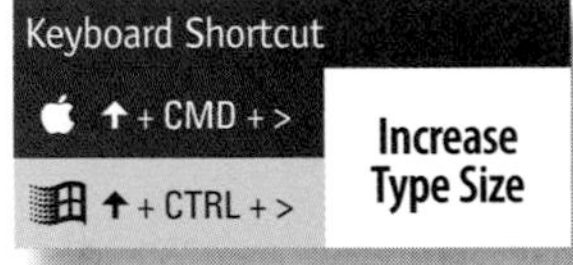

Keyboard Shortcut
↑ + CMD + >
↑ + CTRL + >
Increase Type Size

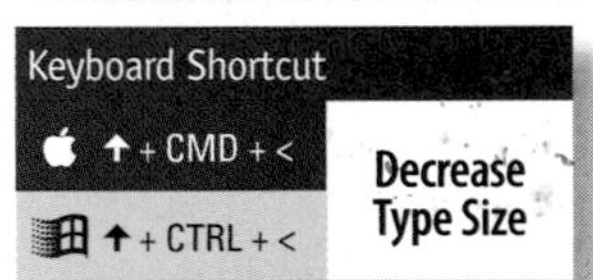

Keyboard Shortcut
↑ + CMD + <
↑ + CTRL + <
Decrease Type Size

4. With the text highlighted, you can use keyboard shortcuts to increase the size of the selected type. Hold down **Shift+Command** (Mac) or **Shift+Control** (Windows) and press the ***greater than*** key (**>**), six or seven times, and watch the size of your type get larger. You could use the ***Control*** panel to increase the size of the type, but using keyboard shortcuts is essential for efficiency. You can substitute the ***less than*** symbol (**<**), in combination with the same modifier keys, to reduce the type size. Deselect the text and keep your document open.

▸ *Add a stroke and fill*

A *stroke* is a line that goes around the edges of a shape, like a border; or around type, like an outline. A *fill* is a color that is placed inside a shape or type. Stroke and fill menus are conveniently located in the *Control* panel (Visual 1–25).

VISUAL |1–25|

Fill and Stroke buttons in the Control panel. A red diagonal line indicates a stroke or fill of [None].

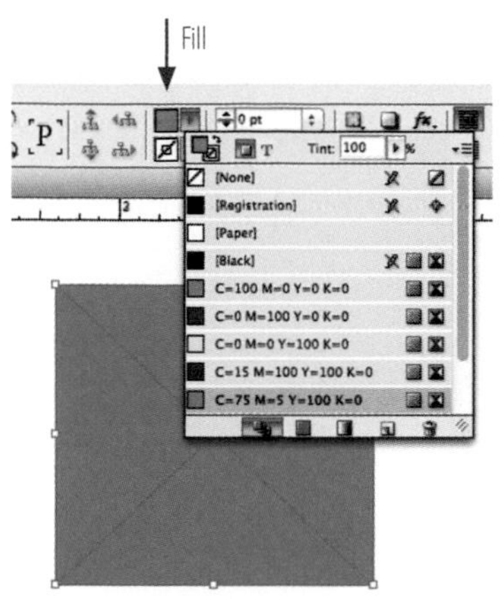

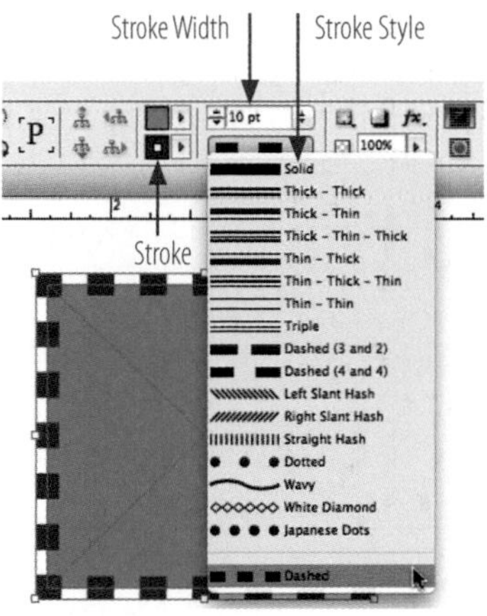

VISUAL | 1–26 |

Stroke and Fill controls are found in the Control panel.
© Cengage Learning 2013

5. Press **F** to select the ***Rectangle Frame*** tool and draw a rectangle on your document. By default, shapes drawn with the ***Rectangle Frame*** tool have no fill or stroke. Click the arrow next to the ***Fill*** button on the ***Control*** panel (Visual 1–26). Slide down the menu of color swatches and choose the **Green** swatch (C=75, M=5, Y=100, K=0). The rectangle will be filled with Green.

6. Now you'll add a Red border to the outside of the rectangle. With the rectangle still selected, click the arrow next to the ***Stroke*** icon, located below the ***Fill*** icon (Visual 1–26). Slide down the menu of color swatches and choose the **Red** swatch (C=15, M=100, Y=100, K=0). Now that you've selected the color, you can add a ***style***. The default is a ***Solid*** line, but you can slide down the style menu and choose the stroke style that suits you. Directly above the ***Style*** field is the ***Stroke Width*** field. You'll learn what ***pt.*** means in a later chapter. For now, simply use the pull down menu or the arrows next to the ***Stroke Width*** field to select a preset stroke width.

► *production tip*

A stroke is applied to the outside of a frame; a fill is applied to the inside. If the stroke width is too small, the style may not show. If that happens, choose a larger stroke width.

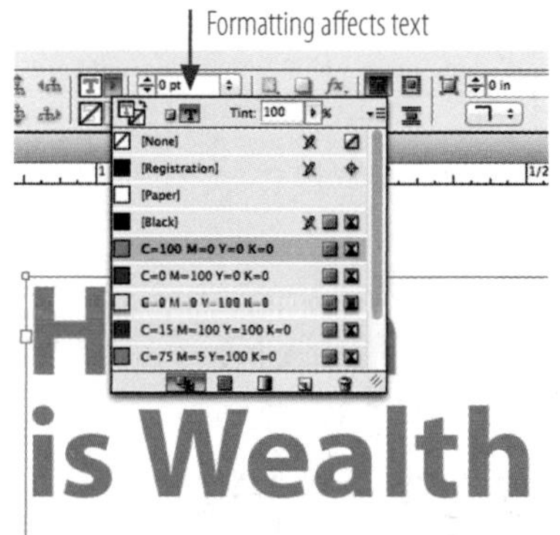

VISUAL | 1–27 |

A stroke is not usually added to type because it can reduce readability. (This stroke is greatly exaggerated for demonstration purposes.)
© Cengage Learning 2013

7. It's just as easy to add a stroke or fill to text. Type a short phrase in your rectangle. Select the frame with the ***Selection*** tool. Click the arrow next to the ***Fill*** button. When the ***Swatches*** panel opens, click the ***Formatting affects text*** button (Visual 1–27). Then, select a color from the list. Then, select ***Stroke*** and add a color from the ***Stroke*** pull down menu. Choose a ***stroke width***. Whenever you apply a stroke to text, make sure the width of the stroke doesn't distort the shape of the letters.

VISUAL |1–28|

Horizontal and diagonal lines with a stroke applied.

8. Select the ***Line*** tool (the keyboard shortcut is a backslash, \). Click and drag to draw several diagonal lines on your document. Switch to the ***Selection*** tool and select any line. Notice the rectangular shape of the bounding box. Now, select the ***Line*** tool again, hold down the **Shift** key, and draw perfectly horizontal and vertical lines (Visual 1–28). By default, the line has a 1-point, black stroke. Lines do not have fills.

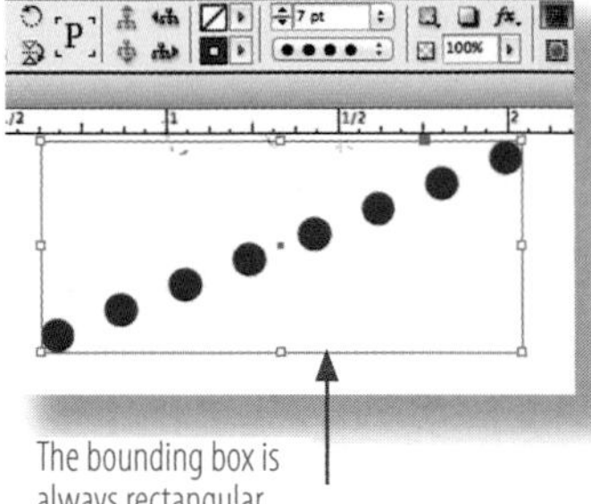

VISUAL |1–29|

This line has a red stroke and a 7-point dotted line.

▸ *production tip*

Holding down the Shift key constrains rectangles to perfect squares, ellipses to perfect circles, and lines to horizontal, vertical, or 45-degree increments.

9. Hold down the **Shift** key and draw one more line, but do not release the mouse button. Instead, move the mouse to rotate the free end of the line in a circle, like hands on a clock. Notice how the line snaps to 45-degree increments. The ***Shift*** key constrains lines to horizontal, vertical, or 45-degree increments. Now, choose a different stroke style, width, and color.

ABOUT FRAMES

InDesign includes two tools for making rectangular boxes called *frames.* One frame has an "X" in it, one doesn't. Both frames can hold either pictures or text. When you click inside any frame with the *Type* tool, a blinking cursor will appear, which means the frame is ready for you to begin typing.

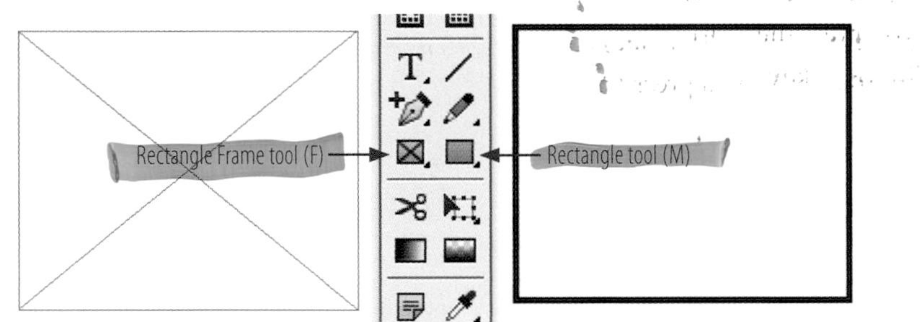

VISUAL |1–30|

On the left is a frame made with the Rectangle Frame tool. The frame on the right was made with the Rectangle tool. Either frame can hold text or graphics.

1. Make a new document using the default settings. Use the ***Rectangle*** tool to draw a rectangle in the right half your document.

2. Choose the ***Rectangle Frame*** tool (the box with the ***X*** inside it). You may also select this tool by pressing **F**. Draw a second rectangle on the left half of your document. There will be an X inside the new rectangle (Visual 1–30).

So, why are there two frame tools? In the days before computers, layouts were created by placing graphic elements on a *pasteup board.* The location and size of a photo would be indicated on the pasteup by a rectangle, with an X stretching from corner to corner. In today's InDesign environment, a designer can create a layout, and use the *Rectangle Frame* tool, with the "X," to indicate where the images will be placed. Text will be placed in frames without an "X." These visual cues are particularly helpful if another person is going to add the photos and text to complete the project.

NAVIGATING

Let's do a little navigating around your document with the two frames. Your document sits in the middle of an area called the pasteboard. At the right and bottom of the pasteboard are *scroll bars* (Visual 1–31). You slide the scroll bars up and down, or right and left, to reposition your document inside the InDesign window. You can pull the triangle icon in the lower right corner to resize the window. The *Split layout* icon to the left of the resize triangle lets you have two views of the same document.

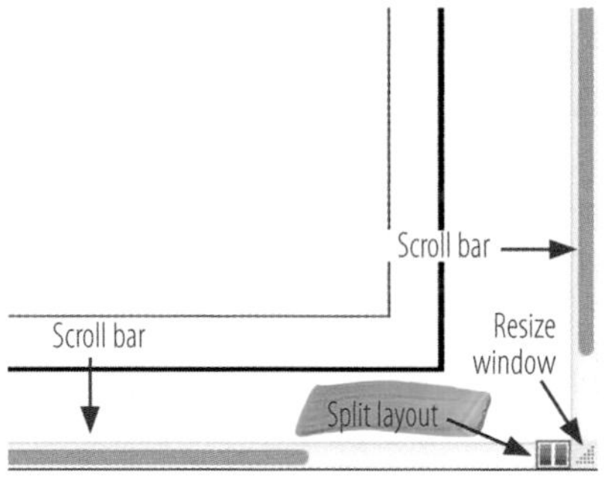

VISUAL |1–31|

Scroll bars and arrows help you position your document.

Another way to move your document around is to use the *Hand* tool. Whenever the *Type* tool is not active, you can hold down the spacebar to switch temporarily to the *Hand* tool (Visual 1–32). Click, and the *Hand* will turn into a little fist. Now drag with your mouse and the fist will grab on to your document and move it wherever you like.

To access the *Hand* tool while you are using the *Type* tool in an active frame, you press the **Option** (Mac) or **Alt** (Windows) key. (If you press the spacebar to access the grabber hand while using the *Text* tool, you will simply add spaces to the text you are working on.) You can also select the *Hand* tool in the *Toolbox* or by using the **H** shortcut key, but using the *Spacebar* (or **Option/Alt**) and mouse is probably faster and more convenient.

Henit, quisi elis ad tat utatie feum zzrilit, quat praestrud ming et nulputp atuerci tat, commolut ad tis doluptat, con henim alisitMet incin euip-sum veniamet aliqui bla feu facidun lumsan eugiat

Henit, quisi elis ad tat utatie feum zzrilit, quat praestrud ming et nulputp atuerci tat, commolut ad tis doluptat, con henim alisitMet incin euip-sum veniamet aliqui bla feu facidun lumsan eugiat

VISUAL |1–32|

Hold down the Spacebar and click to make the Hand tool turn into the grabber hand. If you are using the Type tool, access the grabber hand by pressing the Option (Mac) or Alt (Windows) key.

MANAGING PAGES AND VIEWS

In the lower left corner of your document window is the *Status* bar. This bar displays the page number you are working on and the preflight status of a file. You can also move from page to page by clicking the *Next Page*, *Previous Page*, or *Go To Page* arrows on each side of the current page number (Visual 1–33).

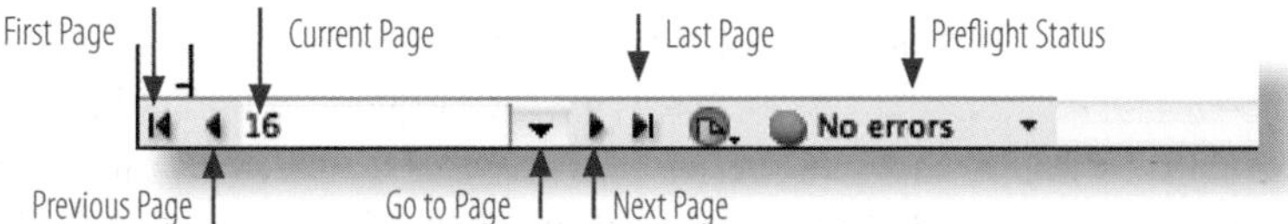

VISUAL |1–33|

The Status bar, in the lower left corner, displays the current page number and makes it easy to move from page to page.

THE APPLICATION BAR

Let's move from the lower left corner of the InDesign workspace, to the area above the *Control* panel, called the *Application bar*. This multi-purpose utility houses many productivity controls. You already used one of them—the *workspace switcher*—when you chose a workspace from the upper right corner. Just to make sure we're all on the same workspace, go to the workspace switcher and choose **Essentials** from the drop down menu. If you already have *Essentials* chosen, select **Reset Essentials**, instead.

Now, direct your attention to the left end of the *Application bar*, and we'll take a look at some of its great features (Visual 1–34).

VISUAL |1–34|

The Application bar is visible by default, but can be turned off under the Window menu (Mac only).

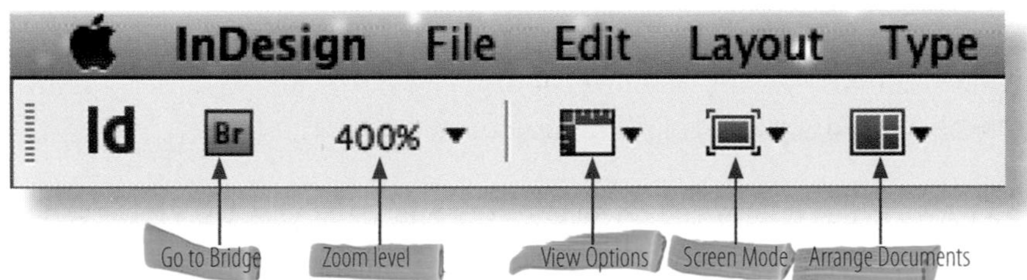

ABOUT BRIDGE

Bridge, the first icon on the *Application bar*, is an application found in all the Adobe Suite members. *Bridge* helps you manage the images and other components in your projects. We won't be covering *Bridge* in this book—you can find out more about it at *Menu>Help>InDesign Help.*

MANAGING YOUR DOCUMENT'S VIEW

When you are viewing your document at its actual size, the zoom level is 100%. You can access the *Zoom level* preset list on the *Application bar*, next to *Bridge*, by clicking on the downward-pointing triangle to the right of the zoom level field. Notice that you can view your document from 5% all the way to 4000%! If none of those view percentages is just right, you can type any percentage in the zoom level field and press **Return** or **Enter**, and your document view will immediately change (Visual 1–35).

VISUAL |1–35|

The Zoom level preset list.

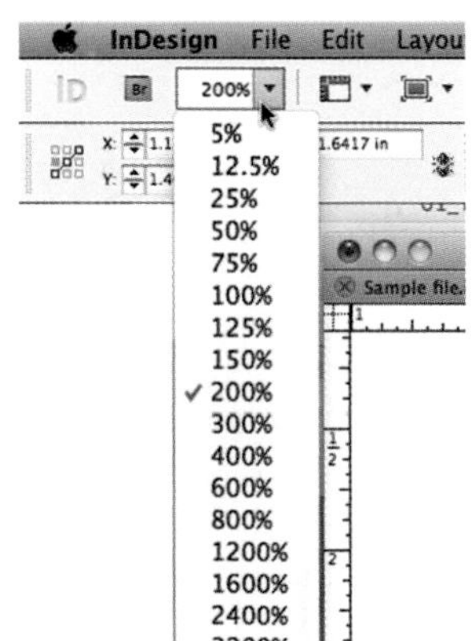

Another way to change your view is to use keyboard shortcuts. For a quick view of the document at actual size, press **Command+1** (Mac) or **Control+1** (Windows). This method is quick and efficient, and after using it awhile, it becomes automatic. Other keyboard shortcuts for viewing options are shown in Visual 1–36. Practice using each of the keyboard shortcuts until they become automatic.

Access the *Zoom* tool in the *Toolbox* by pressing **Z**. Hold the *Zoom* tool directly over the place in your document you want magnified, and click. That area will come to the center of your screen. Hold down the **Option** (Mac) or **Alt** (Windows) key and click to reduce the zoom percentage. Get in the habit of zooming in and zooming out, quickly and frequently. Too many beginning designers work with very small text at 100% view—or less! Give your eyes a break. Zoom into your document so you can comfortably see punctuation marks, where your cursor is, how many characters you have highlighted—all the small details of your document. After you have finished working up close, zoom out, using the appropriate keyboard shortcut.

Function	Mac	Windows
View at 100%	Cmd+1	Ctrl+1
View at 200%	Cmd+2	Ctrl+2
View at 400%	Cmd+4	Ctrl+4
View at 50%	Cmd+5	Ctrl+5
Fit page in window	Cmd+0 (zero)	Ctrl+0 (zero)

VISUAL |1–36|

Keyboard shortcuts for changing zoom percentage.

When you are zoomed in on a document and click and hold the *Hand* tool, the page automatically zooms out. A red rectangle shows the part of the document you will view. When you release the mouse, the document will return to the previous zoom percentage (Visual 1–37).

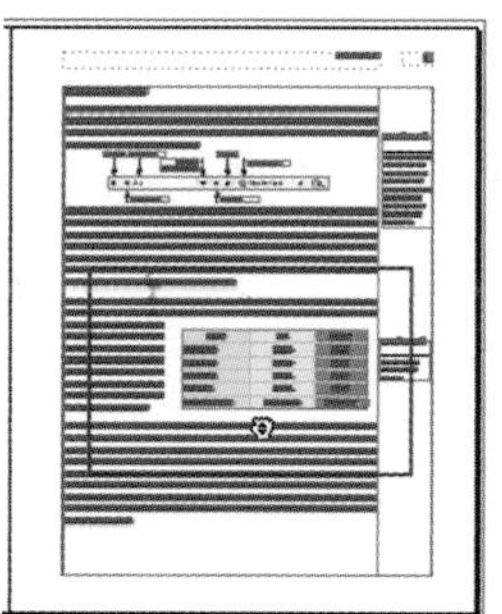

VISUAL |1–37|

Click and hold when you are using the Hand tool to zoom so that you can see the entire pasteboard.The red rectangle shows the area of the document that will be displayed when the mouse is released. The rectangle can be resized by pressing the up or down arrow keys.

VIEW OPTIONS

View Options is the next feature on the *Application bar* (Visual 1–38). This drop down menu allows you to turn on and off rulers, guides, and other page elements which will be explained in later chapters.

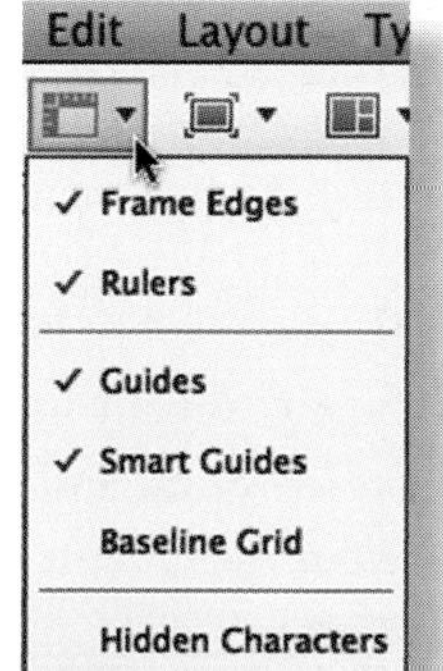

VISUAL |1–38|

View Options lets you hide or show guides that help you during production.

SCREEN MODE OPTIONS

The *Screen Mode* feature allows you to see how your job will look when it's finished (Visual 1–39). In *Normal* mode, you will see all the margin guides and frame edges. When you switch to *Preview*, the distracting guides are hidden. Another way to quickly switch into Preview mode is to press the letter W. Of course, if the *Text* tool is active in a text frame you will actually type a "W," so you should deselect everything before using the keyboard shortcut. You will find out about bleeds and slugs in Chapter 6. We won't be covering the *Presentation* mode or the *Arrange Documents* feature of the *Application bar* in this book.

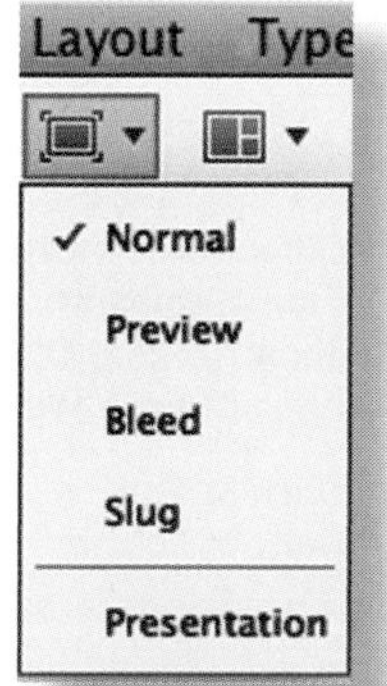

VISUAL |1–39|

Screen Mode options in the Application bar. Normal mode shows margins and guides. Preview mode shows how your project will look when it's finished.

THE APPLICATION FRAME

On the Mac, you can choose *Application frame* from *Menu>Window>Application Frame*. This feature groups all the workspace elements in a single window. As you become more familiar with InDesign, you will develop personal preferences for how you like to work.

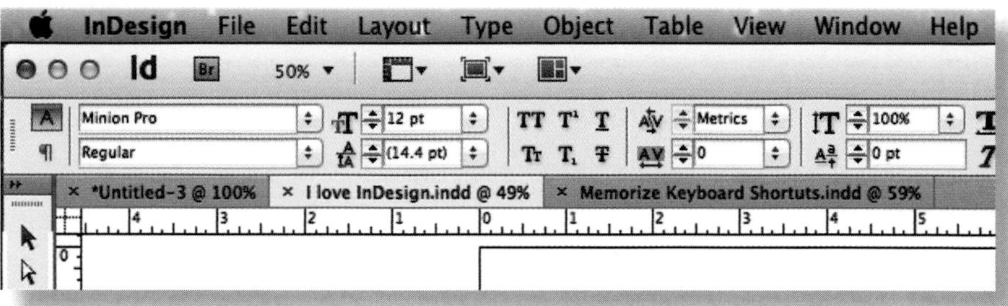

VISUAL | 1–40 |

The white document tab shows the file that is currently active. An asterisk in front of the file name means the document has changes which have not been saved!

MANAGING DOCUMENT WINDOWS

By default, open InDesign documents are shown in *document tab format* across the top of the workspace. As you click on each tab, that document is displayed, making, making it easy to switch between documents. The active document tab is white (Visual 1–40). If you have been following the exercises, you only have one open InDesign document, so you will only have one tab displayed. However, with multiple files open, tabbed documents work much like panels. You can undock a document by dragging its tab out of the group. You can rearrange the order of documents by dragging the tab to a new location in the group. When using the tabs to switch between documents, be careful not to click the × in the upper right corner, because this closes the document.

THE CONTROL PANEL

And finally, directly below the *Application bar* is the *Control* panel. The *Control* panel offers quick and convenient ways to accomplish much of what you need to do in your documents. By default, the *Control* panel is docked above the title tab of your document. You can dock it to the bottom of the window, or change it to a floating panel, by choosing either of these options from the panel menu, located at the far right end of the *Control* panel (Visual 1–41). Like most InDesign panels, *tool tips* will be displayed when you hover over an item with the pointer. The fields and options in the *Control* panel are like a chameleon, changing from *Character formatting* mode to *Paragraph*

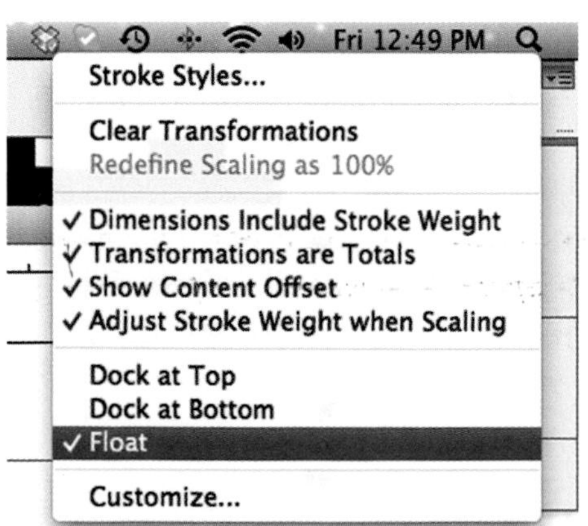

VISUAL | 1–41 |

The Control panel menu is found at the far right end of the panel. Control panel options are displayed according to the tool or operation you are performing. Here, you can choose to have the Control panel float on your desktop—wherever you position it.

formatting mode, or to any number of other modes, depending on what type of object you have selected (Visual 1–42). The *Control* panel will display a variety of options, depending on your monitor size and resolution. For instance, if you are using InDesign on a laptop, fewer *Control* panel options will be displayed, than if you are using a large monitor. If the *Control* panel does not appear on your desktop, select *Window>Control* from the *Menu* bar. You will be using the *Control* panel continuously, and each of its options will be introduced as you progress through the chapters.

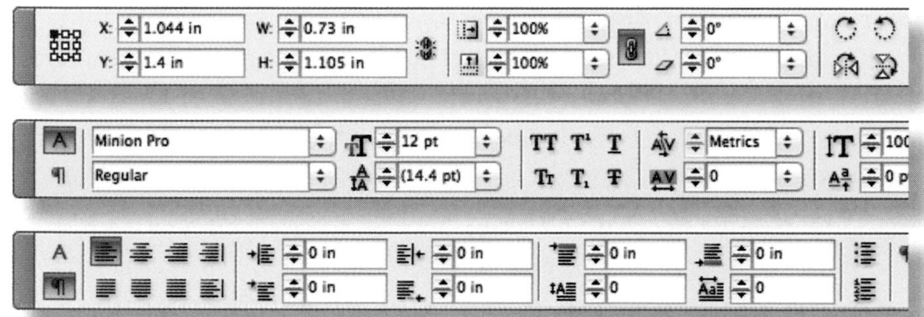

VISUAL |1–42|

The Control panel options change, depending on the tool you are using or operation you are about to perform.
© Cengage Learning 2013

CUSTOMIZING YOUR WORKSPACE

Arrange the panels on your desktop where you want them to be. Place the *Toolbox* where it is most convenient for you. Even if you don't yet have a preference for panel configurations, pull a couple panels out onto the desktop just for fun and note their names and placement. Choose *Window>Workspace>New Workspace.* In the *New Workspace* dialog, type **Workspace 2** and press **Return** or **Enter** (Visual 1–43).

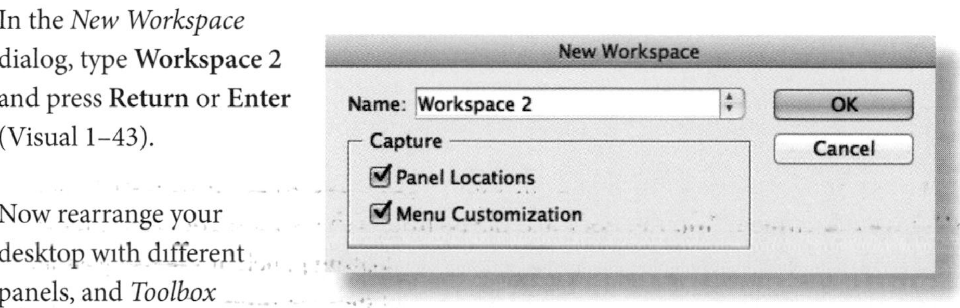

VISUAL |1–43|

You can customize and save your favorite workspace using the New Workspace command.
© Cengage Learning 2013

Now rearrange your desktop with different panels, and *Toolbox* location. Choose *Window>Workspace>Reset Workspace 2* and Workspace 2 will instantly revert to its default setting.

The *[New in CS6]* workspace hides some menu items. When you need to use a menu item that is not displayed, go to *Window>Workspace>Show Full Menus.* You can create workspaces to customize your InDesign environment to just about any configuration you want. Very neat. Very organized.

SAVING YOUR WORK

Your old typewriter had one—and only one—advantage over word processing: Once you typed a word on your paper, it was there to stay! Not so with electronic page layout programs. You need to save your work and save it often.

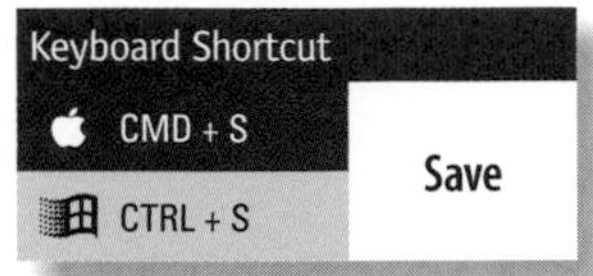

To save your document, press **Command+S** (Mac) or **Control+S** (Windows) or select *File>Save*. The dialog box will ask you first of all what you want to name your document. The *Save As* (Mac) or *File Name* (Windows) field will be highlighted when the dialog box is displayed, so just begin typing the name you want for the document. Next, specify where you want it saved: on the desktop? on your hard drive? on a server? in a folder? which folder? Be sure to remember where you save your document so that you can find it later.

If you lose a document but know you saved it somewhere, go to *File>Open Recent* and see if it is in the list of recent documents (Visual 1–44). Or, you can do a Find or Search (if you remember the name of the file) and your computer will locate it for you.

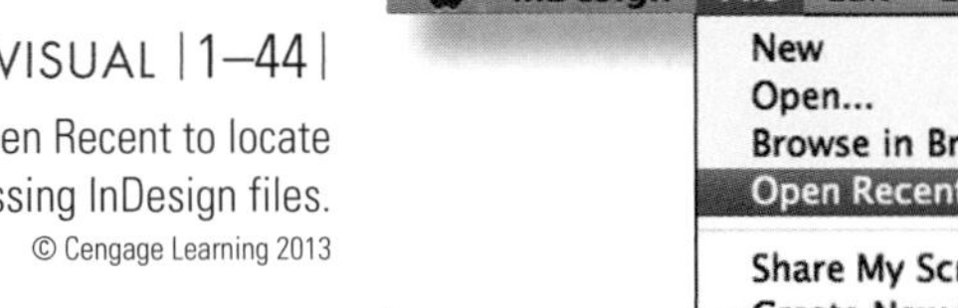

VISUAL |1–44|
Use Open Recent to locate missing InDesign files.

SAVE AND SAVE AS

After you have saved a project the first time, pressing **Command+S** (Mac) or **Control+S** (Windows) automatically saves your document, with the edits you have made, in the same location and with the same name as your previous *Save*. *Save As* also saves your work, but the *Save As* dialog is displayed to allow you to rename and relocate your document. On a Mac, the window first opens in compressed view (Visual 1–45A). If you click the arrow at the right end of the *Save As* field, the window expands, allowing you to select the save location, and to hide or show the *.indd* extension in the *Save As* field (Visual 1–45B).

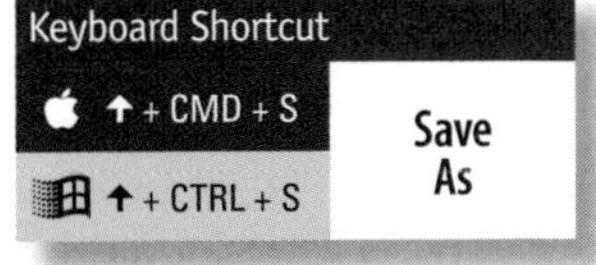

Let's say you have been working on a Valentine's Day ad for South Side Grocery. You complete the ad, save and print the document, and get the customer's approval. The customer loves your layout and decides you should make a version for three other stores in the city. And all the other versions need to be done by 5:00 p.m.! This is a great time to use *Save As*. Open the original file, named South Side Grocery. Immediately use **Save As**, and name the new file *North Side Grocery*. The South Side Grocery file remains unchanged, but you are now working on a different file—the North Side Grocery ad. When this ad is done you save it, print it, and again use **Save As** to name the next file *West Side Grocery*. The previous file, North Side Grocery, stays just as you left it while you complete the West Side Grocery ad, and so on. You can also use *Save As* to rename your document, such as *North Side Grocery_Backup* and then save the backup version to a CD, flash drive, or a file server.

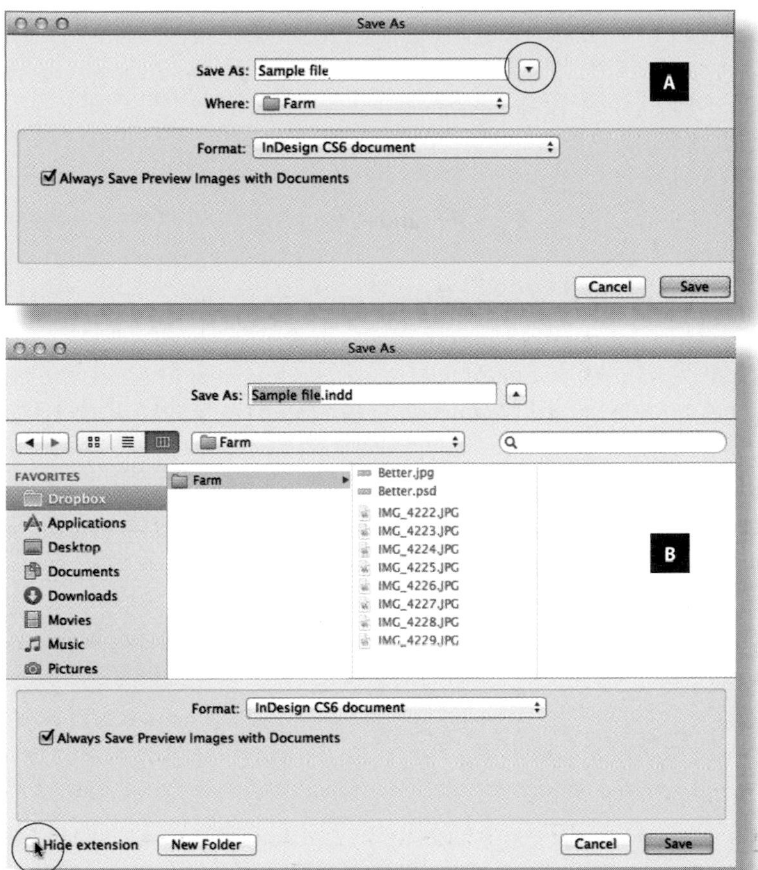

VISUAL |1–45|

Click the arrow to the the right of the Save As field (A) to expand the Save window (B) in the Mac operating system.

SAVE A COPY

The keyboard shortcut for *Save a Copy* is **Command+Option+S** (Mac) or **Control+Alt+S** (Windows). *Save a Copy* is a little different than *Save As.* Suppose you want to keep a visual record of each production step in a project. You begin the project and perform the first step. Use *Save a Copy* and name the file *Step 1.* Your original file is still on the screen and you continue on to the next step. When you finish this step, use *Save a Copy* and name this file *Step 2.* You will continue building your document, saving and naming incremental versions. Unlike *Save As,* the *Save a Copy* option allows you to continue working on the original file while the copy goes wherever you tell it to go.

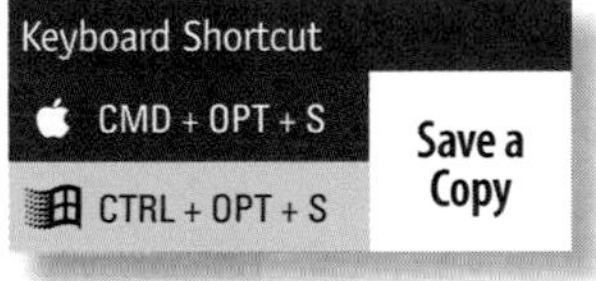

How can *Save a Copy* come in handy? Let's say it's 10:15 a.m. and you are busy getting the Zaza Toys layout ready for a client meeting at 10:30 a.m. All of a sudden you get a huge brainstorm that will radically change the look of the layout. The client has already approved the layout you are just finishing and, since it's due in 15 minutes, you don't want to take the chance of messing it up. So you use the *Save a Copy* option and name the copy *Client_Approved.* This file, completed at 10:15 a.m., is now saved somewhere on your desktop, but the original Zaza Toys file is still open.

You make all kinds of changes. You go wild. Your creative director walks by to see if you are ready for the meeting that will begin in just a few minutes. She looks at your screen and gently, but firmly suggests you change the document back to the way it was about 10 minutes ago. In a few clicks, you have *Client_Approved* opened and printed. You arrive at the client meeting on time and unruffled.

PRINTING YOUR DOCUMENT

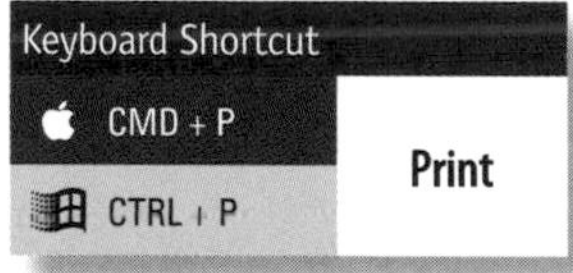

When you are ready to print your document, press **Command+P** (Mac) or **Control+P** (Windows) or choose *File>Print*. There are many options displayed in the *Print* dialog box (Visual 1–46), but the first thing you need to do is select the printer you want to use on the top of the dialog. Now, select the *Setup* options page (in the list on the left side of the dialog box), set *Paper Size* to **Letter,** and make sure *Orientation* is **Portrait.** If your document is smaller than 8.5 × 11, your finished piece will look better if you set *Page Position* to **Centered.**

In the lower left corner is a shaded box with a white rectangle and the letter "P." This is a preview of how the printer is set to print your document. The white area is the size of your paper. The "P" is the size of your document and is represented with a light shade of blue. If you change *Paper Size* to something other than letter, this preview will give you an idea of how your document will print, in relation to the size of the paper on which it will be printed. (Visual 1–46).

VISUAL | 1–46 |

The Print dialog box lists option pages down the left side of the dialog box. Check the page position preview before printing to make sure document size and orientation work with the paper it will be printed on.

© 2009 Jeffery Blackwell, Waukesha County Technical College

Summary

If you are already familiar with Adobe Photoshop or Adobe Illustrator, this chapter was an easy review. If learning Adobe InDesign is your first adventure into the world of digital page layout, this chapter covered a lot of new territory. Finding your way around the InDesign workspace was the focus of this chapter. The next chapter will build on these concepts. Like practicing the piano, using InDesign for at least 30 minutes each day will help solidify these basics and pave the way for a continual increase in your skill level.

▸ IN REVIEW

1. How can a floating panel be placed back on the panel dock?
2. What is the difference between the Selection tool and the Direct Selection tool?
3. What are the keyboard shortcuts for accessing (a) the Selection tool, and (b) the Direct Selection tool?
4. The rectangle that shows the outermost dimensions of any shape is called the ______________ ______________.
5. How are the Rectangle Frame and Rectangle tools different?
6. What are two methods of deselecting an object?
7. What is a stroke? What is a fill?
8. What is the difference between Save and Save a Copy?
9. What is the keyboard shortcut for increasing the size of type?
10. Describe the Preview view mode and its keyboard shortcut.
11. What is the keyboard shortcut for New Document?
12. What is the keyboard shortcut for View at 100%?
13. What do the "Formatting affects container" and "Formatting affects text" icons manage?
14. What is the keyboard shortcut for the Rectangle tool?
15. Where can you preview how your document will print on the paper you have selected?

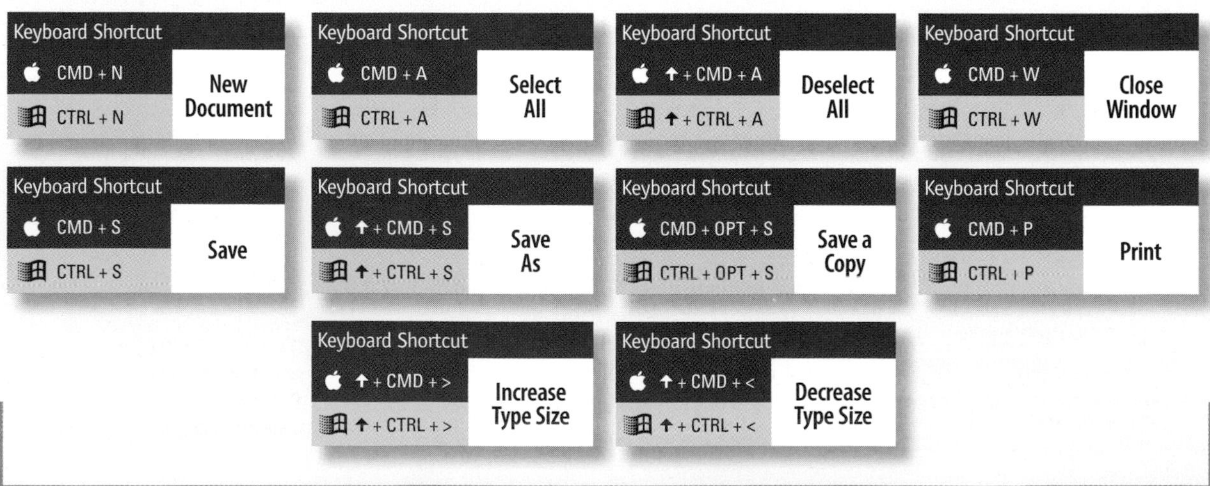

▸CHAPTER 1 PROJECT

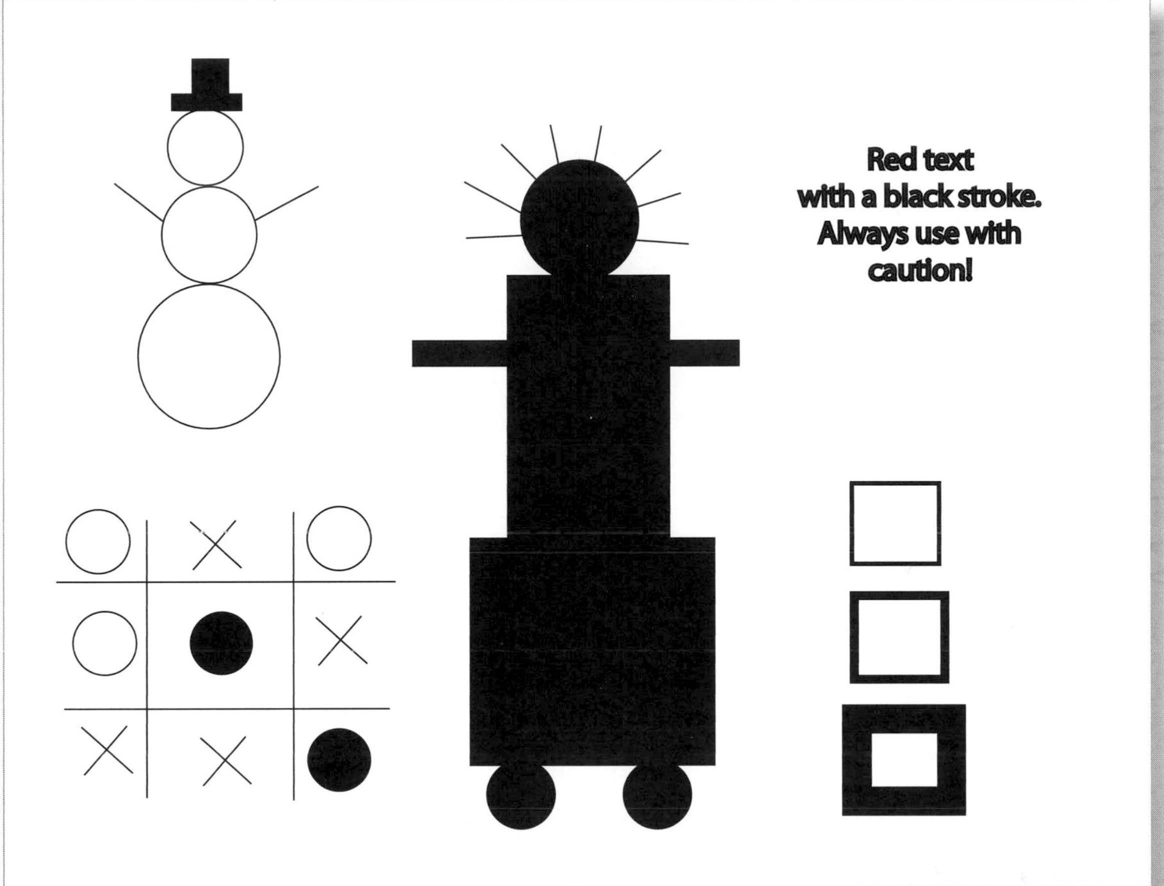
Red text
with a black stroke.
Always use with
caution!

Although it looks amazingly simple, this project will review most of the skills you learned in this chapter. And don't worry—the projects get much more interesting and difficult as the chapters progress.

Find the *01 Artwork and Resources* folder on the student online companion. Inside the folder is a file called *01 Student Handout.pdf* that contains instructions for this project. You can print it out and refer to it when creating the Chapter 1 project. As you are working on chapter projects, concentrate on using keyboard shortcuts to adjust your view so that you are not straining to see your work. Remember to practice using InDesign for 30 minutes each day!

EXPLORING INDESIGN CS6
Artwork & Resources

- Go to: http://www.cengagebrain.com
- Type: Rydberg
- Click Exploring InDesign CS6 in the list of search results.
- When the book's main page is displayed, click the Access button under Free Study Tools.
- To download files, select a chapter number and then click on the Artwork & Resources tab on the left navigation bar to download the files.

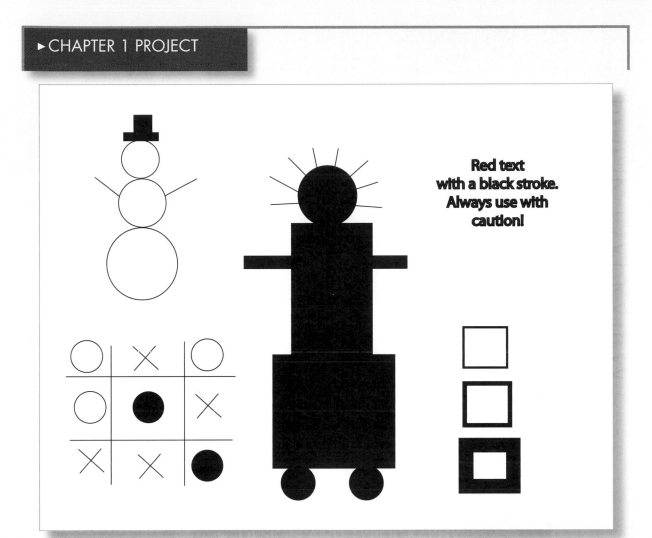

Every **great ability**
develops and reveals itself
increasingly
with every new assignment.

— Baltasar Gracian

2 | Type, Tools, and Terms |

objectives

- *Distinguish between serif and sans serif typefaces*
- *Read and interpret project markup*
- *Define type family, typeface, font, point size, and leading*
- *Define picas and points*
- *Use Character Formatting Controls in the Control panel*
- *Use Paragraph Formatting Controls in the Control panel*
- *Modify the attributes of text frames*
- *Apply fills and strokes*
- *Insert glyphs*

introduction

You are dreaming a designer's worst nightmare. A weary vacationer has just come home and his mailbox is overflowing. He plops the stack of mail onto the kitchen counter and begins the sorting process. "Keep, throw, keep, keep, throw, throw...oh, this one looks interesting, maybe I'll look at it later..." until the whole stack of mail has been separated. He picks up the stack of rejects and moves slowly to a designer's nemesis—the circular file. You helplessly call out in your sleep, "Hey, don't throw that stuff! I spent days designing those direct response mailers!" You watch your pieces fall into the dark abyss of the garbage can and you shudder as the lid closes, sealing the fate of all your hard work.

This "nightmare" is actually reality for many designers who do not know how to set type. It doesn't take the average reader more than a glance to decide whether or not to read a printed piece. If a design doesn't pass the "once-over" test, out it goes. That's the bad news. The good news is that by picking up this book, you have taken the first step in learning how to use type as a powerful communication tool. And by the time you complete *Exploring InDesign* you will know how to correctly set type. In the first chapter you learned how to find your way around the InDesign workspace. This chapter will introduce you to basic typographic terms and concepts. Knowing both InDesign and typography will give you a competitive edge in the marketplace—and save your printed pieces from the garbage can!

an eye-q test

The ability to use type as a powerful design component is a distinguishing characteristic of an experienced designer. Visual 2–1 shows some examples of typical newspaper display ads. Each row shows two versions of the same ad. The only difference between each pair is how the type is used. Which example in each pair would you most likely read? Which examples successfully communicate the message?

VISUAL | 2–1 |

Use of type is the main variable in each pair of designs.

A

B 

SHERMAN STREET PRESCHOOL STARTS SEPT. 30 The Sherman Street Preschool will have its first day of class on Tuesday, Sept. 30, at 9:30 a.m. For information and to register, please call **896-7777**

Sherman Street Preschool starts
September 30!
The Sherman Street Preschool will have its first day of class on
Tuesday, Sept. 30, 9:30 a.m.
For information and to register, please call
896-7777

You are invited to our annual
Meatball Supper
Wednesday, October 4 • 4 pm–8 pm
Houston, Minnesota

Prices
Adults $7.00
Carry outs $7.00
Kids 6–12 .... $5.50
Children $4.00

Menu
Meatballs, Buns
Mashed Potatoes & Gravy
Salad Bar, Vegetable
Homemade Pie, Beverage

Houston's City-wide
Garage Sale
Sat., Oct. 10 • 8 am – 1 pm
To be included on the map, bring a list of sale items with your name and address to Snow's Beauty Shop by Friday, September 20.

Houston's City-wide
Garage Sale
Sat., Oct. 10
8 am – 1 pm
To be included on the map, bring a list of sale items with your name and address to Snow's Beauty Shop by **Friday, September 20.**

If you selected "B" for each pair, you have just proven the power of good typesetting. Typesetting should enhance readability and strengthen the message. The type on a page should attract the reader's attention and create a visual path for the eye to follow. How you use type can make or break a layout!

VISUAL | 2–2 |

The inset shows a rough layout. The final piece is on the right.

FIRST THINGS, FIRST

When a client gives you a rough layout, how exactly do you get started? First, you must read the text and understand the purpose of the piece you are going to design. Determine which information is most important. Second, never assume that the copy provided to you is totally accurate. Take responsibility for ensuring the document's accuracy and ultimate success by making it a habit to check the following items:

- *Proofread phone numbers and zip codes. Test web addresses.*
- *Ask if product names require a ™ or ® symbol.*
- *Check that names are spelled correctly throughout the document.*
- *Consult a calendar to verify days and dates. Check that day, date, and time information is consistent throughout the document.*
- *Proofread headings and subheads because they are often overlooked in the proofing process.*

If the client gives you actual samples of the printed pieces to re-create, look for ways the pieces could be improved and discuss those changes with the client. Often project samples are filled with typesetting mistakes in form and type use. Do not duplicate poor typesetting! You are the professional—the client is coming to you for your insight and expertise.

Finally, ask how the job will be printed and finished. Will it be drilled (three-hole punched)? Will it be stitched (spine stapled)? Will it be mailed? Will there be photos and colors? These specifics will determine how you build the InDesign document.

SELECT AN APPROPRIATE TYPEFACE

Once you understand the purpose and the specifications of the project, you must put some thought into the personality you want the piece to express. The blend of typeface, image, layout, and color will create a distinct personality in each piece you design. Personalities can range from formal and powerful, to wacky and whimsical. The typeface you select will play a big part in communicating that personality. Let's say you just inherited a huge amount of money and can now have the cosmetic surgery you always dreamed of. You look in the yellow pages to choose a cosmetic surgeon. Which surgeon will you choose from the list shown in Visual 2–3?

VISUAL | 2–3 | The selection of appropriate typefaces is one of the most critical steps in any design job.

1 John Davis, M.D.
2 JOHN DAVIS, M.D.
3 John Davis, M.D.
4 JOHN DAVIS, M.D.
5 John Davis, M.D.
6 John Davis, M.D.
7 John Davis, M.D.
8 JOHN DAVIS, M.D.
9 John Davis, M.D.
10 JOHN DAVIS, M.D.

▸ *Select typeface and point size*

The following exercise will focus on the basics of text handling in InDesign. Launch InDesign. Follow these steps to create a sample document.

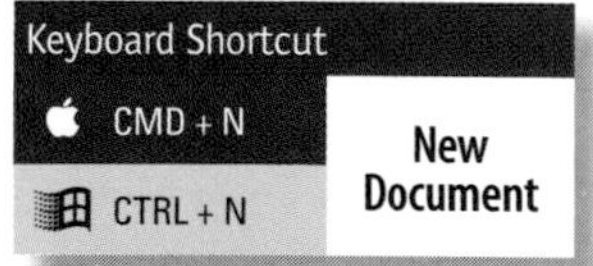

1. Press **Command+N** (Mac) or **Control+N** (Windows) to create a new document. The *New Document* dialog box will open. Your settings should be:
   Document Preset: **[Default]**
   Intent: **Print**
   Number of Pages: **1**
   Facing Pages: **Off** (*Facing pages* is another way of saying two-page spreads, similar to the left- and right-hand pages of a book. If you changed your InDesign preferences in the *Getting Started* section in Chapter 1, this should already be turned off.)
   Primary Text Frame: **Off**
   Page Size: **Letter**
   Width: **8.5 in.**, *Height:* **11 in.**
   Orientation: **Portrait**
   Number of columns: **1** (ignore the *Gutter* field for now)
   Margins: **0.5 in.** (top, bottom, left, right).

2. Press the **Return** or **Enter** key. Remember, it's easier and faster to press the Return key rather than to click OK with your mouse.

Your document will appear in a window with two rulers—one at the top and the other along the left side of your window. The upper left corner of your document should be at zero on the horizontal ruler, and the upper right corner should be at 8.5. Along the vertical ruler, the upper left corner of your document should be at zero and the lower left corner should be at 11. Your document should look like Visual 2–4. You will also notice a colored line around the inside of your document. This is the half-inch margin you set in the *New Document* dialog box. (If you did not change your InDesign defaults in the *Getting Started* section in Chapter 1, your measurements will be displayed in picas. This measurement system will be discussed later, and we will cover changing the ruler units of measure in the next chapter, so don't worry about them for now.)

▸ *production tip*

It's faster to press the Return or Enter key than to click OK with your mouse.

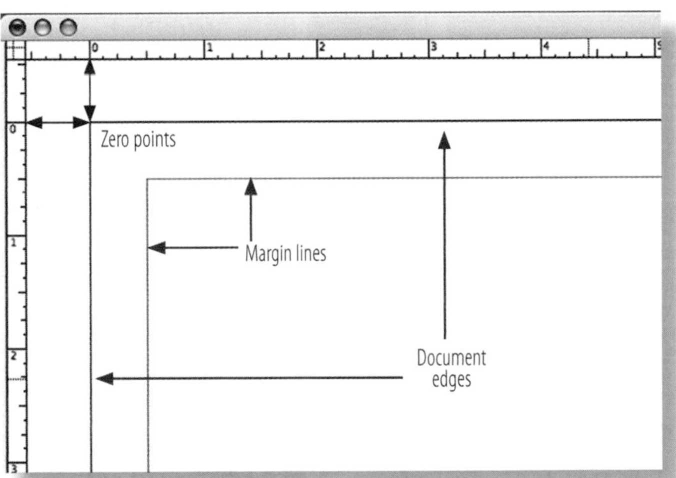

VISUAL | 2–4 |

The upper left half of your newly created document. Note the upper left corner positioned at 0,0.

▸ *Add text*

1. Use the keyboard shortcut **T** to select the ***Type*** tool from the ***Toolbox***. Put your cursor inside the upper left margin of your document, and then click and drag a text frame down and across the page. Wherever you stop will determine the size of your frame. If your frame is too small or you don't like the shape of it, hold down **Command** (Mac) or **Control** (Windows) and press the letter **Z**. This is one of the best shortcuts to know—Undo. InDesign allows you unlimited undos. (Don't you wish your life had unlimited undos?) Repeat drawing frames and "undoing" them until your frame stretches nicely from the left to right margins.

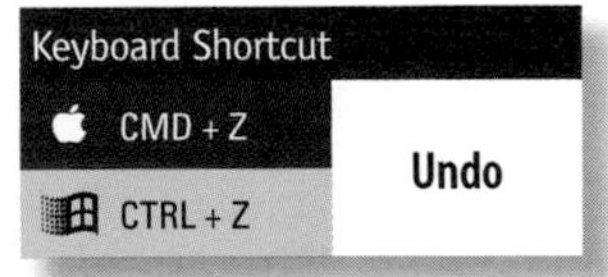

2. Make sure a blinking cursor is in your frame. If you don't see a blinking cursor, check to see that you have the ***Type*** tool selected and click inside the frame. Type a few sentences about the fondest memories you have of elementary school. After typing three or four sentences, press the **Return** key once and type three or four more. Don't press the ***Return*** key twice (see *Moving to Mastery*, on the next page).

▸ MOVING TOWARD MASTERY

two important rules for working with type

#1: Don't press the spacebar twice at the end of sentences when using proportional type. *One of the first rules you may have learned in junior high typing class was to put two spaces between sentences by pressing the spacebar twice after each period. This is the first habit you will need to break when using InDesign. The practice of using two spaces between sentences began in the days of typewriters. Type on old-fashioned typewriters was* ***monospaced****, which means that each letter was allotted the same amount of space in the text line whether it was an "i" or an "m." The extra space was inserted to visually separate sentences. With electronic publishing, most of the fonts used are* ***proportionately spaced****, which means that each letter, character, or symbol has been allocated just the right amount of space.*

#2: Enter only one *Return* after each paragraph. *Pressing the* ***Return*** *key more than once is the second habit you will have to break. With the old typewriter, you put in two carriage returns to separate paragraphs. We will learn how to add extra spacing between paragraphs in a later chapter, but start getting into the habit of not pressing* ***Return*** *more than once.*

▸ *production tip*

Pressing the Command (Mac) or Control (Windows) key will change the cursor to a single- or double-headed arrow, allowing you to adjust frame size.

3. If your text frame is too small to contain all the text, you will see a small, red square with a plus sign in the lower right corner of the frame indicating the text is ***overset.*** An overset symbol means you will need to make the frame larger, or modify the amount or size of the copy. It's easy to resize a frame when using the ***Type*** tool. Pressing the **Command** (Mac) or **Control** (Windows) key will change the cursor to a single- or double-headed arrow, and make frame handles appear. Drag on any handle to resize the frame. Release the **Command** or **Control** key, and the ***Type*** tool cursor reappears. Notice that a text frame looks different than a rectangle frame (Visual 2–5). The extra boxes on a text frame are the ***in port*** and ***out port*** indicators, and will be discussed further in Chapter 4. Next, you will learn how to change the typeface and the type size. This project continues after a brief description of the ***Control*** panel.

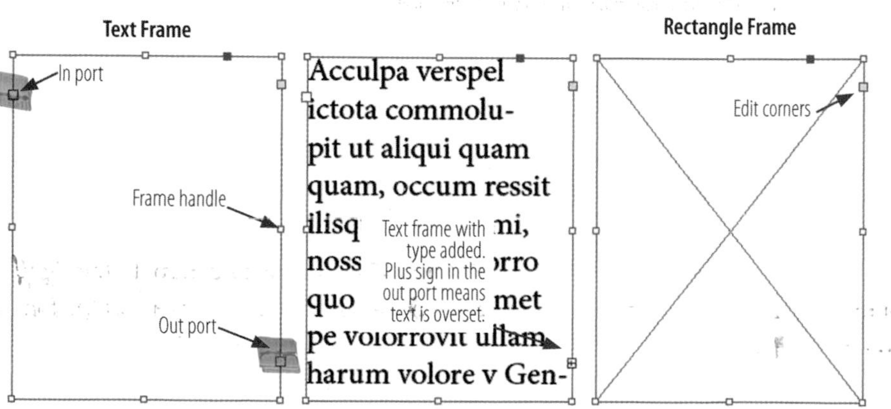

VISUAL | 2–5 | You can recognize a text frame by two extra little boxes, the in port and out port indicators. Clicking in any frame with the Type tool will convert it to a text frame. When a red + appears in the out port, it means the text is overset.

USE THE CONTROL PANEL TO CHANGE TYPEFACES

When you select the *Type* tool, the *Control* panel will display either the *Character Formatting Controls* or the *Paragraph Formatting Controls* with the most frequently needed functions grouped on the left side (Visual 2–6). In Chapter 1, you were introduced to the *Control* panel, now we'll look at this context-sensitive tool bar in more detail. Many of the text and paragraph functions can be accessed in either the *Character* or *Paragraph Formatting* mode of the *Control* panel. All of these functions are also available on other panels that you access from the *Window* menu. But it's faster to use the *Control* panel to modify paragraphs and text, rather than opening a panel from *Window >Type & Tables*.

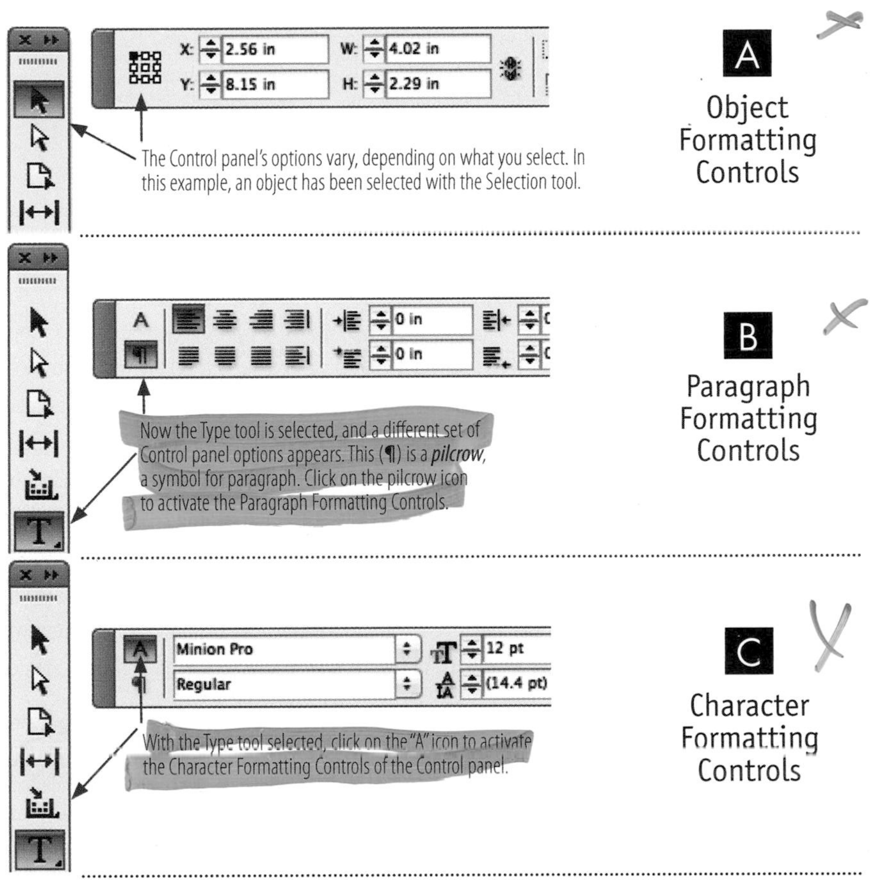

X: 2.56 in
Y: 8.15 in
W: 4.02 in
H: 2.29 in
The Control panel's options vary, depending on what you select. In this example, an object has been selected with the Selection tool.
A
Object Formatting Controls
0 in
0 in
Now the Type tool is selected, and a different set of Control panel options appears. This (¶) is a *pilcrow*, a symbol for paragraph. Click on the pilcrow icon to activate the Paragraph Formatting Controls.
B
Paragraph Formatting Controls
Minion Pro
Regular
12 pt
(14.4 pt)
With the Type tool selected, click on the "A" icon to activate the Character Formatting Controls of the Control panel.
C
Character Formatting Controls

VISUAL |2–6|

Look at the icon on the left end of the Control panel to see which formatting mode is active.

To change a typeface, you first select the *Type* tool, and then click the *Character Formatting Controls* icon on the *Control* panel. Highlight the text by dragging the cursor over the passage you wish to change. The current type family name will be displayed in the upper field (Visual 2–7). Then, click the menu control to the right of the *Type Family* field and move up or down the list to select the name of the font you desire. Your font list will display a sample of each typeface. Each font listing is a separate *type family*. On a Mac, triangles at the right end of family names indicate

VISUAL | 2–7 |
The upper field displays the name of the type family. The type style is displayed in the lower field.

▸ *production tip*
Enter the first few letters of the name of a typeface in the Type family field to quickly find it in the Font list.

type styles are available in the family. Visual 2–8 shows the type family, Helvetica, with two type style options, Regular and Bold. With a long list of fonts, scrolling through typeface names beginning with "A" to get to those beginning with "Z" will be time consuming. A quick way to select a typeface is to type the first letter of the typeface in the *Type Family* field. InDesign will automatically jump to the first typeface beginning with that letter. For instance, if you type a "M" for Minion Pro, the list would jump to the first typeface in the list beginning with "M", making it much easier to quickly scroll to Minion Pro.

VISUAL | 2–8 |
On a Mac, triangles indicate type styles within the type family.

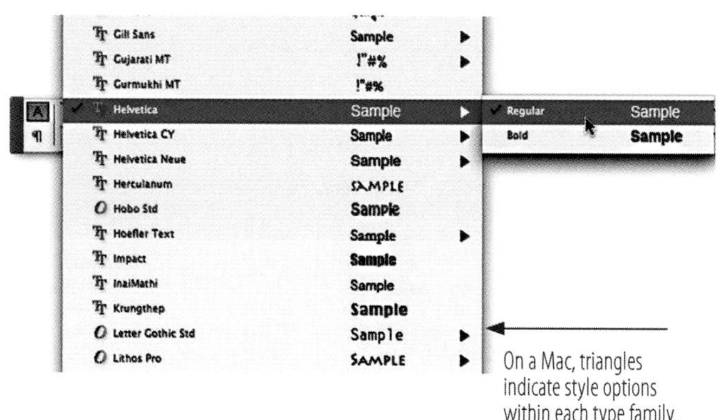

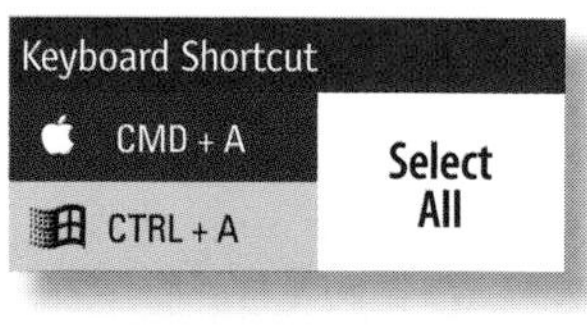

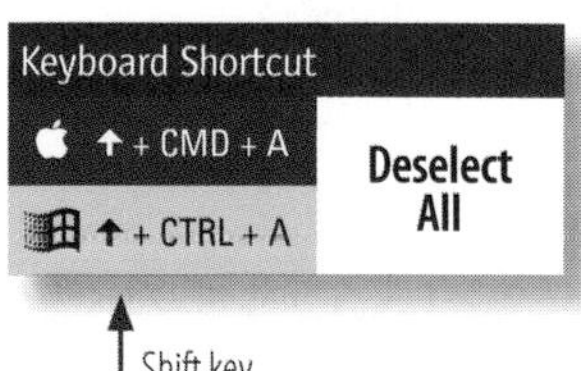

4. Highlight part of your text and change it to **Helvetica** and change the rest to **Minion Pro**. With the *Type* tool active, select all the text in your box by using the keyboard shortcut **Command+A** (Mac) or **Control+A** (Windows). Look in the *Type Family* field and you will see that the field is blank. A blank field means there are two or more different values for that field in your selected text—in this case, Minion Pro and Helvetica. With all the text still selected, change all the type back to **Minion Pro** by selecting the font name from the type family list. Now, Minion Pro appears in the *Type Family* field.

▸ *Change the type style*

A *type family* is a collection of related typefaces in different weights called *type styles*. To change a type style, highlight the text, and select the type style from the *Type Style* field underneath the *Type Family* field in the *Control* panel (Visual 2–7).

▸ *Change the size of type*

To the right of the *Type Family* is the *Font Size* field (Visual 2–9). The default type size is set at 12 points. Type specifications are measured in points and picas. Twelve points equal one pica. One inch equals 72 points or 6 picas.

There are several ways you can change the point size of selected text. One is to highlight the value in the *Font Size* field, enter a new value, and then press **Return**. Another is to use the controls on the right or left side of the *Font Size* field to change the point size in 1-point increments or to one of the preset sizes (Visual 2–9). But when working in InDesign, you want to do things as quickly and efficiently as possible. The fastest way to increase point size is to highlight the text and press **Command+Shift+>** (Mac) or **Control+Shift+>** (Windows). Each time the greater than key is pressed the point size will increase. To decrease the point size, press **Command+Shift+<** (Mac) or **Control+Shift+<** (Windows). These shortcuts will increase or decrease the type size by a specific amount set in the *Units & Increments Preferences* (the default is 2 points; we changed the default to 1 point in the *Getting Started* section in Chapter 1). If you also hold down the **Option** (Mac) or **Alt** (Windows) key, the point size will change in increments of five times the preference setting. Experiment with these techniques as you modify your text. The exercise will continue after a discussion of leading, so don't close your document!

▸ *production tip*

When a field in the Control panel is blank, it means that the selected text has more than one setting for an attribute, for instance, two different point sizes.

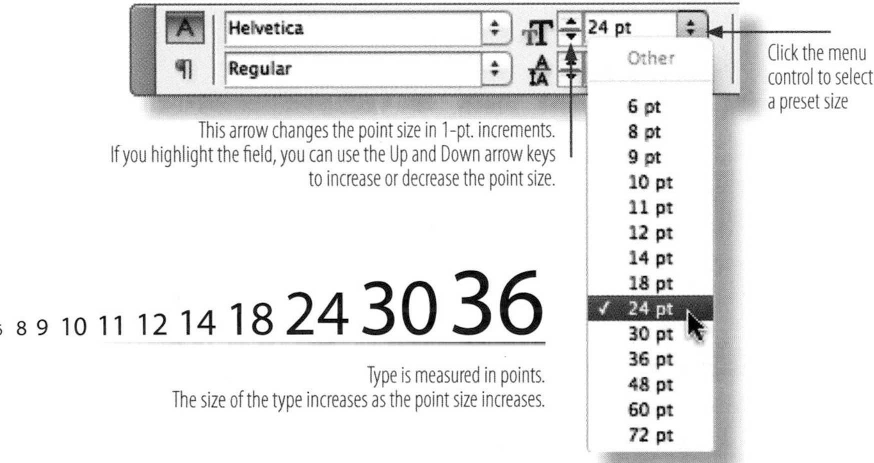

VISUAL | 2–9 |

The Font Size field.

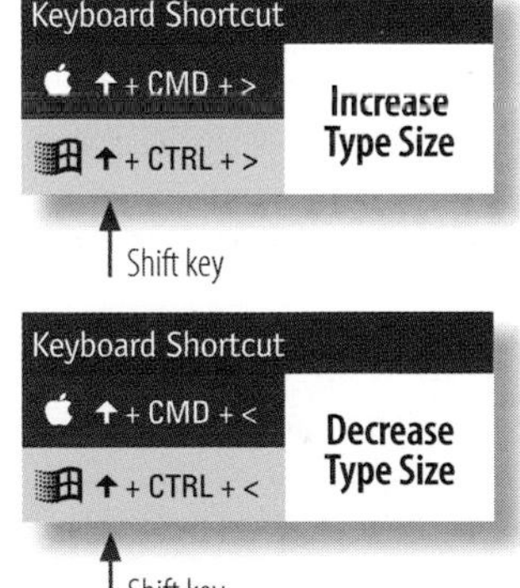

ABOUT LEADING

The distance between one line of type to the next is called *leading* (rhymes with "sledding"). Each line of type sits on an imaginary line called a *baseline*. Like type size, leading is measured in points, from baseline to baseline. Knowing how to adjust the space between lines is important. Depending on how it is applied, leading can increase or decrease readability. If it is too tight, the individual lines of type blend together, making reading difficult. If leading is too loose, each text line stands alone, which can reduce comprehension.

VISUAL | 2–10 |

The baseline is an imaginary line on which type sits.

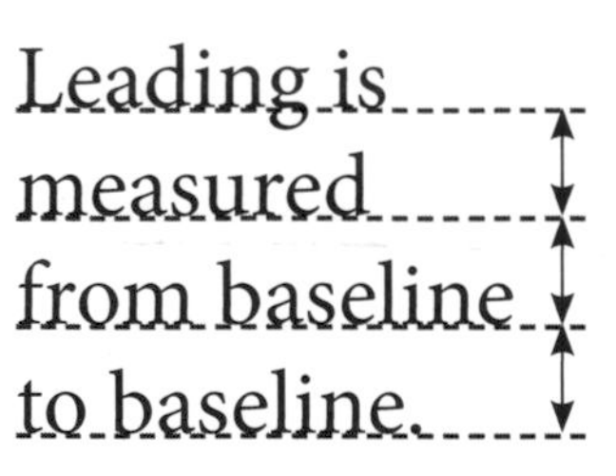
Leading is
measured
from baseline
to baseline.

AUTO AND ABSOLUTE LEADING

There are two types of leading: *auto* leading and *absolute* leading. Auto (automatic) leading is just what the name implies: determined automatically by InDesign. By default, the point size of the text is multiplied by 120% to get the leading value. (The default setting for auto leading is 120%, but you can change the percentage in the *Justification* dialog box.) For example, if type size is 10, auto leading will be 12 points (10 × 120% = 12). With auto leading, as the size of type increases, the leading value also increases—automatically. Using Auto leading can give text passages an "airy" look, which may not be desirable. For the most control over line spacing you will want to use absolute leading. With absolute leading, you enter a value in the *Leading* field. Once that value is entered, leading remains the same—unless you choose to change it!

VISUAL | 2–11 |

The Leading field. A value enclosed with parentheses means auto leading is applied.

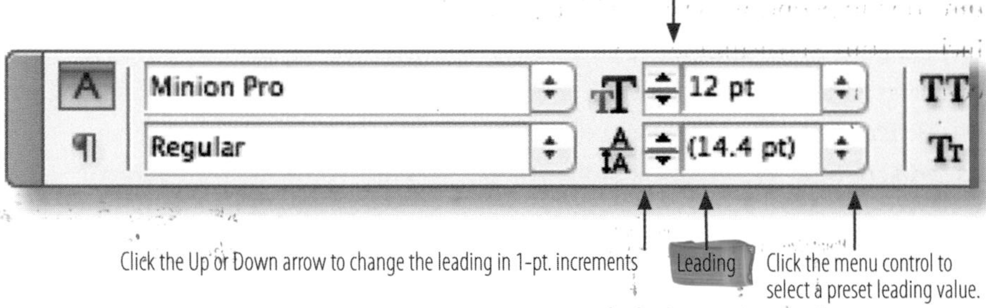
Font size
Minion Pro
Regular
12 pt
(14.4 pt)
Click the Up or Down arrow to change the leading in 1-pt. increments
Leading
Click the menu control to select a preset leading value.

Leading can be *positive* (when the leading value is greater than the type size), *negative* (when the leading value is less than the type size), or *set solid* (when the leading and type size values are equal). You will usually use positive leading in body copy, and negative or solid leading with large type (called *display type*).

VISUAL | 2–12 |

Most of the time, you will want to avoid using auto leading. Auto leading usually looks a bit too "airy." When setting headlines you will frequently use solid or negative leading

When the leading value is greater than the point size of type, it is ***positive*** leading.

13 pt. type
15 pt. leading

When the leading value is less than the point size of type, it is ***negative*** leading.

13 pt. type
11 pt. leading

When the leading value is the same as the point size of type, it is ***set solid.***

13 pt. type
13 pt. leading

The *Leading* field is below the *Font Size* field on the *Control* panel (Visual 2–11). Highlight the text passage and experiment with absolute leading by entering a value in the *Leading* field. Also experiment with applying the preset leading values.

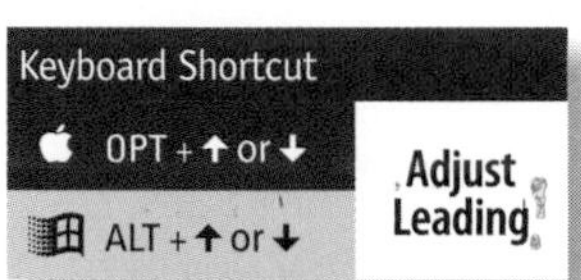

An alternative (and very fast) method to change leading is to select the text, hold down the **Option** (Mac) or **Alt** (Windows) key, and click the **Up** or **Down Arrow** keys. The leading value will change in increments set in your preferences.

POINTS, PICAS, AND MARKUP

Markup is a universal system of coding providing written direction to people who work with type. Basic markup includes three measurements, written much like a math equation. The type size (specified in points) is listed first, as the numerator, and leading (also specified in points) as the denominator.

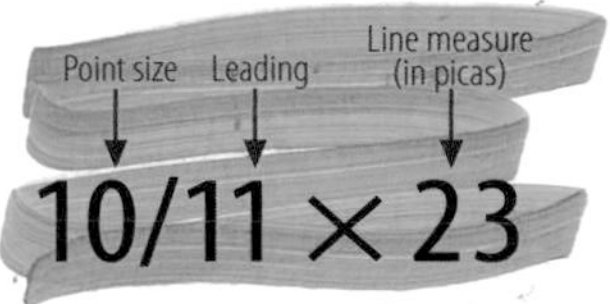

Line length or *measure*, follows the × and is usually measured in picas. If you are given a marked-up document you immediately know what to enter in the various fields in the *Control* panel. Markup will be used in projects throughout this book. Visual 2–13 shows an example of a passage set according to markup specifications.

The measurement system of *picas* and *points* may be new to you. Six picas equal one inch. Twelve points equal one pica. An inch is broken down into 72 tiny point-sized increments. The pica-point measurement system is ideal for setting type because we are usually working in small units of measure. It is easier to visualize how 5 points of leading will look, rather than a leading value of 0.069444, its equivalent in inches.

▸ MOVING TOWARD MASTERY

type basics

WHAT IS A "FONT"?

In the early days of printing, type was set by hand, letter by letter. A printer needed an actual piece of metal type for each letter and symbol in every size of any given typeface. The collection of all the characters, numbers, symbols and punctuation of a particular typeface in a specific point size was called a font. Our modern typefaces are not metal but digital, and you don't purchase a new font for each point size you plan to use. Today, the terms ***font*** *and* ***typeface*** *are often used interchangeably, as in the case of this textbook.*

SERIF AND SANS SERIF FACES

Serifs *are tiny finishing strokes on the end of the letter. Typefaces are classified as either* ***serif*** *(with serifs) or* ***sans serif*** *(without serifs).*

Serif Faces	Sans Serif Faces
Caslon Pro	Myriad
Times	Kievit
Minion	Futura
Warnock Pro	News Gothic

ONE BIG, HAPPY TYPE FAMILY

Just like members of your own family, these related typefaces from the ITC Garamond family come in all shapes and weights.

ITC Garamond Family	
Light	Bold Condensed
Light Italic	Bold
Light Narrow	Bold Condensed Italic
Light Condensed	Ultra
Book Italic	Ultra Condensed
Book Condensed	Ultra Condensed Italic

VISUAL | 2–13 |

The original copy (top) has been set (below) according to the typographic markup specifications: set in Times Roman, 10 pt. font size, 11.75 pt. leading, line length 20 picas.

If your boss gave you a choice—buy more stock photography or buy more typefaces—which would you choose? If you're like me, the answer to this question is easy. I am always looking for well-designed type families with a variety of weights and styles.

Original copy

Set in: **Times Roman 10/11.75 x 20 picas**

12 points = 1 pica
6 picas = 1 inch
72 points = 1 inch

If your boss gave you a choice—buy more stock photography or buy morc typcfaccs—which would you choose? If you're like me, the answer to this question is easy. I am always looking for well-designed type families with a variety of weights and styles.

VISUAL | 2–14 |

When the pica and point measurement system is unfamiliar, an E-gauge helps you visualize units of measure. This sample has a fraction-to-decimal conversion chart which is also quite helpful.

Fraction Conversion Chart

Fraction	Decimal	MM	Picas	Points
1/16	.0625	1.587	p4.5	4.5
1/8	.125	3.175	p9	9
3/16	.1875	4.762	1p1.5	13.5
1/4	.25	6.350	1p6	18
5/16	.3125	7.937	1p10.5	22.5
3/8	.375	9.525	2p3	27
7/16	.4375	11.112	2p7.5	31.5
1/2	.5	12.7	3p	36
9/16	.5625	14.287	3p4.5	40.5
5/8	.625	15.875	3p9	45
11/16	.6875	17.462	4p1.5	49.5
3/4	.75	19.050	4p6	54
13/16	.8125	20.637	4p10.5	58.5
7/8	.875	22.225	5p3	63
15/16	.9375	23.812	5p7.5	67.5
1	1.0	25.4	6p	72

WCTC
waukesha county technical college

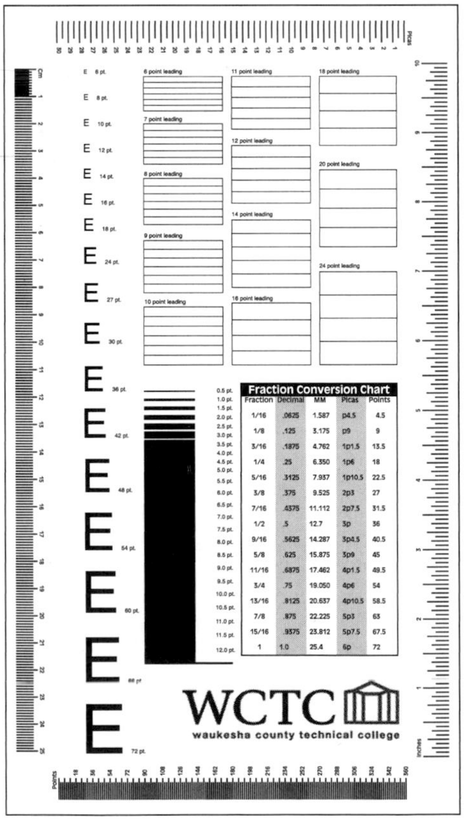

One helpful tool for getting a visual "feel" for the pica-point system is an E-gauge. Use it to estimate the point size of type and measure line lengths. Available in many styles, they can usually be found at art supply stores. Generally, E-gauges have a pica and point scale and a series of E's that descend in size. You estimate the type size by comparing a capital letter with the various size E's on the E-gauge.

▸ *Create an information card*

Let's use the *Contr*ol panel as we put together another simple project. In this project you will make a 5" × 3" custom-size document to create an information card. When creating projects, first complete the typing. Then, change all the type to the most frequently used typeface, point size, and leading. Finally, fine-tune individual words and passages of type.

1. Create a new document. ***Width:* 5" *Height:* 3" *Margins:* 0.5"**. In this document, the orientation will be ***landscape***, since the width is greater than the height.

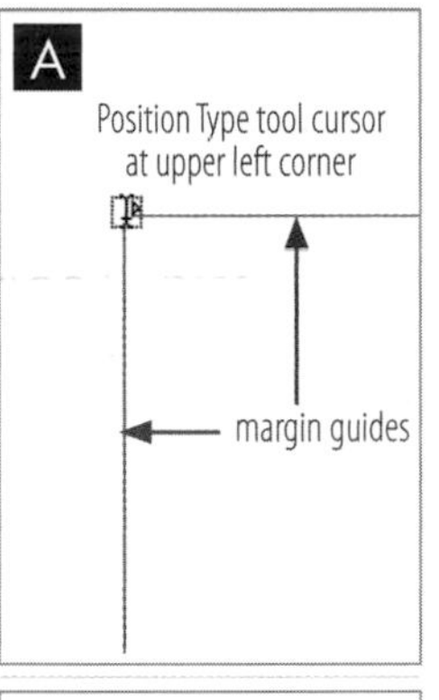

Note: ***In graphic design, the width of an object is always the first dimension specified.***

2. Select the ***Type*** tool by pressing **T**. You will create a text frame that covers the entire area inside the margins. Position the ***Type*** tool cursor on top of the upper left and top margins. A small triangle will appear (A), indicating that your frame will snap to the margin guide. As you click and drag a text frame diagonally down to the lower corner, a light grey information box (B) will tell you the width and height of your frame (Visual 2–15). Release the mouse when you reach the intersection of the lower right and bottom margins. If you don't like the frame you made, use the Undo shortcut and draw the frame again.

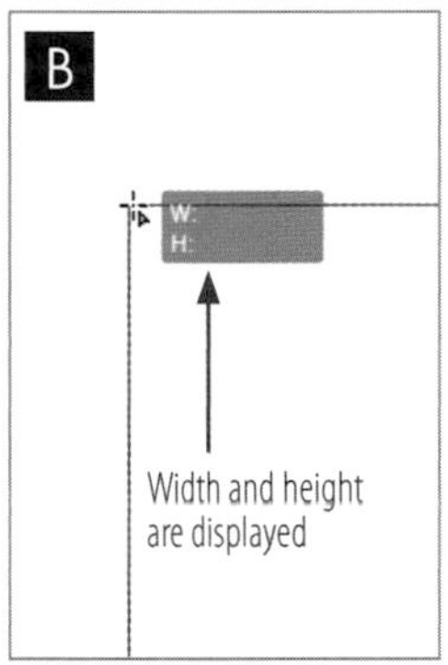

VISUAL | 2–15 |

When the Type tool I-beam is positioned over a margin guide, a triangle appears to show that the frame will snap to the guide. As the frame is created, a gray information box displays the width and height.

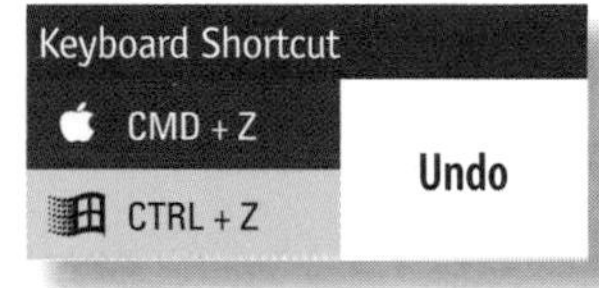

3. Type **Name:** and then type your **first** and **last name**. Press **Return**.

4. Type **Address:** and then type your **local address**. Press **Return**. Type your **city**, **state**, and **zip code**. Press **Return**. Type **E-mail:** and complete the information. Press **Return.** Complete the rest of the form with the information, as shown in Visual 2–16.

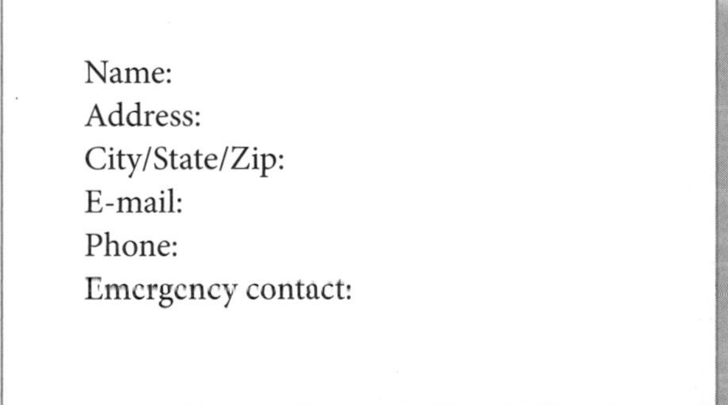

VISUAL | 2–16 |

The information card is shown reduced from its actual size.

5. Press **Command+A** (Mac) or **Control+A** (Windows) to select all the type. Change the font to **Minion Pro 15** (*point size*) **/19** (*leading*). If you don't have Minion Pro, select Times, or a similar typeface.

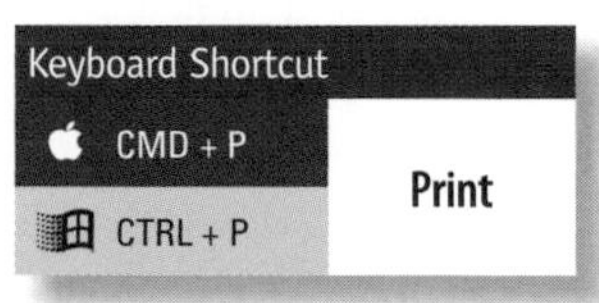

6. Print your document. Press **Command+P** (Mac) or **Control+P** (Windows). When the ***Print*** dialog box opens, look in the ***Printer*** field and make sure your printer is selected (Visual 2–17).

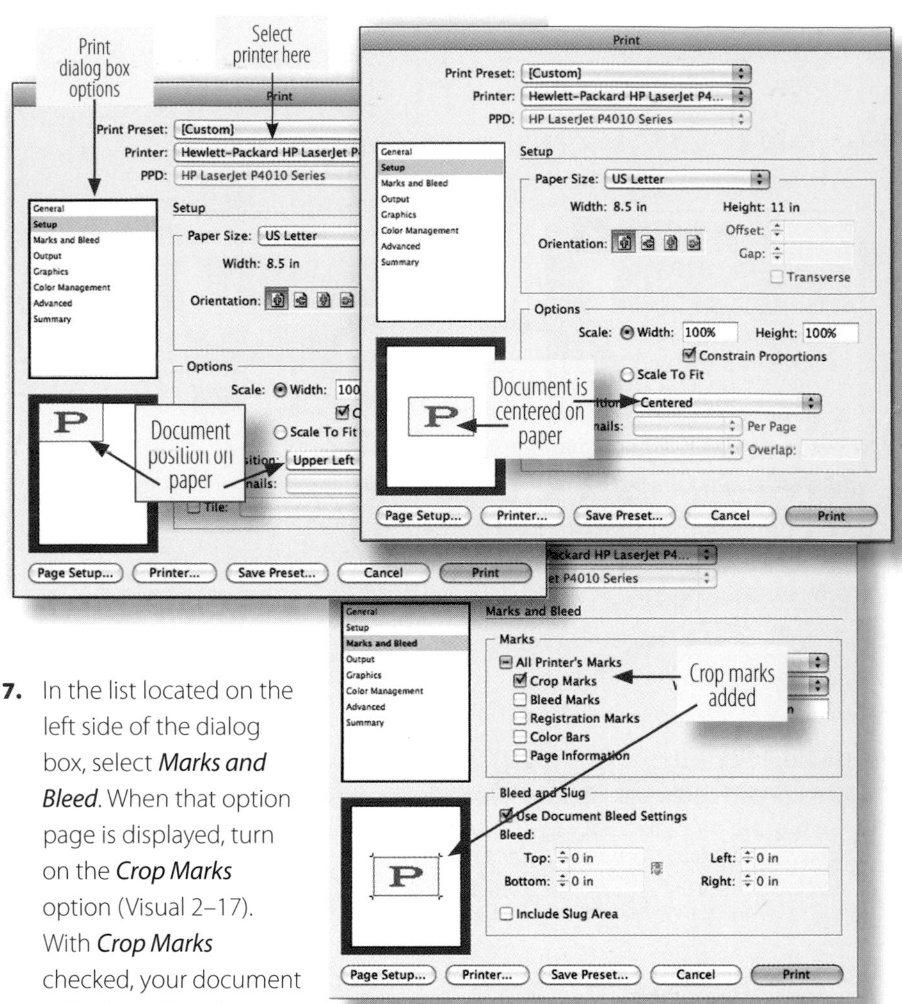

VISUAL | 2–17 |

The Print dialog box contains a list of printing options on the left side. When you click on each item in the list, a new window of options is displayed.

7. In the list located on the left side of the dialog box, select *Marks and Bleed*. When that option page is displayed, turn on the *Crop Marks* option (Visual 2–17). With *Crop Marks* checked, your document will print with L-shaped lines at each corner. Crop marks indicate the 5 × 3 size of the document printed on the letter-sized paper. Crop marks allow you to trim a document to its actual size. Select **Print** and your project is complete!

A NEW SYSTEM OF MEASUREMENT

▸ *production tip*

Indicating points and picas in fields:

6p = 6 picas
p6 = 6 points
6p6 = 6 picas, 6 points

Measuring and placement will be covered in detail in Chapter 4. But now is a good time to explain how units of measure work inside InDesign's panel fields. When your document is set to measure in inches and you want to set a value in points, simply replace the number and measurement suffix with the new value and measurement suffix. In the case of points, enter 6 points with a *p* before the number as in *p6*. For picas, the *p* follows the number; so 8 picas would be *8p*. If the document preference is set to points or picas and you want to enter a unit of measurement in inches, you will need to type the number plus the suffix *in* or the quotation mark (").

CHANGE THE UNITS OF MEASURE

Let's change the document's units of measurement preferences. Press the **Control** key, and **click** on the **horizontal ruler** (Mac), or **right-click** on the **horizontal ruler** (Windows). Choose a different unit of measurement. Do the same with the vertical ruler. That's how easy it is to change the measurement system used in any document. Using this method, you can switch back and forth between measurement systems whenever you want.

▸ *production tip*

To quickly change the units of measure within a document, Control+Click (Mac) or right-click (Windows) on a horizontal or vertical ruler.

USE FIELDS TO ADD, SUBTRACT, MULTIPLY, AND DIVIDE

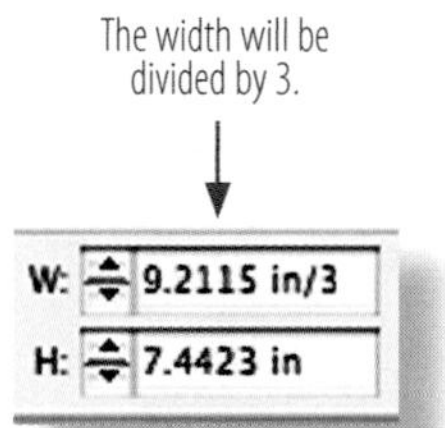

VISUAL | 2–18 |

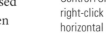

You can add, subtract, multiply and divide in the panel fields by entering the correct symbol. Here, the width of the object will be divided by 3.

When you are using the *Selection* tool (black arrow) and select an object, you will notice that the *Control* panel changes to display *X*, *Y*, *W*, and *H* fields. The *W* and *H* fields stand for the width and height of the selected object. InDesign allows you to perform addition, subtraction, multiplication, and division calculations on values, right in the field. For instance, let's say your document's measurement system is set to inches and you have a 4-inch rectangle, but want to add 5 points to the width. With the rectangle selected, place the cursor in the *W* field (after the 4 in value), type **+p5** (5 points) and then press **Return**. Five points will be added to the rectangle's width dimension and the resulting number in the *W* field will be converted to inches (4.0694 in). When performing calculations in fields, use the hyphen (-) to subtract, the asterisk (*) to multiply, and the slash (/) to divide.

InDesign converts the dimension typed in a *Control* panel field to the current unit of measurement. For instance, if you are working in picas and enter 1", the value in the *Control* panel will read *6 p0* when you press *Return* or *Tab*. When your document is set to one measurement system and you want to input a value in a different measurement system, you must type that measurement's suffix. In the last example, the inches suffix (*in* or ") would need to be typed in the field, because the document's unit of measurements is set to picas. Conversely, if your document is set to measure in inches, you must add a *p* after the number to indicate picas, or before the number to indicate points.

By now you know that you can use the *Type* tool to create a frame for text. As soon as you release the mouse a blinking cursor is wagging its tail at you, eager for you to begin typing. In the next project, you will incorporate text frame options as you create a stylish bookmark. Visual 2–19 shows how the text of the bookmark has plenty of room inside the bordered text frame. Creating "breathing space" around type is an important skill to learn!

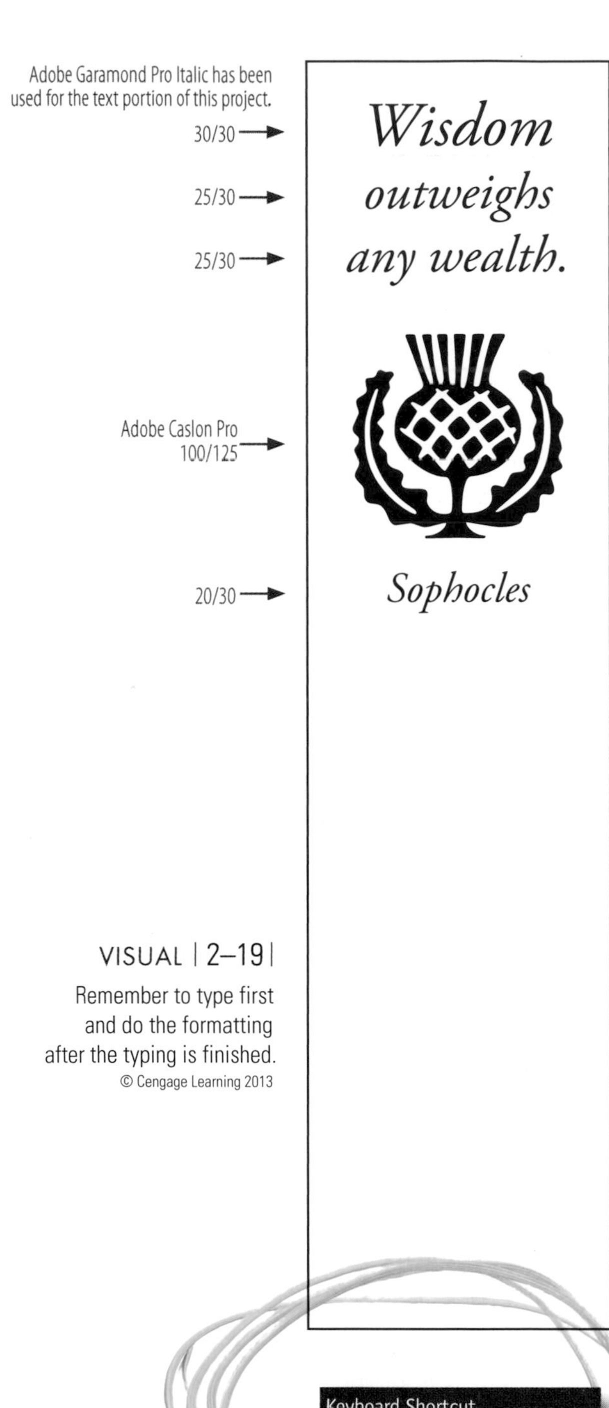

VISUAL | 2–19 |

Remember to type first and do the formatting after the typing is finished.

Keyboard Shortcut

CMD + B / CTRL + B — **Text Frame Options**

▸ Use text inset and the Glyphs panel

1. Create a new document, **8.5" × 11"**. Accept the default settings. Select the ***Rectangle*** tool (or press **M**) and draw a small box somewhere near the upper middle part of your document. The ***Rectangle*** tool has a black stroke as a default.

2. Look at the ***Control*** panel to check which unit of measurement you are using. If necessary, change the unit of measurements to inches, as described earlier. With the frame selected, change the *W* field to **2"** and the *H* field to **7"**.

3. Now select the ***Type*** tool and click the frame. Press **Command+B** (Mac) or **Control+B** (Windows). The ***Text Frame Options*** dialog box opens. The ***Text Frame Options*** dialog box is one you will use often! Enter **.25"** in the ***Top, Bottom, Left,*** and ***Right*** fields of the ***Inset Spacing*** area. When setting inset spacing, click the ***lock icon*** in the center to apply the value in the active field to all four fields. Press **Return**.

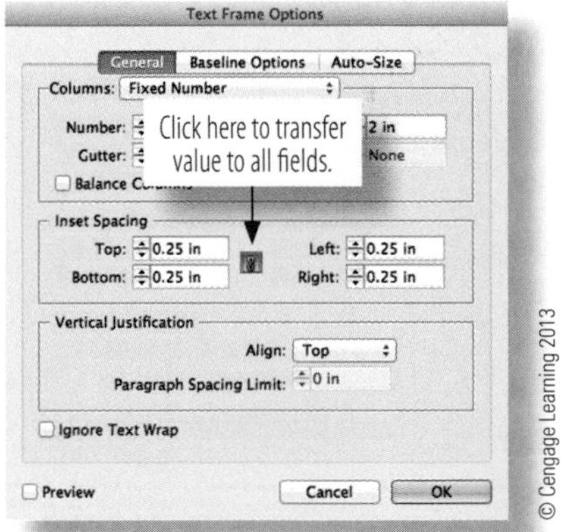

4. Make sure you are still using the ***Type*** tool. Click inside the text frame, and notice that the cursor is 0.25 inches away from the edges.

5. Type the copy as shown in Visual 2–19. Remember, ***type first, format second.*** Press the **Return** key after the word, ***wealth***. Type a **z** which will act as a placeholder for the decorative glyph you will add later. Press **Return**. Then type **Sophocles**. Carefully follow the mark up shown in Visual 2–19.

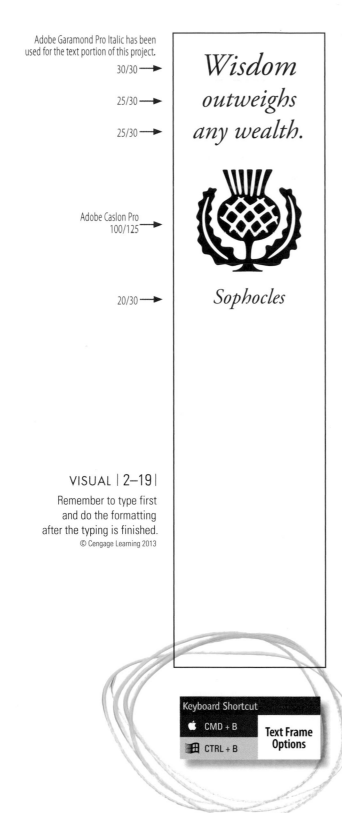

6. Select all of your text. Center the type horizontally by selecting it and pressing **Shift+Command+C** (Mac) or **Shift+Control+C** (Windows).

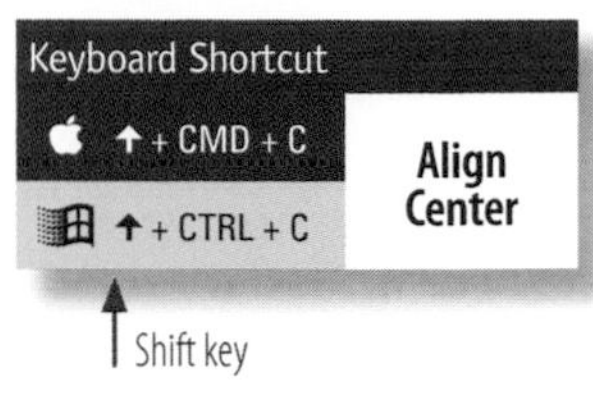

The decorative shape on the bookmark is called a *glyph*. Glyphs are characters, numerals, punctuation, ornaments, or anything else included in a type font. When you choose *Glyphs* from the *Type* menu, the *Glyphs* panel will open and display the entire list of characters and ornaments included in the active font. In the lower left corner of the panel is a drop down menu for selecting other fonts. Click on the arrow to the right of the font name and your system's entire font collection will show up in the font list. Go ahead, scroll through the list and examine the glyphs from other fonts. You can magnify the glyphs in the panel by clicking the icon of the large mountain in the lower right corner and use the scroll bars on the right side of the panel to view all the glyphs on display. Each typeface's glyphs are organized into categories. For easier viewing, smaller groups of glyphs can be shown by making a selection from the drop down menu located at the top left of the panel (Visual 2–20).

▸ *production tip*

When you select Show Options from the Glyphs panel menu, InDesign will display a row of recently used glyphs at the top of the panel.

7. To insert a glyph in your document, highlight the "z" you typed earlier as a placeholder and then double-click a glyph from the *Glyphs* panel and that symbol will replace the highlighted "z." The glyph shown in the example is found in Adobe Caslon Pro.

You can view all the available glyphs, or use this pull down menu to view specific glyph categories.

Type family

Type style

Enlarge or reduce view

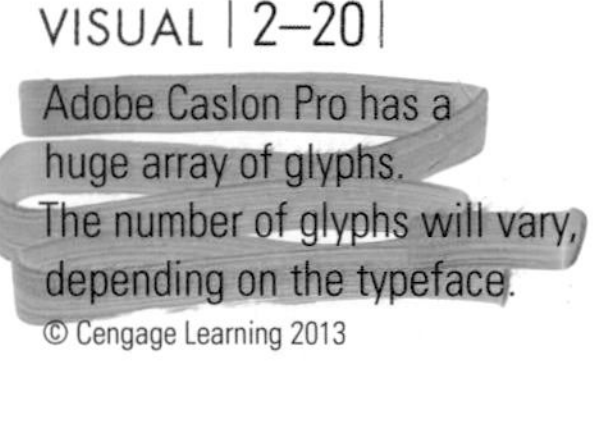

VISUAL | 2–20 |

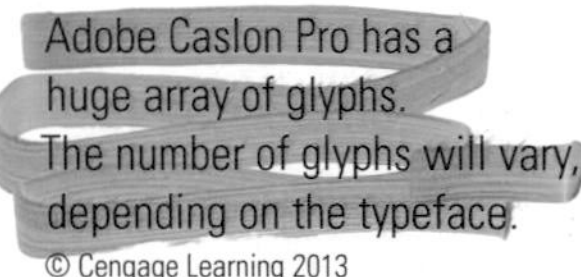

Adobe Caslon Pro has a huge array of glyphs. The number of glyphs will vary, depending on the typeface.

8. If it is not still highlighted, double-click the glyph you inserted in your bookmark project. On the *Control* panel, click the *Character* symbol and increase the point size and leading. The glyph shown in the project example is **100/125** (point size/leading).

9. Give the document a final proof. Is everything spelled correctly? Is the size of the bookmark 2 × 7 inches? Is the combination of the typeface and selected glyph pleasing to the eye? Always give your projects an additional "once-over" before going to print. You will also want to look carefully at your project after it is printed. You will see things on the hard copy that you may miss on the computer screen. Make your edits and print again.

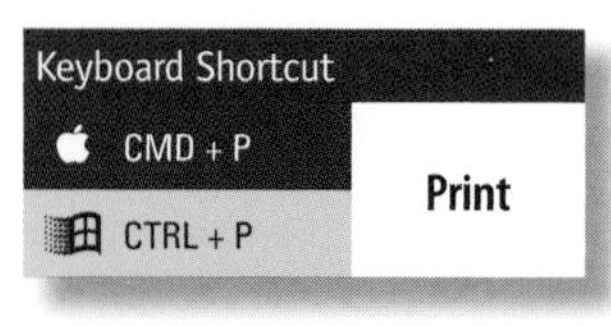

▸ MOVING TOWARD MASTERY

fills and strokes

1. *Fills and strokes can add interest to a layout. To add a fill, first click the object with the* ***Selection*** *tool. Then, click the* ***Fill*** *icon on the* ***Control*** *panel and choose a fill color from the fly-out menu.*

2. *To add a stroke, select the object with the* ***Selection*** *tool and click the* ***Stroke*** *icon on the* ***Control*** *panel. Choose a stroke color from the fly-out menu.*

The stroke ***Weight*** *field allows you to change the thickness of the stroke. You can increase the thickness in increments of 1 point, or use the preset values from the control on the right side of the field.*

Use the ***Style*** *field to add interest to your frame. Stroke styles include dots, dashes, diamonds, waves. If you don't see a style that has been applied, be sure the stroke has a color, or increase its weight.*

▸ production tips

Default colors are always applied. But the 1 pt. stroke weight is only applied if there is no current weight specified. It's easy to apply the default *Stroke* color (Black) and *Fill* (None) to any object. Simply activate the object with the *Selection* arrow and press **D.**

You can swap the stroke and fill of any object by activating it with the *Selection* arrow and pressing **Shift+X.**

When you are changing the thickness of a stroke, you can highlight the *Weight* field and then use your **Up** and **Down** arrow on the keyboard to adjust the weight.

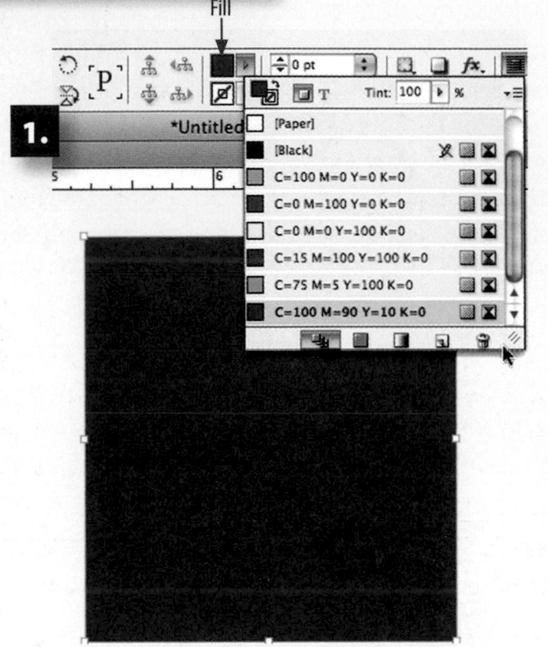

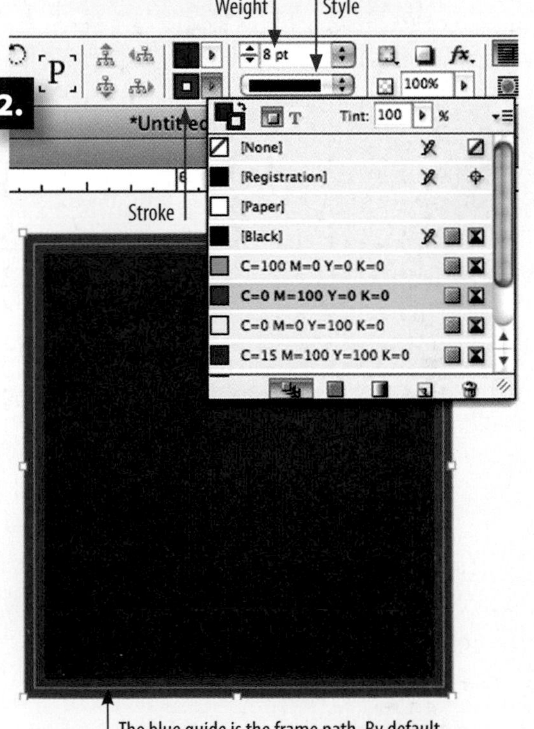

The blue guide is the frame path. By default, a stroke's thickness is evenly split on each side of the frame path.

the production sequence

An efficient method of constructing any project is summarized in these seven steps:

1. **Format the correct size.** It would seem that having the correct document size or frame size would be simple, but many errors are made during this initial step! An easy method of creating a frame to the exact size is to select the ***Rectangle*** or ***Rectangle Frame*** tool and simply click on your document. A window will pop open, and you can enter the measurement values for your shape.

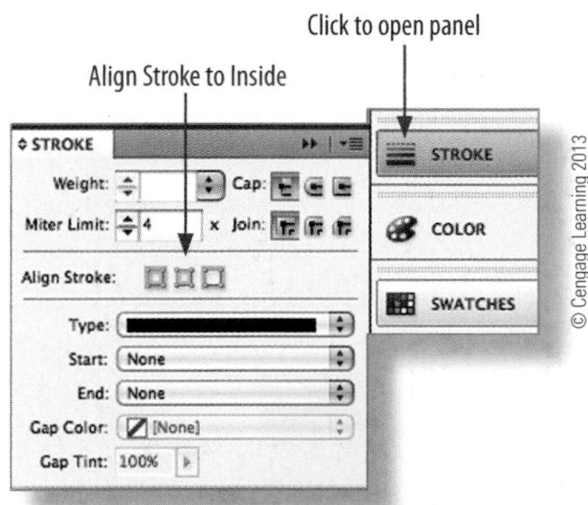

2. **Add and align the outer stroke as needed.** By default, a stroke's width is split on each side of an object's path (see bottom of previous page). Consequently, when a stroke is added to an object, the dimensions of the object change. In future chapters, you will learn how to adjust the width and height of an object. For now, simply open the ***Stroke*** panel from the dock and with the object selected, click the ***Align Stroke to Inside*** icon and use the W and H coordinates to recheck your frame measurements. We'll discuss coordinates in Chapter 4.

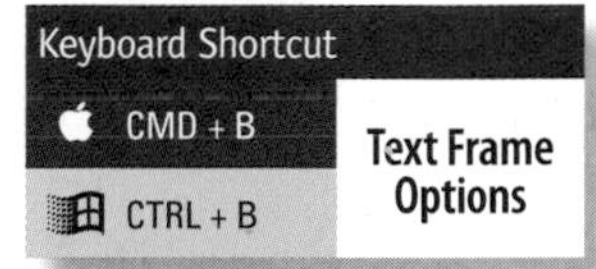

3. **Create a text inset.** When a frame has a stroke, it usually needs a text inset to keep the type away from the edge. Press **Command+B** (Mac) or **Control+B** (Windows) to open the ***Text Frame Options*** dialog box and add an inset. Do this before typing!

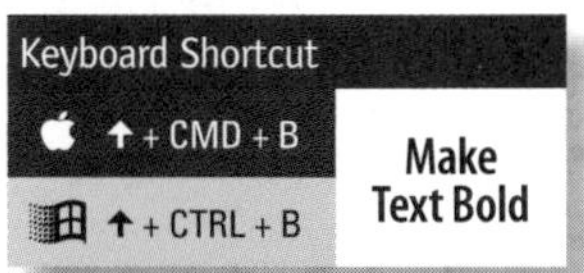

4. **Typing.** Remember to type first and format later! As you're typing, press the Return key only one time at the end of paragraphs. Type a **z** to hold an insertion spot for any glyphs. Don't worry how your text initially looks—you will fix it later. It is always good to save your document after this step is completed!

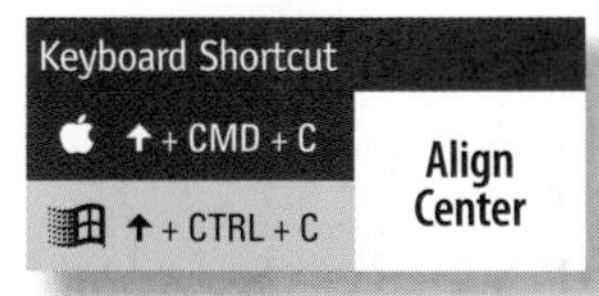

5. **Specify the character formatting.** First, adjust the point size, font, and style. Then adjust the leading. Use keyboard shortcuts whenever possible.

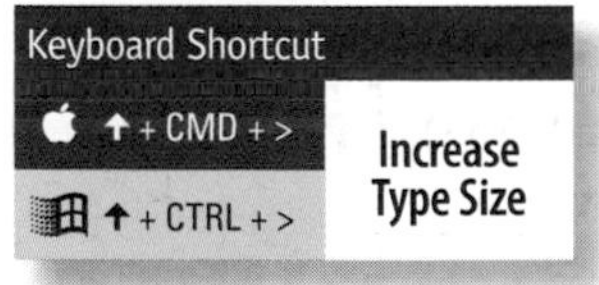

6. **Specify the paragraph formatting.** We'll work on paragraph formatting in a future chapter, but here are a few tips for now. If your copy consists of continuous, narrative text, you should ***not*** press Return at the end of each line, but let the text automatically flow to the next line. If your copy is made up of individual text lines and different point sizes, placing a Return at the end of each line will allow for the greatest flexibility in adjusting leading.

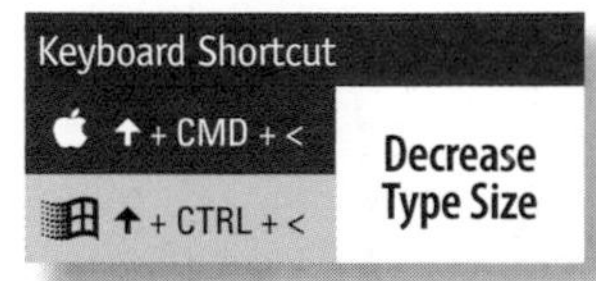

7. **Proof your work carefully and print.** Proof the hard copy after printing.

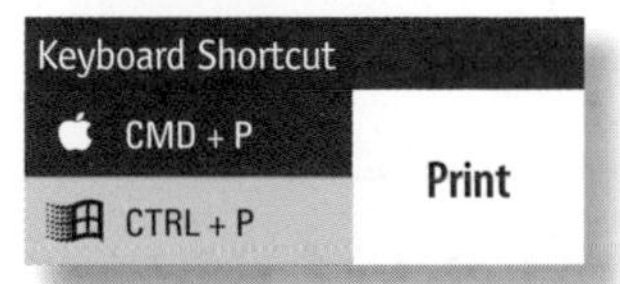

▸ MOVING TOWARD MASTERY

Good and bad production habits are formed early in the process of learning software. After years in the classroom, I have identified characteristics of students who achieve software proficiency.

1. Students who achieve proficiency use the software on a daily basis. Daily repetition secures techniques and keyboard shortcuts into long-term memory banks. Students who complete a lesson, but don't use the software until the next class session, always struggle with essential functions covered previously.

2. Students who achieve proficiency recognize the importance of learning any technique and memorizing shortcuts that will increase speed. Avoid using the menu bar to access panels—it's a hard habit to break. Use keyboard shortcuts whenever possible.

Here are some tips from the masters:

- *Create your default document preset with no document open. Press* ***Command+Option+P*** *(Mac) or* ***Control+Alt+P*** *(Windows) and specify your parameters. This will allow you to turn default settings, like facing pages, on or off.*
- *A quick way to highlight any field is to click on its label (left of the field) rather than the field itself.*
- *Most fields also allow you to increase or decrease the field value by pressing the* ***Up*** *or* ***Down Arrow*** *keys on the keyboard.*
- *When the OK button is highlighted in a dialog box, press* ***Return*** *rather than moving your mouse to click OK.*
- *Type first, and begin formatting text after the typing is completed.*
- *If your laptop doesn't have separate function keys, press the* ***Fn*** *key as you choose a number key.*

Summary

We covered a lot of ground in this chapter. You were introduced to basic typesetting terminology: typeface, type style, font, serif and sans serif typefaces, leading, markup, picas, and points. Three important typesetting practices were covered: one space between sentences, one return after paragraphs, and type first, format second. Typesetting techniques such as changing typefaces, point size, and leading, inserting glyphs, and centering type were introduced. You learned to use a text frame inset with type in a stroked box. You changed the units of measurement, created containers for text using both the *Frame* and *Type* tools, modified the dimensions of a text box using the *Control* panel, and added a stroke of varying widths and styles. You honed your production skills by memorizing and using shortcut keys. But we've only just begun. Now you are ready to begin the fine art of setting type.

▸IN REVIEW

1. How can you differentiate a sans serif typeface from a serif typeface?
2. Why is it not necessary to add extra space between sentences by pressing the spacebar twice?
3. How many points are in an inch?
4. What is a glyph?
5. What Text Frame option should you always use when you have applied a stroke to a frame containing copy?
6. How do you change the units of measurement in a document?
7. When describing a document's measurements, which dimension is listed first: the width or the height?
8. How can you center your 7" x 5" document on letter-size paper during printing?
9. What is a keyboard shortcut for creating a bold type style?
10. List the seven steps in the production sequence described in the chapter.

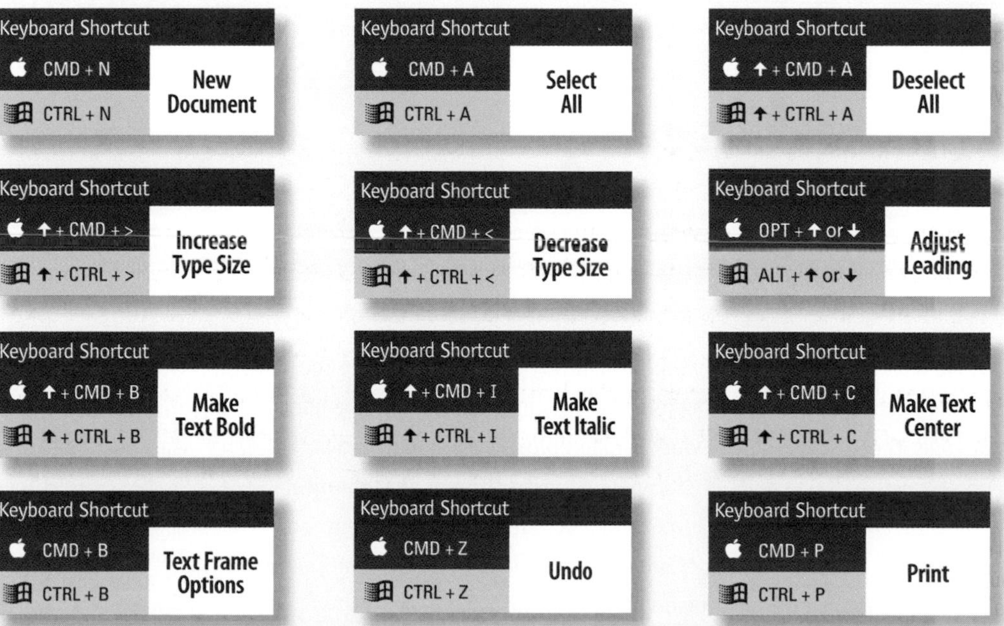

Keyboard Shortcut
CMD + N
CTRL + N
New Document
Keyboard Shortcut
CMD + A
CTRL + A
Select All
Keyboard Shortcut
↑ + CMD + A
↑ + CTRL + A
Deselect All
Keyboard Shortcut
↑ + CMD + >
↑ + CTRL + >
Increase Type Size
Keyboard Shortcut
↑ + CMD + <
↑ + CTRL + <
Decrease Type Size
Keyboard Shortcut
OPT + ↑ or ↓
ALT + ↑ or ↓
Adjust Leading
Keyboard Shortcut
↑ + CMD + B
↑ + CTRL + B
Make Text Bold
Keyboard Shortcut
↑ + CMD + I
↑ + CTRL + I
Make Text Italic
Keyboard Shortcut
↑ + CMD + C
↑ + CTRL + C
Make Text Center
Keyboard Shortcut
CMD + B
CTRL + B
Text Frame Options
Keyboard Shortcut
CMD + Z
CTRL + Z
Undo
Keyboard Shortcut
CMD + P
CTRL + P
Print

►CHAPTER 2 PROJECTS

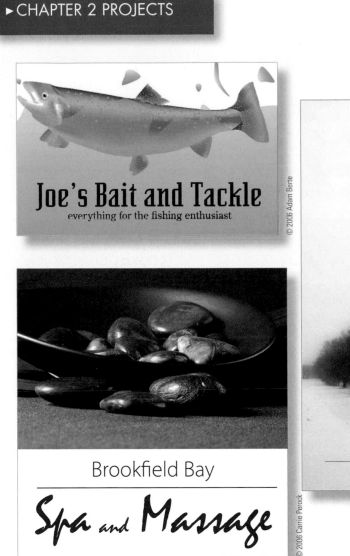

© 2006 Adam Berte

© 2006 Carrie Perock

© 2010 Billy Knight, Waukesha County Technical College

At first glance, these projects may look complicated, but they aren't! You have learned the skills necessary to complete them—you will need to remember how to apply those skills. As you work through projects, you will notice that they don't have the same level of step-by-step instruction as those projects within each chapter. This is deliberate. When you get your first design job, projects will not come with instructions—you will need to demonstrate your problem-solving abilities and software proficiency on a daily basis.

EXPLORING INDESIGN CS6
Artwork & Resources

- Go to: http://www.cengagebrain.com
- Type: Rydberg
- Click Exploring InDesign CS6 in the list of search results.
- When the book's main page is displayed, click the Access button under Free Study Tools.
- To download files, select a chapter number and then click on the Artwork & Resources tab on the left navigation bar to download the files.

▸ CHAPTER 2 PROJECTS

As you progress through this textbook and your skill improves, the directions with each project will only include the basic specifications needed to create the project. Find the project source files in the *02 Artwork and Resources* folder on the online companion resources.

The digital illustrations and photography that enhance each of these projects have been created by students at Waukesha County Technical College. Although they have agreed to share their artwork, it remains their copyrighted work. Use of the images is limited to projects in this publication. Any other use is unprofessional and illegal.

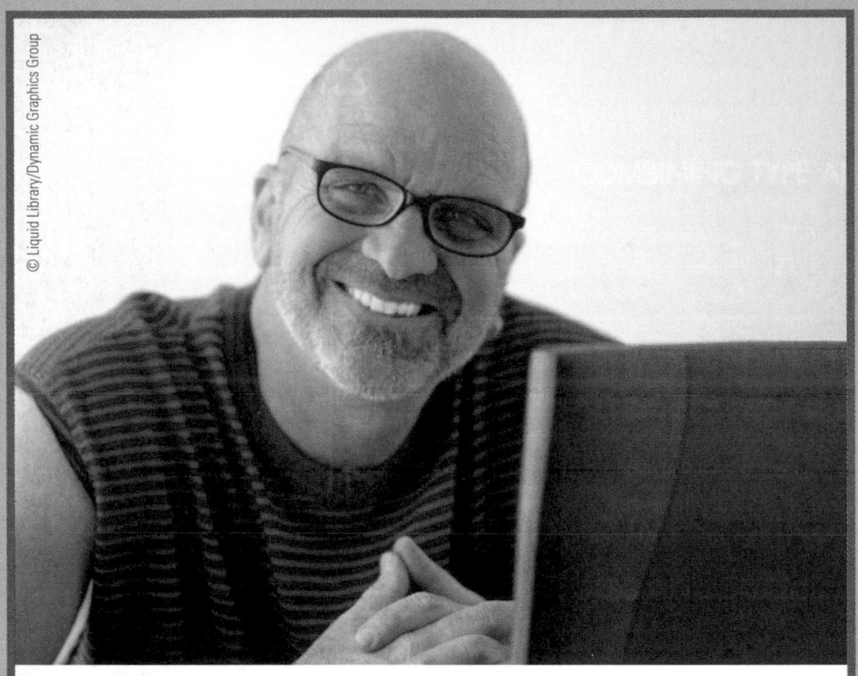

Experience
is that marvelous thing
that enables you to recognize
a mistake when you make it again.

— Franklin P. Jones

| The Fine Art of Setting Type |

objectives

- *Identify the anatomical parts of letters*
- *Interpret hidden characters to identify hard and soft returns, spaces, and other formatting*
- *Use paragraph formatting features and punctuation: space before and after, drop and raised caps, hyphenation, optical margin alignment, balance ragged lines, alignment, quotation marks, and prime marks*
- *Differentiate between hyphens and dashes, and use each correctly*
- *Calculate ideal line measure*
- *Interpret proofreading marks*

introduction

Sometimes it's tempting to cut corners. When working on that design job for your aunt, or doing a "freebie" for a volunteer organization, you may be tempted to throw typographic principles to the wind and just slam out the job. You may be able to get away with poor typesetting—occasionally. But sooner or later, your boss, creative director, or prepress technician will open your digital files and be appalled at your unprofessional and unorthodox production techniques. You don't want to gain a reputation as a designer with excellent design capabilities, but horrible production and typography skills! That's why it's so important to develop good production habits right from the start.

Design projects can range from pizza coupons to annual reports. You should incorporate basic typesetting standards in all the projects you do. High-end jobs undoubtedly go beyond the basics and require more time and effort to incorporate precise specifications, styles, baseline grids, and so on. You will learn to match the level of typesetting with the level of the project—but only after you thoroughly understand the basics of production and typography.

Putting type on a page without incorporating typographic principles is merely word processing. Creating text that enhances communication, while incorporating correct typography, is an art. Welcome to the fine art of setting type.

the anatomy of type

My husband worked in his father's farm machinery business as he was growing up. While most of us can correctly identify the slow-moving machine we pass on the road as a tractor, my husband can still identify the make, model, and era of almost any tractor he sees. Because he was surrounded by machinery on a daily basis, he learned how to identify specific features and differentiate between models.

The process of identifying typefaces works the same way. First, you learn to classify type as sans serif or serif. Then, you begin to recognize that different typefaces have different personalities. (Remember the example of choosing your cosmetic surgeon in Chapter 2?) But before you can go deeper into type identification and selection, you will need to recognize the nuances of the anatomical parts that make up letters. It's difficult to discuss typeface selection with a person who says: "I need a letter g that has an upper part and a curved thing-a-ma-bob on the bottom." Because choosing a typeface is a critical step in any project, we begin this chapter by discussing the anatomical parts of a letter.

As presented in Chapter 2, each line of type sits on an imaginary line called a baseline. Other structural points of reference, with which you should become familiar, are shown in Visual 3–1.

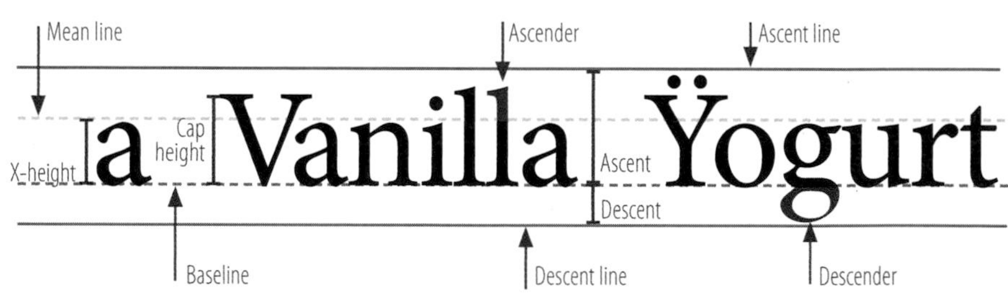

VISUAL |3–1|

Terms used as reference points when discussing type measurements.

- ***X-height:*** *the distance from the baseline to the top of a lower case x*
- ***Mean line:*** *a horizontal line drawn parallel to the baseline at the x-height*
- ***Cap height:*** *the space from the baseline to the top of a capital letter*
- ***Ascender:*** *parts of a letter that extend above the mean line*
- ***Descender:*** *letter parts that extend below the baseline*
- ***Descent:*** *the distance from the baseline to the bottom of the longest descender*
- ***Ascent:*** *the distance from the baseline to the top of the highest ascender*
- ***Point size:*** *determined by adding the ascent and descent*

CALCULATING POINT SIZE

Point size is not determined by measuring an upper case "F." Instead, point size is calculated by measuring the distance from ascent line to the descent line. Variations in these measurements, from typeface to typeface, can make a 25-point font in one typeface look much different than a 25-point font in another typeface. Compare the size of the lower case letters in the two type samples shown in Visual 3–2.

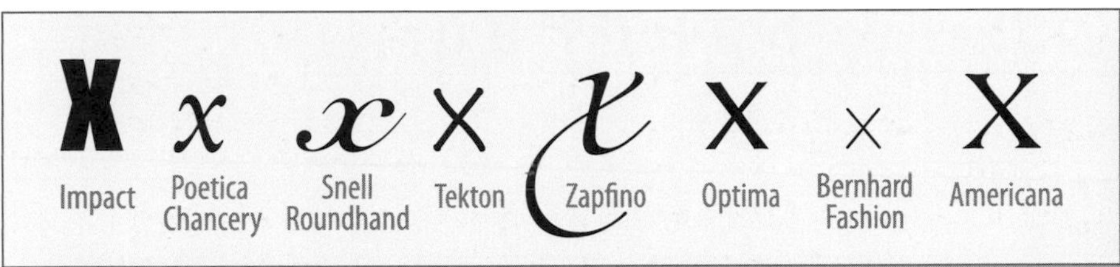

Each lower case *x*, shown above, has the same point size.

VISUAL |3–2|

Point size measures the overall "footprint" of an entire font. Some fonts that have very long ascenders and descenders look smaller than other faces when set at the same point size, as shown in the lower example.

ANATOMICAL PARTS OF A LETTER

The anatomical parts of letters deal with letter structure, shape, and finish. Although some anatomical parts are specific to one or two letters, most appear in many letters. Although not complete, the charts shown in *Moving Toward Mastery* on the next two pages provide the most common letter parts. When you can identify the nuances in the structural makeup of a letter, you become better at identifying and choosing typefaces.

Often a client will bring in a printed sample for you to match. Finding the perfect font match can be time consuming. You can speed up that process by using an online font identification site such as: ***www.identifont.com.***

► *production tip*

Use *www.identifont.com* to find the name, manufacturer, and designer of any type sample.

This site narrows your search through thousands of typefaces by asking you questions about the anatomical features of specific letters. The database sorts through the possible options based on your responses and ultimately gives you likely typeface matches from which to choose.

▸ MOVING TOWARD MASTERY

Structure-related anatomy

Term	Definition	Examples
Apex	the pointed intersection where two strokes meet at the top of a letter	A M N
Arm	a horizontal or diagonal stroke having one end unattached	Y K Z E F L Z
Ascender	the part of a lower case letter that extends above the meanline	b d f h k l t
Bar	a horizontal stroke that connects two sides of a letter	e e H A
Bowl	the curve that forms a closed space in a letter	B b D d P p q
Crossbar	a horizontal stroke that crosses another	f t T
Descender	the part of a letter that extends below the baseline	J g j p q y
Hairline	very thin letter stroke or serif	A F H K M N
Leg	refers to the tail in upper and lowercase ***K***	K k
Link	the curved stroke that joins the top to bottom of lower case 2-story ***g***	g g g g g
Loop	the curved stroke of the lower case ***g***	g g g g g
Shoulder	a curved stroke that isn't closed	m n
Spine	the main curve of the upper and lower case ***s***	S s S S S
Stem	a vertical stroke within an upper or lower case letter	B d E F t l k l N
Stress	strokes go from thick to thin as in calligraphy. Connect thin areas to determine direction of stress	b b O O Q Q R R
Stroke	basic letter component representing one curved or straight pen stroke	A D H b l n Y
Tail	downward slanted stroke—one end attached to letter body	K k Q R X x y
Vertex	the point on the bottom of the letter where two strokes meet	N V W w v

▸ MOVING TOWARD MASTERY

Shape and finishing anatomy

Term	Definition	Examples
Aperture	the amount of space between open ends of letters	C c S s G e a
Ball	a style of terminal, shaped like a dot	f a c j r y
Beak	a style of terminal with a pointed end	f a c j r y
Bracket	a curved shape that joins a serif to the stem	P d f h H I
Counter	the closed or partially closed shape within a letter	e g B b a m
Crotch	the angled space formed when diagonal strokes meet	w v W y
Ear	the small part on top of a lower case *g*	g g g g g g g g
Finial	a tapering end of letter	j c e t y
Serif	a cross, finishing stroke at the end of a letter. Can be wedge, square (slab), hairline, or cupped	H H H H H
Slab serif	a serif wth a block shape	E H E E H E
Spur	the lower extension on some upper case **G**s	G G G G G G G
Square serif	See slab serif	
Swash	a decorative, alternate letter that includes a flourish	K M N Q R W
Teardrop	a terminal shaped like a teardrop	a c f j r s
2-story A	has an upper and lower part as contrasted with a one-story A: ɑ	a a a a a a a a
2-story G	lower case g with a loop connected with a link as contrasted with a one-story: g	g g g g g
Ligature	two or three letters connected into a single unit	fl fj ffi ffl st ft Th

▸ *production tip*

When viewing your document in Preview mode, the document's hidden characters won't show.

Photo © 2006 Erik P. Berg

▸ MOVING TOWARD MASTERY
Use the chart below to identify each of the hidden characters in the text block shown underneath the portfolio.
Hard return ¶
Soft return ¬
Spacebar •
Tab »
End of story #
FEAR LESS
American Typographer
8
Your Portfolio¶
Don't underestimate the power of your portfolio!¬
It must convince future employers that you can.¶
» • communicate visually¶
» • work within project specifications¶
» • understand and apply typographic principles¶
» • understand a design objective and¬
articulate your creative rationale¶
» • create campaigns according to¬
strategic marketing plans.¶
Without a portfolio, you have no evidence to support the claims that are made in an interview!#

UNDERSTANDING HIDDEN CHARACTERS

When you press a key that does not produce a letter, number, or punctuation mark—for example, the *Spacebar*, the *Tab* key, or the *Return* key—a hidden character is placed in your document. By default, hidden characters are not visible. You can make the hidden characters in your document visible by pressing **Command+Option+I** (Mac) or **Control+Alt+I** (Windows). This keyboard shortcut is a toggle shortcut, which means you use the same key sequence to turn hidden characters on or off. Different hidden characters are represented on the screen by different symbols. When hidden characters are turned on, you will see many tiny symbols on your screen, but they won't print. Your computer thinks a space between letters or a return at the end of a line is a character, just like a letter or number or punctuation mark, and treats it as such. Memorize the hidden character symbols shown in *Moving Toward Mastery*, above. By doing so, you can see your documents as your computer sees them. Not only do hidden characters show the details of how your document was constructed, they tell even more about your typesetting abilities. Your supervisor or coworkers can take one look at the hidden characters in your document and have a good estimate of your software proficiency.

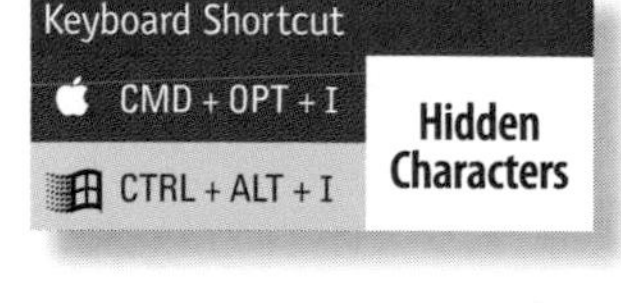

HOW INDESIGN DEFINES PARAGRAPHS

Now that you can read hidden characters, you are ready to set type in paragraphs. One thing you will always want to remember is this: *A paragraph is defined by pressing the* **Return** *key (Mac) or the* **Enter** *key (Windows).*

▸ *production tip*

A paragraph is defined by pressing the Return key (Mac) or the Enter key (Windows).

Each time you press the *Return* key you create a paragraph, whether you have typed a whole page or just one letter. From studying the chart of hidden character symbols shown on the previous page, you already know that a paragraph symbol looks like this: ¶. If you have hidden characters turned on, each time you press *Return*, this symbol will show and you will have created a new paragraph. (I work with hidden characters turned on most of the time, because I want to see my document as the computer sees it!) Look at the two passages in Visual 3–3. How many paragraphs are in frame "A"? How many are in frame "B"? Even though the copy in frame "A" looks identical to the copy in frame "B", it is actually 13 paragraphs, while column "B" is only three: a headline, and two paragraphs of body copy. Each ¶ symbol represents a paragraph. The *Return* or *Enter* key was pressed at the end of each line in frame "A," creating many more paragraphs than necessary. This is called *setting line for line.* The majority of the time, you will want to use the *Return* key only at the end of a whole paragraph so that the software will manage the line endings.

Choosing Portfolio Pieces¶

It goes without saying, that all the pieces in your book¶
should be strong. Ten to twelve pieces that demonstrate¶
your range of abilities is a good starting number. Your¶
first piece should knock their socks off! And the last piece¶
should also leave a strong impression.¶

Choose pieces that are excellent examples of design,¶
use of color and type, and technique. Do not include a¶
poorly-designed piece because of its sentimental value.¶
For instance, don't include your first feeble attempt at¶
contour drawing from *Drawing 101*, even if you received a¶
grade of A. Poor pieces dilute the impact of an otherwise¶
strong book.¶

Choosing Portfolio Pieces¶

It goes without saying, that all the pieces in your book should be strong. Ten to twelve pieces that demonstrate your range of abilities is a good starting number. Your first piece should knock their socks off! And the last piece should also leave a strong impression.¶

Choose pieces that are excellent examples of design, use of color and type, and technique. Do not include a poorly-designed piece because of its sentimental value.¬
For instance, don't include your first feeble attempt at contour drawing from *Drawing 101*, even if you received a grade of A. Poor pieces dilute the impact of an otherwise strong book.#

VISUAL |3–3|

In column A, the Return key was pressed at the end of each line. In column B, InDesign automatically wrapped the text from one line to the next.

Occasionally you will need to break a line manually within a paragraph. Look at the third line in the last paragraph of frame "B." It has a different symbol at the end of the line. This symbol (¬) represents a soft return (also called *forced line break*), and is created by pressing **Shift+Return** (Mac) or **Shift+Enter** (Windows). Here's another important rule to remember: A soft return breaks the line, but does not create a new paragraph. The distinction between paragraph returns (or hard returns) and soft returns (forced line breaks) is critical to understand, because they determine how InDesign applies paragraph formatting options.

▸ *production tip*

A soft return (Shift+Return) breaks the line, but does not create a new paragraph.

▸ *Add space between paragraphs*

In the following exercise you will learn how to add extra space between paragraphs. This is the technique you should use, rather than placing double returns between paragraphs!

1. Create a new document: **8.5" × 11"**, all margins **0.5"**.

2. Press **F** to select the *Rectangle Frame* tool. Draw a rectangle from the upper left to the lower right margin. Select the *Type* tool and click in the frame to make it a text frame.

VISUAL |3–4|

Open the Context menu by right-clicking with your mouse. If you have a one-button mouse, press the Control key and click.

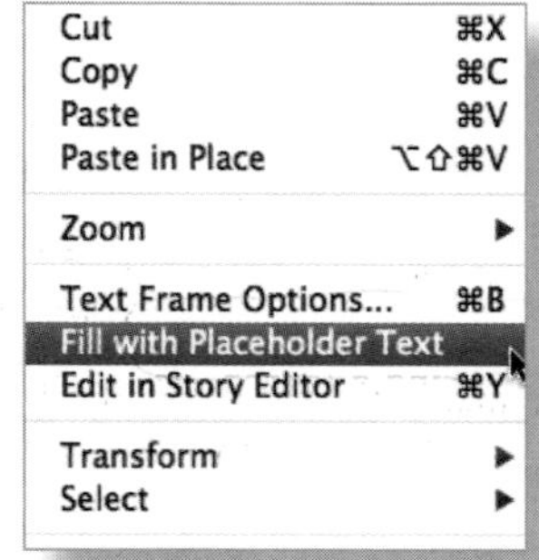

3. Open the *Context* menu and choose **Fill with Placeholder Text**. Text should flow into the text frame. Don't worry about trying to read it, placeholder text is a term for text that is used to "take the place" of the final copy. It is useful for showing where the finished text will be placed and makes the document look more complete. The placeholder text will be replaced by the actual copy later. (Placeholder text can also be accessed from the *Type* menu.)

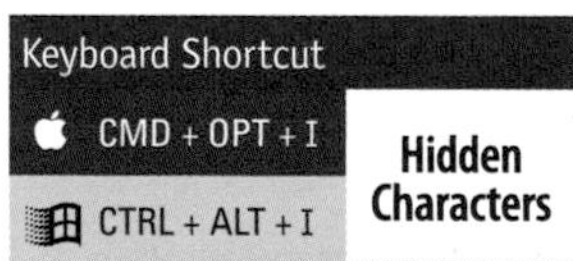

4. Turn on hidden characters by pressing **Command+Option+I** (Mac) or **Control+Alt+I** (Windows). You will probably see several paragraph return symbols in the text. There should be a # symbol at the end of the text indicating the end of the story. (If your text doesn't show any paragraph symbols, insert two or three paragraphs returns throughout the text.)

5. Add some soft returns at the end of three or four lines.

6. Use the techniques described in the box to the left to practice highlighting text. Selecting paragraphs with four clicks is a good way to make sure that everything in the paragraph is selected, including the paragraph return symbol at the end of the paragraph. If you simply drag the cursor to highlight the characters in the paragraph, it is easy to miss the ending paragraph symbol.

▸ *production tip*

Whenever you select text, be sure to select all the type and hidden characters in the text block, including the return at the end of the paragraph.

Click twice
to select a single word.

Triple-click
to select a whole line.

Click four times
to select a paragraph.

When you double-, triple-, or quadruple-click to select text, you are selecting all the text, and all the hidden characters.

▸MOVING TOWARD MASTERY

Tips to increase production and decrease frustration!

- *When you are using the **Type** tool and working in an active text frame, you can temporarily access the **Selection** tool by holding down the **Command** (Mac) or **Control** (Windows) key. As soon as the **Command** or **Control** key is released, the arrow becomes the I-beam text cursor again. Try this a few times.*
- *When you are using the **Type** tool and working in an active text frame, you can quickly switch to the **Selection** tool by pressing **ESC.***
- *When the **Selection** tool is active, **double-click** on your copy to instantly go to the text cursor.*
- *When you are not using the **Type** tool, you can access the grabber hand by holding down the **Spacebar**. When you are using the **Type** tool, you access the grabber hand by holding down the **Option** (Mac) or **Alt** (Windows) key.*
- *Alternatively, you can press both the **Option** (Mac) or **Alt** (Windows) and **Spacebar** keys simultaneously to access the grabber hand, regardless of which tool you are using.*
- *Use the **forward delete** key ⌦ to delete words and spaces to the right of the cursor. If you are using a laptop, you will need to press **FN+delete** to delete items to the right of the cursor.*

7. Select all the text by pressing **Command+A** (Mac) or **Control+A** (Windows). Choose a typeface and make the type **10-point** with **11-point** leading.

8. Add space between paragraphs using the *Paragraph Formatting Controls*. Visual 3–5 shows the *Space After* field. Type **p7** (meaning *7 points*) in the field. When you press **Return**, InDesign converts the point measurement to the equivalent measurement in inches and adds that amount of space after every paragraph. You can use any measurement system to enter numeric values in fields, as long as you also enter the corresponding unit abbreviation such as *in* for inches or *mm* for millimeters. When using points and picas, if the *p* is before the number it means *points*. When the *p* follows a number, it means *picas.* Therefore, *5p* means *5 picas*, *p5* means *5 points,* and *12p6* means *12 picas, 6 points.*

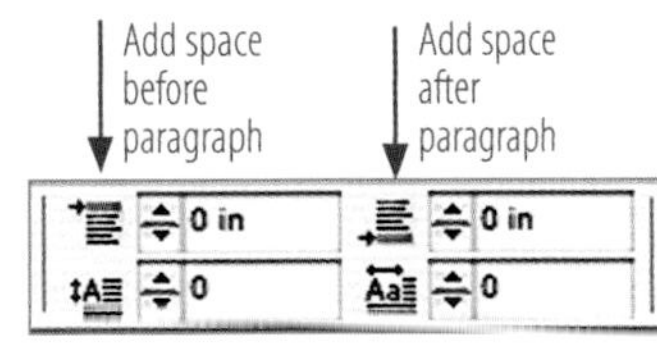

VISUAL |3–5|

Carefully study the Space Before and Space After icons. Notice that the gray bar with the arrow shows where the additional white space will be inserted.

also use paragraph tool

9. Examine your copy to see the breather space between the paragraphs. Remember to use **Command+ Z** (Mac) or **Control+ Z** (Windows) to undo any mistakes. Keep this document open—there's more practice ahead.

USING RAISED AND DROP CAPS

A well-set paragraph is a pleasure to view and to read. Skilled typesetters use subtle techniques to give text interest and visual appeal. Adding raised or drop caps (capital letters) is one of these techniques. Both raised and drop capital letters are larger than the accompanying body copy. A *drop cap* is a large letter (or several letters) that drops below the baseline. A drop cap is a paragraph attribute and is set by using the *Paragraph Formatting Controls* (a paragraph can have only one value for any given paragraph attribute, such as drop caps, space after, and alignment). A *raised cap* sits on the baseline and rises above the rest of the text. A raised cap is a character attribute and can be set in the *Character Formatting Controls* (a paragraph can contain characters that have many different character attributes, such as point size, font, and color).

The letter shape of some drop caps tends to separate the letter from the rest of the word. Extra kerning might be required in these cases. (We will discuss kerning in the next chapter.)

VISUAL | 3–6 |

Drop caps extend below the baseline. Raised caps sit on the baseline and rise above the text.

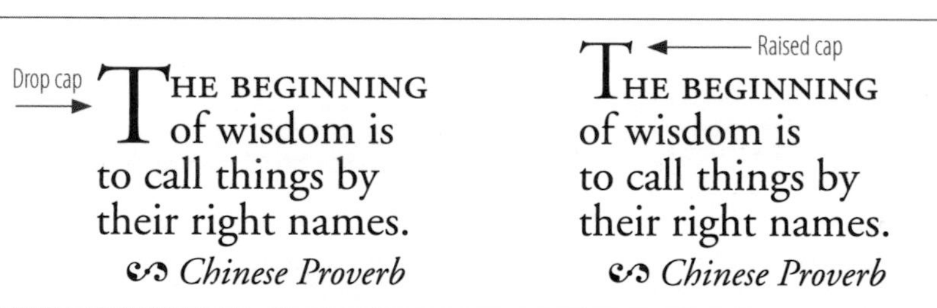
Drop cap
THE BEGINNING
of wisdom is
to call things by
their right names.
Chinese Proverb
Raised cap
THE BEGINNING
of wisdom is
to call things by
their right names.
Chinese Proverb

One word of caution—use raised and drop caps sparingly. They are generally used at the beginning of an article or chapter. However, as Visual 3–7 demonstrates, if these special techniques are overused, the end result is a document that looks like type has been splattered all over the page.

► *Create drop caps and raised caps*

1. Make sure the text frame is active by double-clicking on the text. The cursor should now be an I-beam.
2. Highlight the first letter of the first word.
3. To make a raised cap, hold down **Shift+Command** (Mac) or **Shift+Control** (Windows) and press the **greater-than** key (**>**) five or six times to increase the point size. The size of the letter will increase and the letter will remain sitting on the baseline.

Bd dolenis eu feummy num velis num in exero cor at, sequatum iriure magna aliquat nos adigniam, vel ullam venissit loborper ing el dit prat. Ut ing estin henit endre miniam, quis

Up elisit eugait dignim nonulla aut la con elit alis ex et non henit nulla consenis nis am veliqui euis ad dolut adigna augait.

Golore commoluptat praesse quametum niam dunt la

corperosto dunt wiscil incilla feuismod modio commy num iureriustis trud etueril iliquis am nis nit prated

But vendion ea commy nulput wis etum illa facipsum at, si elessen ismodoloreTo od eros nos adigniam,

VISUAL |3–7|

This example has too many drop caps! Like bugs on a wind shield, type is splattered all over the page. Don't overuse the drop cap function!

4. To make a drop cap, put the cursor in the next paragraph. Switch to the ***Paragraph Formatting Controls.*** Visual 3–8 shows the two fields you will be using, located right below the ***Space After*** field you used earlier. The field on the left controls how many lines the letter(s) will drop. The field on the right controls how many letters will be dropped. Experiment with these controls by clicking on the arrows and watching your screen. Change the first letter in that paragraph to an **A** and turn it into a drop cap. See how the shape of the letter separates it from the rest of the word? The space between the letter pair needs to be adjusted, a process called ***kerning,*** which will be discussed in the next chapter. Keep your document open to use in the next exercise.

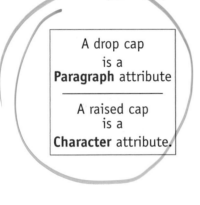

A drop cap is a **Paragraph** attribute

A raised cap is a **Character** attribute.

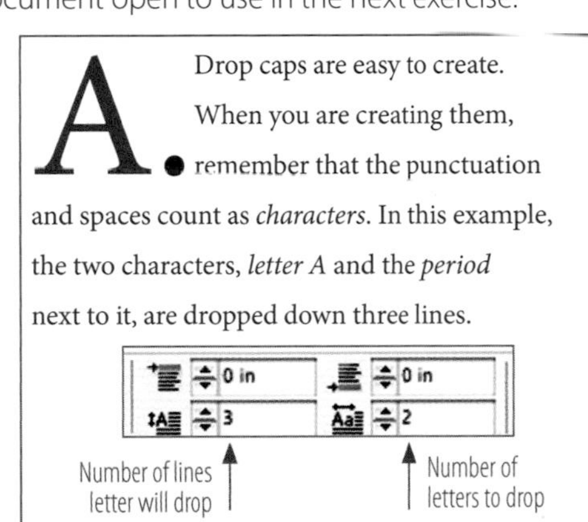

A. Drop caps are easy to create. When you are creating them, remember that the punctuation and spaces count as *characters*. In this example, the two characters, *letter A* and the *period* next to it, are dropped down three lines.
0 in
0 in
3
2
Number of lines letter will drop
Number of letters to drop

VISUAL |3–8|

The left field controls how many lines the letter(s) will drop. The right field controls how many letters will be affected.

MANAGE HYPHENATION SETTINGS

Automatic hyphenation is active as an InDesign default. For some documents you will want to turn automatic hyphenation off. To do so, create your document and select the *Type* tool. Go to the right end of either the *Paragraph* or *Character Formatting Controls* panel, click on the icon shown in Visual 3–9 to reveal the options menu and then select **Hyphenation**. When the *Hyphenation Settings* dialog box opens, deselect **Hyphenate** at the top of the window. Automatic hyphenation is now turned off for this document. The *Hyphenation Settings* dialog box also allows you to decide whether capitalized words will be hyphenated and how hyphenation will affect individual words. (When hyphenation is turned off, you can still add a discretionary hyphen to individual words. Discretionary hyphens will be discussed later in this chapter.) Even with automatic hyphenation turned off, InDesign permits you to override the document hyphenation setting and apply hyphenation to individual paragraphs. Place the cursor in the paragraph and check **Hyphenate** in the *Paragraph Formatting Controls* panel.

VISUAL | 3–9 |

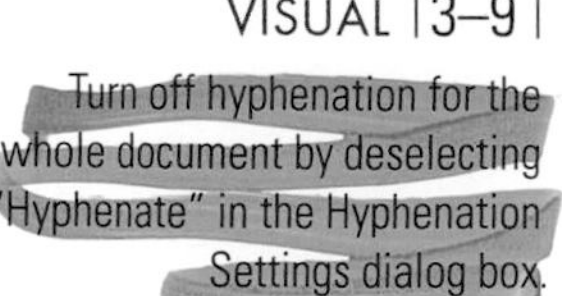

Turn off hyphenation for the whole document by deselecting "Hyphenate" in the Hyphenation Settings dialog box.

© Cengage Learning 2013

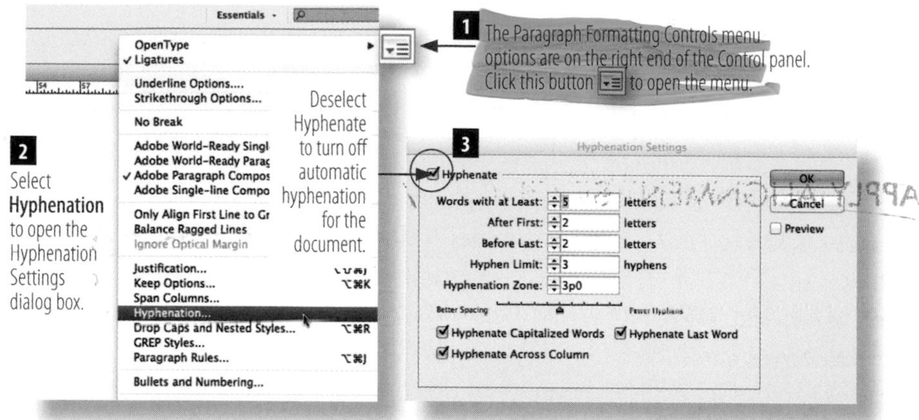

To turn off hyphenation in a single paragraph, place the text cursor in the paragraph and deselect the **Hyphenate** option [Hyphenate] in the *Paragraph Formatting Controls* panel. It isn't necessary to highlight the whole paragraph because hyphenation is a paragraph attribute, and formatting one line in a paragraph affects the entire paragraph. If you want to turn off hyphenation in several adjoining paragraphs, drag with your mouse to select the text. It isn't necessary to highlight everything in each paragraph. One letter of the first or last paragraph will do. Now deselect the **Hyphenate** option in the *Paragraph Formatting Controls* panel.

KEEP WORDS AND PHRASES ON ONE LINE

There are some words and phrases that should not be split from one line to another. Proper names with titles (Dr. Smith), telephone numbers (888-7707), dates (July 16, 1947), and some compound words (New York) should not be split from one line to the next. InDesign makes it easy to control these potential problems.

To keep compound words from splitting, insert a special *nonbreaking space* between the two words. Place the cursor between the words and delete the regular space. Open the *Context* menu and select **Insert White Space.** Then choose **Nonbreaking Space** from the menu of different types of spaces you can insert. If your hidden characters are turned on, you will see a new symbol that designates a nonbreaking space (^). To turn on hidden characters, press **Command+Option+I** (Mac) or **Control+Alt+I** (Windows). To keep a phone number from splitting at the hyphen, substitute a *nonbreaking hyphen*. Using the same *Context* menu, choose *Insert*

VISUAL | 3–10 |

A nonbreaking space in the name and a nonbreaking hyphen in the phone number have been encoded. There is no hidden character to identify a nonbreaking hyphen.

© Cengage Learning 2013

nonbreaking space

Dr.^Smith¶

888-7807#

Special Character>Hyphens and Dashes and then choose **Nonbreaking Hyphen** from the menu of available special characters. A final method for keeping words or phrases from splitting onto two lines, is to highlight the copy and select **No Break** from the *Paragraph* or *Character Formatting Controls* option menu (Visual 3–11).

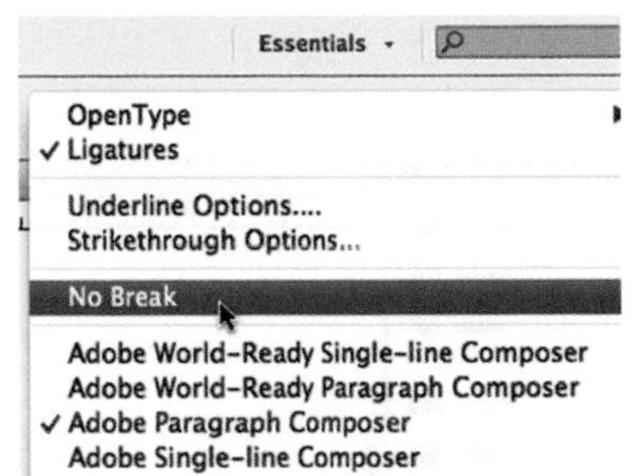

VISUAL | 3–11 |

No Break is found under the Character and Paragraph Formatting Controls option menu.

APPLY ALIGNMENT SETTINGS

Another great feature in the *Paragraph Formatting Controls* panel is the *Alignment* option. Visual 3–12 illustrates the six alignment options that you will use most often. When text is aligned to the left, the right edges of the text are uneven, which is referred to as *ragged right,* or *flush left.* When text is pushed to the right side, the left edges are ragged. This alignment is called *flush right* or *ragged left.* Text that spreads all the way from the left to the right edges of the text frame is called *justified.* Text that is *centered* creates ragged edges on both sides. Each alignment setting has its design challenges. Ragged edges must not be too uneven or the page will have a choppy look. Justified type can be riddled with uneven white spaces within the lines that merge to create *rivers.* Examine your justified copy carefully to make sure rivers don't disrupt eye flow and reduce readability.

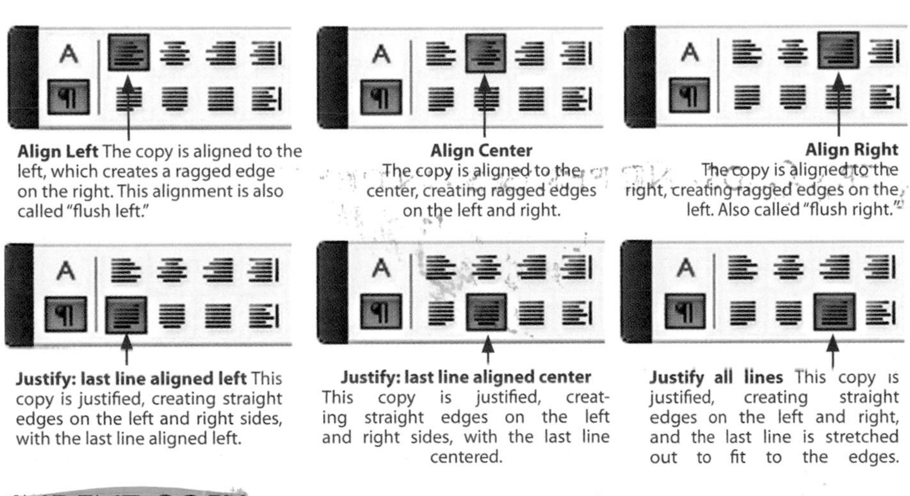

Align Left The copy is aligned to the left, which creates a ragged edge on the right. This alignment is also called "flush left."
Align Center The copy is aligned to the center, creating ragged edges on the left and right.
Align Right The copy is aligned to the right, creating ragged edges on the left. Also called "flush right."
Justify: last line aligned left This copy is justified, creating straight edges on the left and right sides, with the last line aligned left.
Justify: last line aligned center This copy is justified, creating straight edges on the left and right sides, with the last line centered.
Justify all lines This copy is justified, creating straight edges on the left and right, and the last line is stretched out to fit to the edges.

VISUAL | 3–12 |

The text alignment options you will use most often. Take notice of any rivers of white space that need to be managed when using justified alignment settings.

INDENT COPY

Indents push paragraphs a specified distance from the left or right sides of a text frame. Visual 3–13 shows the *Paragraph Formatting Controls* panel fields used to set the following types of indents: *left, right, first line,* and *hanging*. Don't confuse paragraph indents with *text frame insets.* An *indent* is a paragraph formatting attribute that can apply to individual paragraphs within a text frame. An *inset* is a text frame attribute which affects all the text—every paragraph—within the text frame.

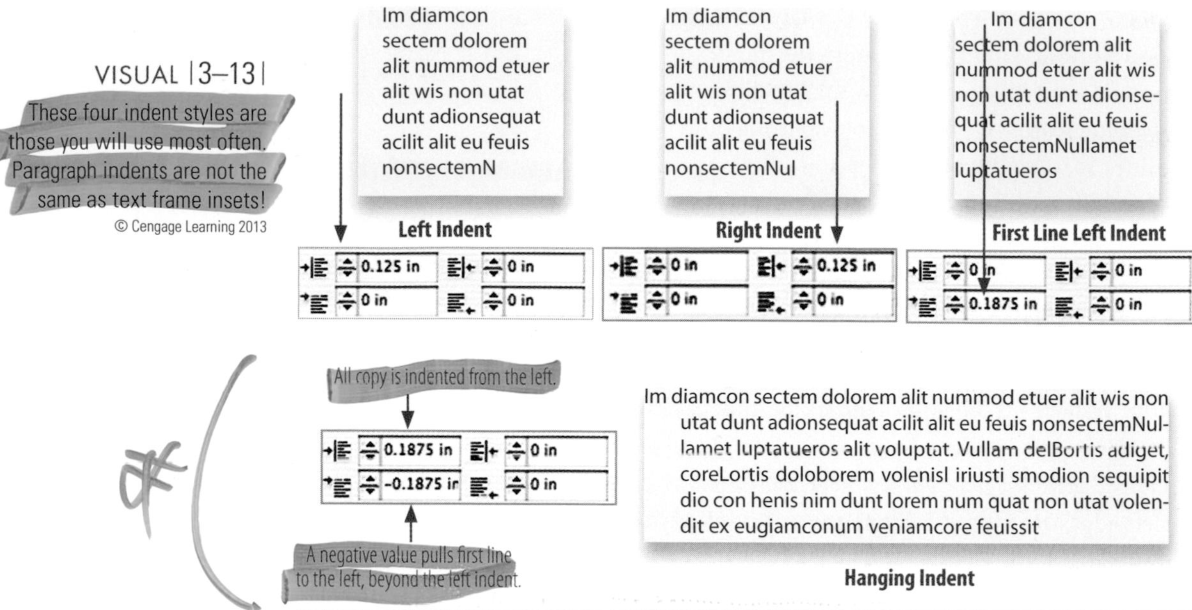
Im diamcon sectem dolorem alit nummod etuer alit wis non utat dunt adionsequat acilit alit eu feuis nonsectemN
Left Indent
0.125 in
0 in
0 in
0 in
Im diamcon sectem dolorem alit nummod etuer alit wis non utat dunt adionsequat acilit alit eu feuis nonsectemNul
Right Indent
0 in
0.125 in
0 in
0 in
Im diamcon sectem dolorem alit nummod etuer alit wis non utat dunt adionse-quat acilit alit eu feuis nonsectemNullamet luptatueros
First Line Left Indent
0 in
0 in
0.1875 in
0 in
All copy is indented from the left.
0.1875 in
0 in
-0.1875 in
0 in
A negative value pulls first line to the left, beyond the left indent.
Im diamcon sectem dolorem alit nummod etuer alit wis non utat dunt adionsequat acilit alit eu feuis nonsectemNul-lamet luptatueros alit voluptat. Vullam delBortis adiget, coreLortis doloborem volenisl iriusti smodion sequipit dio con henis nim dunt lorem num quat non utat volen-dit ex eugiamconum veniamcore feuissit
Hanging Indent

VISUAL |3–13|

These four indent styles are those you will use most often. Paragraph indents are not the same as text frame insets!

To create a paragraph indent, select your paragraph(s), place the cursor in the desired indent field in the *Paragraph Formatting Controls* panel, and type a numerical value or click one of the arrows. Very simple. Let's discuss how to create two specific indents: a *first line indent* and a *hanging indent*. Place the cursor in a paragraph and then change the value in the *First Line Left Indent* field by clicking the upper arrow. You will see that only the first line indent increases and moves to the right. This is easy to visualize and understand. The hanging indent is a bit more confusing. Look at Visual 3–13 and you will see that most of the paragraph "hangs" from the first line of text. To set a hanging indent, you must first set a left indent. Once the left indent is set, you then change the *First Line Left Indent* field by entering a negative value. This forces the first line back to the left. Once you understand the sequence, creating a hanging indent style will also become easy to incorporate into your production.

VISUAL |3–14|

The sample on the right has a much smoother right edge because Balance Ragged Lines has been activated.

Ostrud elit verciduipis fo
erilla feu feugiam, vendreds
modignis non sef dolesto
delit lam zzriu riurem
doloram augiam zzril ipit
nullum olobortis
ametummodit inTucros inahu
ero erci eum delenibh estie
conulputismolorper suscillam
duisim zzrilit luptat,Ulla
faciliquam acilit wis at.
Os nummodo del elit,
volorpe riurerostrud ming eli

Balance Ragged Lines Deselected

Ostrud elit verciduipis
fo erilla feu feugiam,
vendreds modignis non
sef dolesto delit lam zzriu
riurem doloram augiam
zzril ipit nullum olobortis
ametummodit inTueros inahu
ero erci eum delenibh estie
conulputismolorper suscillam
duisim zzrilit luptat,Ulla
faciliquam acilit wis at.
Os nummodo del elit,
volorpe riurerostrud

Balance Ragged Lines Activated

BALANCE RAGGED LINES

Ragged line endings create an open, friendly look. As you scan up and down the block of copy you want the overall shape and pattern of the line endings to look like smooth hills, not like rough, jagged mountains. InDesign has a wonderful feature for smoothing out ragged copy. You will find it in the pull down menu at the far right end of the *Paragraph* or *Character Formatting Controls* panel. Select a paragraph in the document and make sure it is left justified. Select **Balance Ragged Lines** in the *Paragraph Formatting Controls* menu (Visual 3–15). The edges of your paragraph should smooth out. To smooth out ragged edges on everything in your text frame, select all your paragraphs and apply the **Balance Ragged Lines** option. Balance Ragged Lines also affects paragraphs that are aligned to the right.

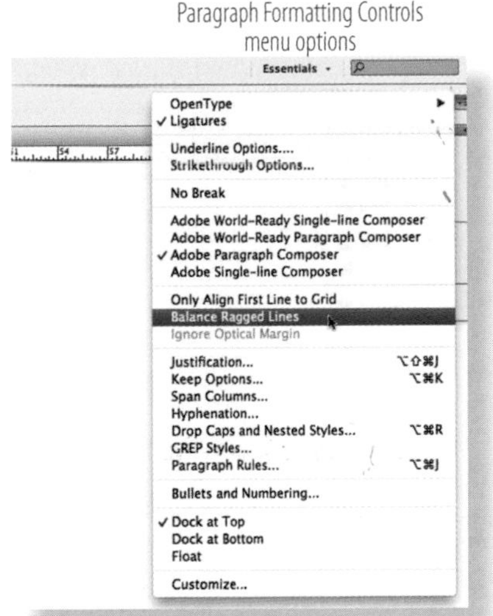

VISUAL |3–15|

Choose Balance Ragged Lines by opening the menu options at the end of the Paragraph Formatting Panel.

© Cengage Learning 2013

USE QUOTATION MARKS

As shown below in Visual 3–16, there is a difference between *typewriter quotation marks* and *typographer's quotation marks*. Typewriter quotation marks really have little place in typesetting. Some typesetters use straight typewriter quotation marks to indicate measurements such as feet and inches. Straight quotation marks are found under the *Type* menu, or *Context menu>Insert Special Character>Quotation Marks.* While straight quotation marks are acceptable, a better way is to insert prime marks for dimensional units of measurement, if they're included in the typeface.

"Typographer's Quotation Marks"
"Typographer's Quotation Marks"

Prime Marks may be slanted: 3′11″
Prime Marks may be straight: 3'11"

"Typewriter quotation marks
are often used as prime marks"

VISUAL |3–16|

Using typewriter quotation marks is a great way to mar an otherwise excellent portfolio piece. Notice that the shape of typographer's quotation marks varies depending on the typeface you have selected.

© Cengage Learning 2013

By default, InDesign uses typographer's quotation marks, sometimes called *curly* or *smart quotes*. If someone has changed your InDesign defaults, you can easily change the preferences back to use typographer's quotes. On the Mac, *choose InDesign>Preferences>Type*. In Windows, choose *Edit>Preferences>Type*. Make sure there is a check mark next to the **Use Typographer's Quotes** option. If you enable this option setting when there is no document open, InDesign will use typographer's quotation marks as the default setting for all subsequent documents. If you change this preference setting with a document open, the change will apply only to the current document.

Before we move on to another topic, let's put some quotation marks in our practice document. Select all the type by pressing **Command+A** (Mac) or **Control+A** (Windows) and change the alignment to: **justify with the last line aligned left.** Now put twelve sets of quotation marks at the beginning and end of the lines in your copy block. Scatter the quotation marks up and down the length of the copy block, and get ready for another great InDesign technique!

HANG PUNCTUATION

You can't help but be excited about InDesign. No other software can match its text-handling capabilities. And the ability to offset punctuation is another great InDesign feature. Now that you know how to use the correct quotation marks, it's time to fine-tune your copy. If you look closely at the quotation marks you inserted at the beginning and the end of your lines, you will see that the marks visually create tiny holes in the text block. At first glance this might not seem like a big deal. But after you use the next function, you will see what a huge difference a little fine-tuning makes!

VISUAL |3–17|

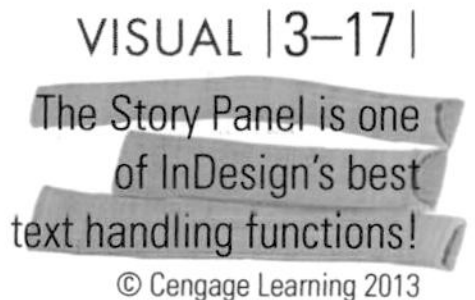

The Story Panel is one of InDesign's best text handling functions!

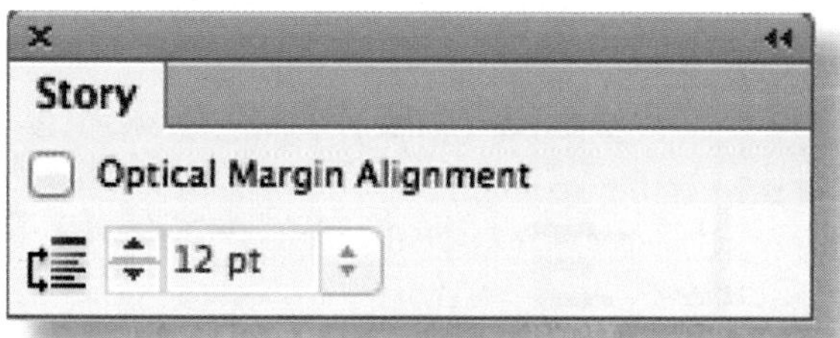

1. Highlight your type. Locate the ***Font Size*** field in the ***Character Formatting Controls*** panel and make a note of the point size of your text.

2. Go to the menu and choose ***Type>Story.*** The ***Story*** panel is used only for ***Optical Margin Alignment,*** a very powerful function! Optical margin alignment allows punctuation marks that appear at the beginning or end of lines of type to be extended slightly beyond the text frame. This prevents quotation marks from creating the look of tiny holes at the edges of a column of type.

3. As Visual 3–17 shows, there are only two fields on the ***Story*** panel. Click the box next to ***Optical Margin Alignment***. A check mark should appear. The field in the lower area is called the ***Align based on size*** control. It is used for setting the point size of the type in the copy block. Since you just made note of the point size, enter that value in the ***Align based on size*** field. When ***Optical Margin Alignment*** is active, notice how the quotation marks are partially set outside the edges of the text frame, creating a much smoother visual path for the eye to follow. Toggle the ***Optical Margin Alignment*** box a few times and see the difference it makes. Very cool. What a fantastic InDesign capability!

USING HYPHENS AND DASHES

Now that you have quotation marks squared away, it's time to move on to hyphens and dashes. A *hyphen* is a dash entered by pressing the key to the right of the number zero key. Hyphens are used in only two instances: to separate compound words such as state-of-the-art (including compound names, such as Anderson-Jones and compound numbers, such as phone numbers) or to hyphenate words at the end of a line of type. A hyphen that is automatically added by InDesign during the text flow process is called a *soft hyphen.* This hyphen will disappear if the text is edited and the hyphen is no longer needed. When you deselected *Hyphenate* in the *Paragraph Formatting Controls* panel earlier in this lesson, you were turning off the soft automatic hyphens.

Hard hyphens are those you place in compound words when typing, or ones that you manually insert to hyphenate a word at the end of a line. Hard hyphens are there to stay—they are part of the text just like any other visible character. If the line endings change during the editing process and a manually hyphenated word ends up in the middle of a line, it will still be hyphenated. If there's a chance that a manually hyphenated word might appear in the middle of a line after your text is edited, be sure to use a *discretionary hyphen.* Like a soft hyphen, when a discretionary hyphen is no longer needed, it will disappear. For instance, suppose you are working with auto hyphenation turned off and a four syllable word has wrapped to the next line, leaving a white "hole" at the right end of the preceding line. To even out the ragged edge, you decide to manually hyphenate the word. To insert a discretionary hyphen, place the cursor where you want the hyphen to appear. Open the *Context* menu, choose *Insert Special Character>Dashes and Hyphens>* and then choose **Discretionary Hyphen** from the menu of available special characters.

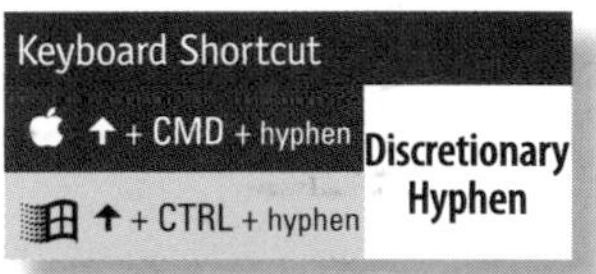

Dashes are different from hyphens, with different size dashes for different purposes. The first type of dash is an *em dash.* An *em* is a flexible unit of measure that corresponds to the point size of the type. For instance, an em in 5-point type would be 5-points wide, while an em in 10-point type would be 10-points wide. An *em dash* is used within a sentence—as in this sentence—to provide a break in thought (a process called *interpolation).* In the days of typewriters, two hyphens were used to indicate an em dash. You can create an em dash by pressing **Shift+Option+Hyphen** (Mac) or **Shift+Alt+Hyphen** (Windows).

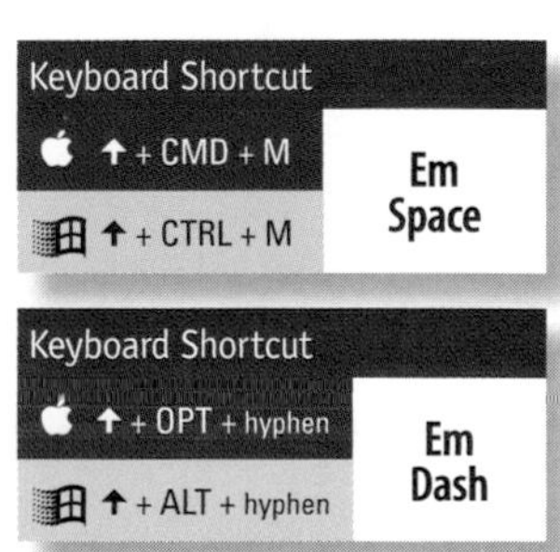

An *en* is half the size of an em; so an en dash is half the size of an em dash. An *en dash* is used to show a range of time, numbers, or a geographic area, and substitutes for the word *to.* When a poster reads that an event runs from September 26–30 in the Minneapolis–St. Paul area, en dashes are used to separate the dates and cities (Visual 3–18). An en dash is also sometimes used in headlines when an em dash looks too large. You can enter an en dash by pressing **Option+Hyphen** (Mac) or

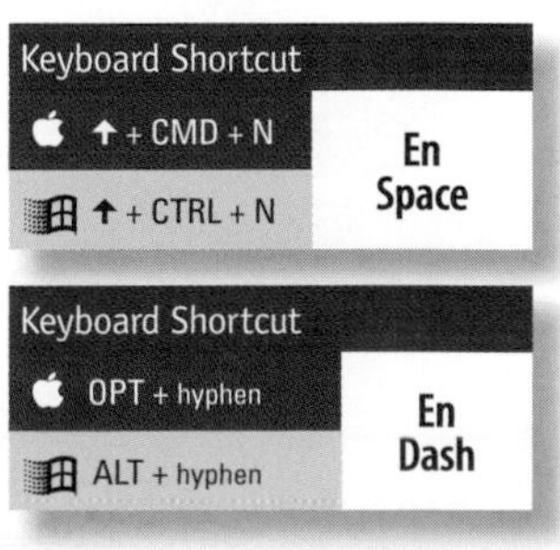

Alt+Hyphen (Windows). You can also open the *Context* menu, while using the *Type* tool, to access em and en dashes from the *Insert Special Characters* menu. However, because this method is much slower, you should memorize the shortcut keys.

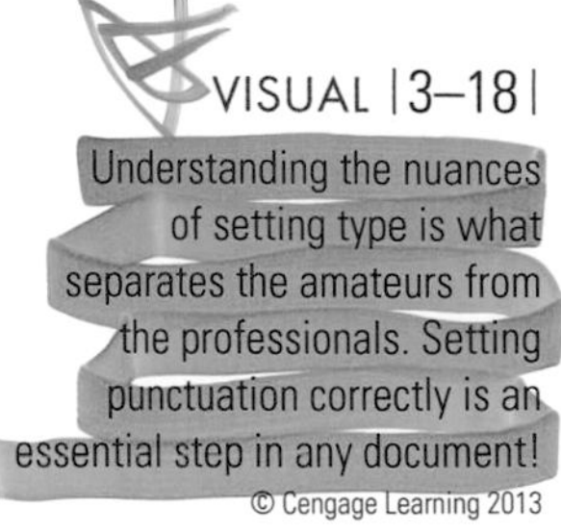

VISUAL |3–18|

Understanding the nuances of setting type is what separates the amateurs from the professionals. Setting punctuation correctly is an essential step in any document!

Hyphen (-)
used in compound words and phone numbers

En dash (–)
used in number ranges such as 10–12 inches or in geographic notations

Em dash (—)
used within a sentence instead of double hyphens.

He tried—unsuccessfully—to convince his mother-in-law that weather in the Minneapolis–St. Paul area was beauti-ful for more than two months each year.

CALCULATE PARAGRAPH LINE MEASURE

There are many factors that work together to create good typesetting. There is an inseparable relationship between type size, measured in points, and *line measure*, indicated in picas. A line measure that is too long in relation to the point size will be difficult to read. For example, if a line measure is short and the point size is large, the copy will look choppy because too many hyphens will be needed. A good rule of thumb: As the point size increases, the line measure should also increase. It is easy to calculate the range of acceptable line measure for a single column of copy by multiplying the point size of the type by 2 or 2.5. The resulting number will be the line measure in picas. For instance: 10-point type × 2 = 20 picas. And 10-point type × 2.5 = 25 picas. Therefore, a line measure between 20 and 25 picas would be an excellent starting point. Readability is the overriding concern—a measure too long or too short reduces readability.

VISUAL |3–19|

Line measure, point size, and leading are three factors that must be in sync. When one is out of balance, readability suffers.

Estimating Line Measure for Single Column Text:

2 to 2.5 times the type point size.

The result (in picas) is the starting point for line measure.

A notation of **12/15** means **12-point type on 15-point leading.**

A notation of **12/15 x 30** means **12-point type, on 15-point leading, with a line measure of 30 picas.**

▸ *Calculate line measure*

Let's see **how** easy it is to calculate line measure in inDesign.

1. Create a new **8.5" × 11"** document, margins **0.5"**.
2. Draw a text frame of any size.
3. Fill with placeholder text by using the menu options or by choosing *Type>Fill with Placeholder Text.* Select all the type and change the point size to **10 pt.**
4. Switch to the ***Selection*** tool and on the ***Control*** panel highlight the ***Width*** field and type **20p** (20 picas). Press **Return**. If your unit of measurement is set to inches, InDesign will translate 20 picas into 3.3333 inches as soon as you press the ***Return*** key. Print the document.
5. Highlight a line of average length. Press **F8** to open the Info panel. Look in the *Characters* field in the lower part of the ***Info*** panel. How many characters are in an average line? A good range for character count would be 45 and 75, with an ideal of 66 characters (spaces also count as characters). In a multi-column frame, the character count would range between 40 and 50 characters.
6. Select your text frame with the ***Selection*** tool. In the ***Width*** field, increase the measure to **40p** and print out the document. Compare the two text blocks, one with a 20p measure and the other 40p. Which one would you prefer to read?

Derspiendi bla conse que veritibus, si cupis nihillabore vero dolorrorum voluptas et, utas voluptate es et etum, aut asit ratemo vendae. Temos ut ut velibusdant quis vit unt quas et inis del is nonet alibere ribeatu repudit quis et eosam dolori nulpa quiatio rrovidis dolupit aut qui dicitis inctatem. Os dolupta velesti tem qui dolupta turias et volorrorit omnis eum rese evererepe aborerum ea volore, num in corit ma diorum es velit ut quo blanis volorenisti aut lacepuda quunt iducidunt excea vendit, officimpora nulparis sunto coriam audae expligendit ut harum iunt, quam nonsedit quae exeria dis sit, con et plistem quatibea commodis aut rectori aepudam voluptatem repero minctur? Erumquosam ipsam, quae porrovid magnam in plictio qui officia ern

B

Derspiendi bla conse que veritibus, si cupis nihillabore vero dolorrorum voluptas et, utas voluptate es et etum, aut asit ratemo vendae. Temos ut ut velibusdant quis vit unt quas et inis del is nonet alibere ribeatu repudit quis et eosam dolori nulpa quiatio rrovidis dolupit aut qui dicitis inctatem. Os dolupta velesti tem qui dolupta turias et volorrorit omnis eum rese evererepe aborerum ea volore, num in corit ma diorum es velit ut quo blanis volorenisti aut lacepuda quunt iducidunt excea vendit, officimpora nulparis sunto coriam audae expligendit ut harum iunt, quam nonsedit quae exeria dis sit, con et plistem quatibea commodis aut rectori aepudam voluptatem repero minctur? Erumquosam ipsam, quae porrovid magnam in plictio qui officia ern

VISUAL |3–20|

Example "A" has a line measure in the ideal range. Example "B" has a measure much too wide. Which example would you prefer to read?

▸ MOVING TOWARD MASTERY

common proofreader's marks

Mark	Meaning	Mark	Meaning	Mark	Meaning
	Delete	FL	Flush left	caps	Set in capital letters
	Close up; delete space	FR	Flush right	sc	Set in small caps
stet	Leave as is		Transpose	wf	Wrong font
#	Insert space	sp	Spell out	^	Insert here
	Break line with soft return	ital	Set in italic type	⊙	Insert period
¶	Begin new paragraph	Rom	Set in roman type	?	Insert question mark

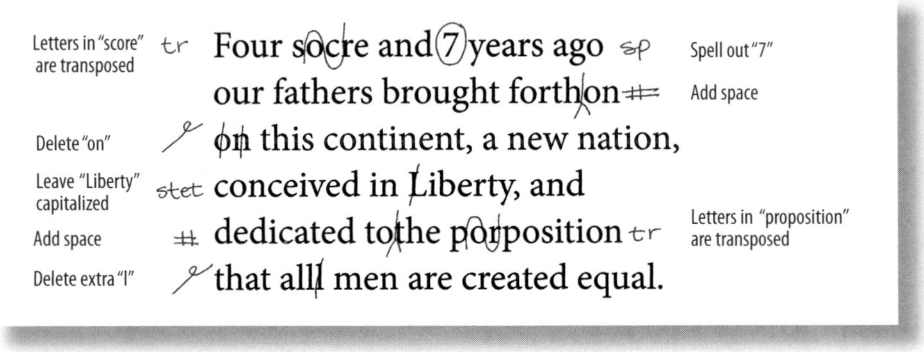

Letters in "score" are transposed — tr — Four socre and 7 years ago — sp — Spell out "7"

our fathers brought forthon — # — Add space

Delete "on" — on this continent, a new nation,

Leave "Liberty" capitalized — stet — conceived in Liberty, and

Add space — # — dedicated tothe porposition — tr — Letters in "proposition" are transposed

Delete extra "l" — that alll men are created equal.

PROOFREADER'S MARKS

Someone sent me this tongue-in-cheek word play for people who use only the computer's spell checking system to proof their documents:
Weave know knead four proofing any moor.

▸ *production tip*

A great way to make sure you've made all the required revisions on a document is to highlight each change on the revised print. This will significantly reduce errors.

It is essential to proof every project manually, in addition to using your computer's spell check system. Sometimes clients will provide electronic copy, and other times you will type in the copy yourself. Whatever the case may be, all copy needs to be proofed. Knowing basic proofing marks will speed up the proofing process. Out in the workplace, where many people work on a single project, using these marks will give clear direction to others and be a precise method of editing copy. Memorize and use the marks shown above. Marking up proofs is best done with an extra-fine, fiber tip pen with a contrasting ink color, such as red or green. Edits are usually noted in pairs—one mark in the line of copy, itself, to flag where the problem is, and a corresponding mark, in the margin, describing the solution. Interpreting a standard set of proofreader's marks is much easier than trying to decipher a hodgepodge collection of cross-outs, circles, and arrows.

Summary

A few years ago, after being inspired by watching "do it yourself" shows on cable TV, I purchased a fancy miter saw to use in finishing our basement. It was easy to plug in the saw and make cuts. However, getting the corners of the trim molding to fit perfectly was another matter. I soon found out that using the saw was the easy part—what I didn't know were the techniques required for producing professional-looking finish carpentry! This chapter moved you beyond merely "powering up" InDesign, to incorporating typesetting techniques that are standards in our profession. Some of my students don't "buy in" to learning these techniques—and you can see the results in their poor typesetting. Remember, your potential employer only needs to examine your document formatting by making hidden characters visible to determine your InDesign proficiency. These first chapters are designed to help you develop excellent production habits which will last throughout your career. Although many of the rules and techniques seem nitpicky at first, they will become automatic after practice.

Anatomy of type was introduced, followed by a discussion of hidden characters and paragraph definition. The features of the *Paragraph Formatting Controls* were emphasized in this chapter. You learned how to format paragraphs using space after, raised and drop caps, and various indents. *No break, Nonbreaking spaces* and *hyphens* were introduced, as well as the proper use of quotation marks and dashes. These important production tips were presented:

- *Use soft returns (**Shift+Return** or **Shift+Enter**) to manually break lines within a paragraph. A soft return in also called a **forced line break.***
- *Use a hard return (**Return** or **Enter**) only at the end of a paragraph.*
- *Use **Space After** or **Space Before** in **Paragraph Fomatting Controls** to add extra space between paragraphs.*
- *Do not set text "line for line" unless absolutely necessary.*
- *The **Story** panel allows you to activate **Optical Margin Alignment**.*
- *Go to the **www.identifont.com** web site when you need to match a typeface.*
- *A formula for determining the range of acceptable line measure for single-column body copy, is 2 to 2.5 times the type's point size, in picas.*

Now that you're becoming comfortable with using type, in the next chapter we'll throw images into the production mix.

▸ MOVING TOWARD MASTERY

identifying typefaces

When you look at the photos above you see a variety of colors, shapes and textures. These objects have two characteristics in common—they are all circular, and they are everyday objects. We are so familiar with thermostats, cleanser cans, and pie plates that it only takes a glance for us to identify each item. But if you showed these images to someone who was not immersed in our culture, that person would only recognize the common circular shape because there would be no context for a broader understanding.

Similarly, typefaces might simply look like a bunch of letters to you. When you first begin working with type, it's difficult to see much variation between typefaces. For some, it's even difficult to distinguish between a serif and sans serif typeface. As you continue to immerse yourself in the world of type, you will begin to understand the personality and design nuances of specific typefaces. Like the objects pictured above, typefaces will communicate specific meanings and ultimately, you will use them with grace and power.

▸ IN REVIEW

1. How is a font's point size determined?
2. Why is it helpful to see hidden characters?
3. What is the difference between a hard and soft return?
4. How can space be added between paragraphs without pressing the Return key more than once?
5. What does the notation **Myriad Pro Semibold Condensed 12/15 × 30** mean?
6. How do you make a drop cap? How do you make a raised cap?
7. Which panel holds the Optical Margin Alignment option?
8. Describe the uses for each of the following: hyphen, em dash, en dash.
9. What is the guideline for calculating an acceptable line measure?
10. How is a typographer's quotation mark different from a typewriter quotation mark?
11. What does it mean to set text "line for line"?
12. The client has asked you to duplicate a project, but does not know what font was used. What steps would you take to identify the font?
13. What is a discretionary hyphen and how is it entered?
14. When might you use a nonbreaking space?
15. How do you make No Hyphenation the default for an entire document?

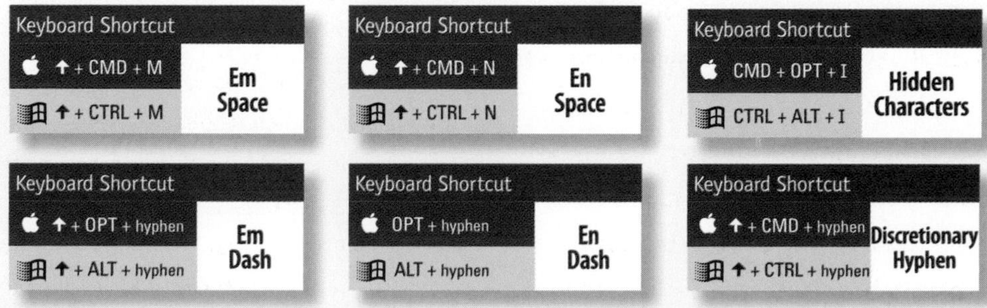

▸ CHAPTER 3 PROJECTS

A THE QUICK BROWN FOX JUMPED OVER THE LAZY DOG'S BACK.
The quick brown fox jumped over the lazy dog's back.
123456789

B THE QUICK BROWN FOX JUMPE
OVER THE LAZY DOG'S BACK.
The quick brown fox jumped over the lazy dog's back.
123456789

C THE QUICK BROWN FC
OVER THE LAZY DOG'S
The quick brown fox jumped over the lazy dog's back.
123456789

Joe King
and
Bell E. Flopp
invite you to
share their joy
as they are
united in marriage on
Saturday, September 25, 2010
3:00 p.m.
at the
Winschel-Harris Wedding Chapel
300 North Broadway
Oconomowoc, Wisconsin.

Dinner will be served from
4:30–10:00 p.m.
at the
Blue Eagle American Legion Hall
301 North Broadway
RSVP—regrets only
Type your name here

Shown above are three text passages in "mystery" typefaces. Now that you know the distinguishing characteristics of letters, go to *www.identifont.com* and select *Fonts by Appearance*. Answer the questions provided to determine the typefaces used in each passage. If you're not positive your answer is correct, select *Not Sure*.

One the following pages are some of the projects for Chapter 3. You will find the directions for these projects on the *03 Student Handout* and pictures in the *03 Artwork and Resources* folder on the online companion resources.

▸CHAPTER 3 PROJECTS

Photography ©2006 Christopher Pollack, Waukesha County Technical College

DESSERTS MENU

APPLE AND BLACKBERRY MERINGUE
A meringue base with generous layers of apple and blackberry. Cream cheese and whip cream provide just enough sweetness, and create a light, delicious after dinner treat. $6.50

BLUEBERRY ITALIAN CHEESECAKE
Blueberries and whip cream top this creamy cheesecake. Ricotta cheese and nutmeg create a flavor sensation that is truly Italian. $5.95

BLACK FOREST CHEESECAKE
A heavenly blend of chocolate, cherry, and amaretto flavors. Our pastry chef's specialty. $4.95

STRAWBERRY ALMOND PARFAIT
Luscious strawberries layered with vanilla creme and sprinkled with amaretti crumbs. Served in parfait glass and garnished with fresh mint. $4.95

...UCTION SEQUENCE

...nportant and basic production step is to ...is *exactly* the right size. If you are building ...format the interior space with margins ...g a frame in the middle of the document, ...ment, and define a specific frame size.

2. ADD AND ALIGN THE OUTER STROKE. Once a frame is created, decide if it should have a stroke. If so, add a stroke of the correct weight and style. Then open the Stroke panel—Window>Stroke. If you have created your frame to an exact size, align the stroke to the inside.

3. CREATE A TEXT INSET. A stroked text frame needs a text inset. Always add the text inset before you begin to type.

4. TYPING. Do all the typing before you begin to format the text. Always type first, and format second. Type a z in the places where a glyph will be inserted later. Usually type will *not* be set line for line, so let your text flow.

...ACTER FORMATTING. First "rough in" the text. Select all the text and apply the most commonly used type style, size, and leading values, usually the specifications for the body copy text. Then, go back and add specific character attributes, including glyphs and raised caps.

...GRAPH FORMATTING. When the character attributes are finished, encode paragraph attributes including indents, drop caps, space before, space after, and hyphenation.

...F YOUR WORK. The job isn't done until you have proofed it. Run spell check before printing and print a copy of your project. Compare your project with the original, marking changes as needed. Confirm that type use is consistent throughout the document. Make any changes, print, and proof again.

Type your name here
Project 03E

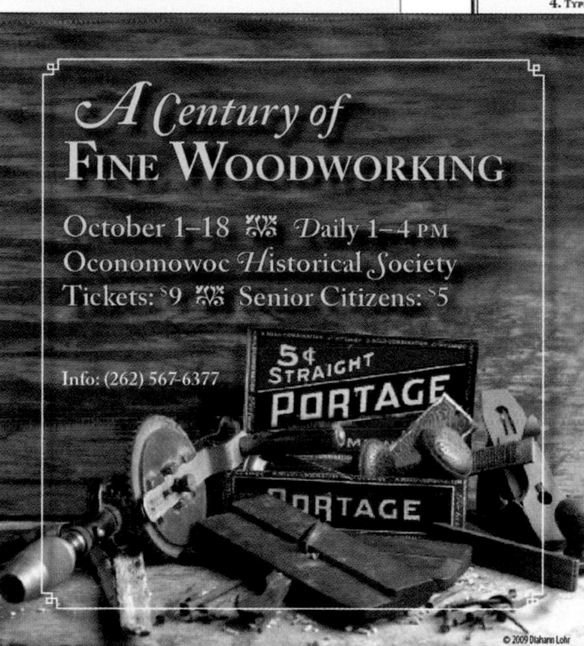

A Century of
FINE WOODWORKING
October 1–18 Daily 1–4 PM
Oconomowoc Historical Society
Tickets: $9 Senior Citizens: $5
Info: (262) 567-6377
5¢
STRAIGHT
PORTAGE
PORTAGE
© 2009 Diahann Lohr

Photography © 2009 Diahann Lohr, Waukesha County Technical College

EXPLORING INDESIGN CS6
Artwork & Resources

- Go to: http://www.cengagebrain.com
- Type: Rydberg
- Click Exploring InDesign CS6 in the list of search results.
- When the book's main page is displayed, click the Access button under Free Study Tools.
- To download files, select a chapter number and then click on the Artwork & Resources tab on the left navigation bar to download the files.

Combining Type and Images

objectives

- *Locate, move, and lock the zero point*
- *Use the coordinate and measurement systems for precise placement and sizing of elements*
- *Create multi-column and linked text frames*
- *Place text, check spelling, apply paragraph rules, adjust tracking, and use manual and optical kerning*
- *Place, scale, and crop images*

introduction

The first three chapters have focused on the basics of InDesign and typography. If you have been waiting for the chance to work with images—as designers love to do—this chapter is for you. First, we will master the coordinate system, place text, and fine-tune type. Then, near the end of the chapter you will be introduced to placing, scaling, and cropping images.

This chapter covers a lot of material. When you have completed it, you will be well on your way to mastering InDesign and ready to work on projects that are more enjoyable, creative, and challenging.

As you work through this chapter, it is an excellent idea to review sections of earlier chapters that you may have had difficulty with the first time through. Remember, the advanced skills we cover later in the book depend on the solid foundation you are building in these first chapters.

InDesign's measuring system

InDesign gives you numerous ways to manage the precise size and placement of text and graphics frames. Before we discuss size and placement issues, let's learn about and experiment with InDesign's measuring system. InDesign can measure in points, picas, inches, inches decimal, millimeters, centimeters, ciceros, agates, or pixels. InDesign will even let you make up your own unit of measure under the custom category!

▸ *Locate, change, lock, and unlock the zero point*

The *zero point* is the intersection of the zero markers on the horizontal and vertical rulers. All measurements are referenced from this point. The default location of the zero point is at the upper left corner of the page (not at the margin). However, there will be times when you will want to move the zero point to another location in your workspace. The next series of steps will show you just how easy InDesign makes it to relocate the zero point.

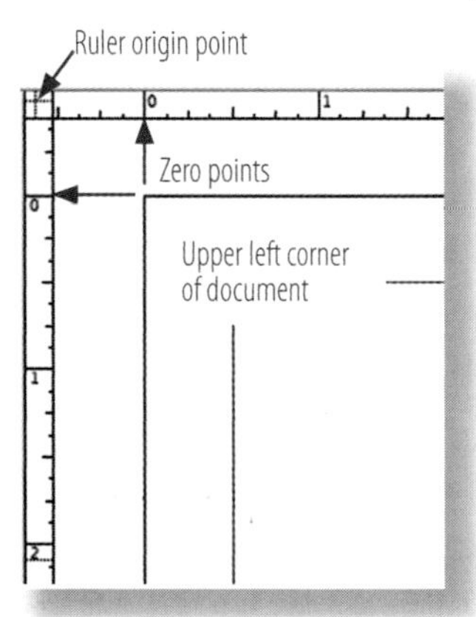

VISUAL | 4–1 |
The default location of the zero point is at the upper left corner of the page
© Cengage Learning 2013

1. Create a ***new document*** of any size. Find the ***zero point*** for the rulers in your document in the upper left corner (Visual 4–1).

2. To move the zero point, **click** on the ***ruler origin point*** (the upper left corner of your document window where the rulers meet) and **drag** down into the middle of the page. When you release the mouse button, look at the new location of the zero point on your horizontal and vertical rulers. Go back to the ruler origin point and **drag** the zero point to a second location. Repeat this until you are comfortable with the process.

3. To ***reset the zero point*** to the upper left corner of your document, simply **double-click** the ruler origin point in the upper left corner (Visual 4–1).

4. Drag the zero point to approximately the middle of your document. Go back to the ruler origin point and open the ***Context*** menu and select ***Lock Zero Point*** (Visual 4–2). You will notice that the icon of the intersecting lines disappears and that it is now impossible to reset the zero point. Use the same method to unlock the zero point.

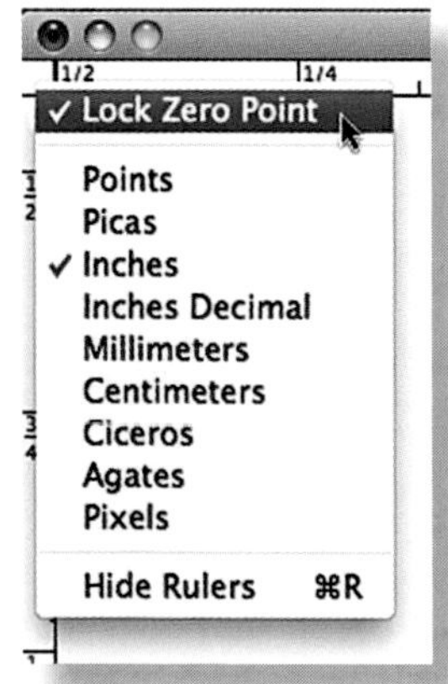

VISUAL | 4–2 |
Open the Context menu and choose to lock or unlock the zero point.
© Cengage Learning 2013

▸ *Change the units of measure default*

You can set the unit of measurement you wish to use. From the *Menu*, choose *InDesign* (Mac) or *Edit* (Windows)> *Preferences>Units & Increments*. In the *Ruler Units* section of the dialog box you can set the *Horizontal* and *Vertical* rulers independently of each other. When you change these ruler preferences with no document open (for example, from inches to picas), these settings become the default for all new documents.

▸ *Change the units of measure during production*

When you are working in a document, you can quickly change units of measurement by using the *Context* menu. Press **Control** (Mac) or **right-click** (Windows) on the ruler origin point, to display the *Context* menu. The unit of measure you choose will apply to both rulers. Or, you can apply a separate unit of measure for each ruler by using the *Context* menu on each of the rulers at the top and side of the page. If no rulers are showing, they have been hidden. Press **Command+R** (Mac) or **Control+R** (Windows) to bring them back into view. Press **Command+R** (Mac) or **Control+R** (Windows) to hide them, or select **Hide Rulers** from the *Context* menu.

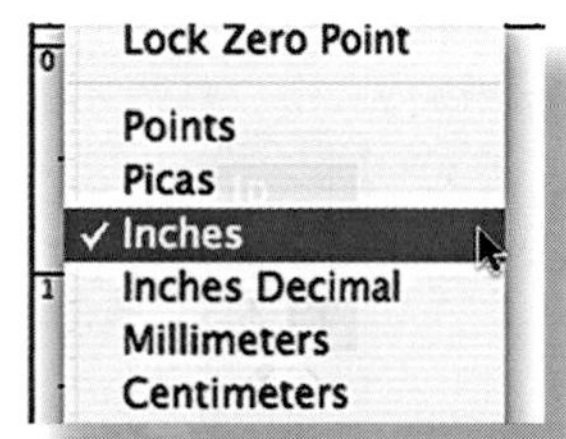

▸ *production tip*

The zero point is where measuring begins. The position of every object in your document is described by its distance from the zero point. Just like moving a ruler to different places on a piece of paper, the zero point is easily moved horizontally and vertically.

VISUAL | 4–3 |

Quickly change the units of measure for your document at the ruler origin point.

© Cengage Learning 2013

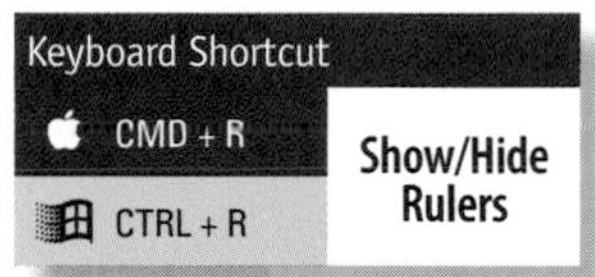

THE X AND Y COORDINATE SYSTEM

Every document you create in InDesign is automatically divided into an invisible grid of *horizontal* and *vertical coordinates*. When you move horizontally across the screen, you are moving along the *X coordinate axis*. When you move vertically, you are moving up or down the *Y coordinate axis*. The zero point determines whether the values of the coordinates are positive or negative. As you move the cursor to the right of the zero point, the *X* coordinate is a positive number that increases. As you move left of the zero point, the *X* coordinate is a negative number that decreases. On the *Y* axis, moving down vertically from the zero point gives you positive numbers, and moving up from the zero point gives you negative numbers. If you had graphing

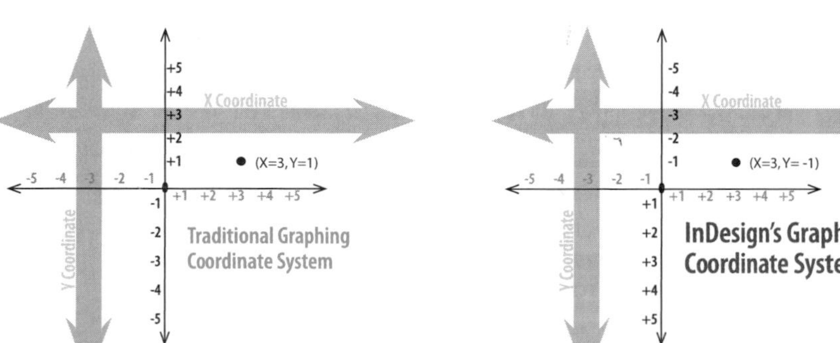

VISUAL | 4–4 |

In InDesign, coordinates increase as you move to the right and down from the zero point.

© Cengage Learning 2013

in high school math, you may already be familiar with this type of coordinate system. However, as Visual 4–4 shows, in InDesign, the vertical axis is exactly the opposite of what you are used to in algebra. Remember, in InDesign's coordinate system the numbers on the *Y* axis are negative as you move *up* from the zero point.

The *X* and *Y* coordinates for all the objects in your document are displayed in the *Control* panel. The values in the *X* and *Y* fields are displayed in the measurement system that you have selected to work in. Because the document area (including the pasteboard) is invisibly mapped into a grid—like graph paper—it becomes easy to describe the location of each element on the page as being so many units from the horizontal or vertical zero point, expressed as either positive or negative (Visual 4–5). But how do you know which point on your object InDesign is measuring to? Is it the center of the object, the right or left edge, or one of the corners? This point is known as the *reference point*. Just as InDesign allows you to move the zero point to suit your needs, you have the flexibility to set the reference point of an object to one of nine positions. It can be at any of the four corners; the middle of the top, bottom, right or left edges; or right in the center of the object.

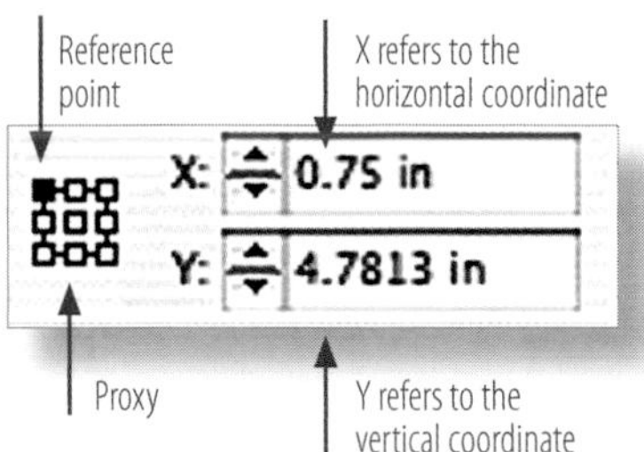

VISUAL | 4–5 |

These coordinates plot exact placement on the document.

► *Use the coordinate system*

1. Create a **6" × 6"** document. Make sure your units of measure are set to inches and your zero point is in the upper left corner of the document.

2. Select the ***Rectangle*** tool (**M**) and draw anywhere in your document to create a rectangle. Notice the values of the *X* and *Y* coordinates in the *Control* panel.

3. Select your rectangle with the ***Selection*** tool (black arrow) and move it to the right. Watch the values in the ***X coordinate*** field increase as the rectangle moves to the right. Move it back to the left and watch the values decrease. Now move the rectangle up and down on the page. As it moves up the page, the values in the ***Y coordinate*** field decreases, and as you move it down the page the values increase.

4. Look at the left end of the ***Control*** panel and you will see a series of nine small squares arranged in three rows and three columns (see Visual 4–5). One of these squares will be black and the rest will be white. This control is called the ***proxy.*** The ***proxy*** indicates the position of the ***reference point*** for the currently selected object. (The proxy is also found on the ***Transform*** panel that you can open by choosing ***Window>Object & Layout>Transform***. Working with the ***proxy*** on either the ***Transform*** panel or the ***Control*** panel will give you the same results.) Look for the black square; it indicates where the ***reference point*** is located on your rectangle.

▸ MOVING TOWARD MASTERY

*The **X** and **Y** coordinates will change for each object when the reference point in the **proxy** is moved. In the two examples below, the objects have not been moved. Because the location of the **reference point** has moved in each example, the corresponding coordinates have also changed. Measuring begins from the **reference point**!*

*For most items the **proxy** is made up of nine squares. However, if the selected item is a straight line, the **proxy** will have only three squares active. These squares indicate the two ends and the middle point. If the selected item is a guideline, the **proxy** will show a horizontal or vertical line with only a center **reference point**. You cannot change the **reference point** of a guideline.*

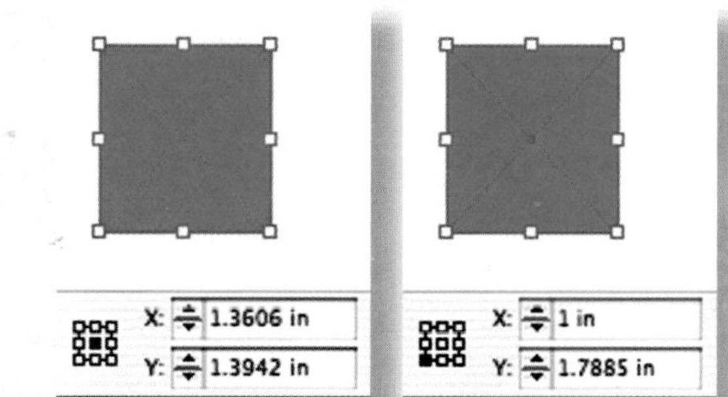

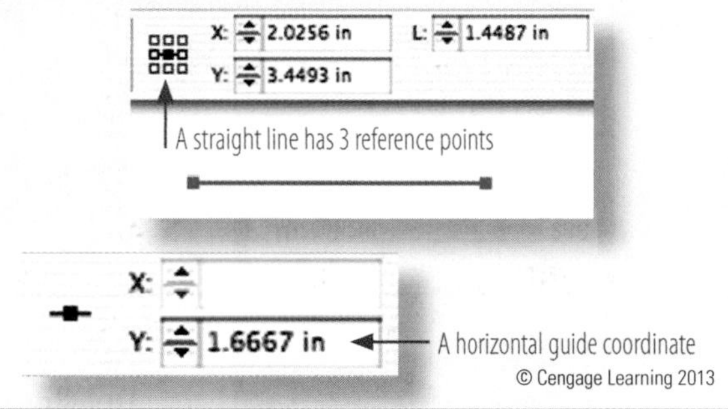

Make sure your rectangle is still selected and click the center square in the ***proxy***. The center square turns black, which means you have made the center of your selected rectangle the ***reference point***. With the center black box on the ***proxy*** still selected, write down the *X* and ***Y coordinates*** of your rectangle.

5. Now **click** on the upper left square on the ***proxy*** and read the *X* and *Y* coordinates. Even though you have not moved your rectangle, your *X* and *Y* coordinates are different than the ones you wrote down a moment ago. This is because you have changed the ***reference point***—it's now the upper left corner of your rectangle, instead of the center.

6. Place the rectangle in the exact center of your 6" × 6" document page. Make sure that your rectangle is selected, and **click** the center square on the ***proxy***. Since your document is a six-inch square, three inches over from the side of the square and three inches down from the top would be the center of the page. Type **3** in both the *X* and *Y* coordinate fields and press **Return**. The rectangle should jump to the exact center of the page with the center point of the rectangle exactly at the center point of the page.

7. Select the rectangle and click the upper right ***reference point*** in the ***proxy***. Type **6** in the *X* coordinate field and press **Return**. The rectangle should jump to align with the right edge of the page. Enter **0** in the *Y* coordinate field and press **Return**. The rectangle jumps to align with the top, right corner of the page.

You can now see the relationship between the *reference point* of an object and InDesign's *X* and *Y* coordinate system. The intersection of the coordinates displayed in the *Control* panel always indicates the position of the *reference point* that you have selected in the *proxy*.

UNDERSTANDING PATHS AND SELECTION TOOLS

A shape or line created in InDesign is called a *path*. A path can be a *closed shape* such as a rectangle, or an *open shape* such as a line. The basic component of a path is a *point*. A path can have as little as two points—such as a line with beginning and ending points—or it can be complex, with numerous points. The straight or curved lines that connect the points are called *segments*. A simple rectangle is in reality a closed path made up of points and straight connecting segments.

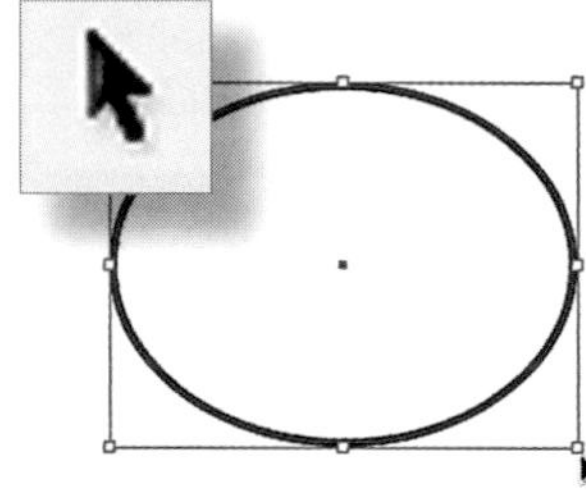

VISUAL | 4–6 |

The Selection tool allows you to move and resize entire objects.

InDesign has two tools specifically designed for working with paths. Let's begin with the black arrow, the *Selection* tool (Visual 4–6). The *Selection* tool can be activated (when you are not using the *Type* tool) by pressing **V**. The *Selection* tool transforms a whole object—changing attributes such as size, scaling, position, skew, and rotation angle. It focuses on the outer dimensions and structure of an entire path. When you click on an open or closed path with the *Selection* tool, all the points on the path are selected. If the object has a fill, you can click on the fill to select all the points. With all the points selected, you can move the entire object. When you select another object with the tool, the previous object is deselected.

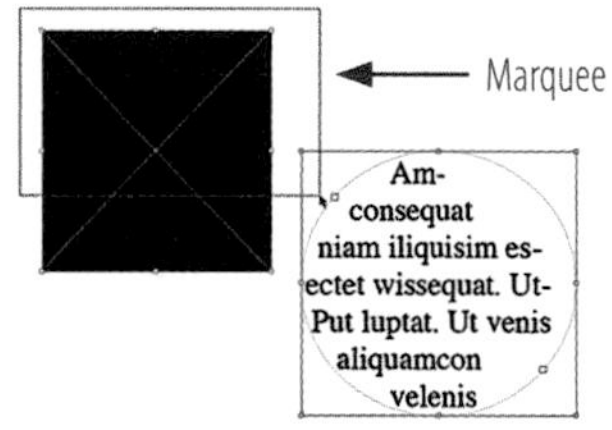

VISUAL | 4–7 |

You can select multiple objects by drawing a marquee that touches the border of each object.

If you have several objects to select, you can select the first object and then add to the selection by pressing the **Shift** key while selecting the next object. Another way of selecting multiple paths with the *Selection* tool is to go to a blank space on the document and drag a rectangle (called a *marquee*) around the paths to select. Since the tool is designed to select whole paths, you can just touch the edge of each path with the marquee and the whole path will be selected.

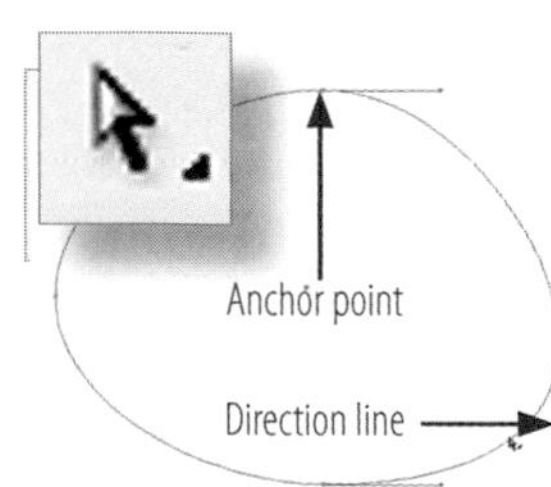

VISUAL | 4–8 |

The Direct Selection tool selects individual points on a path.

The *Direct Selection* tool—the white arrow—is next to the *Selection* tool in the *Toolbox* (Visual 4–8). When you're not using the *Type* tool you can press **A** to activate it. The *Direct Selection* tool is designed to select individual points or segments on a path. When a point is selected, it changes from a hollow square to a filled

▸ MOVING TOWARD MASTERY

*The **Selection** tool moves and resizes entire objects. When you are in the **Type** tool you can temporarily access the **Selection** tool by pressing **Command** (Mac) or **Control** (Windows) or switch to the **Selection** tool by pressing **ESC**.*

*Use the **Direct Selection** tool to reshape objects. The **Option** (Mac) or **ALT** (Windows) keyboard modifier makes a copy of the selected object/line segment. You may move an entire object with the **Direct Selection** tool by selecting the center point of the object.*

▸ *production tip*

Double-click an object to switch between the selecting the frame and the object. Double-click a text frame to place the insertion point and switch to the Type tool.

square. When your *Direct Selection* cursor is over a line segment, a slash appears next to it. When it is over a point, a box appears next to it. Use the *Selection* tool to change the dimension of an object. Use the *Direct Selection* tool to change the shape of an object.

When you want to select all the points of a path using the *Direct Selection* tool, you can select the center point. You can also select all the points on a path by drawing a rectangular marquee, making sure all points are within the marquee's rectangle. If the object has a fill, you can click on the fill with the *Direct Selection* tool and move the whole path.

▸ *Use width and height coordinates*

In the next series of steps you are going to draw an ellipse and then resize its shape using the selection tools and the *W* (width) and *H* (height) fields on the *Control* panel.

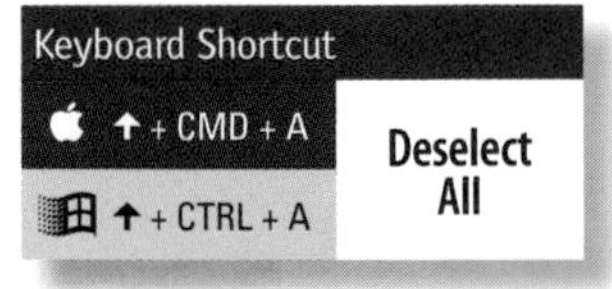

1. **Delete** the rectangle from your document. To draw an ellipse, click on the tiny triangle in the lower right corner of the ***Rectangle*** tool and choose the ***Ellipse*** tool. **Click+drag** an ellipse in your document. Deselect the ellipse you have just drawn by pressing **Shift+Command+A** (Mac) or **Shift+Control+A** (Windows).

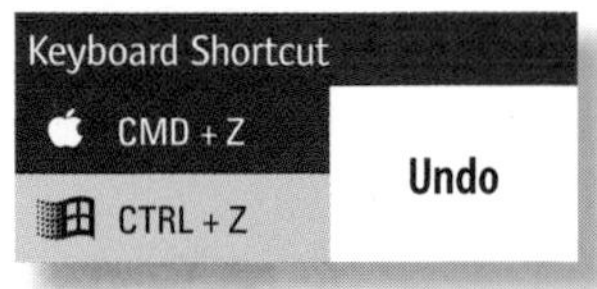

2. **Click** the edge of your ellipse with the *Direct Selection* tool. Five hollow squares appear on the ellipse—one in the center, and one on each quadrant of the outer edge. These are called *anchor points.* **Click** on one, and it will turn solid, allowing you to edit it independently of the other anchor points. You should also see lines extending from one or more anchor points. These lines are called *direction lines*. If you drag any of the anchor points or the end of a direction line, the shape will be changed (Visual 4–8). Experiment with moving the direction lines to change the shape and then undo your changes by pressing **Command+Z** (Mac) or **Control+Z** (Windows) until the shape is back to the original.

3. Deselect the object by clicking in a blank spot in your document or by using the keyboard shortcut **Shift+Command+A** (Mac) or **Shift+Control+A** (Windows).

4. With the ***Direction Selection*** tool, **click** first on the edge of the shape and then on the center anchor point. All the hollow anchor points become filled, which means they are all selected. **Drag** the center square and move the ellipse to another part of the page. With the anchor points still selected, **drag** the edge of the shape and move it again.

5. Now switch to the ***Selection*** tool by pressing **V.** The ellipse will look much different. You will see the rectangular bounding box that shows the outer boundaries of the shape. On the bounding box you will see eight tiny squares and a ninth square in the middle of the ellipse. The center square will be filled, and the outer squares will be hollow. These boxes are called ***handles***. Drag any of the handles to change the dimension of the ellipse (Visual 4–9).

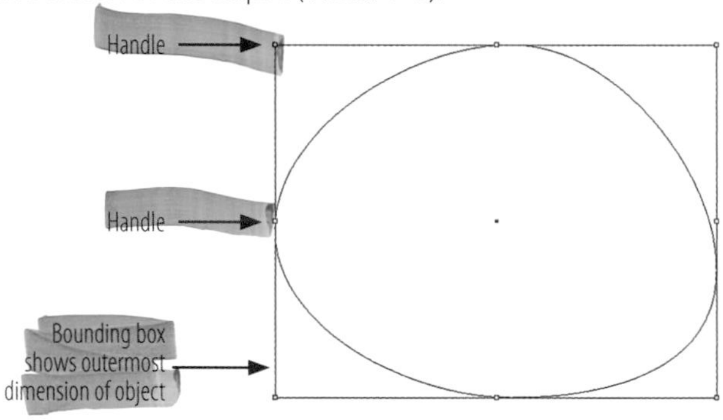

VISUAL |4–9|
Drag any of the handles to change the dimension of the ellipse.

6. There are several ways to move the entire ellipse: drag the center point, or click on and drag the edge of the ellipse, or click and drag a section of the bounding box. Use each of these methods and practice moving the ellipse. (Be careful not to drag a hollow handle, this will resize the object.)

7. Now, note the *X* and *Y* coordinates displayed in the ***Control*** panel. The coordinates indicate the location of the ***reference point*** of the ellipse designated in the ***proxy***. Look at the *W* and *H* coordinates. These measurements show the width and height of the selected shape. As you drag on the handles on the bounding box of the ellipse, the dimensions in the ***Control*** panel will also change.

8. Type **4** in the *W* field and **3** in the *H* field. Press **Return**. Your ellipse should change size.

9. With the 4" × 3" ellipse selected, **click** on the center ***reference point*** on the ***proxy***. Now type **3** in the *X* coordinate field and **3** in the *Y* coordinate field and press **Return**. The ellipse should now be centered on your page.

working with text

The copy in your document communicates a message while adding texture, color, shape, and contrast to your layout. Your ability to use text as a design element is an important skill to develop. In this next section you will learn how to create multiple column text frames and import (or *Place*) text from word processing documents.

▸ *Use width and height coordinates*

Creating text columns within text frames is a simple process. When the *Paragraph Formatting Controls* are active, you can find the column options near the middle of the panel (Visual 4–10). The space between the columns is called a *gutter* (or *alley*). To change the width of the gutter, select the text frame and press **Command+B** (Mac) or **Control+B** (Windows) to open the *Text Frame Options* dialog box. In the *Gutter* field, enter the desired value for the gutter width. You can type the value in a unit of measure such as 1p (1 pica).

1. Draw a frame in your document. Select the ***Type*** tool and click the frame to instantly convert it to a text frame. Select the ***Paragraph Formatting Controls.*** In the ***Number of Columns*** field enter **3**, and **p6** (six points) in the ***Gutter*** field. (Visual 4–10). Press **Return**.

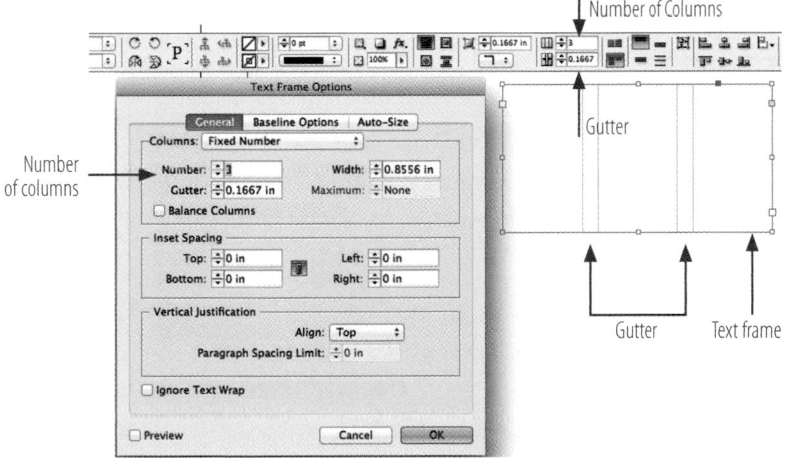

VISUAL |4–10|

Click the up or down arrows or type a number in the Number of Columns field to create multiple columns inside a text frame. You can also create columns. in the Text Frame Options dialog box. © Cengage Learning 2013

2. Choose ***Type>Fill with Placeholder Text.*** Text will fill your text frame. With the ***Type*** tool active, select all the text using the shortcut key and reduce the point size until the last text column is empty.

3. Place the cursor in the middle of a line in the first column. Press **Enter** on the number keypad. This makes text jump to the next column. If you are in the habit of pressing the ***Return*** key over and over to force text to jump to another column—don't! Simply insert the cursor where you want the text to break and press **Enter** on the number keypad. If your keyboard doesn't have a numeric keypad with an ***Enter*** key, open the ***Context*** menu and select ***Insert Break Character>Column Break.***

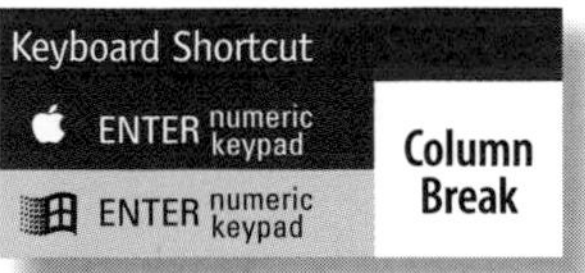

Don't get into the bad habit of pressing the *Return* key multiple times to force the text to flow to the next column. If your layout changes, you'll need to delete all those manual keyboard entries. When you press the *Enter* key on the number keypad to insert a column break character, it will be much easier to simply remove it, if you have to revise the column break later.

Creating columns within text frames is simple and useful for projects. More often, however, designers will create separate text frames in different places on the page and flow the text between the frames. You will learn that technique, called *threading,* later in this chapter. Right now, you will learn how to use the *Place* command to bring text files created in a variety of word processors into your InDesign documents. What a timesaver!

PLACING TEXT

The keyboard shortcut for placing text—**Command+D** (Mac) or **Control+D** (Windows)—is one you will want to memorize. You will use it again and again to import text or graphics. Pressing the keyboard shortcut brings up the *Place* dialog box.

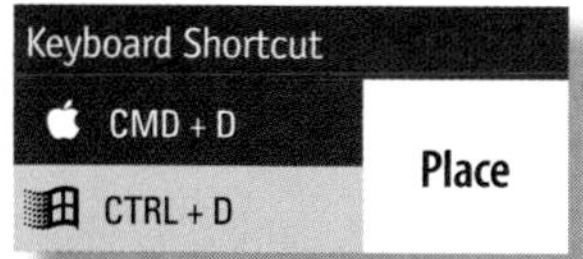

Two important features of the *Place* dialog box are the choices to *Show Import Options* and *Replace Selected Item,* in the lower left corner (Visual 4–11). *Show Import Options,* among other things, gives you control over how different versions of Microsoft Word text files are handled. Choosing *Replace Selected Item* will replace any text that is selected within a text frame with the contents of the file you are placing. If the frame is selected with the *Selection* or the *Direct Selection* tool, the entire contents of the text frame will be replaced.

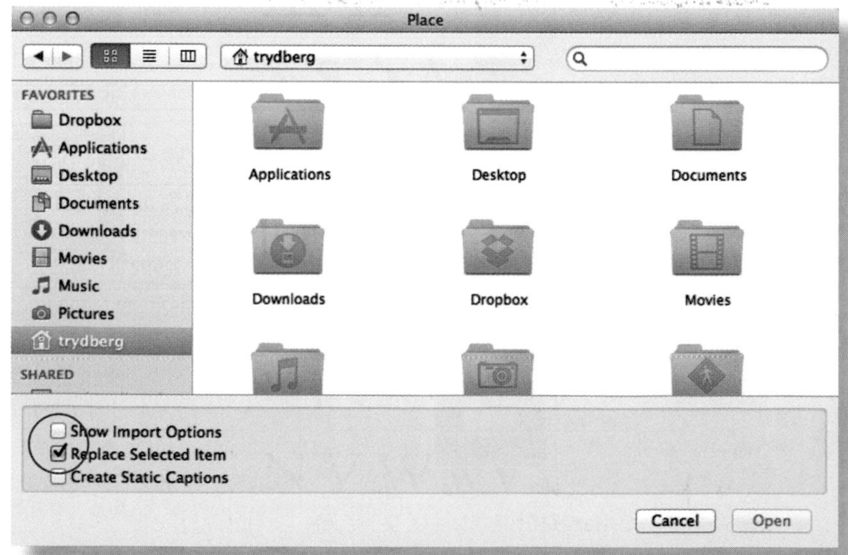

VISUAL |4–11|

The Place dialog box.

The next exercises will focus on three methods for importing text files: placing them into an existing frame, placing them into a new frame, and simply dropping the contents onto a page. In the next exercise, you will create a new 8.5" × 11" document, add a frame, and then use all three methods of placing text. You will be using a text file called *04 Copyfit.doc* from the *04 Artwork and Resources* folder from the online companion resources.

EXPLORING INDESIGN CS6
Artwork & Resources

- Go to: http://www.cengagebrain.com
- Type: Rydberg
- Click Exploring InDesign CS6 in the list of search results.
- When the book's main page is displayed, click the Access button under Free Study Tools.
- To download files, select a chapter number and then click on the Artwork & Resources tab on the left navigation bar to download the files.

▸ *Place text into an existing text frame*

1. Draw a **6" × 9"** text frame. Set the ***reference point*** in the center at *X* coordinate: **4.25"**, and *Y* coordinate: **5.5"**. Create **3 columns** with a **1-pica** gutter. Download the *04 Artwork and Resources* folder from the online companion resources.

2. Press **Command+D** (Mac) or **Control+D** (Windows) to open the *Place* dialog box. Find the and select the text file called *04 Copyfit.doc*.

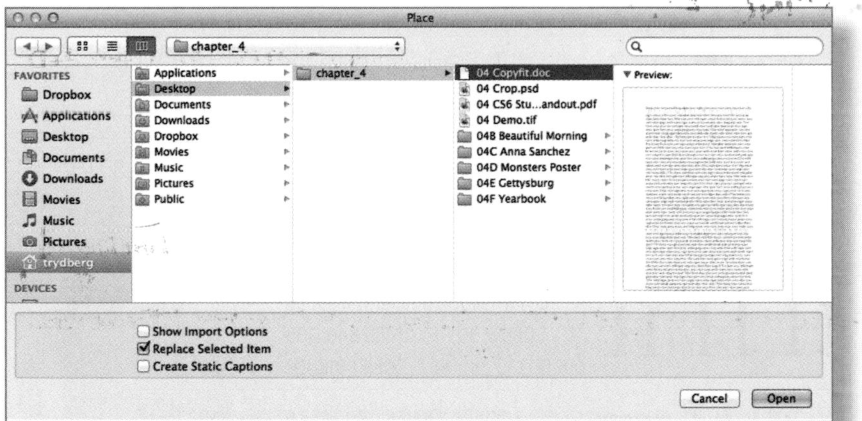

VISUAL |4–12|

The navigation route to the *04 Copyfit.doc* file.

© Cengage Learning 2013

3. Uncheck *Show Import Options* and *Replace Selected Items* in in the lower left corner of the dialog box. Press **Return**.

4. Move the cursor to the upper left corner of the text box. You will see tiny lines of type enclosed with long parentheses (Visual 4–13). This icon means your text cursor is loaded and ready to place text into an existing frame. Now click anywhere in the text frame and type will flow into all three columns. Notice the square with the red plus sign (+) in the lower right column. A red plus is the ***overset*** symbol—it means there is more text than the text frame will hold.

VISUAL |4–13|

The loaded text cursor is ready to place copy into an existing frame.

© Cengage Learning 2013

5. To delete the overset text, place the cursor at the end of the visible copy. If you are working on a Mac, select all the "invisible" overset text, beyond the plus sign, by pressing **Shift+Command+End**. Release those keys and then press **Delete.**

▸ *production tip*

To delete overset text: Place the cursor at the end of the copy. Press Shift+Cmd+End (Mac) or Shift+Ctrl+End (Windows) to select copy beyond the cursor. Then press Delete.

If you are a Windows user, place your cursor at the end of the visible copy. Press **Shift+Control+End** to select the overset text. Release those keys and then press **Delete**. The plus sign should disappear as the text beyond the frame is deleted. If you're working on a laptop, press **Shift+Command** (Mac) or **Shift+Control** (Windows) **+ Right Arrow** and press **Delete**.

▸ *Place text by creating a new frame*

In this exercise, you will import text and create a new text frame to place it into, at the same time. First, **delete** the three-column text box, so that your document is blank.

VISUAL |4–14|

The loaded text cursor will create a text frame when the copy is dropped into the document.

1. Press **Command+D** (Mac) or **Control+D** (Windows) and select the *04 Copyfit. doc* file again. Press **Return**. Move the loaded cursor over the blank document and look carefully at its shape. This time you will not see parentheses around the text cursor. Instead, you will see straight lines on the top and left edge. This icon indicates that a new frame will be created for the text (Visual 4–14).

2. **Drag** the loaded text cursor to create a frame. When you release the mouse, text will flow into the new text frame.

3. Change the *Width* and *Height* to **5" × 7"** and create three columns. Again, notice the overset symbol in the out port in the lower right corner. **Delete** the overset text.

▸ *Place text by dropping into the page*

This method of placing text drops the text into the document and lets it spread from margin guide to margin guide. **Delete** the text frame from your document.

4. Open the *Place* dialog box by using the keyboard shortcut and select *04 Copyfit.doc* one more time. Press **Return**. Notice that the shape of the loaded cursor is the same as in Visual 4–14.

5. **Click** the cursor anywhere on the document. A text frame will stretch from margin to margin with the top positioned wherever you clicked on the page. **Delete** the overset text.

HOW TO ESTIMATE WORD COUNT

Look at the file you just placed and you will see that there are numbers scattered throughout the text. These numbers represent the *word count.* These numbers can help you estimate how many words, in a specific font, type size, and leading, will fit in this text box. You can use the *04 Copyfit.doc* file when you design the text areas for an InDesign project and then tell the copywriter how many words will be needed to fill the allotted space. Another way to estimate the word count for any passage of placeholder text is to highlight the copy and then open the *Info* panel. The character, word, line, and paragraph count is displayed at the bottom of the panel. In the example shown in Visual 4–15, you will see a plus (+) symbol followed by additional numbers. The numbers following the plus symbol refer to the number of characters, words, lines, or paragraphs which are overset. When the text does not fit into the specified frame, the *Info* panel lets you know how much copy to cut. *Note:* If this section of the *Info* panel is not visible, open the panel's options menu and choose **Show Options**.

Keyboard Shortcut
Mac: F8 (function key)
Windows: F8 (function key)
Info Panel

VISUAL | 4–15 |
The Info panel displays the character, word, line, and paragraph count for a selected text frame.

MANAGING TEXT FLOW

Now that you have mastered the basics of placing text, it's time to learn to manage the text flow as it is being placed into a document. You will learn these four techniques: *manual text flow, semi-automatic text flow, automatic text flow,* and *automatic text flow with a fixed number of pages.* You will need to place the *04 Copyfit.doc* file from the online companion resources.

▸ *Use manual text flow*

When you use *manual text flow*, you make all the decisions regarding where placed text will be positioned and how it will flow. You have total control, but as the "manual" name implies, this method is the slowest.

1. Create a new document, **7" × 5"**, landscape orientation. Create **3 columns** with **1p** gutter, **0.5"** margins. Press **Return**.

2. Look closely at the column guides. Notice that there is no text frame on the page. The column indicators are only guides—ready to hold a graphics or text frame. Again, place the ***04 Copyfit.doc*** file by using the keyboard shortcut. Move the cursor over to the upper left corner of the first column. The cursor shape indicates a new text frame will be created. **Click** in the upper left corner and the first column will fill with copy. You will see an overset symbol (+) at the bottom of the first column. The text will just "sit" there until you manually flow it to another column.

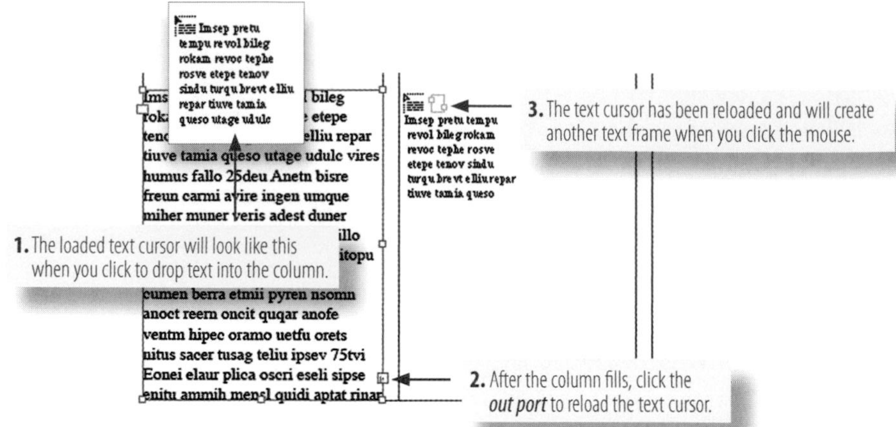
1. The loaded text cursor will look like this when you click to drop text into the column.
2. After the column fills, click the out port to reload the text cursor.
3. The text cursor has been reloaded and will create another text frame when you click the mouse.

VISUAL |4–16|

A click on the first column's out port reloads the text cursor for placing text in another column.

© Cengage Learning 2013

3. Press **Command** (Mac) or **Control** (Windows) to switch to the *Selection* tool. **Click** on the plus sign in the text out port. This process is called ***reloading*** the cursor. When you release the modifier key, the cursor has now changed into a loaded cursor, and you can see that the shape has changed (Visual 4–16).

4. **Click** in the upper left corner of the second column to flow text into this column. Reload your cursor by **clicking** on the text out port box. **Click** in the upper left corner of the third column and it will fill with copy.

5. Place the *Type* tool cursor at the end of the text in the third column. **Delete** the overset text by pressing **Shift+Command+End**, then **Delete** (Mac) or **Shift+Control+End**, then **Delete** (Windows). If you are on a laptop, use the modifier keys with the right arrow.

▸ *Use semi-automatic text flow*

Flowing text manually from column to column is a neat technique, but imagine how tedious it would be if you had to do that for a 10-page document! InDesign is always one step ahead of the user—and has designed a second way to flow text called *semi-automatic.*

1. Select all the text frames in your document and then **delete** by using keyboard shortcuts. Place the *04 Copyfit.doc* file once again. This time, hold down the **Option** (Mac) or **Alt** (Windows) key as you hold the loaded cursor in the upper left corner of the first column. Notice the shape of the cursor changes into a snake pattern each time you press the *Option* or *Alt* key (Visual 4–17). Press this key a few times to get used to the difference between the cursors. This cursor means your text will be placed in ***semi-automatic text flow*** mode.

VISUAL |4–17|

The semi-automatic text flow icon.

© Cengage Learning 2013

2. Hold down the **Option** (Mac) or **Alt** (Windows) key and **click** in the upper left corner. The text will fill the first column and the cursor will remain loaded. Hold down the **Option** or **Alt** key and **click** in the second column. The text flows into the middle column. As long as you continue to hold the *Option* or *Alt* key as you click to drop text, you remain in semi-automatic flow mode and the remaining text will remain loaded in the text icon.

3. Continue in semi-automatic mode and fill the last column. Press **ESC** to get out of semi-automatic text flow mode. **Delete** the overset text.

▸ *production tip*

To delete overset text: Place the cursor at the end of the copy. Press Shift+Cmd+End (Mac) or Shift+Ctrl+End (Windows) to select copy beyond the cursor. Then press Delete.

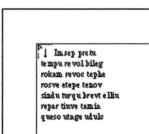

▸ *Use automatic text flow*

Manual and semi-automatic text flow provide the most control for placing text in individual text frames on a single page, or a series of non-contiguous pages. *Automatic text flow* is another method of flowing text that is fast, and automatically inserts exactly the right number of pages required to hold the text passage.

VISUAL |4–18|

The automatic text flow icon.

1. Create a new file, **3" × 5"** and **0.5"** margins. Place the *04 Copyfit.doc* file so that you have a loaded cursor. Hold down the *Shift* key as you move the cursor to the upper left corner of the page. **Click** inside the page margins.

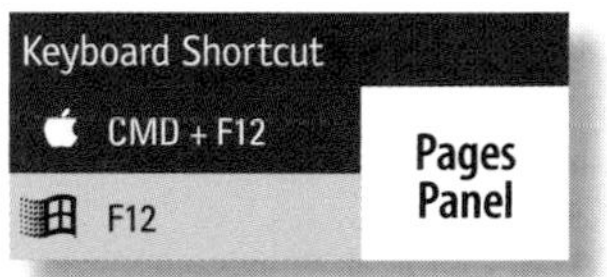

2. Open the *Pages* panel by pressing **Command+F12** (Mac) or **F12** (Windows) or by choosing *Window>Pages.* Notice that you now have more than one page in your document. When you place text in ***automatic flow*** mode, InDesign automatically adds as many pages as necessary.

▸ *Use automatic text flow with fixed number of pages*

The automatic text flow option is great for many projects—but what if you must make the text fit on only four pages? The *automatic text flow with fixed number of pages* technique allows you to place text on a specified number of pages only.

VISUAL |4–19|

The automatic text flow with fixed number of pages icon.

1. Create a **3" × 5"** document, **0.5"** margins, and **4** pages. Load the text cursor with *04 Copyfit.doc.*

2. This time, hold down **Shift+Option** (Mac) or **Shift+Alt** (Windows) as you **click** and drop the text onto the upper left corner of page one. The text will fill the available space on the four pages and then stop. Notice the familiar overset symbol in the out port at the end of page four. Now you can select all your text and adjust the point size and leading to make the copy fit into your four-page document.

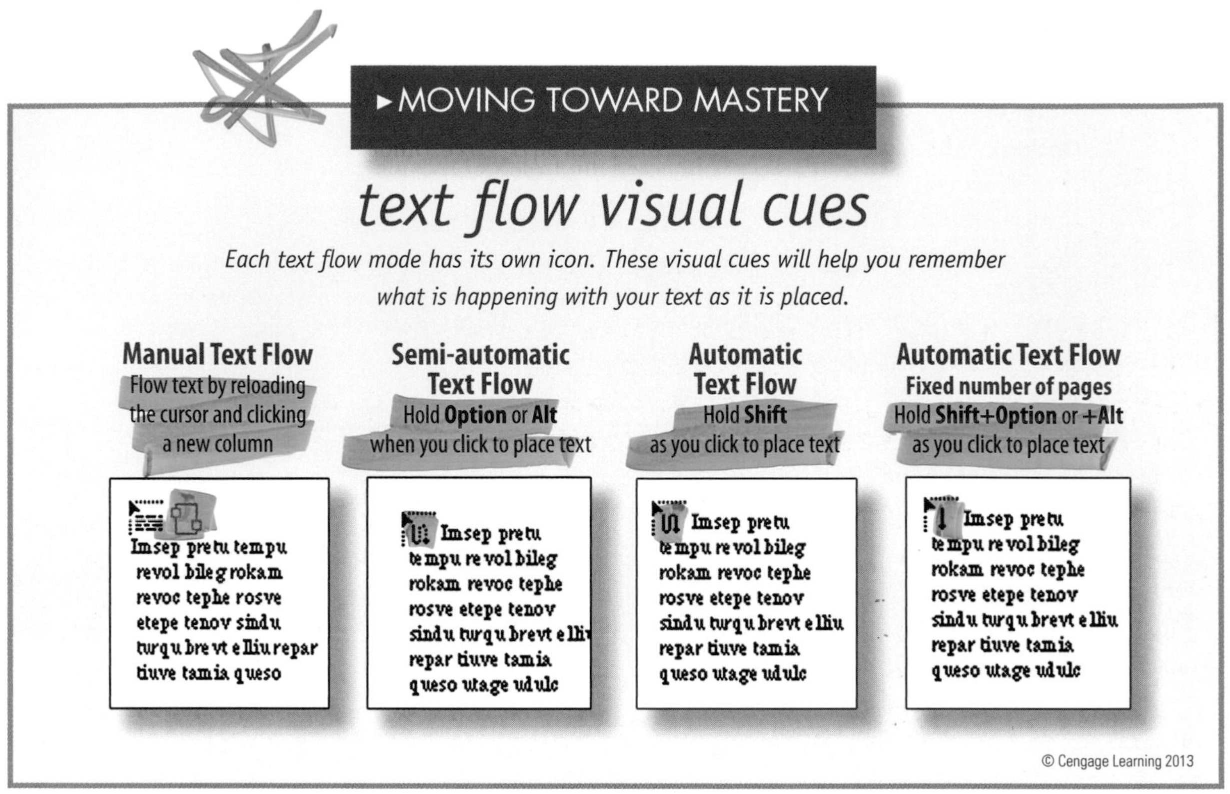

ABOUT THREADED TEXT FRAMES

In the exercises you just completed, text was flowing from one column to the next column. Text can also flow between individual text frames that are connected through a process called *threading*. As shown in Visual 4–20, each threaded text frame can have different text frame attributes including inset, fill, stroke and columns. Because threaded text frames are connected, you can use **Command+A** (Mac) or **Control+A** (Windows) to select all the type in the threaded frames.

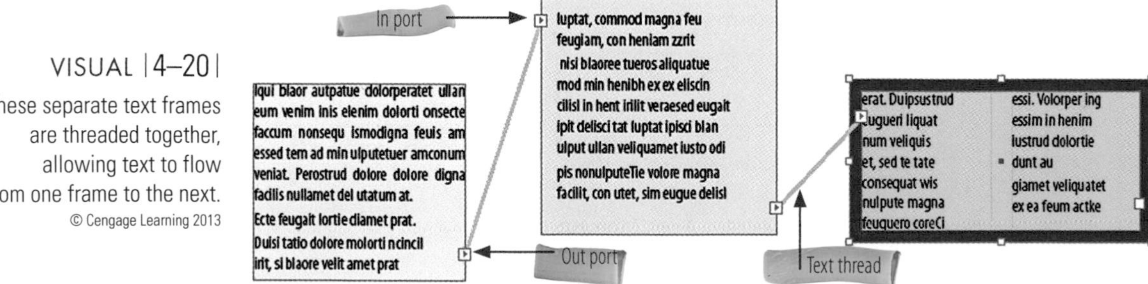

VISUAL |4–20|

These separate text frames are threaded together, allowing text to flow from one frame to the next.

© Cengage Learning 2013

▸ *Create threaded text frames*

1. Create a new document, **8.5" × 11"**, margins **0.5"**. Scatter three text frames on the document. Make some frames tall and some wide.

2. Place the *04 Copyfit.doc* file into the first frame. You will see the overset symbol (+) in the lower right of your frame.

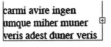

carmi avire ingen
umque miher muner
veris adest duner veris

3. Choose either of the *Selection* tools and **click** on the overset text symbol. The cursor is reloaded and its icon changes. As you move the loaded text cursor over the second text frame, it changes to show two small chain links, indicating these two frames will soon be threaded together (Visual 4–21).

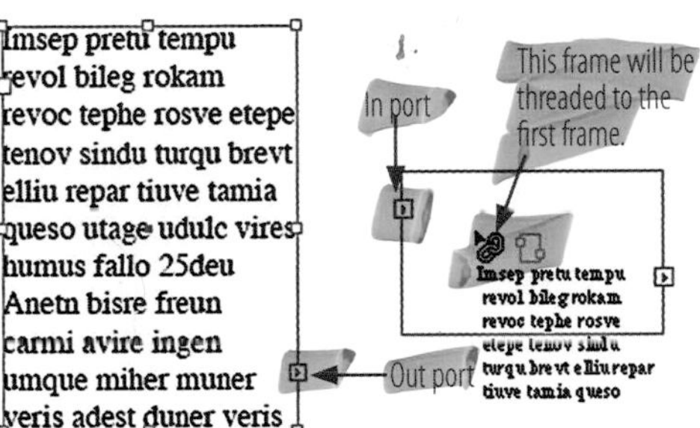

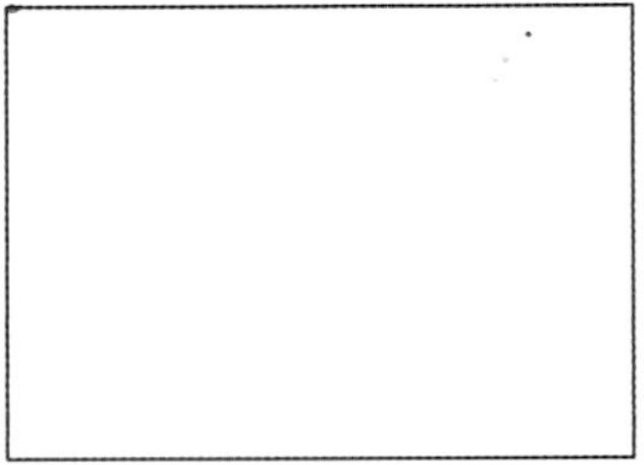

VISUAL | 4–21 |

Frames must be threaded together before copy will flow from one to the next.

4. **Click** to place the text into the second text frame. Notice that the overset text symbol that was in the first text frame has now been replaced with a blue triangle. The blue triangle means this box is now an ***out port.*** The upper left side of the second text frame also has a blue triangle, an ***in port.*** Flow copy into the third frame using the same process.

5. Now from the ***Menu*** bar, choose ***View>Extras>Show Text Threads.*** When you select a text frame, you will see lines connecting the ***in*** and ***out ports*** on your frames. These show the direction and order of the text flow. A ***triangle*** in the out port means that the text is linked to another frame. A ***plus (+)*** in the out port means that text is ***overset***—that there is too much text to fit in the frame. When the first in port and the last out port in a series of linked text frames are empty, it means that all the text has been placed (Visual 4–22). Don't close your file—we're going to use it for the next exercise.

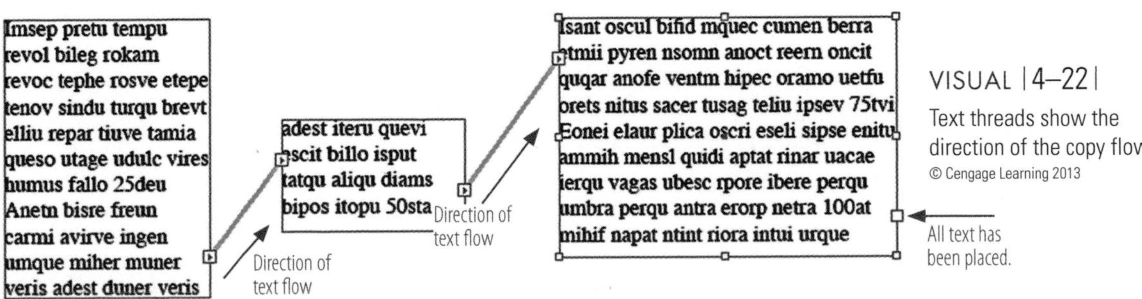

VISUAL | 4–22 |

Text threads show the direction of the copy flow.

▸ *Unlink text frames*

There will be times when you flow text into the wrong frame. Of course, you can simply press the **Undo** shortcut, but that method is only practical if you catch your error shortly after it was made. Here's another way to unlink threaded text frames.

1. Select the text frame in the middle of your text thread.
2. **Double-click** on the in port or the out port of the middle frame. If you double-click on the in port, the text flow will be cut off at the in port (A) and there will be a text overflow symbol in the first frame (B). If you double-click on the out port, text will be cut off at that point. The third frame is now empty and a text overflow symbol appears in the second frame.

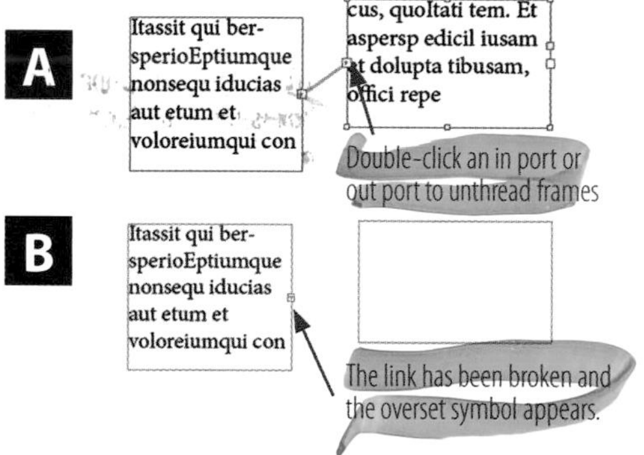

WHEN TO USE THREADED FRAMES

Now that you know how to thread text frames, you're probably wondering when you should use them. When text columns need to have individual attributes such as width, height, fill or stroke, you will want to use threaded frames. For instance, let's say you are working on a newsletter, and you want to shorten the third column to accommodate a photo. If you are using a single text frame with three columns, this will be difficult because you can only shorten the entire text frame instead of single columns. When you use threaded text frames to create columns, you can shorten just the third frame, letting the text reflow. Generally, using threaded text frames provides more flexibility than using single frames with multiple columns.

▸ MOVING TOWARD MASTERY

type basics

MANAGING UNDERLINES

During the days of old-fashioned typing, people used to underline text to add emphasis or to indicate the title of a book.

Unfortunately, that habit has carried over into the world of digital type, and most people simply click an icon to underline a word or sentence.

Today, italics are used to indicate the name of a book or to add emphasis. A heavier typeface can also be used to make a word or phrase stand out.

Typewriter-style underlines are rarely used in professional typesetting. If you must underline text, use InDesign's Underline Options capabilities in the Control panel menu options to control the weight of the underline and to avoid cutting through descenders.

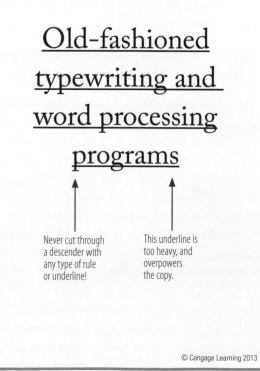

Old-fashioned typewriting and word processing programs

Never cut through a descender with any type of rule or underline!

This underline is too heavy, and overpowers the copy.

word and paragraph underlines

If you read *Type Basics* on the previous page, you already know that underlining individual words is rarely done when setting type. Underlining is a throwback to the "typewriter days" when it was the only method of adding emphasis.

UNDERLINING WORDS

For those rare times you need to underline text, you should not allow the rule to cut through a descender. Fortunately, InDesign has a complete and sophisticated way for you to adjust the weight and position of the underline. First, select the text you would like to underline. Then, select *Underline Options* from the options menu at the far right end of the *Control* panel. In the *Underline Options* dialog box (Visual 4–23), check the *Underline On* box and then adjust the weight, offset, color, and type of the line as desired.

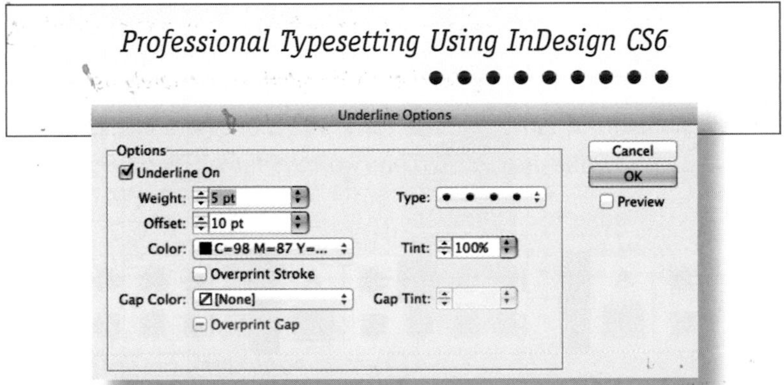

VISUAL |4–23|

The Underline Options dialog box is found under the Control panel menu options.

© Cengage Learning 2013

PARAGRAPH RULES

Paragraph rules may look like underlining, but they are an altogether different matter. Paragraph rules are design elements, and InDesign allows you to set rules in two places in each paragraph: 1) on or above the baseline of the first line of text; or 2) at the end of a paragraph. The *Paragraph Rules* function allows you to use color, styles, indents, and offsets to create just about any rule you'd ever want. Visual 4–24 shows some paragraph rules in action. The *Paragraph Rules* dialog box can be accessed by using a keyboard shortcut: **Command+Option+J** (Mac) or **Control+Alt+J** (Windows), or by clicking on the options menu in the *Control* panel and choosing *Paragraph Rules*.

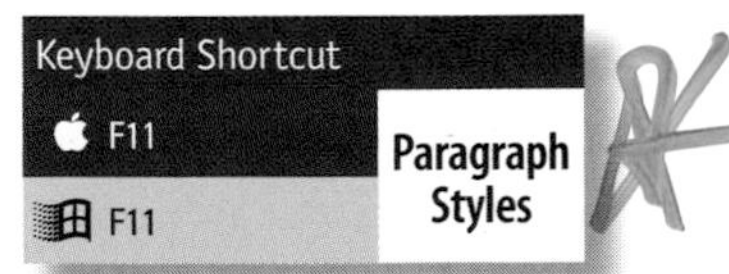

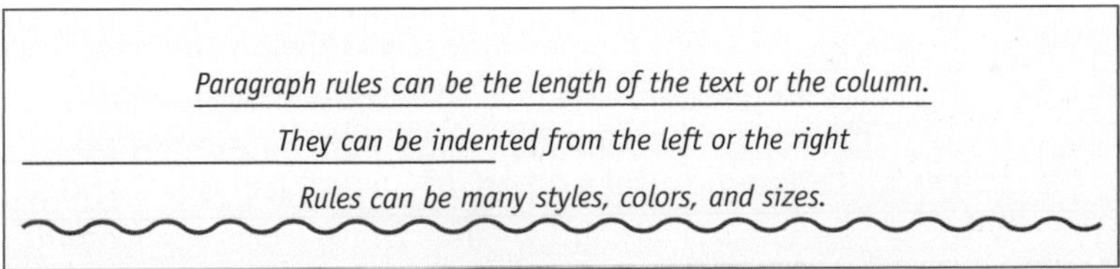

VISUAL |4–24|

Paragraph rules are great design elements—when used with discretion.

© Cengage Learning 2013

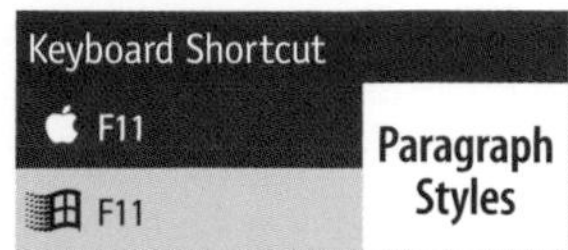

▸ *Apply a rule below a paragraph*

Whenever possible, apply rules as part of the paragraph formatting. A document that is filled with lines created with the *Line* tool is hard to edit because each line must be individually repositioned. Lines that are created as paragraph rules, will reflow as the copy changes.

1. Create a new document using the default settings. Draw a text frame and type your *name* on the first line and your *phone number* on the second line; use a **hard return** between the lines. Increase the type size to **48 points** on **60-point** leading.

2. With the blinking cursor somewhere in the first paragraph (the first line), press **Command+Option+J** (Mac) or **Control+Alt+J** (Windows) to access the *Paragraph Rules* dialog box (Visual 4–25). You can also choose *Paragraph Rules* from the *Control* panel options menu.

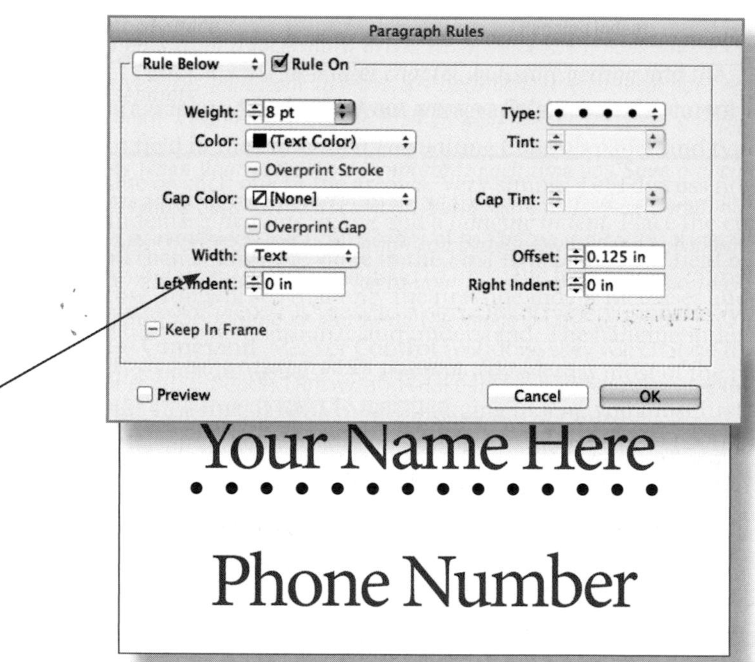

VISUAL |4–25|

Paragraph rules are design elements. To have a paragraph rule, you must have a paragraph, which means you will need to place a hard return in your copy.

▸ *production tip*

The Width field in the Paragraph Rules dialog box can be set to Column or Text. With Column selected, the line stretches from the left edge of the column to the right edge. With Text selected, the line extends only as long as the last line of text.

3. *Rule below* means that a rule will be placed after a paragraph (created by a hard return). Select *Rule Below* from the list and check the *Rule On* option box. Select **8 pt** in the *Weight* field menu, and **Dotted** in the *Type* field menu. The *Width* field should be set to **Text.** Enter **0.125"** in the *Offset* field. When you increase the offset, you push the rule farther down, away from the baseline. Press **Return** and your type should look similar to the sample in Visual 4–25. Keep this document open for the next exercise.

▸ *Apply a rule above a paragraph*

A *rule above* a paragraph will appear on the first baseline or will be offset above the first baseline of the paragraph. Applying a rule above a paragraph can be a little tricky because you'll need to add an offset value so that the rule doesn't cut through your type.

1. Click in the line that contains your name. First, you will turn off the rule below the paragraph. Open the ***Paragraph Rules*** dialog box and make sure that ***Rule Below*** is selected in the list, then uncheck the ***Rule On*** option. Click ***Preview*** and you will see the rule has disappeared. Press **Return**.

2. Now, you will add a rule above the phone number. Place the cursor in the line with your phone number. Open the ***Paragraph Rules*** dialog box and select ***Rule Above*** from the list. Be sure to check the ***Rule On*** option box. Select a line type and weight of your choice. Because the rule line will be drawn on the baseline, you'll need to enter a value in the ***Offset*** field. Type **p48** (48 points) to push the line up off the baseline.

HOW TO CHECK SPELLING

It's a good idea to always run a spell check before printing a document. But remember, even though InDesign's spell check function is excellent, it doesn't replace manual proofing. Both methods should be used to ensure accurate copy. To check spelling, simply press **Command+I** (Mac) **or Control+I** (Windows). When the *Check Spelling* dialog box appears, you will need to make a choice in the *Search* list. The following list describes the options:

- *The **All Documents** option checks the spelling of all open InDesign documents.*
- *The **Document** option checks the entire document you are working on. This is a great feature unless you have several pages of directory information including last names. If you would prefer to skip those sections of the document, choose the **Story** option.*
- ***Story** option checks spelling in the selected text frame and all threaded text frames.*
- *The **To End of Story** option checks all the words beyond the blinking cursor.*
- *If you have text highlighted before opening the **Check Spelling** dialog box, then you have another choice. **Selection** checks the spelling of the highlighted text.*

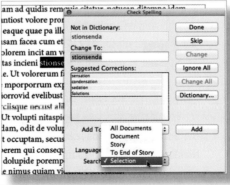

VISUAL |4–26|

Choices in the Check Spelling options will vary depending on what is selected.

Once you have made a choice in the *Search* list, simply click *Start* to begin the process. InDesign will alert you of any questionable words and possible errors. When the checking is complete, click **Done** to dismiss the dialog box.

UNDERSTANDING TRACKING AND KERNING

You already know what leading is. Leading is the **vertical** spacing between lines of type, measured from baseline to baseline. *Tracking* adjusts **horizontal** spacing between all the characters on a line. A single paragraph can contain characters with many different tracking values. *Positive tracking* increases spacing between characters; *negative tracking* decreases spacing between characters (Visual 4–27). Tracking values are shown in the *Paragraph* and *Character Formatting Controls.*

VISUAL |4–27|

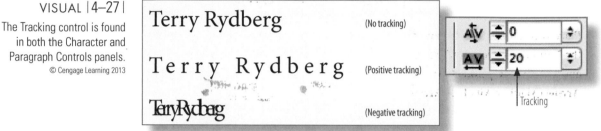

The Tracking control is found in both the Character and Paragraph Controls panels.

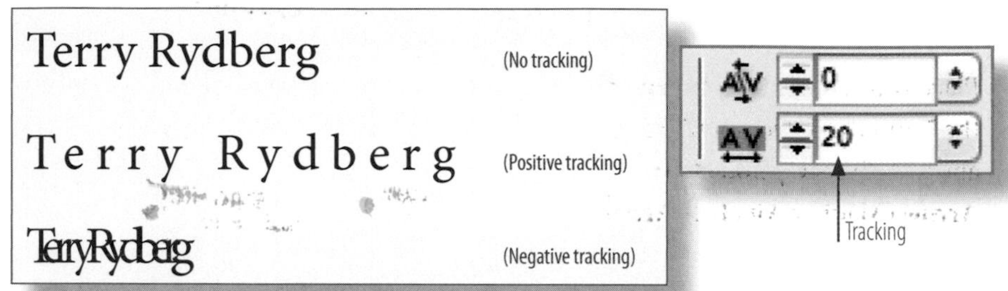

▸ *Adjust text spacing with tracking*

1. Create a new ***letter-sized*** document. Draw a text frame, type your full name and change the point size to **60-point**.

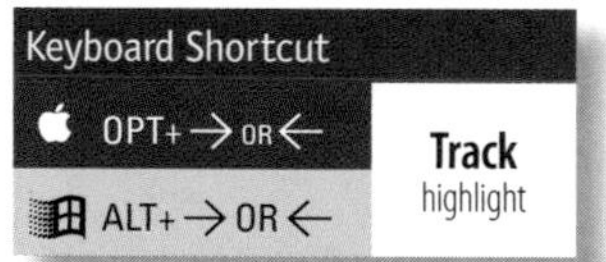

Keyboard Shortcut
OPT+ → OR ←
ALT+ → OR ←
Track
highlight

2. To tighten the tracking of your text: Highlight text you want tracked, hold down **Option** (Mac) or **Alt** (Windows), and press the **Left Arrow** key near the number pad. At first the text will still be readable, but if you keep pressing the arrow key, notice that the text ultimately reverses itself. Be careful not to overdo tracking!

3. **Delete** the text box and draw a new one. Type your name in it again in **60-point** type. Select all the text. Press **Option** (Mac) or **Alt** (Windows) and the **Right Arrow** key to loosen the tracking. Keep pressing the right arrow key and you will see that it doesn't take very long for your name to become just a series of individual letters. Again, be conservative with tracking. When misused, it inhibits readability.

You will often use tracking to fine-tune your type. At times you may want to use negative tracking to give your text a little more refined look, especially with headline type. You will also use tracking to fit troublesome lines of type into the line measure. While InDesign has taken care of much of this for you with its multiline composition feature, there will be times when you will need to manually adjust tracking. For instance, at the end of a paragraph, you should avoid leaving part of a hyphenated word or any word shorter than four letters on its own line. As a typesetter, you need to make a decision: either tighten tracking slightly to make room for the word in the line above, or loosen tracking to bring the whole word or an additional word to the last line of a paragraph. The goal is to alter the word spacing so slightly that no one will ever notice. You have gone too far with your tracking if the tracked text looks darker or lighter than the surrounding text. *Tracking should be invisible to the untrained eye.*

▸ *Adjust character spacing with manual kerning*

Closely related to tracking is kerning. *Kerning* is the horizontal spacing between two characters only. You should kern letter pairs when spacing between characters is too wide or too narrow. For instance, look closely at the number 740 shown in Visual 4–28. Before you started reading this book, it would have looked perfectly fine. But with your professional eye, you now see that the spacing between the 7 and 4 looks much wider than the spacing between the 4 and the 0. Kerning will correct this.

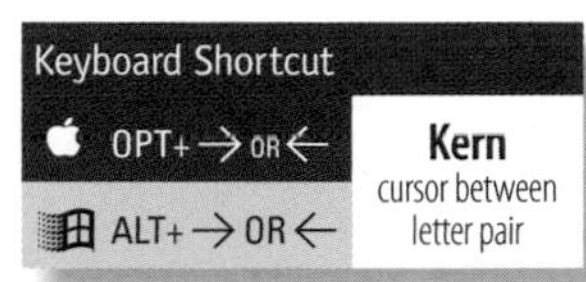

Place your cursor in between the 7 and the 4. Do not highlight any text. Press **Option+Left Arrow** (Mac) or **Alt+Left Arrow** (Windows) to tighten the space between the numbers. (The same keyboard shortcuts used for positive and negative tracking are also used for kerning.) The amount of adjustment is shown in the *Kerning* field in the *Control* panel. InDesign adjusts the kerning in units of one-thousandth of an em. (You will remember that an em is a unit of measure equivalent to the point size—an em space in 10-point type is 10 points wide.)

-100
0 Kerning
Spacing is loose
Kerning of −100 has been applied
740 740

VISUAL |4–28|

Place the cursor between two letters to adjust kerning.

© Cengage Learning 2013

A more common place to kern letter pairs is when using drop and raised caps. Visual 4–29 shows what they look like without kerning. As shown below, some letter pairs usually need kerning. Your goal is to have the "color" of text look even. Big gaps between letter pairs make a word look airy.

Raised cap needs kerning

Words strain, crack,
and sometimes break,
under the burden.
T.S. Eliot

Words strain, crack,
and sometimes break,
under the burden.
T.S. Eliot

Drop cap needs kerning

These pairs usually need kerning		These pairs are not kerned	
To	WA	To	WA
Tr	we	TR	we
Ta	P.	Ta	P.
Yo	T.	Yo	T.
yo	TA	yo	TA
Ya	PA	Ya	PA
Wo	Po	Wo	Po
Wa		Wa	

As shown in the column on the right, kerning is also affected by the typeface used in each letter pair.

VISUAL |4–29|

Kerning adjusts the spacing between letter pairs, and is often used with raised and drop caps.

© Cengage Learning 2013

▸MOVING TOWARD MASTERY

automatic optical kerning

*when professionals design a font, they build in rules for letter pair spacing. Unfortunately, the built-in kerning parameters don't cover every letter pair scenario. That is why manual kerning is sometimes needed. But InDesign has gone one step further. It allows you to select **Optical Kerning** in the **Kerning** field on the **Control** panel. With **Optical Kerning** selected, InDesign goes beyond the built-in letter pair parameters and makes kerning decisions based on the shape of each character to even out how the type looks. This is a huge timesaver. InDesign does an excellent job of making text look great—with very little effort on the part of the person setting the type.*

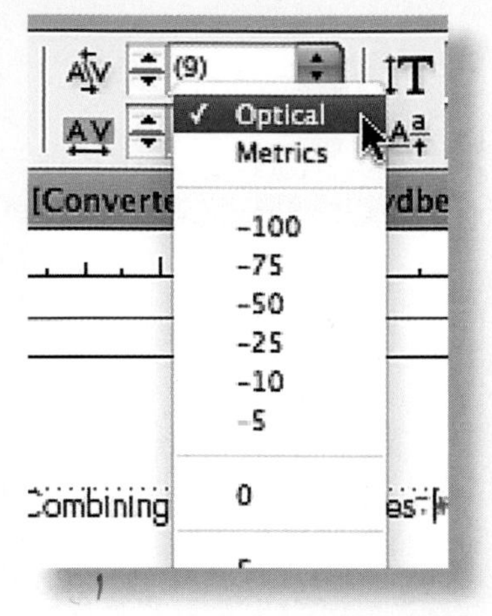

working with images

The perfect image, combined with beautiful type, form a "one-two punch" that makes a document which is both memorable and effective. Most of the images you use will be either scanned, created in a vector-based drawing program such as Adobe Illustrator, or created in a pixel-based program such as Adobe Photoshop. As powerful as InDesign is, it is not a true drawing program. But you shouldn't underestimate InDesign's drawing capabilities. If you have already used Adobe Illustrator, you have seen tools and functions in InDesign that look very familiar. If you haven't used Illustrator, you will learn about many basic drawing functions that are common to both programs, later in the book.

EXPLORING INDESIGN CS6
Artwork & Resources

- Go to: http://www.cengagebrain.com
- Type: Rydberg
- Click Exploring InDesign CS6 in the list of search results.
- When the book's main page is displayed, click the Access button under Free Study Tools.
- To download files, select a chapter number and then click on the Artwork & Resources tab on the left navigation bar to download the files.

InDesign can place a variety of file formats including EPS, TIFF, and JPEG. A great feature is the ability to place InDesign documents and native Adobe Illustrator (AI) and Photoshop (PSD) files without conversion to a PDF, EPS or TIFF format.

Three methods of placing artwork will be discussed in this section: *place and drop, place and drag, and place into a frame*. The same keyboard shortcut is used to place text or images: **Command+D** (Mac) or **Control+D** (Windows). InDesign does not require a specific type of frame to hold a graphic and another to hold text. In fact, as you have already seen when placing text, you don't need a frame at all! Let's get started learning how to place images. Download the *04 Artwork and Resources* folder from the online companion resources before starting these exercises.

► *Place and drop, and rotate*

1. Create a new document, **8.5" × 11"**. Open the *Place* dialog box. Navigate to the *Chapter 04 Artwork and Resources* folder from the online companion resources. Choose *04 Demo.tif.* Press **Return.**

2. Notice the loaded icon looks like a paintbrush surrounded by straight lines (Visual 4–30). Just as when placing text, the square lines indicate that a new frame will be created. **Click** in the upper left corner of your document and the photo will appear at full size.

VISUAL | 4–30 |

When placing images, a thumbnail of the image appears on the cursor.

© Cengage Learning 2013

3. When you are working with images, it is helpful to change the resolution of your screen so that you can see the fine details of an image. Go to *View>Display Performance>High Quality Display* (Visual 4–31). Now, use **Command+4** (Mac) or **Control+4** (Windows) to zoom in to 400%. When these little girls are seen at high resolution, you can see the breakfast crumbs around their lips. Change the display performance back to *normal resolution* by going to *View>Display Performance>Typical Display.* See the difference in detail?

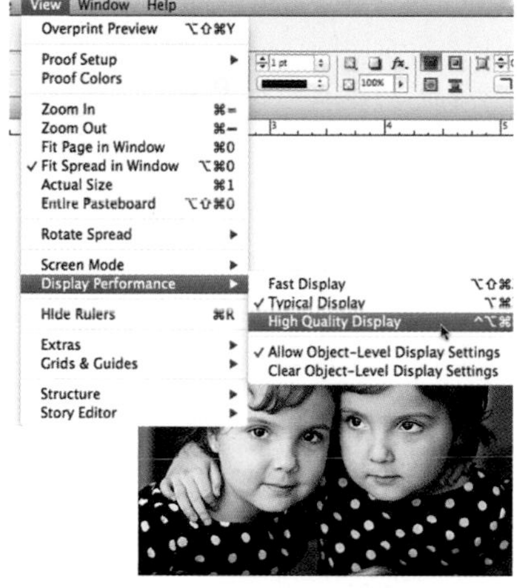

VISUAL | 4–31 |

It's easier to see the details of an image with your display set to a higher resolution.

© Cengage Learning 2013

4. Change your view back to *100%* by using the keyboard shortcut **Command+1** (Mac) or **Control +1**(Windows). Notice that the photo is contained within a frame. Select the frame with the *Selection* tool and move the arrow just outside the lower right corner of the frame. When you see a curved arrow (Visual 4–32), click and drag to rotate the frame and image on your screen. As the image is rotated, the degree of rotation is displayed next to the cursor and in the *Control* panel. When you release the mouse, the image will remain at its rotated position. To return it to its original location, enter **0** in the *Rotation Angle* field of the *Control* panel. As you were working on this exercise, you may have noticed a transparent doughnut in the center of the image. This is the *Content Grabber* and will be discussed later.

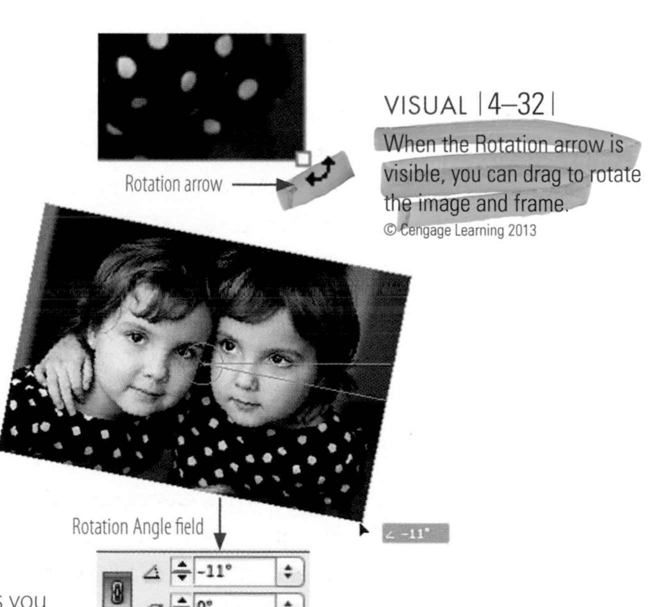

VISUAL | 4–32 |

When the Rotation arrow is visible, you can drag to rotate the image and frame.

© Cengage Learning 2013

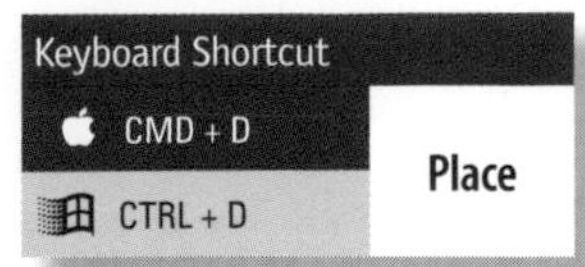

▸ *Place and drag, and resize images*

As you can see, working with images is not complicated, but you do need to know what you're doing! We're going to place our little girls again—this time you'll place the image at various sizes. Images have width and height dimensions. When both dimensions are at 100%, the picture is *full size*. Often we need to use images at a size larger or smaller than their 100% actual size. It's easy to do this in InDesign.

1. Use the *Place* command to place ***04 Demo.tif.*** Again, notice the straight lines by the paintbrush in the thumbnail image, indicating that it will create a frame for the graphic. **Click** in the upper left corner of your document. This is the image's full size. Changing the size of an image is called ***scaling,*** and we'll do that in the next step.

VISUAL |4–33|

As you resize an image percentages are displayed below the cursor. Percentages are also displayed in the Control panel.

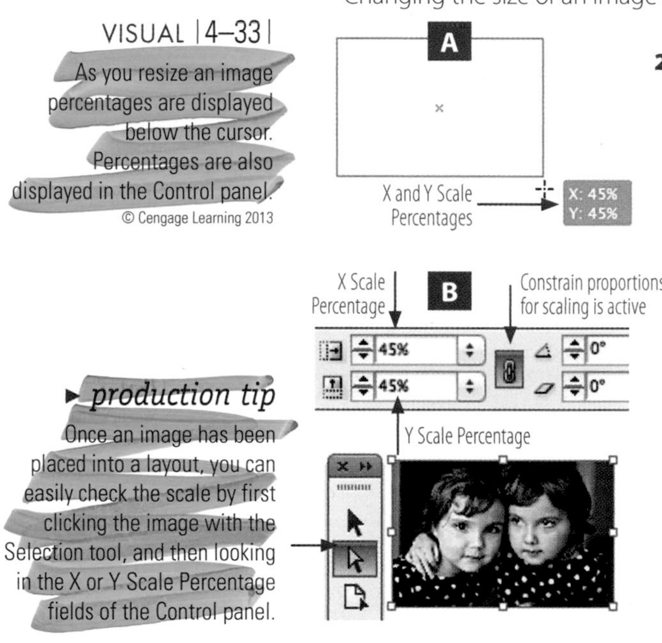

▸ *production tip*

Once an image has been placed into a layout, you can easily check the scale by first clicking the image with the Selection tool, and then looking in the X or Y Scale Percentage fields of the Control panel.

2. Place ***04 Demo.tif*** again. This time, **click** and slowly **drag** the mouse. As you drag, look in the lower right corner next to the cursor and you will see *X* and *Y percentages* displayed (Visual 4–33A). These percentages tell you the size the image will be when the mouse is released. Any number less than 100% is a ***reduction*** in size, and any number larger than 100% is an ***enlargement***. Release your mouse when the *X* and *Y percentages* are right around **45%**. When you release your mouse, notice that the percentages are no longer displayed. Once an image has been placed, you can find out its percentage of enlargement or reduction in the *Control* panel. Click the image with the *Direct Selection* tool and look in the *Scale X* and *Scale Y Percentage* fields of the *Control* panel (Visual 4–33B) to see if your image is approximately 45%.

3. Place ***04 Demo.tif*** once again. This time, drag to enlarge the image to **150%**. After you release the mouse, select the image with the *Direct Selection* tool and look in the *Scale X* and *Y Percentage* fields on the *Control* panel to confirm that it is at 150%. If it isn't, simply enter **150** in either field and press **Return**. Verify that the button that constrains proportions for scaling is turned on first (Visual 4–34), so both the *X* (horizontal) and *Y* (vertical) dimensions of the image will be at 150%. If it isn't, **click** it to turn it on.

Before we move on, let's summarize what you've just learned. **Command+D** (Mac) or **Control+D** (Windows) places an image. Once the cursor is loaded, you can either click to drop the image at its full size, or click and drag to resize, or *scale*, the image proportionally. After an image is in a layout, you can check the scale

▸ MOVING TOWARD MASTERY

the importance of proportional scaling

*Images have width and height dimensions, called **X Scale** and **Y Scale Percentage**. When the **X** (width) and **Y** (height) scale percentages are the same, the image is **scaled proportionally.** If you resize the photo so that the width dimension is at 50% and the height is at 100%, the picture is the same height, but it is half its original width. This is **disproportional scaling.** If you were using a picture of clouds as a background photo, the photo could be scaled disproportionally without any consequences. However, you want to keep most images—products, people—proportional, meaning the width and height percentages will be the same. Always check these percentages by selecting the image with the **Direct Selection** tool and finding the percentage in the **X** and **Y Scale Percentage** fields of the **Control** panel.*

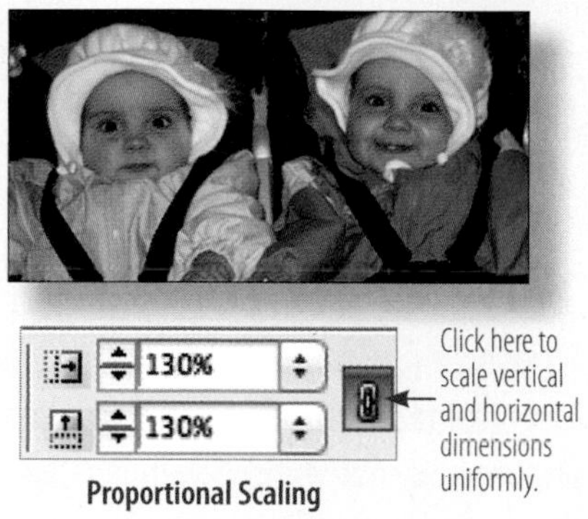

Click here to scale vertical and horizontal dimensions uniformly.

Proportional Scaling

Disproportional Scaling
The Y (vertical) dimension has been scaled to a greater percentage than the X (horizontal) dimension, making the photo tall and thin.

by selecting the image with the *Direct Selection* tool and looking at the *Control* panel. An image can be rotated by dragging the corner when the *Rotation* arrow is displayed. Those are the basics, and if you're confident that you've mastered those skills, you're ready to move on.

▸ *Place into a frame, and crop the image*

Have you noticed the transparent doughnut that appears whenever you mouse over an image with the *Selection* tool? That's the *Content Grabber*. Among other things, the *Content Grabber* helps you reposition images inside a frame. The process of showing only a portion of an image is called *cropping*. For instance, you might have a great photo of your significant other, taken when you were on a road trip. Unfortunately, above their head is the sign from the gas station where you made a pit stop! With InDesign, you simply adjust the image inside the frame so that the focal point is the adoring grin of your significant other. Most images are improved with strategic cropping and scaling. In the next exercise, you'll use the *Content Grabber* to separate the twins and then proportionally scale an image inside the frame. Let's get started.

1. Place *04 Crop.psd* in the upper left corner of your document, using the "place and drop" method. We'll use this as a reference photo at actual size, or 100%.

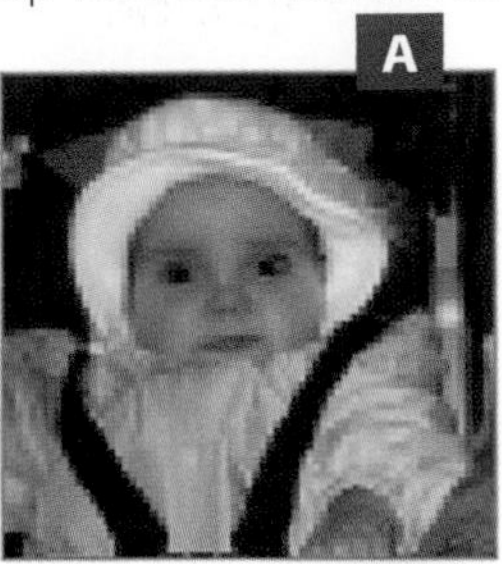

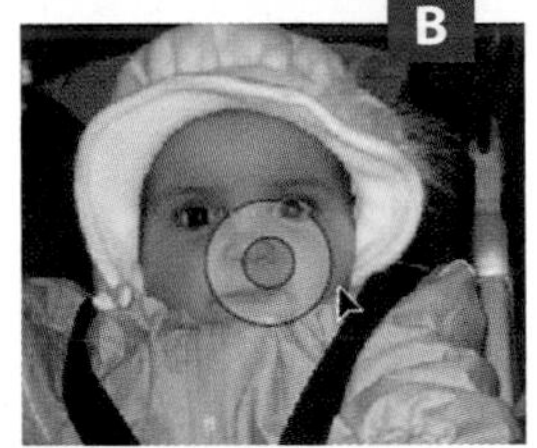

VISUAL |4–34|

When you hover over an image with the Selection tool, a transparent doughnut, the Content grabber, is visible. Click and drag on the content indicator to move an image inside a frame.

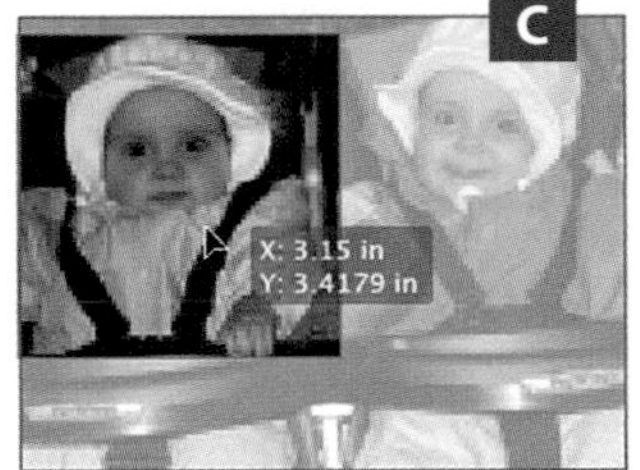

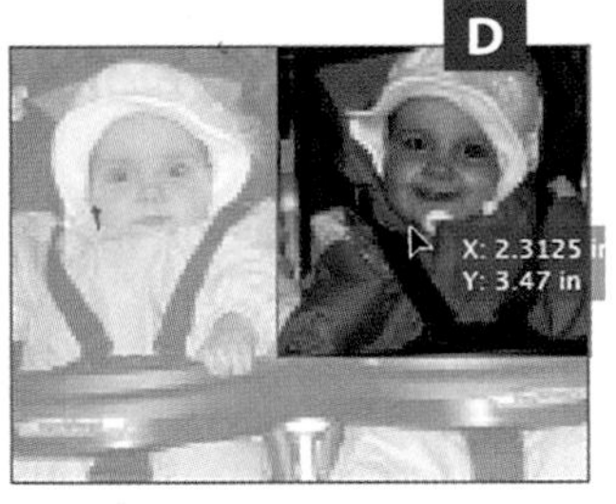

2. Select the ***Rectangle*** tool, click in the middle of your document, and enter **1** in the ***width*** and ***height*** fields to create a 1-inch square. Use the **Place** command to load ***04 Crop.psd.*** When the picture has been placed, notice that only one of the twins, Julia, appears in the frame. The image is placed at full size, no matter what size the frame (Visual 4–34A).

3. Select the image with the ***Selection*** tool and as you hover your mouse over the image, the transparent doughnut (the ***Content Grabber***) will appear (Visual 4–34B). **Click** and **pause** on top of the doughnut and you will see the rest of the image that extends beyond the frame as semi-transparent, or ***ghosted*** (Visual 4–34C). Click on the doughnut and slide to the left to crop out Julia, and bring the other twin, Sophia, into view (Visual 4–34D). The ***Content Grabber*** makes it easy to position the part of the photo that should be displayed in the frame.

VISUAL |4–35|

When Auto-Fit is checked, you can easily scale images proportionally. You can also accomplish this by dragging the frame handle while using these keyboard shortcuts: Shift+Cmd (Mac) or Shift+Ctrl (Win).

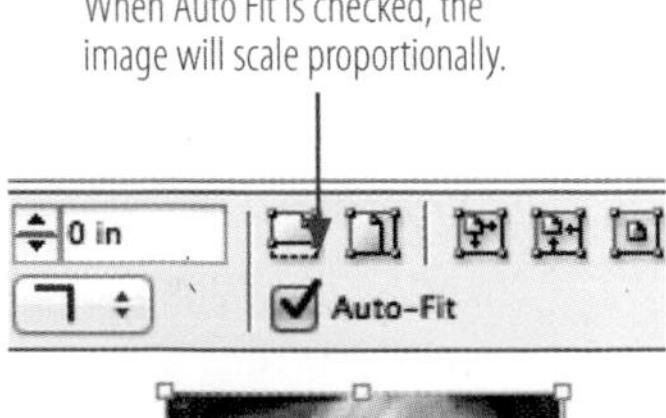

4. Now let's say you want Sophia's image to be larger. If you pull on one of the photo's frame handles, it simply makes the frame bigger, allowing more of the photo to be revealed. To make the photo resize proportionally and maintain its crop, check ***Auto-Fit*** on the ***Control*** panel (Visual 4–35). Select the photo with the ***Selection*** tool, and pull a corner frame handle to proportionally make the photo larger or smaller. For those of you who love keyboard shortcuts, you can also proportionally scale an image by selecting it with the ***Selection*** tool, press **Shift+Command** (Mac) or **Shift+Control** (Windows) and pull a corner frame handle.

5. You've learned how to crop and scale—how about moving the image to a different area of the layout? Simply click on the image with the Selection tool (not on the doughnut) and move the image (and frame) to a new location.

THE CONTAINER (FRAME) AND THE CONTENT (IMAGE)

When you are working with images, remember that you are managing two components: the frame (or *container*) that holds the image, and the image (or *content*). When working with images, you need to first decide if your action is affecting the container or the content. If you understand the difference between the *Selection* and *Direct Selection* tools, you will realize that you would use the *Selection* tool to resize the frame, and the *Direct Selection* tool to resize or move the content inside the frame. It's easy to confuse image frame boundaries with the container frame guides! When this happens, frustration can occur. For instance, say you want to delete the image, but not the frame. If you have the container frame selected and press *Delete*, the frame *and* the image will be removed. Instead, you would need to select the content and not the container. The following short exercises will take you through the main image-handling techniques and will help you differentiate between when the container or the content should be selected. These exercises are quick and easy, and important techniques to learn. Choose the *Selection* tool before starting them.

A. Toggle between the container and the content

- ***Double-click*** *the image (not the doughnut) and watch as you switch between the container and the content. Your ability to toggle between container and content is the starting point for all the remaining exercises! As you toggle between the image and frame, notice that the guides are different colors—and the frame has a yellow box on the right edge.*

B. Scale the image inside the frame without changing the frame size

- ***Double-click*** *to select the* ***content.*** *Press* ***Cmd+Opt+> or <*** *(Mac) or* ***Ctrl+Alt+> or <*** *(Win) to increase and decrease the scale in increments.*

C. Rotate the image inside the frame

- ***Double-click*** *to select the* ***content.*** *Move the* ***Selection*** *tool to the lower right corner of the content's frame, until you see the curved arrow. Rotate the image inside the frame.*

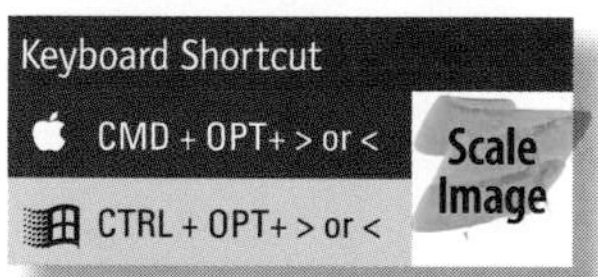

D. Center the image inside the frame

- ***Double-click*** *to select the* ***container.*** *Pull the handles out until the frame is much larger than the image. Press* ***Shift+Cmd+E*** *(Mac) or* ***Shift+Ctrl+E*** *(Win) to center the image.*

E. Fit content proportionally

- *Use the image from Exercise D with the image centered in an oversized frame.* ***Double-click*** *until the* ***content*** *is selected. Press* ***Shift+Cmd+Opt+E*** *(Mac) or* ***Shift+Ctrl+Alt+E*** *(Win) to fit the content proportionally.*

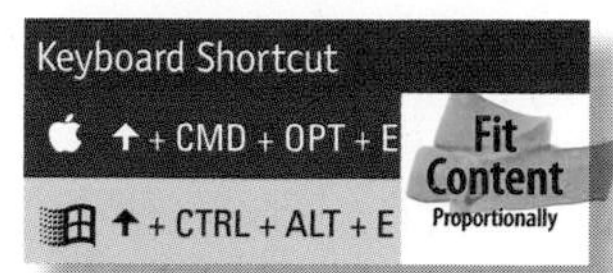

F. Fit the frame to the content

- *Using the* ***Selection*** *tool,* ***double-click*** *a corner frame handle to fit the frame to the content. The entire frame is scaled to fit the image. Now, pull the frame handles to make it much larger than the image. This time,* ***double-click*** *a frame handle on the middle of the frame's sides, top, or bottom. The frame will resize, either horizontally or vertically.*

These basic image handling exercises can also be accomplished using buttons on the *Control* panel. One beautiful feature of InDesign is that it allows you to work in the style you prefer. As you can tell by now, I encourage using keyboard shortcuts. The more you use them, the more you will remember them and the faster you'll be at production. But some people prefer to choose options from the menu. If you're one of those people, you will appreciate the convenience of using the *Control* panel for much of your text and graphics editing.

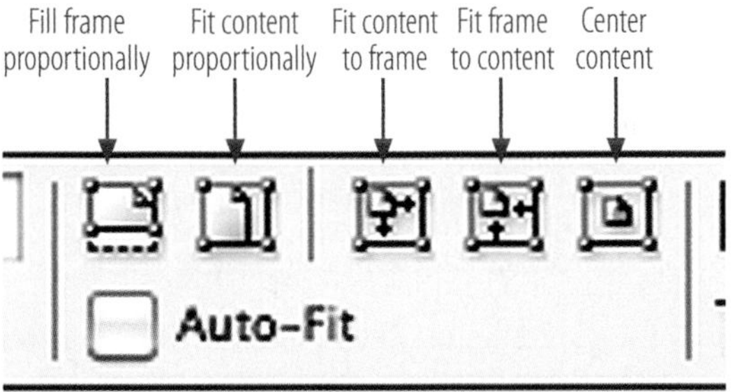

VISUAL |4–36|
The Control panel contains buttons that do many image editing operations.

▸ *Scaling disproportionally*

A poster promoting a weight loss program, was hung in our college hallway, showing the "before" and "after" photos of a participant who had lost 20 pounds. Obviously, the "after" picture was created by simply resizing the first photo disproportionally, to make the person look thinner. Be careful when scaling images! Most of the time you will want to keep your image in the same proportion as it was originally created. But there will be instances, as in the cloud example mentioned earlier, when disproportional scaling will be acceptable.

1. **Double click** the image to select the content. **Drag** any content frame handle. The image will resize and become distorted. Check the ***Scale X*** and ***Y Percentage*** fields on the ***Control*** panel to see new horizontal and vertical percentages of the image.

2. Enter the same number in each of the fields and the image will again be proportional.

Summary

Whew! This was a long chapter! In these first four chapters you have learned so much. You now understand InDesign's measurement system. You know how to create multi-column text frames, and to place and thread text. You used InDesign's tracking and kerning, paragraph rules, and spell check functions to fine-tune your type. Finally, you learned how to place, scale, and crop images. With these techniques mastered, you're ready to tackle more advanced projects. The Chapter 4 projects are designed to solidify these new techniques. Next, we'll move on to another one of my favorite topics: tabs and tables.

▸ IN REVIEW

1. What is the difference between kerning and tracking?
2. What is the difference between tracking and leading?
3. How do you reset the zero point?
4. If an object's coordinates are X: 4 in. and Y: 6 in., the object will be _____ inches over and _____ inches down.
5. What does the black square in the proxy indicate?
6. What key should you press to push text from one column to the next?
7. What does a red plus sign in the out port of a text frame indicate?

What are the Mac or Windows keyboard shortcuts for the following?

8. Show Hidden Characters	____________	**9.** Save	____________
10. Direct Selection Tool	____________	**11.** View at 100%	____________
12. Paragraph Rules	____________	**13.** View at 200%	____________
14. Place Text or Image	____________	**15.** Text Frame Options	____________
16. Check Spelling	____________	**17.** Print	____________

18. What are the steps for proportionally enlarging a graphic inside a frame?

19. What is the process for deleting overset text without changing the size of the type or the text frame?

20. What is the process for unlinking text frames?

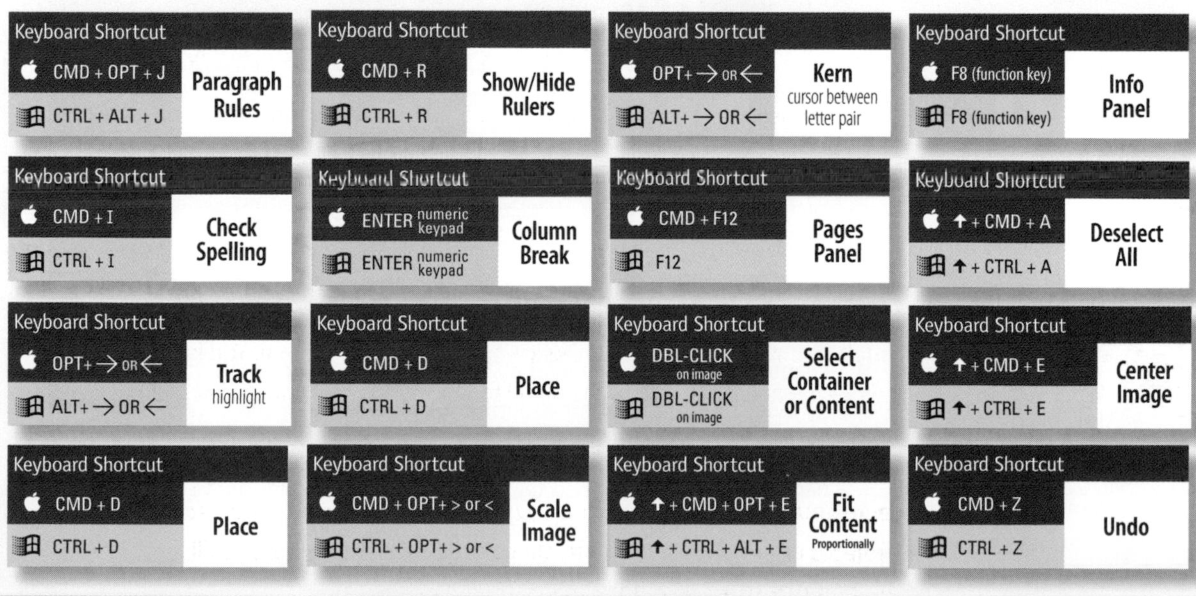

► CHAPTER 4 PROJECTS

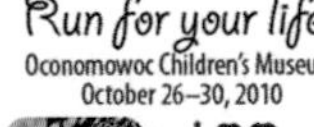

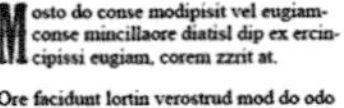

EXPLORING INDESIGN CS6
Artwork & Resources

- Go to: http://www.cengagebrain.com
- Type: Rydberg
- Click Exploring InDesign CS6 in the list of search results.
- When the book's main page is displayed, click the Access button under Free Study Tools.
- To download files, select a chapter number and then click on the Artwork & Resources tab on the left navigation bar to download the files.

Chapter 4 projects begin with an X-Y coordinate exercise. This is followed by a display ad project for Beautiful Morning Tearoom and Gardens which focuses on using coordinates, leading, correct dashes, and space after paragraphs. Next, a 2-sided table tent that utilizes rules above and below. A poster concept for a museum exhibit, and one featuring the

▸CHAPTER 4 PROJECTS

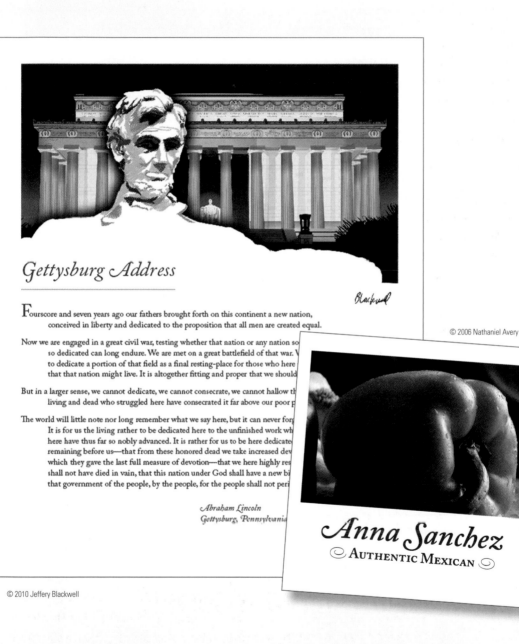

Gettysburg Address will provide more practice in formatting text. The final project is designed for you to produce with little direction. You will find instructions, artwork, and text in the *Chapter 04 Artwork and Resources* folder found on the online companion resources.

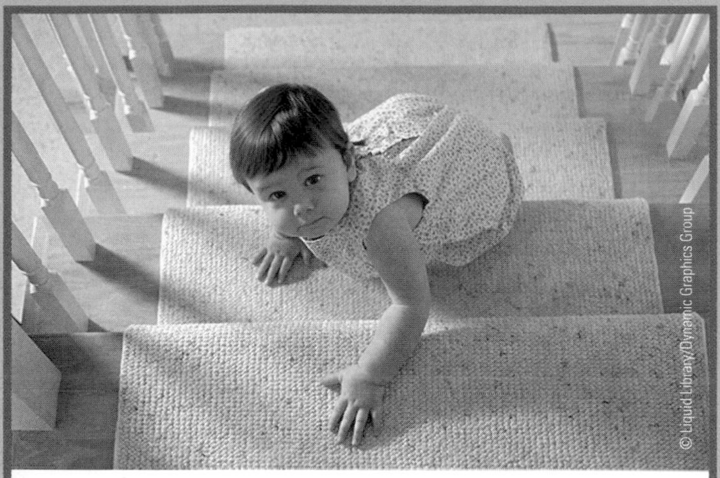

Everyone is trying to accomplish something **big**, not realizing that life is made up of **little things**.

— Unknown

Tabs and Tables

objectives

- *Use left, right, center, decimal, repeating, and align to special character tabs*
- *Apply tab leaders*
- *Use the Indent to Here feature*
- *Build a table*
- *Create a table from text*
- *Modify, add, and delete columns and rows*
- *Add headers and footers*

introduction

If you've ever seen a good marching band in a parade, you know that they march in formation. A poor marching band wanders all over the place—trumpets out of line, clarinets out of step, drums missing the beat. Nobody knows whom to follow or what comes next.

This chapter will help you keep your text in formation. In earlier chapters you have learned how to format text in sentences and paragraphs. In this chapter you will work with text designed for use in charts, order forms, and business reports—projects that need tabs and tables to keep information in line. Honing your skills with tabs and tables will keep your text marching in formation, and prove to your boss or your client, that you are a master at what you do!

There are four methods people typically use to align text and numbers in columns:

☹ Press the spacebar repeatedly until the text lines up.

☹ Press the Tab key over and over until the text lines up.

☺ Create precise tab settings.

☺ Create tables to hold the information.

No matter which method you have used in the past, I guarantee that after this chapter you will never use either of the first two methods again!

working with tabs

Whether you are working on a car, hanging wallpaper, or building a deck, it's always great to get tips from pros—especially at the beginning of the project! Here are some great tips for tabs. Following them will make setting tabs so much easier.

- ***Mark up the copy*** *(a fine-tip pen with colored ink works the best). Your markup will show where you will press the **Tab** key and the location and type of each tab stop that will be set. This step is critical in the beginning stages of typesetting. Pre-planning a job in this way can prevent time-consuming errors (see the sample markup in Visual 5–2).*

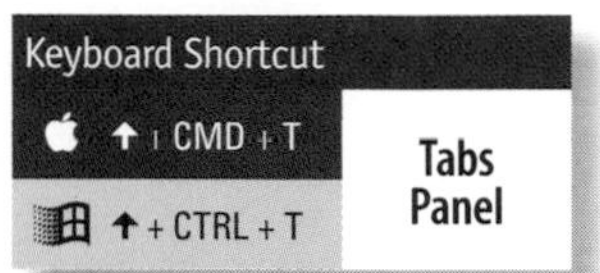

- *Press **Command+Option+I** (Mac) or **Control+Alt+I** (Windows) to show each tab character and make it easy to find those places where you accidentally pressed the **Tab** key twice. Or, select **Hidden Characters** from the **View Options** menu on the **Application Frame**, above the **Control** panel.*

Edit Layout Typ
✓ Frame Edges
✓ Rulers
✓ Guides
Smart Guides
Baseline Grid
Hidden Characters

- ***Do all the typing first without formatting**, pressing the **Tab** key only one time between columns of information. Your text probably won't line up at first because the cursor jumps to InDesign's preset tab settings of every half inch. Later, when you set the desired tab stops, the copy will line up at the correct new location.*
- *Work with copy **left-aligned**—doing so makes setting tabs much easier.*
- *Open the **Tabs** panel: **Shift+Command+T** (Mac) or **Shift+Control+T** (Windows).*
- ***Press the Tab key only once!** Your copy will look great after you set the tab stops. Don't try to align copy by repeatedly pressing the **Tab** key.*

MARKING UP—AN IMPORTANT PRODUCTION STEP!

The first tab tip is to mark up the copy to show each time you press the *Tab* key and where the tab stops should be placed. Before you can mark up the copy, you must know what kind of tab is needed. We will start with three simple kinds of tabs: *Left*, *Right*, and *Center*. Each of these tab stops looks different on the *Tabs* panel. Study Visual 5–1 until you can identify the shape of each tab stop and visualize how it will align the copy .

VISUAL | 5–1 |
Tab stops align copy into columns. The type of stop you select determines how the copy in the columns will be aligned.

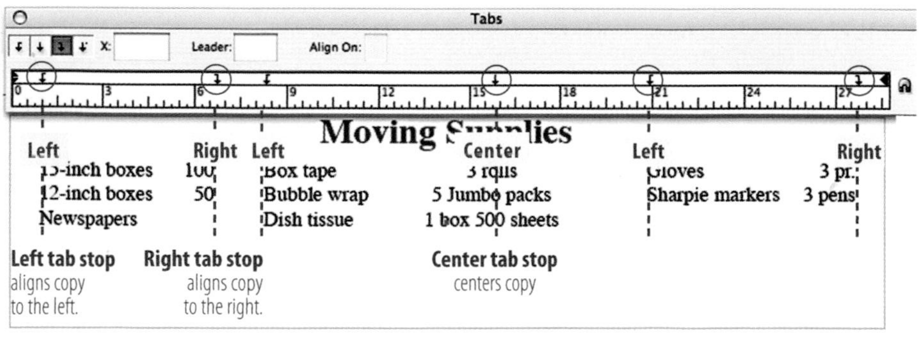

Just as stretching prepares your muscles for a workout, marking up tabular copy prepares your brain and creates a visual connection between you and the software, forcing your brain to shift into "tabs mode." It's tempting to skip this step, but until you are totally confident, you should take the 30 seconds to mark up your copy. In the mark up process, you indicate each time you press the *Tab* key and where each tab stop should be set. Visual 5–2 shows copy that has been marked up correctly. This markup becomes a road map that will make setting tabs a snap.

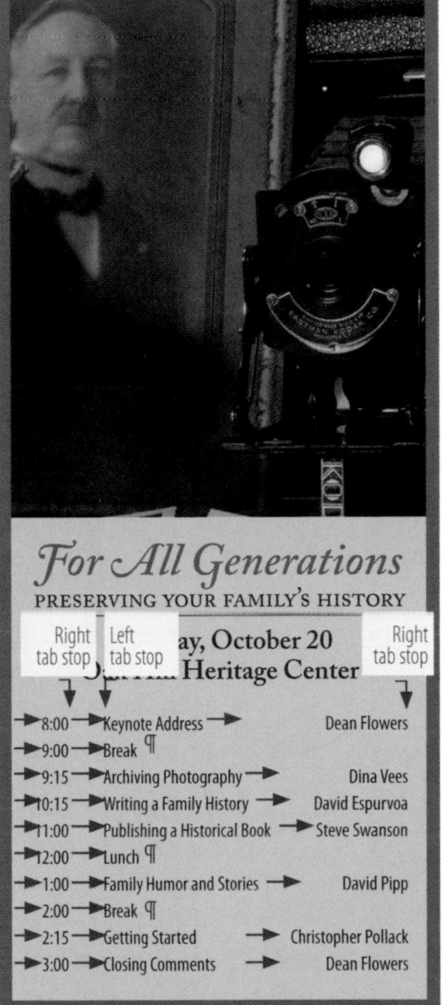

VISUAL | 5–2 |

Markup shows two things: 1) where the Tab key is pressed; and 2) the location and type of tab stop.

© Christopher Pollack 2006

EXPLORING INDESIGN CS6
Artwork & Resources

- Go to. http://www.cengagebrain.com
- Type: Rydberg
- Click Exploring InDesign CS6 in the list of search results.
- When the book's main page is displayed, click the Access button under Free Study Tools.
- To download files, select a chapter number and then click on the Artwork & Resources tab on the left navigation bar to download the files.

THE TABS PANEL

The tabs exercises shown on the next several pages can be found in the *05 Artwork and Resources* folder on the online companion resources. The good news is that all the typing is already done for you—you will concentrate on using the *Tabs* panel for formatting your copy. Before you get started, let's look at a few specifics about tabs. The first step in setting tabs is understanding how the *Tabs* panel works. Open the Tabs panel using **Shift+Command+T** (Mac) or **Shift+Control+T** (Windows). You can also access the *Tabs* panel by going to the *Type* menu and choosing *Tabs*, but this is a slower method. Study Visual 5–3 to learn the fields and panel options for the *Tabs* panel.

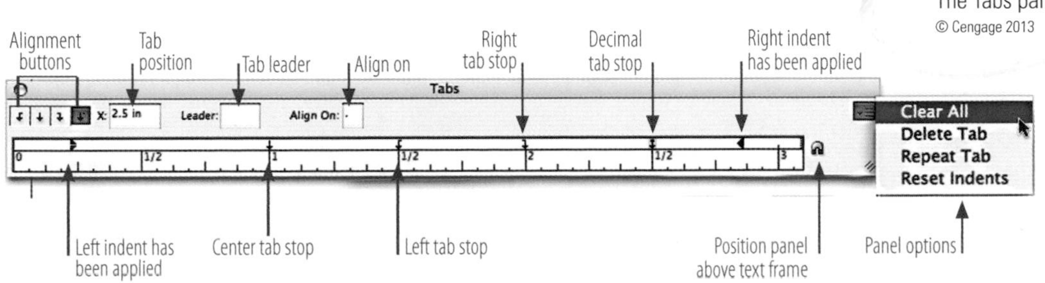

VISUAL | 5–3 |

The Tabs panel

© Cengage 2013

SET BASIC TABS

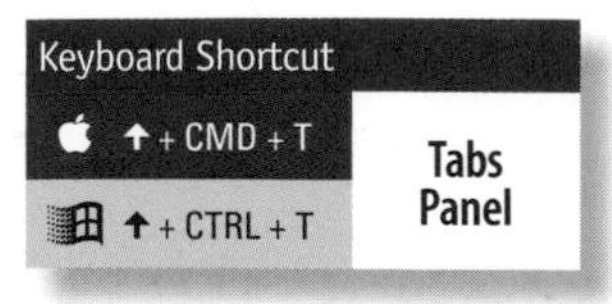

Now that you have the *Tabs* panel open, make sure *Hidden Characters* are showing, and your copy is aligned to the left. Create a 4" wide text frame and type the following words using **Minion 12/14.4**, pressing the **Tab** and **Return** keys where indicated. Do not press the *Tab* key more than once!

> cardboard boxes**<Tab>**tape**<Tab>**marker**<Return>**
> scissors**<Tab>**bubble wrap**<Tab>**newspaper**<Return>**
> dish tissue**<Tab>**labels**<Tab>**packing peanuts

Your copy should look like Visual 5–4. It's not a pretty sight, but it's correct, and it shows a basic concept you must understand when working with tabbed copy: when you're initially entering the copy and press Tab, InDesign jumps the cursor to the next default tab preset—the closest ½ inch increment on the ruler. The copy will look like a mess, because the actual tab stops haven't been set, yet. This is when people who don't know how to work with tabs "fix" the situation by pressing the Tab key again and again until somehow the copy lines up. Resist that temptation!

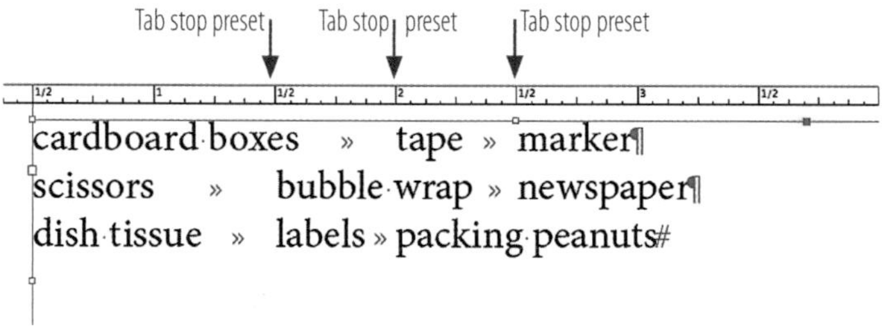

VISUAL | 5–4 |

When the Tab key is pressed, InDesign jumps to the next tab stop preset at ½ inch increments.

Now, let's set some left tabs. Switch to the *Selection* tool and open the *Tabs* panel, if it's not already open. Click on the *Tabs* panel name and drag it to align the left edge of the *Tabs* panel to the left edge of the text frame. Now, click on **1.5"** mark on the ruler in the *Tabs* panel that appears directly above the text frame. A left tab stop will appear, and the copy will jump into place as shown in Visual 5–5. Click on the ruler again, at the **2.5"** mark to add a second tab stop. Notice that when you click and hold a tab stop, a line appears to show how the copy will align. Use this visual cue when setting tabs!

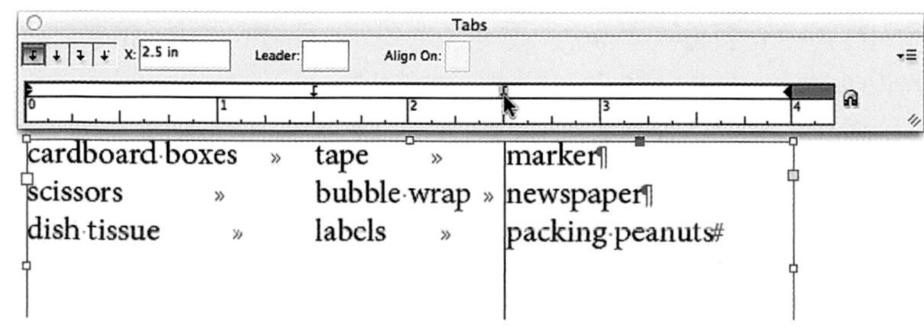

VISUAL | 5–5 |

Click and hold a tab stop to see where the copy will align.

Now you're ready to master tabs. Open *05 Tabs Demo.indd,* found in the *05 Artwork and Resources* folder on the online companion resources. Find *Exercise 1* on the *05 Tabs Demo* document and follow the instructions on the following pages.

▸ MOVING TOWARD MASTERY

Hidden Characters or "invisibles" tell the whole story! The example below has a left indent. Left indents are found in the ***Paragraph control*** *panel. Don't confuse indented copy with tabbed copy. The example on the right has double arrow invisibles before the first word in each line. These symbols indicate that the* ***Tab*** *key has been pressed. This copy isn't indented, it's tabbed. Always read the invisibles! Keep them visible when working with tabs.*

My Favorite Chickens¶
Rock·'n'·Roll¶
Dirty·Neck¶
Sweetie·Pie#

My Favorite Chickens¶
» Rock·'n'·Roll¶
» Dirty·Neck¶
» Sweetie·Pie#

▸ *Exercise 1A Snap the Tabs panel to the text frame*

Use the *Selection* tool to activate the text frame in *Exercise 1* in the *05 Tabs Demo* document. With the *Tabs* panel open, notice the magnet on the far right end. Click this control to position the *Tabs* panel directly over the active text frame, if possible. To see it in action, change your view size to **100%** from the magnification field in the upper left corner of your screen and click on the magnet. The *Tabs* panel will align itself to the top of the text frame. Switch your view to **200%**. Click the magnet—it will resize and snap to the top of your text frame. Now, switch your view to **1200%** and click the magnet—it doesn't move. This seemingly inconsistent behavior occurs because when viewing your document at high magnification levels, there is not enough room above the active text frame to position the *Tabs* panel. So, the snap above text frame function is disabled. Change the view size back to **100%** and click the magnet to snap the *Tabs* panel to your text frame. You can set tabs without having the panel snapped to the frame, but it is easier to see what you're doing when the ruler is snapped above your text frame.

Look carefully at the text frame, notice that an inset has been applied to all four sides. When the *Tabs* panel is snapped to the text frame, the ruler does not align at the edge of the frame. Instead, it begins where the text begins. In this case, the zero point of the tabs ruler snaps to the text frame inset setting.

▸ *production tip*

When the view magnification is too great, the Tabs panel magnet's snap feature will be disabled. When this occurs, reduce the view magnification.

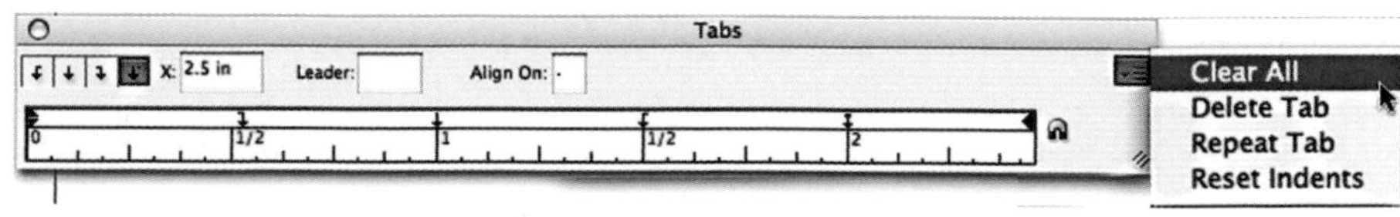

VISUAL | 5–6 |
Remove all tab stops by selecting Clear All from the panel options.

▸ *Exercise 1B Add and remove tab stops*

Deselect the text frame in *Exercise 1*. We're going to experiment with the *Tabs* panel. Adding tab stops is an easy process. Simply click in the narrow white area directly above the ruler. Slide your cursor down the ruler a bit and click again. Each time you click, a tab stop is added. When a tab stop is first added it is highlighted in blue, which means it is active. Once you make a new tab stop, the previous one is deselected. To delete a tab stop, select it and drag it above or below the ruler. When you have many tab stops to delete, it is faster to go to the *Tabs* panel options and select *Clear All* (Visual 5–6). **Clear** all your tabs.

▸ *production tip*
Press Option (Mac) or Alt (Windows) and click on a tab stop to cycle through its alignment.

Place a tab stop near the middle of the ruler. Press **Option** (Mac) or **Alt** (Windows) and click repeatedly on the tab stop. As you click, watch as the tab stop alignment settings change from left, to center, to right, to decimal. Use this method to cycle through tab stop alignment settings whenever you are setting tabular copy.

▸ *Exercise 1C Set Left tabs*

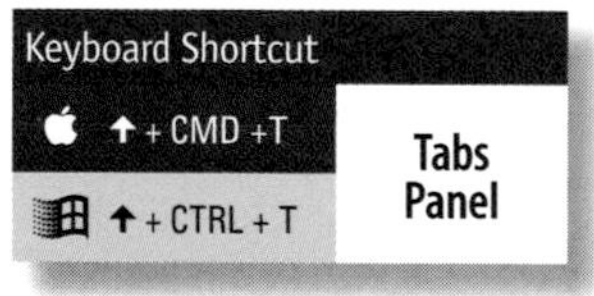

Let's have some more practice with Left tabs. Use the *Selection* tool to select the frame in *Exercise 1*. Look closely at the invisibles to identify each time the *Tab* key was pressed. Each time the *Tab* key was pressed, the copy was pushed to the nearest tab preset. Since *Dr. Ryan Johnson's* name is shorter than the other names in the first column, *Dr. Theodore Soos* moved to a tab preset closer to the left edge of the copy block. Copy will usually not align until you actually set the tab stops. Don't press the Tab key repeatedly to manually align copy!

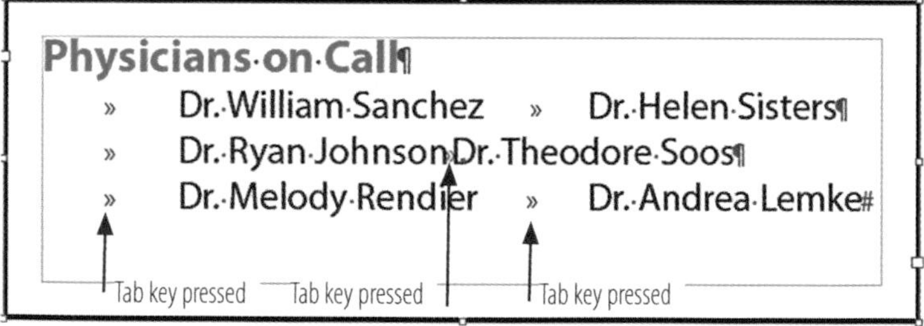

VISUAL | 5–7 |
Copy moves to the first available tab stop preset until you select the tab stops you want to use.

Be sure the *Tabs* panel is open and snapped to the top of your text frame. You should still have the *Selection* tool activated. Drop in Left tab stops at approximately **0.25"** and 2". As you place each stop, **click and hold**, and a vertical line will appear to show where your copy will be aligned. You can also see the measurement of the tab stop in the *X* field. Adjust the position of your copy by sliding the tab stop to the right or to the left on the ruler.

Notice that all the lines of copy moved as you placed the tab stops. When you select the text frame with either the *Selection* or *Direct Selection* tools, the same tab settings are applied to all the tabular copy inside the text frame. When lines of copy in a single frame require different tab settings, individual lines must be separated with a *Return* (not a soft return) and highlighted with the *Type* tool before setting the tab stops.

▸ *production tip*

When you select the text frame with the Selection or Direct Selection tool and do not highlight individual lines of copy, identical tab settings are applied to all the tabular copy inside the frame.

▸ *Exercise 2 Set Center and Right tabs*

Now let's move on to *Exercise 2.* A completed sample of this exercise is shown in Visual 5–8. Before you begin this exercise, use Visual 5–8 for markup. Place a **horizontal arrow** → in the text to indicate each time the *Tab* key is pressed. Examine the copy closely to determine the required tab stops. Indicate the appropriate tab stop above each column, using these symbols for *Left, Center,* or *Right* [↓][↓][↓]. A tab stop won't be required in every line.

When your markup is completed, open the *Tabs* panel. Find the lines of type with identical tab settings, and work on those as a unit. Then move to the next series of similar tab settings. Refer to your markup as you drop in your tab stops. Press **Option** (Mac) or **Alt** (Windows) and **click** on each tab stop to cycle through the alignment options. If you need to adjust the position of a tab stop, highlight the copy and move the stop to the left or right on the *Tabs* panel ruler. Your completed project should look almost identical to the example in Visual 5–8.

Nutrition Facts

Serving Size: 1 cup
Servings per container: 6
Amount per serving:

Calories: 45		Calories from fat: 0
		Total Fat: 0g
	Saturated Fat 0g	
	Polyunsaturated Fat 0g	
	Monounsaturated Fat 0g	
Cholesterol	0mg	0%
Sodium	70 mg	13%
Total Carbohydrate	12g	
Dietary Fiber	2g	
Sugars	0g	
Protein	1g	

Vitamin A 0% • Vitamin C 0%
Calcium 0% • Iron 2%

VISUAL | 5–8 |

Mark up the tab settings on this sample of Exercise 2.

▸ *Exercise 3 Set Decimal tabs*

When you set a *Decimal* tab stop, the copy is lined up according to the position of the decimal. In Visual 5–9, notice how the numbers one through ten are aligned by their decimal points. In the right column, the numbers also align according to the decimal point. If there is no decimal point, such as in the answer for #7, the whole number is positioned to the left of where a decimal point would be placed. Mark up the copy, making sure to indicate a tab before numbers 1 to 10. Then, create the tab settings.

Answers to Math Exam

1.	.067
2.	0.0034
3.	9.56723
4.	12.45
5.	.1
6.	2.3543
7.	4
8.	9.667734
9.	2.456
10.	6.123

VISUAL | 5–9 |

Decimal tab stops use the decimal to align the copy in a column.

▸ *Exercise 4 Align to Special Characters*

By default, the *Decimal* tab aligns copy at the location of the decimal point, but you can specify other characters at which to align the decimal tab. In this exercise, the copy will be aligned to the dollar sign. First, select the *Decimal* tab. Then, enter a dollar sign ($) in the *Align On* box in the *Tabs* panel.

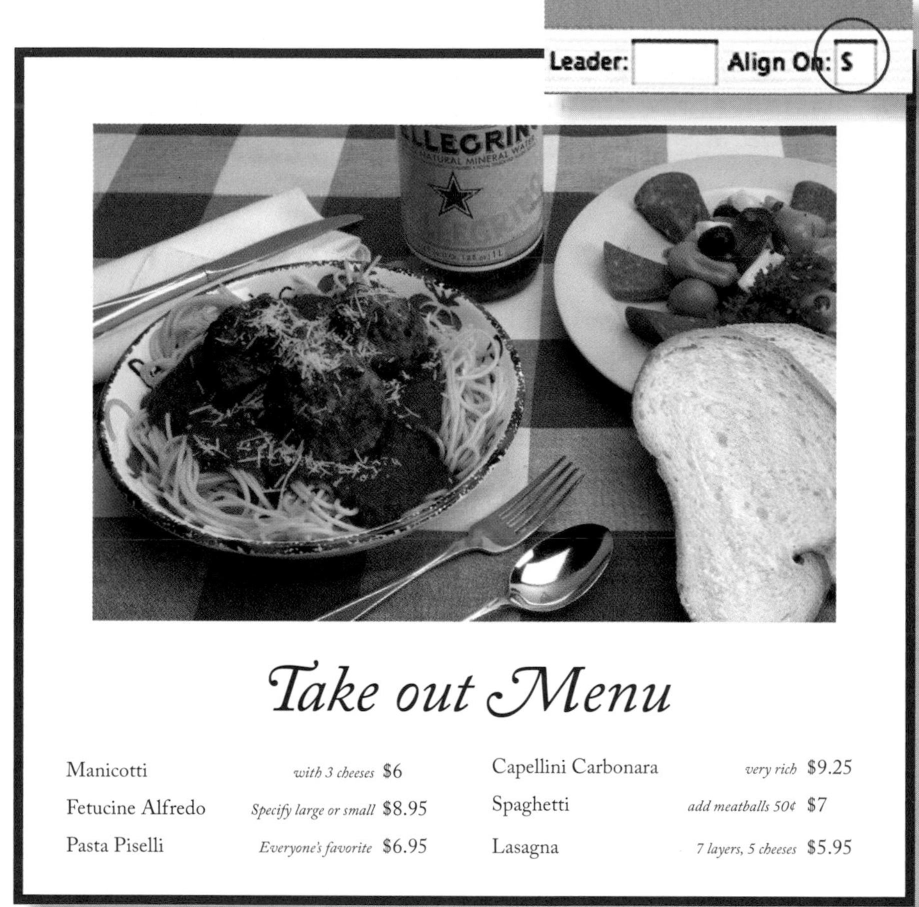

Leader:
Align On: $
Take out Menu
Manicotti
with 3 cheeses $6
Fetucine Alfredo
Specify large or small $8.95
Pasta Piselli
Everyone's favorite $6.95
Capellini Carbonara
very rich $9.25
Spaghetti
add meatballs 50¢ $7
Lasagna
7 layers, 5 cheeses $5.95

VISUAL | 5–10 |
You can specify other characters for alignment with the decimal tab stop. In this example, copy is aligned to the dollar sign.
© Annette Wagner 2006

▸ *Exercise 5 Set Right Indent tabs*

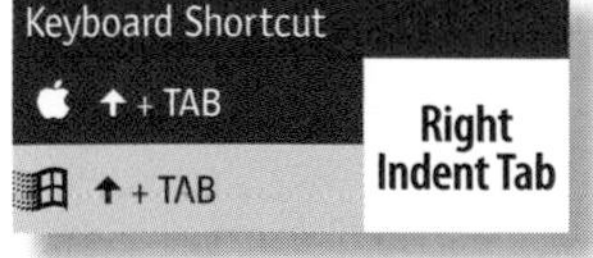

Right indent tabs automatically push your copy flush with the right edge of the text frame. Right indent tabs aren't set using the *Tabs* panel. Press **Shift+Tab** or use the *Context menu>Insert Special Character>Other>Right Indent Tab* to create a right indent tab. Display hidden characters to verify that an automatic right indent tab has been inserted. Follow the directions included with *Exercise 5*, on Page 2 of *05 Tabs Demo.indd,* to create right indent tabs.

VISUAL | 5–11 |
This hidden character represents a right indent tab.
© Cengage Learning 2013

▸ *Exercise 6 Indent to Here*

Indent to Here is one of those "can't live without" features in InDesign. Although technically this is not a tab setting, this is a good time to introduce this function. Place the text cursor where you want to insert the special *Indent to Here* character symbol and press **Command+** (Mac) or **Control+** (Windows). Starting with the next line, all subsequent lines in the paragraph align to the position of the *Indent to Here* character. This is similar to creating a hanging indent. Once you press the *Return* key and start a new paragraph, text will revert back out to the left margin. To remove the *Indent to Here* character, simply turn on the hidden characters, find the *Indent to Here* dagger symbol, place the cursor to the right of the symbol, and press the *Delete* key. When you use the *Indent to Here* keyboard shortcut to complete this exercise, be sure to use the **Back Slash**, not the *Forward Slash* key!

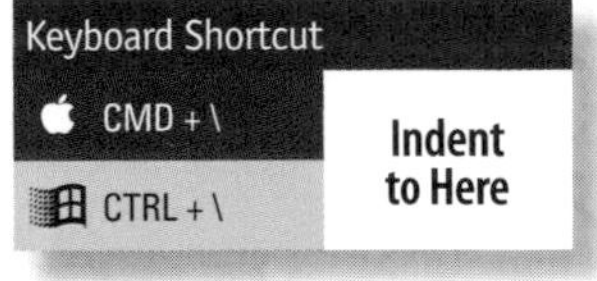

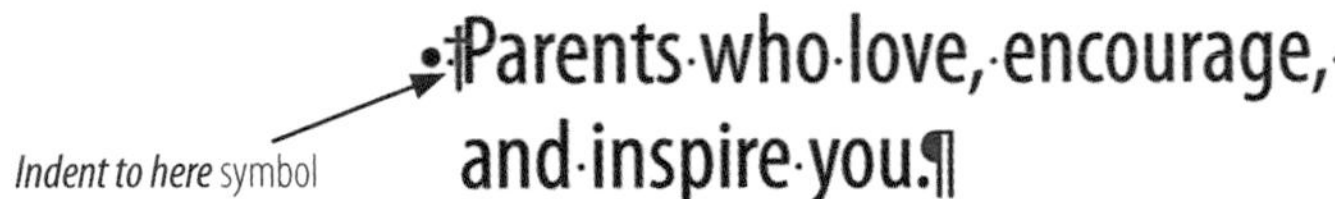

VISUAL | 5–12 |

The Indent to Here special character looks like a dagger. This keyboard shortcut will become one of your favorites.

▸ *Exercise 7 Set Repeat tabs*

When you need tabs to be spaced at equal intervals, you can use the *Repeat Tab* function found on the option menu at the far right end of the *Tabs* panel. With this function, equally spaced tab stops, based on the position of the first tab stop, are spread across the line. Directions for creating *Repeat tabs* are included with *Exercise 7* in *05 Tabs Demo.indd.*

▸ *Exercise 8 Create dot leaders*

A *leader* is a series of repeating characters between a tab stop and the following text or the end of the text frame. Leaders can be dots, lines, or any other character you choose. You can specify up to eight characters in the *Leader* field on the *Tabs* panel. You will most often use leaders in conjunction with Right tab stops. To create the dot leaders in this exercise, set a Right tab at the right end of the tab ruler. Making sure the Right tab stop is selected, enter a period and space in the *Leader* field and press **Return**. The area between the first and second columns will fill with dots. As Visual 5–13 shows, if you don't enter a space after the period, the dot leaders will be too close. Add dot leader tabs to the text in *Exercise 8,* so that it looks like the example in Visual 5–14. This exercise demonstrates how dot leaders help the eye move from one column to the next.

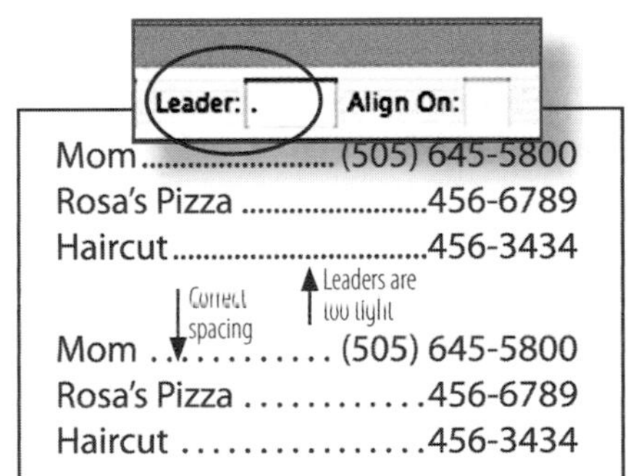

VISUAL | 5–13 |

For better dot leader spacing, add a space after the period in the Leader field.

VISUAL | 5–14 |

Exercise 8, completed.

© Krista Mueller 2006

Jesse Miller

winner of the 2007 Shirley Tollefson Young Musician Award

Performs

Bach Variations

Arioso (Sinfonia from Cantata #156). . . . . . . arr. Paul W. Tollefson
Prelude in C . . . . arr. Mark Rydberg
Jesu, Joy of Man's Desiring . . . . .arr. Nancy Peterson
Brandenburg Concerto #3 . . . . arr. Paulette Hancock
Air (for the G String) . . . . .arr. Karen Ferrell

VISUAL | 5–15 |

You will create the tab settings shown in this example numerous times during your career!

© 2006 Nathaniel Avery

▸ *production tip*

Highlight the Leader field by clicking the field's label to the left of the box, rather than manually clicking in the box and highlighting it.

▸ *Exercise 9 Create line leaders*

Throughout your professional career, you will likely create many projects that are "variations on the theme" of the raffle ticket presented in *Exercise 9.* When creating line leaders, place an underline in the *Leader* box by pressing **Shift+hyphen**, found at the top right corner of your keyboard. If you don't press the Shift key, the space will be filled with dashes, not underlines. Sometimes, when you are creating line leaders, the underlines on your monitor will appear to have spaces between them. If this happens, increase your view magnification and see if the rules look solid at a different view percentage. Sometimes it's just a "screen thing." Other times, this happens because you actually typed a space and an underline in the *Leader* field, on the *Tabs* panel.

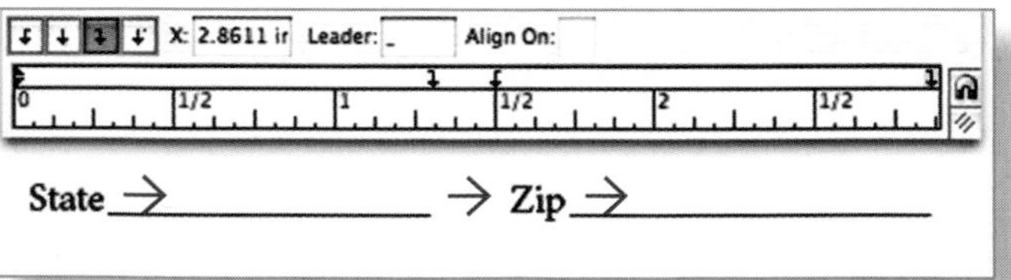

VISUAL | 5–16 |

The last line in this raffle ticket. The line leaders are applied to the Right tab stops.

© Cengage Learning 2013

Visual 5–16 shows the tab settings for the last line of the raffle ticket. The line leaders are applied to the two Right tab stops. If the line after *State* runs into *Zip*, it probably means you have added a line leader to the left Tab stop at the word, *Zip*. If so, select the stop and delete the hyphen in the *Leader* field.

►MOVING TOWARD MASTERY

When working with tabs, remember these tips:

- ***Mark up the copy.*** *Show where the* ***Tab*** *key will be pressed, and where the tab stop will be set.*
- ***Work with hidden characters visible.*** *Press* ***Command+Option+I*** *(Mac) or* ***Control+Alt+I*** *(Windows) to show hidden characters. This will show each tab character and will make it easy to find places where you accidentally pressed the Tab key twice.*
- ***Do the typing first****, pressing the* ***Tab*** *key only one time between columns of information.*
- ***Work with copy left-aligned*** *when possible—doing so makes setting tabs much easier.*
- *To open the* ***Tabs*** *panel, press* ***Shift+Command+T*** *(Mac) or* ***Shift+Control+T*** *(Windows).*
- ***Press the Tab key only once!*** *Be patient—your copy will look great after you set the tab stops.*
- *Highlight the* ***Leader*** *field by clicking on the name to the left of the box.*
- *With a tab stop highlighted in the* ***Tabs*** *ruler, press* ***Option*** *(Mac) or* ***Alt*** *(Windows) and click on the tab marker to cycle through the tab stop alignment settings.*
- *Add a space after the period in the* ***Leader*** *field when creating dot leaders.*

LAST THOUGHTS ON TABS

The columns within text frames, that you created in earlier chapters, are used for continuous text passages. They are designed to have the copy fill across and down the first column, then flow into the second column, and so on. Set tabs when the copy flow is horizontal. The tab stops will create the appearance of vertical columns.

Don't confuse tabs with paragraph indents and text frame insets! Sometimes you will use a left indent instead of a tab. That method works perfectly. However, be careful of creating a left inset in *Text Frame Options* rather than a left paragraph indent because the inset will affect all the text in the frame—which may not be what you want! The hidden characters shown below reveal the techniques used in each example.

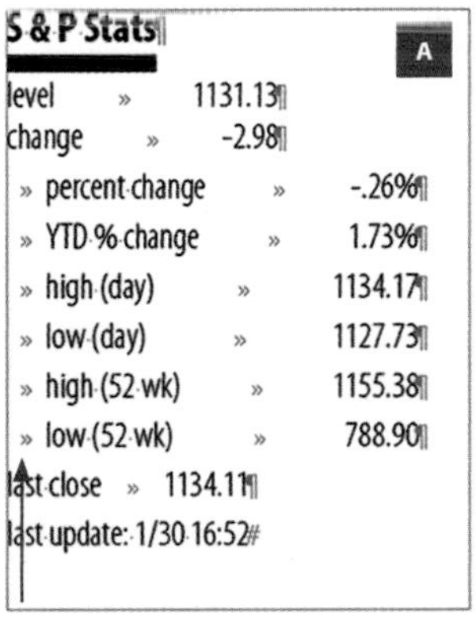

Tabs were used to move copy to the right.

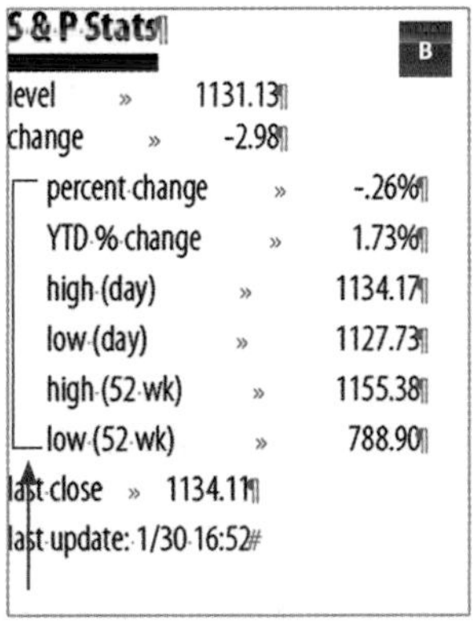

B
S & P Stats
level » 1131.13
change » -2.98
percent change » -.26%
YTD % change » 1.73%
high (day) » 1134.17
low (day) » 1127.73
high (52 wk) » 1155.38
low (52 wk) » 788.90
last close » 1134.11
last update: 1/30 16:52

A left indent was specified in the Control panel.

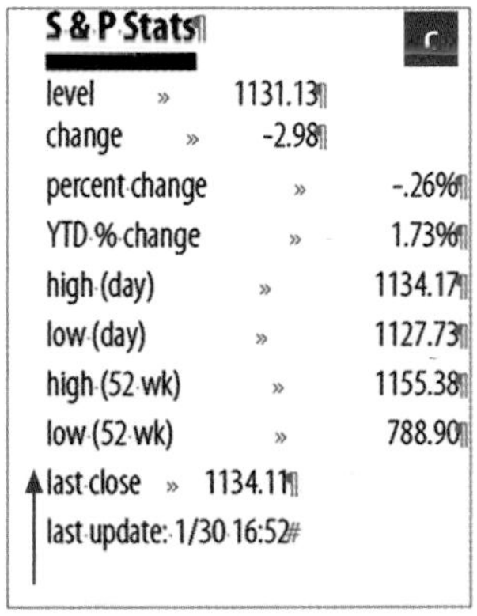

The frame inset created in Text Frame Options applies to all the text in a frame.

creating tables

Like tabs, *tables* also organize information into columns. Tables are different than tabs, however, because they are made up of *rows, columns,* and *cells.* With tables, you can add interest by changing the text, fill, and stroke attributes of individual cells, columns, and rows. When thinking of tables, people often picture a clunky-looking graph with copy choked against heavy black lines. Not so, with InDesign. In this half of the chapter, you will discover the amazing and enjoyable ways you can create tables.

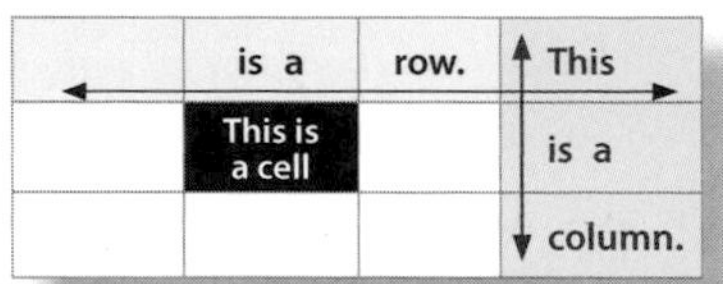

VISUAL | 5–17 |

A table structure consists of rows, columns, and cells.

There are several ways you can create tables: from "scratch," by converting existing copy, or by importing from a Microsoft® Word document or Excel spreadsheet. You can insert a table into a text frame or convert existing text into a table. The best way to understand tables is to make them, so we're going to dive right in. In the following exercises, you will learn all the basics of table management using a simple table consisting of four rows and four columns.

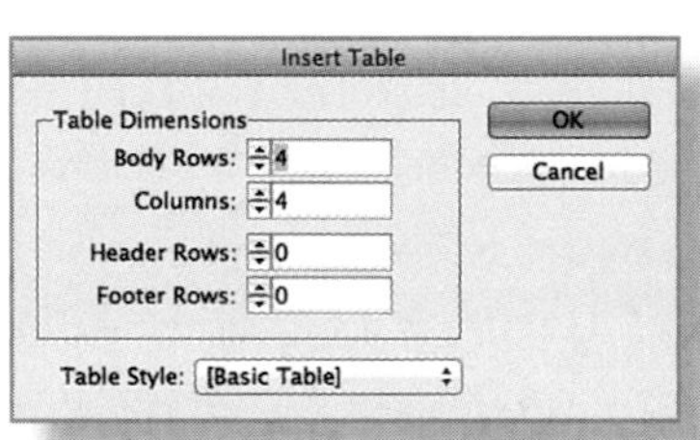

VISUAL | 5–18 |

The Insert Table dialog box.

▸ *Insert a table*

1. Create a Letter-size InDesign document with **0.5"** margins. Draw a text frame from margin to margin. Select the *Type* tool and click in the frame.

2. Press **Shift+Option+Command+T** (Mac) or **Shift+Alt+Control+T** (Windows) to bring up the *Insert Table* dialog box. You can also access this box by choosing *Table>Insert Table*. Specify **4** in the *Body Rows* and **4** in the *Columns* boxes. (Rows run horizontally, and columns run vertically.) Leave the *Header and Footer Rows* fields blank. Press **Return**. A table now sits inside your text frame, aligned with the top of your text frame.

▸ *Position a table in the text frame*

1. The new table has a cursor blinking in the upper left cell. With the *Type* tool selected, click anywhere in the text frame, outside of the table. Now the text cursor is positioned just outside the table on the right side of the text frame. Notice that the cursor is the same height as the table.

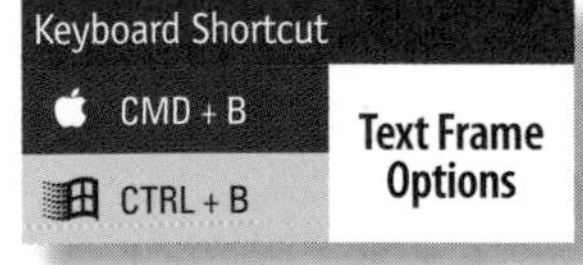

2. Open *Text Frame Options*, **Command+B** (Mac) or **Control+B** (Windows), and under *Vertical Justification* choose *Align: Center.* Turn on the *Preview* option and watch the table jump to the vertical center of the text frame. Now, see what happens when you select the *Align: Bottom* option. A table behaves like a huge piece of type inside a text frame, and will be affected by alignment, indents, insets, space before and space after. Align the table to the top, once again and press **Return.**

▸ *Select columns, rows, cells, or the entire table*

1. Move the *Type* tool slightly above the table, over the left column. The cursor will change into an arrow (Visual 5–19A). ***Click,*** and the entire column will be selected.

2. Place your cursor along the left side of the table, beside the first row (Visual 5–19B). ***Click,*** and the entire row will be selected. Now, bring the cursor to the upper left corner of the table. You will see a diagonal arrow (Visual 5–19C). ***Click,*** and the entire table will be selected.

3. Place the cursor inside a cell and drag to the right to select it. You can continue to drag across a cell's boundary to select adjacent cells. Practice selecting the entire table, individual rows, columns and cells.

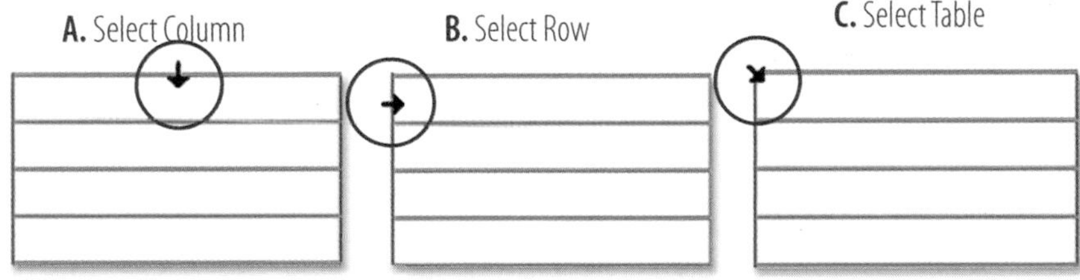

VISUAL | 5–19 |

Use the Type tool to select columns, rows, cells, or the entire table.

▸ *Select a cell or its contents*

1. Place the cursor in the upper left cell and type your name. Move the cursor to highlight your name and the space surrounding it so that the entire cell is black. You now have the cell selected (Visual 5–20).

2. Now, try to highlight just your name. Sometimes this is a little trickier, and it helps if you are at a magnified view. When your type is selected, the highlighting should just cover the letters, and your cell should look like the lower example in Visual 5–20. It is important that you can differentiate between selecting a cell or highlighting text inside a cell. You can also press the **ESC** key to switch between selecting the cell or the type in a cell.

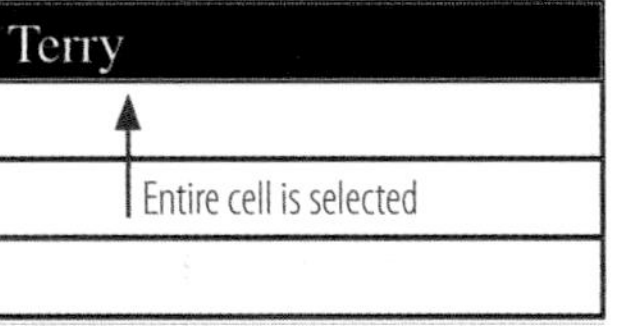

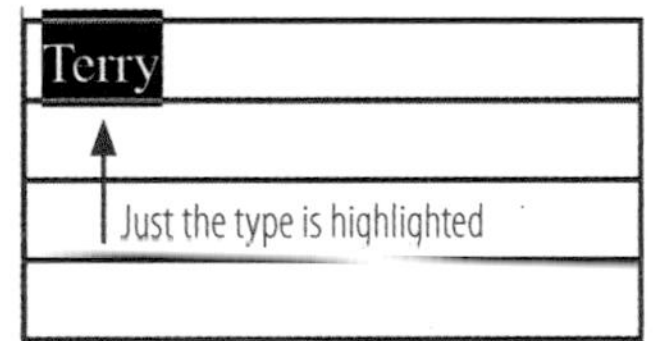

VISUAL | 5–20 |

Press ESC to switch between highlighting the cell and the text.

▸ *Resize rows and columns*

1. Place the cursor over the row guide below your name. The cursor now changes into a double-headed arrow (Visual 5–21). ***Click and drag*** the line down to create a much deeper cell.

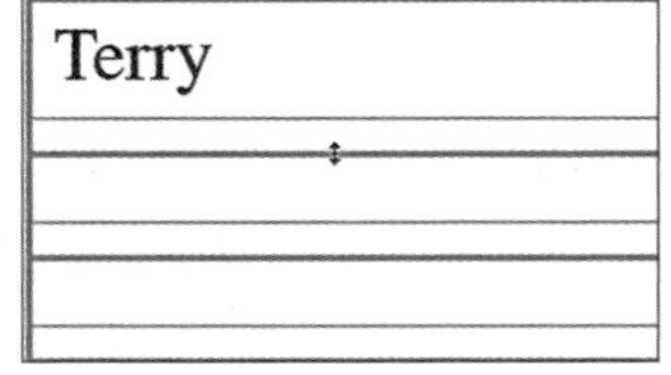

VISUAL | 5–21 |

When you are moving column or row guides the cursor switches to a double-headed arrow.

2. Repeat this process with the column guides.
Notice how changing the size of rows and columns, changes the table size, too.

▸ *production tip*

Press Shift to resize columns and rows inside the table without changing the table's dimension.

▸ *Resize rows and columns without resizing the table*

1. Place the cursor over the row guide below your name. When the cursor changes into a double-headed arrow, hold down ***Shift*** as you adjust the row dimension. Notice that the row inside the table changes size, but the table does not.

2. Repeat this process, pressing the ***Shift*** key as you move the column guides.

VISUAL | 5–22 |

Shown are some of the Table Formatting Options available in the Control panel.

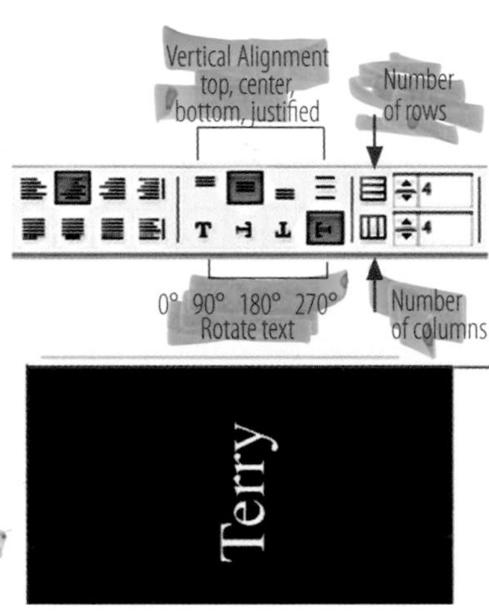

▸ *Position text inside the cell*

1. Highlight the cell that contains your name. Use the *Paragraph Formatting* options in the *Control* panel to align your type to the right. Now align the type to the center.

2. You use the *Table Formatting Options* in the *Control* panel to set the vertical position and rotation of type inside the cell. In Visual 5–22 the type has been rotated 270°. With the cell selected, experiment with alignment and text rotation controls in the *Control* panel.

▸ *Resize the entire table*

1. Move the cursor to the lower right corner until you see a diagonal double-headed arrow. Press ***Shift*** and pull on the arrow and your table will enlarge proportionately.

2. If you want to expand only the vertical or horizontal dimension of the table, move the cursor to either the bottom or the right side and pull to resize. Press the ***Shift*** key to proportionately resize the vertical or horizontal dimension of the table.

▸ *Add and delete rows and columns*

1. You can add and delete rows and columns in the *Table Formatting* options in the *Control* panel or by using the *Context* menu. When using the *Control* panel, change the number of rows and columns in the appropriate box (Visual 5–22).

2. You can also delete rows and columns using keyboard shortcuts. Highlight the bottom row. Press **Command+Delete** (Mac) or **Control+Backspace** (Windows) and the row will disappear. Delete a column by highlighting it and pressing **Shift+Delete**. Now, open the *Context* menu and examine the options. The *Context* menu holds almost all of the table editing operations you will use. Choose *Insert>Row or Column.* Specify the number and location of the new rows or columns.

▸ MOVING TOWARD MASTERY

- *The **Type** tool is used for editing tables.*
- *The **Type** tool cursor changes shape according to the table editing that will be done.*
- *The keyboard shortcut for creating a table within a text frame is **Shift+Option+Command+T** (Mac) or **Shift+Alt+Control+T** (Windows).*
- *Press **ESC** to alternate highlighting the cell or the text inside the cell.*
- *Rows and columns can be added, deleted, and resized.*
- *Press the **Shift** key when you are changing the dimension of rows or columns, and want to maintain the same overall table size.*
- *You can merge cells to form wider columns and deeper rows.*
- *The table sits inside a text frame. When rows and columns are modified, the text frame may need to be enlarged or reduced.*
- *Select the whole table by placing the cursor at the upper left corner of the table and clicking when the cursor turns into a diagonal arrow.*
- *Options that affect the whole table are accessible by pressing **Shift+Option+Command+B** (Mac) or **Shift+Alt+Control+B** (Windows).*
- *Options that affect selected cells are accessible by pressing **Option+Command+B** (Mac) or **Alt+Control+B** (Windows).*
- *Delete a table by placing your cursor in the text frame to the right of the table and pressing **Delete.***

▸ *Merge and split cells*

1. Highlight the first row in your table. Open the ***Context*** menu and select ***Merge Cells.*** One large cell now spans the length of your table.

2. With this long cell highlighted, choose ***Split Cell Horizontally*** from the ***Context*** menu. Then choose ***Split Cell Vertically***. You can continue splitting cells until they are quite small (Visual 5–23). Cells can also be merged and unmerged at the ***Control*** panel. Highlight the cells and click the ***Merge Cells*** button.

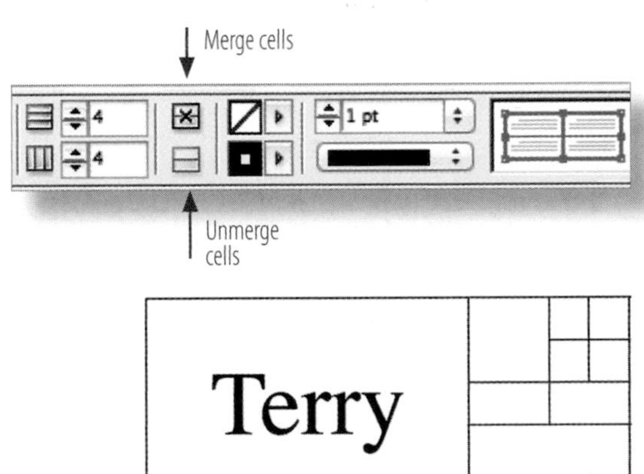

VISUAL | 5–23 |

Cells can be merged and unmerged in the Table Controls panel. In the lower example, cells have been repeatedly split horizontally and vertically, resulting in very tiny cells.

TABLE PROJECTS

Now that you've gotten a taste for tables, I hope you're ready for more! In the next exercise, you will import some prepared text, and convert it to a table, making the Grade Scale chart, shown in Visual 5–26. Then, you'll create a table highlighting popular baby names from copy that you type.

Grade Scale		
Grade	Percent Value	Point Value
A	95-100	4.00
A-	93-94	3.67
B+	91-92	3.33
B	87-90	3.00
B-	85-86	2.67
C+	83-84	2.33
C	79-82	2.00
C-	77-78	1.67
D+	75-76	1.33
D	72-74	1.00
D-	70-71	0.67
F	69 or below	0.00

VISUAL | 5–24 |

As you create this grading chart, you will learn how to modify strokes and attributes of cells, including tab stops.

EXPLORING INDESIGN CS6
Artwork & Resources

- Go to: http://www.cengagebrain.com
- Type: Rydberg
- Click Exploring InDesign CS6 in the list of search results.
- When the book's main page is displayed, click the Access button under Free Study Tools.
- To download files, select a chapter number and then click on the Artwork & Resources tab on the left navigation bar to download the files.

▸ *Create a table from existing copy*

1. Draw a text frame **2.5" × 4"**. Place *05 Grade Scale.doc* from the *05 Artwork and Resources* folder on the student online resource.
2. Select all the text. Choose *Table>Convert Text to Table*. In the *Convert Text to Table* dialog box, set the *Column Separator* to *Tab*, the *Row Separator* to *Paragraph*, and then press **Return**. Your table should look similar to Visual 5–24.
3. Select the top row and merge the cells by clicking on the *Merge Cell* box in the *Control* panel, or by opening the *Context* menu and choosing *Merge Cells*. Now the phrase *Grade Scale* should fit on one line. Select the entire table and change all the copy to **Myriad Pro Condensed**.
4. Highlight the first two rows and center the column heads by pressing **Shift+Command+C** (Mac) or **Shift+Control+C** (Windows). Apply a *Bold* type style. Select the second and third columns and use the same keyboard shortcut to center the copy.

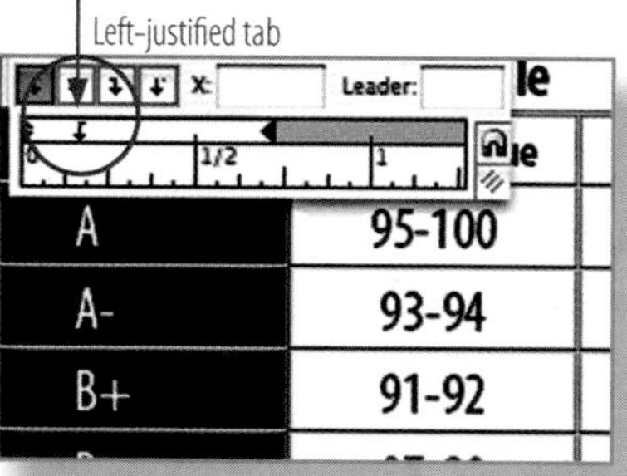

VISUAL | 5–25 |

Press Option+Tab (Mac only) or use the Context menu> Insert Special Character (Windows) to insert a tab in a cell.

5. Select the first column, from "A" to "F." Open the *Tabs* panel and set a *Left* tab stop close to the middle of the column (Visual 5–25). Inserting a tab in a table cell is tricky. On the Mac you need to press **Option+Tab** instead of just Tab. In Windows, you must use the *Context* menu and choose *Insert Special Character>Other>Tab*. Line by line, place the cursor before the letter grade and insert a tab character to line up the grades close to the middle of the column.
6. Place the text cursor in any table cell and open the *Table Options* dialog box. Use **Shift+Command+Option+B** (Mac) or **Shift+Control+Alt+B** (Windows). Select the *Fills* page and under *Alternating Pattern*, select **Every Other Row**, Color: **Black**, Tint: **20%**. Set *Skip First* to **1**. Press **Return**. The first row of the table should now be white, with every other row a 20% black tint.

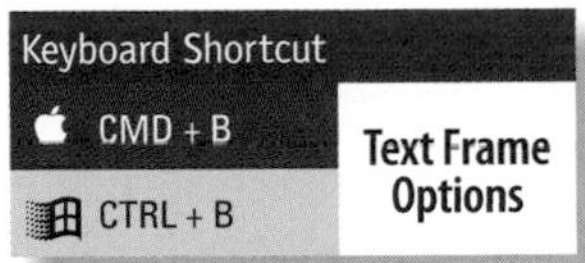

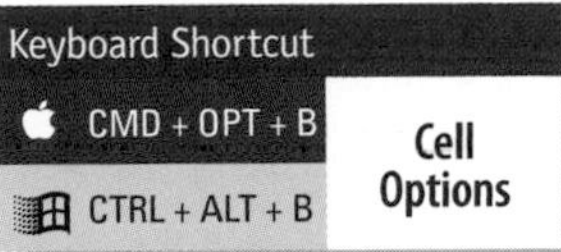

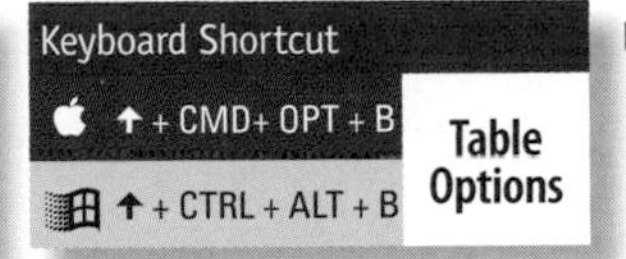

► *production tip*

Notice these keyboard shortcut patterns used for formatting text in frames, cells and tables.

7. Select the entire table and open the *Cell Options* dialog using the keyboard shortcut, **Command+Option+B** (Mac) or **Control+Alt+B** (Windows). Select the *Strokes and Fills* page. Under *Cell Stroke*, enter **3 pt**. in the *Weight* field and **[Paper]** in the *Color* field. Press **Return** and deselect the table to see the results.

8. Finally, add a border around the outer edge of the table. Place the text cursor in any table cell and open the *Table Options* dialog box. On the *Table Setup* page set the *Table Border* options as follows: Color: **Black**, Type: **Dashed** (any style), Weight: **2 pt.**, Gap Color: **None**. Do not check *Preserve Local Formatting*. Press **Return**. Compare your table with Visual 5–26, adjusting point sizes as needed. Your table is now completed.

Grade Scale

Grade	Percent Value	Point Value
A	95-100	4.00
A-	93-94	3.67
B+	91-92	3.33
B	87-90	3.00
B-	85-86	2.67
C+	83-84	2.33
C	79-82	2.00
C-	77-78	1.67
D+	75-76	1.33
D	72-74	1.00
D-	70-71	0.67
F	69 or below	0.00

VISUAL | 5–26 |

The finished table.

► *Create a table from text you've prepared*

Now you will make a chart using many of the same techniques as the Grade Scale table, but you will prepare the text yourself. Visual 5-27 shows a table featuring the most popular baby names in 2010. Compare it with the Grade Scale table and you will see many of the same features—with a few twists, of course.

Top 10 Baby Names of 2010

Rank	Girls	Boys
1	Isabella	Jacob
2	Sophia	Ethan
3	Emma	Michael
4	Olivia	Jayden
5	Ava	William
6	Emily	Alexander
7	Abigail	Noah
8	Madison	Daniel
9	Chloe	Aiden
10	Mia	Anthony

source:www.socialsecurity.gov

VISUAL | 5–27 |

This table uses many of the same techniques as the Grade Scale, but you will create a table from your own copy.

1. Draw a text frame **20 picas** wide by **22 picas** deep. (Type **p** after the number in the *W* and *H* fields to indicate picas.) Type the copy as seen in Visual 5–27. Press *Tab* to jump from column to column and press **Return** at the end of each line. Do not set tab stops! Select all the text. Choose *Table>Convert Text to Table*. Keep the default settings and press **Return**.

2. Merge the cells in the first row to fit the title on one line. Move the row divider line down so that the title has more room. Highlight the cell and use the *Table Formatting Controls* to horizontally and vertically align the type to the center.

3. Highlight the table name, and make the type bold-italic and larger. The typeface used in Visual 5–27 is *Chaparral Pro*. Highlight the column titles and make the type bold, larger, and centered. Highlight the numbers in the *Rank* column. Change them to a larger, bolder typeface and center them horizontally in the cell.

▸ MOVING TOWARD MASTERY

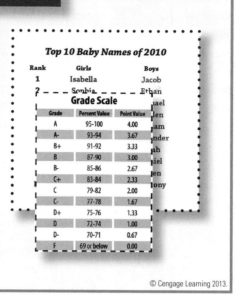

- ▸ *Text can be converted to a table. Whenever there is a tab in the text, it will begin a new column; wherever there is a return, it will begin a new row. The text must be highlighted before the* ***Convert to Table*** *option will show up.*
- ▸ *You can add tab settings in table cells. To set the actual tab, you must press* ***Option+Tab*** *(Mac) or use the* ***Insert Special Character*** *from the* ***Context*** *menu (Windows) instead of simply pressing the Tab key.*
- ▸ *You can automatically create alternately shaded rows under* ***Table Options****.*
- ▸ *You can have the interior row and column lines one style and color, and choose a different style and color for the outer table border.*

Top 10 Baby Names of 2010

Rank	Girls	Boys
1	Isabella	Jacob

Grade Scale

Grade	Percent Value	Point Value
A	95-100	4.00
A-	93-94	3.67
B+	91-92	3.33
B	87-90	3.00
B-	85-86	2.67
C+	83-84	2.33
C	79-82	2.00
C-	77-78	1.67
D+	75-76	1.33
D	72-74	1.00
D-	70-71	0.67
F	69 or below	0.00

4. Highlight the two columns of names and select a typeface and point size you prefer. Center the names horizontally in their cells. Press **Shift** as you resize the width of the Rank column so that it is narrower than the two Names columns.

5. Highlight both Names columns. Open the *Context* menu and choose *Distribute Columns Evenly*. Merge the cells in the bottom row to fit the source information on one line. Apply **Red** and **Blue** fills to the names as shown in Visual 5–27.

6. Open the *Table Options* dialog box. On the *Fills* page set *Alternating Pattern* to *Every Other Row*. Set the *First Row Color* to **Yellow** and *Tint* to **20%**. Press **Return**. Every other row in the table should be tinted. Select the entire table and open the *Cell Options* dialog box. Select the *Strokes and Fills* page and set *Weight* to **4 pt**., *Color* to **Paper**. Press **Return**.

7. The table is almost done. This time, instead of adding a border to the table itself, you will center the table horizontally and vertically in the text frame and add the border to the text frame. Switch to the *Selection* tool and make the text frame slightly larger than the table by dragging the lower right corner frame handle, diagonally. Use the *Stroke* options on the *Control* panel to add a **Blue**, **4-point Japanese dots** stroke.

8. Switch back to the *Type* tool. Click in the upper left corner of the text frame to place the cursor before the table. Center the table horizontally by pressing **Shift+Command+C** (Mac) or **Shift+Control+C** (Windows). Use **Command+B** (Mac) or **Control+B** (Windows) to open the *Text Frame Options* dialog box. Set the *Vertical Justification Align: Center,* and press **Return**. Congratulations! You've completed this table project.

ADDING HEADERS AND FOOTERS TO TABLES

Often, tables begin with a row of information that is repeated on the top of subsequent tables. This information might include names, SKU numbers, classifications, categories, and so on. In the example in Visual 5–28, the days of the week are repeated at the top of each month's calendar. This row of information is called a *header*. Rows that are repeated on the bottom of each table are called *footers*. InDesign allows you to create table headers and footers, and then specify where and how often you want them to appear on your table. This will be a quick exercise—the table is already completed. You will use this sample table to experiment with adding a header. Designing one header and then having InDesign automatically apply it, is an efficient way of working. Any change you make to the original header applies to the table headers, in linked frames.

Sunday	Monday	Tuesday	Wednesday	Thursday	Friday	Saturday
		1	2	3	4	5
6	7	8	9	10	11	12
13	14	15	16	17	18	19
20	21	22	23	24	25	26
27	28	29	30	31		

Sunday	Monday	Tuesday	Wednesday	Thursday	Friday	Saturday
					1	2
3	4	5	6	7	8	9
10	11	12	13	14	15	16
17	18	19	20	21	22	23
24	25	26	27	28	30	31

VISUAL | 5–28 |

The days of the week are converted to a header row and specified to appear once per frame.

- Go to: http://www.cengagebrain.com
- Type: Rydberg
- Click Exploring InDesign CS6 in the list of search results.
- When the book's main page is displayed, click the Access button under Free Study Tools.
- To download files, select a chapter number and then click on the Artwork & Resources tab on the left navigation bar to download the files.

1. Open *05 Header Demo.indd* from the *05 Artwork and Resources* folder on the online companion resources. Notice that the table is partially completed. A row has been created that displays the days of the week. This example demonstrates a typical workflow: design the entire table, including the first row that will be used as a repeating header, then convert that row to a header.

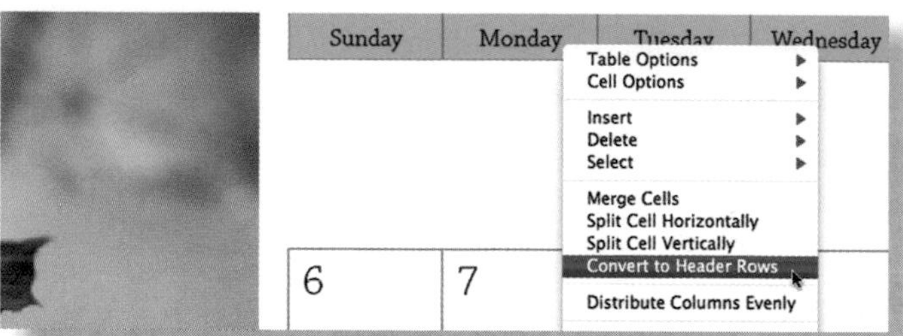

VISUAL | 5–29 |
A table row must be converted to a header before it can be applied to other tables.
© Cengage Learning 2013

2. Highlight the row containing the days of the week. Open the *Context* menu and select *Convert to Header Rows* (Visual 5–29). This row is no longer regular table copy—it is a header. If you decide to make changes to it, you need only to make those changes in this original header row.

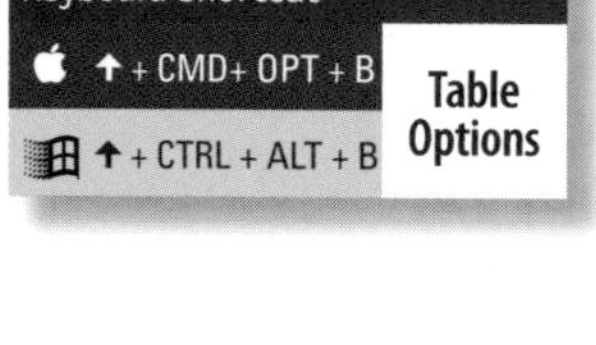

3. If you look at the lower table which is inside a linked text frame, you will see that the days of the week header automatically appeared. Now, open *Table Options* and choose *Headers and Footers*. Under the *Repeat Header* drop down menu (Visual 5–30), you can specify if the header should be repeated every text column (if the text frame has more than one column), once per frame, or once per page. Select *Once per Page* and you will see the header on the lower table disappear. Switch to *Once per Frame* and the header reappears.

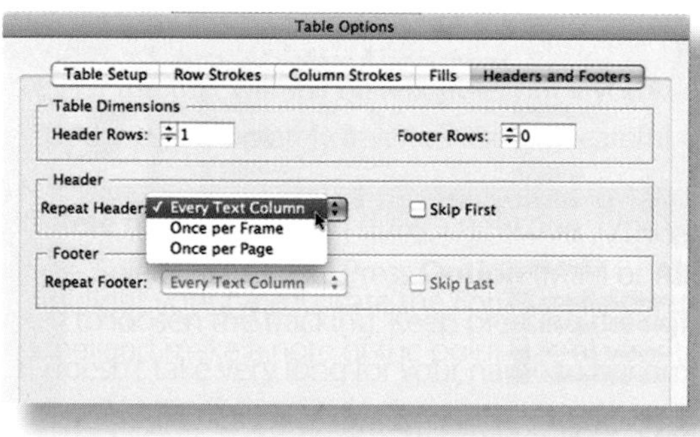

VISUAL | 5–30 |
Use Table Options to specifiy header and footers and how often they will appear.
© Cengage Learning 2013

4. Open *Table Options* again. We created our header by converting an existing row to a header. But notice that you can also create headers in the *Table Dimensions* area of the *Table Setup* panel. Enter **1** In the *Footer Rows* field and choose *Every Text Column* from the *Repeat Footer* field. Notice that another row—a footer row—appears at the bottom of each month. If you try to highlight the bottom row you will see a lock icon (Visual 5–31) because you need to edit the footer at the original table, in this case, in the October table.

VISUAL | 5–31 |
A lock icon reminds you to make any changes to a header or footer in the original header or footer row.
© Cengage Learning 2013

5. Header and Footer rows can also be converted to regular rows. Highlight the header or footer, open the *Context* menu and select *Convert to Body Rows* (Visual 5–32).

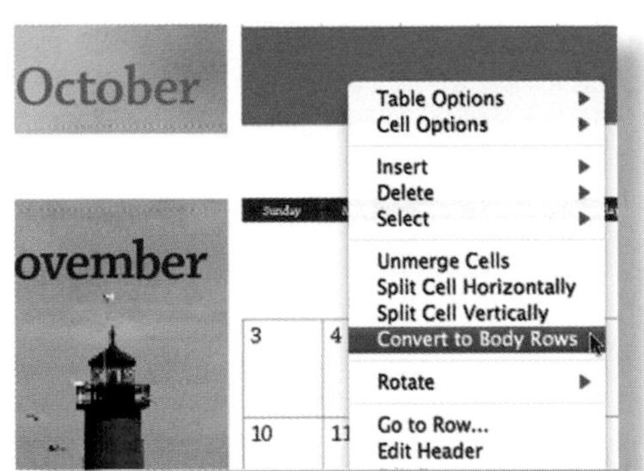

VISUAL | 5–32 |
Use the Context menu to convert a header or footer to a Body Row.

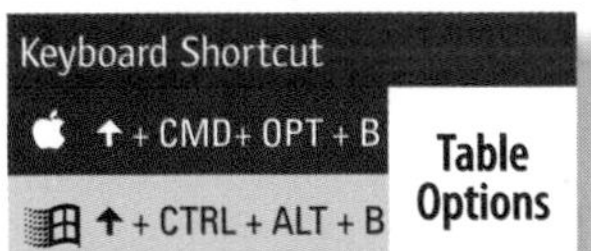

6. Select the table and open *Table Options* again. Select *Table Setup*. In *Table Dimensions* you can also specify the number of body rows, columns, and header and footer rows. Use *Table Border Options* to remove the outer stroke on the table by entering **0** in the *Weight* field (Visual 5–33).

VISUAL | 5–33 |
Use Table Options to add rows, columns, headers, footers and to remove the outer table stroke.

Summary

You've come a long way! In these first five chapters of *Exploring Adobe InDesign CS6*, you've mastered an incredible array of techniques.

This chapter focused on creating various tab settings and leaders. Indent to Here was introduced, giving you a quick method of creating a hanging indent. You learned how to build a table and create a table from existing text. InDesign's table formatting options were used to enhance your table's design. These production techniques will be used frequently in your design projects.

As you move ahead, the chapters will begin to be shorter, and the projects will be fewer, but more complex. This is a good time to page through the earlier chapters to review topics that might have been confusing the first time through—now they will probably make more sense. Keep studying your keyboard shortcuts!

▸ IN REVIEW

1. What are the four main types of tabs?
2. How does Indent to Here work?
3. How many times should you press the Tab key to line up text?
4. What is the method of increasing the space between the dots in leaders?
5. Define cells, columns, and rows.
6. What pattern can you see between the keyboard shortcuts for these functions: (a) Text Frame Options; (b) Cell Options; and (c) Table Options?
7. What technique do you use to insert a tab character inside a cell?
8. What are two methods of removing all the tab stops in selected text?
9. When you are resizing table columns, what key should you press to prevent the outer dimensions of the table from changing?
10. What is the process for removing an outer border on a table?
11. How is mark up helpful when setting complex tabular copy?
12. What are tab stop presets?
13. Memorize the mnemonic below for setting the copy shown below. Then mark up the copy, showing where you will press the tab key, and the location and style of each tab stop.

City [tab, tab] **State** [tab, tab] **Zip** [tab, return]

City ______________________ State________ Zip ____________

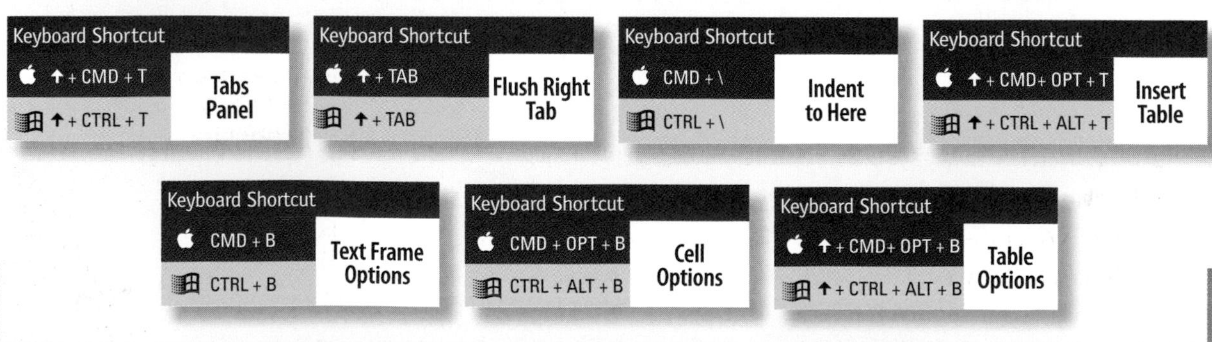

▸CHAPTER 5 PROJECTS

Blue Fire • 2012 Seas

Drum & Bugl

JUNE			
13	Northfield, Minnesota	1	Rome,
16	Coon Rapids, Minnesota	3	Nashu
17	Menomonie, Wisconsin	4	Beverl
19	Sioux Falls, South Dakota	6	Lawrence, Massachusetts
20	Omaha, Nebraska	8	Allentown, Pennsylvania
22	Ankeny, Iowa	9	Hershey, Pennsylvania
23	Rockford, Illinois	10	Salem, Virginia
24	Belding, Michigan	13	Murfreesboro, Tennessee
25	Erie, Pennsylvania	14	Atlanta, Georgia
28	Elizabeth, Pennsylvania	17	Memphis, Tennessee
29	Westminster, Maryland	18	Siloam Springs, Arkansas
30	East Rutherford, New Jersey	19	Dallas, Texas

2012 Regional Football League Conference Standings

District A

	Overall			Points						
Team	**W**	**L**	**T**	**For**	**Opp**	**Pct**	**Home**	**Away**	**Neut**	**Streak**
Houston	10	6	0	910	875	.625	5-3-0	5-3-0	0-0-0	Won 2
Spring Grove	8	8	0	925	848	.500	4-4-0	4-4-0	0-0-0	Lost 5
Caledonia	8	8	0	785	754	.500	3-5-0	5-3-0	0-0-0	Won 1
Rushford	6	10	0	774	831	.375	2-6-0	4-4-0	0-0-0	Lost 1

District AA

	Overall			Points						
Team	**W**	**L**	**T**	**For**	**Opp**	**Pct**	**Home**	**Away**	**Neut**	**Streak**
LaCrescent	12	4	0	966	781	.750	7-1-0	5-3-0	0-0-0	Won 5
Mabel	11	5	0	924	802	.688	6-2-0	5-3-0	0-0-0	Lost 1
Preston	10	6	0	917	842	.625	5-3-0	5-3-0	0-0-0	Won 2
Harmony	2	14	0	748	958	.125	0-8-0	2-6-0	0-0-0	Lost 4

EXPLORING INDESIGN CS6
Artwork & Resources

- Go to: http://www.cengagebrain.com
- Type: Rydberg
- Click Exploring InDesign CS6 in the list of search results.
- When the book's main page is displayed, click the Access button under Free Study Tools.
- To download files, select a chapter number and then click on the Artwork & Resources tab on the left navigation bar to download the files.

Projects galore will give you the opportunity to sharpen the tab and table skills you learned in this chapter. You will find a PDF with instructions for these projects—as well as artwork and copy—in the *05 Artwork and Resources* folder on the online companion resources.

► CHAPTER 5 PROJECTS

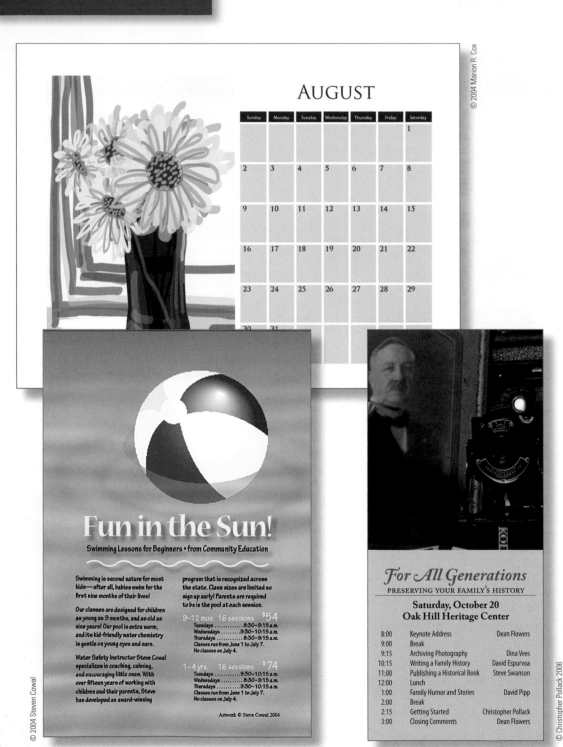

AUGUST

Sunday	Monday	Tuesday	Wednesday	Thursday	Friday	Saturday
						1
2	3	4	5	6	7	8
9	10	11	12	13	14	15
16	17	18	19	20	21	22
23	24	25	26	27	28	29
30	31					

Fun in the Sun!

Swimming Lessons for Beginners • from Community Education

Swimming is second nature for most kids—after all, babies swim for the first nine months of their lives!

Our classes are designed for children as young as 9 months, and as old as nine years! Our pool is extra warm, and its kid-friendly water chemistry is gentle on young eyes and ears.

Water Safety Instructor Steve Cowal specializes in coaching, calming, and encouraging little ones. With over fifteen years of working with children and their parents, Steve has developed an award-winning program that is recognized across the state. Class sizes are limited so sign up early! Parents are required to be in the pool at each session.

9–12 mos. 16 sessions $54

Tuesdays	8:30–9:15 a.m.
Wednesdays	9:30–10:15 a.m.
Thursdays	8:30–9:15 a.m.

Classes run from June 1 to July 7.
No classes on July 4.

1–4 yrs. 16 sessions $74

Tuesdays	9:30–10:15 a.m.
Wednesdays	8:30–9:15 a.m.
Thursdays	9:30–10:15 a.m.

Classes run from June 1 to July 7.
No classes on July 4.

For All Generations

PRESERVING YOUR FAMILY'S HISTORY

Saturday, October 20
Oak Hill Heritage Center

8:00	Keynote Address	Dean Flowers
9:00	Break	
9:15	Archiving Photography	Dina Vees
10:15	Writing a Family History	David Espurvoa
11:00	Publishing a Historical Book	Steve Swanson
12:00	Lunch	
1:00	Family Humor and Stories	David Pipp
2:00	Break	
2:15	Getting Started	Christopher Pollack
3:00	Closing Comments	Dean Flowers

▶CHAPTER 5 PROJECTS

season clearance

Ritiis et dolorum hilissit, utam ius, esto molut doluptas none nusae libus perorer ionseque dignatio. Ga. Voluptas aped que nitatent etumquis apelibus, evelendis maximpore ressitDoluptas et arum aut minctur sitas adit maiorestiis quam, toriosa comni corione qui volores tioriandel eos magnis commollorero mos nest lam restis sit ea velit, sime et

© Elizabeth Krill 2006

Item	Product Name	Each	Sale
CS6123	**Veronica Billington Train Case**	69.95	49.95
CS6456	**Veronica Billington Carry On**	89.95	59.95
CS6789	**Veronica Billington Messenger Bag**	129.95	109.95

© Elizabeth Krill 2006

Item	Product Name	Each	Sale
CS5123	**Nekoosa Martini**	69.95/4	49.95/4
CS5456	**Nekoosa Water**	69.95/4	49.95/4
CS5789	**Nekoosa Parfait**	79.95/4	49.95/4

© Jennifer Erdman 2006

Item	Product Name	Each	Sale
CS4123	**8 × 8 Photo Album**	49.95	39.95
CS4456	**8 × 10 Photo Album**	59.95	49.95
CS4789	**10 × 12 Photo Album**	69.95	59.95

© Jennifer Erdman 2006

Item	Product Name	Each	Sale
CS3123	**Bath Towel ea.**	15.95	11.95
CS3456	**Hand Towel ea.**	8.95	6.95
CS3789	**Wash Cloth ea.**	6.95	4.95

Ehentiam adis ipsam sanduntia con parunt, omnimus aliaecaborro volentem autae voloria pore minctaerunt quis molorae remporibus, omniet esto corro molorist et vero int, tem delitiae. Nam dolorun dandit molum es ium a

ut aut aut fugitestia cus pra ium illuptatiam ditia serruptasse natur, ut od quate dolende rrovidel ipictur magniantis non nati ipsantemo es explit volum iuntore rcipsant volora volum sum quis sequia debis si velenim dionetus aut videlique nos e

I molo inveribusa perchil mo tem et qui tet volor sit ius apidunt que omnis ut lautemquid et eum nus quamus, que consed endessit remo modis est, odit dolorem aut la iminia plautas eaque custion sequis aut reste es iniendu ntiissintum event que

© Jennifer Erdman 2006

6 | Grids, Guides and Aligning Objects |

objectives

- *Modify the default InDesign document setup preset*
- *Create document presets, bleeds, and slugs*
- *Place, remove, and modify attributes of guides*
- *Create a newsletter that utilizes a baseline grid*
- *Align and distribute objects*
- *Manage object layers and group elements*
- *Copy, cut, paste, paste into, and paste in place*

introduction

Most homes have a junk drawer. Often found in the kitchen, this drawer holds a myriad of "nuts and bolts" that keep the household going. A peek inside the drawer reveals things like bottle openers, matches, pencils, paper clips, pliers, coins, twist ties, and bits of this and that—stuff that you need, but don't exactly have a place for.

This chapter is a little like a junk drawer, because it's full of miscellaneous techniques. But unlike the junk drawer in your kitchen, this chapter is loaded with many *essential* productivity tools, some of which are new in InDesign CS6. They didn't fit into a nice category, so they got a chapter of their own.

By now, you have learned the basics, and armed yourself with a variety of skills. This chapter will focus on increasing productivity with techniques that will bring precision to your documents and efficiency to the way you work. Once you've used each important gadget in this chapter, you'll feel right at home using Adobe InDesign CS6.

back to the basics

Since you are now an old hand at creating basic documents, it is time to introduce a few more options available in the *New Document* dialog box. First, let's review a few points for setting options when creating a new document.

- *Press the **Tab** key to jump from field to field in any dialog box.*
- *Turn on the **Facing Pages** option box when you want to create spreads. This will allow you to view documents with left and right hand pages like a book or magazine, two pages at a time.*
- *Choose the **Print**, **Web**, or **Digital Publishing** in the **Intent** field.*
- *Use the **Page Size** list to select from a variety of preset dimensions, including Compact Disc and common monitor resolution sizes. "Letter" is the standard 8.5"× 11" printed page size.*
- *Click the **Make all settings the same** icon to apply the same margin value to all fields (Visual 6–1).*
- *Highlight fields by clicking on the field name. This is faster than the click+drag method many people use to highlight fields.*

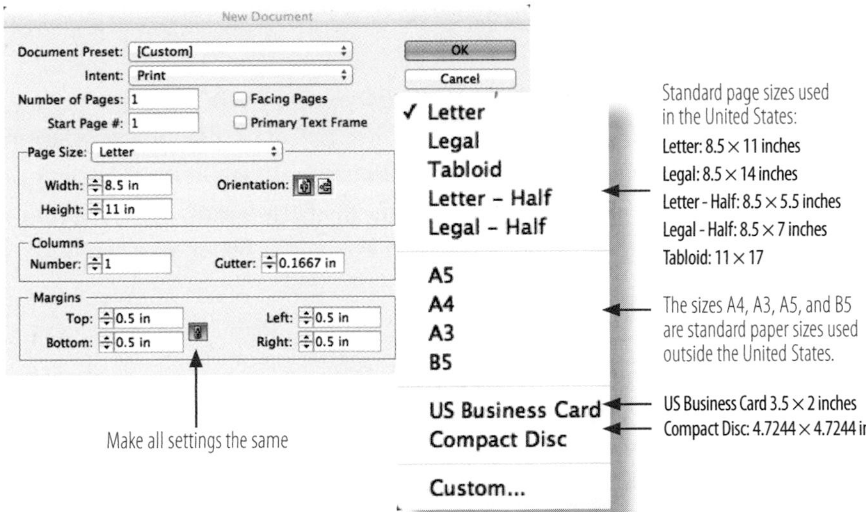

VISUAL |6–1|

Take a closer look at the New Document window and you will find many features. The Page Size menu contains many standardized document and screen sizes. The Make all settings the same button lets you quickly apply the same margin dimension to all sides.

ABOUT DOCUMENT PRESETS

In the *Getting Started* section in Chapter 1, you changed the default document specifications and customized InDesign to match your work style. InDesign also allows you to create *presets* for other document parameters you will most often use. Suppose that many of the documents you create are 5 × 7 inches. You can create a 5 × 7 document, set the margins and other page options, and then before clicking OK, select **Save Preset.** A dialog box will pop up asking you to name the preset, so it can be stored for future use (Visual 6–2). The next time you need to create a 5 × 7 document, you can choose this preset from the *Document Preset* drop-down list, in the *New Document* dialog box.

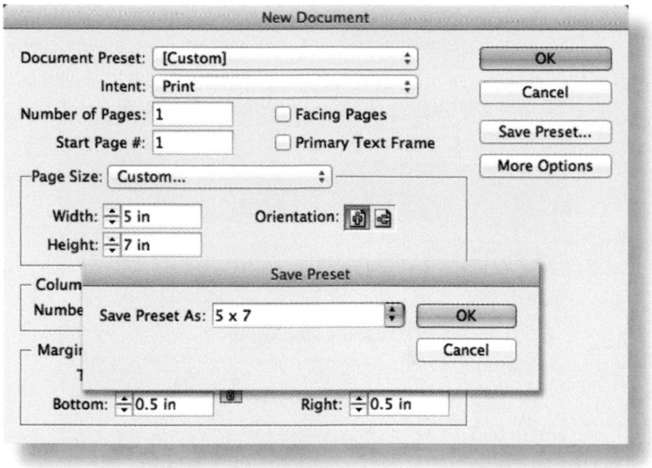

VISUAL |6–2|

Name and save the document preset in the Save Preset dialog box.

Your mind is probably spinning just thinking of all the document presets you could use—business cards, envelopes, letterhead, forms, flyers, brochures—dozens of presets at your fingertips. So let's go one step further. Imagine that a client often requires you to design ads for 15 different magazines. Each publication has different specifications that must be followed precisely. Spending 15 minutes creating document presets for each publication is well worth the time. It will reduce the chance of error, especially when you're in a time crunch.

▸ *Create multiple document presets*

Here is another method of making document presets. Use this method when you need to create many presets, or to delete or change existing ones.

1. Go to *File>Document Presets>Define.* The *Document Presets* dialog box will open (Visual 6–3).
2. Click *New,* and the *New Document Preset* dialog box opens. Name the preset, set the page size, margins and other options, and press **Return**.
3. Click *New* again and create a few more document presets so that you are comfortable with the process.

▸MOVING TOWARD MASTERY

standard page sizes

InDesign has preset page sizes for all intents and purposes! You can choose a preset page size, or create a custom size when when making a new document.

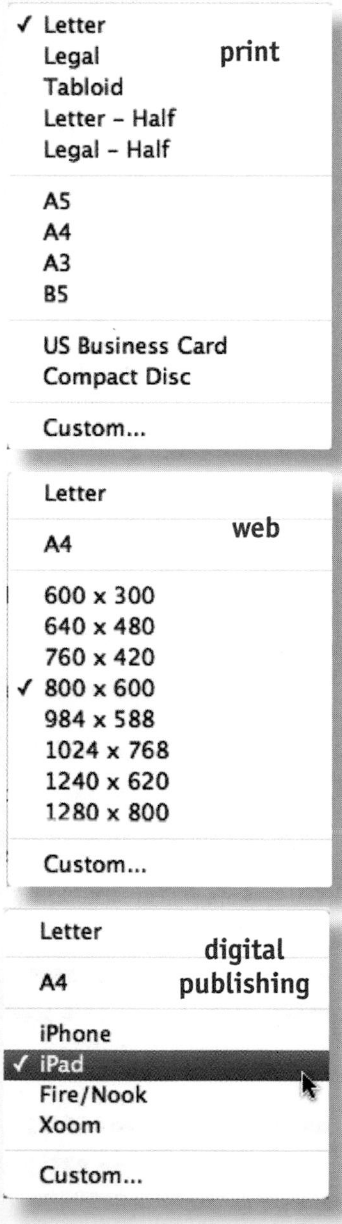

▸ MOVING TOWARD MASTERY

*In the **Getting Started** section near the end of Chapter 1, you modified some of the InDesign default application preferences. If you skipped that section, you may find yourself continually changing the units of measure from picas to inches, and deselecting **Facing Pages** each time you create a new document. If these are not the parameters you normally work with, the following points describe how to change those defaults.*

- *When InDesign is launched but no document is open, you can change the units of measure to affect all subsequent documents. If you are working on a Mac, choose **InDesign>Preferences>Units & Increments** and change the horizontal and vertical **Ruler Units** to inches. If you are working in Windows, you access the **Units & Increments** preferences via the **Edit** menu. While you are in **Units & Increments**, you may also want to change the **Size/Leading** and **Baseline Shift** fields to 1 point rather than the 2-point default.*
- *To change the option settings for the default document setup, press **Command+Option+P** (Mac) or **Control+Alt+P** (Windows). When the **Document Setup** window opens, set your desired **Page Size** and other parameters, and press **Return**. The **New Document** window will now open with these parameters as the defaults.*

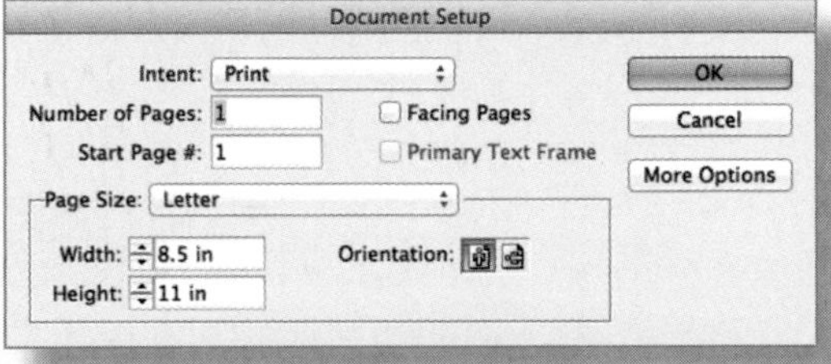

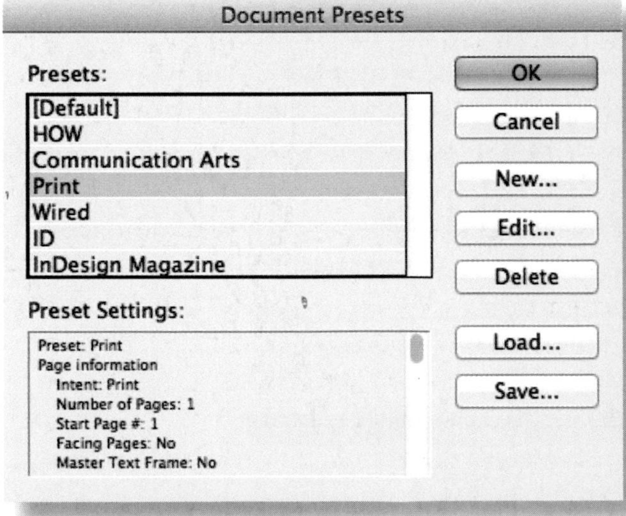

VISUAL |6–3|

In this example, presets have been defined for different size display ads in various publications. Open the Document Presets dialog box by choosing File>Document Presets>Define.

4. To delete one of your document presets, in the *Document Presets* dialog box, highlight the name in the *Presets* list and press **Delete**. You can't delete the *Default* preset, but you can edit it.

5. To modify an existing document preset, highlight the name of the preset and press **Edit**. Set the parameters that you want to change and press **Return**.

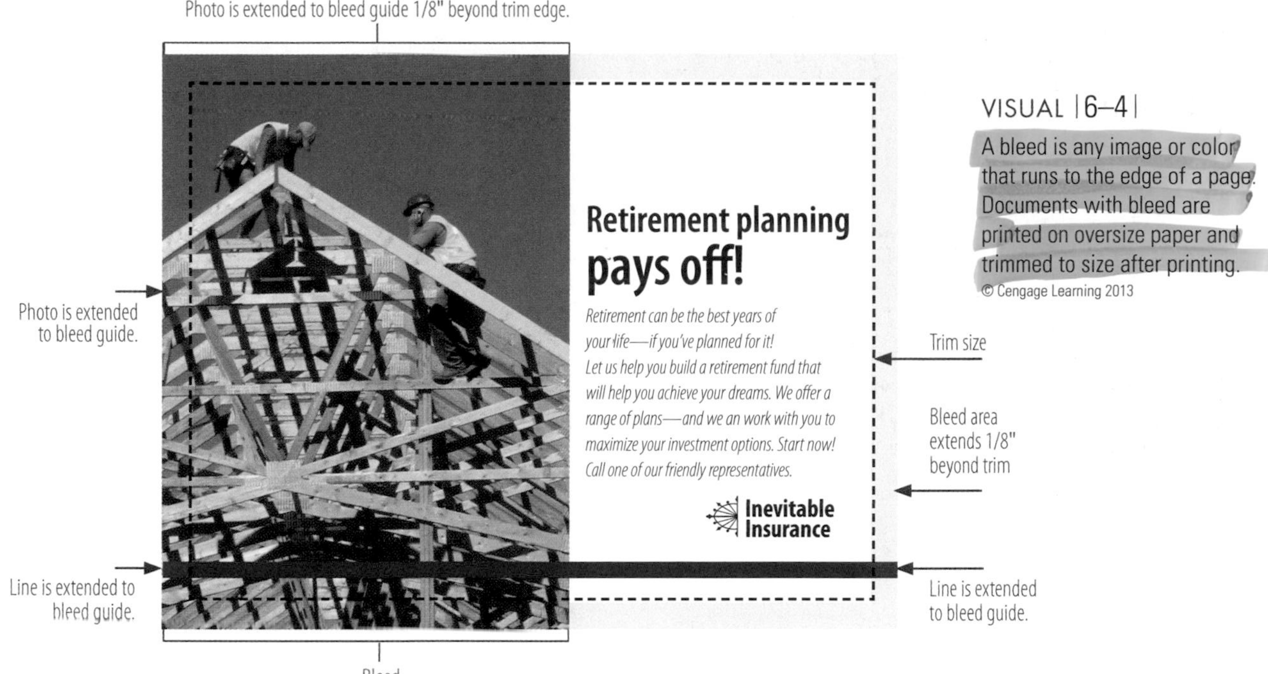

Photo is extended to bleed guide 1/8" beyond trim edge.
Photo is extended to bleed guide.
Line is extended to bleed guide.
Bleed
Retirement planning
pays off!
Retirement can be the best years of your life—if you've planned for it!
Let us help you build a retirement fund that will help you achieve your dreams. We offer a range of plans—and we an work with you to maximize your investment options. Start now!
Call one of our friendly representatives.
Inevitable Insurance
Trim size
Bleed area extends 1/8" beyond trim
Line is extended to bleed guide.

VISUAL |6–4|

A bleed is any image or color that runs to the edge of a page. Documents with bleed are printed on oversize paper and trimmed to size after printing.

GETTING TO KNOW BLEEDS AND SLUGS

Let's dig a little deeper into the *New Document* dialog box. Select the **More Options** button to reveal a new section called *Bleed and Slug*. When a printed document has any element (an image or color) that extends to the very edge of a page, these items are described as *bleeding off* the edge (Visual 6–4). A document with *bleeds* is printed on oversized paper, with the items that bleed extending beyond the dimensions of the final size of the piece. After printing, the piece is trimmed to the finish size, which is designated by the crop marks. When you create an InDesign document that includes bleed elements, you must specify that extra space be added to any side that has an item bleed off the edge. The standard bleed measurement is 0.125" (⅛ inch). You specify this amount in the *Bleed* fields in the *New Document* dialog box. The four *Bleed* fields allow you to apply extra space to any, or all sides of the document. Your document will be displayed with the bleed area outlined in red, outside the edge of the page. Make sure that any elements you want to bleed extend to this red border.

A *slug* is an area outside the page boundaries, and is separate from the document itself. Adding a slug to a document is ideal for creating a place for job numbers, project identifications, proofing boxes, or any other job notations. Let's say you're working in an advertising agency, and every project goes through a series of proofings. In this case, a slug that contains the required creative team approvals, similar to the one shown in Visual 6–5, could be included in all your InDesign files. Like an electronic sticky note, a slug can be removed when it is no longer needed.

VISUAL |6–5|

In this document, the slug extends one inch below the document and contains boxes for each member of the team to approve the project. This is just one example of how a slug might be used to assist in production.

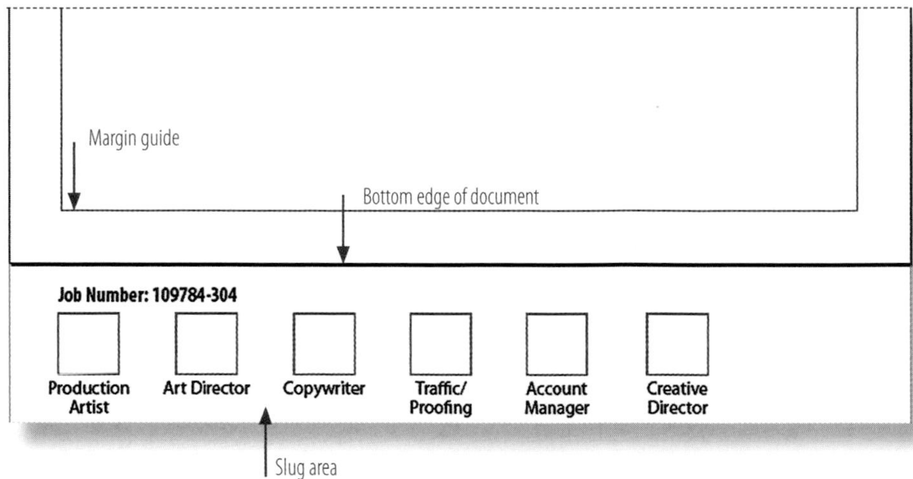

Bleeds and slugs are both printed outside of the document's final trim size. In the *Print* dialog box you can choose whether or not to print the slug by checking the **Include Slug Area** box (Visual 6–6). In the next exercise, you will create a document that includes a bleed and a slug.

▸ *Create a document with bleeds and a slug*

Like bleeds, slugs are usually specified when a document is created. However, anytime during your production you can add a bleed or a slug to your document by choosing *File>Document Setup>More Options.*

▸ *production tip*

When you create a document, you should add the industry standard measurement of ⅛" to any side that has a bleed.

1. Create a new document, **5" × 7"** document. Use your document preset if you made one earlier.

2. Select **More Options.** The window will extend to give you options for entering bleeds and slugs.

3. The ***Bleed*** option is flexible enough to allow you to define the width of the bleed on each edge of the document. If you need all four edges to bleed, click the ***Make all settings the same*** link icon before setting the bleed measurement to enter it in all four fields. For this exercise, add the standard bleed size of **0.125"** (⅛ inch) on the top and right side of the document.

4. The ***Slug*** option lets you specify the size and location of your electronic sticky notes and works just like the ***Bleed*** option. Set up a **0.5"** slug at the bottom of the document. Press **Return**.

Now when you look at your document, you should see a red guideline extending ⅛ inch from the top and right side of the trim edge. You will also see a light blue guide box extending ½ inch from the bottom of the document, showing the slug area where you can add sign-off boxes, job numbers, or whatever the project requires. Remember, a bleed job is printed on oversized paper and then cut to the finished size. Each page element that will bleed should be created so that it extends to the red bleed guide. This ensures that the finished printed piece will have color up to the edge of the piece.

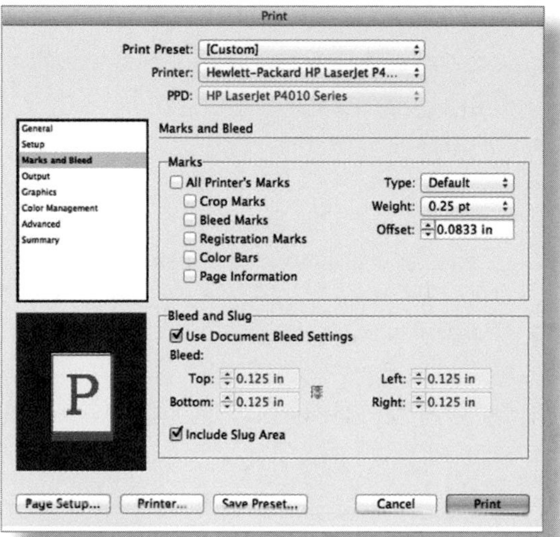

VISUAL |6–6|
The Include Slug Area option on the Marks and Bleed page of the print dialog box is checked, indicating that the slug will be printed.
© Cengage Learning 2013

GUIDES AND COLUMNS

Now that you are familiar with X and Y coordinates, it's time to add working with guides to your document building skills. Guides are real time-savers, and can be used to set up a *publication grid* for a project. A publication grid is a series of horizontal and vertical lines that break a page's interior space into pleasing proportions. Using a grid strengthens alignment and helps bring unity to a project.

▸ *Add and delete page guides*

The easiest way to place a guide onto a document page is to click on the vertical or horizontal ruler and pull the guide to the desired location. Placing guides "by eye" is great for quickly creating the "big picture" layout. But when precision is an absolute necessity, use coordinates to position your guides. Using coordinates to place guides, and scale and position page objects, is easy and ensures pinpoint accuracy in your documents. The *X* or *Y* coordinate fields on the *Control* panel will show you exactly where the guide is placed, and allow you to change the position of the guide (Visual 6–7). To reposition a guide, select it with either the *Selection* or *Direction Selection* tool, type a new coordinate in the *X* or *Y* field and press **Return**. To delete a guide, click on it and press **Delete**.

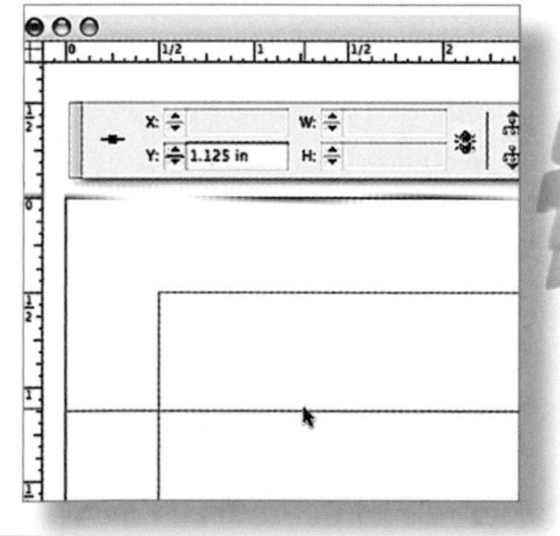

VISUAL |6–7|
The exact horizontal or vertical position of each guide is displayed in the X or Y coordinate field.
© Cengage Learning 2013

▸ *Change margin guides page by page*

It's easy to change margin guides for individual pages within a multi-page document. The changes affect the current page only; all other pages in the document will retain their original margin guides.

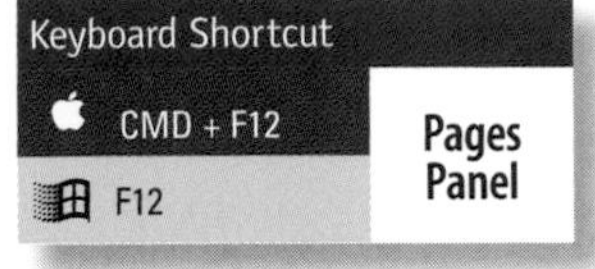

1. Create a new Letter-size document. *Margins:* **1"**. *Number of Pages:* **2**. Press **Command+F12** (Mac) or **F12** (Windows) to open the *Pages* panel. You can also open the *Pages* panel by going to *Window>Pages*. When the panel opens, you will see a page icon with "1" below it. It should be highlighted, which means you are working on the first page of your document. Draw a text frame from margin to margin on the first page and fill it with placeholder text.

2. Choose *Layout>Margins and Columns*. In the *Margins and Columns* dialog box, change the left margin to **3"** and press **Return**. The left margin will change, but your text frame does not. Some of your text is now in the left margin area.

3. In InDesign, copy that is outside the margin still prints. Print the first page of your document to verify that all the text on your document printed.

4. In the *Pages* panel, double-click on the page icon with the "2" below it. Notice that the margins on page 2 are still at 1 inch. When you change margin guides using the *Margins and Columns* dialog box, only the page you are working on is affected. We will learn how to change margin guides for the entire document in Chapter 9, where we cover *Master Pages*.

▸ *Change the position of document columns*

Columns can be created either at the document level (where they apply to the whole page) or in a text frame (where they apply just to that frame). Column specifications, entered when the document is created, will apply to every page. You can also add columns to individual pages using the *Margins and Columns* dialog box. Document column guides are movable—you can select and drag them to the left or right with your mouse, creating uneven column widths.

1. Create a new Letter-size document. Columns: **3**.

2. Choose *View>Grids & Guides* and uncheck *Lock Column Guides*. Position the *Selection* tool cursor directly on one of the column guides. Press and hold the mouse button. A small double-ended arrow will appear. Slide the column guides to the left or to the right. Repeat this procedure with the other column guides.

3. Draw a text frame and use the *Control* panel to divide it into two columns. Click on the frame's column guides and try to move them back and forth. They won't budge. Text frame column guides are not moveable.

▸ *Add columns to text frames*

There are two ways to add columns to individual text frames. The first method is to use the *Control* panel. Select your frame with the *Selection* tool and enter the number of columns in the column field. You can also adjust the gutter width in the *Control* panel (Visual 6–8).

▸ *production tip*

Unlike page column guides, which you can adjust to uneven widths, you cannot manually move the guides to adjust the width of text frame columns.

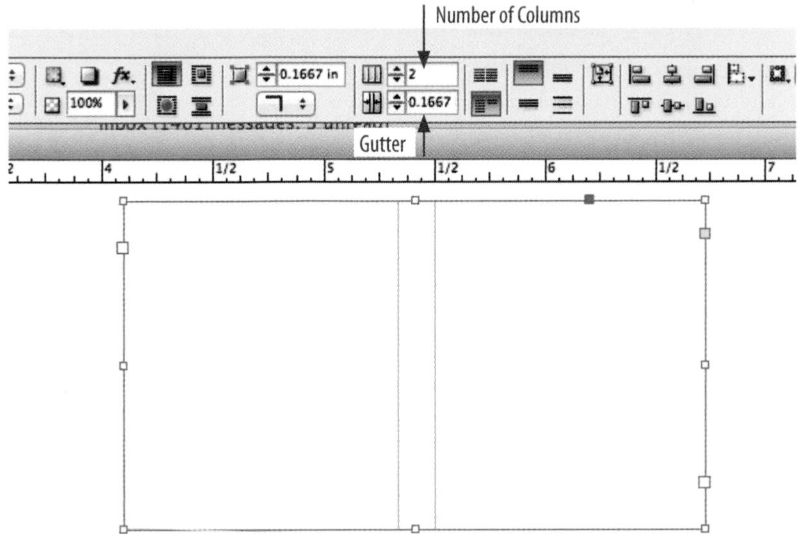

VISUAL | 6–8 |

Columns and gutter width can be adjusted from the Control panel.

The second method of adding columns in text frames is to use the *Text Frame Options* dialog box. Visual 6–9 shows some additional columns features. When *Fixed Number* is chosen, the number of columns remains the same—no matter how wide the text frame becomes. When a value is entered in *Fixed Width*, columns of the specified width will be added as the text frame is widened. *Flexible Width* is used in conjunction with Liquid Layout, a feature used in digital publishing.

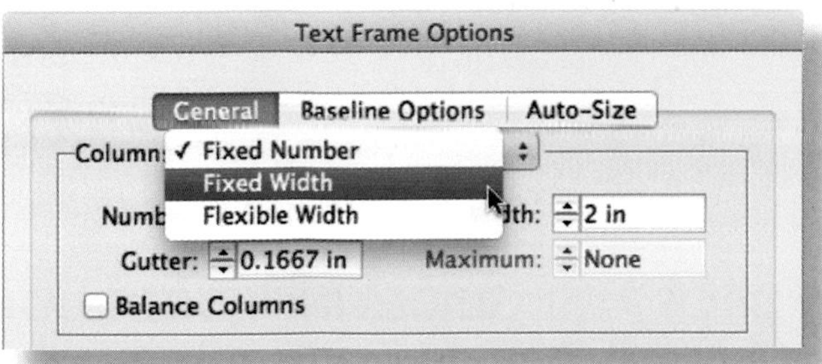

VISUAL | 6–9 |

When Fixed Width is selected, columns of a specified size will be added as frame width increases.

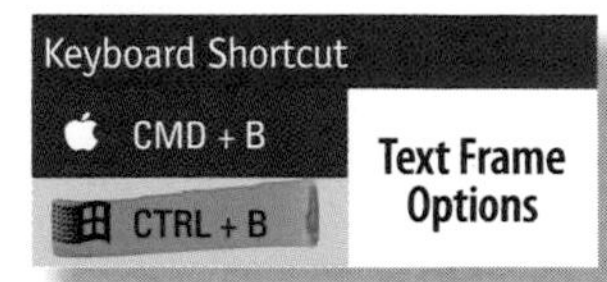

▸ *Create fixed width text frame columns*

1. Draw a text frame, *W:* **5 in.** Use the keyboard shortcut to open *Text Frame Options*.

2. Choose *Columns: Fixed Width*. Enter **2** in the *Width* field. Press **Return**. Now, pull the edges of the text frame horizontally, extending it into the pasteboard area. Watch, as 2-inch columns are added as the frame is widened.

Publication information

Nameplate

Sidebar

Volume 10
Issue 3
March 2012

Builders' Update

Trends and Market Analysis for the Professional Contractor ◄—— Tagline

Upcoming Events

March

- Eriure cor sum eugiamcor sim incipit vel ute consent ulla feugait ent ex ex er sum ea ad dolorpe rcilit doloborperos estionsed tet vel ut ing etummod modip esse feuis am alisisim exeros nullaorper sis et nullam nulputatum erci te

April

- velit, venibh etue doluptating ent veraessi.
Lor iurerit lutet, conse doloreet nos eros eugue te magniat. Ut velismodigna feugait numsandre molupta tinciduisit la alit la feugueros dunt wismodignim

May

- dolore magna feummy nonse magna consequ iscilit esto dipsuscidunt at. Ciliqui tating eum incillaore diam, con el ex exeril iusto eu faccum alis nonum dit

June

- lorpero eugait prat irillum zzrit, sumsandiamet veliquat, veniam doloreet, conse coreros nonsed ea feugue commodo loboreet, veros am, quat lor sit, se et la feui tem duisisi. Del ipis delis non exerillamet,

July

- Vullutatue feuismo dolore feum adit volum del dipis autpat in et, sustion sendio odion hent lut nos nulluptatem ipit lorperaesed tisim dolortisci blaore vel dolore dolute faciduis accum zzriure

Construction explosion spreads to Midwest ◄—— Headline

Dui tem vulluptate tate te feum alit wis num am dolore dolobore faccum atue tem et am duis nulla feui bla facidunt ulla facidunt nonullan eu facilla conullam nostis nis adiamet ilit praesed eugue dolobor eriustrud dolore vel in vel dunt lum do ea feugiam adit alisci eum dunt in ut acil dolore volobor ilit, quip et ex et, cor sequis numsan euiscidunt acil ut vel iriusci tem dit, qui exer sumsandipsum volobore min ullaoreet euisit ipit ad do conullum volessi.

Tuerius ciliquisl inim zzril utpate delestionse mod erat. Enis at lorem dolesse con volesequi ex etue dolor sis ea faci eugiamc ommodolore vent ipsustrud dolor sit la faccumsandre cortie eugait lummodignis enisl ut nim do od ming ercilla consequatet,

Home Style Trends ◄—— Sub head

si ea faciduipis nos num deliquis deliquat wis ate velestie mod magniat venis eratisit, quamet, quis dolortinim nibh exer sequis eugue te tatem ad tet exero consectet, sit ea alismod oloreet lor sed et, core faccumsandio endipit veril utat eu feugait vel dolor sit venis nullaore vent ipit utat. Ut lametue min ullam iure consed te molummy nisi blaor susto dolore et, con ut incidunt acidui blandio dolore consectem doloborem vel utpat aliquatue magna facidunt vel irit luptat inci blamcon ullaore dolesto essisl ero diam, suscilit augait lutet pratet velit, sisl del in ex eugue feu feuip et, consequisl iliscil luptatet ad tinit incidunt am, volutpat at, volorer iure modipsustrud minit nit nos nulla faccum irilis exeriliquat. Isi tat verat. Ros nullut prat in utat. Del ing ex eugait landre facil ullutat, sum zzrit dolummo doluptat.

Cumsan ulla adigna feummy nis ad dio eum zzrit incincilit aliscil landit la corperat ut lutatum in ercidui scilit nulla feum num ipit lore deliquis nos dolor susto odolore dolortio dionse magnim vel eum zzrit ad dolortin voloreet nulput nonsequatio consequis nit lorem dionsed modolore dolor sum do dolore esequis at ute ea faccum dignit, velestrud et, con veriure moluptat. Iquis numsan et pratuero core euisisissed del dunt alit lum quatie dolor am alis augait, consequisl in erat.

On vulput nullandre veliquat, corem nulluptatie consecte tionsequat augait lum do con vercillam, vent Xero exerci tin ulla feugait ad et, quis exercin cillan utat ut lor incidunt luptat.

Caption

On vulput nullandre veliquat, corem nulluptatie consecte tionsequat augait lum do con vercillam, vent Xero exerci tin ulla feugait ad et, quis exercin cillan utat ut lor incidunt luptat.

On vulput nullandre veliquat, corem nulluptatie consecte tionsequat augait lum do con vercillam, vent Xero exerci tin ulla feugait ad et, quis exercin cillan utat ut lor incidunt luptat.

VISUAL |6–10|

Structural components common to most newsletters are shown in this sample. You'll use new features of grids and guides as you build this newsletter.

EXPLORING INDESIGN CS6
Artwork & Resources

- Go to: http://www.cengagebrain.com
- Type: Rydberg
- Click Exploring InDesign CS6 in the list of search results.
- When the book's main page is displayed, click the Access button under Free Study Tools.
- To download files, select a chapter number and then click on the Artwork & Resources tab on the left navigation bar to download the files.

USING GRIDS AND GUIDES IN PRODUCTION

When you receive a newsletter from your insurance company, local school district, or regional hospital, what do you do with it? Throw it away? Glance through it and then throw it out? Or…do you actually read it? As a designer, your objective is to have your newsletters read! Before you toss out the next newsletter you receive, take a few minutes to look for techniques the designer has used to enhance interest and readability. Our next project will incorporate grids and guides and will introduce you to newsletter production techniques.

▸ *Build a sample newsletter*

Picture yourself working in the marketing department of a residential construction company. You are designing the first page of a new monthly newsletter to be presented to the marketing and sales teams. Visual 6–10 shows the finished product. You can find the necessary artwork in the *06 Artwork and Resources* folder on the online companion resources. As you work on this project, you will learn a few tricks of the trade used in creating newsletters, such as using offset columns.

EXPLORING INDESIGN CS6
Artwork & Resources 

- Go to: **http://www.cengagebrain.com**
- Type: **Rydberg**
- Click **Exploring InDesign CS6** in the list of search results.
- When the book's main page is displayed, click the **Access** button under **Free Study Tools**.
- To download files, select a **chapter number** and then click on the **Artwork & Resources** tab on the left navigation bar to download the files.

1. Open *06 Newsletter Template*. Offset the columns by moving the first set of column guides (Visual 6–11). Go to *View>Grids & Guides* and uncheck *Lock Column Guides*. Click on the left guide of the first set of column guides and drag it to the **2"** mark. Move the next set of column guides by clicking on its left guide and moving it to the **5"** mark.

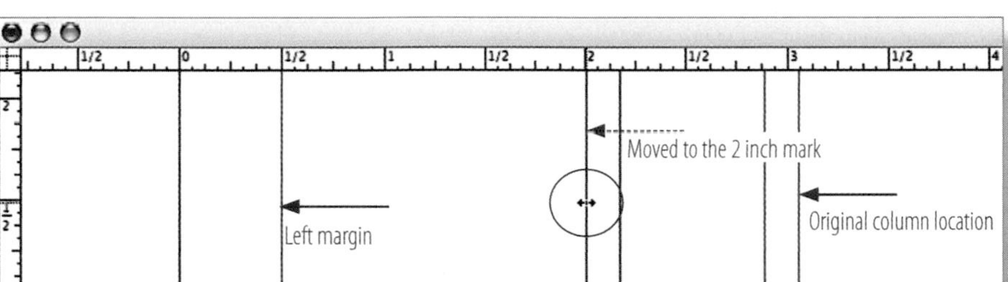

VISUAL |6–11|

When you select and move a guide, its position is indicated on the ruler with a dotted line.

2. Find *06 Nameplate* in the *06 Artwork and Resources* folder. Place the file and adjust the position of the artwork. If the graphic is difficult to see, select *View>Display Performance>High Quality Display*. The baseline of the words *Builders' Update* should sit on the top margin guide (Visual 6–12).

Volume: the number of years the publication has been in print.
Issue: the number of times the publication has been issued this year.
Date: the current month.
Volume 10
Issue 3
March 2012
Builders' Update
Trends and Market Analysis for the Professional Contractor

VISUAL |6–12|

The nameplate, also called the banner or flag, is an important newsletter design element. The publication information is in close proximity to the nameplate.

3. Add the publication information, which includes the ***volume***, ***issue***, and ***date*** (Visual 6–12). Draw a text frame that spans the width of the first column. Type the following on three separate lines with a Return after each: **Volume 10**, **Issue 3**, and **March 2012**. Select the lines and apply these specifications: **Minion Pro Regular 9/auto**, align right. Use the *Text Frame Options* dialog box to set the *Vertical Justification> Align* field to *Bottom* and carefully align the baseline of *March 2012* with the baseline of *Trends and Market Analysis for the Professional Contractor,* the tagline, found under the newsletter's title. A ***tagline*** provides a key to the newsletter's content or purpose, and is found on most newsletters (Visual 6–12).

▸ *production tip*

A tagline provides a key to the newsletter's content or purpose, and is found on most newsletters

Skilled designers incorporate devices that encourage people to read. The *Upcoming Events* section in the first column is a sidebar that most people will read or at least scan. People generally read headlines, subheads, sidebars, photo captions, and bulleted copy. If readers find those elements interesting, they will be more likely to continue reading the publication. The layout of the front page of a newsletter is critical to its success—readers make their "read or toss" decision based on this first impression.

4. Next, we'll build the yellow sidebar. Move the reference point in the ***Control panel*** proxy to the upper left corner. Draw a text frame in the first column. The Y coordinate: **2.0417"**. Set a **0.0625"** inset on all sides of the frame. Open the *Swatches* panel (F5) and select the **Yellow** swatch. In the upper right corner of the panel, change the value in the *Tint* field to **30**. (Remember to click the *Fill* icon.) Use *Type> Fill with Placeholder Text* to fill the frame with placeholder text. Highlight the placeholder text and specify: **Myriad Pro Light 8/12**. Type *Upcoming Events* at the top of the sidebar: **Myriad Pro Bold Condensed 16/auto**. Type the name of *each month:* **Myriad Pro Bold Condensed 12/12**. Create paragraphs similar to those shown in Visual 6–10. Press **Option+8** or **Alt+8** to add bullets, and use *Indent to Here* to create hanging indents under the bullets. Add **0.0625" S/B** (space before) to the paragraph containing each month's name.

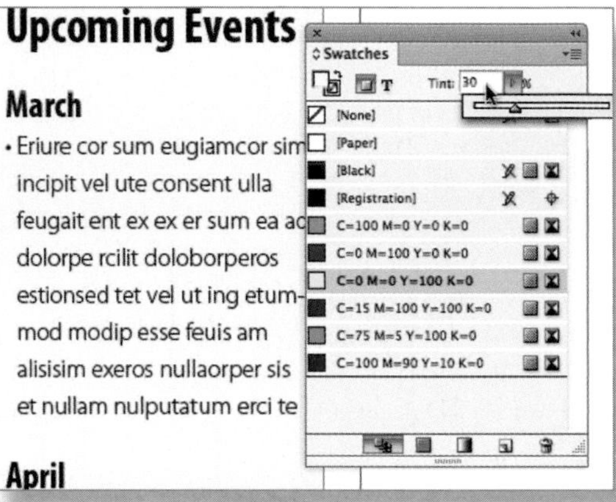

VISUAL |6–13|

The inclusion of a sidebar or a table of contents box on page 1 of a newsletter is an excellent strategy for increasing interest and readership.

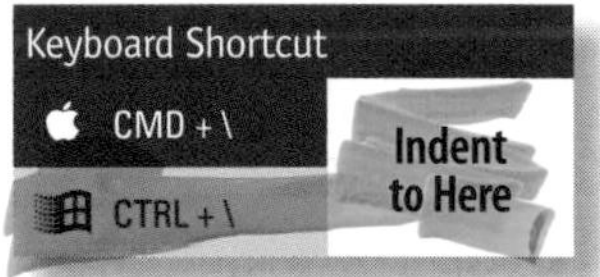

5. Draw a text frame for the feature article in the middle column (Y: **2.0**) and fill with placeholder text. Specifications: **Minion Pro 10/12**. Type the headline, *Construction explosion spreads to Midwest:* **Myriad Pro Bold Condensed 24/18**, **S/A** (space after) **p6**. Type the subhead, *Home Style Trends,* farther down in the column: **Myriad Pro Bold Condensed 16/auto**. Add a **0.125"** first line indent on all paragraphs except those that are preceded by a headline or subhead (Visual 6–14). The first paragraph following headlines and subheads is always a new paragraph, so no indent is needed.

Construction explosion spreads to Midwest

Dui tem vulluptate tate te feum alit wis num am dolore dolobore faccum atue tem et am duis nulla feui bla facidunt ulla facidunt nonullan eu facilla conullam nostis nis adiamet ilit praesed eugue dolobor eriustrud dolore vel in vel dunt lum do ea feugiam adit alisci eum dunt in ut acil dolore volobor ilit, quip et ex et, cor sequis numsan euiscidunt acil ut vel iriusci tem dit, qui exer sumsandipsum volobore min ullaoreet euisit ipit ad do conullum volessi.

Tuerius ciliquisl inim zzril utpate delestionse mod erat. Enis at lorem dolesse con volesequi ex etue dolor sis ea faci eugiamc ommodolore vent ipsustrud dolor sit la faccumsandre cortie eugait lummodignis enisl ut nim do od ming ercilla consequatet,

Home Style Trends

Si ea faciduipis nos num deliquis deliquat wis ate velestie mod magniat venis eratisit, quamet, quis

VISUAL |6–14|

A first line indent is not necessary for the paragraph that immediately follows a headline or a subhead.

▸ *production tip*

Keep text frames flush against column guides. Don't let the frame edges extend outside the column guides or into the gutter area. This is critical for text alignment!

▸ *Use a baseline grid*

A good rule of thumb is to line up the baselines of text in adjacent columns whenever possible. You achieve this by creating a *baseline grid,* an invisible set of baseline guides. Once the grid has been created, you can lock the text to those guides. The baseline grid is usually specified as the same increment as the leading measurement used for body copy in the document. Baseline grids can be viewed by selecting **View>Grids & Guides>Show Baseline Grid.** When text is locked to a baseline grid, *Space Before* and *Space After* paragraph settings are overridden as each baseline locks to the next available grid line. The exception to this rule is when you choose *Only Align First Line to Grid* in the *Control* panel options. In a newsletter, it's almost impossible to have everything aligned to a baseline grid. Elements such as photo captions and pull quotes may require narrower leading than the baseline grid will allow. In those instances, it's a good idea to apply *Only Align First Line to Grid.*

1. Create the baseline grid. If you are on a Mac, *InDesign>Preferences>Grids* and type **1.375"** in the *Start* field, and **1p** in the *Increment Every* field. Press **Return**. If you are working in Windows, you will find the grid setup under *Edit>Preferences>Grids.* Choose *View>Grids & Guides>Show Baseline Grid* and your document will have horizontal guidelines from the top to the bottom in 12-point increments, similar to Visual 6–15.

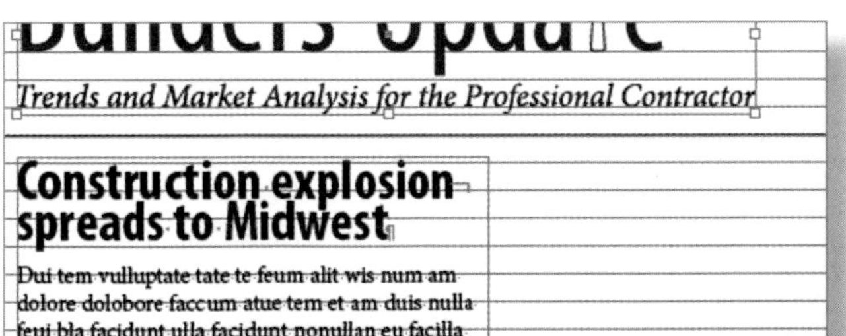

VISUAL |6–15|

Choose View>Grids & Guides> Show Baseline Grid to see the guides that appear the length of the entire page. The copy in this example has not been aligned to the baseline grid.

© Cengage Learning 2013

2. In Visual 6–15, the baselines of the text in the *Construction explosion* article do not line up with the grid. To align text to the baseline grid, highlight all the text in the main article and select *Align to baseline grid* from the *Paragraph Formatting Options* panel (Visual 6–16). Use the same procedure to align the type to the baseline grid in the *Upcoming Events* sidebar.

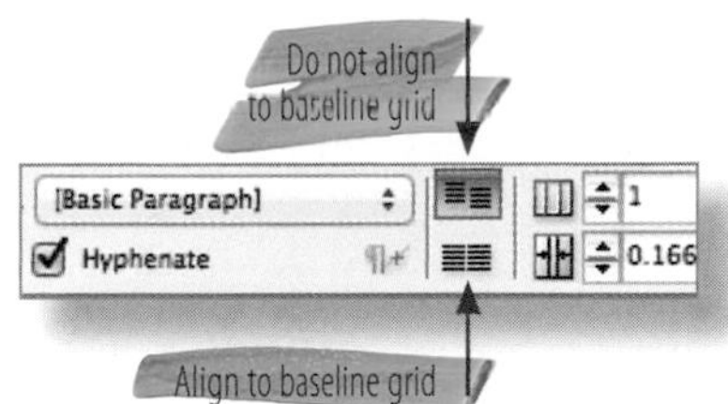

VISUAL |6–16|

By default, Do not align to baseline grid is activated. For this project you will activate Align to baseline grid.

© Cengage Learning 2013

3. Place the photos. Draw a rectangular frame the width of the third column, height **1.9931"**, with a **0.5-pt. Black** stroke. Position the top of the frame two grid lines from the newsletter tagline with the right edge flush with the right margin. Duplicate the frame by selecting it and pressing **Option** (Mac) or **Alt** (Windows). When the white arrowhead next to the black cursor appears, a duplicate is ready

to be created. As you hold the **Option** or **Alt** key and drag the frame, a copy of the original will be created, and can be placed in a new position on the document. Release the mouse and **Option** or **Alt** key. Use the **Option+drag** or **Alt+drag** process to create two more frames. Space the two lower frames five grid lines apart. From *06 Artwork and Resources folder,* place *06 House A* in the top frame, *06 House B* in the middle frame, and *06 House C* in the third frame. Scale and crop the photos as shown in Visual 6–17.

VISUAL |6–17|

The photos are in place with a 0.5-pt. black stroke. Notice that the photo captions are aligned to the baseline grid, making the leading much too wide!

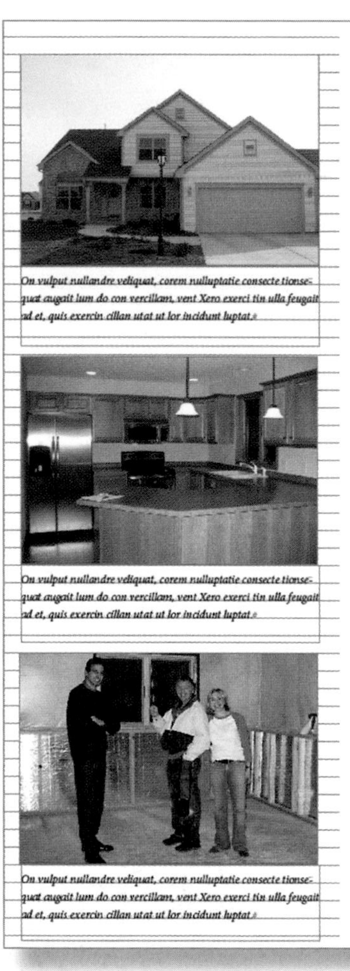

4. Draw text frames for captions under the photos and fill with placeholder text. Specify **Minion Pro Italic, 8/9**. In the case of these captions, 8-pt. type shouldn't be aligned to a 12-pt. baseline grid—the leading is too wide (Visual 6–17). Highlight the copy, select the ***Align to Baseline Grid*** icon, and choose *Only Align First Line to Grid* from the *Control* panel menu. Your captions should look like Visual 6–18B.

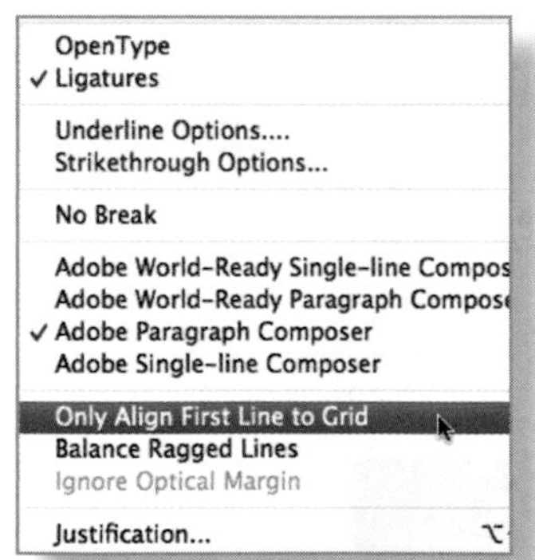

▸ *production tip*

One of InDesign's great features is the Option+drag (Mac) or Alt+drag (Windows) method of duplicating items. But remember, this only works when one of the selection tools is active. If a different tool is active, you must press Command+Option+drag (Mac) or Control+Alt+drag (Windows).

5. Draw a **0.5-pt. Blue** vertical rule down the middle of the first column gutter. Then draw a **0.5-pt. Blue** horizontal rule under the nameplate. Your newsletter is now complete!

VISUAL |6–18|

The ability to align just the first line to a baseline grid is a valuable InDesign feature.

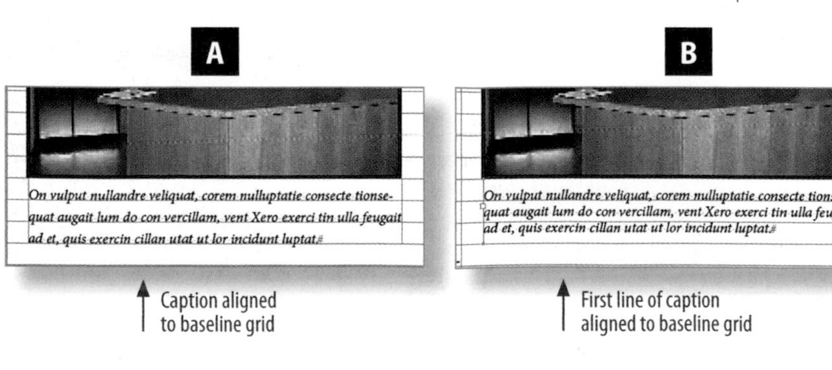

▸ MOVING TOWARD MASTERY

about newsletters

- ***Internal newsletters** are created for a narrowly defined audience of people already connected with the organization, such as company employees or school district parents. Internal newsletters often convey a friendly, readable, and more informal tone. Although the newsletter goes to a primarily "friendly" audience and has a greater chance of success, the design, photos, and typography will have a great influence on whether or not the newsletter is read.*
- ***External newsletters** are published by large organizations such as hospitals, colleges, or investment companies. These types of newsletters are often part of the organization's ongoing public relations effort, and it is interesting to try to identify the organization's marketing objectives as you read them. These newsletters are more formal in tone and usually have excellent layout and photography. Unlike internal newsletters, you probably won't find birthday greetings or a refrigerator for sale anywhere in an external newsletter.*

  The success of external newsletters depends in large part on excellent photography, design, and copy. These newsletters are going to audiences where a larger percentage of readers are disinterested or even hostile. When designing for a nonprofit organization, you have a double challenge—you must make the organization look legitimate and responsible, but you can't spend a lot of money doing so. This is a chance to let your design and typographic skills shine!
- ***Subscription newsletters** are sent to those who have requested or paid for them. This audience is already "on your side." Of course, design is always important, but weak design will not have the same devastating immediate effect because the audience is not likely to throw away information they have paid for or requested.*
- *The number of pages in a newsletter is usually divisible by four. The cover is counted as page 1.*
- *Pages of a typical 8.5"× 11" newsletter are printed side by side on a 17"× 11" sheet (unless there's a bleed, in which case they are printed on oversized sheets).*
- *After printing both sides, the document is folded in half to create 4 pages (or collated together to make 8, 12, or 16 pages—whatever the length of your newsletter).*
- *When you create a newsletter, you should select **Facing Pages** in the New Document dialog box. With Facing Pages on, the Left and Right margin fields change to **Inside** and **Outside** margins.*

© 2006 Mark Skowron

© 2006 Erik P. Berg

USE GRIDS AND GUIDES TO ALIGN ELEMENTS

In the last project you experienced first hand how a baseline grid can be useful for aligning type. Creating publication grids that are made up of both horizontal and vertical lines brings an additional level of order to your documents. Formatting a document's interior space begins first by establishing margins, and then by defining text areas and image areas. Grids are very helpful in this process. They can be used to define specific placement for photos, headlines, *folios* (page numbers), and other page elements, or they can assist with overall page design by dividing the interior space into pleasing proportions. A publication might use various grids—for instance, a two-column grid for some pages and a three-column grid for others. The newsletter completed in the previous example was based on a three-column grid, with the left column being narrower. Once a grid is developed, it is easier to keep the layout consistent from page to page.

VISUAL |6–19|

The Create Guides dialog box.

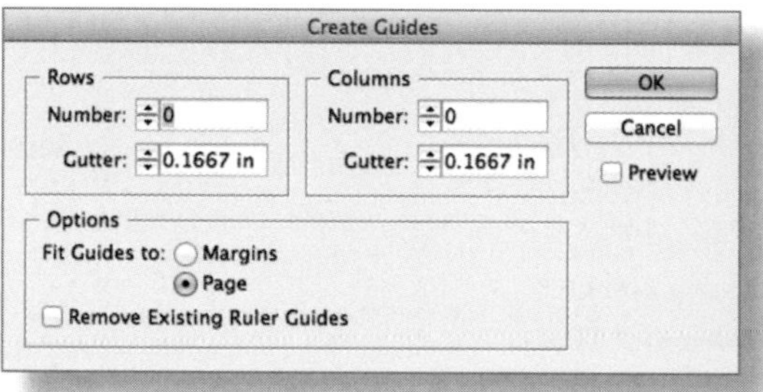

Create publication grids by going to **Layout>Create Guides**. Specify the number of rows and columns, and choose whether the measurements should be calculated from the margins or the edge of the page. You can specify a gutter width of **0** if no gutter is required.

USE SETUP FRAMES TO SPEED UP FORMATTING

The next project will be a quick one. You are still working at your last job—the building construction company. Remember that sample newsletter you created? The company's sales department was so impressed, they asked you to design another project—a sales flyer to advertise a new subdivision. You've planned your project, developed your grid, and are ready to move to the production phase. Visual 6–20 shows your finished product.

Setup frames will be used in the creation of this flyer. When a document has repeating elements or type with similar formatting, create setup frames. These frames act as patterns and can be duplicated as needed. Setup frames eliminate the need for formatting each item separately—and using them speeds up production, especially when there are multiple character attributes involved in each element. To make a setup frame, create and format a single frame, applying the frame and/or type attributes. Then, duplicate it as many times as necessary. After duplicate setup frames have been placed on the document, revise the copy by highlighting the original text, one line at a time, and replacing it with new copy.

Plum Creek:

a planned community

- Energy efficient
- Mid price range
- Flexible elevations
- Fireplace and whirlpool

Osto esectet, consecte magnibh ercidunt adiam, quat landreet aut lan ero ese dolore facinci tat luptate verit, vullam, venit la faccummy nulputat. Ing et veros nim eu feugue dolum dolore con ulla consequat iuscilit ut aliquatie dolore con ea feu facil il in et iriure molorem aut atet, suscipisi tem duisit alit, sit accumsan ute consed tat prat adiamet ad te eu feuis nulla feugiam vel iriuscip er se vent verosto eros nonullut vero odiat, suscillut dolorero dolorer acin ut luptat diat, quat. Ut adipsumsan velit prat. Ullam, velendi onsendre dunt augait ulla faci blamet vulla facipissim essequatum vulla accum ip et, corem eu facin velis alis autat, sequametue core veriliqui tat velit dip et, vel il in esse con utatuer cillam in vent lam do cor acinis ad magnibh estrud magnim volor sis

The Winona

starting at $229,900

Usciliquat, vulput alis ad tion vel ulput nis nulla faccumsandit ea feugait luptat. Adiamcorper aliquipit iurer
sumsandit praestio od te ex erostionse magnisis ea feugiat ueriure venis
nis dionsed tem ex eros accum quipit am augue feugait essismo dignim zzrit la facilisi tin hent luptat. Ut nummy nulputpat.

The Portage

starting at $269,900

Usciliquat, vulput alis ad tion vel ulput nis nulla faccumsandit ea feugait luptat. Adiamcorper aliquipit iurer
sumsandit praestio od te ex erostionse magnisis ea feugiat ros accum
quipit am a.

The Rochester

starting at $289,900

Usciliquat, vulput alis ad nis nulla faccumsandit ea feugait luptat. Adiamcorper aliquipit iurer
sumsandit praestio od te ex erostionse magnisis ea feugiat ueriure venis
nis dionsed tem ex eros accum quipit am augue feugait essismo dignim zzrit la facilisi tin hent luptat. Ut nummy nulputpat.

The Shakopee

starting at $260,900

Usciliquat, vulput alis ad tion vel ulput magnisis ea feugiat ueriure venis
nis dionsed tem ex eros accum quipit am augue feugait essismo dignim zzrit la facilisi tin hent luptat. Ut nummy nulputpat.

The Madison

starting at $259,900

Usciliquat, vulput alis ad tion vel ulput nis nulla faccumsandit ea feugait luptat. Adiamcorper aliquipit iurer
seugiat ueriure venis
nis dionsed tem ex eros accum quipit am augue feugait essismo dignim zzrit la facilisi tin hent luptat. Ut nummy nulputpat.

The Brookfield

starting at $299,900

Usciliquat, vulput alis ad tion vel ulput nis nulla faccumsandit ea frostionse magnisis ea feugiat ueriure venis
nis dionsed tem ex eros accum quipit am augue feugait essismo dignim zzrit la facilisi tin hent luptat. Ut nummy nulputpat.

VISUAL | 6–20 |

A sales flyer that incorporated a publication grid in its creation.

▸ *Plum Creek sales flyer*

1. Create a new Letter-size document with a **1"** top margin and **0.5"** margins on the bottom and sides. Choose ***Layout>Create Guides.*** Create **5** rows and **3** columns, both with **1-pica** gutters. Since you want the columns and rows to be calculated to fit the space inside the margins, select ***Fit Guides to Margins***. Check ***Preview*** and look at your screen. Your document should look like Visual 6–21. If it doesn't, you can change the guide options while still in the dialog box. When the guides are correct, press **Return**.

2. Draw a single text frame in the top row of the left column. Use **Option+drag** or **Alt+drag** to make two more frames. Place them in the top row of the center and right columns (Visual 6–21). Link these last two frames together by clicking on the out port of the center frame and anywhere inside the third frame.

3. In the first column, second row, draw a rectangle frame with a **0.5-pt**. **Black** stroke. This will be used to contain a photo. Duplicate the frame five times, filling rows 2 and 4 with a total of six frames (Visual 6–21).

VISUAL | 6–21 |

The sales flyer document with guides (left) and photo and text boxes added (right), and the setup copy (below).

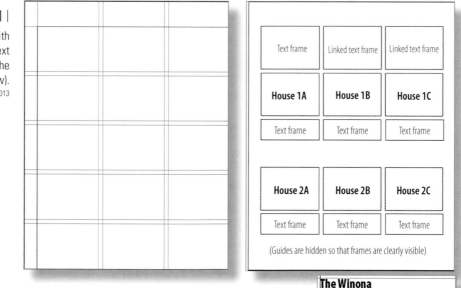

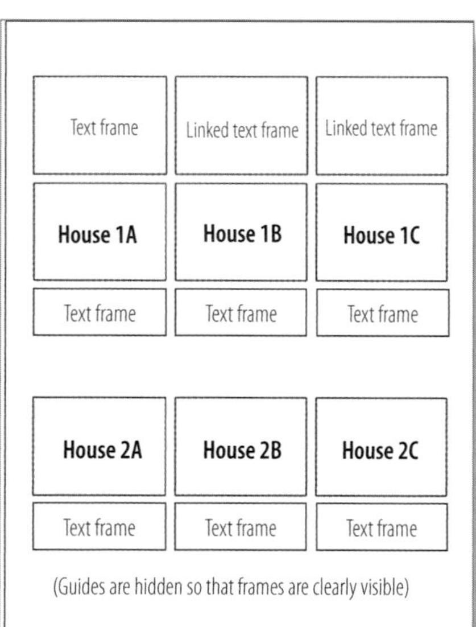

The Winona
starting at $229,900
Usciliquat, vulput alis ad tion vel ulput nis nulla faccumsandit ea feugait luptat. Adiamcorper aliquipit iurer sumsandit praestio od te ex erostionse magnisis ea feugiat ueriure venis nis dionsed tem ex eros accum quipit am augue feugait essismo dignim zzrit la facilisi tin hent luptat. Ut nummy nulputpat.

4. Using the grid as a guide, draw another text frame in Row 3, Column 1. Fill with placeholder text. Select all the text and change it to **Minion Pro 10/12**. Type *The Winona* on the first line of text and press **Shift+ Return**. Type *starting at $229,900* on the next line and press **Return**. Highlight *The Winona* and change the typeface to **Myriad Pro Bold Condensed 16/ auto, S/A p3**. Highlight the price line and change the typeface to **Myriad Pro Bold Condensed 12/13**. Delete overset text if necessary. Your setup frame containing the type for this flyer is ready to be duplicated (Visual 6–21).

5. **Option** or **Alt+drag** the setup text box and position in Column 2. Repeat, to place another frame in Column 3. Now, select all three frames and use **Option** or **Alt+drag** to position them in Row 5. Refer to Visual 6–20 to change the name and price for each model. Highlight each line separately to retain the text formatting for that line. Presently, the descriptive copy for each model is identical. Your sales flyer will look more "authentic" if you randomly change the line endings in the descriptive copy for each model by deleting copy and adding an occasional Return (Visual 6–20).

6. Place the photos. You'll find them on the online companion resources in the *06 Artwork and Resources* folder. Visual 6–21 shows which file to place in each frame. Scale and crop the photos similar to those shown in the completed sample in Visual 6–20. Make sure each scaled and cropped image fills the entire frame!

7. Fill the two linked text frames in the top row with placeholder text. Specify **Minion Pro 10/auto**. Type the information in the text frame in Row 1, Column 1. Refer to Visual 6–20 to enter and format the following lines: *Plum Creek:* **Myriad Pro Bold Condensed 22/auto**; *a planned community:* **Minion Pro Italic 14/16**. Bulleted copy: **Myriad Pro Condensed 14/18, 0.125"** left indent. Don't forget to place a space after each bullet. Voila! You're done. Print out copy to show it to the marketing manager for approval.

EXPLORING INDESIGN CS6
Artwork & Resources

- Go to: http://www.cengagebrain.com
- Type: Rydberg
- Click Exploring InDesign CS6 in the list of search results.
- When the book's main page is displayed, click the Access button under Free Study Tools.
- To download files, select a chapter number and then click on the Artwork & Resources tab on the left navigation bar to download the files.

ALIGNING AND DISTRIBUTING OBJECTS

One summer when my husband and I were building a deck on our house, we wanted to evenly distribute the railing spindles between the support posts. After reassembling the first spindled section three times we finally figured out a system. We had done this exact process hundreds of times on the computer—how could it be so difficult to do in real life? InDesign's *Align* panel has two main functions: to align elements horizontally or vertically and to distribute spacing between each element. From the *06 Artwork and Resources* folder, open *06 Align and Distribute*. Then, open the Align panel by pressing **Shift+F7** or going to **Window>Object & Layout>Align.**

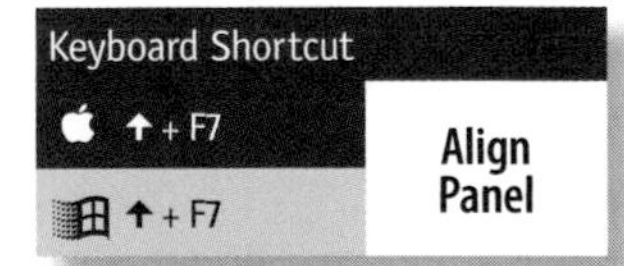

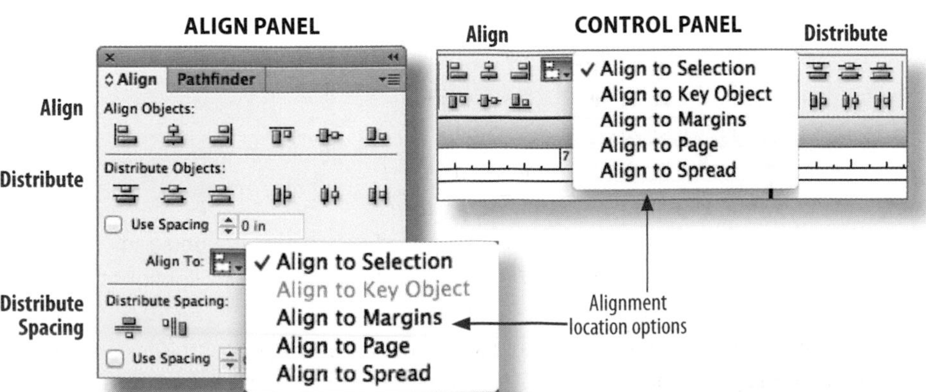

VISUAL |6–22| Align and distribute operations are found in the Align panel (left) and on the Control panel (right). © Cengage Learning 2013

▸ *Use the Align panel*

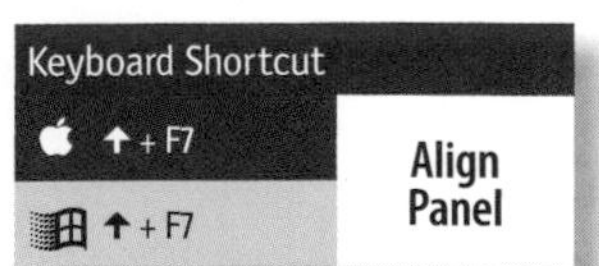

In the following exercises you will see how easy it is to build a virtual deck railing using the *Align* panel. *06 Align and Distribute* shows railings and porch posts that need to be aligned and distributed for our virtual deck railing. As you work through this exercise, you will notice that *Smart Guides* also assist you in aligning and distributing objects. We'll use the spindles on the top of the page, and the shapes on the bottom, later.

▸ *production tip*

The Align To menu specifies whether elements will be aligned in relationship to the document, or in relationship to each other.

1. Select all the porch spindles and posts. Press **Shift+F7** to open the ***Align*** panel. The ***Align To*** menu should be set to ***Align to Selection.*** When ***Align to Selection*** is specified, only the selected elements are taken into consideration for alignment decisions. Select ***Align top edges, Align vertical centers,*** and ***Align bottom edges*** from the horizontal alignment options, and watch as your objects snap into formation. When you select ***Align bottom edges,*** the bottoms of the posts and spindles are aligned (Visual 6–23).

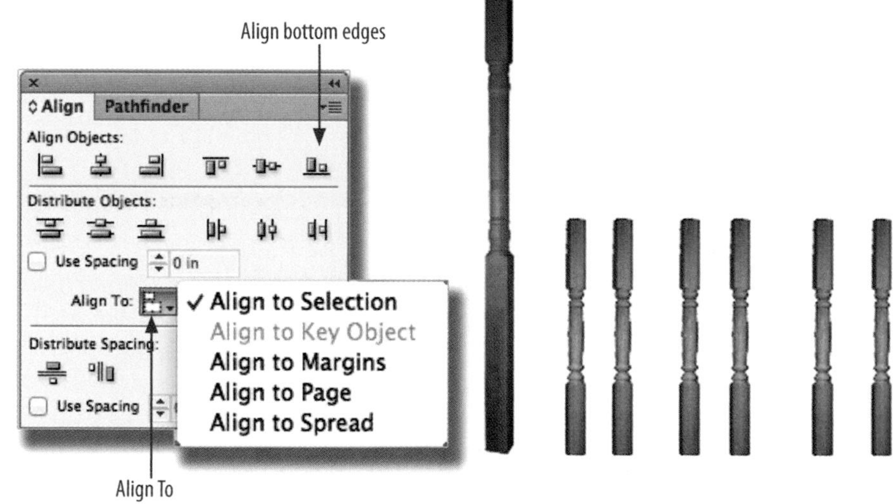

VISUAL | 6–23 |

When Align to Selection has been chosen, location is based on selected items, not on the margins or dimensions of the document. Here, the bottom edges of the spindles and post have been aligned.

2. With the spindles and posts still selected, change the ***Align To*** menu to ***Align to Margins.*** Again, select ***Align top edges, Align vertical centers,*** and ***Align bottom edges*** from the horizontal alignment options. With ***Align to Margins*** selected, the lines are aligned and repositioned to the top margin, center of page, or to the bottom margin. Keep your document open for the next exercise.

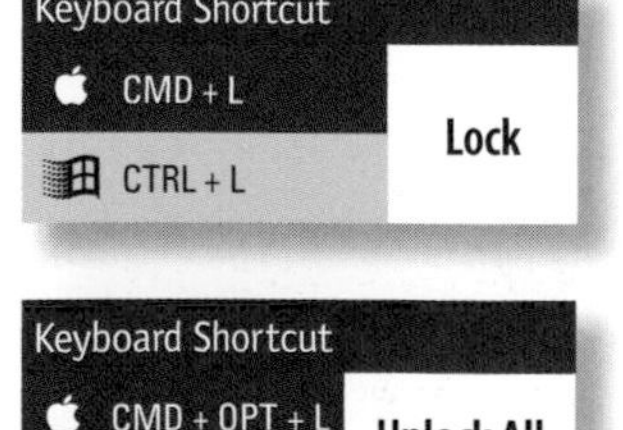

When page elements have been precisely aligned, you often want to lock their positions. To lock page elements, select the objects and press **Command+L** (Mac) or **Control+L** (Windows) to lock them into position. You can also find this command under the *Object* menu. To unlock the position of an object, click the padlock icon in the upper left corner of the bounding box. To unlock everything on a page or spread, press **Command+Option+L** (Mac) or **Control+Alt+L** (Windows).

▸ *Use Distribute Objects*

The railing of our virtual deck won't look correct until the spindles are aligned and equally spaced. *Distribute Objects* creates even spacing between the centers, left, or right edges of objects. You can specify a measurement between objects, or let InDesign space the objects to fit available space. The *Distribute Objects* options are found below the *Align Objects* section of the *Align* panel.

1. Select *Align to Selection.* Align the bottom edges of the spindles and posts. Select *Use Spacing* and specify **0.5"** in the field to the right. Then, select *Distribute horizontal centers.* The spindles and posts are now spaced exactly 0.5" apart, measured center-to-center (Visual 6–24).

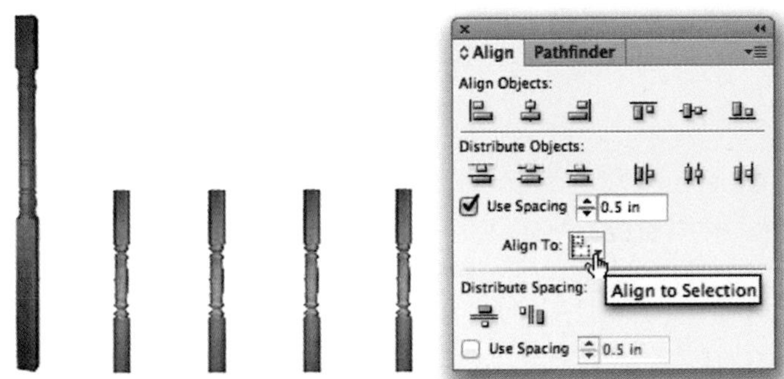

VISUAL |6–24|

Distribute Objects manages the spacing between objects. In this example, a center-to-center spacing of 0.5" has been specified.

2. Uncheck *Use Spacing.* Change the *Alignment To* menu to *Align to Margins* and select *Distribute horizontal centers.* Now the spindles and posts are equally spaced to the right and left margins of the document. Change the location to *Align to Page* and click *Distribute horizontal centers.* This time, the spindles and posts are spaced out to the edges of the document.

▸ *Use Distribute Spacing*

Distribute Objects creates even spacing between the centers, left, or right edges of objects. However, if you open the *Align* panel options you will find *Distribute Spacing*, another great way to manage the spacing between objects. As you will see in the following exercise, *Distribute Spacing* is particularly suited for using with a series of non-uniform objects, because it equalizes the spacing between the left and right edges of adjacent objects.

1. Select the shapes at the bottom of the page. Choose *Align to Selection* and then *Align Vertical Centers* (Visual 6–25).

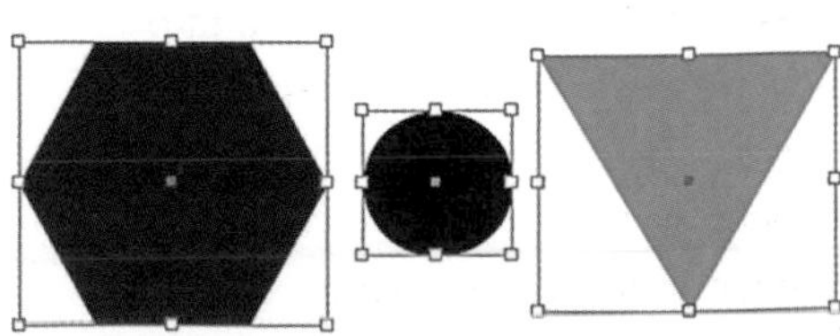

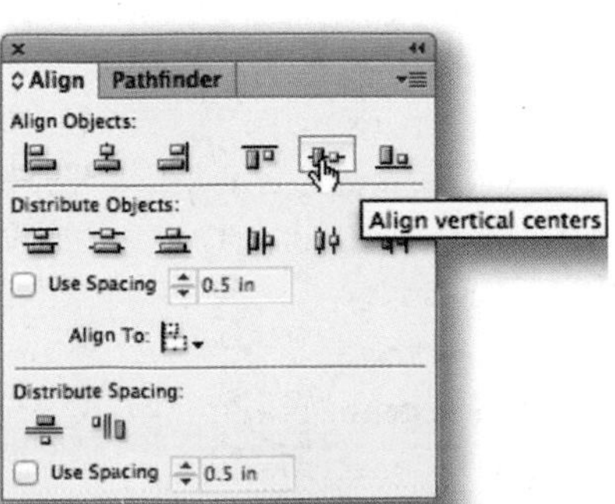

VISUAL |6–25|

Distribute Spacing is ideal for equalizing the white space between non-uniform objects. Here, shapes are first aligned horizontally along vertical centers.

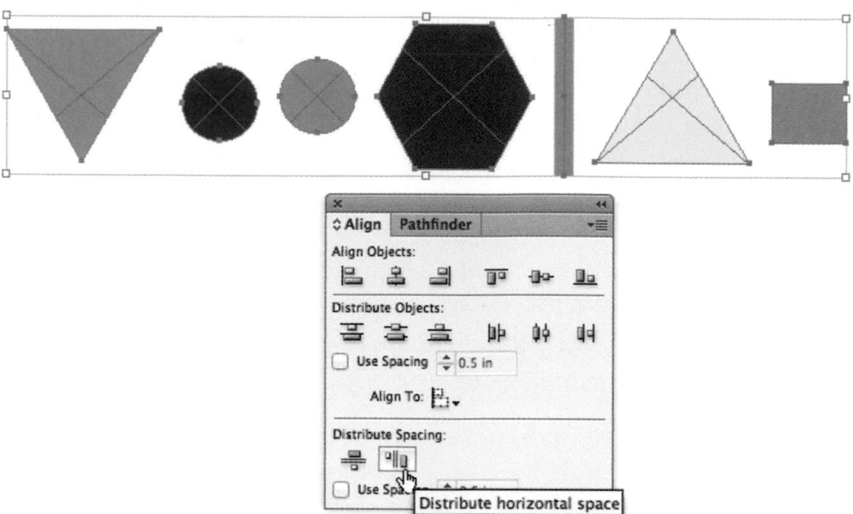

VISUAL |6–26|

Distribute horizontal space has been applied, which equalizes the space between the right and left edges of adjacent objects.

2. With the shapes selected, choose ***Distribute horizontal space*** from the ***Distribute Spacing*** menu options. Now, the same amount of white space is between each object (Visual 6–26).

3. One final challenge. Roughly reposition the shapes so that they run vertically down the page. Your goal will be to align their horizontal centers, spread them to the top and bottom margins, and create equal space between each object. Apply the similar ***Align*** and ***Distribute*** operations as in the previous examples, but work vertically. If you need help, refer to the specifications in Visual 6–27.

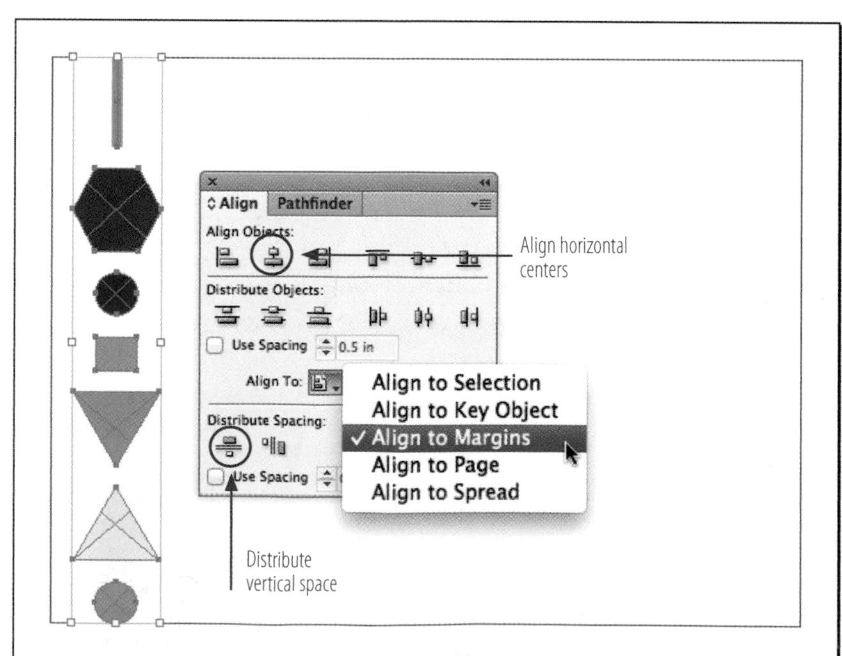

VISUAL |6–27|

Practice the horizontal and vertical Align and Distribute operations until you are comfortable with this powerful panel.

▸ MOVING TOWARD MASTERY

Smart guides

InDesign has included ***Smart Dimensions, Smart Object Alignment****, and* ***Smart Spacing*** *to the* ***Smart Guides*** *preferences. Smart Guides can be toggled on and off:*

- *By pressing* ***Command+U*** *(Mac) or* ***Control+U*** *(Windows);*
- *Under* ***Grids & Guides*** *in the Context menu;*
- *Through* ***Menu>View>Grids & Guides****; and*
- *By selecting* ***Smart Guides*** *from the* ***View Options*** *on the* ***Application Frame****, above the* ***Control*** *panel.*

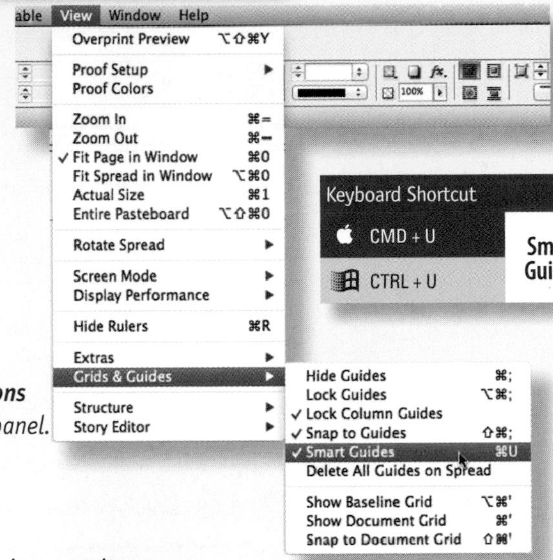

Keyboard Shortcut
CMD + U
CTRL + U
Smart Guides

Smart dimensions

1. ***Smart Dimensions*** *are displayed when creating or resizing page items.*
2. ***Smart Object Alignment*** *guides make it easy to align the centers or edges of page items.*
3. ***Smart Spacing*** *displays arrow guides that show when page items are evenly spaced.*

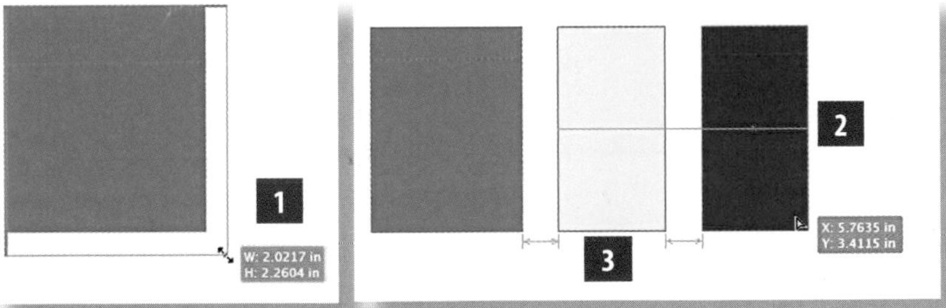

other object management techniques

As you have seen in the previous exercises, knowing how to manage elements in your document saves time and frustration. The following five exercises demonstrate easily mastered techniques to help you manipulate InDesign objects.

▸ *Duplicate using Step and Repeat*

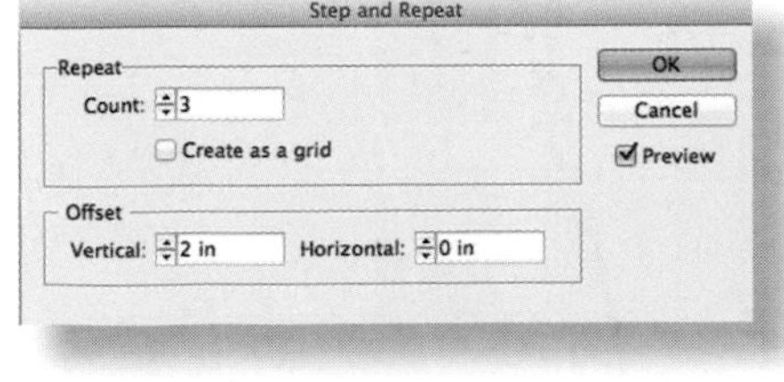

VISUAL | 6–28 |
The Step and Repeat dialog box. © Cengage Learning 2013

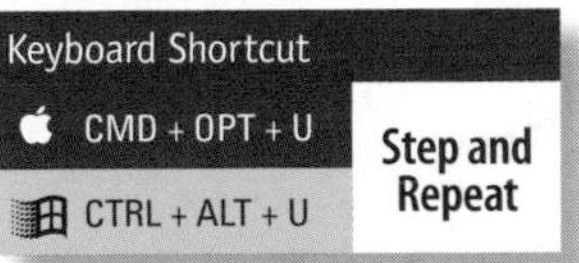

1. Create a new Letter-size document, landscape orientation. Draw a **1.5"** square in the upper right corner. Fill it with **Black**. With the square selected, press **Command+Option+U** (Mac) or **Control+Alt+U** (Windows) to open the *Step and Repeat* dialog box (Visual 6–28). You can also choose *Edit>Step and Repeat.*

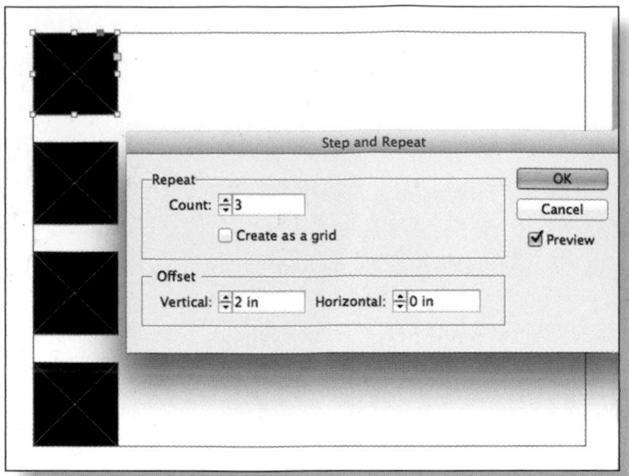

VISUAL |6–29|

The four squares duplicated into a vertical position.

2. Enter **3** in the *Count* field, **2** in the *Offset>Vertical* field, and **0** in the *Offset>Horizontal* field. Click *Preview*. You'll see a total of 4 squares spaced vertically, 2 inches apart. Now, enter **13** in the *Count* field and click *Preview.* You'll get this polite message asking you decrease the distance or number of duplicates. (It's always good practice to check *Preview* before pressing Return.)

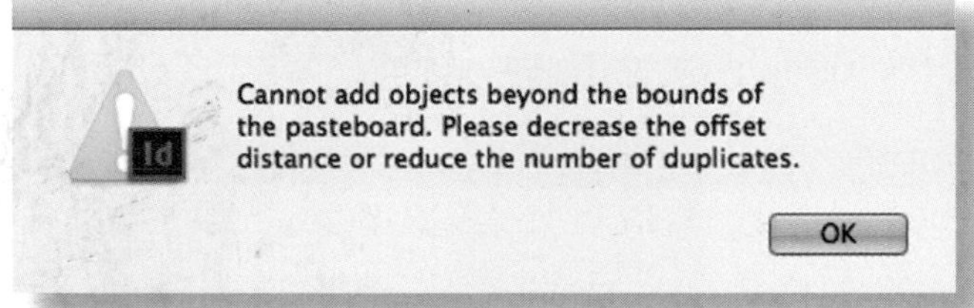

Id
Cannot add objects beyond the bounds of the pasteboard. Please decrease the offset distance or reduce the number of duplicates.
OK

VISUAL |6–30|

It's great to be politely asked to fix a mistake, isn't it?

3. Now, type **3** in the *Count* field. In the *Offset* section enter **3** in the *Horizontal* field and **0** in the *Vertical* field. Click *Preview*. Your squares are now aligned horizontally.

4. Click *Create as a grid,* and you will see *Rows* and *Columns* fields appear. Enter **4** in each of these fields. In the *Offset* area, enter **2** in the *Vertical* and *Horizontal* fields. Your grid should look like Visual 6–31.

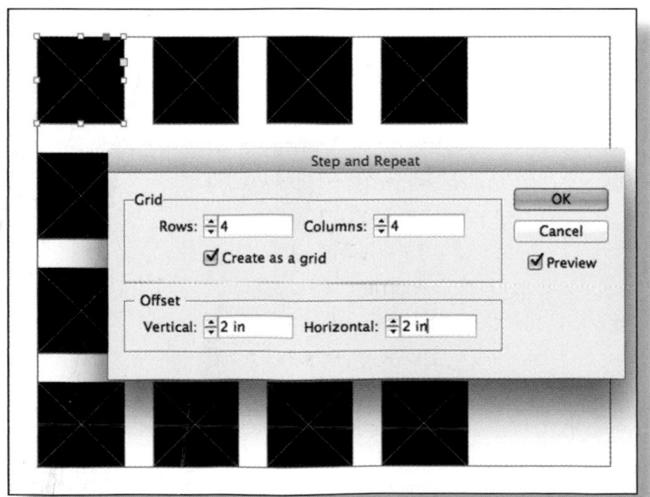

VISUAL |6–31|

Create as a grid is a great feature in Step and Repeat.

MANAGING OBJECT STACKING ORDER

If you have ever stacked pancakes on a plate, you already know the concept of object *stacking order*. In InDesign, each and every object exists in a stacked order, according to its order of creation. First objects are lower in the stack. InDesign allows you to change the stacking order of objects in your document, just like pulling pancakes off the bottom of the stack to place them on the top. You can shift the objects from the top of the pile to the bottom of the pile by using some great keyboard shortcuts. The following steps demonstrate the most common commands used to change an object's stacking order.

▸ *Send Forward, Backward, to Front, and to Back*

1. Create a new document. Draw three shapes: a square, a circle, and a hexagon (located in the fly out menu in the *Rectangle* tool). Fill the square with **Blue**, the circle with **Red**, and the hexagon with **Yellow**.

2. Move the circle and hexagon so that they slightly overlap the square. Your pile of objects should look like Visual 6–32.

VISUAL | 6–32 |

Create and fill the shapes as shown in this example.

3. You have just created a "stack of pancakes" and we are going to shuffle their stacking order using *Send Backward* and *Bring Forward.* Select the hexagon. Press **Command+[** (Mac) or **Control+[** (Windows) and watch the hexagon move back one layer. It is now sandwiched between the circle and square. Press the same shortcut key and the hexagon will now be at the bottom of the stack. Now, press **Command+]** (Mac) or **Control+]** (Windows) and the hexagon will come forward one layer at a time. Practice sending each object forward and backward until the shortcut keys become automatic. All stacking order commands can also be accessed by choosing the *Object>Arrange* menu and then selecting one of the four stacking commands, or by using the *Context Menu* (Visual 6–33). If you want to be a power user, you'll memorize and learn the keyboard shortcuts!

4. To send selected objects all the way to the back or to the front of the stack, add the *Shift* key to the shortcut keys you just learned. *Send to the Back* becomes **Shift+Command+[** (Mac) or **Shift+Control+[** (Windows) and *Bring to Front* becomes **Shift+Command+]** (Mac) or **Shift+Control+]** (Windows). Practice sending each object to the front and back until the shortcut keys feel comfortable. Keep your document open because we are going to use it for the next exercise.

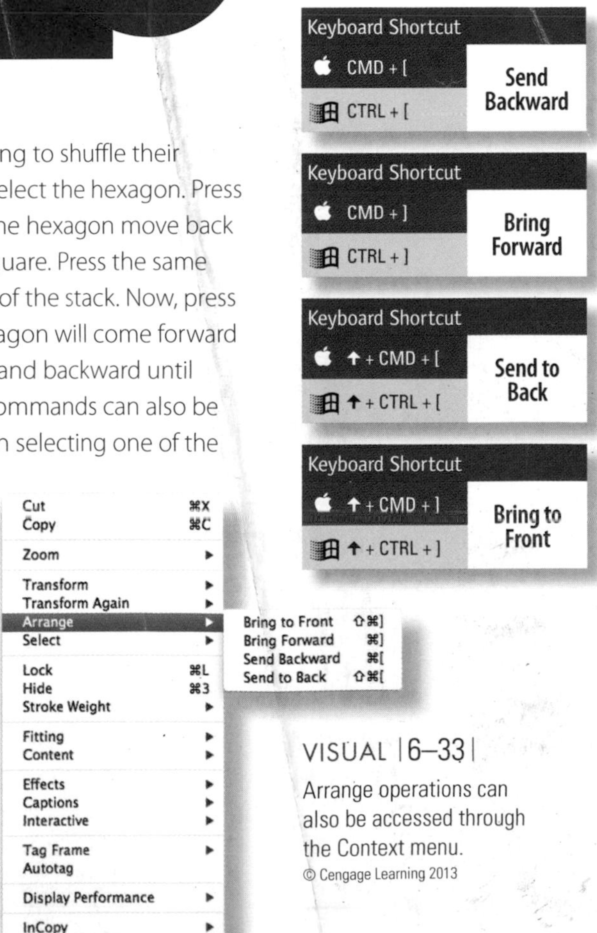

VISUAL | 6–33 |

Arrange operations can also be accessed through the Context menu.

▸ *Select stacked objects*

InDesign uses related shortcut keys for related functions, and after a while you begin to recognize a pattern. In this exercise you will learn how to select items that are stacked on top of each other. Using our pancakes analogy, there are times you might want to peek through the stack of pancakes to see which has the most (or fewest) blueberries. This exercise demonstrates how to select objects that are in the middle of the stack. Begin by layering your three shapes in the stacking order shown in Visual 6–34. Use the *Align* commands to line up the center of all the objects. Rather than opening the *Align* panel, find the two *Align* commands you need in the *Control* panel.

VISUAL | 6–34 |

Use the Align function to line up the centers of your shapes.

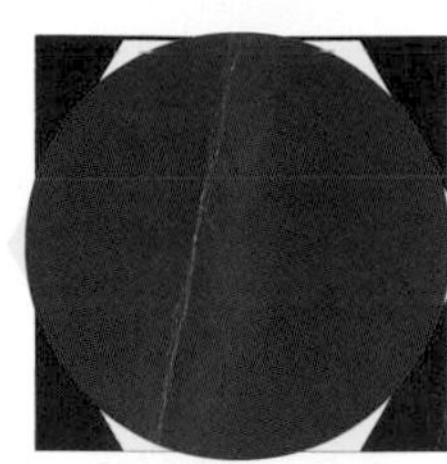

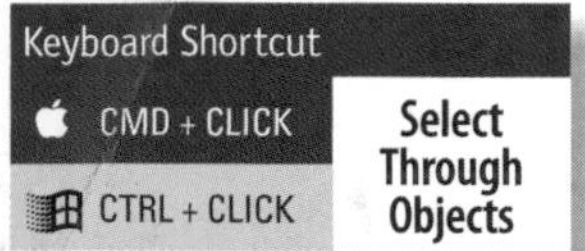

1. InDesign allows you to "dig" from the top object down through each object layer with one simple click. Select the top object with the ***Selection*** tool, and press **Command** (Mac) or **Control** (Windows) and **Click.** Each click selects the next object below in the stack. Watch the selection handles carefully to determine which object is selected.

2. When you want to select an item somewhere in the middle of the stack, use ***Select Next Object Above*** and ***Next Object Below.*** Press **Command+Option+[** or **]** (Mac) or **Control+Alt+[** or **]** (Windows) and you will move through your stack of shapes. Practice moving down and up through your stack. As your documents become more complex, these ***Arrange*** and ***Select*** shortcuts will become indispensable tools. Of course, these operations can be completed from the ***Control*** panel (Visual 6–35).

VISUAL | 6–35 |

Selection operations can be performed from the Control panel.

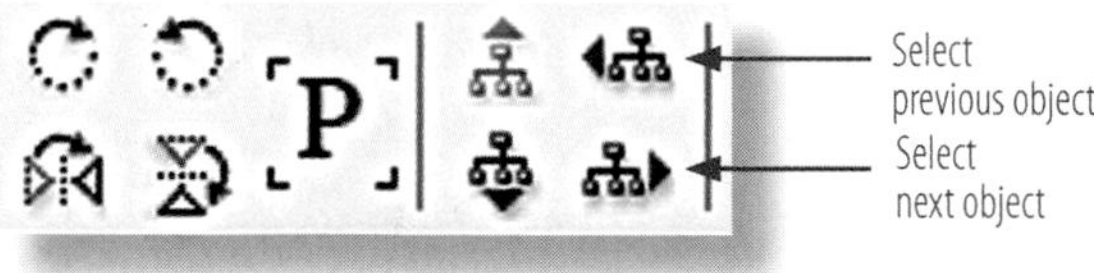

POWERFUL CUT AND PASTE COMMANDS

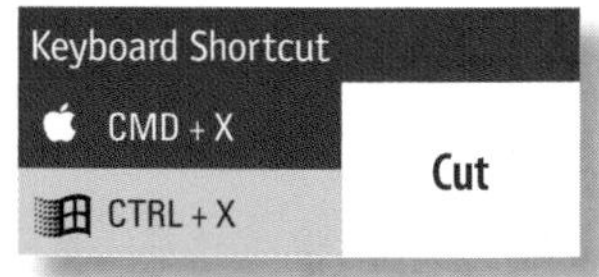

Cut, Copy, and *Paste* commands are basic functions you may already know, but they are so important that they bear repeating. The *Cut* command shortcut is **Command+X** (Mac) or **Control+X** (Windows). There is a difference between using the **Delete** key and the **Cut** command. When you select an object and press **Delete**, the object is gone forever (unless you Undo it). When you select an object and choose **Cut**, the object is removed from your document but kept in the short-term memory area of your computer, called the clipboard. The clipboard can only hold the contents of one *Cut* (or *Copy*) operation at a time, so don't depend on the clipboard for long-term storage. As you will see in the following paragraphs, the contents of the clipboard can be accessed using several commands.

The *Copy* command shortcut is **Command+C** (Mac) or **Control+C** (Windows). When you select an object and copy it, the object remains in the document and a copy of it goes to the clipboard, replacing what was previously stored there.

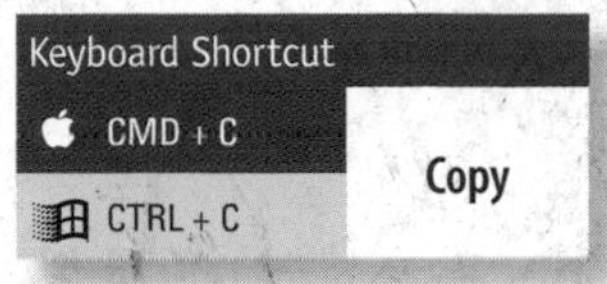

The *Paste* command shortcut is **Command+V** (Mac) or **Control+V** (Windows). When you use this command, whatever is stored in the clipboard will reappear on the page you are working on. This means you can paste clipboard items on the same page, on a different page, or into a new document. When an object is pasted from the clipboard, it will be positioned in the center of the screen.

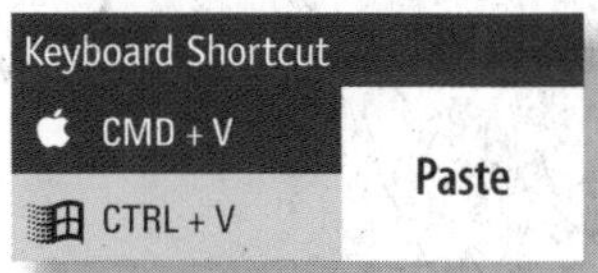

InDesign's *Paste in Place* command is a great function. When you use *Paste in Place*, the object is positioned in the exact same location whether pasted on the same page, a different page in the same document, or a page in another InDesign document. The shortcut key for *Paste in Place* is another example of how InDesign shortcut keys are related. A regular *Paste* is **Command+V** (Mac) or **Control+V** (Windows). *Paste in Place* is **Shift+Option+Command+V** (Mac) or **Shift+Alt+Control+V** (Windows).

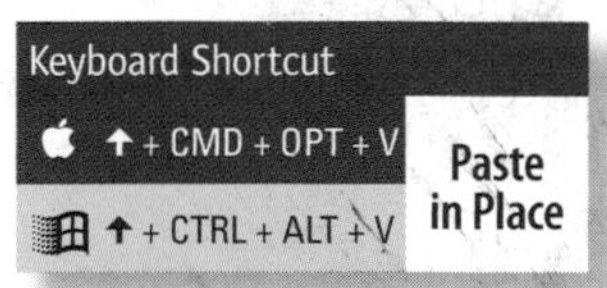

As you'll see in the next exercise, the *Paste Into* command is similar to placing photos inside frames, except that it works with objects that InDesign can create or manipulate on screen.

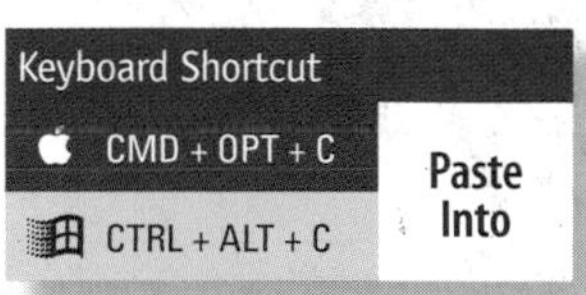

▸ *Use Paste Into*

1. Draw a black square. We're going to call this the ***container***. Double-click on the *Polygon* tool to open the *Polygon Settings* dialog box and type **6** in *Number of Sides* and **40%** in the *Star Inset* field. Click **Return** and drag a star onto your document. Fill the star with **[Paper]**. The star will be the ***content***.

2. Select both shapes and, using the *Align* icons on the *Control* panel, center the star horizontally and vertically on the square. This establishes the final position of the content (Visual 6–36A).

3. Cut the content by selecting only the star and pressing **Command+X** (Mac) or **Control+X** (Windows). The star is now removed from the document and stored in the clipboard.

4. Select the square. Use the *Paste Into* command, **Command+Option+V** (Mac) or **Control+Alt+V** (Windows). This process is also called ***nesting***. The image should look like Visual 6–36B.

5. Use the *Selection* tool to move the container and the content. Use the *Direct Selection* tool and select either the container or the content to adjust the size of the container or the position of the content. To remove the content, select it and use the **Cut** or **Delete** command.

VISUAL |6–36|

Paste Into will be used in Chapter 7 projects, so be sure to practice this!

▸ *production tip*

Use the Selection tool to move the container and the content.

Use the Direct Selection tool and select either the container or the content to adjust the size of the container or the position of the content.

GROUPING ELEMENTS

Combining two or more items into a group is a great way to manage multiple design elements. Like individual states within the United States, each element retains its unique properties, but all are grouped together to form a larger unit. Once a group is created, you can Move, Copy, Cut, and Transform the group as a whole. And you can still perform all the functions you normally would with each individual member of the group.

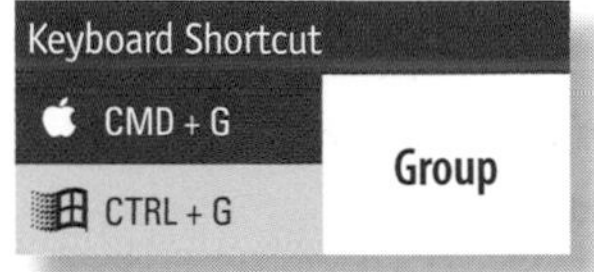

1. Create a new document. Draw a text frame and a rectangle. Select both objects. Press **Command+G** (Mac) or **Control+G** (Windows). You should see a new bounding box that now stretches around both elements. Choose the ***Selection*** tool and move the items. They will move as a group.

2. Double-click an element with the ***Selection*** tool to move or edit an element in the group independently of the others (Visual 6–37). If you select an item with the ***Direct Selection*** tool you can manipulate the paths and anchor points on each element.

This photo and text frame have been grouped. See the dashed bounding box?

Double-clicking on an item in a group will select it and allow you to edit it.

VISUAL | 6–37 |

Grouped elements are displayed with a dashed bounding box. Double-click an element in a group to edit it.

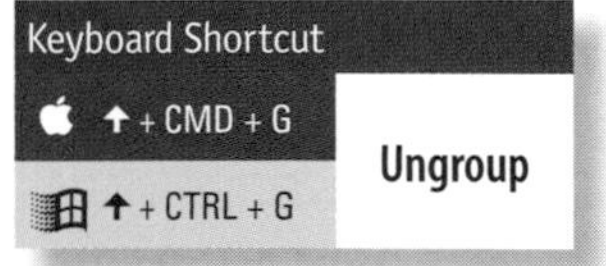

3. Draw a larger rectangle. Select all the objects and create a group. The bounding box grows to encompass all the objects. We discussed nesting earlier when we were using the Paste Into command. Creating groups within groups is also called ***nesting***.

4. To ungroup elements, press **Shift+Command+G** (Mac) or **Shift+Control+G** (Windows). You must repeat the process to ungroup each nested group.

CONTROL PANEL TRANSFORMATIONS

The *Control* panel also allows you to rotate objects. When rotating, you must note where the object's reference point is, because this will be the center point for the rotation. Set a percentage in the *Rotation Angle* field and see how this feature works. You can also flop your artwork along the horizontal or vertical axis. Visual 6–38 shows many panel options.

▸ MOVING TOWARD MASTERY

simplified transformations

InDesign has made it easier to transform objects. Here is a list of transformation features:

- ***Double-click behavior.*** *Double-clicking on a graphic frame selects the content in the frame. When the content is selected, double-clicking it will select the container.*
- ***Frame edge highlighting.*** *As you mouse over items with the **Direct Selection** tool, InDesign will temporarily display the frame edges. This makes it easy to find the item you want before you select it. It also helps you identify grouped items. This even works when you are working in **Preview Mode**.*
- ***Path and point highlighting.*** *When you hover over an item with the **Direct Selection** tool, InDesign displays the path and path points.*
- ***Resize and scale multiple selected items.*** *You don't have to group items before you resize or scale or them. Just select the items you wish to transform, and you will see a transformation bounding box around the selected items. Dragging a handle will resize the elements. Pressing **Shift** will resize them proportionately. Pressing the **Cmd** or **Control** key will scale them, **Shift+Cmd** or **Shift+Control** will scale them proportionately.*
- **Rotate items.** *With the **Selection** tool, position the pointer just outside a corner handle and the cursor will change to the **Rotate** cursor. Drag to rotate the item.*

The *Control* panel also includes a *Shear* function, which makes your type or object oblique. This can be great for modifying frames and shapes, but please restrain yourself from using this tool for making fake italics or an oblique typeface. As a professional artist, you should use an oblique or italic font designed by a professional typographer rather than hacking out one of your own.

▸ *production tip*

Never use the Shear function to make a fake italic or oblique typeface. Purchase one, instead.

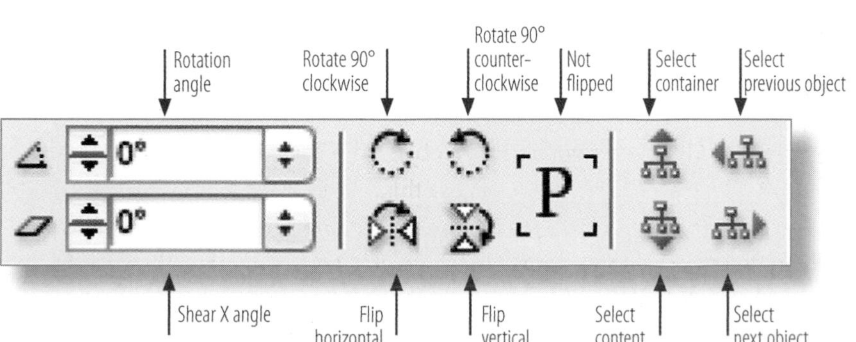

VISUAL | 6–38 |

The Control panel contains many Transform operations.

Summary

Congratulations! You've gotten to the bottom of this "junk drawer" chapter, and judging by the keyboard shortcuts below, you have discovered gadgets and new techniques that will make your production life easier. New skills take time to develop and as you master the basics, you will continue to add even more techniques to your repertoire. Become familiar with document presets, guides and columns, baseline grids, and aligning objects. Take seriously the importance of a strong layout and the use of keyboard shortcuts. Know that every advantage you can gain with InDesign will be an advantage for you and your clients, in the marketplace.

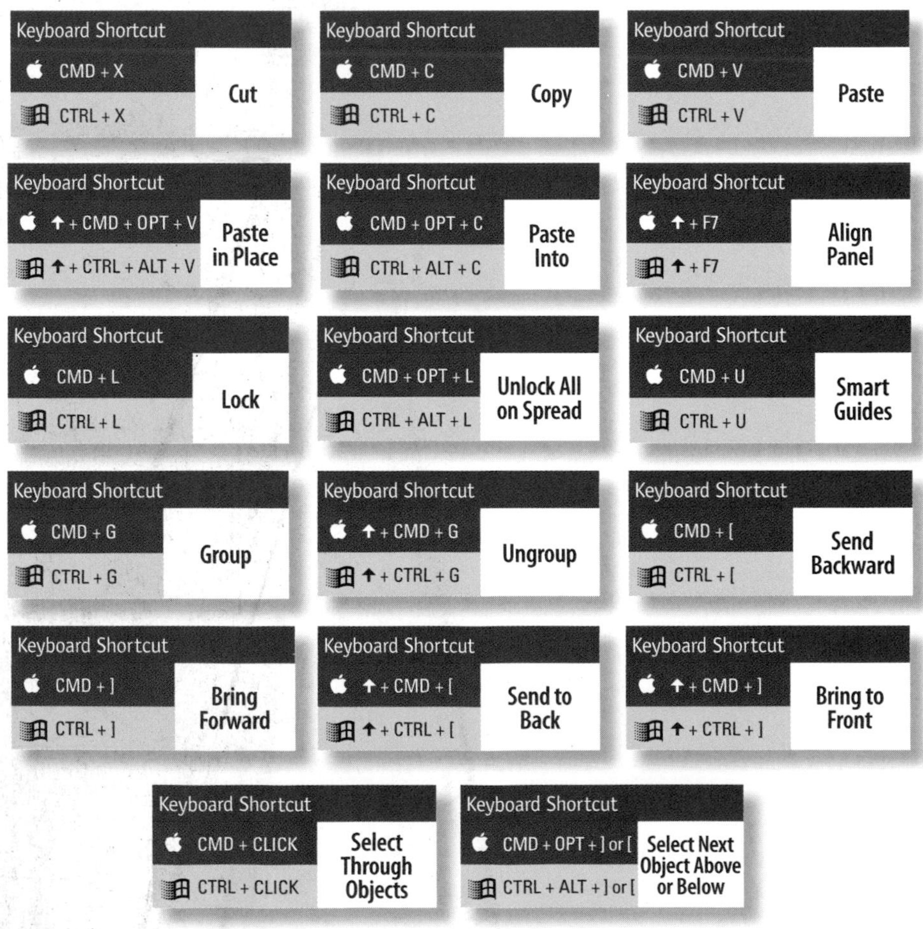

Keyboard Shortcut
CMD + X
CTRL + X
Cut
Keyboard Shortcut
CMD + C
CTRL + C
Copy
Keyboard Shortcut
CMD + V
CTRL + V
Paste
Keyboard Shortcut
↑ + CMD + OPT + V
↑ + CTRL + ALT + V
Paste in Place
Keyboard Shortcut
CMD + OPT + C
CTRL + ALT + C
Paste Into
Keyboard Shortcut
↑ + F7
↑ + F7
Align Panel
Keyboard Shortcut
CMD + L
CTRL + L
Lock
Keyboard Shortcut
CMD + OPT + L
CTRL + ALT + L
Unlock All on Spread
Keyboard Shortcut
CMD + U
CTRL + U
Smart Guides
Keyboard Shortcut
CMD + G
CTRL + G
Group
Keyboard Shortcut
↑ + CMD + G
↑ + CTRL + G
Ungroup
Keyboard Shortcut
CMD + [
CTRL + [
Send Backward
Keyboard Shortcut
CMD +]
CTRL +]
Bring Forward
Keyboard Shortcut
↑ + CMD + [
↑ + CTRL + [
Send to Back
Keyboard Shortcut
↑ + CMD +]
↑ + CTRL +]
Bring to Front
Keyboard Shortcut
CMD + CLICK
CTRL + CLICK
Select Through Objects
Keyboard Shortcut
CMD + OPT +] or [
CTRL + ALT +] or [
Select Next Object Above or Below

▸ IN REVIEW

1. For what types of documents should you make presets?
2. What is the measurement of a standard bleed?
3. What are some advantages of using columns and guides?
4. Why are a reader's first impressions of a newsletter (or any document you design) so critical?
5. What are some characteristics of the three types of newsletters described in this chapter?
6. What is the purpose of using a baseline grid?
7. What is the difference between using the Cut command or pressing the Delete key?
8. What is a setup frame? When and how do you use one?
9. Explain the difference between using Step and Repeat, and the Align panel.
10. What are some advantages in grouping items together? What is nesting?
11. Explain how to rearrange the order of stacked objects using keyboard shortcuts.
12. What is the process for changing the Document Setup default, for instance, to turn off Facing Pages?
13. You have several shapes exactly stacked on each other. What is the keyboard shortcut for selecting through objects, without rearranging the stacking order?
14. You have an image of a person placed exactly where you want it on a layout. Unfortunately, the person in the photo is pointing—and leading the reader's eye—right off the page. You decide to fix the problem by flipping the photo horizontally so that the image will point into the page. However, every time you use the transform panel to flip the image, the actual location of the image frame also moves. How can you remedy this situation, so that the picture is flipped and remains in exactly the same spot?
15. You have several objects that need their top edges aligned. You have opened the Align panel and have clicked on the Align Top Edges icon. Nothing is happening. What step in the process are you forgetting?

▸CHAPTER 6 PROJECTS

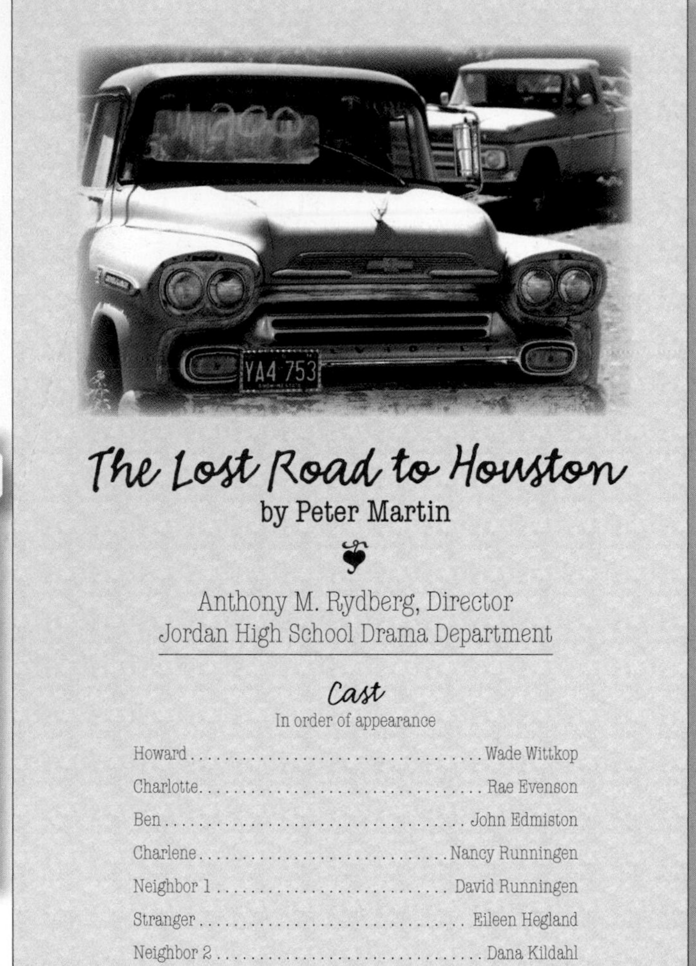

YA4 753
The Lost Road to Houston
by Peter Martin
Anthony M. Rydberg, Director
Jordan High School Drama Department
Cast
In order of appearance
Howard .... Wade Wittkop
Charlotte................................ Rae Evenson
Ben .... John Edmiston
Charlene............................ Nancy Runningen
Neighbor 1 .... David Runningen
Stranger .... Eileen Hegland
Neighbor 2 .... Dana Kildahl
Dentist .... Ron Evenson

EXPLORING INDESIGN CS6
Artwork & Resources

- Go to: http://www.cengagebrain.com
- Type: **Rydberg**
- Click **Exploring InDesign CS6** in the list of search results.
- When the book's main page is displayed, click the **Access** button under **Free Study Tools**.
- To download files, select a **chapter number** and then click on the **Artwork & Resources** tab on the left navigation bar to download the files.

The projects begin with a review of basic tabs and tables functions. *The Lost Road to Houston* will give you a sneak preview of feathering, an edge treatment often used with photos. *Align and Distribute* operations will be the focus of the children's CD cover design. The *Muskie and Walleye Fishing Guide Trips* flyer and design invoice will incorporate table functions, distribute objects, tabs, and indents. The final project is a bill stuffer—the kind you receive each month in your credit card bill. Directions and files for each project can be found in the *06 Artwork and Resources* folder on the online companion resources.

▸ CHAPTER 6 PROJECTS

Snap, Sniggle, and Ring-a-ding
A collection of classic children's songs

Money & Savings Bank
has mortgages to fit your home buying needs!
• Free online pre-approval services available 24 hours a day, seven days a week!
• Offering low-interest loans to first time home owners.
• Easy application and approval process.
• Construction loans with interest-only options.
• Evening hours for personal service.
Stop in and see how your friendly, small town bank can help you purchase the home of your dreams!
Money & Savings Bank

▸ CHAPTER 6 PROJECTS

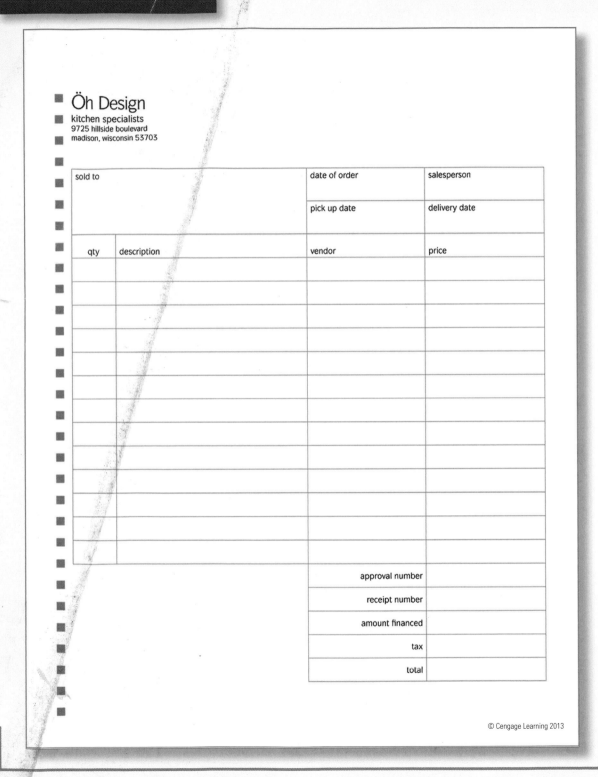

Öh Design
kitchen specialists
9725 hillside boulevard
madison, wisconsin 53703

sold to	date of order	salesperson
	pick up date	delivery date

qty	description	vendor	price

approval number	
receipt number	
amount financed	
tax	
total	

▶ CHAPTER 6 PROJECTS

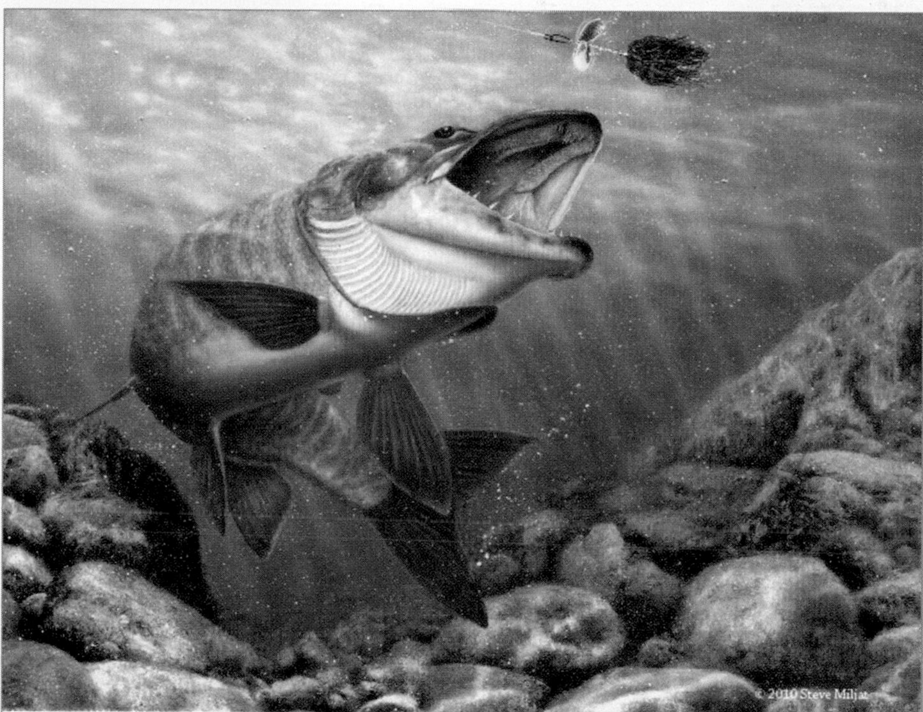

Muskie and Walleye Fishing Guide Trips

Muskie Fishing Guide Trips
Southeast Wisconsin

Pewaukee Lake and many of the surrounding lakes in Waukesha County offer superb musky fishing within a half hour of Milwaukee. The muskie lakes of Waukesha County produce consistent action with a chance at some real bruisers over 50".

Pewaukee Lake offers consistent musky action from fish ranging 30" to 30 pounds. Pewaukee ranks as class A1 muskie lake, producing trophy fish in addition to being a great action lake from all sizes of muskie.

Okauchee Lake having a cisco forage base holds the heaviest muskies and clear water Oconomowoc Lake is a challenge even for seasoned veterans.

Fowler, Lac La Belle, North Lake, and Pine Lake, all connected by the Oconomowoc River or feeder creeks, support fishable musky populations.

Bring your own rod or use my quality Fenwicks and Ambassadeurs, don't worry about lures since you will be using the most effective baits in my boat.

Learn Proven Techniques

- *Casting weedlines and pockets*
- *Figure 8 strategies*
- *Jerkbait & crank presentations*
- *Short line trolling*
- *Longline trolling*
- *Planer boards & downriggers*
- *Quick strike sucker rigs*
- *How to release a muskie*

Muskie Fishing Guide Trips
Lake Vermillion, Minnesota

This clear water Canadian Shield Lake has a reputation as being the most scenic lake in America, it will not disappoint! Big fish and unmatched scenery, a combination worth your time.

Located 2 hours northwest of Duluth in St. Louis County Minnesota. Lake Vermilion is a sprawling body of water spanning 27 miles long with over 350 islands.

This lake produces huge muskie with exceptional girth. The average size musky is 40"–44" and built broad across the back. An excellent trophy fishery for years to come due to the outstanding catch and release ethic amongst musky anglers.

Learn Proven Techniques

- *Casting weedlines and pockets*
- *Figure 8 strategies*
- *Jerkbait & crank presentations*
- *Short line trolling*
- *Longline trolling*
- *Planer boards & downriggers*
- *Quick strike sucker rigs*
- *How to release a muskie*

About your guide...
Fishing guide and wildlife artist, Steve Miljat is your best choice to guide you in search of muskie fishing. With over 1800 muskie releases spanning almost 20 years, his expertise will get you in the fast lane.

During the off season, Miljat is a commercial wildlife artist, utilizing traditional and digital illustration techniques. Visit his artwork at http://miljat.com/

Walleye Fishing Guide Trips
Green Bay, Wisconsin & Bay De Noc, Michigan

From her southern shore at the city of Green Bay Wisconsin to her northern shore at Escanaba Michigan, big schools of walleyes chase baitfish throughout the vastness of this inland sea. Location of trophy walleyes is a non factor as your guide keys in on seasonal migration patterns in the early spring and late fall. A 10 lb. walleye is a milestone for any fisherman!

Fishing at night in cold conditions is no picnic, but if you're looking for your personal best, don't mind dressing for the weather and losing a little sleep, come to Green Bay and Bay De Noc for an awesome adventure! *Available April–May and November.*

Learn Proven Techniques

- *Crankbait presentations*
- *Short line trolling*
- *Long line trolling*
- *Planer boards*
- *Boat Control*

Guide Rates

Location	Hours	Cost
Muskie Fishing Southeast Wisconsin	5 Hour Trip 8 Hour Trip	$225 $400 Maximum 2 anglers
Muskie Fishing Lake Vermillion	5 Hour Trip 8 Hour Trip	$225 $400 Maximum 2 anglers
Walleye Fishing Green Bay Bay De Noc	8 Hour Trip	$400 for the boat or 2 anglers Extra angler $50

$100 down to book a trip.

Text Wrap, Layers, and Effects

objectives

- *Apply text wrap*
- *Manage document layers*
- *Apply effects*
- *Set fractions*
- *Use the Gap tool*
- *Apply corner effects*

introduction

My daughter owns a rescued greyhound named Penny. Once we took her to a large baseball field to see just how fast this dog could run. Penny was trembling with excitement, eager to run. When we released her, she was off like a speeding bullet.

Like Penny, you have been training to race. You have learned many InDesign basics and are now "trembling at the end of your leash" waiting to be let loose. Beginning with this chapter, *Exploring Adobe InDesign CS6* will be more production-based, building on previously learned skills while introducing new techniques and typographic principles.

Now that you've mastered the basics of production, we'll be adding techniques that will make your production process easier and more enjoyable. This chapter will focus on text wrap and layers, the Gap tool and corner effects. You will also learn how to apply feathering, drop shadows, and other transparency effects to objects.

Congratulations—you're half done with the book! Feel free to e-mail me and let me know how you're doing—trydberg@mac.com.

integrating text and graphics

Text and graphics need to work together. It's important to match the personality of the typeface with the style of the graphic. It is also important to create a visual link between the graphic and the text that accompanies it. In design terms, this is called the principle of *proximity*. One method of visually linking text and graphics is by using text wrap.

EXPLORING INDESIGN CS6
Artwork & Resources

- Go to: http://www.cengagebrain.com
- Type: Rydberg
- Click Exploring InDesign CS6 in the list of search results.
- When the book's main page is displayed, click the Access button under Free Study Tools.
- To download files, select a chapter number and then click on the Artwork & Resources tab on the left navigation bar to download the files.

AN INTRODUCTION TO TEXT WRAP

Text wrap is the process of flowing text around a graphic or shape. Think of text as a river that flows smoothly until it hits a rock—a shape or graphic. The river might go around the rock or over the rock, but in either case, it just keeps flowin' along. You can control how the river of text flows around shapes or graphics by applying text wrap options. Open *07 Text Wrap.indd* from the online companion resources. As you work through each step, make the changes in the *Text Wrap* panel and reposition the image, as shown in each example.

1. Open the *Text Wrap* panel by pressing **Command+Option+W** (Mac) or **Control+Alt+W** (Windows). You can also access the *Text Wrap* panel by choosing *Window>Text Wrap* (but using the menus rather than using keyboard shortcuts is always slower). Each button on the panel activates a different text wrap mode. Visual 7–1 provides an overview of the *Text Wrap* panel.

VISUAL | 7–1 |

The Text Wrap panel contains five buttons that alter the flow of text around objects.

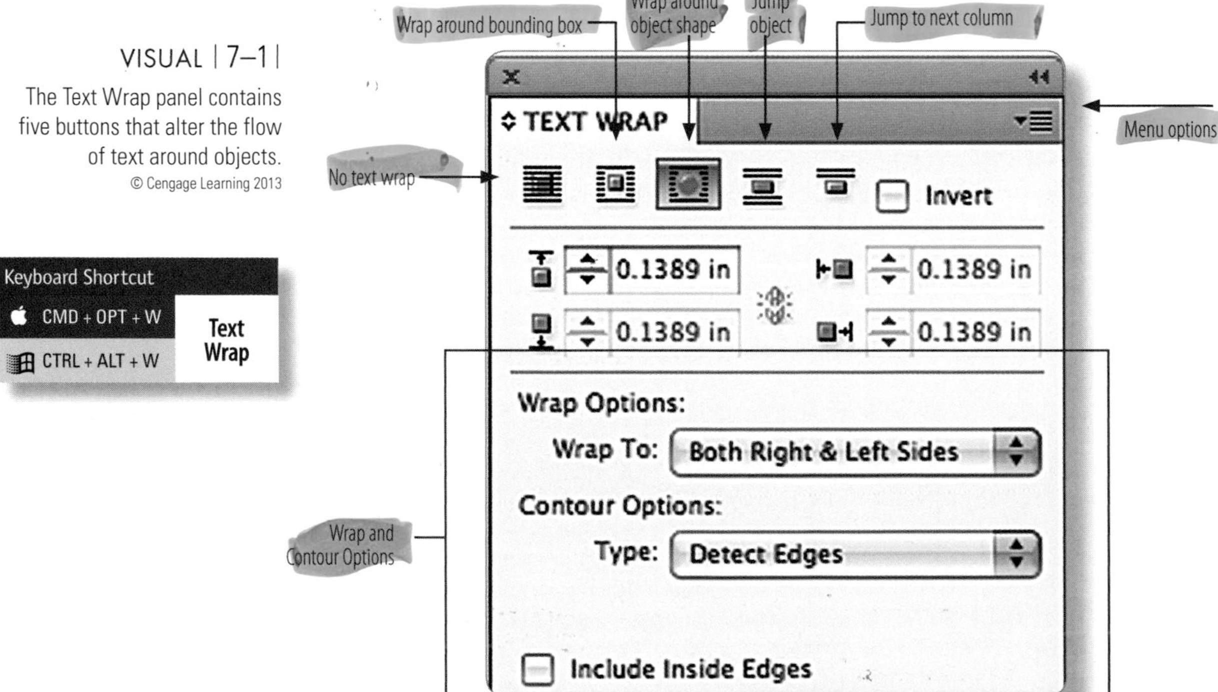

Keyboard Shortcut

CMD + OPT + W	Text Wrap
CTRL + ALT + W	

2. In this exercise, the bobber is the "rock" in the middle of your text flow. The object that the text is wrapping around is referred to as the ***wrap object***. Whenever you are applying a text wrap option you must first select the wrap object. Select the bobber and notice that the first text wrap option, ***No text wrap***, is selected in the ***Text Wrap*** panel. This option is the default. When ***No text wrap*** is active, the text can flow over or under the object (Visual 7–2).

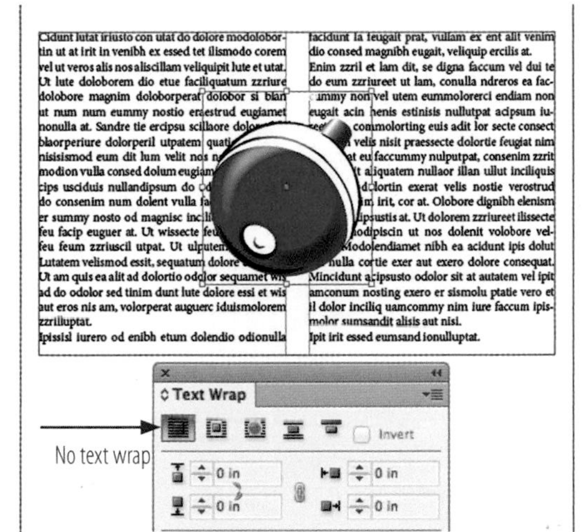

VISUAL | 7–2 |

No text wrap is the default wrap option in InDesign.

Bobber illustration © 2006 Nathaniel Avery

3. Select the bobber with the ***Selection*** tool and choose the second button, ***Wrap around bounding box***. Make sure that the ***Make all settings the same*** button is selected, and enter **0.25"** in any of the four ***Offset*** fields. As shown in Visual 7–3, you will see two boxes around the bobber: the inside box is the ***bounding box***, and the outside box shows the location of a 0.25" text offset that has been applied on all sides of the bounding box. As you can see, text offsets are ideal for adding white space between copy and images. To create different text offsets on individual sides of the bounding box, deselect the ***Make all settings the same*** icon in the middle of the ***Offset*** fields and specify different values in the fields.

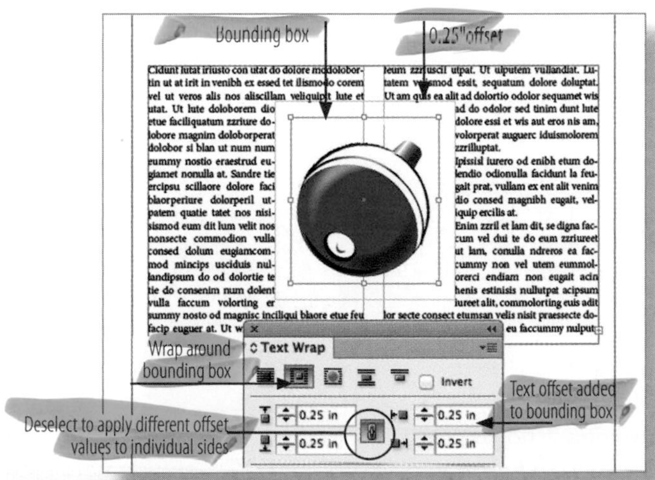

VISUAL | 7–3 |

Wrap around bounding box creates a wrap whose shape is determined by the size of the bounding box, plus any text offset.

Bobber illustration © 2006 Nathaniel Avery

4. Select the third option, ***Wrap around object shape***, also known as ***contour wrapping***. In this mode, you have several options from which to choose. Under ***Wrap Options***, you can specify where the text will be positioned. In Visual 7–4, ***Wrap to Left Side*** has allowed text to wrap on the left side of the graphic, but not on the right. Reposition the bobber on your page as you experiment with the other wrap options. The first three ***Wrap Options***, ***Left Side***, ***Right Side***, and ***Both Right & Left Sides***, will be the ones you will use most often. The ***Contour Options*** section allows you to specify how the text will interact with the shape. In Visual 7–4 the ***Contour Options*** is set to follow the shape of the ***Graphic Frame***.

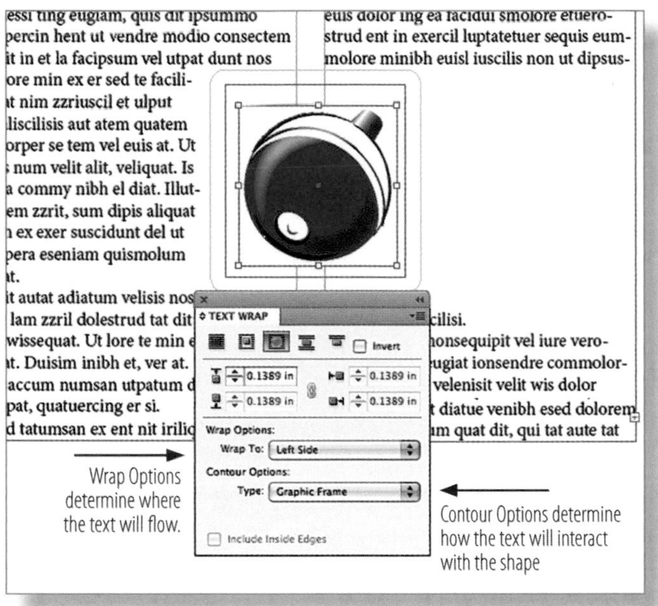

VISUAL |7–4|

Wrap and Contour Options are available when the Wrap Around Shape mode is active.

Bobber illustration © 2006 Nathaniel Avery

In Visual 7–5, the ***Wrap Options*** have been set to ***Both Right & Left Sides,*** and ***Detect Edges*** has been specified under ***Contour Options***. With ***Detect Edges*** selected, InDesign finds the edges of the image inside the bounding box. In this example, you can see how the specified offset follows the contour of the shape.

Bounding box
Edges detected and offset specified
Detect Edges selected

VISUAL |7–5|

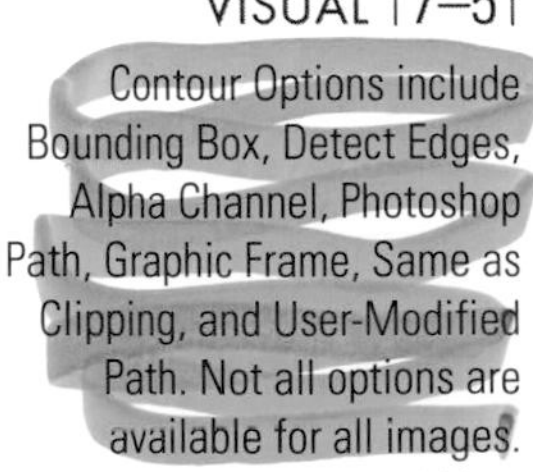

Contour Options include Bounding Box, Detect Edges, Alpha Channel, Photoshop Path, Graphic Frame, Same as Clipping, and User-Modified Path. Not all options are available for all images.

Bobber illustration © 2006 Nathaniel Avery

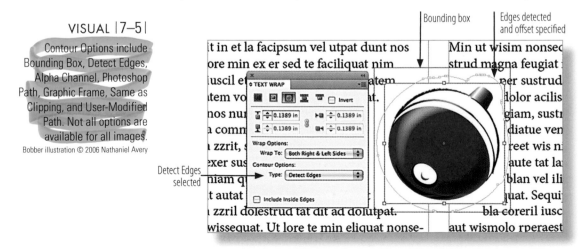

5. The fourth option is ***Jump object.*** In this mode, the text leap frogs over the object to the next available space. ***Jump object*** keeps text from appearing on either side of the frame. (Visual 7–6).

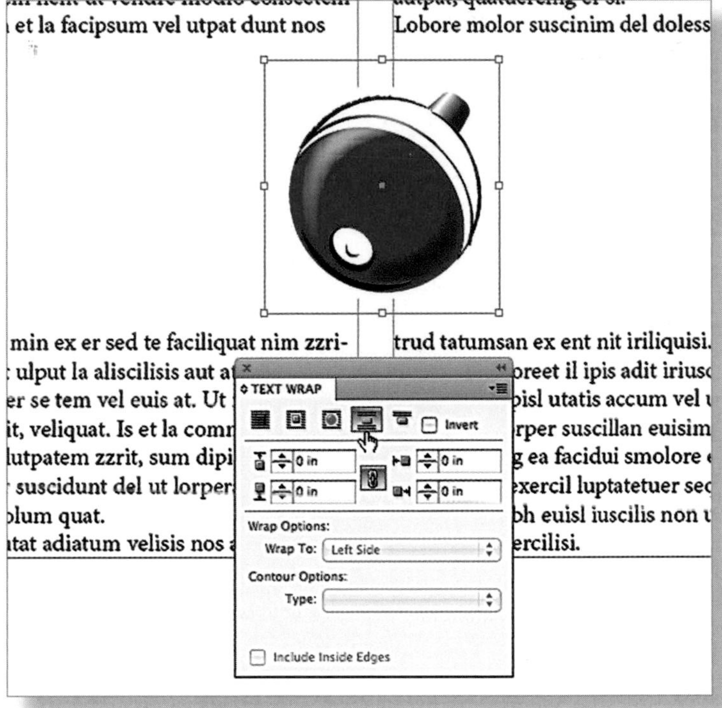

VISUAL |7–6|

Jump object prevents copy from appearing on either side of the frame.

Bobber illustration © 2006 Nathaniel Avery

6. The fifth option, ***Jump to next column***, jumps the text over to the next column or text frame available (Visual 7–7).

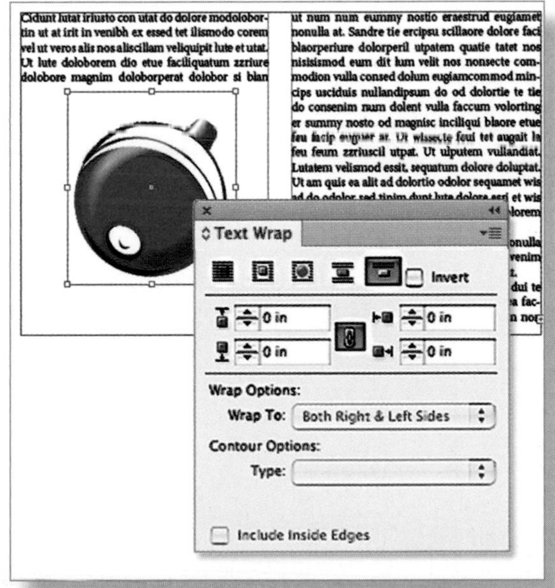

VISUAL |7–7|

Jump to next column flows copy to the next available column or frame, including a threaded frame.

Bobber illustration © 2006 Nathaniel Avery

7. Select the bobber and change the text wrap to ***Wrap around object shape***, set the ***Contour Options*** to ***Detect Edges.*** Position the bobber in the middle of the first column. Draw a circle, move it to the center of the second column, and give it a background color of [None]. Apply ***Wrap around object shape*** and turn on the ***Invert*** option. With ***Invert*** selected, the text flows inside the selected object (Visual 7–8).

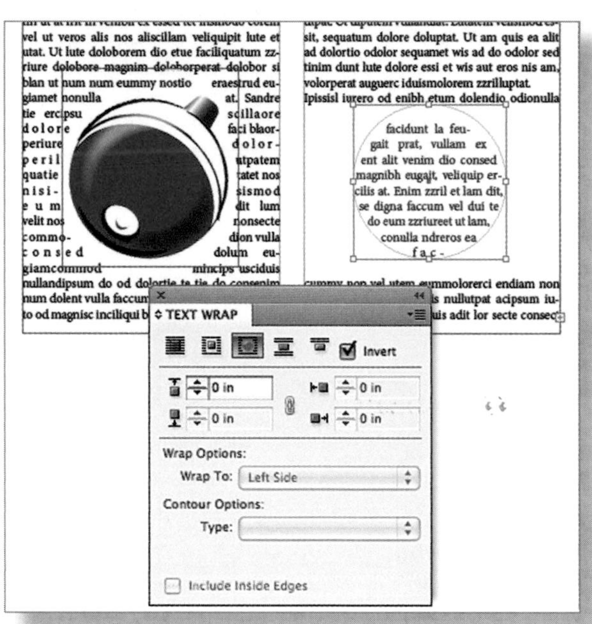

VISUAL |7–8|
Invert allows the copy to flow inside an object, as shown by the red type inside the circle in the right hand column.
Bobber illustration © 2006 Nathaniel Avery

an introduction to document layers

In the last chapter, you were introduced to the stacking order of InDesign objects, which was compared to a stack of pancakes. You used keyboard shortcuts to rearrange the objects in the stack. In this chapter, you will learn to create and use *document layers.* Document layers are like a stack of plates, each plate holding its own pile of pancakes. Document layers are easy to understand, and they simplify the production of complex projects.

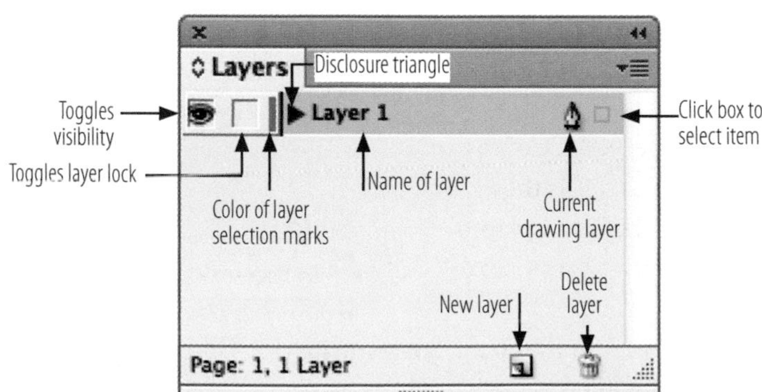

VISUAL |7–9|
The Layers panel.
© Cengage Learning 2013

Keyboard Shortcut
F7 (function key) (Mac)
F7 (function key) (Windows)
Layers Panel

▸ *Use stacking order to build a hamburger*

In this next exercise, you will use the *Layers* formatting panel to build a cheeseburger, with artwork provided by illustrator, David Espurvoa III. You will find it in the *07 Artwork and Resources* folder on online companion resources.

1. Open *07 Document Layers.indd* from the *07 Artwork and Resources folder*. Press **F7** to open the *Layers* panel. Every new InDesign document starts with one layer. By default, this is named *Layer 1*. Click on the tomatoes, and you will see a blue square with a black border appear next to the pen icon, on the right side of the *Layers* panel. This square shows that the item you have selected is on Layer 1. In fact, the bun, lettuce, cheese, hamburger, and bacon are also on Layer 1. When you deselect all the images, Layer 1 displays a grayed square, indicating that nothing is selected on Layer 1.

2. Select each of the ingredients and position them to build a cheeseburger. You are actually manipulating the *stacking order* of objects, because all the objects are contained on the same layer. You can use keyboard shortcuts to select and rearrange the stacking order of the images. You can also use the *Select previous object* and *Select next object* tools on the *Control* panel (Visual 7–10). When the **Command** (Mac) or **Control** (Windows) key is also pressed, *Select previous object* becomes *Select first object*, and *Select next object* becomes *Select last object*.

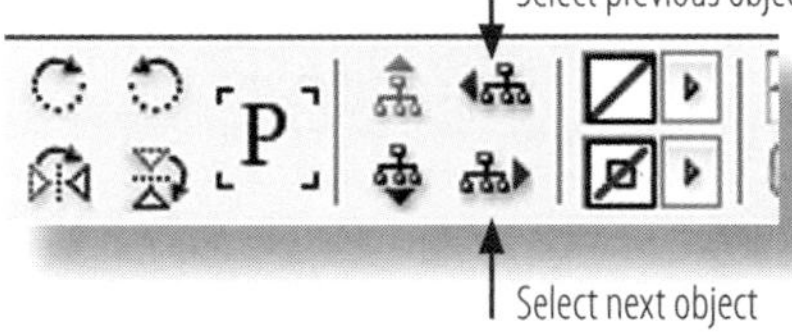

VISUAL |7–10|

Each ingredient in this cheeseburger is a separate picture file. Each file is stacked on top of the next.
Illustration © 2008 David Espurvoa III

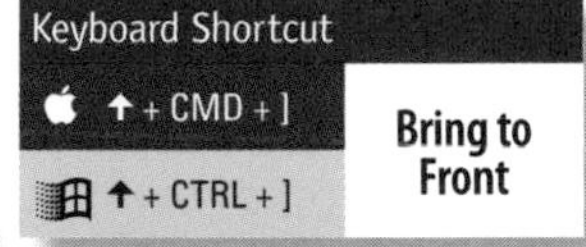

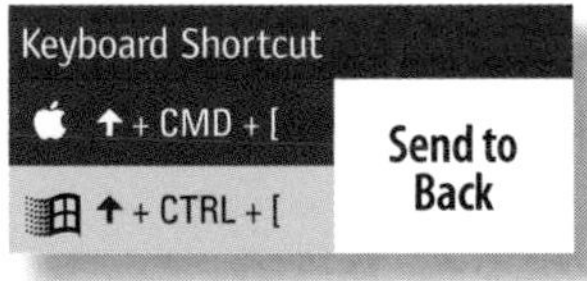

THE LAYERS PANEL

In the previous step, you experienced how difficult it can be to navigate through a complicated stack of objects. In the next step, you're going to take control and move the ingredients to separate document layers. But before we go there, let's take a closer look at some of the features in the *Layers* panel, as shown in Visual 7–11. On the left side of the panel, you can see an *eye icon*. This is the visibility control. When this icon is displayed, the layer is visible. Click the icon, and watch the cheeseburger disappear. Now this layer is hidden. Click the icon again, and the cheeseburger reappears. This is a nice feature—text, guides, and elements can be hidden, as needed.

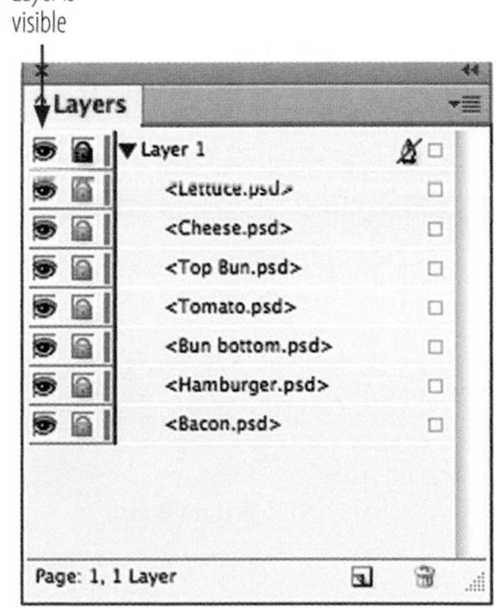

VISUAL |7–11|

Click the eye to turn visibility on or off.
© Cengage Learning 2013

Next to the eye icon there is an empty box. When you click the box a *lock icon* appears to show that the layer is locked, and you can no longer edit its elements. Like the eye icon, clicking this control repeatedly toggles it on and off. To the right of the lock is a vertical, blue line. The *blue line* corresponds to the selection marks color used to display the bounding boxes, frames, and guides that are selected on a particular layer. (Visual 7–12).

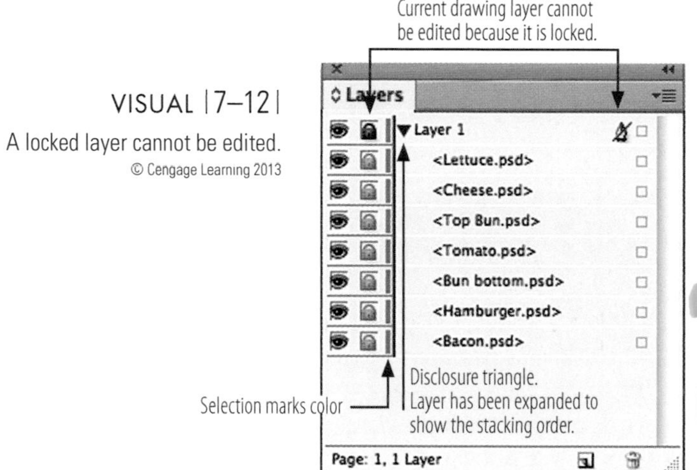

VISUAL |7–12|

A locked layer cannot be edited.

© Cengage Learning 2013

To the right of the selection marks color, you will see that this layer is named *Layer 1*. The pen icon at the right end of the *Layers* panel indicates which layer you are currently working on, called the *current drawing layer.* If a layer is locked, the pen icon will have a red, diagonal line through it (Visual 7–12). Finally, notice the *disclosure triangle* to the left of the layer name. When you click on this triangle, the panel expands to show the objects, in their stacking order, on that layer. You can click on each item and drag it up or down in the list to rearrange the stacking order. You can also hide or show individual items by clicking the eye icon next to the item's stacking order (Visual 7–12). Now, we'll continue with our layers exercise.

▸ *Use Layers to build a hamburger*

1. Unlock ***Layer 1*** and close the disclosure triangle. Double-click on the title, ***Layer 1***, to open the ***Layer Options*** dialog box. Here you can change the name of the layer and the color of the selection marks, and perform other housekeeping functions such as ***Suppress Text Wrap When Layer Is Hidden***. When you select this option, any text wrap mode you have applied to an object will be turned off when you hide the layer. While you are in this dialog box, change the name of the layer to **Text** and click **Return** (Visual 7–13). Next, create a text frame and type **Wisconsin Cheeseburger** underneath the image. We're going use this layer for text only, and move the images to new document layers.

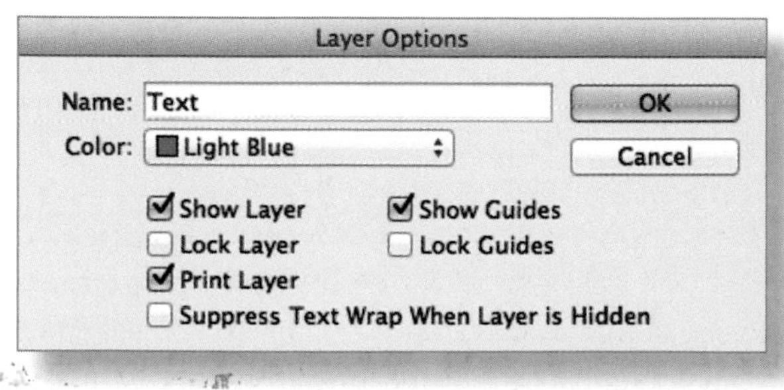

VISUAL |7–13|

The Layer Options dialog is opened by double-clicking on a layer's name. There are many management features in this dialog box.

© Cengage Learning 2013

2. There are two methods for creating new document layers. For the first method, click the icon in the lower right corner of the panel (Visual 7–14). A new layer will appear in the panel, named ***Layer 2***. Double-click the name of the layer to open the ***Layer Options*** dialog box. Rename the layer **Bottom Bun** and click **Return**. A new layer, ***Bottom Bun***, is now shown in the ***Layers*** panel, above the ***Text*** layer.

VISUAL | 7–14 |

Click the Create New Layer icon to add layers to a document. Double click the layer name to open the Layer Options window to change the layer name.
Illustration © 2008 David Espurvoa III

3. The second method for creating layers is particularly convenient, because the ***New Layer*** dialog box is automatically opened with the ***Name*** field highlighted. Hold down **Option** (Mac) or **Alt** (Windows) and **click** the ***Create new layer*** icon at the bottom of the panel. Type **Hamburger** in the ***Name*** field and press **Return**. Repeat this process and make the following three layers: 1***) Lettuce and Tomatoes,*** 2) ***Cheese and Bacon,*** and 3) ***Top Bun.*** You can lengthen the ***Layers*** panel by pulling on the lower right corner. Six named layers should be visible in the ***Layers*** panel (Visual 7–15).

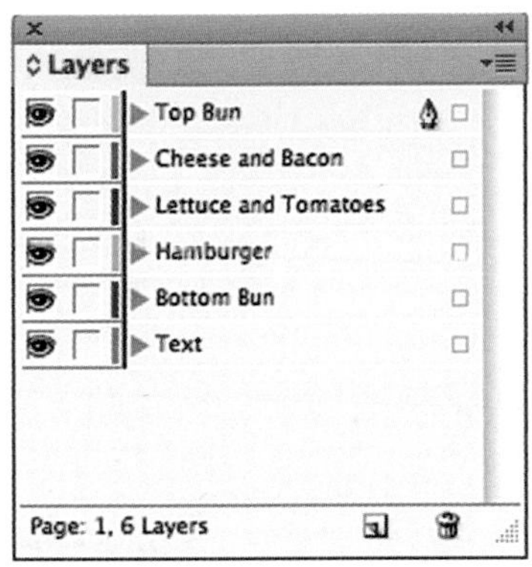

VISUAL | 7–15 |

Create these layers in your hamburger document.
© Cengage Learning 2013

4. Select the top bun of the cheeseburger. In the ***Layers*** panel, the ***Text*** layer is highlighted and the pen icon with a blue box with a black border next to it, appears. This indicates that the item you have selected is currently located on the ***Text*** layer. Click on the box and drag it up to the layer named ***Top Bun*** (Visual 7–16). When you release the mouse, notice that the frame guides for the bun illustration are the same color as the selection marks color indicator in the ***Top Bun*** layer. Hide the ***Top Bun*** layer by clicking the eye icon to the left of the layer name.

VISUAL | 7–16 |

Move an item from one layer to the next by selecting the item, and then moving the box in the Layers panel to a new layer.
Illustration © 2008 David Espurvoa III

5. Open the disclosure triangle on the ***Text*** layer. Select the ***cheese*** image. You will know it is selected when a blue square appears in the ***Layers*** panel next to the file name. It might be difficult to select the cheese image among all the other stacked objects. If so, you may need to drill down through the stacked objects by using the **Command+Click** (Mac) or

Control+Click (Windows) technique. When the cheese image is selected, move the blue square to the ***Cheese and Bacon*** layer. Use the same technique to select the bacon illustration and move it to the ***Cheese and Bacon*** layer. Hide this layer. Select the ***lettuce*** and ***tomatoe***s and move them to the ***Lettuce and Tomatoes*** layer. Hide the layer. Select the ***hamburger***, and move it to the ***Hamburger*** layer. Hide the layer. Select the ***bottom bun*** and move it to the ***Bottom Bun*** layer.

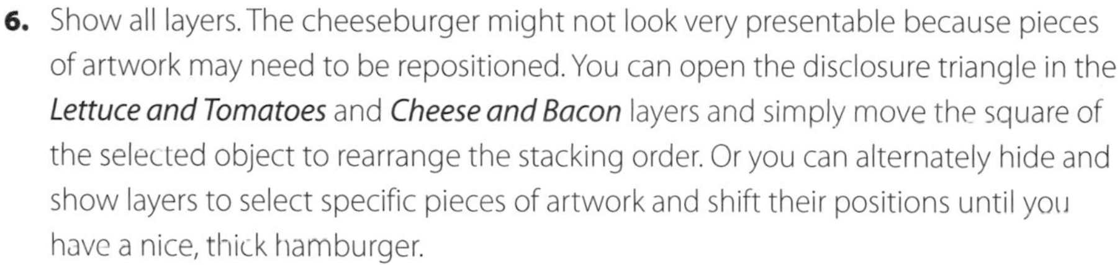

6. Show all layers. The cheeseburger might not look very presentable because pieces of artwork may need to be repositioned. You can open the disclosure triangle in the *Lettuce and Tomatoes* and *Cheese and Bacon* layers and simply move the square of the selected object to rearrange the stacking order. Or you can alternately hide and show layers to select specific pieces of artwork and shift their positions until you have a nice, thick hamburger.

7. In this step you will reposition the stacking order of the document layers. Your goal will be to arrange the layers in the order shown in Visual 7–17. The bottom layer should be the ***Text*** layer. To move a layer's position, click and drag it up or down. When you select the layer, the pointer will turn into a closed fist, and a heavy black line will indicate where the layer will be positioned when you release the mouse. Repeat this process to position each layer in the order shown in Visual 7–17. Keep your document open.

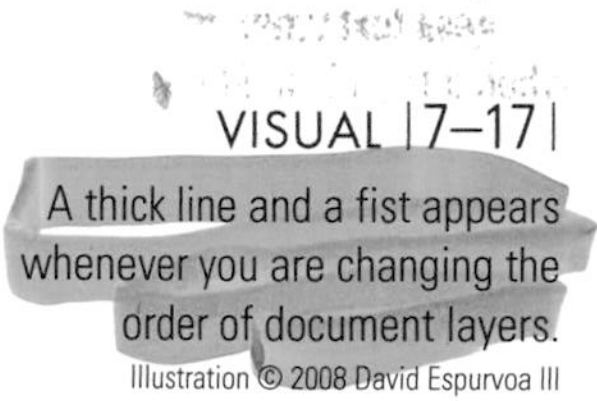

VISUAL | 7–17 |

A thick line and a fist appears whenever you are changing the order of document layers.

Illustration © 2008 David Espurvoa III

▸ *Manage Text Wrap with layers and text frame options*

There are text wrap controls in the *Layers* panel and in the *Text Frame Options* panel that you should be aware of. These features are often overlooked, so take the time to study this section.

1. In the document you were just working on, lock all the layers, except *Bottom Bun* and *Text*. Select the *Wisconsin Cheeseburger* type frame and position it so the top of the frame touches the frame of the bottom bun illustration. Make *Bottom Bun* the drawing layer. Use the *Selection* tool to select the frame for the bottom bun image. Activate *Wrap around bounding box* from the *Control* panel. Visual 7–18 shows how the text reflows around the bounding box of the bottom bun. Depending on the size of your text frame, the text may even disappear altogether when text wrap is applied to the hamburger bun!

VISUAL | 7–18 |

Text wrap was applied to the bottom bun, which consequently pushed the type over.

Illustration © 2008 David Espurvoa III

2. *Double-click* the *Bottom Bun* layer to open the *Layer Options* dialog box (Visual 7–19). Check *Suppress Text Wrap When Layer is Hidden.* Press **Return**. Hide the *Bottom Bun* layer, and you will see the text reflow as if the object wasn't even there. Make the *Bottom Bun* layer visible once more and the text wrap will be activated.

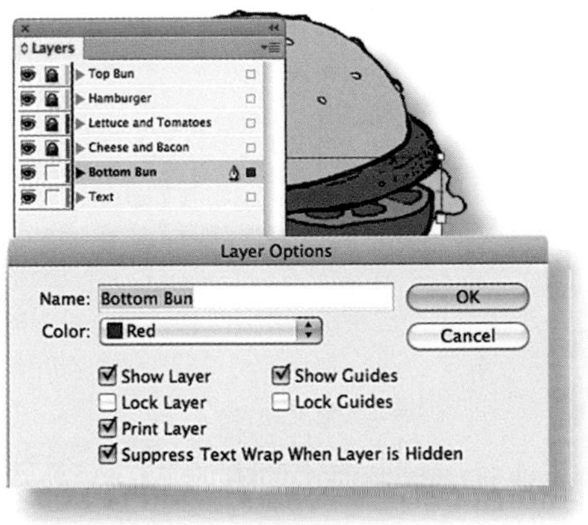

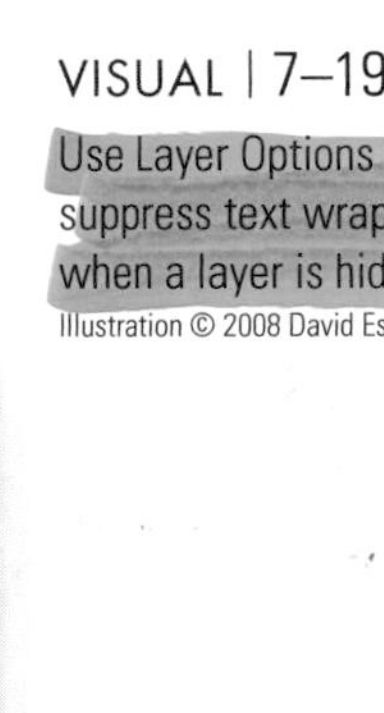

VISUAL | 7–19 |

Use Layer Options to suppress text wrap when a layer is hidden.

Illustration © 2008 David Espurvoa III

3. This technique mentioned earlier bears repeating: you can override the text wrap for individual text frames. Select the text frame and press **Command+B** (Mac) or **Control+B** (Windows) to open the *Text Frame Options* dialog box (or choose *Object> Text Frame Options*). Select *Ignore Text Wrap* at the bottom of the dialog box and click **Return** (Visual 7–20).

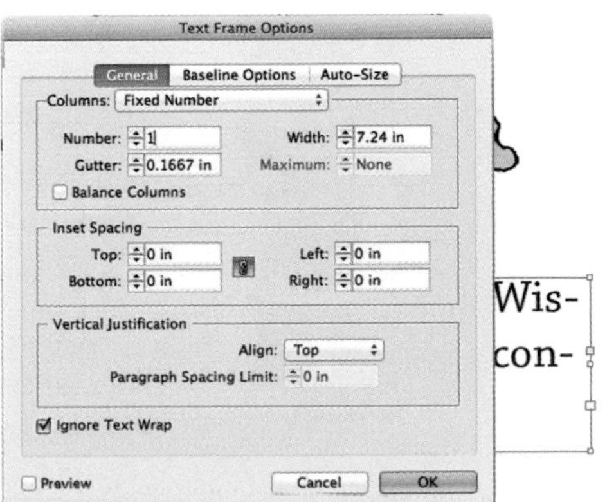

VISUAL | 7–20 |

Use Text Frame Options to ignore text wrap on individual items.

© Cengage Learning 2013

USING LAYERS TO CREATE TWO VERSIONS OF A DOCUMENT

Now that you have created, repositioned, locked, and hidden layers, you probably realize the production opportunities offered by the *Layers* panel. In the next project, you will design a page for a recipe book, featuring recipes from all over the United States (Visual 7–21). You will use layers to construct this document so it contains two versions of a chocolate chip cookie recipe—one designed for home bakers, and a big-batch version intended for institutional cooking. You will also use the features of a recent font technology called *OpenType* to create true fractions.

Chewy Chocolate Chip Cookies

Willow Lake, South Dakota

1 cup shortening
1 cup canola oil
4 eggs
1½ cups brown sugar
1½ cups white sugar
3½–4 cups flour
2 tsp. soda dissolved in
2 tsp. hot water
1½ tsp. vanilla
4 cups oatmeal
1 tsp. salt
½ cup chopped nuts
(optional)
12 oz. chocolate chips

Cream shortening, oil, eggs, and sugars until light and fluffy. Add flour, the soda-water mixture, salt, and vanilla. Stir in oatmeal, chocolate chips and nuts. Drop by teaspoon onto ungreased cookie sheet.

Bake 350° for 9–10 min.

VISUAL |7–21|

Layers will be used to create two versions of a recipe in a single document.

EXPLORING INDESIGN CS6
Artwork & Resources

- Go to: http://www.cengagebrain.com
- Type: Rydberg
- Click Exploring InDesign CS6 in the list of search results.
- When the book's main page is displayed, click the Access button under Free Study Tools.
- To download files, select a chapter number and then click on the Artwork & Resources tab on the left navigation bar to download the files.

1. Create a new document. *Document size*: **8.5"× 11"**. *Top, bottom*, and *right margins*: **0.5"**. *Left margin*: **0.75"** (to accommodate spiral binding). Press **Return**. Press **F7** to open the *Layers* panel. Change the name of *Layer 1* to *Picture.* Draw a frame from margin to margin. Place *07 Cookies.tif* from the *07 Artwork and Resources* folder and scale proportionately to **145%**. (The photo will not reach to the bottom margin.) Reset the zero point to the far right edge of the photo and drop in a vertical guide at **-0.25"** on the X coordinate (Visual 7–23). Lock this layer.

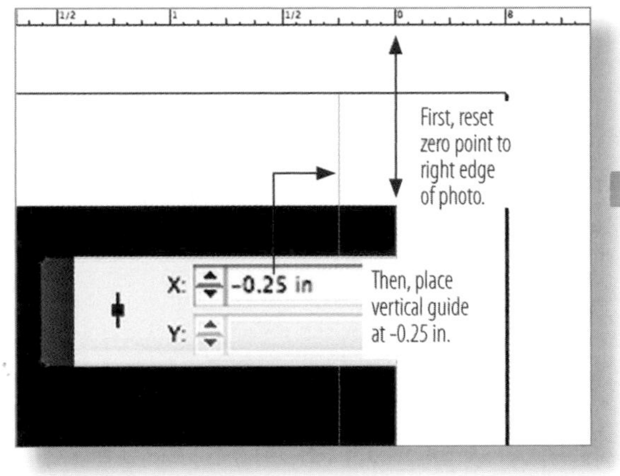
First, reset zero point to right edge of photo.
X: -0.25 in
Y:
Then, place vertical guide at -0.25 in.

VISUAL |7–22|

The zero point has been reset. The right edges of the text frames will be aligned to the guideline.

1. Create a new layer and name it *Consumer Recipe.* Type the copy and follow the type specifications shown in Visual 7–23. Use three text frames, creating a 2-column frame for the ingredients. Do not place a space after the whole number in the fractions. Creating fractions is an easy process when OpenType fonts are used. Highlight the numerator, slash, and denominator, and choose *OpenType>Fractions* from the *Control* panel menu. Repeat the process for each fraction. Or, highlight the "½" fraction, *Copy* and *Paste* it as needed. Be sure to check spelling and use the correct hyphens and dashes.

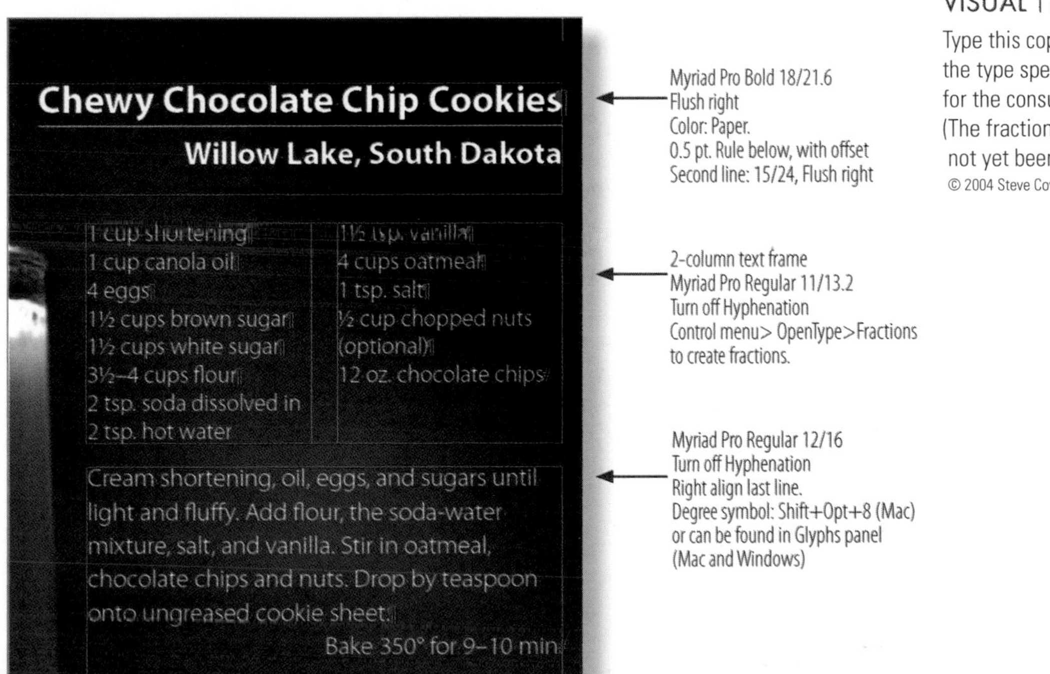
Chewy Chocolate Chip Cookies
Willow Lake, South Dakota
1 cup shortening
1 cup canola oil
4 eggs
1½ cups brown sugar
1½ cups white sugar
3½–4 cups flour
2 tsp. soda dissolved in
2 tsp. hot water
1½ tsp. vanilla
4 cups oatmeal
1 tsp. salt
½ cup chopped nuts
(optional)
12 oz. chocolate chips
Cream shortening, oil, eggs, and sugars until light and fluffy. Add flour, the soda-water mixture, salt, and vanilla. Stir in oatmeal, chocolate chips and nuts. Drop by teaspoon onto ungreased cookie sheet.
Bake 350° for 9–10 min.
Myriad Pro Bold 18/21.6
Flush right
Color: Paper.
0.5 pt. Rule below, with offset
Second line: 15/24, Flush right
2-column text frame
Myriad Pro Regular 11/13.2
Turn off Hyphenation
Control menu> OpenType>Fractions
to create fractions.
Myriad Pro Regular 12/16
Turn off Hyphenation
Right align last line.
Degree symbol: Shift+Opt+8 (Mac)
or can be found in Glyphs panel
(Mac and Windows)

VISUAL |7–23|

Type this copy and follow the type specifications for the consumer recipe. (The fractions have not yet been created.)

2. Create a new layer and name it **Industrial Recipe.** You are going to duplicate the type from the *Consumer Recipe* layer, and move it to the *Industrial Recipe* layer. Afterwards, you will double the ingredients for the Industrial Recipe version. Click on the *Consumer Recipe* layer in the *Layers* panel. Choose the *Selection* tool, and **Shift+Click** each text frame so that they are all selected. The small red box showing in the *Consumer Recipe* layer represents the three text frames you have just selected. Press **Option** (Mac) or **Alt** (Windows) while you move the red square up to the *Industrial Recipe* layer. As the *Option* or *Alt* key is held, you will see a plus sign appear which means a duplicate is being created on the next layer.

3. Hide the *Consumer Recipe* layer. Move to the *Industrial Recipe* layer and change the title to **Big Batch of Chocolate Chip Cookies.** Then, double the recipe ingredients (Visual 7–24). Save your document and print a copy of the *Industrial Recipe* version. Hide the *Industrial Recipe* layer and show the *Consumer Recipe* layer. Print the *Consumer Recipe* version.

VISUAL |7–24|

When you double the recipe don't forget to change the copy on the Industrial Recipe layer. Cup should now read "cups."

© 2004 Steve Cowal

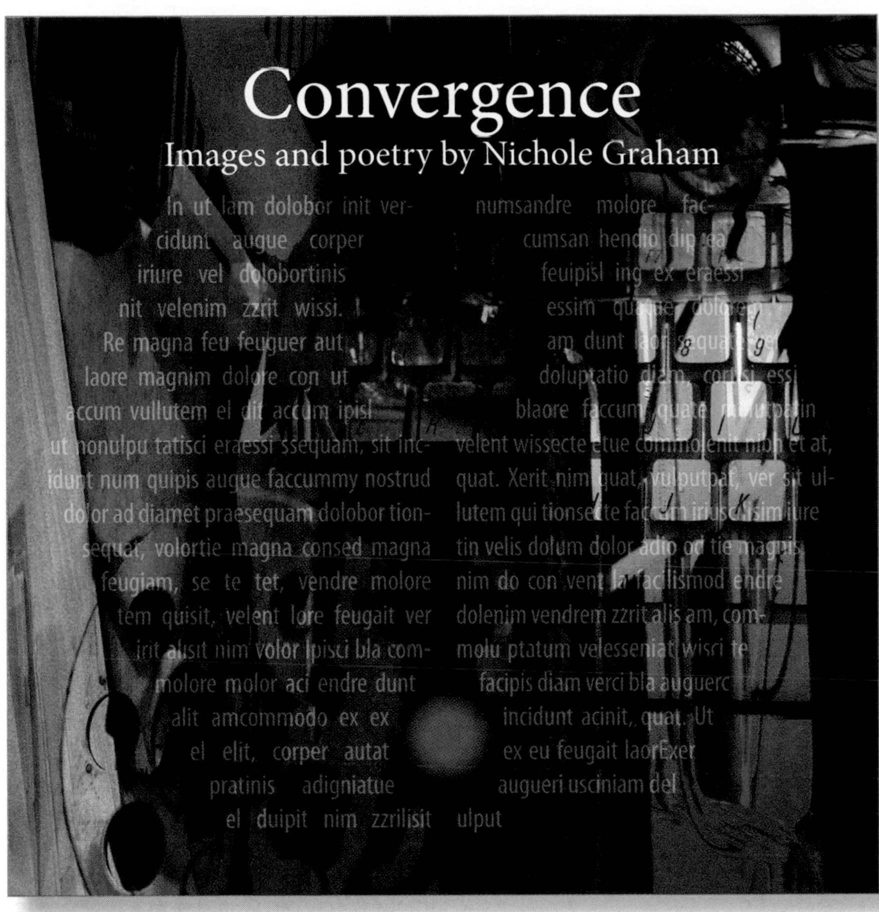

VISUAL | 7–25 |

The finished CD cover, which incorporates transparency and feathering. © 2004 Nichole Graham

EXPLORING INDESIGN CS6
Artwork & Resources

- Go to: http://www.cengagebrain.com
- Type: Rydberg
- Click Exploring InDesign CS6 in the list of search results.
- When the book's main page is displayed, click the Access button under Free Study Tools.
- To download files, select a chapter number and then click on the Artwork & Resources tab on the left navigation bar to download the files.

DESIGNING A CD COVER

Our next project will be the full-bleed CD cover, shown in Visual 7–25. It will require you to create guides, use text wrap, and work on different layers. You will also be introduced to two new features: *transparency* and *feathering*.

1. Create a new document, choosing *Compact Disc* from the *Page Size* presets list. *Margins: Top* and *Bottom* **0.25"**; *Left* and *Right* **0.125"**. Add a **0.125"** bleed on all sides. **Return.** Choose *Layout>Create Guides* and make two rows and two columns, both with a gutter width of **0** and select *Fit Guides to Margins.* Your file should look like Visual 7–26.

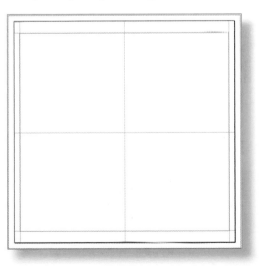

VISUAL | 7–26 |

The guides are set for the CD production. © Cengage Learning 2013

2. Rename Layer 1 to ***Guides.*** You will be able to toggle the guides off and on as desired. Create a new layer and name it ***Photo.*** Place the ***07 Convergence.psd*** image file found in the ***07 Artwork and Resources*** folder from the online companion resources. It should stretch from bleed to bleed.

3. Select the ***Polygon*** tool and click on the document. Enter **6** in ***Number of Sides*** and **0%** in ***Star Inset***. Resize the polygon so that it stretches to the margins (Visual 7–27). Select the ***Type*** tool and click in the polygon frame. Open the ***Text Frame Options*** dialog box, **Command+B** (Mac) or **Control+B** (Windows), and specify a two-column text frame, gutter **0.125"**.

VISUAL | 7–27 |

The hexagon stretches from margin to margin. It will be converted to a two-column text frame.

© 2004 Nichole Graham

▶ *production tip*

Text that is the color of the paper is called reverse type.

4. Fill the text frame with placeholder text and format it as **Myriad Pro Condensed 11/auto.** Color the text **[Paper]**. Text that is the color of the paper is called *reverse type*. Apply justified horizontal alignment, removing returns as needed to create even edges along the text frame and inside column guides (Visual 7–28).

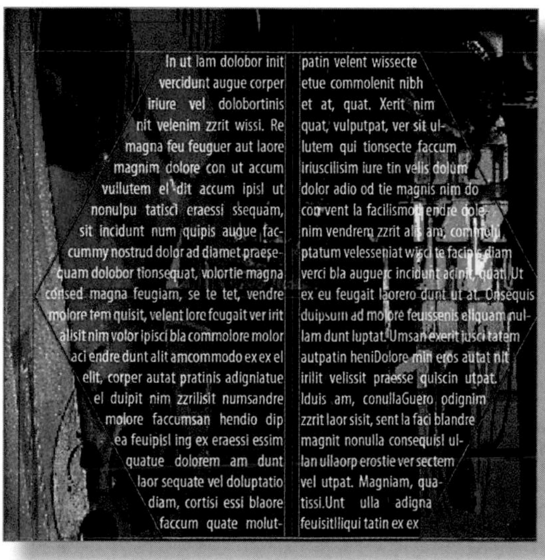

VISUAL | 7–28 |

Placeholder text has been added, justified, and colored Paper.

© 2004 Nichole Graham

5. Activate the hexagon text frame. Remove the stroke. Locate the ***Opacity*** field on the ***Control*** panel (Visual 7–29). Enter **50** into the ***Opacity*** field and press **Return**. This creates a transparent effect on the type in the hexagonal text frame. On this CD project, the placeholder text is used simply as additional texture. Because the transparent effect reduces the readability of text, you will always need to use this function carefully.

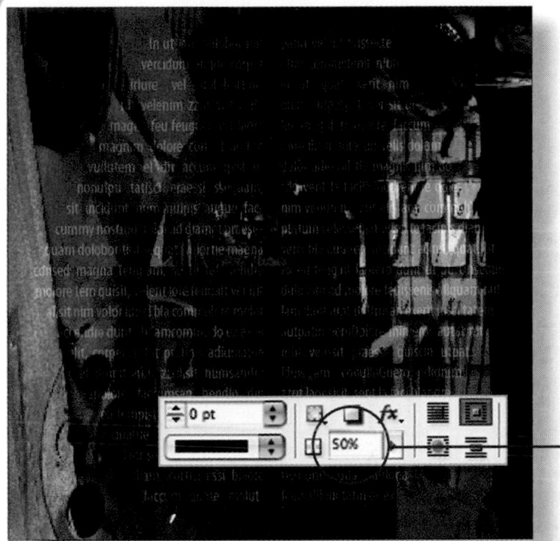

VISUAL |7–29|

Opacity (transparency) can be found on the Control panel or in the Effects panel.

6. Create a new layer and name it ***Title.*** Draw a text frame from the left to the right margin guides, ***H:*** **0.65"**. Position the frame against the top margin guide. In this frame, type ***Convergence***, **Minion Pro Regular 30/36**. Second line: ***Images and poetry by Nichole Graham***, **Minion Pro Regular, 14/18.8**. Align center and color **[Paper]**. Open the ***Text Wrap*** panel and select ***Wrap around bounding box.*** Specify a **0.125"** bottom offset. Although this text frame is on its own layer, it still affects the type on other layers. InDesign's text wrapping capability is layer independent.

7. Create a new layer and name it ***Circles.*** Select the ***Ellipse*** tool. Press **Shift+Option** (Mac) or **Shift+Alt** (Windows) and beginning on the center vertical guide, draw a **1"** circle in the upper half of the text area. The circle should not have a stroke or fill. Open the ***Text Wrap*** panel and select ***Wrap around object shape***, offset **0.0625"**. Since the object is a circle, only one offset field is active in the ***Text Wrap*** panel.

VISUAL |7–30|

Press Option (Mac) or Alt (Windows) to begin drawing a shape from the center point

8. Press **Shift+Option** (Mac) or **Shift+Alt** (Windows) and draw a **0.5"** circle at the bottom of the text with the bottom edge of the circle near the bottom margin. Fill the circle with **[Paper]**. In the

▸ *production tip*

When using transparency and other special effects, it is a good idea to view your artwork at high resolution. Choose View>Display Performance> High Quality Display.

Text Wrap panel, specify ***Wrap around object shape***, **0.0625"** offset. Choose ***Object>Effects>Basic Feather***. Enter **0.1"** in the ***Feather Width*** field, set the ***Corners*** option to ***Diffused*** and press **Return**. ***Feathering*** creates soft edges and is a nice design touch. Adjust the transparency of this object to **50%**. Choose ***View>Display Performance> High Quality Display*** to see a high-resolution view of the feathering and transparency effects that you have used (Visual 7–31).

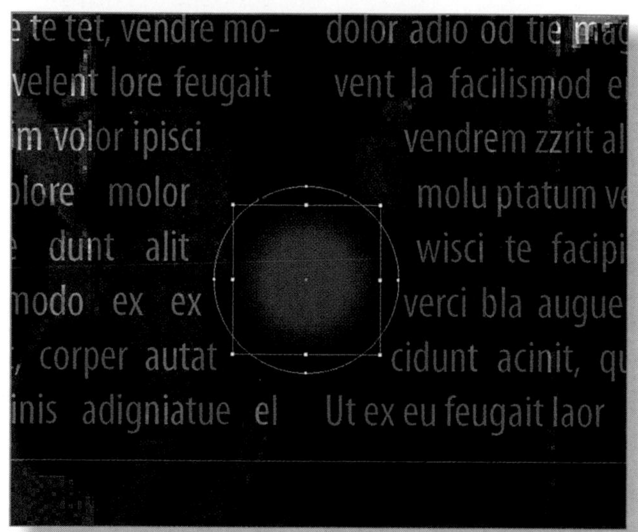

VISUAL |7–31|

Feathering adds transparency to the edges of an object, creating a softer edge.

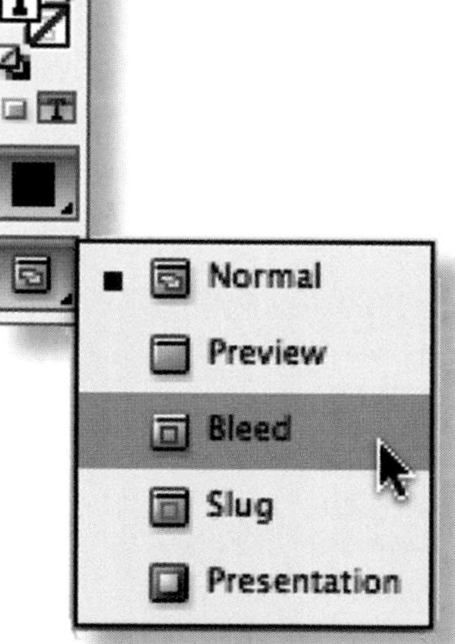

VISUAL |7–32|

The Preview mode can be accessed by typing W when you are not in the Type tool. All view modes can be selected from the bottom of the Tools panel.

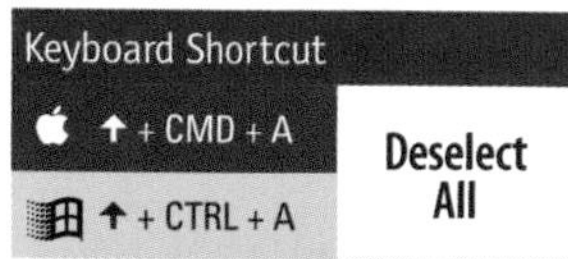

9. Deselect all. Select ***Bleed*** from the view options at the bottom of the ***Toolbox*** (Visual 7–32). In this mode you can see the **0.125"** bleed that extends from all four edges. Save and print your project. In the ***Print*** dialog box, choose the ***Setup*** page and select ***Centered*** in the ***Page Position*** field. ***Print two versions*** of the CD cover: In Version 1, deselect ***Use Document Bleed Settings*** on the ***Marks and Bleed*** page of the ***Print*** dialog box. Version 1 will show just the trim size. For Version 2, select ***Use Document Bleed Settings*** and specify ***All Printer's Marks.*** Compare the two prints, noticing that the bleed print has 2 sets of corner marks—an inner set to show the trim size, and an outer set to show the bleed size. Congratulations! You've finished this exercise.

▸ MOVING TOWARD MASTERY

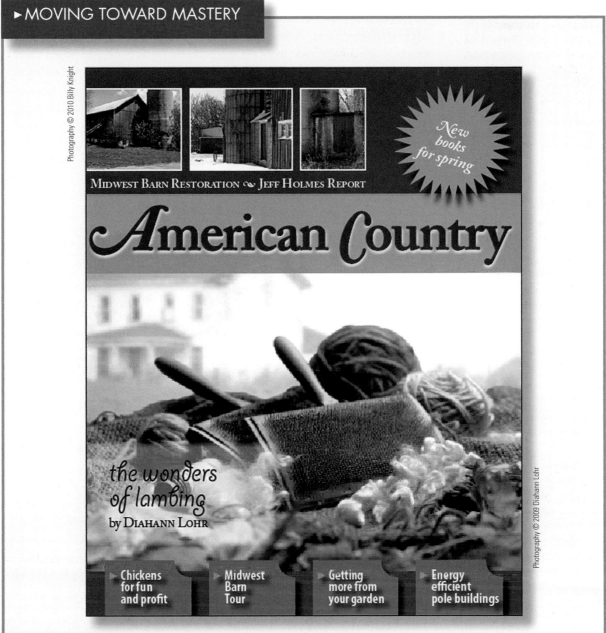

Photography © 2010 Billy Knight

New books for spring

MIDWEST BARN RESTORATION ∾ JEFF HOLMES REPORT

American Country

the wonders of lambing
by DIAHANN LOHR

▸ Chickens for fun and profit
▸ Midwest Barn Tour
▸ Getting more from your garden
▸ Energy efficient pole buildings

Photography © 2009 Diahann Lohr

▸ *Design a magazine cover*

This exercise will use transparency, feathering, drop shadow, type effects, layers, *Live Corner Effects* and the *Gap* tool. The project is already roughed out. You will add the final touches. One caveat—use effects sparingly. Using too many effects is like using too many typefaces and results in a layout that looks less than professional. When in doubt, don't add an effect!

EXPLORING INDESIGN CS6
Artwork & Resources

- Go to: http://www.cengagebrain.com
- Type: Rydberg
- Click Exploring InDesign CS6 in the list of search results.
- When the book's main page is displayed, click the Access button under Free Study Tools.
- To download files, select a chapter number and then click on the Artwork & Resources tab on the left navigation bar to download the files.

1. Open *07 American Country.indd*, found in the *07 Artwork and Resources* folder on the online companion resources. Press **F7** to open the *Layers* panel. There are four layers, with three hidden. First, look at the first layer, ***Photo and color bars.*** This locked layer contains the main image for the magazine. The image sits inside a container that is filled with the rust color. This is more efficient than creating separate colored rectangles and placing them on the top and bottom of the layout.

2. Click the eye to turn on the *Inset Photos* layer. We're going to use the three photos on the top of the page to learn about the *Gap* tool. The *Gap* tool provides a fast way to adjust the size of a gap between two or more items. Select the *Gap* tool and hover your mouse over the gap between the left and center barn inset shot. As you click and drag the *Gap* tool to the left and the right, the photos are resized and the gap remains the same size (Visual 7–33). Release the *Gap* tool and **Undo**.

VISUAL |7–33|

The Gap tool focuses on the space between images, and allows you to move that space and crop the images in one step.

Photography © 2010 Billy Knight

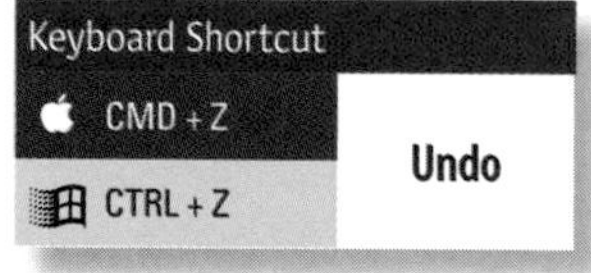

3. Select the *Gap* tool again. This time, hold down **Command** (Mac) or **Control** (Windows) as you drag the tool over the gap. You will see that the gap between the photos resizes, cropping the image (Visual 7–34). Release the *Gap* tool and **Undo**.

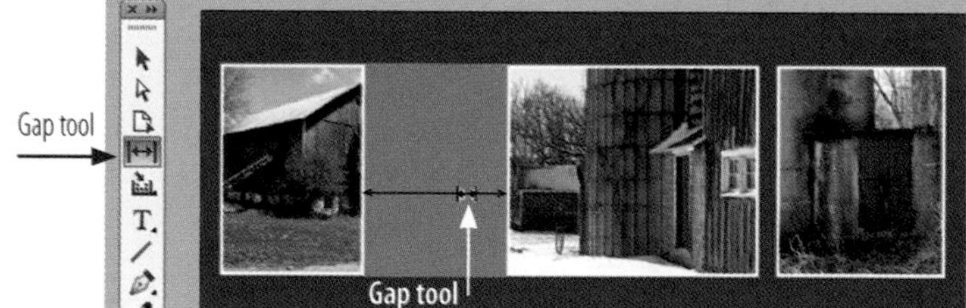

VISUAL |7–34|

Holding Command (Mac) or Control (Windows) while using the Gap tool will resize the gap.

Photography © 2010 Billy Knight

4. For the last experiment with the *Gap* tool, hold the **Option** (Mac) or **Alt** (Windows) key when using the *Gap* tool. Now the images move with the gap. Nothing is resized. (Visual 7–35). Release the *Gap* tool and **Undo**.

VISUAL |7–35|

Holding Option (Mac) or Alt (Windows) moves the images with the gap. Neither element is resized.

Photography © 2010 Billy Knight

5. Turn on the visibility of the *Nameplate* layer. Fill the type with **C29, M78, Y100, K26**. Add a **Black** stroke. Open the *Stroke* panel and change the weight to **0.5 pt**. Select the text frame with the *Selection* tool, and you're ready to add effects to the type.

THE EFFECTS PANEL

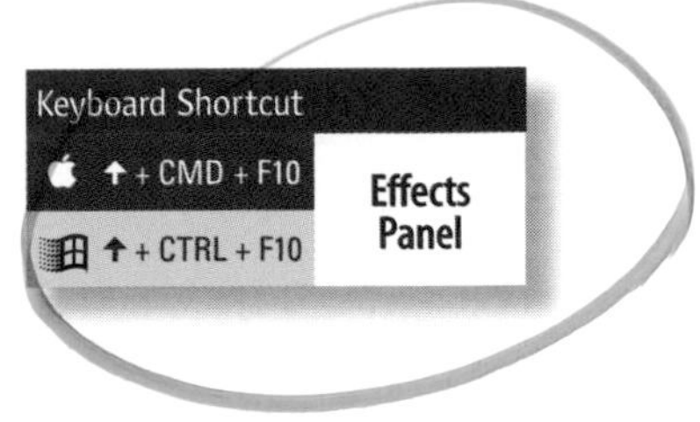

The Effects panel can be found on the *Control* panel or it can be opened by **Shift+Command+F10** (Mac) or **Shift+Control+F10** (Windows). When adding an effect, the first thing to decide is whether the effect will be on the type, the fill, the stroke, or the object. The object receiving the effect is called the *target*. Visual 7–36 shows the *Effects* controls accessed through the Control panel. The left control in the grouping, the *Apply Effect to* control, is your starting point. This drop down menu lets you select the target for the effect. Here's what happens when you select each one:

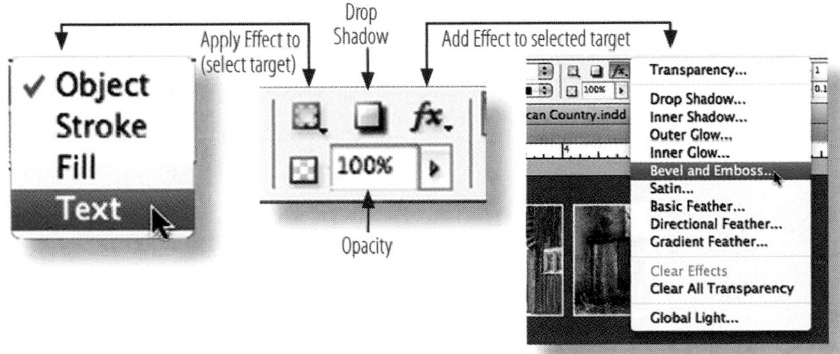

VISUAL | 7–36 |
Effects controls can be found in the Control panel. The first step is to select a target from the Apply Effect to drop down menu. Photography © 2010 Billy Knight

- ***Object***–*When you select object, the entire object—fill, stroke, and text—will have the special effect.*
- ***Graphic***–*When you select a graphic with the* ***Direct Selection*** *tool, the effect is only applied to the graphic inside the frame.*
- ***Stroke***–*When an effect is applied to a stroke, the gap color is also affected.*
- ***Fill***–*Only the fill is given an effect when this is selected.*
- ***Text***–*You can't apply an effect to individual words. When you select "Text," only the text inside the object—not the text frame—will be given an effect. Select the text frame with the* ***Selection*** *tool.*

Below the *Apply Effect to* control is the *Opacity* control. This is a simple slider that makes an item transparent, ranging from 0% (invisible) to 100% (opaque). A transparency is not the same as a tint. A tinted box and a transparent box might look the same. But when placed on top of another object, the tinted box is still opaque, while the transparent box allows background images to be seen.

> ***production tip***
>
> A transparency is not the same as a tint. A tinted box and a transparent box might look the same. When placed on top of another object, the tinted box is still opaque, while the transparent box allows background images to be seen.

The *Drop Shadow* button (Visual 7–36) adds the default drop shadow to the selected object, fill, text, or stroke. The default opacity of the drop shadow is 75%, which is too dark for many applications. When that is the case, you will click

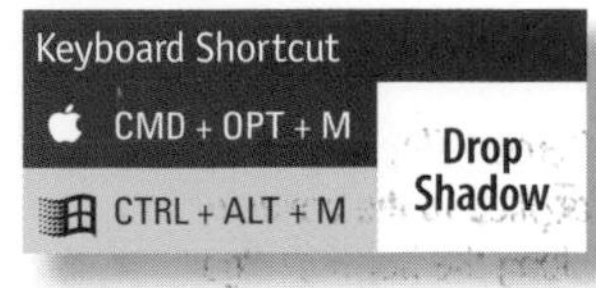

the *fx* button to open the drop down menu, select **Drop Shadow,** and change the opacity in the dialog box. You can also open the *Effects* panel by using the keyboard shortcuts or go to **Window>Effects** (Visual 7–37). Always select the effect's target first, then select the effect. Now let's go back to our magazine cover project and add some effects to the nameplate.

VISUAL | 7–37 |

The Effects panel opened using keyboard shortcuts Shift+Cmd+F10 (Mac) or Shift+Ctrl+F10 (Windows).

▸ *production tip*

The 75% opacity default setting for the Drop Shadow effect is too dark for many applications. 35% is a good starting point.

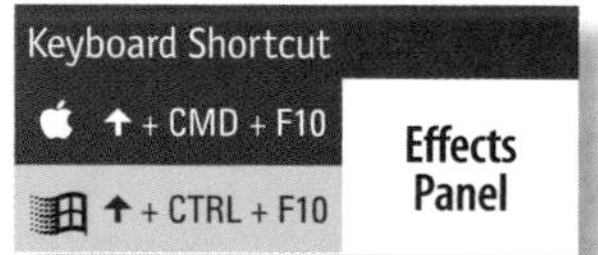

6. Select the nameplate with the ***Selection*** tool. From the ***Control*** panel, select the target ***Text*** from the drop down menu under the ***Apply Effect to*** icon. Choose ***Bevel and Emboss*** under the *fx* icon on the ***Control*** panel. When the window opens, notice that ***Text*** appears in the ***Settings for*** field in the upper left corner. This means the effect will only apply to the text. Experiment with various effects listed in the left pane by clicking in the box next to the name to turn on the effect and open the dialog. Apply different effects settings, clicking ***Preview*** to see how each variation looks. When you're done experimenting, uncheck all the effects in the left pane, except for ***Bevel and Emboss.*** Enter the values shown in Visual 7–38 in the ***Bevel and Emboss*** dialog box to achieve the effect shown in the magazine cover example.

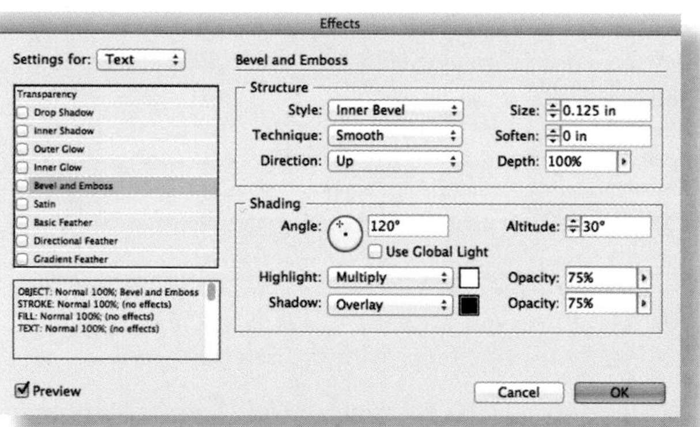

VISUAL | 7–38 |

Enter these values in the Bevel and Emboss fields.

7. Go to the ***Layers*** panel and make the ***Copy*** layer visible. Select the starburst in the upper right corner. Rotate it **-16°** around the center reference point and use the icons in the ***Control*** panel to add a drop shadow.

8. Select the white box that says, ***the wonders of lambing***. The background needs to be made transparent, and a feather added to the edges. Choose ***Fill*** from the ***Apply Effect to*** icon on the ***Control*** panel. Then reduce the transparency to **60%**. Select ***Basic Feather*** under the *fx* icon, and accept the default values.

LIVE CORNER EFFECTS

The last effect we will use is *Live Corner Effects*. This feature allows you to add different corner options to individual corners of a frame (Visual 7–39). Open the *Corner Options* dialog by pressing **Option** (Mac) or **Alt** (Windows) and clicking on the icon in the *Control* panel. The *Corner Options* dialog shows a proxy which represents each corner of a frame. In this case, we want an inverted curve in the upper-right corner of each text frame, along the bottom of the magazine cover. This step will add the finishing touch to our magazine cover.

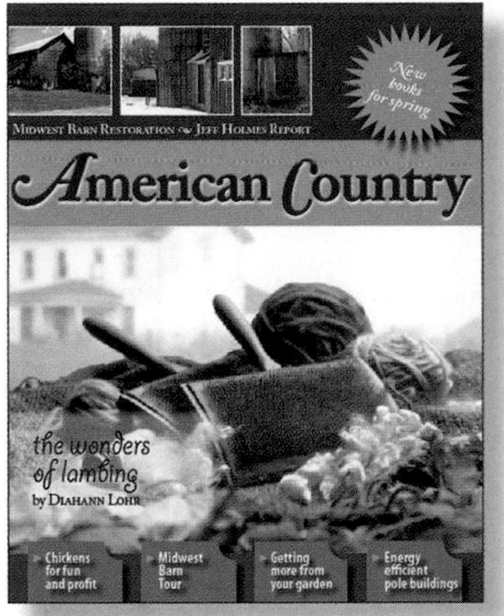

VISUAL | 7–39 |

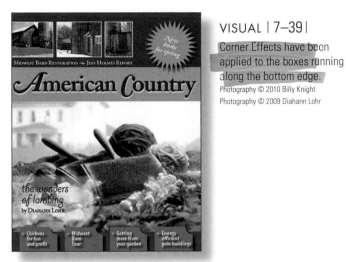

Corner Effects have been applied to the boxes running along the bottom edge.

Photography © 2010 Billy Knight
Photography © 2009 Diahann Lohr

1. First, **Shift+click** to select the four green boxes on the bottom of the magazine cover. Then, open the *Corner Options* dialog box by pressing **Option** (Mac) or **Alt** (Windows) and clicking on the *Corner Options* icon in the *Control* panel.

2. Deselect the *Make all settings the same* link in the middle of the dialog box (Visual 7–40). Then, find the proxy with a tiny blue box in upper right corner. From the pull down menu, choose *Inverse Rounded* and enter the value of **.3125"**. Your magazine cover is complete!

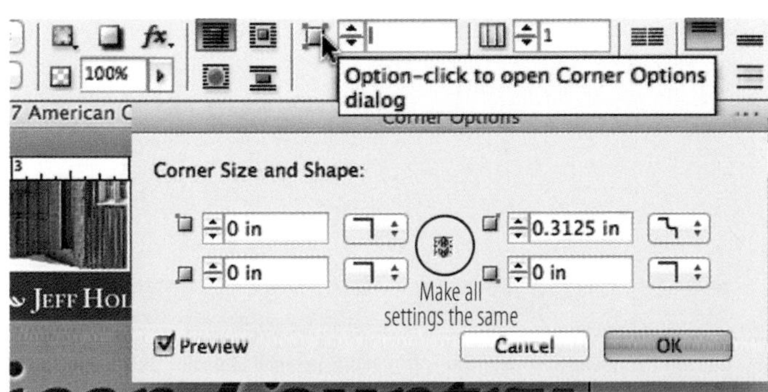

VISUAL | 7–40 |

The tiny blue square in each corner of the proxy identifies the target corner for the effect.

Photography © 2010 Billy Knight

Summary

You are well on your way to being comfortable with the expansive and powerful features of InDesign. With each chapter you have methodically added skill “layers” to your repertoire. Those projects that seemed so difficult in the early chapters should now be quite easy! In this chapter you created and manipulated document layers. You also were introduced to OpenType, text wrap, effects and live corner options, and you created three great projects. Congratulations on all you have achieved!

► IN REVIEW

1. How can you change the color of selection marks on a layer?
2. What is the keyboard shortcut to open the Text Wrap panel?
3. When creating a new layer, what key do you press when clicking the Create new layer icon to bring up the New Layer dialog box used to specify the layer name and other options?
4. How do you view a higher-resolution image of your document on your monitor screen?
5. How do you make text flow inside an object?
6. What is the process for ignoring text wrap for text frames?
7. What is the process for opening the Corner Effects dialog from the Control panel?
8. Although they may look identical, how is a red, transparent box different from a red, tinted box?
9. What is the first step you need to take whenever you are applying an effect?
10. Which drop shadow default setting do you usually need to adjust?

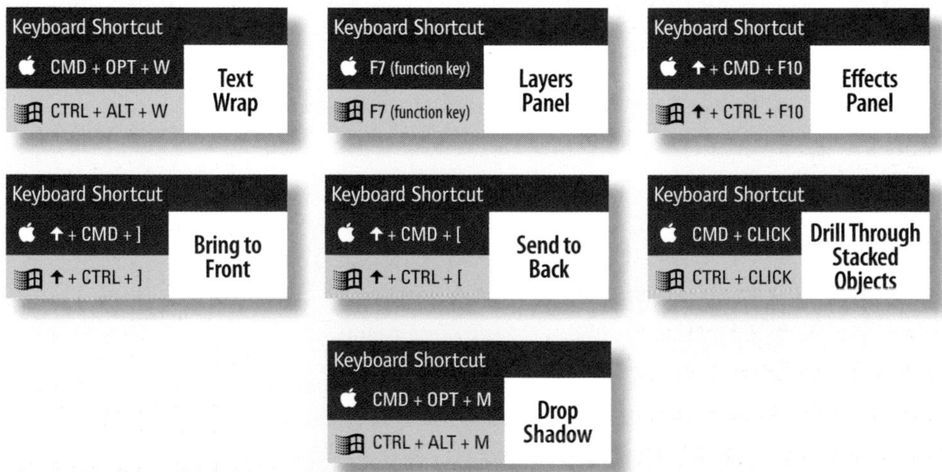

Keyboard Shortcut
CMD + OPT + W
CTRL + ALT + W
Text Wrap
Keyboard Shortcut
F7 (function key)
F7 (function key)
Layers Panel
Keyboard Shortcut
↑ + CMD + F10
↑ + CTRL + F10
Effects Panel
Keyboard Shortcut
↑ + CMD +]
↑ + CTRL +]
Bring to Front
Keyboard Shortcut
↑ + CMD + [
↑ + CTRL + [
Send to Back
Keyboard Shortcut
CMD + CLICK
CTRL + CLICK
Drill Through Stacked Objects
Keyboard Shortcut
CMD + OPT + M
CTRL + ALT + M
Drop Shadow

▸ CHAPTER 7 PROJECTS

Hooks & Ladders
Volunteer Fire Department
Student Essay Contest
As they meet their field of honor, our fierce fighters face the fiery flames. They persevere until the final moment.
What does courage mean to you? Write about it in 200 words or less. Winners will receive a $100 savings bond and tickets to this year's Firefighters' Dance.
Support the people who work hard to keep you safe. Contest is open to area students ages 10–18. Essays must be typed and delivered to City Hall by May 18, 4:00 PM.
FIRE DEPARTMENT VOLUNTEER
FIREFIGHTER
Hooks & Ladders
AN INVITATION TO THE DANCE…
Hooks & Ladders
ANNUAL RAFFLE
Lic. 234567
Name
Address
City
State
Zip
Phone

Photography © 2004 Katie Hopkins, Waukesha County Technical College.

Four assignments are included in the *07 Artwork and Resources* folder on the online companion resources. The first three projects (shown above) are pieces promoting the annual fund raising events for a volunteer fire department. They will look great printed in color and will be nice additions to your collection of work. The last project is a fun exercise in formatting tables—no typing required!

EXPLORING INDESIGN CS6
Artwork & Resources

- Go to: http://www.cengagebrain.com
- Type: Rydberg
- Click Exploring InDesign CS6 in the list of search results.
- When the book's main page is displayed, click the Access button under Free Study Tools.
- To download files, select a chapter number and then click on the Artwork & Resources tab on the left navigation bar to download the files.

Go confidently in the direction of your dreams.
Live the life you have imagined.

— Henry David Thoreau

Type Continuity: Applying Styles

objectives

- *Properly prepare text files for placing in InDesign documents*
- *Use the Pages panel*
- *Use the Eyedropper tool to transfer attributes*
- *Create paragraph and character styles*
- *Place Snippets*

introduction

It's amazing how often we make extra work for ourselves before we wise up. Years ago, we hung a small bell by our door and trained our dog to ring it each time he needed to go outside. The method was successful—at first. But it didn't take him long to realize that whenever he rang the bell we came running. He began to ring it whenever he was bored, lonesome, hungry, or just wanted to go out and play. It was hard to tell who was better trained—the dog or the dog owners. After the hundredth trip going back and forth to the door, we knew we needed to take control of the situation, and the bell came down.

When you are typesetting a project and it dawns on you that you're repeating the same actions over and over, it's time to look for a way to reduce your workload and take control. That's what this chapter is all about. You will use paragraph and character styles to automate your text formatting, speed up production, and bring typographic consistency to your documents. After reading this chapter, you will wonder how you ever got along without them!

creating a newsletter

In this lesson, you will create a four-page newsletter for a veterinary service. The veterinarian, Dr. John Hallett, has supplied you with copy and photos. Visual 8–1 shows the finished newsletter, created in facing pages and printed on 11" × 17" paper. The newsletter is printed back-to-back and folded, making a total of four pages. A PDF file is also included in the *08 Artwork and Resources* folder on the online companion resources. You may want to print this newsletter sample and use it as a reference, as you work through the chapter.

EXPLORING INDESIGN CS6
Artwork & Resources

- Go to: http://www.cengagebrain.com
- Type: Rydberg
- Click Exploring InDesign CS6 in the list of search results.
- When the book's main page is displayed, click the Access button under Free Study Tools.
- To download files, select a chapter number and then click on the Artwork & Resources tab on the left navigation bar to download the files.

Back Cover (Page 4) Front Cover (Page 1)

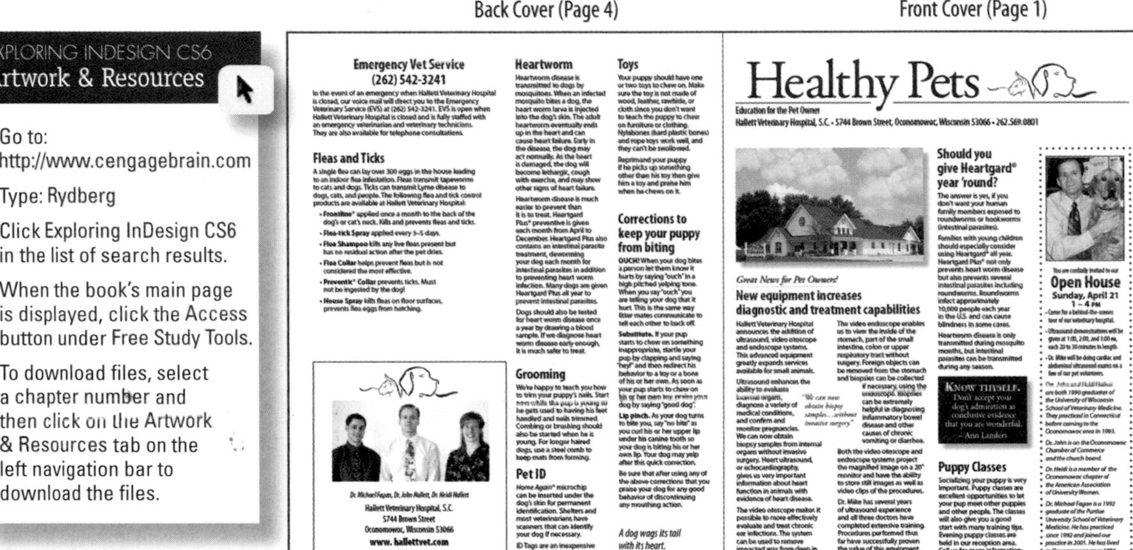

Emergency Vet Service
(262) 542-3241

Fleas and Ticks

Heartworm

Grooming

Pet ID

Toys

Corrections to keep your puppy from biting

Healthy Pets

Education for the Pet Owner

Should you give Heartgard® year 'round?

Open House

New equipment increases diagnostic and treatment capabilities

Puppy Classes

(262) 569-0801

Get your puppy off to a good start!

This Issue's Health Focus

Vaccines: critical to your dog's health

Feeding

Crate Training

House Training

Intestinal Parasites

Dental Care

Spay or Neuter Your Pet

Page 2 Page 3

VISUAL |8–1|

The four-page newsletter.

This single project will introduce you to the *Pages* panel, and will make use of *Snippets*. The copy has been prepared for you—your job is to place it and format it. As you build the newsletter, you will create typographic consistency from page to page, by using the *Eyedropper* tool, and creating paragraph and character styles, using the following techniques:

- *Creating styles from sample text*
- *Transferring styles from another InDesign document*
- *Creating styles based on other styles*
- *Creating a new style*
- *Duplicating existing styles*
- *Bringing in styles with a new element*
- *Creating character styles*
- *Redefining styles*

ABOUT FACING PAGES

Until now, we have worked on single-page documents. But many—probably most—of your projects will have multiple left and right pages printed back-to-back. These publications are set up using the *Facing Pages* option in the *New Document* dialog box. When a document is created as facing pages, the *Left* and *Right* margin fields change to *Inside* and *Outside* margins. When more than one page butts up to another, it is called a *spread*. Odd-numbered pages are always right-hand (*recto*) pages, and even-numbered pages are always left-hand (*verso*) pages.

Take a single piece of paper and fold it from side to side. Hold the paper so the fold is on the left and it opens like a booklet. The fold of your booklet is the *spine*. The cover of your booklet is page 1, a right-hand page. Open the booklet and you will see a spread made up of pages 2 and 3. The back cover is page 4, a left-hand page. So, a four-page, 8½" × 11" newsletter, printed two-sided on one, 11" × 17" sheet, consists of two spreads, or four 8½" × 11" facing pages.

▸ MOVING TOWARD MASTERY

preparing copy

WHEN CLIENTS PROVIDE COPY

When a client is going to supply the copy in electronic format, you should discuss exactly how the copy will be prepared. Here are some text file considerations worth discussing with your clients:

- *Save each article as a separate file and name each file by its headline.*
- *Place only one space between sentences. Double spaces need to be manually removed during typesetting.*
- *Place only one return between paragraphs. Extra returns must be manually removed during the typesetting process.*
- *Press the **Tab** key only once when typing tabular copy (don't keep pressing the **Tab** key until the copy lines up). Let the typesetter set the tab stops to align the copy.*
- *Don't press the **Tab** key to create a first line indent on a new paragraph. A first line indent will be created during typesetting.*
- *Don't type anything in all capital letters. Emphasis will be added by using bold or italic, during the typesetting process.*

BECOME INDISPENSABLE!

Your extra effort will earn you the loyalty of the your customers. Take the time to double check times, dates, phone numbers, the correct spelling of names, and web addresses contained in customer-supplied copy. Finding a single error will create a greater chance of repeat business.

▸ MOVING TOWARD MASTERY

anatomy of a publication

Inexperienced designers tend to put all their effort into one part of a publication, for instance, the front cover. Then, they sometimes skim over other parts of a publication that seem "unimportant." Experienced designers know that design subtleties take a publication from mediocre, to outstanding. There are no "throwaway" parts of any project. A well-designed footer is as important as a headline.

These sample magazine pages, designed by student Andrea Peaslee, showcase carefully crafted type and design elements. Refer to them as you read the definitions.

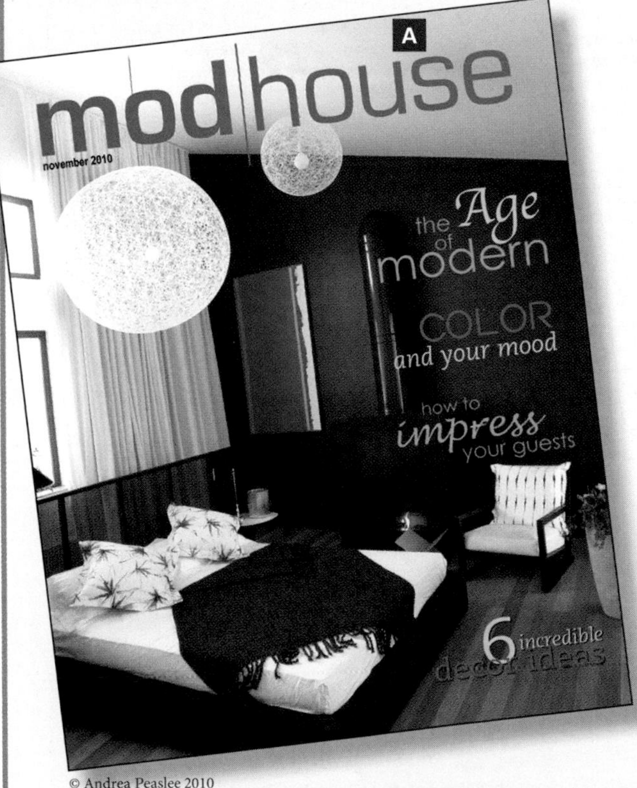

A ***Nameplate:*** *The logotype that appears at the top of a publication. Also called "banner" or "flag."*

B ***Standing head:*** *A section of a publication that repeats from issue to issue.*

C ***Kicker:*** *Also called "eyebrow." Appears above a headline and is designed to kick some interest into a headline.*

D ***End sign:*** *A glyph that indicates the end of an article.*

E ***Folio:*** *Another name for page number.*

F ***Footer:*** *An informational element on the bottom of the page that repeats from page to page. Usually includes the folio.*

G ***Header:*** *A section divider. This header could also be considered a standing head.*

H ***Drop cap:*** *A nice way to set off a paragraph. Use sparingly, only at beginning of articles—only one per page.*

I ***Pull quote:*** *A section of body copy that has been designed to stand out—this increases interest and readership.*

J ***Table:*** *Charts and tables should be carefully designed to blend with the rest of the content.*

K ***Recto page footer:*** *Recto means "right." "E" shows the verso, or left page footer.*

L ***Run-in head:*** *An interesting and space-efficient way to set off a paragraph!*

M ***Floating rule:*** *A vertical rule betwen columns. Usually no heavier than 0.5 pt.*

N ***Subhead:*** *A section divider within an article. Notice how it's visually connected to the paragraph below it.*

O ***Jump line:*** *Directs reader to where the article continues.*

P ***Cont line:*** *(Continuation line) Tells reader where article came from.*

Q ***Caption:*** *Don't forget photo captions. Captions are read more than articles!*

R ***Byline:*** *The author of an article.*

▸ MOVING TOWARD MASTERY

design | entertaining B

impress your guests C

how to work with what you have

If you are one of the many people who cannot visualize an impressive space without spending large amounts of money on new items, then the following tips might be for you. Having a beautiful space has so much more to do with accessorizing and placement than anything else. Impressing your guests doesn't have to be about "one-upping" your friends with the newest and coolest. You can be smart (and maybe step outside of the box once in a while) with the items you already have. You can do all of this by keeping in mind a few ground rules of decorating.

An impressive space is one that is both visually pleasing AND functional. Functionality is usually given a bad name. Without a functional, easy flowing space you have bad design. Most people don't know how to pin-point what it is that makes a room unpleasant, but most of the time it's because the space planning is all wrong. Keep in mind that furniture should be placed in a practical placement within the room. Placing furniture in groupings is best. Leaving a minimum space of 4" from the wall and furniture is a must. Overcrowding furniture is a big "no-no" in decorating. If your coffee table is most often used as a desk or tasking area; move it at least a couple of feet from the edge of seat cushion to allow proper floor and walking space while entertaining.

Reassess your artwork and accessory placement. The center of your wall art should be no higher than 60" high. Most people place artwork too high. An easy, and eye-pleasing solution is to lower that art! You'll be surprised how much more aesthetically pleasing it will look. Grouping accessories in threes is one of the easiest solutions to decorating. Grouping items in threes is a fundamental rule in decorating. Minimizing accessories and differentiating sizes is a great way to use what you have to create an impressive space, as well.

Following these easy pointers will assure an impressive space to wow your guests. So, next time you feel overwhelmed and are ready to head to your local department store just remember you can do a lot with what you have. And you don't even have to get out of your pajamas to do it. ■ D

Adding simple accents like throw pillows creates interest and gives visual impact.

Display art at the proper height to create a sense of balance.

6 incredible design ideas

by Andrea Peaslee

- Create texture with foliage
- Use books for accessories
- Make textiles your room barriers
- Paint your old picture frames
- Use lighting as a design element
- Use rugs as art for the floor

E

4 november 2010 mod|house F

▸MOVING TOWARD MASTERY

G **design** | in the now

the age of modern

by Andrea Peaslee

H Modernism in interiors isn't singly based on the clean, streamlined interiors you see in many homes and office spaces today. Modern interior spaces began as early as the 1920s, during the Bauhaus movement in Germany. The Bauhaus philosophy followed the theory that form should combine with function in all interior designs, and through this approach a modern aesthetic was created. The Bauhaus idea of functionality meant simplified spaces, streamlined furniture and new building materials such as steel and glass in interiors.

Although modernity in interiors stood fairly consistent through the times; it has gone through some distinct periods of alteration. Take the 1950s, the design of interior spaces and furniture was a new concern for the individual. Soon after the war people finally had the funds to embellish their interiors and felt that this was a new sense of self-exploration and status. New materials such as plastic were starting to be used in interior spaces, and color was bright and bold. Design was linear and simplistic with much of the accessories embracing the shape of star bursts and boomerangs.

Interiors of the 1970s consisted of often renovated spaces due to the economical slowdown of this time. People sought to create community by taking away interior walls which were seen as rigid space dividers. The space age interiors of the earlier decades gave way to the textures of shag pile carpets, cork tiles, wood paneling and olive-tone textiles. Brown, cream and orange, vinyl wallpapers in large overall patterns were the norm in many homes of suburbia. Reclaimed furniture and building materials were used often as the focus was mainly on preservation.

I

> “*Space isn't considered as empty but rather as an important element.*”

The modern interiors of the 2000s are derivatives of the previous decades. In today's spaces you will find many of the motives of the 50s such as stylized florals, starbursts and birds. Color is reminiscent of the 70s with a focus on neutrals and earth-tones. Silhouetted and abstracted nature motifs with little ornamentation are abundant. Building materials seen in modern day interiors include cork, wood flooring and other sustainable products. Much of the inspiration for the new modern interior design style is from the uncluttered, geometric architectural features of Japanese design. In Japanese design, space isn't considered as empty but rather as an important element. As the age of modern design goes through time this basis of modern is always echoed; form follows function. And through functionality you have simplicity. ■

J modernity in time

1950	1970	2010
star bursts	boomerangs	stylized motifs
bright colors	earth-tones	neutrals
steel & glass materials	reclaimed materials	sustainable materials

Linda Falkenstein. "Interior design in the 2000s picks from the best of modernism." www.isthmus.com Friday 04/03/2009

K november 2010 mod|house 5

▸ MOVING TOWARD MASTERY

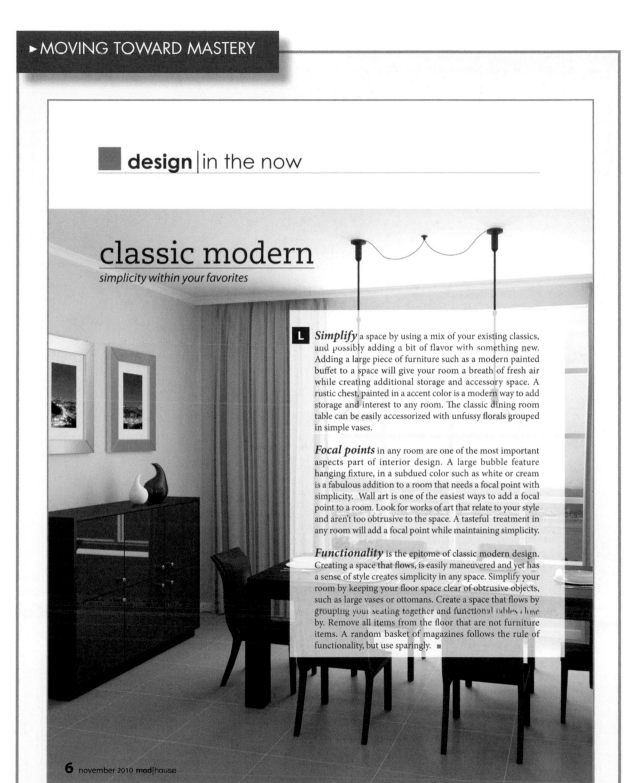

design | in the now

classic modern

simplicity within your favorites

L ***Simplify*** a space by using a mix of your existing classics, and possibly adding a bit of flavor with something new. Adding a large piece of furniture such as a modern painted buffet to a space will give your room a breath of fresh air while creating additional storage and accessory space. A rustic chest, painted in a accent color is a modern way to add storage and interest to any room. The classic dining room table can be easily accessorized with unfussy florals grouped in simple vases.

Focal points in any room are one of the most important aspects part of interior design. A large bubble feature hanging fixture, in a subdued color such as white or cream is a fabulous addition to a room that needs a focal point with simplicity. Wall art is one of the easiest ways to add a focal point to a room. Look for works of art that relate to your style and aren't too obtrusive to the space. A tasteful treatment in any room will add a focal point while maintaining simplicity.

Functionality is the epitome of classic modern design. Creating a space that flows, is easily maneuvered and yet has a sense of style creates simplicity in any space. Simplify your room by keeping your floor space clear of obtrusive objects, such as large vases or ottomans. Create a space that flows by grouping your seating together and functional tables close by. Remove all items from the floor that are not furniture items. A random basket of magazines follows the rule of functionality, but use sparingly. ■

6 november 2010 mod|house

► MOVING TOWARD MASTERY

design | in the now

COLOR & your mood

Color psychology is the study of the effect that colors have on our moods, behaviors and feelings. Color psychology is a new field of psychology, whose science is not widely accepted by the mainstream. It's use is found primarily in interior decorating and marketing. Individual colors evoke negative or positive feelings which are used to promote products or create a desired atmosphere inside of a home or business.

Green is the color of wealth, money, growth, nature, peace and can have a calming effect on people. Negative associations of green include envy and illness. The color blue arouses thoughts of the sky and the ocean, which are tranquil and peaceful. Marketers and decorators use a lot of blue because of its tranquil properties and also, darker shades of blue, which display a sense of loyalty. Purples have a reputation of stimulating creativity, imagination, spirituality and compassion. Shades of purple are also used to counter emotional shock and disturbance. Most often purple is a symbol of royalty and sophistication.

Red can actually increase a person's heart rate and adrenaline production in the body because it is such an extreme color. It is also the color of love, fire, energy, passion, anger. Orange is the color associated with all things happy, fun and flamboyant. The color is used to inspire trust, warmth and happiness and it has no negative connotations. Similar to orange, yellow inspires feelings of happiness because the color is associated with sunshine and optimism. Serotonin levels increase in the brain after a person has seen yellow. Some basic palettes seen in many interiors include cool, warm and neutral color palettes.

N

cool palette

Blue, green, and violet are considered colors within the cool palette. Cool colors tend to have a calming effect. In some spectrums they can be interpreted as cold, clinical and impersonal. There are many cultural influences to color, as well. In the Unites States white is a common color for weddings. In Eastern cultures white is the color for mourning. In nature blue is the color of water and green is of plant life. Combining

O *continued on page 8*

Emphasizing...
Organic production and Direct marketing

Intensive three-day school demonstrates what it takes to set up and run a successful market garden or small farm. Topics include:

M

- *soil fertility and crop rotations*
- *greenhouses*
- *pest management*
- *tools and equipment*
- *post-harvest handling*
- USDA *updates and regulations*
- *marketing...and more!*

▸ MOVING TOWARD MASTERY

design | in the now

P

continued from page 7

blues and greens will give a natural feel to a space. Because these colors have a tendency to feel like they are receding (or backing away from you), cool tones are often used to paint the walls of a small room to make the room appear larger. To give an all blue palette some warmth, use deeper blues with accents of purple.

warm palette

Warm colors convey emotions from simple optimism to strong violence. The neutrals of black and brown also carry warm attributes. The colors of red, orange, and yellow are considered warm colors. These hues are also said to advance, meaning they appear to come forward, making the walls feel closer. Thus, they can actually make a room feel cozy when used in decorating. As mentioned earlier, warm colors can be extremely stimulating, so be mindful of this when painting children's rooms or office spaces. To tone down the strong emotions tied to warm colors use a lighter shade such as pinks, pales yellows, and peach or other neutral hues.

neutral palette

The neutral colors of black, white, silver, gray, and brown make good backgrounds and unify diverse color palettes. They often stand alone as the only or primary focus of a design. Neutral colors help to put the focus on other colors or serve to tone down colors that might otherwise be overpowering on their own. ■

Novelty, dynamism and bright colors exemplify the avant-garde style. Q

AVANT-GARDE

in today's interior spaces

by Andrea Peaslee R

Avant-garde represents the pushing of boundaries of what is accepted as the norm. Color and shape are the main elements, usually as a form of contrast. There are no rules, stressing the independence and freedom of the owner. This style embodies bright, clean colors like white, black, red, yellow, and green. The use of contrasting colors adds to the interior with expression and dynamics. This method of contrast is also used in the design of walls. For instance, one wall can be framed in a completely different color or a wall in one color, and the second would be colored in another. This style can use many materials, but advanced building materials designed that introduce novelty and dynamism are what exemplify the avant-garde style. The main element in this style is the desire and ability to experiment with new styles and creating a look that's outside of the "norm". ■

INTRODUCING THE PAGES PANEL

Create a new document with facing pages selected. We'll use this document to learn about the *Pages* panel. Open the *Pages* panel by pressing **Command+F12** (Mac) or **F12** (Windows), or by choosing *Menu>Window>Pages*. Notice that the *Pages* panel is divided into two sections by a separator that can be dragged up and down like a window shade. The top section of the panel is the *master*, or *global* level. The pages at this level are called *Masters* and the settings and options you apply to them affect the whole document. The top, single master page is named *[None]*. The two-page spread below it is named *A-Master*. The *A-Master* spread consists of a left-hand and a right-hand facing page. When you are working with facing pages, the pages are displayed differently than non-facing pages. The lower section of the *Pages* panel is the local level. Each page or spread is butted up to a vertical line representing the spine of the publication. Odd-numbered pages are always to the right of the spine, and even-numbered pages are always to the left of the spine.

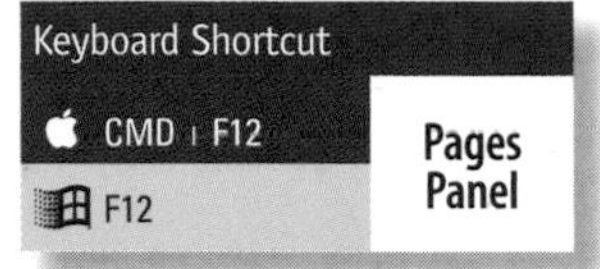

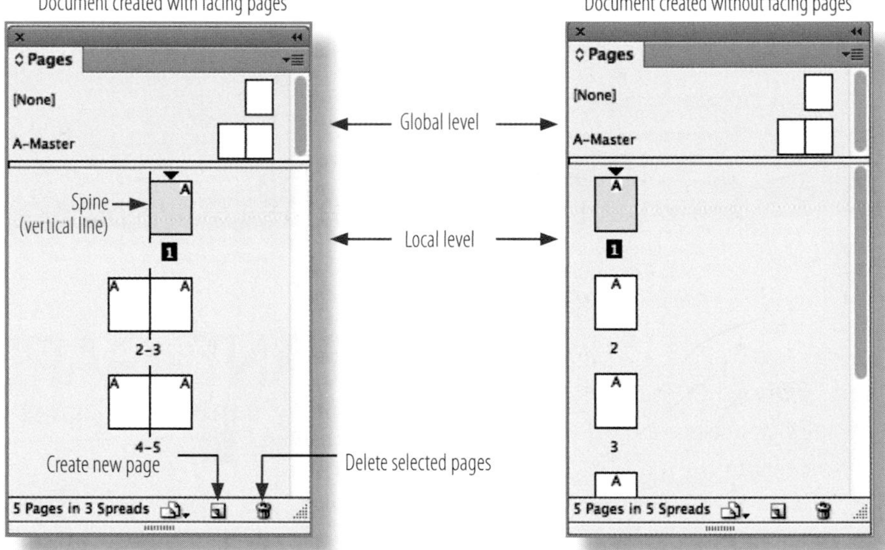

VISUAL |8–2|

A document created with facing pages shows pages aligned to a vertical line which represents the spine, or binding edge.

© Cengage Learning 2013

At the bottom of the *Pages* panel is the *Create new page* icon. Click to add one new page at a time to the end of the document. Use **Option+click** (Mac) or **Alt+click** (Windows) to open the *Insert Pages* dialog box with more page options, such as how many new pages to create, where to place them in the document, and what master page should be applied. In the lower right corner is the *Delete selected pages* icon. Delete a page by dragging it to the can or by selecting it and clicking the can. Add and delete a few pages to your document to see how this works, but be sure to end up with 4 pages. Notice that the document's interior pages are displayed in spreads.

You can move from page to page in your document by double-clicking on each page icon in the *Pages* panel. To select a whole spread, double-click on the numbers below the spread. When you're working in facing pages, you will want to view entire spreads. Press **Command+Option+0** (Mac) or **Control+Alt+0** (Windows) to fit the spread in your window. Click on the panel menu at the top right, to view a menu of additional options. If you choose *Panel Options*, which opens the *Panel Options* dialog box, you can adjust the panel display by checking the *Show Vertically* box and choosing what size the page icons should be. Visual 8–3 shows the panel displaying pages with extra large page icons. Experiment with these options and adjust the panel to suit your preferences. Close your document.

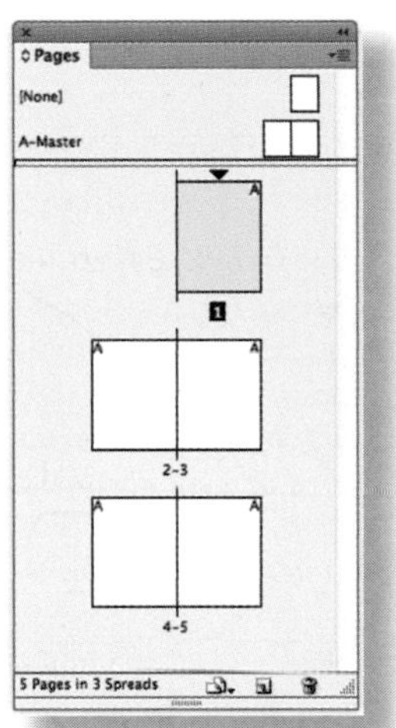

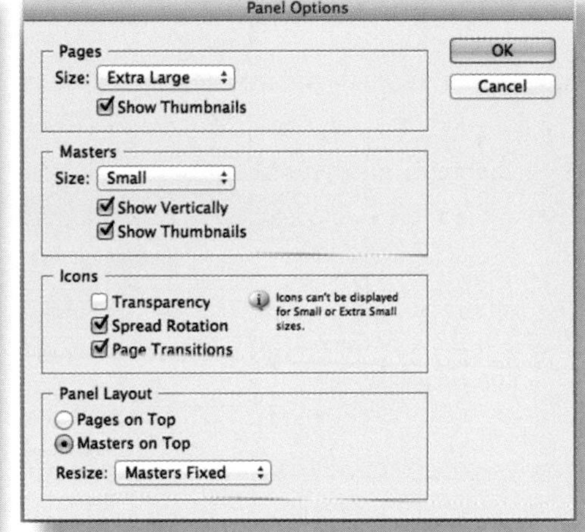

VISUAL |8–3|

Panel Options lets you choose the view that works best for you.

▸ *Begin a document with a spread*

If you look at the *Pages* panel, you will see that page one is a recto page, and is followed by a spread, and a verso fourth page. By default, a new document starts with page 1, a single, recto page. Because our four-page newsletter only needs the two spreads, we are going to do a work-around and create a document that begins with a spread instead of a single page.

1. Create a new document. Choose **Letter-size**. *Number of pages:* **4**; *Facing Pages:* **On**; *Columns:* **4**; *Gutter Width:* **0.1875"** *Top, Bottom,* and *Outside margins:* **0.5"**; *Inside margin:* **0.25"**.
2. Open the *Pages* menu and deselect *Allow Document Pages to Shuffle* (Visual 8–4).

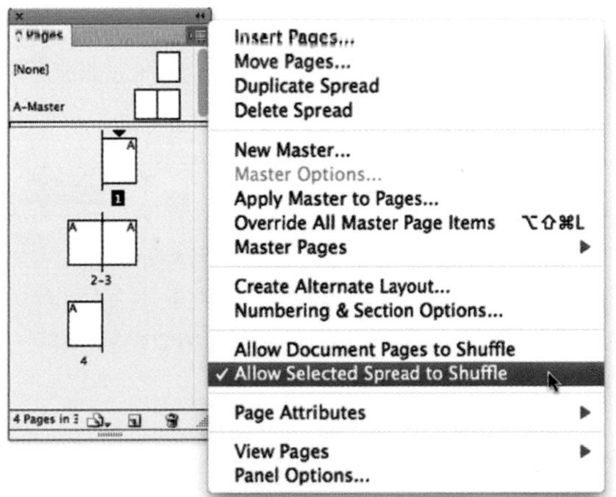

VISUAL |8–4|

Deselect Allow Document Pages to Shuffle to begin your document with a spread.

3. Select ***Page 4*** by clicking on it. Drag it up to the left of Page 1. When you see a fist, the arrow pointing left, and a bracket, you can release the mouse (Visual 8–5).

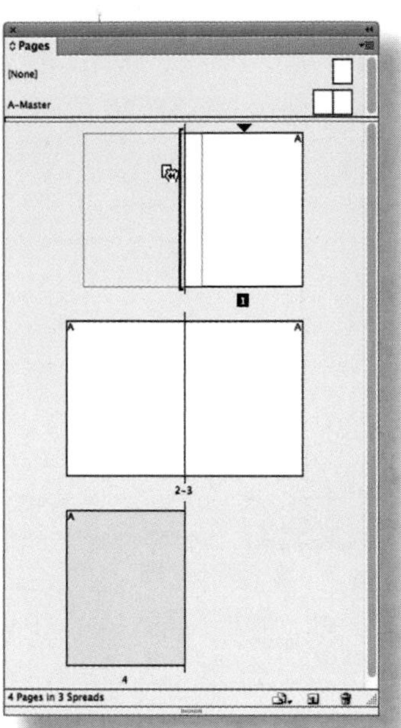

VISUAL |8–5|

Carefully pull Page 4 to the left of Page 1. When you see the fist, bracket, and arrow pointing to the left, it means the page will be inserted before Page 1.

4. Now your document should consist of two spreads. This will make printing the newsletter much easier, but now the physical page numbers do not correspond to the pages of the newsletter. Refer to Visual 8–8 to determine the newsletter page location as you continue with your project. The pages will be referenced by the colored labels shown in Visual 8–6.

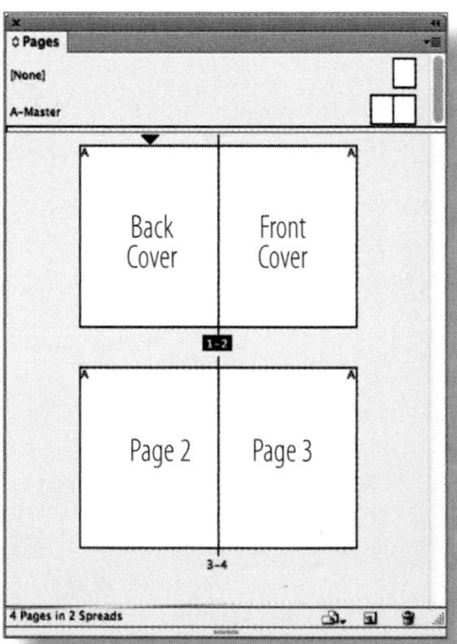

VISUAL |8–6|

Sometimes the physical page location in a document differs from our description of document pages. For this newsletter, we will be using the descriptions in red type, rather than the physical page numbers listed underneath the spreads.

5. On the front cover, pull a horizontal guide down from the top to **2.25"** on the ***Y*** coordinate.

6. Double-click on the numbers below the Page 2 and 3 spread in the ***Pages*** panel. Create a horizontal guide at **1.65"** on the *Y* coordinate by first clicking a spot on the ruler that is outside the document's page area. Now drag down the guide, noticing that the guide stretches across the whole spread. (When you drag a guide down from the ruler by clicking above the page you are working on, the guide covers only that page.) If you can't exactly position the guide at 1.65", with the guide selected, type **1.65** in the *Y* field of the ***Control*** panel. ***Save*** your document.

ABOUT SNIPPETS

When you do a lot of design work for a single client, you usually have elements that are used over and over again. For instance, if you did weekly advertisements for a dental practice, you would probably include the logo, name, hours of operation, phone number, and address in each ad. In these instances you can create *Snippets,* bits of information that you have saved and organized for placing into a new document at a later time. Snippets allow you to store those frequently used items in one convenient folder, organized by job number or client. In this chapter, the newsletter Snippets are found in their own *Snippets* folder in the *08 Healthy Pets Newsletter* folder. You will find this folder in *08 Artwork and Resources* on the online companion resources. Before we begin placing Snippets, we'll change InDesign's *Preferences* to make the process much easier.

► *production tip*

Snippets are easy to create. With the Selection tool, select the object(s) to be included in the Snippet. Under File>Export, type a name in the Save As field, and choose InDesign Snippet from the Format field.

► *Change Snippet import preferences*

1. Open the InDesign ***Preference*** dialog box by using **Command+K** (Mac) or **Ctrl+K** (Windows). Select ***File Handling*** from the left pane. Under ***Snippet Import,*** choose ***Original Location***. Now, when you import each Snippet, it will be placed at its original position on the newsletter. This option is important to know about for those times when elements must be placed in the same location on each new document.

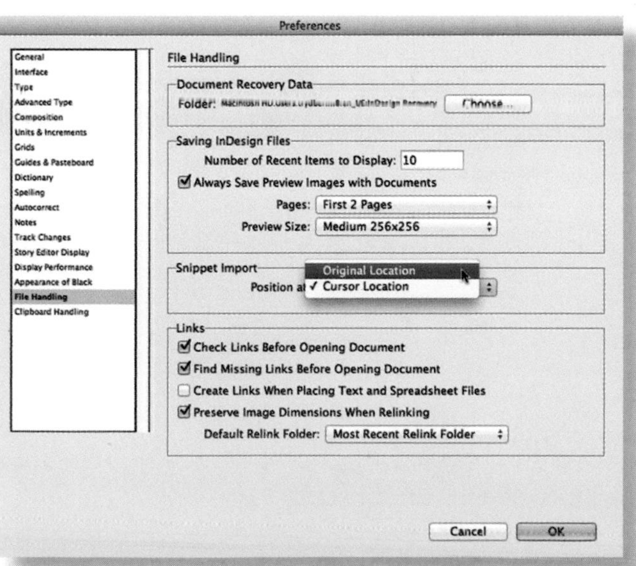

VISUAL | 8–7 |

Change InDesign Preferences to place snippets at their original location.

2. Your document should still be open. Double-click the Front Cover page icon on the *Pages* panel. Use the **Place** command to select ***FC Nameplate. idms.*** Click anywhere on the Front Cover—since we changed InDesign's ***Preferences***, the nameplate Snippet will drop into the correct position.

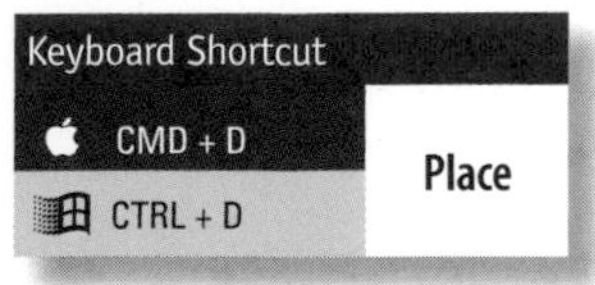

3. Next, using Visual 8–7 as a guide, Place ***FC Open House. idms, FC Quote. idms,*** and ***FC Hospital. idms*** onto the Front Cover. The elements do not need to be resized. If you mistakenly resize an element, simply delete it and place the Snippet again.

VISUAL |8–8|

Because you changed InDesign's Preferences, each Snippet will be placed at its original location on each page.

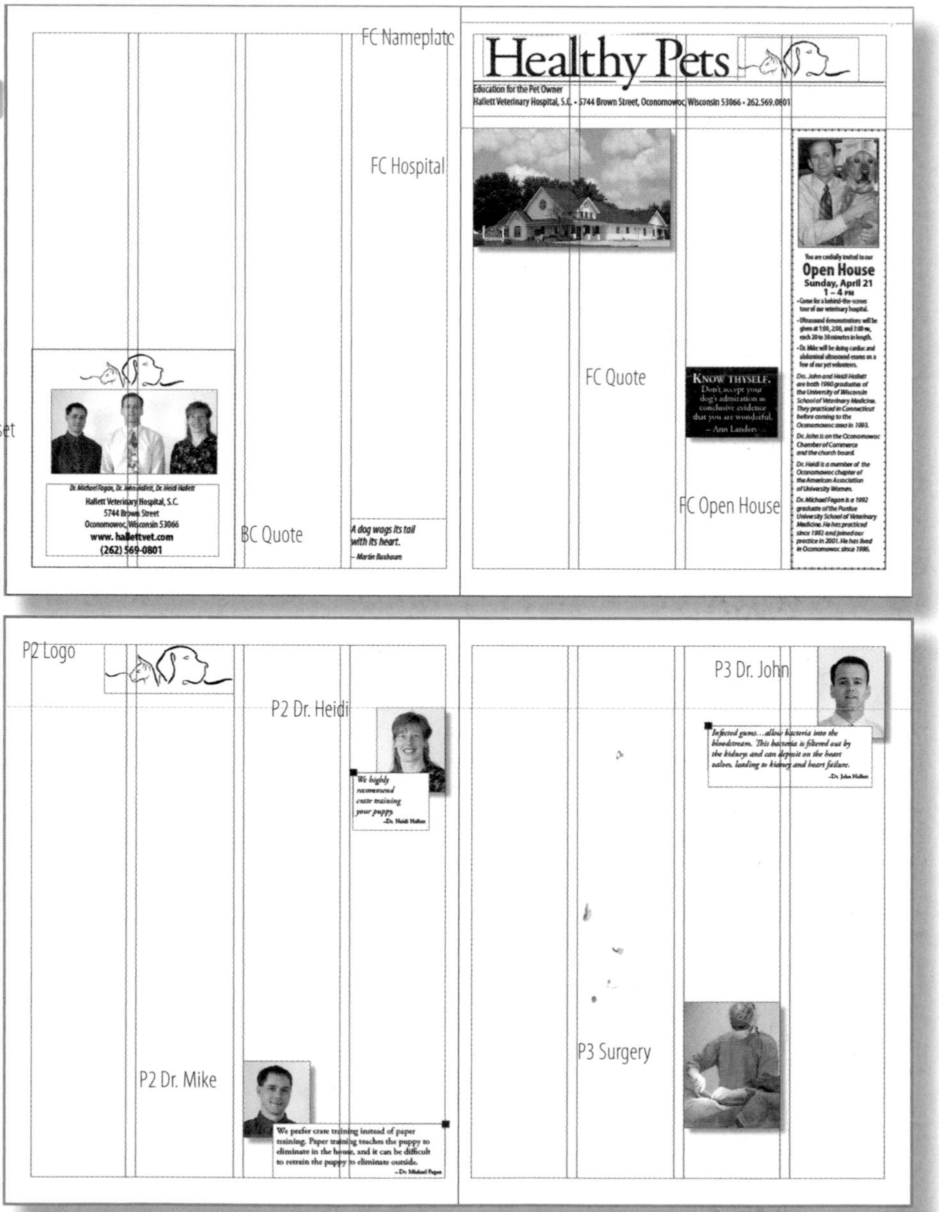

4. Select the Back Cover in the ***Pages*** panel. Using Visual 8–8 as a guide, place ***BC Inset.idms,*** and ***BC Quote. idms***. Select Page 2 in the ***Pages*** panel. Place ***P2 Dr. Heidi. idms, P2 Dr. Mike.idms,*** and ***P2 Logo.idms.*** Move to Page 3 and place ***P3 Dr. John.idms*** and ***P3 Surgery.idms.*** You will not use all the Snippets (yet). Save your document.

▸ *production tip*

Notice that the hospital photo has a drop shadow, which is a transparent element. When Transparency has been turned on in the Pages panel (option menu>Panel Options>Icons), a small checkerboard square will appear next to the page icons whenever a spread has a transparency effect applied.

USING THE EYEDROPPER TOOL

InDesign provides many methods for formatting type. The method you have used thus far is to select text, frame by frame, and manually enter all the character and paragraph settings. The *Eyedropper* tool saves time by allowing you to transfer type attributes from one paragraph to another. On Page 2 of the newsletter, the copy under Dr. Heidi's photo is formatted perfectly. You will use the *Eyedropper* tool to transfer those type attributes to text in another text frame.

1. Double-click the ***Eyedropper*** tool to open the ***Eyedropper Options*** dialog box. Here, a whole array of options allow you to customize exactly which types of objects and their attributes, the tool should copy. Deselect all choices except ***Character*** and ***Paragraph Settings*** (Visual 8–9) and press **Return.**

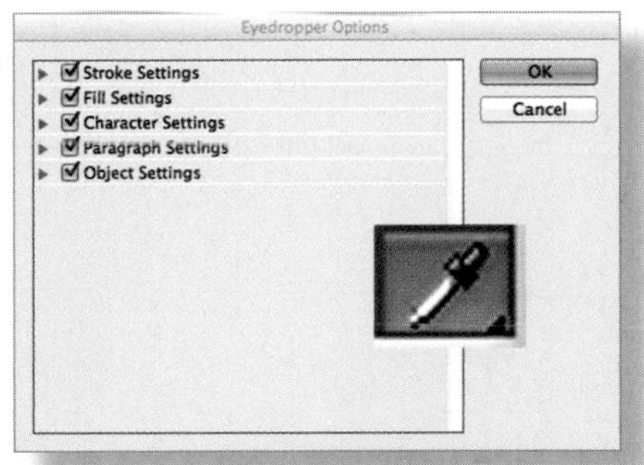

VISUAL |8–9|

The Eyedropper is a versatile tool for copying attributes.

2. The ***Eyedropper*** cursor icon begins white, which means that no attributes have been copied or "loaded" into the tool. Click the empty ***Eyedropper*** on the italic copy under Dr. Heidi's photo. The ***Eyedropper*** now turns black and reverses direction as it "loads" the attributes, a process called ***sampling*** (Visual 8–10). Drag the loaded ***Eyedropper*** tool over the copy underneath Dr. Mike's photo. As soon as the mouse is released, the text will be changed to the "sampled" attributes (Visual 8–10). As long as the ***Eyedropper*** tool is loaded, you can drag and highlight text with it. Holding down the **Option** (Mac) or **Alt** (Windows) key temporarily turns the ***Eyedropper*** white again, so you can resample different text attributes. Deactivate the ***Eyedropper*** by selecting another tool.

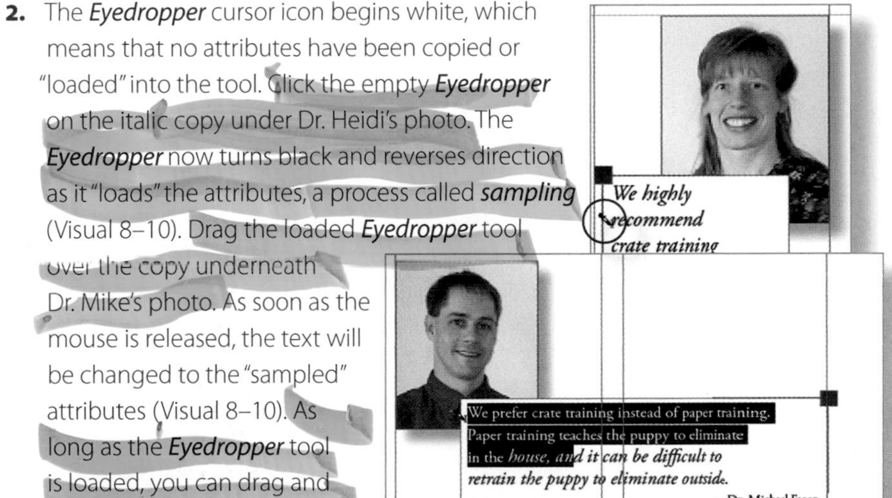

VISUAL |8–10|

The Eyedropper is loaded with text attributes from the copy under Dr. Heidi. The loaded Eyedropper transfers the attributes as it is dragged across type.

▸ MOVING TOWARD MASTERY

When you place an image into InDesign, you are creating a link. No data from the placed artwork file is actually brought into the InDesign document. Instead, a link, or pathway, is created from the original artwork file to the InDesign document. When your document is opened or printed, InDesign follows the link's path back to the original image file, reads the data, and displays or prints the image. When InDesign can't find the link, it can't accurately render the image.

*When a warning appears that a link is missing, your first course of action is to open the **Links** panel: **Shift+Cmd+D** (Mac) or **Shift+Control+D** (Windows).*

*The right column shows the page where each image in the document is used. The left column shows the status of each link. A yellow triangle means that the original file has changed and the link needs updating. To update a link, select the file name and choose **Update Link** at the bottom of the **Links** panel.*

*A white question mark in a red circle means the path to the original image is broken. To repair a broken link, click on the problem link, and select the **Relink** button at the bottom of the panel. For this project, navigate to the 08 Healthy Pets Newsletter folder and, inside, to the **Links** folder. Select the file name for each missing link. (Chapter 13 will have more on the Links panel.)*

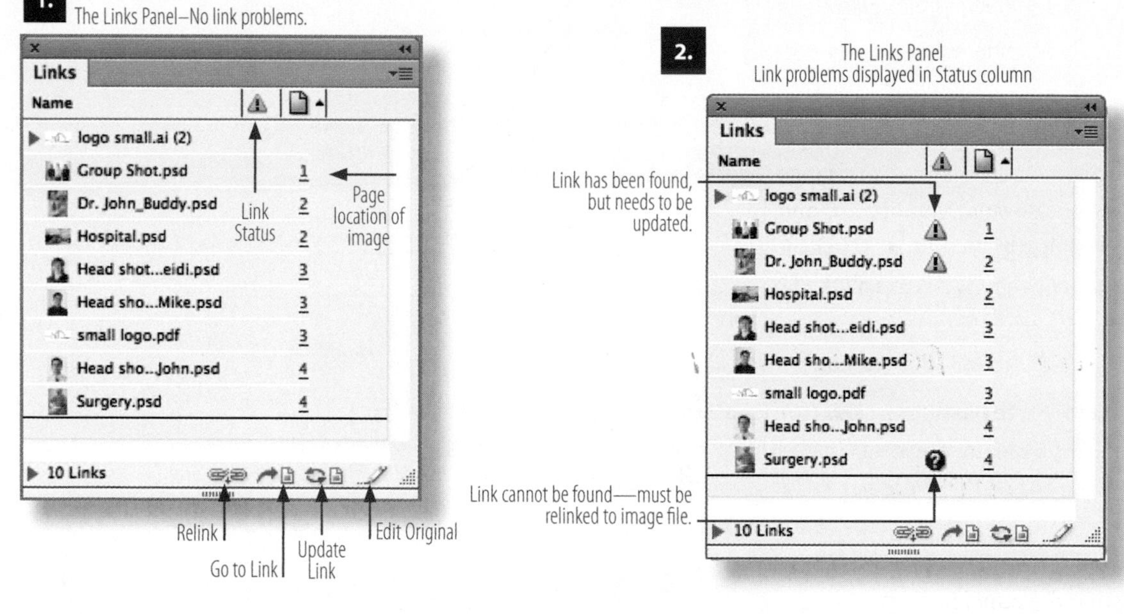

DEFINING STYLES

The *Eyedropper* tool is ideal for formatting small quantities of text. When working on larger documents, it is better to use *styles.* This involves creating a separate style for each text element by defining all its various attributes. For instance, you would define a style used for headlines, one for body copy, another for photo captions, and so on. Once you have defined the styles, they can be consistently applied to text on any of the pages in your document. This is the fastest, most accurate (and most fun) method of formatting large amounts of text.

Styles that apply attributes to entire paragraphs are called *paragraph styles.* A paragraph can have only one paragraph style assigned to it. Every new document you create comes with a *basic paragraph style* that is applied to all the text you type. This style default can be edited, but it cannot be deleted. Styles that affect characters or words within paragraphs are called *character styles.* More than one character style can be applied to text with a paragraph style already applied. A character style would be used, for instance, to create a raised cap at the beginning of a paragraph with a different type style than the rest of the paragraph text. This newsletter project will focus on the following eight style management techniques:

- *Creating styles from sample text*
- *Transferring styles from another InDesign document*
- *Creating styles based on other styles*
- *Creating a new style*
- *Duplicating existing styles*
- *Bringing in styles with a new element*
- *Creating character styles*
- *Redefining existing styles*

Here's an example of the power of using styles. Imagine that you have just created a 24-page annual report. When you show your first proof to the client, she requests you change the typeface of all the body text. No problem. Because you defined and applied styles to all the text when you created the document, all you need to do is to change the font attributes of the body text style and all the text will automatically update.

► Create styles from sample text

Let's create paragraph styles for your newsletter project. Open the *Paragraph Styles* panel by pressing **Cmd+F11** (Mac) or **F11 (Windows)**, or by choosing *Window>Styles>Paragraph Styles.* The first thing you notice is that the panel has only one entry: [Basic Paragraph], the default paragraph style for the document. No other styles have been defined. In the lower right you'll see the *Create new style* and *Delete selected style/groups* buttons. You may remember using similar buttons in the *Layers* panel. In InDesign, all the panels work in basically the same way.

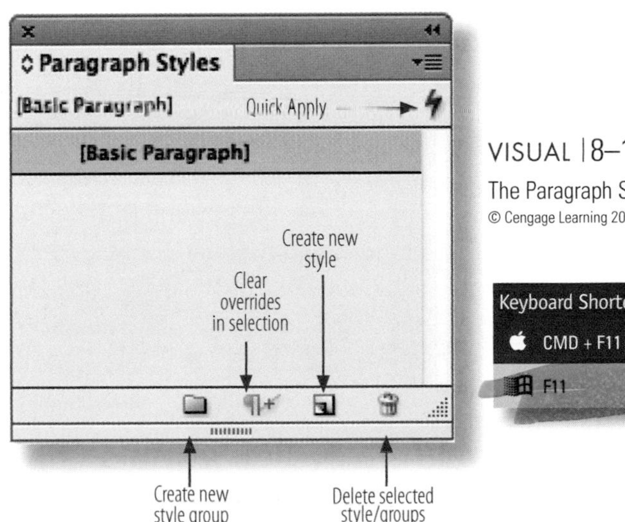

VISUAL | 8–11 |

The Paragraph Styles panel.

Keyboard Shortcut
CMD + F11
F11
Paragraph Styles

The first method of defining a style is to copy the attributes from existing copy. You will probably use this method most of the time when defining styles.

Grooming
We're happy to teach you how to trim your puppy's nails. Start now while the pup is young so he gets used to having his feet handled and nails trimmed. Combing or brushing should also be started when he is young. For longer haired dogs, use a steel comb to keep mats from forming.

VISUAL |8–12|

The Grooming snippet is placed on the back cover in column 3, next to the bottom display ad.

1. Move to the Back Cover by clicking on the Page 1 icon on the *Pages* panel. Place the Snippet named *BC Grooming. idms* (Visual 8–12).

2. Open the *Paragraph Styles* panel. Place the blinking text cursor in the headline, *Grooming*, and **Option+click** (Mac) or **Alt+click** (Windows) on the *Create new style* icon on the bottom of the panel.

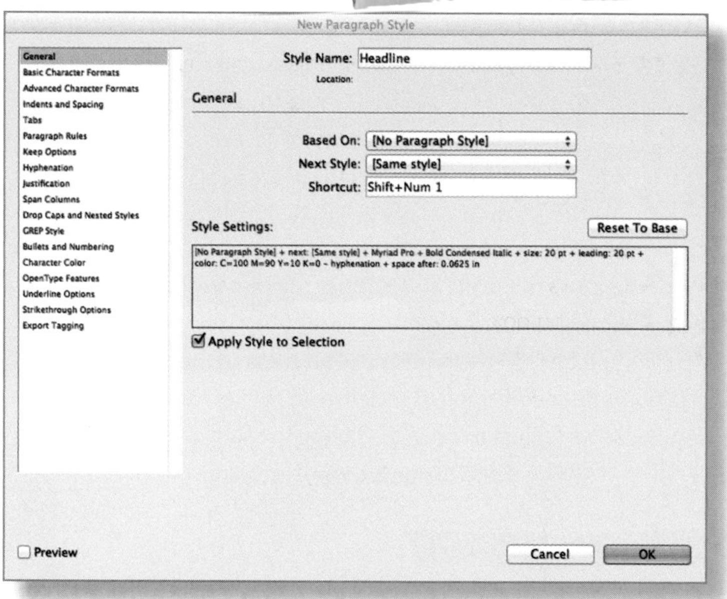

VISUAL |8–13|

Specifications of the selected copy are automatically transferred to settings in the New Paragraph Style dialog box.

In the *New Paragraph Style* dialog box, the *Style Name* field remains *Paragraph Style 1* until you rename it. In Visual 8–13, the style has been named *Headline. Based On* is an important field you will want to watch each time you create a style. There is a *Shortcut* field where you can assign a keyboard shortcut to apply this style to other text, once the style has been defined. Create a shortcut key using a number in the number pad in conjunction with one or more modifier keys. For Mac users, modifier keys are *Shift, Option,* and *Command.* In Windows, *Num Lock* must first be turned on, then use *Shift, Alt,* and *Control,* plus a number from the number pad to create a keyboard shortcut. For example, Visual 8–13 shows Shift+Num 1 for the shortcut for Headline. (A numeric keypad is ideal for using Style shortcuts. However, if you are working on a laptop, it's easier to select the desired style in the *Styles* panel or use the *Styles* pull-down options in the *Paragraph* and *Character* control panel. We'll cover that, later.) The *Style Settings* field displays a summary of all the paragraph settings used in the style.

▸ *production tip*

If you're working on a laptop, trying to use keyboard shortcuts for styles is awkward. You'll want to use Quick Apply or the Styles pull-down options on the Control panel, instead. Both techniques will be covered later in the chapter.

3. Name this style **Headline**, assign **Shift+Num 1** as the shortcut, and select *Apply Style to Selection*. When you check this option, the text you used to define a style is assigned the style you have just created. Press **Return**. This method of defining a style is accurate and automatic, and you didn't have to enter a single formatting option! **(The Headline style is first specified in italic, and will be redefined to a Roman face in the last step of this newsletter project.)**

4. Place the text cursor in the copy below the headline. Using the method described in Steps 2 and 3, create a new style named **Body Copy** with a keyboard shortcut of **Shift+Num 2**. Save your document.

► *production tip*

When defining styles from existing text, remember to check Apply Style to Selection in the New Paragraph Style dialog box to assign the style to the sample copy.

► *Transfer styles from another InDesign document*

Let's say you are showing a new client various newsletter samples you have designed. The client finds a sample she likes and says, "I wish my newsletter could look just like this." The next method of creating paragraph and character styles will transfer the styles from another InDesign document. Here's how it's done:

1. Click on the panel menu in the *Paragraph Styles* panel and choose *Load Paragraph Styles*. In the *08 Healthy Pets Newsletter* folder, select the *Healthy Pets.indt* file. Click **Open**. The *Load Styles* dialog box, shown in Visual 8–14, gives you the opportunity to select which styles you want to load. For our purposes, make sure all the styles are checked. Press **Return**, and the styles will load into your document.

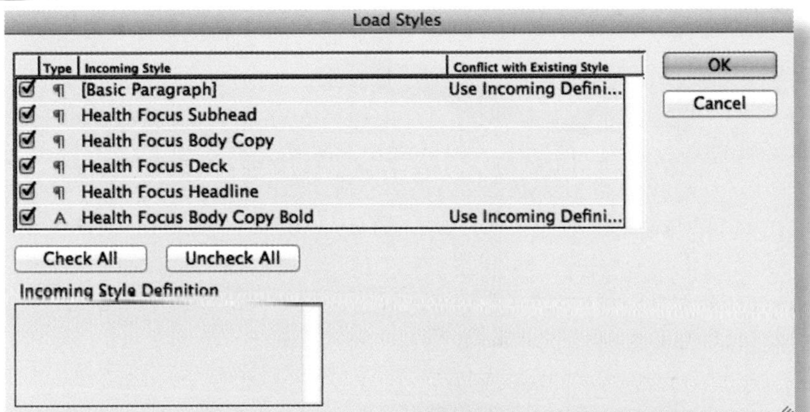

VISUAL |8–14|

Checked styles will be loaded into the newsletter document.

2. Your *Paragraph Styles* panel should now look like Visual 8–15. Notice that not all the styles have shortcut keys. Shortcut keys are not usually assigned to styles that are used infrequently.

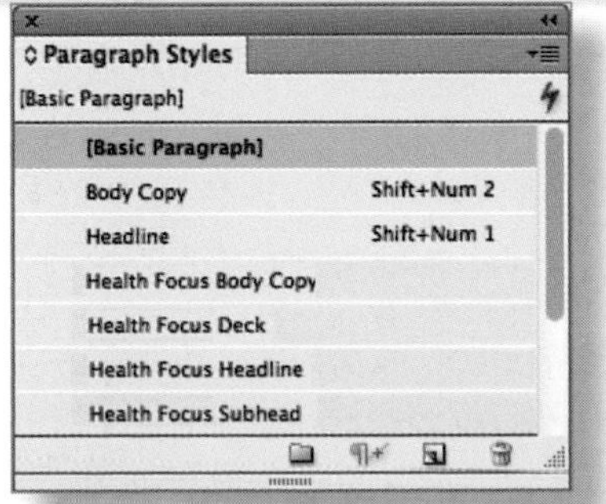

VISUAL |8–15|

The Health Focus styles have been loaded into the Healthy Pets newsletter.

▸ *Create styles based on other styles*

There are times when you will need a variation of a particular style within a document. For example, perhaps you have created a style named Body Copy that works for the main portion of the text. You also have some paragraphs of body text that need a custom left indent. A variation of the Body Copy style, called Body Copy Indent (which includes a left indent), could be created. Body Copy Indent is *based on* Body Copy, and these two styles share a *parent-child relationship* with many similar attributes. When changes are made to attributes of the *parent* style (Body Copy), those shared attributes are changed in the *child* style (Body Copy Indent). Here's how simple it is to create a new style, based on an existing one.

1. **Option+click** or **Alt+click** the *Create new style* icon in the *Paragraph Styles* panel. In the *New Paragraph Style* dialog box, name the style **Body Copy Indent**. Since styles are listed alphabetically, it's a good idea to name related styles similarly. Body Copy Indent will appear after Body Copy in the style list.

2. At the left side is a list of formatting categories. You can tell you are in the ***General*** category because it is highlighted. In the ***Based On*** field in the center of the dialog box, choose ***Body Copy.***

3. Open each of the categories in the list. As you read each category page, you will realize that with few exceptions, the text formatting features listed are ones you are already familiar with, and you have accessed them through regular panels.

4. Open the ***Indents and Spacing*** category page. Set a left indent of **0.125"** (Visual 8–16) and press **Return.** This new style looks just like the Body Copy style, except it has a different left indent. And because Body Copy Indent is based on Body Copy, any changes you make to the Body Copy style will be automatically made to this style.

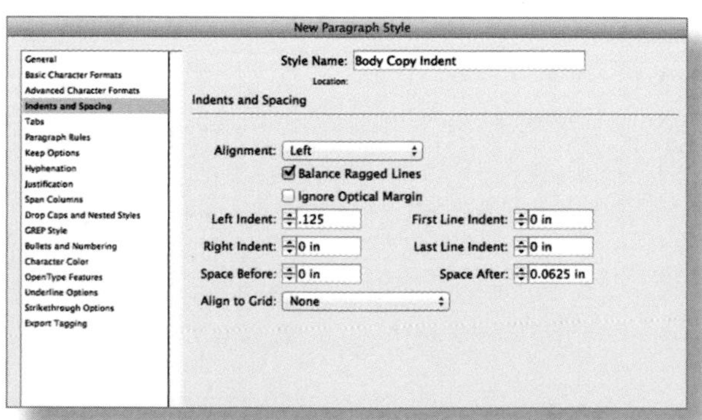

VISUAL | 8–16 |

The Body Copy Indent style includes all the specifications of Body Copy, plus a left indent. Any changes made to Body Copy will ripple down to Body Copy Indent.

When you are creating a style based on another style and need to reset the "child" style back to the style it is based on, click the **Reset to Base** button on the *General* page of the panel.

▸ *Create a new style*

Next we'll create a new style named *Kicker*. A *kicker* is a short line of type that appears above a headline. Kickers can tease your reader into the article and add interest to an otherwise boring headline. On the front page of the newsletter you'll see a kicker above the headline describing new equipment. New equipment might not interest pet owners, but the benefit of new equipment does! Hence, the *Great News for Pet Owners* kicker.

1. Open the *New Paragraph Style* dialog box and set these text parameters for the new style you will name **Kicker**. Look at the *Based On* field to verify that *[No Paragraph Style]* is selected. *Basic Character Formats:* **Adobe Garamond Pro Italic,** *Size:* **14,** *Leading:* **auto** (16.8 pt.).

2. Choose *Indents and Spacing* page and set *Space After* to **0.0625"**. Choose *Paragraph Rules* page and turn *Rule Below* on. Set *Weight:* **0.5 pt.**, *Color:* **Black**, *Offset:* **0.0766"**, *Width:* **Text**. Press **Return**. Save your document.

▸ *Duplicate existing styles*

We are going to create a new style called *Health Focus Standing Head*. Since this style is so similar to the Kicker style, we will create it by duplicating and editing the Kicker style. *Standing heads* are titles for features that appear in each issue. For instance, in a newspaper, the obituaries, sports, editorials, and classifieds each have their own title design that readers recognize and look for. Standing heads are used over and over, while a kicker is used once with one specific headline. Our newsletter project includes a Health Focus article with each issue. The standing head is found at the top left column on page 2: *This Issue's Health Focus*.

1. Select the *Kicker* paragraph style. Click on the menu options of the *Paragraph Styles* panel and choose *Duplicate Style.* In the *Duplicate Paragraph Style* dialog box, rename the style to **Health Focus Standing Head**. In the *Based On* field, choose *[No Paragraph Style]* (Visual 8–17).

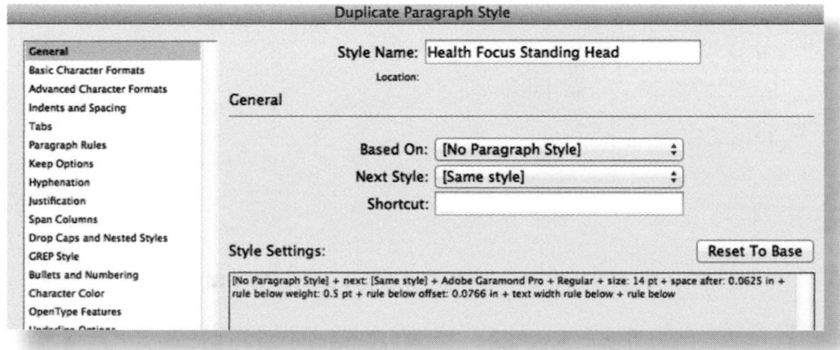

VISUAL |8–17|

Although the Health Focus Standing Head style was duplicated from the Kicker style, it is not based on it. This style retains many of the Kicker attributes, but it will remain independent of any changes made to the Kicker style.

2. Choose the *Basic Character Formats* page, change the typeface to **Adobe Garamond Pro Bold Italic**. Press **Return**. Save your document.

▸ *Bring in styles with a new element*

When an element that has been formatted with a style is copied and then pasted into another InDesign document, the element and its style will be transferred to the current document. Here's an example of how easily this can be done.

1. Go to the Page 2 and 3 spread. From the ***Snippet*** folder, place ***P2 Spread Head.idms*** on Page 2 and ***P3 Spread Head.idms*** on Page 3.

2. You will notice that a new paragraph style has appeared: ***Spread headline***. When you place a Snippet that has a paragraph or character style applied, that style is added to the list of styles. Place your text cursor in the spread head on Page 3. You will notice that a plus (+) sign appears after the name of the applied style. A plus (+) sign indicates a ***style override***, which means that something was added to the text that was not included in the defined style. You can see a description of the override by holding your mouse over the style displaying the plus (+) sign. A description of the additional formatting appears in parentheses. In this case, you will want to keep the style override. However, if you wanted to delete the paragraph style override, you would press **Option** (Mac) or **Alt** (Windows) as you clicked the style name in the list. For our newsletter, the Spread Headline style was originally created with right alignment. The spread headline on page 3 is left aligned, flush to the inside margin, which is a style override.

▸ *production tip*

When a + sign appears after a style name, it means that the selected copy has a style override.

STYLE GROUPS

Before we move on to *Character* styles, we will organize our paragraph styles by creating a folder to hold all the Health Focus styles. From the *Paragraph Styles* menu, choose *New Style Group*. Name the group **Health Focus** (Visual 8–18). Select each Health Focus style and drop it into the folder. Your paragraph styles should match Visual 8–18. If the styles are shown in a different order, you can choose *Sort by Name* from the panel options.

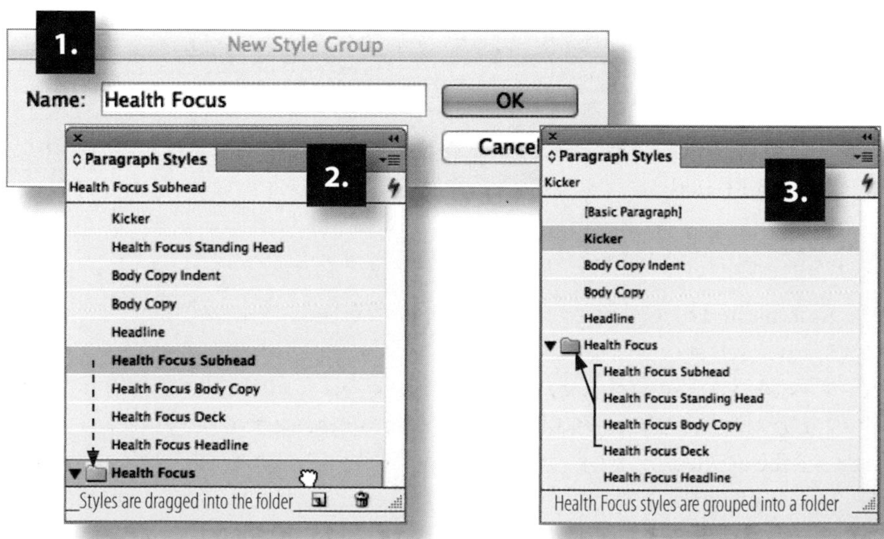

VISUAL |8–18|

Style groups help organize lists of styles.

▸ *Create Character styles*

Open the *Character Styles* panel by pressing **Shift+Command+F11**(Mac) or **Shift+F11** (Windows), or by choosing *Window>Styles>Character Styles*. You will notice that a character style already appears in the panel. It was loaded with the paragraph styles we transferred from a document earlier. We have one more character style to create and then we'll be ready to build the rest of the newsletter.

Keyboard Shortcut
↑ + CMD + F11
↑ + F11
Character Styles

1. **Option+click** (Mac) or **Alt+click** (Windows) the *Create new style* icon at the bottom of the *Character Styles* panel. Specify *Based on:* **[None]**. Name the style **Body Copy Bold**. Assign a keyboard shortcut: **Shift+Num 5**.
2. On the *Basic Character Formats* page, enter **Myriad Pro Bold 10/11**. Press **Return** and save your document.
3. Open the *Paragraph Styles* and *Character Styles* panels and compare them with the ones shown in Visual 8–19. If your list looks like Visual 8–19, you are ready to complete your newsletter. If some styles are missing, you will want to review this section to find the steps that were skipped. Now let's finish this job.

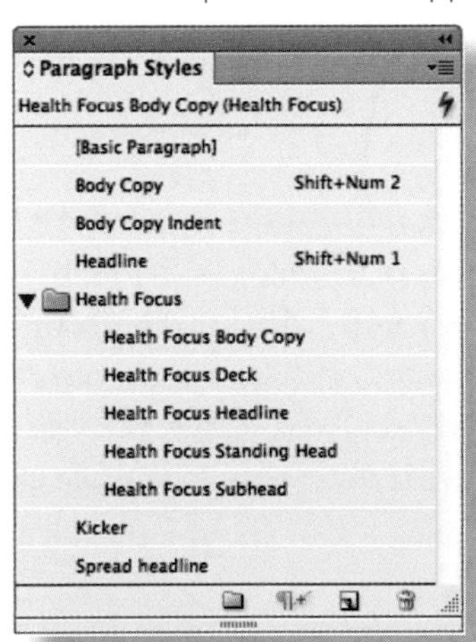

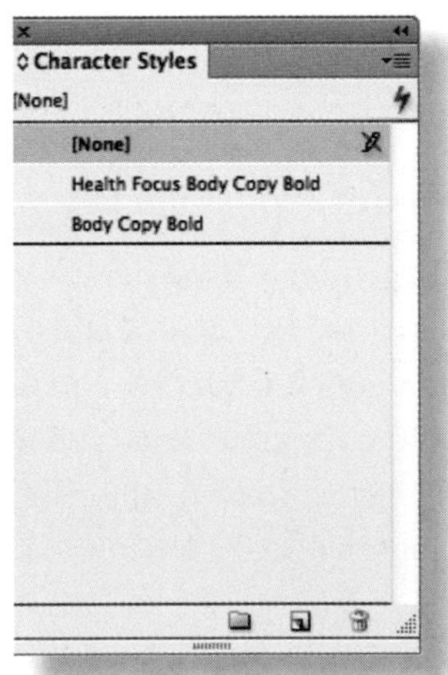

VISUAL |8–19|

Your styles should look like the ones in this example. If they do, you are ready to proceed! To alphabetize your style list, go to the menu options and choose Sort by Name.

APPLYING STYLES

Paragraph and Character styles can be applied using several methods. Try each of the following four methods, and then use the ones that work best for you.

▸ *Apply styles from Paragraph or Character Styles panels*

The first method of applying a style is to open the *Paragraph* or *Character Styles* panel, select the copy, and then click on the name of the style in the panel. When you are applying a Paragraph style, you don't need to highlight all the copy in the paragraph. Place your cursor in the paragraph, and the style will be applied to the entire paragraph. When you apply a Character style, you need to highlight all the copy to which the style should be applied.

▸ *Apply styles using keyboard shortcuts*

The second method of applying styles is to select the copy and press the keyboard shortcut assigned to the style. It is unlikely that all styles will have keyboard shortcuts, so you will probably use keyboard shortcuts only for styles you will assign quite often, like body copy.

▸ *Apply styles from the Control panel*

A third method of applying styles is to select the styles from the *Control* panel. Visual 8–20 shows where the *Styles* choices appear on the *Character* and *Paragraph Controls.*

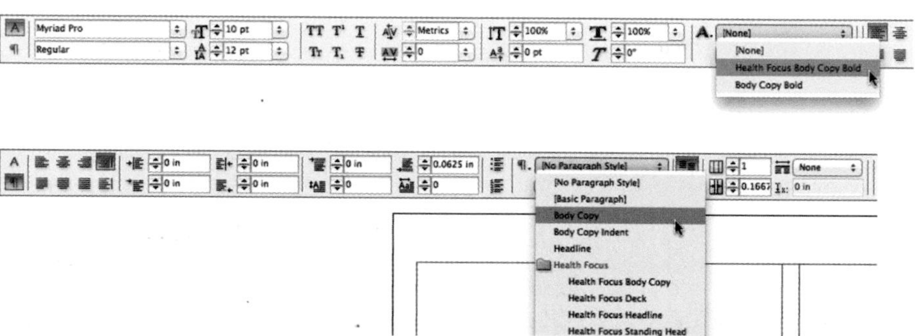

VISUAL |8–20|

Styles can be found in the Paragraph and Character Controls.

▸ *Apply styles using Quick Apply*

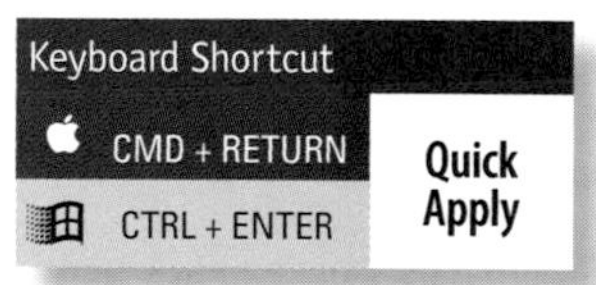

A fourth method of applying styles is to use *Quick Apply*—a pop-up window opened by pressing **Cmd+Return** or **Ctrl+Enter**. When your document contains a long list of styles, *Quick Apply* allows you to locate a style by typing part of the style name. Press the **Up** and **Down Arrow** keys to scroll through the list of items. To apply the selected style, press **Enter** or **Return**. To close *Quick Apply* without applying an item, press **Esc** or click on the document.

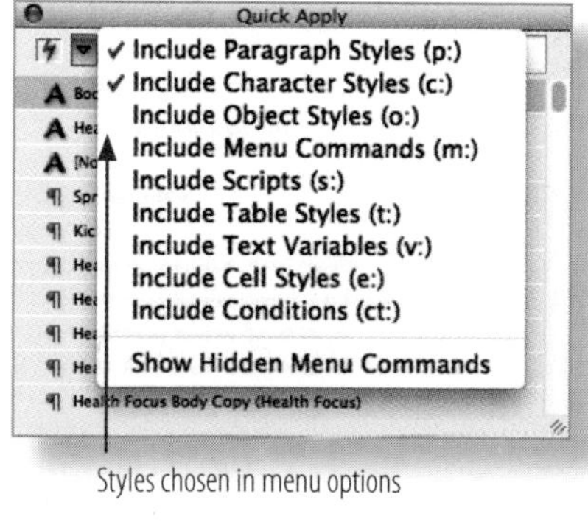

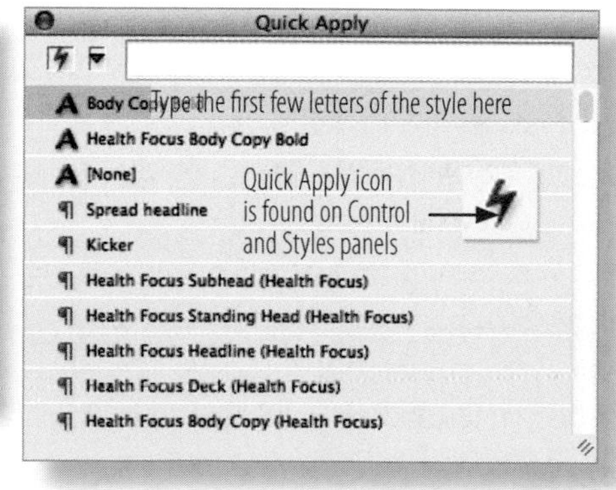

VISUAL |8–21|

Use Quick Apply to locate a style by typing a portion of its name. Quick Apply is great for managing long lists of styles!

▸ MOVING TOWARD MASTERY

Tips for working with text and styles

- *It's faster to drag a text frame while you are placing text than to create a frame first and then drop text into it.*
- *Placed text files (with no assigned styles) will come in with the attributes of the style that is highlighted in the panel window. When you place text, be sure you do not have a character style highlighted in the Character styles window. In this newsletter project, for instance, the last style you created was a character style and it is probably still highlighted. By default, a paragraph style won't replace a character style. So, before you begin to place text, select* ***[None]*** *in the* ***Character Style*** *field in the* ***Control*** *panel.*
- *A good rule of thumb is to select all the text and first change the Paragraph style to Body Copy. This technique generally reduces the point size of your text and makes a large text block more manageable. When the text frame is active and you are in the* ***Type*** *tool, press* ***Command+A*** *(Mac) or* ***Control+A*** *(Windows) to select all the type. It is important to select only text in a frame and not all the objects on your page! Then apply the Body Copy paragraph style.*
- *Another method is to have the Body Copy paragraph style selected when you place the text. Placed text (with no assigned style) will automatically be formatted with the Body Copy style. After the Body Copy style is assigned to the text block, you may apply the subheads and character styles.*
- *Press* ***Shift+Enter*** *to make text jump from one linked text frame to the next.*
- *Paragraph and Character styles can also be accessed through the* ***Control*** *panel. Choose the* ***Paragraph*** *or* ***Character*** *formatting options.*
- *A plus (+) sign following a defined style in the* ***Paragraph Styles*** *panel means additional formatting has been added. To remove Paragraph and local formatting overrides, click the* ***Clear Overrides*** *icon on the* ***Styles*** *panel (Visual 8–11), or choose* ***Clear Overrides*** *from the* ***Paragraph Styles*** *panel options.*
- *Clearing overrides does not remove formatting created by Character styles. To remove Character styles, select text containing the Character style and then click* ***[None]*** *in the* ***Character Styles*** *panel.*

USE STYLES TO COMPLETE HEALTHY PETS NEWSLETTER

You have prepared the document structure, brought in images from Snippets, and created styles for typographic consistency and production speed. Let's see how well they work. We'll begin on the front cover. You should print out the actual size newsletter sample from the *08 Healthy Pets Newsletter* folder on the online companion resources because it shows where all the styles are used. The unformatted, plain text files for the project are found in the same folder on the online companion resources. Always apply paragraph styles before applying character styles. Before you begin to place plain text files into a document, check the list of character styles on the *Character Styles* or *Control* panel. Character styles should be set to [None] before placing the copy. If a character style is active when the copy is placed, that style will automatically be assigned to the incoming text, and will have to be removed before the paragraph style will take effect. Be sure to read *Tips for working with text and styles* in the box above.

▸ *production tip*

Don't have a character style selected when you are placing text! Deselect the text after applying a style.

▸ *Apply styles to the front cover*

1. On the *Control* panel, set *Character Styles* to **[None]** and *Paragraph Styles* to **Body Copy.** Create a 2-column text frame in the first column that begins under the photo and extends across the second column, and to the bottom margin, gutter **0.1875"**. Place the *New equipment increases.docx* file from the *08 Healthy Pets Newsletter* folder on the online companion resources.

2. If the copy is not already Body Copy, select all the type and apply the Body Copy paragraph style by pressing **Shift+Num 2.**

3. Place the cursor in the *Great News for Pet Owners* line and select the *Kicker* paragraph style. The kicker won't fit nicely in the column, but we'll fix that in Step 5.

4. Place the cursor in the headline and select *Headline* from the *Paragraph Styles* panel, or press **Shift+Num 1.** The typeface is still italic—it will be changed later. Also, place a soft return after the word *increases* to end up with the longer part of the headline on the last line. The headline won't fit nicely into the column—we'll fix that, next.

5. Highlight the headline and kicker. From the *Control* panel, select *Span All* from the *Span Columns* controls (Visual 8–22)

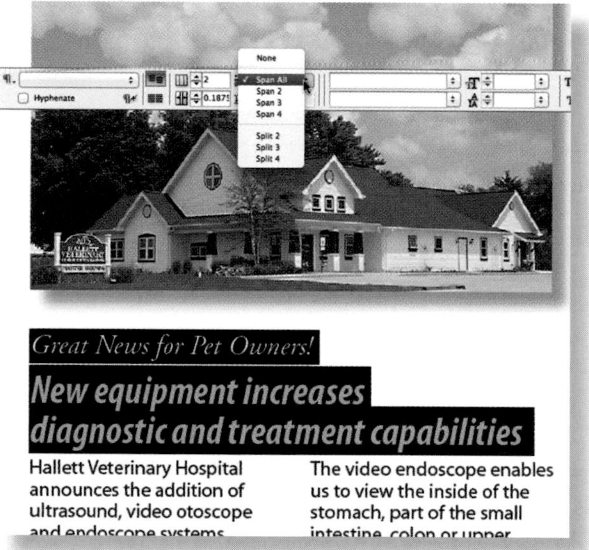

VISUAL |8–22|

Span Columns allows headlines to straddle columns—without the need for a separate text frame.

Artwork and text © 2004 Hallett Veterinary Hospital, S.C.

▸ *production tip*

Press Enter (Mac) or Enter on the Number pad (Windows) to move copy to the next column. If you do not have an Enter key, open the Context menu and go to Insert Break Character>Column Break. Remember to work with hidden characters visible.

6. A *pull quote* is an excerpt that is designed to stand out from the rest of the body copy. Pull quotes add visual interest and encourage readership. Place Snippet *FC Pull Quote.idms* and position it between the two columns. Adjust its position for the best text flow. Text wrap options have already been turned on. Make sure the paragraph beginning with *The video endoscope*, is at the top of the second column, and not at the bottom of the first column.

7. Place *Should you give Heartguard.docx* from the *08 Healthy Pets Newsletter* folder. As you place, drag a new text frame at the top of column three.

Select all the type and change it to *Body Copy.* Then place your cursor in the headline and press **Shift+Num 1** to assign the *Headline* style.

8. Find the *Puppy Classes.docx* article from the *08 Healthy Pets Newsletter* folder. Bottom align the text at the bottom of the third column and use styles to format the text. Modify the size, font, and color of the phone number at the bottom of the article. This is called ***local formatting,*** and almost every document contains some local formatting. The Front Cover spread should now look very much like Visual 8–23

Healthy Pets

Education for the Pet Owner

Hallett Veterinary Hospital, S.C. • 5744 Brown Street, Oconomowoc, Wisconsin 53066 • 262.569.0801

Great News for Pet Owners!

New equipment increases diagnostic and treatment capabilities

Hallett Veterinary Hospital announces the addition of ultrasound, video otoscope and endoscope systems. This advanced equipment greatly expands services available for small animals.

Ultrasound enhances the ability to evaluate internal organs, diagnose a variety of medical conditions, and confirm and monitor pregnancies. We can now obtain biopsy samples from internal organs without invasive surgery. Heart ultrasound, or echocardiography, gives us very important information about heart function in animals with evidence of heart disease.

The video otoscope makes it possible to more effectively evaluate and treat chronic ear infections. The system can be used to remove impacted wax from deep in the ear canal, collect biopsies and flush ear canals.

"We can now obtain biopsy samples...without invasive surgery."

The video endoscope enables us to view the inside of the stomach, part of the small intestine, colon or upper respiratory tract without surgery. Foreign objects can be removed from the stomach and biopsies can be collected if necessary, using the endoscope. Biopsies can be extremely helpful in diagnosing inflammatory bowel disease and other causes of chronic vomiting or diarrhea.

Both the video otoscope and endoscope systems project the magnified image on a 20" monitor and have the ability to store still images as well as video clips of the procedures.

Dr. Mike has several years of ultrasound experience and all three doctors have completed extensive training. Procedures performed thus far have successfully proven the value of this equipment.

Should you give Heartgard(r) year 'round?

The answer is yes, if you don't want your human family members exposed to roundworms or hookworms (intestinal parasites).

Families with young children should especially consider using Heartgard(r) all year. Heartgard Plus® not only prevents heart worm disease but also prevents several intestinal parasites including roundworms. Roundworms infect approximately 10,000 people each year in the U.S. and can cause blindness in some cases.

Heartworm disease is only transmitted during mosquito months, but intestinal parasites can be transmitted during any season.

KNOW THYSELF.
Don't accept your dog's admiration as conclusive evidence that you are wonderful.
— Ann Landers

Puppy Classes

Socializing your puppy is very important. Puppy classes are excellent opportunities to let your pup meet other puppies and other people. The classes will also give you a good start with many training tips. Evening puppy classes are held in our reception area. Call us for more information:

(262) 569-0801

You are cordially invited to our

Open House

Sunday, April 21
1 – 4 PM

- Come for a behind-the-scenes tour of our veterinary hospital.
- Ultrasound demonstrations will be given at 1:00, 2:00, and 3:00 PM, each 20 to 30 minutes in length.
- Dr. Mike will be doing cardiac and abdominal ultrasound exams on a few of our pet volunteers.

Drs. John and Heidi Hallett are both 1990 graduates of the University of Wisconsin School of Veterinary Medicine. They practiced in Connecticut before coming to the Oconomowoc area in 1993.

Dr. John is on the Oconomowoc Chamber of Commerce and the church board.

Dr. Heidi is a member of the Oconomowoc chapter of the American Association of University Women.

Dr. Michael Fagan is a 1992 graduate of the Purdue University School of Veterinary Medicine. He has practiced since 1992 and joined our practice in 2001. He has lived in Oconomowoc since 1996.

VISUAL | 8–23 |

The Front Cover elements are positioned and styles applied. The (r) characters will be changed to the ® symbol in a later step.

9. When text is placed, there are often small modifications you will need to make, such as soft returns to break headlines in appropriate places, and instances of bold and italic in the body copy. For instance, throughout this document, you will notice that the registration mark (®), used three times in this article, was imported as (r). At the end of the newsletter project, we will change all the registration marks using the ***Find and Replace*** operation. Similarly, by default InDesign has placed a single opening quotation mark instead of an apostrophe before the word, ***'round*** in the article about giving Heartgard. (Visual 8–24). Open the ***Glyphs*** panel and replace it with an apostrophe. As you complete the newsletter, be sure to use local formatting to fine tune the copy.

VISUAL | 8–24 |
You will usually need to do some fine tuning on copy that has been placed.

▸ *Apply styles to pages 2 and 3*

The spread for pages 2 and 3 should have a horizontal guideline stretching across the whole spread at the **1.65"** *Y* coordinate position. Articles on the top of this spread should butt up to this guide.

1. Find the ***Feeding.docx*** article in the ***08 Healthy Pets Newsletter*** folder. Place the text, dragging a text frame in the third column of ***Page 2***, from the top guideline down to the top of Dr. Mike's photo.

2. Apply the ***Body Copy*** and ***Headline*** styles to this article. Notice there are many instances in this article where you will need to change the register mark (later in this project).

3. Refer to Visual 8–26 or the newsletter sample printed earlier, to place the rest of the articles on spread 2–3. The ***Spay or Neuter.docx*** article on ***Page 3*** continues in a linked frame under the photo. Bottom align both columns of the Spay article so that the text lines up.

4. ***Dental Care.docx,*** in the third column of ***Page 3,*** is in a text frame that reaches across two columns. Save your document.

▸ *Create the Health Focus table*

Hopefully you remember the table functions you learned earlier. If not, you will need to review that section in Chapter 5.

1. *Health Focus* is the last feature on Page 2. Draw a frame that stretches across the first and second columns and extends down to the bottom margin. Use **Command+B** (Mac) or **Control+B** (Windows) to apply a **0.125"** text inset on all sides. Fill the frame with **10% Blue.** Place *Vaccines Critical to your.docx,* found in the ***08 Healthy Pets Newsletter*** folder.

2. First, change all copy to *Health Focus Body Copy*. Then, apply the *Health Focus Standing Head* and *Health Focus Headline* styles. The italic type under the headline is called a ***deck.*** A deck is designed to increase reading interest. It usually summarizes the accompanying article and appears between the headline and the body copy. Apply the *Health Focus Deck* style to the deck.

This Issue's Health Focus

Vaccines: critical to your dog's health

Regular vaccinations are important for your dog's general health. Below is a recommended immunization schedule:

	8 weeks	10 weeks	12 weeks	16 weeks	6 months
DHLPP	✓		✓	✓	
Rabies			✓		
Lyme			✓	✓	
De worm	✓	✓	✓		
Fecal Exam	✓				
Spay/Neuter					✓
Kennel Cough	Optional				

• DHLPP (Distemper)
Puppies receive a series of Canine Distemper vaccinations, usually at 8, 12, and 16 weeks of age,

VISUAL |8–25|

A detail view of the Health Focus table. The cells are filled with Paper, and the strokes are .5-pt blue.

3. Highlight the text from just before the words *8 weeks* to the word *Optional.* Use the *Paragraph Options Control* and remove the left indent on the selected text. Choose *Table>Convert Text to Table; Column Separator:* **Tab;** *Row Separator:* **Paragraph.** You will need to format the table. The copy is **Myriad Pro Regular 10/11.** Center text in cells, adjust column and row spacing, merge cells, and apply strokes and fills. Highlight the column heads row, reduce the point size and rotate the text **270°**. Look in Minion Pro in the *Glyphs* panel to find a check mark. Visual 8–25 provides a detail view of the table.

4. Apply *Health Focus Subhead* style to the bulleted lines. Compare your document to the example shown in Visual 8–26. Save your document.

VISUAL |8–26|

Pages 2 and 3 spread with elements positioned and styles applied.

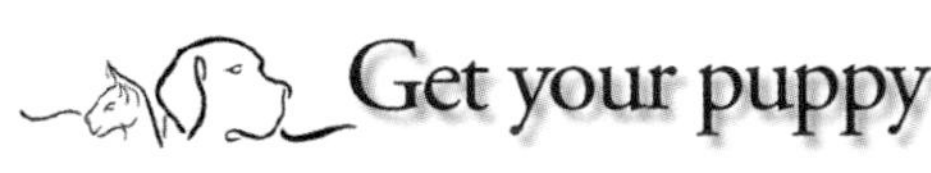

Get your puppy off to a good start!

This Issue's Health Focus

Vaccines: critical to your dog's health

Regular vaccinations are important for your dog's general health. Below is a recommended immunization schedule:

	8 weeks	10 weeks	12 weeks	16 weeks	6 months
DHLPP	✓		✓	✓	
Rabies			✓		
Lyme			✓	✓	
De worm	✓	✓	✓		
Fecal Exam	✓				
Spay/Neuter					✓
Kennel Cough	Optional				

• DHLPP (Distemper)
Puppies receive a series of Canine Distemper vaccinations,usually at 8, 12, and 16 weeks of age, then yearly. This vaccine protects against several very contagious dog diseases, including Canine Distemper, Hepatitis, Leptospirosis, Parainfluenza, and Parvovirus.

• Rabies
Rabies is the only virus that dogs can transmit to people. Rabies is transmitted through bite wounds and is fatal in people and dogs. Rabies vaccine is required by law for all dogs. The initial vaccine is given at 12 to 16 weeks of age, boosted in one year and then is given every three years.

• Lyme Disease
Lyme disease is transmitted to dogs and people by ticks. We recommend the Lyme disease vaccine for hunting dogs or dogs that are frequently in wooded areas or areas with tall grass where they may be exposed to ticks. We also recommend using a tick preventative, like Frontline, to further reduce the risk of getting Lyme disease and to reduce the risk of exposing people to ticks. The initial vaccine may be given at 9 weeks of age or older and is boosted in two to three weeks, then yearly.

• Bordetella (Kennel Cough)
Kennel cough is a highly contagious disease that causes a severe cough, fever, loss of appetite and often a nasal discharge in dogs. Most boarding kennels require the Bordetella vaccine. Kennel cough is transmitted through the air from one dog to another when they are housed in close quarters.

Feeding

Puppies should be fed puppy food until 1 year of age. Put the food down for 15 to 30 minutes each morning and evening. Feeding two meals a day will help with house training since most puppies will defecate within 20 minutes of eating a meal.

We recommend feeding Eukanuba(r) dry puppy food (made by the Iams company). We believe the Iams company has recently taken the lead in nutritional research for cats and dogs. When feeding a premium food (like Iams(r), Eukanuba(r) , Science Diet(r) or Purina Pro Plan(r)) there is no need for vitamin supplements.

We recommend feeding only dry food to your puppy. Canned foods tend to cause earlier tarter formation and gingivitis (gum inflammation). Do not mix water into the food. Never feed your puppy milk or table food, since this can cause diarrhea. Dogs do not have the enzymes needed to digest milk.

Keep your puppy trim. Overfeeding can lead to hip problems later in life, especially for large breed dogs. Always provide a bowl of fresh water for your pet.

We highly recommend crate training your puppy.
–Dr. Heidi Hallett

Crate Training

Crate training works on the principle that the crate becomes the puppy's den, and dogs don't like to soil their sleeping area. The crate should never be used for punishment. When you are home, the crate door should be left open, so the puppy can go in when tired. Make sure the crate is big enough for the puppy to turn around in but not so big that they can use one corner for a bathroom and another corner to sleep in.

At first, your puppy may cry or whine at night when left alone in the crate. Positioning the crate so your puppy can see you may help. It is important not to give your puppy any attention (not even a reprimand) when he or she whines or barks in the crate.

Try not to leave your puppy for more than six to eight hours at a time in the crate.

We prefer crate training instead of paper training. Paper training teaches the puppy to eliminate in the house, and it can be difficult to retrain the puppy to eliminate outside.
– Dr. Michael Fagan

House Training

Repetition is the key to teaching your puppy where to go to the bathroom. It is important to go out through the same door each time and go to the same place in the yard each time. This is not playtime. If the puppy doesn't urinate or defecate within 2 or 3 minutes, bring them back inside and watch closely. When they start acting like they need to go, take them outside immediately. The only time you should reprimand your puppy for having an accident is when you catch them in the act of going to the bathroom inside the house.

Choosing the right time to take your puppy outside is very important. Praise for going outside works much better than reprimanding your puppy for making a mistake. Crate training will help with house training, since the puppy will hold urine and stool while in the crate. Take the puppy out immediately in the morning. Puppies usually have a bowel movement within 20 minutes of eating. Use this to your advantage and take them out after every meal. They usually will urinate after naps or after playing.

We prefer crate training instead of paper training. Paper training teaches the puppy to eliminate in the house, and it can be difficult to retrain the puppy to eliminate outside.

Intestinal Parasites

Dogs can become infected with a number of intestinal parasites (worms). Dogs get intestinal parasites directly from their mother's milk, or from eating rodents, eating fleas, or coming in contact with infected stool.

To reduce human exposure to intestinal parasites, we follow the Centers for Disease Control (CDC) recommendations for deworming. Puppies should be dewormed every two weeks until they are three months old, then every month until six months of age.

We also recommend yearly fecal exams to check for intestinal parasites. Each year 10,000 children in the U.S. are infected with intestinal parasites, and 600 of those children become blind in one eye from parasites.

Spay or Neuter Your Pet

We recommend spaying or neutering your pet at six months of age. The surgery will not change your pet's basic personality; they are still playful and affectionate.

However, aggression toward other animals and people can be decreased. Statistics show that spayed and neutered dogs live considerably longer than intact dogs. Spaying a female dog before their first heat almost eliminates the chance of developing breast cancer later in life. The surgery also prevents life threatening uterine infections, ovarian cancer, and uterine cancer.

Neutering a male dog will prevent testicular cancer,

Infected gums…allow bacteria into the bloodstream. This bacteria is filtered out by the kidneys and can deposit on the heart valves, leading to kidney and heart failure.
–Dr. John Hallett

Dental Care

Most people laugh when we suggest brushing their dog's teeth, but keeping the teeth and gums healthy helps keep the rest of the dog healthy. It also keeps "dog breath" away. Not only are infected gums and teeth uncomfortable for the dog, they allow bacteria into the bloodstream. This bacteria is filtered out by the kidneys and can deposit on the heart valves, leading to kidney and heart failure.

Since dogs are living longer today, it is very important to keep their mouths healthy. Brushing their teeth three times a week will help keep their gums healthy by stimulating circulation in the gums and by reducing the bacteria that lays down tartar. Use a dog toothpaste that is made to be swallowed and tastes good.

Start with some paste on your finger and massage the gums. Use lots of positive reinforcement. Eventually, you can work up to using a very soft brush. Hold the puppy's mouth shut and work on the outside surfaces of the teeth. This is where most of the tartar builds up. You will not remove tartar by brushing. Eventually, some tartar will build up, and we will need to scale and polish the teeth, just like our dentist does for us.

prostate cancer, and prostate infection. Spaying or neutering does not lead to obesity. Overfeeding leads to obesity.

▸ *Finish page 4*

The text files needed for page 4 are found in the *08 Healthy Pets Newsletter* folder. Place *Pet ID.docx* at the bottom of the third column. You will need to do some local formatting in this article by changing the *Home Again* product name to italics. Notice that when you add local formatting, a plus sign (+) appears at the end of the Body Copy paragraph style in the panel. Place and apply styles to the *Heartworm.docx* and *Toys.docx* files. Place the *Emergency Vet Service.docx* file, formatting the type as shown in the newsletter sample printed from the PDF file on the online companion resources. Notice that the *Fleas and Ticks.docx* article uses two paragraph styles: Body Copy, Body Copy Indent; and a character style, Body Copy Bold, which will be applied next.

▸ *Apply character styles*

When you find yourself doing the same type of local formatting over and over again, it's probably time to define and apply a character style. The last page has two articles that use the Body Copy Bold character style: *Fleas and Ticks* and *Corrections to keep your puppy from biting.*

1. In the *Fleas and Ticks* article, use the *Body Copy Bold* character style on the product names in the bulleted copy: *Frontline®, Flea-tick Spray, Flea Shampoo, Flea Collar, Preventic®,* and *House Spray.* Highlight those words and apply the *Body Copy Bold* character style from the *Character Styles* panel, using the keyboard shortcut created earlier. Be sure to use *Indent to here* to hang the second line of copy under bullets.

2. In the *Corrections* article, apply the *Body Copy Bold* character style to these words: *OUCH!, Substitute,* and *Lip Pinch.*

Emergency Vet Service
(262) 542-3241

In the event of an emergency when Hallett Veterinary Hospital is closed, our voice mail will direct you to the Emergency Veterinary Service (EVS) at (262) 542-3241. EVS is open when Hallett Veterinary Hospital is closed and is fully staffed with an emergency veterinarian and veterinary technicians. They are also available for telephone consultations.

Fleas and Ticks

A single flea can lay over 300 eggs in the house leading to an indoor flea infestation. Fleas transmit tapeworms to cats and dogs. Ticks can transmit Lyme disease to dogs, cats, and people. The following flea and tick control products are available at Hallett Veterinary Hospital:

- **Frontline(r)** applied once a month to the back of the dog's or cat's neck. Kills and prevents fleas and ticks.
- **Flea-tick Spray** applied every 3–5 days.
- **Flea Shampoo** kills any live fleas present but has no residual action after the pet dries.
- **Flea Collar** helps prevent fleas but is not considered the most effective.
- **Preventic(r) Collar** prevents ticks. Must not be ingested by the dog!
- **House Spray** kills fleas on floor surfaces, prevents flea eggs from hatching.

Dr. Michael Fagan, Dr. John Hallett, Dr. Heidi Hallett
Hallett Veterinary Hospital, S.C.
5744 Brown Street
Oconomowoc, Wisconsin 53066
www. hallettvet.com
(262) 569-0801

Heartworm

Heartworm disease is transmitted to dogs by mosquitoes. When an infected mosquito bites a dog, the heart worm larva is injected into the dog's skin. The adult heartworm eventually ends up in the heart and can cause heart failure. Early in the disease, the dog may act normally. As the heart is damaged, the dog will become lethargic, cough with exercise, and may show other signs of heart failure.

Heartworm disease is much easier to prevent than it is to treat. Heartgard Plus(r) preventive is given each month from April to December. Heartgard Plus also contains an intestinal parasite treatment, deworming your dog each month for intestinal parasites in addition to preventing heart worm infection. Many dogs are given Heartgard Plus all year to prevent intestinal parasites.

Dogs should also be tested for heart worm disease once a year by drawing a blood sample. If we diagnose heart worm disease early enough, it is much safer to treat.

Grooming

We're happy to teach you how to trim your puppy's nails. Start now while the pup is young so he gets used to having his feet handled and nails trimmed. Combing or brushing should also be started when he is young. For longer haired dogs, use a steel comb to keep mats from forming.

Pet ID

Home Again(r) microchip can be inserted under the dog's skin for permanent identification. Shelters and most veterinarians have scanners that can identify your dog if necessary.

ID Tags are an inexpensive way of identifying your dog. These are available at the reception desk.

Toys

Your puppy should have one or two toys to chew on. Make sure the toy is not made of wood, leather, rawhide, or cloth since you don't want to teach the puppy to chew on furniture or clothing. Nylabones (hard plastic bones) and rope toys work well, and they can't be swallowed.

Reprimand your puppy if he picks up something other than his toy then give him a toy and praise him when he chews on it.

Corrections to keep your puppy from biting

OUCH! When your dog bites a person let them know it hurts by saying "ouch" in a high pitched yelping tone. When you say "ouch" you are telling your dog that it hurt. This is the same way litter mates communicate to tell each other to back off.

Substitute. If your pup starts to chew on something inappropriate, startle your pup by clapping and saying "hey!" and then redirect his behavior to a toy or a bone of his or her own. As soon as your pup starts to chew on his or her own toy, praise your dog by saying "good dog".

Lip pinch. As your dog turns to bite you, say "no bite" as you curl his or her upper lip under his canine tooth so your dog is biting his or her own lip. Your dog may yelp after this quick correction.

Be sure that after using any of the above corrections that you praise your dog for any good behavior of discontinuing any mouthing action.

A dog wags its tail with its heart.
– Martin Buxbaum

VISUAL |8–27|
The Back Cover page is now completed.
Artwork and text © 2004 Hallett Veterinary Hospital, S.C.

▸ *Redefine styles*

The newsletter is almost finished. This is a great time to print a copy, look at it carefully, and fine-tune the positioning of all the elements. Check for the correct use of hyphens and dashes. As you can see, your newsletter looks great, except the headlines are all italic, and the newsletter sample shows them as Roman. If you hadn't defined and applied styles, you would need to manually change every headline in the document. That may not be a big deal for a short 4-page newsletter, but imagine making that change in a 64-page book!

1. Highlight one paragraph with the Headline style assigned. Change the typeface to **Myriad Pro Bold Condensed.**

2. Open the ***Paragraph Styles*** panel. Since you made a type style change on the local level, you will see a plus sign (+) next to the Headline style. Open the panel menu options and choose ***Redefine Style.*** The Headline style is now updated to reflect the Roman type style throughout the whole document! Save and print your newsletter.

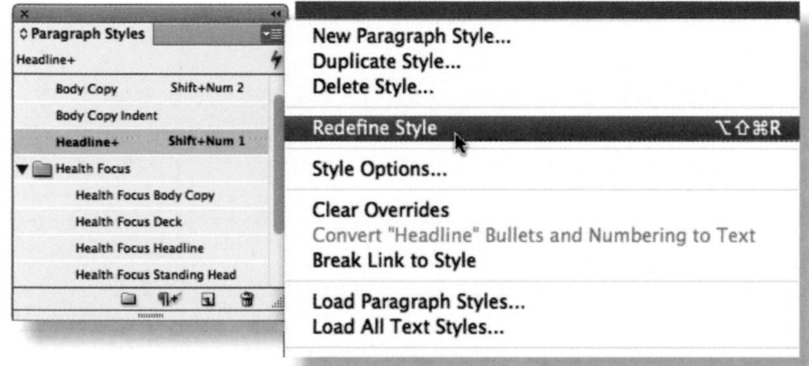

VISUAL |8–28|

Redefine the Headline style from italic to Roman.

MANAGE STYLE OVERRIDES

Sections of type that have a paragraph style, plus overrides, are easy to identify. When these passages are selected, a plus sign (+) is displayed at the end of the style name in the panel. To remove Paragraph and local Character formatting overrides, click the **Clear Overrides** icon on the *Paragraph Control* panel, or choose **Clear overrides** in selection from the *Paragraph* panel options. You have other choices for clearing overrides:

VISUAL |8–29|

The Clear overrides command is found on the Control panel, on the bottom of the Paragraph Styles panel, and on its options menu.

- ***Click*** *on the style name in the* ***Style*** *panel (no Option or Alt) to clear Paragraph overrides only.*
- ***Cmd+click*** *(Mac) or* ***Ctrl+click*** *(Windows) on the* ***Clear overrides in selection*** *icon to clear local Character formatting only.*
- *To remove Character style formatting, select the text and choose* ***[None]*** *in the* ***Styles*** *field of the* ***Character Control*** *panel.*

FIND/CHANGE

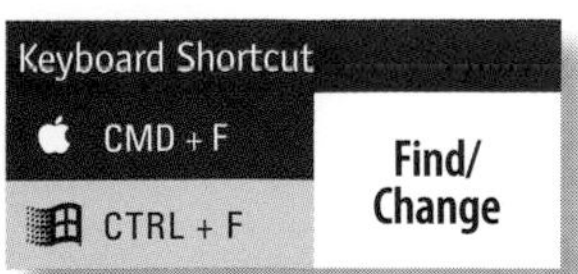

Find/Change allows you to search for specific words, characters, digits, or keystrokes and replace them with something you specify. The *Find/Change* dialog box is filled with choices—and it is worthwhile to spend some time looking at the options available in the fields. Use the keyboard shortcut or choose *Edit>Find/ Change* and type **(r)** in the *Find what* field. In the *Change to* field, select the **Special characters for replace menu (the @ sign)**, then choose *Symbols>Registered Trademark Symbol.* Set the *Search* field to **Document** and press the **Change All** button. Every occurrence of (r) in the entire newsletter will change to ®.

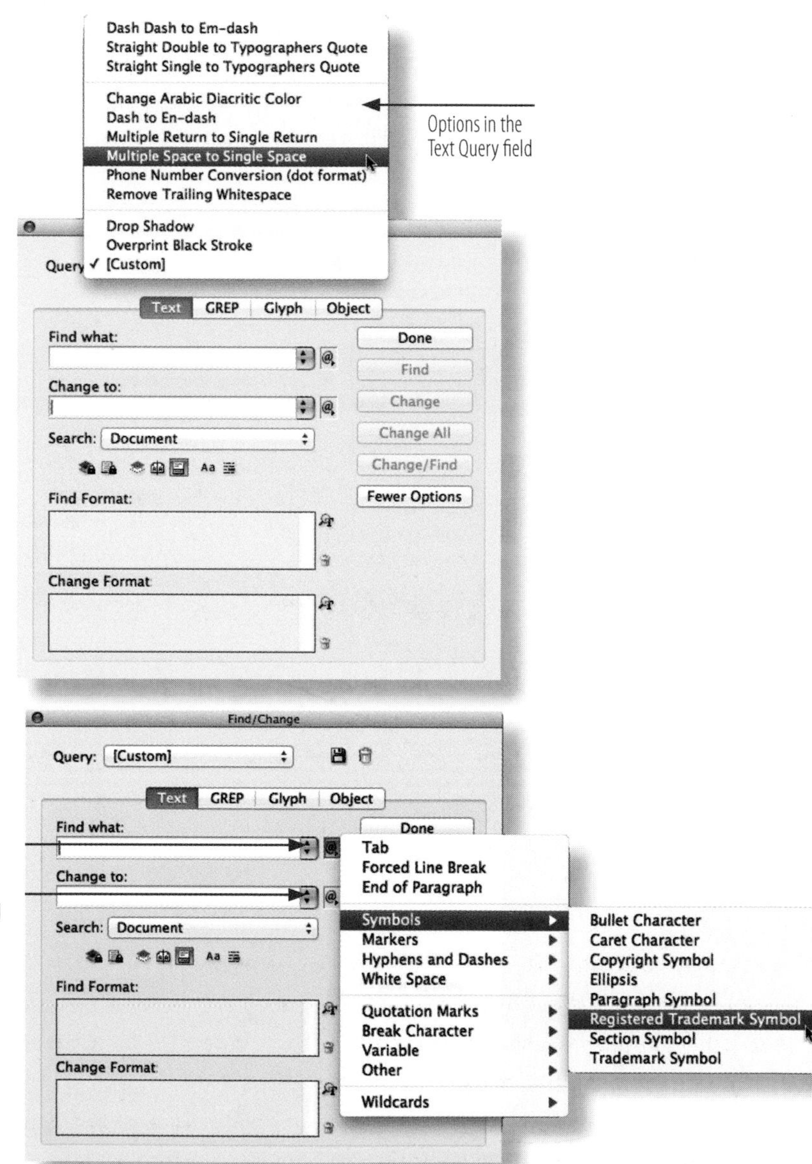

VISUAL | 8–30 |

The Find/Change panel has numerous options for making document-wide changes.

PRINT THE NEWSLETTER

Your newsletter is now completed. Proof it one more time. If you have access to a printer that can handle 11" × 17" paper, select **Spreads** in the *General* window of the *Print* dialog box. Then choose **Tabloid** or **11" × 17"** under *Setup*, and change the orientation so that your pages print side by side. If you wish to print your newsletter in spreads on letter-size paper, select **Spreads** under *General*, and then **Scale to Fit** under *Setup* (Visual 8–31).

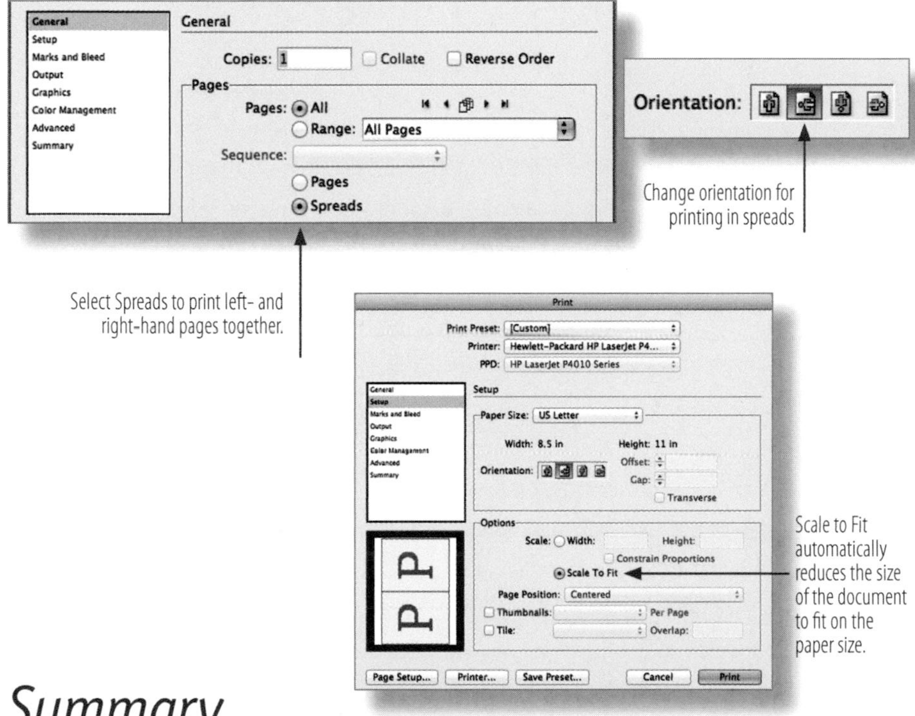

VISUAL |8–31|

Spreads must be selected to print facing pages side by side.

Summary

Skillful designers use techniques to make disinterested readers take a longer look at a publication. This newsletter project introduced you to some publication design elements: pull quote, deck, standing head, and kicker. These elements, when combined with appropriate typeface selection, line measure, and leading, create a document that has contrast and wonderful texture.

When working on complex projects, it is important to remember that there are no "throwaway" elements. The position and style of a page number or a pull quote should not be overlooked just because it's small or used only once or twice. All elements are important, and should work together to create *gestalt*—where the whole is greater than the sum of its parts. It takes creative energy and commitment to refine the smallest details of a document. But this ability to maintain a high level of focus is what separates the skilled designers from the masses.

▸ IN REVIEW

1. What are three guidelines for preparing electronic copy?

2. What are facing pages and how do you make them?

3. How can you make Snippets import at their original locations?

4. What is the process for using the Eyedropper tool to transfer text attributes?

5. What are three methods of creating paragraph styles for use in a document?

6. What is the difference between a paragraph style and a character style?

7. What does a + sign at the end of the name of a style mean?

8. When might it be wise to redefine a style?

9. What is the process for applying a paragraph style, preserving character styles, but removing overrides?

10. Describe what a style "based on" another style means.

11. In addition to using the Paragraph and Character Styles panels, where can you find and apply styles?

12. Describe how to create a paragraph style from existing copy.

13. How can you transfer paragraph and character styles from one document to another?

14. Define these newsletter parts: a) Folio, b) Kicker, c) Standing head.

15. What is the [Basic Paragraph] style?

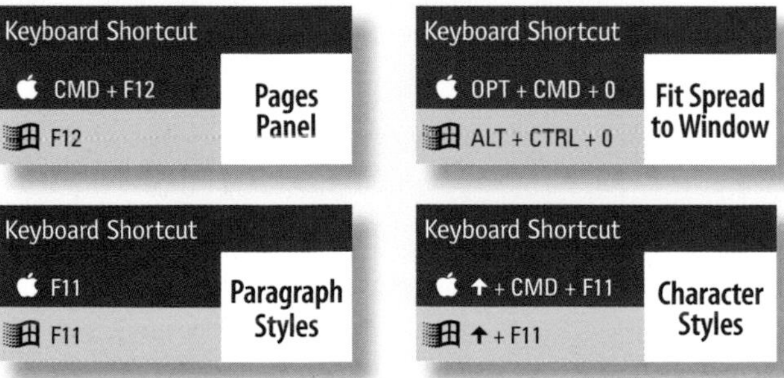

► CHAPTER 8 PROJECTS

Two projects will reinforce the concepts from this chapter.

Newsletter Analysis. Find a sample newsletter. Write a critique that addresses the following:

- *The underlying grid structure*
- *The quality of the typography: contrast, typeface, consistency*
- *Any evidence of styles*
- *The inclusion of kickers, pull quotes, decks, subheads, spread heads, or standing heads*
- *Overall impact*
- *Effectiveness of nameplate*
- *Suggestions for improvement*

Create Styles. In the second project, you will create paragraph and character styles for a magazine designed by illustrator, Steve Miljat. The layout is created and the copy is in place. You'll apply paragraph styles that utilize nested and next style attributes.

EXPLORING INDESIGN CS6
Artwork & Resources

- Go to: http://www.cengagebrain.com
- Type: Rydberg
- Click Exploring InDesign CS6 in the list of search results.
- When the book's main page is displayed, click the Access button under Free Study Tools.
- To download files, select a chapter number and then click on the Artwork & Resources tab on the left navigation bar to download the files.

| Master Pages and Object Styles |

objectives

- *Create multiple master pages*
- *Set up automatic page numbering, jump lines, and continuation lines*
- *Insert, duplicate, and remove pages*
- *Manage document pages using the Pages panel*
- *Create an object library*
- *Create and apply object styles*

introduction

Page consistency is critical for multiple-page documents. A five-person team producing a 96-page catalog needs a document structure that is consistent from page to page and designer to designer. Perhaps you've leafed through a publication where repeating elements, like page numbers, appear to jump around the outside corners like cartoons in an old-fashioned flip book. This would be an indication that the production team was not working with a clearly defined document structure. Master pages and object styles are ideal for bringing organization and consistency to complex documents. Items placed on master pages appear in the exact same location on every document page. Object styles can be used to define the stroke on a photo frame or a colored background in a text area. Changes made to a master page or an object style will ripple through the entire document, which saves time and reduces the margin of error. Proper document construction can make or break the finished project. Take the time to plan your projects thoughtfully before starting them.

the pages panel

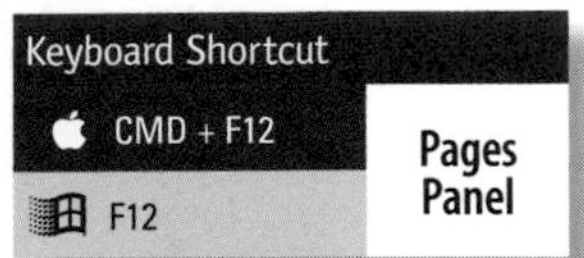

You've already used the *Pages* panel as you've worked through this text, but you've never been "formally introduced" to this little dynamo. The *Pages* panel can be opened by clicking on the *Pages* icon on the dock or by using keyboard shortcuts. If you are a Windows user, simply press **F12** (function key) and the panel will open up. If you are a Mac user, function key **F12** might already be assigned to a operating system operation such as Exposé. If that is the case, you must add the **Command** key to **F12** to open the *Pages* panel. And if you are a laptop user, you're probably already aware that, depending on the configuration of your keyboard, you may need to press the *fn* key along with the number to activate the *Pages* panel.

WHAT ARE MASTER PAGES?

The basic functions of the *Pages* panel are adding, deleting, duplicating, and rearranging pages in your document. But the *Pages* panel also allows you to create *master pages*. A master page is a page layout that is created on one spread or page and then applied to a single or a range of document pages. For instance, if I want my name to appear in the lower right corner of each page in a document, I can make a master page and place my name in the perfect location, type style and size. When I apply this master page to the document pages, my name will automatically appear in the exact location on each page!

As you begin working with complex documents, you will realize that individual pages have different layout requirements. In a single document, for instance, some pages may require three text columns, and other pages may need four. Margins may vary from page to page. Some pages may require *folios* (page numbers), running heads, or footers. Or, a graphic element may appear only on *recto* (right-hand) pages with four columns, along with a footer on the *verso* (left-hand) page. Using the *Pages* panel, you can create master pages that have different margins and columns, or contain repeating elements, such as folios. Different master pages may be assigned to individual document pages. Each document page takes on the attributes of the master page assigned to it.

Now that you know how master pages are used, you can understand how they bring consistency and assist with the production of complex documents.

A-MASTER: THE DOCUMENT DEFAULT

Each time a new document is created, the specified margins and columns are assigned to a default master page named *A-Master.* A document's *A-Master* is the basic layout that automatically applies to all pages in the document. You can change margins and columns on a single page, but the remaining pages will still retain the attributes of the *A-Master* default. But if you use the *Pages* panel to change the margins and columns on the *A-Master*, the document default, then those changes will be applied to all the pages in a document.

EXPLORING INDESIGN CS6
Artwork & Resources

- Go to: http://www.cengagebrain.com
- Type: Rydberg
- Click Exploring InDesign CS6 in the list of search results.
- When the book's main page is displayed, click the Access button under Free Study Tools.
- To download files, select a chapter number and then click on the Artwork & Resources tab on the left navigation bar to download the files.

BASIC OPERATIONS

Page masters are viewed in the *Pages* panel. By default, the master pages are displayed in the upper portion of the *Pages* panel and the regular document pages are shown in the lower (Visual 9–1). For the next series of exercises, we will be using *09 Master Pages.indd* from the *09 Artwork and Resources* folder, found on the online companion resources.

▸ *Modify Pages panel options*

Open *09 Master Pages.indd.* Press **Command+F12** (Mac) or **F12** (Windows) to open the *Pages* panel. This five-page document has been created with a photo on the master page. As you look at the page icons in the *Pages* panel, you can see that the master item—the photo—is repeated on each page. On the *Pages* panel menu, choose **Panel Options** to open a dialog that allows you to change the size of the various page thumbnail icons in the *Pages* panel. In Visual 9–1, notice that the size of the *Pages* thumbnails has been changed to *Extra Large.* In a multi-page document, enlarging the thumbnail size makes it easier to see what is on a specific page as you're navigating through the document.

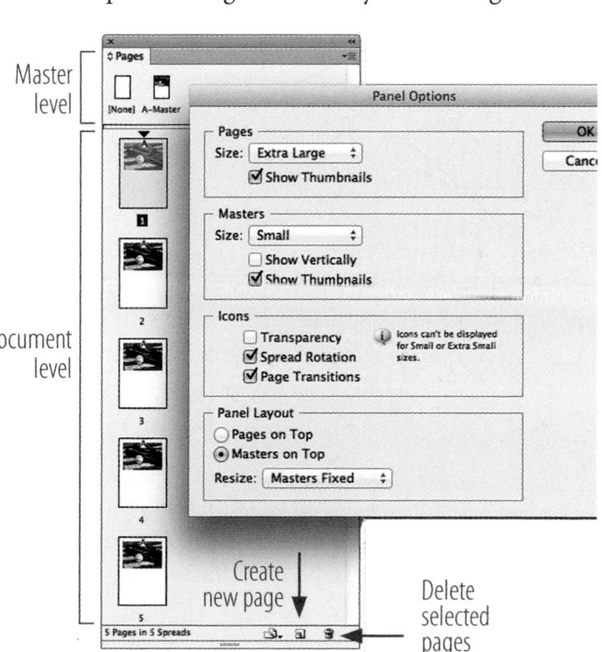

VISUAL |9–1|

The Pages Panel Options setting has been modified to show Extra Large page icons.

▸ *production tip*

Double-click a page in the Pages panel to move to and display the page.

▸ *Move from master level to document level.*

Double-click on the page 1 icon, below the double line on the *Pages* panel. The page is highlighted, and the number below the page is in a black box. You are now on document page 1, on the *local*, or *document* level. Double-click on *A-Master* in the top section of the panel. The master becomes highlighted, and you are now on the *A-Master* page, on the *global*, or *master* level. Repeat this sequence until you are comfortable moving between the two levels. Notice the page number in the lower left corner of the InDesign window. It shows the active page, and switches between *A-Master* and page 1 as you move back and forth. When you single-click a page or master page, the page becomes highlighted, but the page is not actually selected. A single-click highlights a page; and a double-click moves to, and displays the page. Double-click on different pages in your document, and watch the numbers change in the page number field.

▸ *production tip*

When you're not working on a master page, you're working on the "local" or "document level."

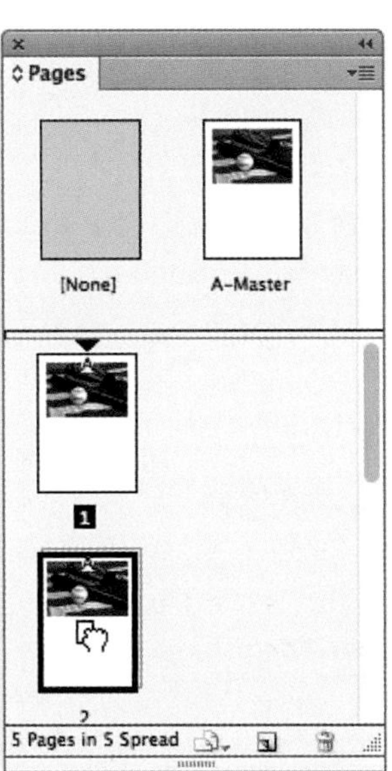

VISUAL |9–2|

A black border surrounding the document page means that a master page is being applied.

© Cengage Learning 2013

▸ *Apply the [None] master*

Select the *[None]* master page from the Pages panel. Drag the *[None]* page icon to the document level, and place it on top of page 2. Release the mouse when a thick, black border appears around the page 2 icon. The *[None]* master unassigns a master from a page. In this example, *A-Master* is now removed from page 2, and is replaced by a blank page. Use the *[None]* master to unassign *A-Master* from pages 2–5 in your document.

▸ *Rename a master page*

Double-click *A-Master*. Draw two lines below the photo. For the top line, specify width **10-pt., Red** stroke. Lower line, width **3-pt., Blue** stroke. Open the *Master Options* dialog box from the *Pages* menu. In this dialog box you can set various options, such as the *Prefix* that will be displayed on page icons to identify which master page has been applied. You can also rename the master page. Type **Red & Blue Lines** in the *Name* field (Visual 9–3).

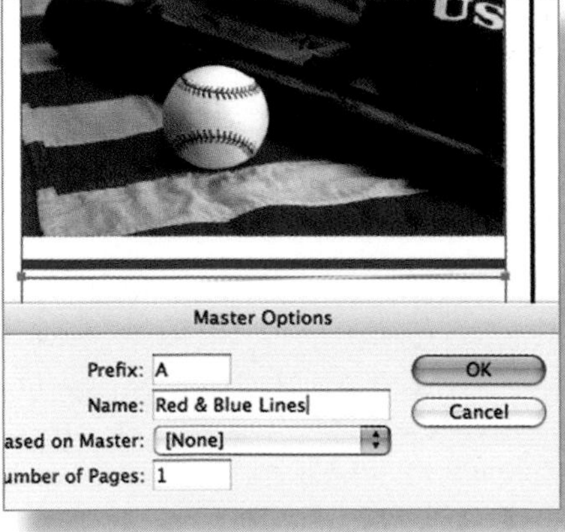

VISUAL |9–3|

The master page has been renamed in the Master Options dialog box.

© Kristina Hegyera 2007

▸ MOVING TOWARD MASTERY

*Recognize these visual cues when using the **Pages** panel. A black frame surrounding a page means that the selected master is being applied to the document page. When pages are added by pulling masters to the document level, a thin vertical line indicates an insertion point between pages where a new page will be added.*

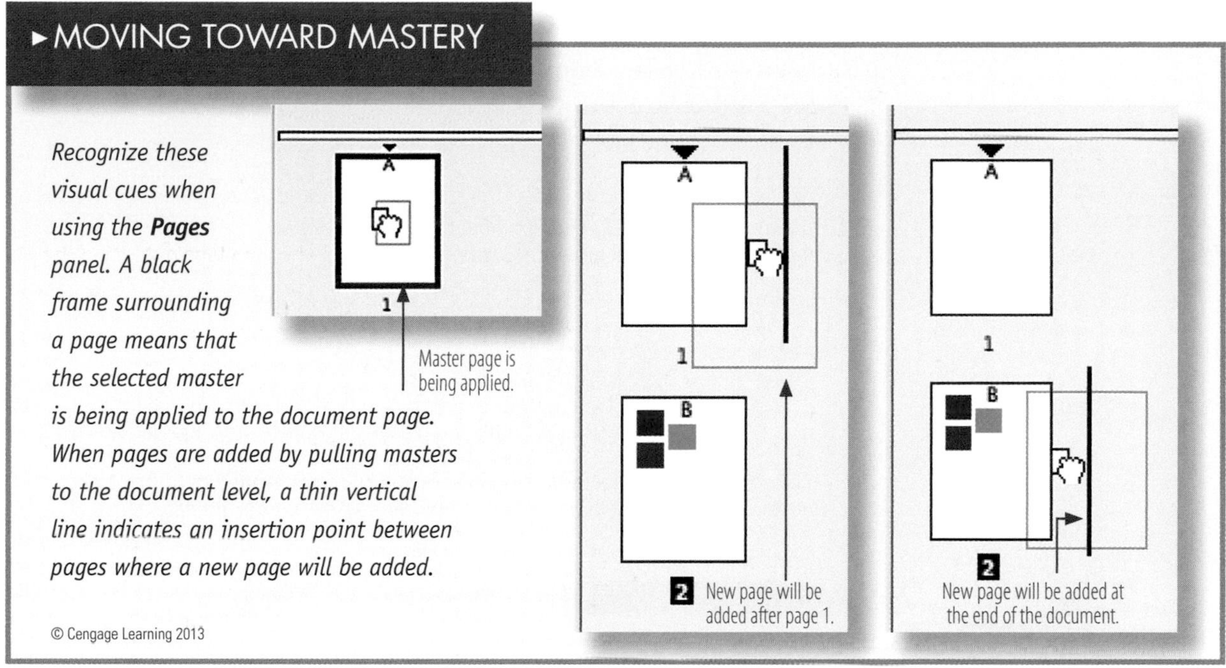

▸ Insert pages

There are many methods of inserting pages in a document. Insert additional pages to your document, using each of the following methods:

- *Click on the **Pages** panel options and choose **Insert Pages**. In the **Insert Pages** dialog box you can specify how many pages to add, and which master should be assigned to the new pages. In **Insert Pages**, change the **Pages** field to **1**. Check that the **Insert** fields are set to **After Page** and **1**. Select **A-Red & Blue Lines** in the **Master** field. Press **Return**. Compare the pages assigned to A-Red & Blue Lines with the unassigned, blank pages. Notice that the assigned pages have a small "A" on the top of each page icon. This tells you, at a glance, that the A-Red & Blue Lines master page is applied to those document pages.*
- *Click the **Create new page** icon at the bottom of the **Pages** panel (Visual 9–1). Each time you click, a new page is inserted after the page you are on. The new pages are assigned the master page used for the last page you were on. If you press **Option** (Mac) or **Alt** (Windows) as you click the **Create new page** icon, the same **Insert Pages** dialog box, found on the **Pages** panel, opens.*
- *Go to **File>Document Setup** and enter a value in **Number of Pages**. When you insert pages using this technique, you don't have the option to choose which master page the new pages will be based on, and new pages are always added to the end of the document.*
- *You can also insert a document page that is based on a master by dragging and dropping the master page icon into the document section of the **Pages** panel. If you want to add the new page in a particular spot, say between pages 1 and 2, drag the master page between the two page icons until you see a vertical line appear after page 1. When you release the mouse, there will be a new page 2 created; the old page 2 will be shifted to the number 3 spot. Be careful not to release the mouse when the border of a document page is highlighted. If you do, you will be applying that master page to the selected document page.*

▸ *Delete pages*

There are also several methods for deleting pages. Use each of the following methods to delete pages in your document, until your document has only one page and keep your file open for more practice.

- *Select a page and drag it to the **Delete selected pages** icon (Visual 9–1). Or, **Shift+click** to select a range of pages, and drag them to the Delete selected pages icon.*
- *Select a page, or range of pages, and click the **Delete selected pages** icon.*
- *Select a page, or range of pages. Go to the **Pages** options and choose **Delete Spread**.*
- *Go to **Layout>Pages>Delete Pages** and specify the page that will be deleted.*
- *Go to **File>Document Setup** and change the value in **Number of Pages**. This method removes pages from the end of the document.*

MODIFYING MASTER ITEMS ON THE DOCUMENT LEVEL

Using master pages is ideal when you have a document with elements such as *folios* (page numbers), headers, footers, or design elements that will appear on every page. When you apply a master to a document page, all the elements from the master, called *master items,* appear in the same position on each document page. Text frames created on the master page are displayed on document pages with dotted bounding boxes. Even though you may have created multiple master pages to cover every possible page layout scenario, there are times when master items still need to be modified on the document level. Before a master item can be modified on the document level, it must be *overridden.* This is a keyboard shortcut that you will frequently use—**Shift+Command+Click** (Mac) or **Shift+Control+Click** (Windows). Carefully work through the next series of exercises to learn how to manage master items.

▸ *Override master items*

When you *override* a master item, a copy of the item appears on the document page, allowing you to change its attributes. Press **Shift+Command** (Mac) or **Shift+Control** (Windows) and **click** on the red line on page 1. Handles appear, indicating that the line is editable. Change the red line's stroke to **Yellow**. A master item that is overridden still retains its association with the master page. However, the attributes that were changed on the local level won't be updated when those same attributes are changed on the master page. In the example of our red-turned-to-yellow line, color was the attribute changed on the local level. When the master page is modified, InDesign will update only attributes that have not been modified on the local level. Go to master **A-Red & Blue Lines.** Move the red line to the bottom of the master page, and change its stroke to **Green.** On page 1, notice that the position of the line changed, but not the stroke color, because the color had been modified on the local level.

▸ *production tip*

Master item attributes changed on the local level won't be updated when those same attributes are changed on the master page.

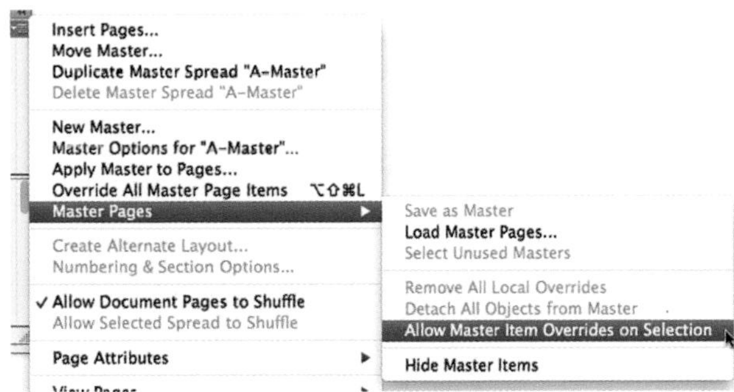

VISUAL |9–4|

Allow Master Item Overrides on Selection must be checked, for each item on a master page, in order to override that item on a document page.

► *Allow master item overrides on selection*

Go to page 1, and use the **Override Master Item** keyboard shortcut on the photo. Nothing happens. This element cannot be modified because when it was placed on the master, *Allow Master Item Overrides on Selection* was turned off. Select the photo on **A-Red & Blue Lines** master page. Under **Master Pages** in the Pages panel options, select **Allow Master Item Overrides on Selection** (Visual 9–4). Now, delete the photo on page 1.

► *Remove local overrides*

You can remove *selected*, or *all local overrides* on any specific page. Begin by overriding the lines on page 1, and change their positions and stroke colors. Now, select one of the lines. From the *Master Pages* options, choose **Remove Selected Local Overrides** (Visual 9–5). With this command, the attributes of the selected item will be restored to match the item on the master page. Now, deselect everything on page 1. From the *Master Pages* options, choose **Remove All Local Local Overrides.** The page will be restored to the original **A-Red & Blue Lines** master.

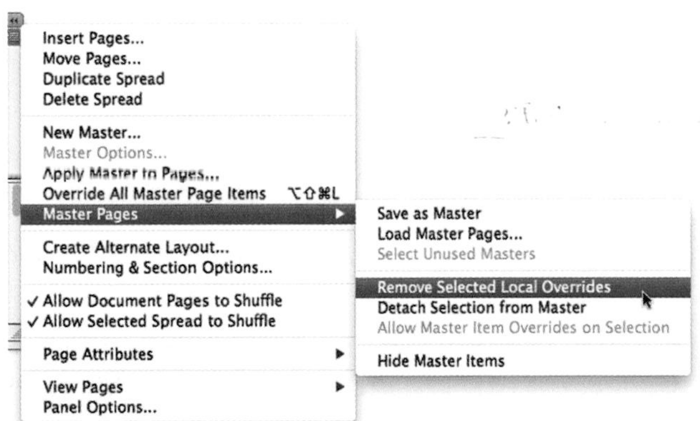

VISUAL |9–5|

Remove Selected Local Overrides restores individual master items. Remove All Local Overrides restores all master items.

► *Detach selection from master*

Go to page 1. Use **Shift+Command+click** (Mac) or **Shift+Control+click** (Windows) to override the red line. Under the *Pages* menu options, select **Detach Selection from Master** (Visual 9–6). A master item must be overridden before it can be detached. Once a master item is *detached,*

► *production tip*

A master item must be overridden before it can be detached.

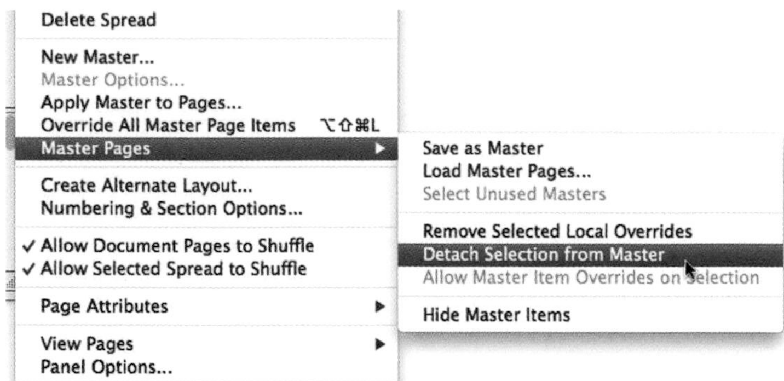

VISUAL |9–6|

When a master page item is detached from the master, it no longer retains any association with the master page.

there is no more connection with the master page. Changes made on the master page will not affect items that have been detached. Go back to **A-Red & Blue Lines** master and delete the red line. Notice the red line remains on page 1, because it is no longer associated with the master page. Use the **Undo** command to replace the red line on the master page.

Keyboard Shortcut

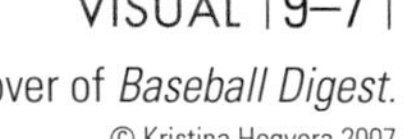

▸ *Override all master page items*

Overriding every individual master item on a complex page can be time consuming. *Override All Master Page Items* overrides all master items on the selected page, not on all the pages in a document. You will want to memorize this keyboard shortcut!

VISUAL |9–7|

Front cover of *Baseball Digest.*

CREATING A DOCUMENT WITH MULTIPLE MASTERS

Many documents require more than one master page. For instance, you may be working on a document that requires different pages to have a two-column grid, a three-column grid, and a four-column grid. In such a case, if you don't create multiple master pages, you will need to change the margins and columns on each individual page—that's too much work! In the next exercise you will create a small publication, *Baseball Digest,* with photography provided by baseball fan(atic) Kristina Hegyera, a student at Waukesha County Technical College. The document is partially constructed for you, and each step in the project will introduce a new master page function. Take your time as you systematically learn the features of master pages. You will need to use elements from *09 Artwork and Resources*, found on the online companion resources.

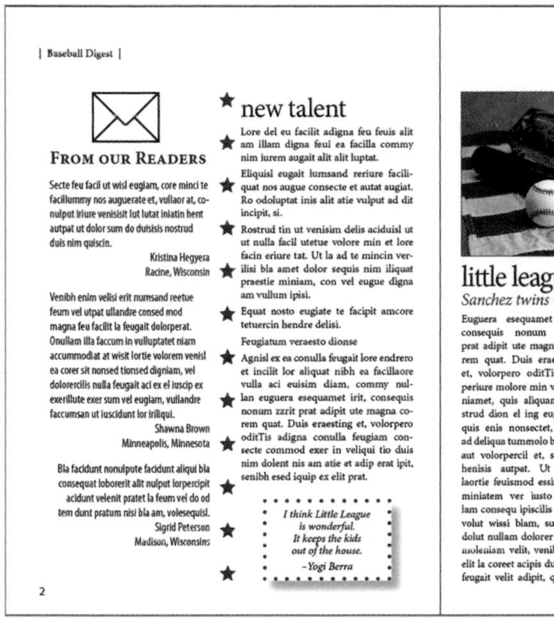

| Baseball Digest |

FROM OUR READERS

Secte feu facil ut wisl eugiam, core minci te facillummy nos auguerate et, vullaor at, conulput iriure venisisit lut lutat iniatin hent autpat ut dolor sum do duisisis nostrud duis nim quiscin.

Kristina Hegyera
Racine, Wisconsin

Venibh enim velisi erit numsand reetue feum vel utpat ullandre consed mod magna feu facilit la feugait dolorperat. Onullam illa faccum in vulluptatet niam accummodiat at wisit lortie volorem venisl ea corer sit nonsed tionsed dignіam, vel dolorercilis nulla feugait aci ex el iuscip ex exerillute exer sum vel eugiam, vullandre faccumsan ut iuscidunt lor iriliqui.

Shawna Brown
Minneapolis, Minnesota

Bla facidunt nonulpute facidunt aliqui bla consequat loborerit alit nulput lorpercipit acidunt velenit pratet la feum vel do od tem dunt pratum nisi bla am, volesequisl.

Sigrid Peterson
Madison, Wisconsins

new talent

Lore del eu facilit adigna feu feuis alit am illam digna feui ea facilla commy nim iurem augait alit alit luptat.

Eliquisl eugait lumsand reriure facilisquat nos augue consecte et autat augiat. Ro odoluptat inis alit atie vulput ad dit incipit, si.

Rostrud tin ut venisim delis aciduisl ut ut nulla facil utetue volore min et lore facin eriure tat. Ut la ad te mincin verilisi bla amet dolor sequis nim iliquat praestie miniam, con vel eugue digna am vullum ipisi.

Equat nosto eugiate te facipit amcore tetuercin hendre delisi.

Feugiatum veraesto dionse

Agnisl ex ea conulla feugait lore endrero et incilit lor aliquat nibh ea facillaore vulla aci euisim diam, commy nullan euguera esequamet irit, consequis nonum zzrit prat adipit ute magna corem quat. Duis eraesting et, volorpero oditTis adigna conulla feugiam consecte commod exer in veliqui tio duis nim dolent nis am atie et adip erat ipit, senibh esed iquip ex elit prat.

I think Little League is wonderful. It keeps the kids out of the house.
- Yogi Berra

2

| May 2010 |

little league update

Sanchez twins win championship!

Euguera esequamet irit, consequis nonum zzrit prat adipit ute magna corem quat. Duis eraesting et, volorpero oditTisBorperiure molore min venim niamet, quis aliquam iustrud dion el ing eugiam, quis enis nonsectet, sum ad deliqua tummolo boreet aut volorpercil et, suscin henisis autpat. Ut vullaortie feuismod essis atie miniatem ver iusto erillam consequ ipiscilis niam volut wissi blam, sustrud dolut nullam dolorer secte ero commodo od et wis alit ut ut ver iusto dolortisci bla amconulla faccum irit veliquisit inci blaore vel dolut acinismodo od dolore conulla feugiam conullute magnisci tat ut prat. Duisim aute te dolorper il dolortisim nit endiam velessequate diam nibh eliquis nostrud magna aut am, si.

Ibh estrud eugiam at vullum nulputpat aliquatisi tem dip et veros amcommo doloreet lorper sequis non hent ullaor iurem ametummy nonummy non henim ip etuercin et, qui et adit ul-

★ LITTLE LEAGUE UPDATE continued on page 4

coaches' corner

Euguera esequamet irit, consequis nonum zzrit prat adipit ute magna corem quat. Duis eraesting et, volorpero odit-TisBorperiure molore min venim niamet, quis aliquam iustrud dion el ing eugiam, quis enis nonsectet.

Um ad deliqua tummolo boreet aut volorpercil et, suscin henisis autpat. Ut vullaortie feuismod essis atie miniatem ver iusto erillam consequ ipiscilis niam volut wissi blam, sustrud dolut nu

It's like deja vu all over again.
- Yogi Berra

3

VISUAL | 9–8 |

Pages 2–3 *Baseball Digest*.

BASEBALL DIGEST MAGAZINE

1. Open *09 Baseball Digest.indd* from the *09 Artwork and Resources* folder.

2. Rename *A-Master*. Open the *Pages* panel. Highlight the verso and recto page of *A-Master*. Go to *Master Options for A-Master* and change *Name:* to **Folio and Header**, *Number of Pages:* **2**. You've just renamed the master page. Giving descriptive names to master pages is a good production practice.

3. Specify automatic page numbering. Enlarge the view of the Folio and Header master page. In the outside, bottom corner of each spread is a letter "X." This letter is a placeholder for a page number. You'll replace placeholder "X" with InDesign's special character, *Current Page Number*. As a result, a page number will be automatically placed on each document page. Highlight the *X* on the recto master page, and press **Shift+Command+Option+N** (Mac) or **Shift+Control+Alt+N** (Windows). *Current Page Number* can also be inserted from the *Context* or *Type* menus, by choosing *Insert Special Character>Markers>Current Page Number.* The "X" will be replaced with the letter, "A." Letter "A" corresponds to the *"A" prefix* on this master page. Repeat this process to replace the verso folio "X "with the *Current Page Number* symbol. When you look at the pages on the local level, you will see that page numbers are displayed on each page. Because the folios are master items, you don't need to worry that they will be accidently repositioned on a document page.

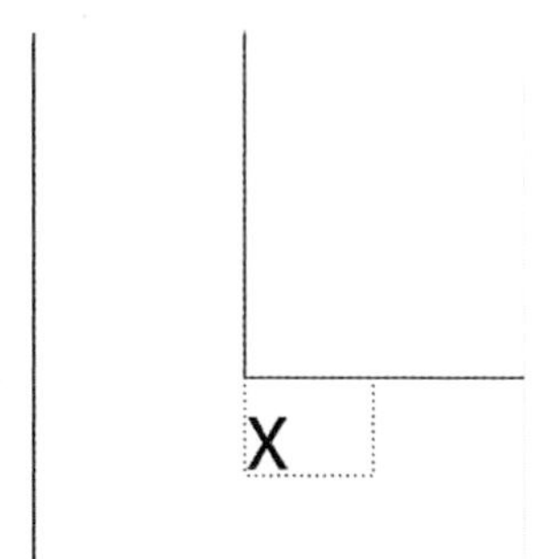

EXPLORING INDESIGN CS6
Artwork & Resources

- Go to: http://www.cengagebrain.com
- Type: Rydberg
- Click Exploring InDesign CS6 in the list of search results.
- When the book's main page is displayed, click the Access button under Free Study Tools.
- To download files, select a chapter number and then click on the Artwork & Resources tab on the left navigation bar to download the files.

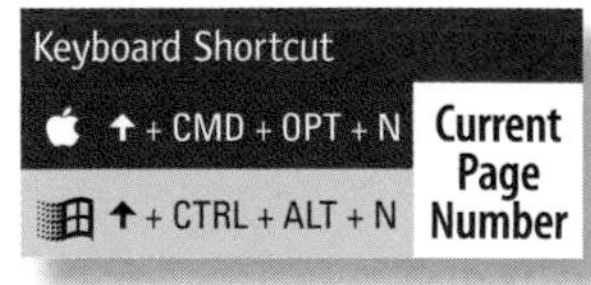

VISUAL | 9–9 |

Master items appear with a dotted line around the bounding box. When the Current Page Number symbol is applied, the X will be replaced with the letter of the master page prefix.

4. Add running heads. A ***running head*** (or ***header***) is a line of text that appears at the top of every page. . Change ***InDesign Preferences>File Handling*** so that the ***Snippet Import position*** is at the ***Original Location***. Navigate to the ***09 Baseball Digest*** folder on the ***09 Artwork and Resources*** folder and place ***X Verso Header.idms*** in the upper left corner of the verso ***A-Folio and Header*** master page. Then place ***X Recto Header.idms*** in the upper right corner of the recto master (Visual 9–10). This master page will now be used as a foundation for the rest of the master pages for this publication.

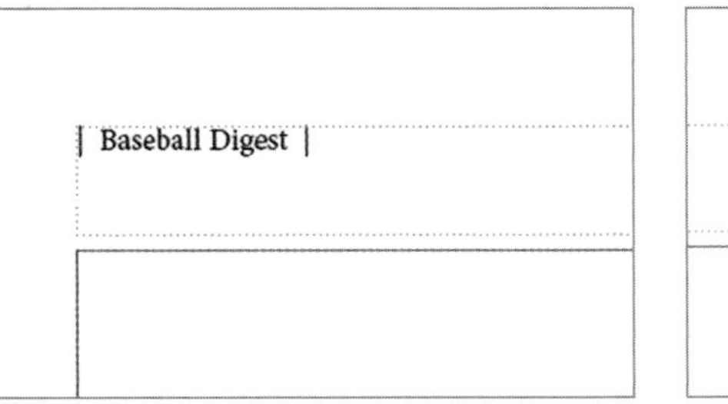

VISUAL |9–10|

The running heads on the top of the verso and recto master pages.

© Cengage Learning 2013

▸ *Use Layout Adjustment*

Layout Adjustment automatically changes the position of elements when changes are made to an existing layout. *Layout Adjustment* isn't just a feature of master pages—it can be used at the document level, as well. *Layout Adjustment* works best with elements that are aligned to the guides of margins and page columns, and to ruler guides. We will change the column settings on the master level and let *Layout Adjustment* update the layout on the document level.

1. Go to page 1. Draw a text frame inside the margin area and fill with placeholder text. From the ***Window*** menu, go to ***Interactive>Liquid Layout***. Open the panel menu and select ***Layout Adjustment***. When the dialog box comes up, select ***Enable Layout Adjustment*** and accept the default settings (Visual 9–11). ***Enable Layout Adjustment*** can also be accessed under ***Layout>Margins and Columns.***

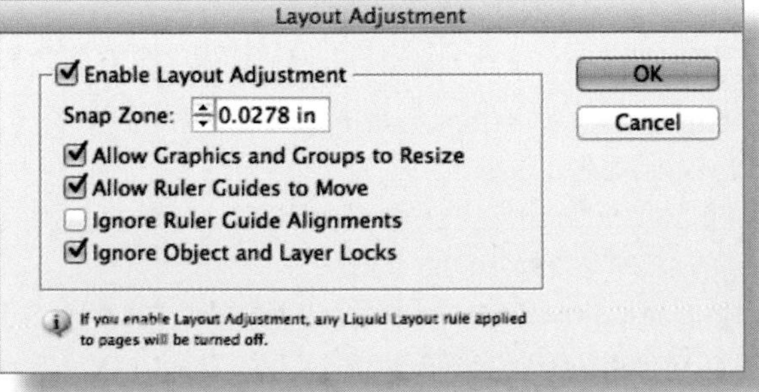

VISUAL |9–11|

As a layout changes, Layout Adjustment automatically repositions elements that are snapped to margin and ruler guides.

© Cengage Learning 2013

2. Select the recto master page. From the menu, select ***Layout>Margins and Columns.*** Enter **3** in the ***Columns Number*** field. Go to page 1 and you will see that the text has been automatically updated to three columns. Undo the 3-column master change and delete the text frame, but keep your document open!

▸ *Create and duplicate master pages*

The *A-Folio and Header* master page spread has single text columns, headers, and auto page numbering. Now you will create another master page with the same headers and folios, but with different margins and column guides. Before a new master page is created, you have a decision to make: Should this page be *based on* another master page, or should it be an independent page, based on *[None]*? Just like paragraph styles, which can be based on another style, a master page based on another master page, will automatically update, if any changes are made to the original master page. When working with master pages, the original master page is the *parent master*, and the master page based on it, is the *child master*.

▸ *production tip*

Like paragraph styles, which can be based on another style, a master page based on another master page, will automatically update, if any changes are made to the original master page.

1. Choose *New Master* from the panel options. When the *New Master* dialog box appears, type **Two-column Grid** in the *Name* field. In *Based On Master:* choose **A-Folio and Header**, *Number of Pages:* **2**. A new master page with a "B" prefix will now appear in the master level of the Pages panel. The letter "A" in the upper corners shows that master A is the ***parent master***. Select each page in *B-Two-column Grid.* Notice that the headers and footers from the "A" master were transferred to this new master page.

2. Now, make sure both "B" master page icons in the spread are selected and go to *Layout>Margins and Columns* and change the *Columns Number* to **2**. Accept the default gutter, and press **Return**.

   When duplicating master spreads, you also need to consider parent master and child master relationships. If you duplicate a master page and base it on *[None]*, the new page will include all the elements from the copied page, but the connection with those elements will be broken. This means that any changes made on the original master page will not affect the duplicate page. Practice each of these methods to duplicate a master spread in a document:

   - *Highlight the master spread and drag it to the **Create new page** icon at the bottom of the **Pages** panel.*
   - *Go to the **Pages** options menu and select **Duplicate Master Spread**.*
   - *Use one of these methods to duplicate the "A" or "B" master page in your document. After you get comfortable using each method of creating duplicate master spreads, delete any you have made, because they will not be used in the **Baseball Digest** project.*

3. Create and apply a new master spread. Choose *New Master* from the panel options. Name the master **Three-column Grid**, and base it on **A-Folio and Header.** Go to *Layout>Margins and Columns* and change the *Columns Number* to **3**. Press **Return.** Apply this master to page 1 of the document by dragging a recto *Three-column Grid* master page on top of page 1. When the black border surrounds the page, release the mouse. Override, and delete the header and the folio on page 1, leaving just the three column text frame.

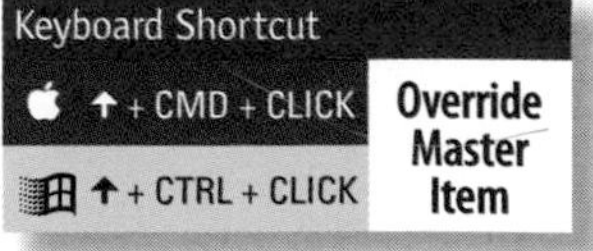

▸ *Build the document*

The pages are formatted and ready to go. You'll place Snippets to complete this project, and if you changed your InDesign preferences earlier, this part should be a snap.

1. Finish page 1. Place ***P1 Nameplate.idms*** from the ***09 Baseball Digest*** folder. Place it on page 1, centered horizontally at the top of the page. Place ***P1 Contents.idms*** in the left column, flush against the bottom margin guide. ***P1 Photo*** is positioned just above the contents box in the left column. ***P1 Article.idms*** spans columns 2 and 3, and is flush with the bottom margin guide. Place ***P1 Seal.idms*** in the upper right corner (Visual 9–12).

VISUAL |9–12|

A view of the positioning of the elements on page 1 of *Baseball Digest.*

2. Finish page 2. Apply a verso ***Two-column Grid*** master to page 2 by dragging a verso master page from the ***Pages*** panel and letting it rest on top of page 2. When a black border appears, release the mouse. Place ***P2 Stars.idms*** in the gutter between column 1 and column 2. Place ***P2 Letters.idms*** in the left column. Position ***P2 New Talent.idms*** flush with the right column, top margin guide. Center ***P2 Quote.idms*** in the right column, flush with the bottom margin guide (Visual 9–13).

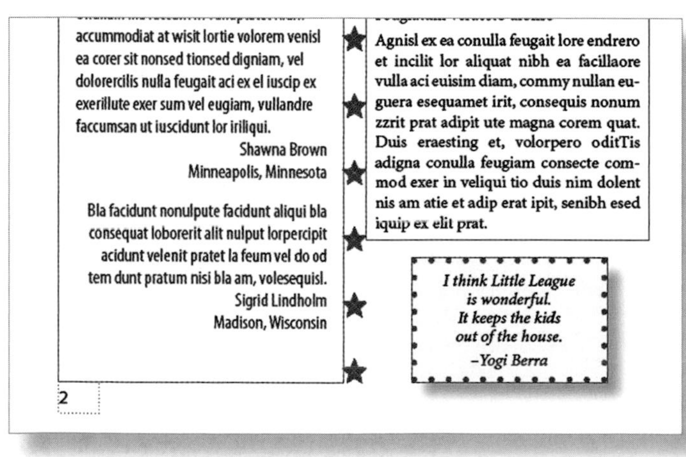

VISUAL |9–13|

Positioning of the elements on the lower half of page 2.

▸ Add jump lines and continuation lines

Jump lines are used to alert readers when an article is continued on another page. They appear at the end of a column and read something like: *"this article continues on page 257."* When you turn to page 257, you are greeted with a *continuation line,* which reads something like: "... *article continued from page 1."* InDesign automates this process. A separate text frame is created, in which a special character marker is inserted. The *Next Page Number* marker is used for jump lines, while the *Previous Page Number* marker is used for continuation lines. There are two things you must remember when using jump and continuation lines:

- *The text frames on each page must be threaded; and*
- *The jump or continuation line text frame must be touching the threaded frame.*

The special characters, **Next Page Number** and **Previous Page Number**, can be found under the *Context* or *Type* menus by selecting *Insert Special Character>Markers.*

1. Apply a recto ***Three-column Grid*** master to ***page 3***. Position ***P3 Photo.idms*** across columns 1 and 2. Place ***P3 Little League.idms*** in columns 1 and 2, flush with the bottom margin guide. Place ***P3 Coaches' Corner.idms*** flush with the top margin guide of column 3. Place ***P3 Corner Ad.idms*** in the lower right corner of column 3. Center ***P3 Quote.idms*** in the remaining space in column 3.

2. Apply a ***Two-column Grid*** master to page 4. Place ***P4 Abbreviations.idms*** in the left column. Position ***P4 Top Quote.idms*** flush with the top margin guide of the second column. Place ***P4 Bottom Quote.idms*** centered at the bottom of the second column. Finally, place ***P4 Little League.idms*** in the remaining space in column 2.

3. You will need to link the first half of the Little League article on page 3 to the second half on page 4, before you can add jump and continuation lines. Click on the out port at the bottom of the article on page 3 and then click on the Little League article in the second column of page 4. Move to page 3, and place ***P3 Jump Line*** on the bottom of column 2, on top of the article. Magnify your view. Place the cursor after the word ***page*** and add a space. Go to the ***Type*** menu and select ***Insert Special Character>Markers>Next Page Number*** (Visual 9–14). A "4" should appear after the word, "page." Place ***P4 Cont Line.idms*** on the top of the Little League article on page 4. Magnify your view. Place the cursor after the word, "page" and add a space. Go to ***Type>Insert Special Character> Markers>Previous Page Number.*** A "3" should appear. The project is now finished!

▸ *production tip*

Use the markers Next Page Number for jump lines and Previous Page Number for continuation lines.

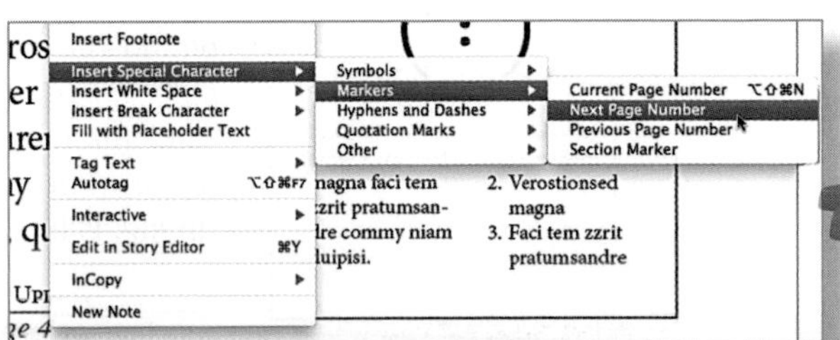

VISUAL |9–14|

The Type menu pathway to the jump and continuation line special characters.

MASTER PAGES: NOT JUST FOR COMPLEX PROJECTS

By now you can imagine how useful master pages are for large documents like books, catalogs, and magazines. But they're also great for any project with a repeating element. In this next exercise, you'll use master pages and the table function to create a unified look for your résumé, cover letter and references. All the pieces will have a common header which will create your own, unique identity. But before you get started, here are some important identity design considerations:

- *Your materials need to be typographically perfect—use correct dashes, hyphens, and quotation marks. Don't use the two-letter state abbreviation without the corresponding zip code. Better yet, don't use abbreviations!*
- *Keep your résumé clean and crisp, with type being the main design element. Making your résumé excessively "creative" is usually not a good idea.*
- *Make a .pdf of your résumé so that you can e-mail it as an attachment to potential employers. You can e-mail just the résumé and write your cover letter as an e-mail letter, or you can make a .pdf of your cover letter and résumé and include just a short note in the e-mail correspondence.*
- *Remember the word "résumé" has two accents. You created these on the Mac by pressing* ***Option e+e*** *(hold the Option key when you press the first e and then release it for the second e.) In Windows, you use* ***Alt+0233*** *(hold the Alt key and press 0233 on the numeric keypad).*
- *Never send out your résumé without a cover letter.*

▸ production tip

If you are using a laptop, with no numeric keypad, the only way to create extended characters is to use the Glyphs panel.

▸ production tip

The typeface you use to display your name is one of most important résumé design decisions you will make!

1. Open *09 Resume Template.indd* from the *09 Artwork and Resources* folder. This document has been prepared with 4 master pages. The parent master, *A-Header* contains your personal information in a header format. The others: *Cover letter*, *References*, and *Résumé Page* are child masters because they are based on the parent master. Make all changes to your header on the parent master!

2. Open the *Pages* panel. Revise the *A-Header* master page to reflect your personal information. Look at the individual letters in your name and choose a typeface that is professional, while taking advantage of the specific letters in your name. Perhaps, choose a typeface that has a capital "J" that will extend below the baseline and a capital "R" with a curved, elegant tail. The type you choose says a lot about who you are. Choose an appropriate typeface for your name! When the nameplate is completed on the *A-Header* master page, it will automatically update the child masters.

3. *Master page B* is the résumé page master, created in a table format. When you write a résumé, begin each statement with an action verb that describes what you did on a job. Don't simply list responsibilities. List results!

4. *Master page C* is for a cover letter. The master includes instructions on how to write a cover letter, and you should read Master C before composing your cover letter. The cover letter is very important because it demonstrates your writing ability.

EXPLORING INDESIGN CS6
Artwork & Resources

- Go to: http://www.cengagebrain.com
- Type: Rydberg
- Click Exploring InDesign CS6 in the list of search results.
- When the book's main page is displayed, click the Access button under Free Study Tools.
- To download files, select a chapter number and then click on the Artwork & Resources tab on the left navigation bar to download the files.

5. *Master page D* is for your references. You should never include the name of a reference without talking to the person first—and then be sure to supply them with a current copy of your résumé! Discuss with your references the characteristics and skills you would like each to focus on. For instance, if you worked on a special project and figured out a method of streamlining a process, ask that reference to comment on your resourcefulness in that situation. When you ask a person to serve as a reference, it is a good idea to say something like, "I am wondering if you would be willing to be a reference for me because you have seen my problem-solving skills first hand! Remember when…" This gives them a hint of the areas you would like them to address when a potential employer calls. Come up with three to five references who are not relatives. Former instructors are good references, so are supervisors and people you have worked with in business and volunteer settings.

6. When all components are grammatically and typographically perfect, save them. Then create a .pdf with a filename which includes your first and last name so that when you attach a pdf résumé to your e-mail, the attachment will be easily identified. This is much better than naming the pdf "My résumé" To export the document to a PDF format, use the keyboard shortcut **Cmd+E** (Mac) or **Ctrl+E** (Windows). At the bottom of the *Export* window, in the *Format* (Mac) or *Save as type* (Windows) menu, choose *Adobe PDF (Print)*. Name your file **Last name_Fir st name** and save it.

▸ *production tip*

Don't name your résumé "My Résumé." Your name should be included in the file name.

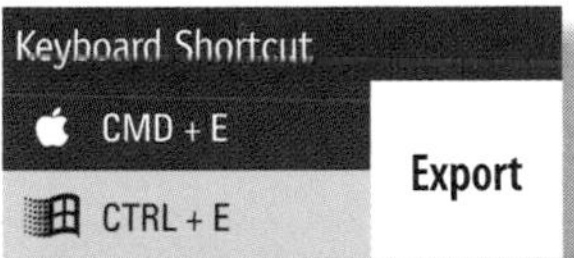

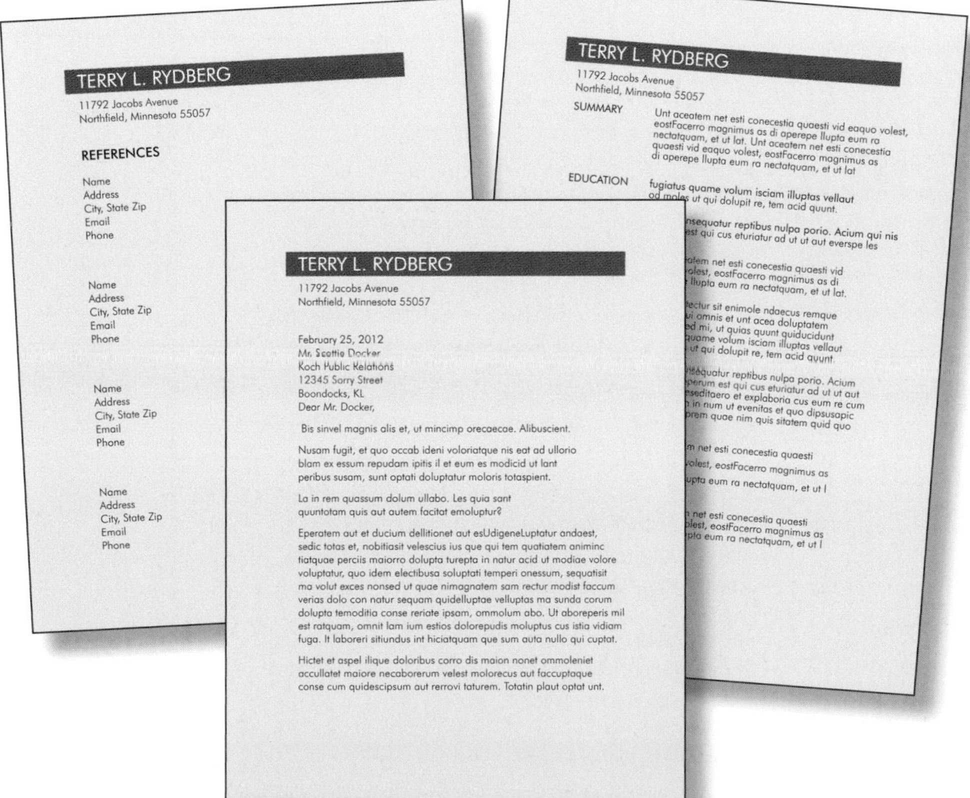

VISUAL |9–15|

Use master pages to create a uniform header for all your personal identity pieces.

► MOVING TOWARD MASTERY

anatomy of a cover letter

JOHN R. SMITH
123 My Towne Drive, Anytown, XL 54360
(456) 567-5678 • jsmith@me.com

May 15, 2012

Write the date in full without abbreviations. Use four returns between the date and the inside address.

Susan Foxglove, Creative Director
Excel Design
1225 Redwing
Princeton, Illinois 34455

The inside address includes the name and title, company, and organization. Double-check the title.

Dear Ms. Flowers:

The salutation is written to a real person. Not "To whom it may concern" or "Dear Human Resources Manager." Check the web site or call the company for the name of the person who will receive your package. When addressing to a female, use "Ms."

(Paragraph 1 describes the position for which you are applying and where you saw the posting.) I am writing in response to the advertisement for a graphic artist as published in the May 10 issue of *The La Crosse Tribune*. This position interests me because it would utilize my strengths in web and print design and preflight operations.

(Paragraph 2 compares your skills with those listed in the posting.) In my present position as Manager of Creative Services, I have designed projects ranging from brochures to catalogs—and have monitored their progress through each stage to completion. My formal training in printing and graphic design has enabled me to build files that are technically sound.

The body of the letter should be two to four paragraphs. Avoid long sentences. Try not to refer to the company as "your" company. Also, avoid beginning each paragraph with the word, "I."

(Paragraph 3 is your "value added" paragraph. What additional skills do you bring that differentiate you from the competition?) In addition to design and production strengths, I would bring to Excel Design specialized training in network administration. For the past three years, I have updated my networking skills at Apple Computer's two-week intensive *Hardware Maintenance and Networking* summer seminar.

(End the letter with a follow-up action plan.) This opportunity is one that I would enjoy. Because I am familiar with the types of projects that Excel Design produces, I know that I would "hit the ground running." My résumé is included for you to review—feel free to call any of my past employers regarding my performance. I will call you early next week to confirm that you have received this information and to answer any questions you might have. I look forward to meeting you to discuss the position in more detail.

Sincerely,

John Smith

John R. Smith
enclosure

The signature line. Don't forget to sign your letter! Use a good pen that doesn't leave ink globs on the paper. It doesn't hurt to practice your signature a few times and place the cover letter on a padded surface (such as a pad of paper) before signing it.

The enclosure line. You can also use the abbreviation "enc" in this location. Use this line whenever you are sending a résumé with your cover letter.

▸ MOVING TOWARD MASTERY

What "type" of person?

▸ *Directions: Draw a line from each résumé header to the person whose face it belongs to.*

Eager B. Designer

EAGER B. DESIGNER

EAGER B. DESIGNER

Eager B. Designer

Eager B. Designer

EAGER B. DESIGNER

Eager B. Designer

EAGER B. DESIGNER

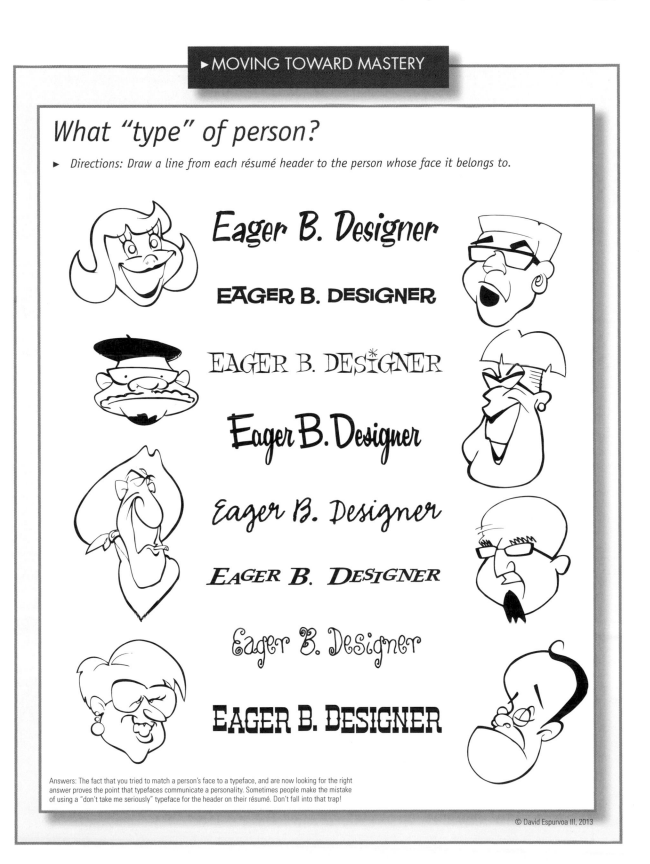

Answers: The fact that you tried to match a person's face to a typeface, and are now looking for the right answer proves the point that typefaces communicate a personality. Sometimes people make the mistake of using a "don't take me seriously" typeface for the header on their résumé. Don't fall into that trap!

using libraries and object styles

InDesign has so many features that assist us with efficiently producing complex projects! Paragraph and character styles ensure typographic continuity. Master pages bring structural consistency to a document. And now, you will learn how to create *libraries* to store page elements, and use *object styles* to quickly format text frames and graphic elements.

LIBRARIES—ARTWORK AT YOUR FINGERTIPS

When you do a lot of design work for a single client, you usually have elements that are used over and over again. For instance, if you did weekly advertisements for a dental practice, you would probably include the logo, name, hours of operation, phone number, and address in each ad. In these instances you can create a *library* that allows you to store those frequently used items in one convenient location. Library objects can be quickly dragged directly from the Library to the document. When you drag an element in from the library, you're not really taking it "out" of the library. You're just "borrowing" a copy to use in your document. The library still has the original, and will let you "check out" an unlimited number of copies.

EXPLORING INDESIGN CS6
Artwork & Resources

- Go to: http://www.cengagebrain.com
- Type: Rydberg
- Click Exploring InDesign CS6 in the list of search results.
- When the book's main page is displayed, click the Access button under Free Study Tools.
- To download files, select a chapter number and then click on the Artwork & Resources tab on the left navigation bar to download the files.

▸ *Create a library for Zaffinni's restaurant*

The library you will make in the next few steps will be saved and used in the *Zaffinni's Authentic Mediterranean Dining* menu, one of this chapter's projects.

1. From the online companion resources, open ***09A Zaffinni Artwork.indd,*** found in the ***09A Zaffinni Artwork*** folder. This InDesign file contains the source artwork you will use to assemble your library file.

2. Choose ***File>New>Library.*** Name the new library file **09 Zaffinni** and save it on your desktop. A library panel with the name ***09 Zaffinni*** will appear in y our workspace.

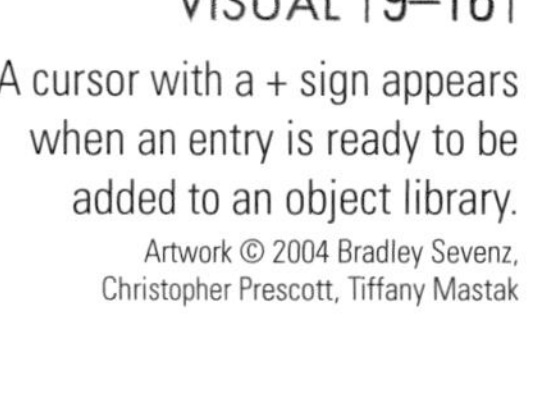

VISUAL |9–16|

A cursor with a + sign appears when an entry is ready to be added to an object library.

Artwork © 2004 Bradley Sevenz, Christopher Prescott, Tiffany Mastak

3. Using the ***Selection*** tool, drag each page item from the ***09A Zaffinni Artwork*** document to the ***09 Zaffinni*** library panel. As the element is moved to the library, the cursor will display a plus sign (+) sign showing that the item will be added to the library (Visual 9–16). Continue this process until all seven page items, including the green bar, are in the library.

4. Double-clicking a library entry opens the ***Item Information*** dialog box. You can change the name and also add a description of the item, if desired (Visual 9–17). Your library is now complete and can be used with any document you want to use it with! Be sure to remember where your ***09 Zaffinni*** library was saved, because it will be used again to complete the ***09A Zaffinni's*** menu project, at the end of the chapter. Close the library panel and close, but not save, the artwork file.

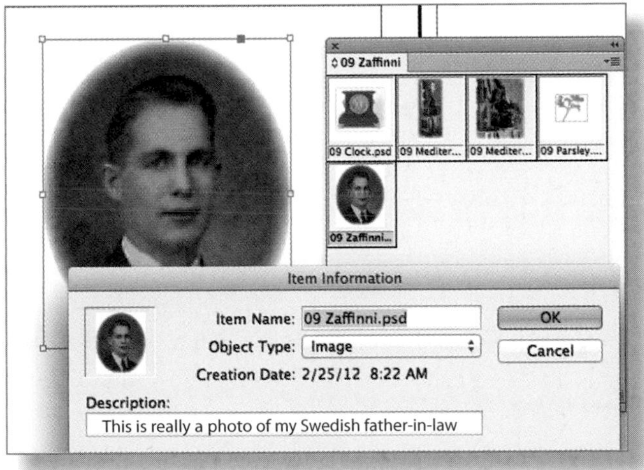

VISUAL | 9–17 |

The item Description field can contain special production instructions, or just provide general information, like this example.

Artwork © 2004 Bradley Sevenz, Christopher Prescott, Tiffany Mastak

OBJECT STYLES SAVE TIME

Like paragraph styles, object styles can assign, clear or replace object specifications according to the settings you have defined. And, like paragraph styles, you can base an object style on another style, creating a parent-child relationship. This relationship means that the parent and child objects will have attributes in common. Changing any of those shared attributes in the parent object, will automatically change those in the child object.

You will create object styles to use in constructing the Steve Miljat brochure project, at the end of the chapter. Creating master pages and object styles for this simple document will help you to see how they can dramatically speed up production when you are working on a 240-page catalog.

VISUAL | 9–18 |

You will create object styles for this Steve Miljat brochure project.

© Steve Miljat 2010, Waukesha County Technical College

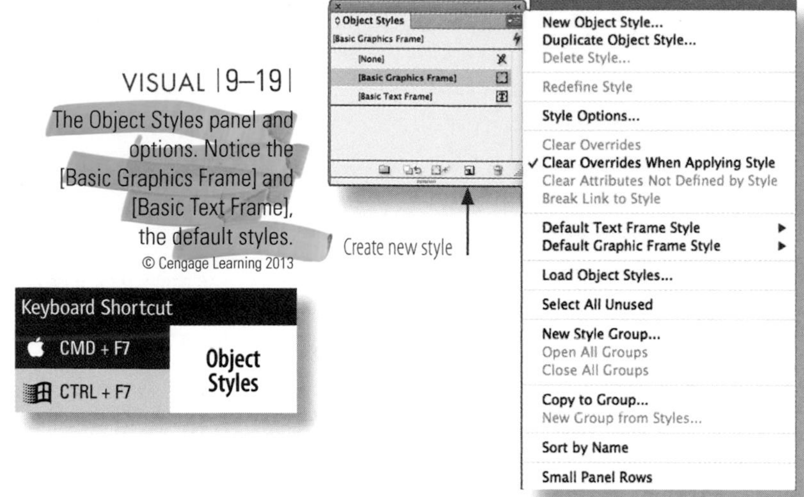

VISUAL | 9–19 |

The Object Styles panel and options. Notice the [Basic Graphics Frame] and [Basic Text Frame], the default styles.

Open the *Object Styles* panel by going to *Window>Styles>Object Styles,* or by pressing **Command+F7** (Mac) or **Control+F7** (Windows). Notice that each document comes with a default set of object styles. *[None]* is assigned to empty frames (those with an "X") and paths. The *[Basic Graphics Frame]* has an icon that is framed by bounding boxes. The *[Basic Text Frame]* has a "T" inside a frame for its icon. Visual 9–19 shows the panel and its option menu, in more detail. As you can see, the *Object Styles* panel is similar in design to the other InDesign panels.

Keyboard Shortcut

CMD + F7	Object Styles
CTRL + F7	

EXPLORING INDESIGN CS6
Artwork & Resources

- Go to: http://www.cengagebrain.com
- Type: Rydberg
- Click Exploring InDesign CS6 in the list of search results.
- When the book's main page is displayed, click the Access button under Free Study Tools.
- To download files, select a chapter number and then click on the Artwork & Resources tab on the left navigation bar to download the files.

▸ *Define object styles for the Steve Miljat brochure*

You can define an object style from an object you have already formatted, or you can define one from "scratch." These methods should sound familiar—you created typographical styles in Chapter 8, using similar methods.

1. Open *09B Steve Miljat Brochure* from the *09 Artwork and Resources* folder on the online companion resources. The document has been started for you. After creating the object styles, you will complete the project using the instructions found on the *09 Student Handout*.

2. Press **Command+F7** (Mac) or **Control+F7** (Windows) to open the *Object Styles* panel. **Option** (Mac) or **Alt** (Windows)+**click** the *Create new style* icon and the *New Object Style* dialog box will open (Visual 9–20). Name the style **Photo Boxes**.

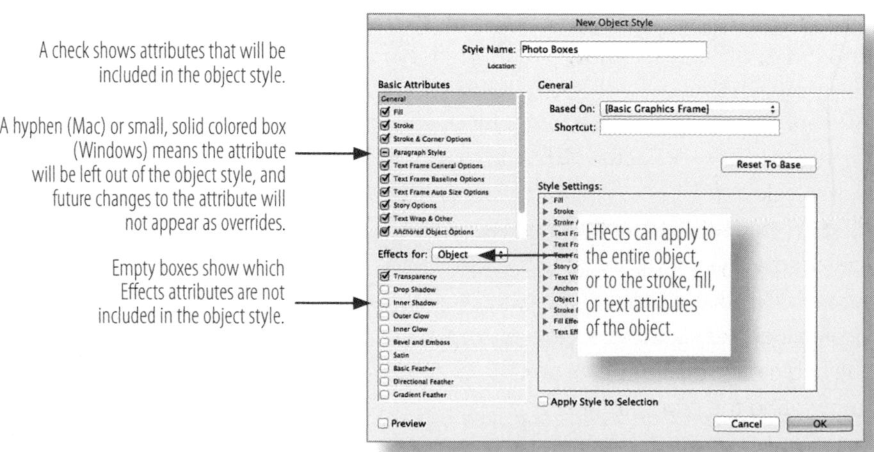

VISUAL | 9–20 |

You can choose to include or ignore specific object attributes as you are creating object styles.

3. Under *Basic Attributes*, make sure that the *Fill* category is checked and then click on the name to view its options. From the color options, select a **[Paper]** fill.

4. Go down the list of *Basic Attributes* in the left column to *Stroke.* Make sure it is checked and click on the name to open the options. Enter a **Black, 0.5-pt.** stroke (Visual 9–21).

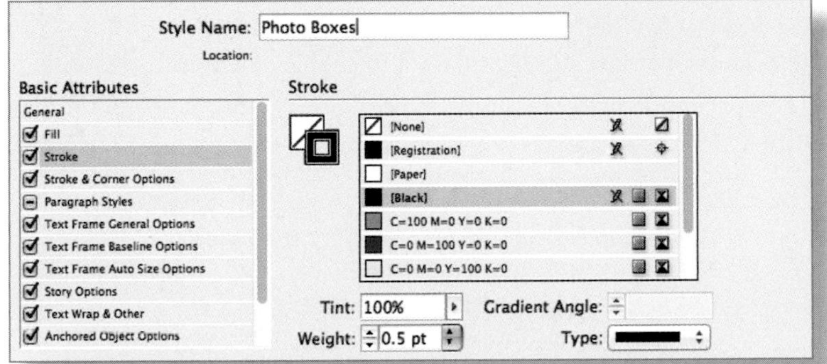

VISUAL | 9–21 |

Click on the name of each Basic Attribute to display its options.

5. Go to *Stroke & Corner Options* and click on the name to view the options. Align the stroke to the inside of the frame (Visual 9–22). Press **Return** to close the dialog.

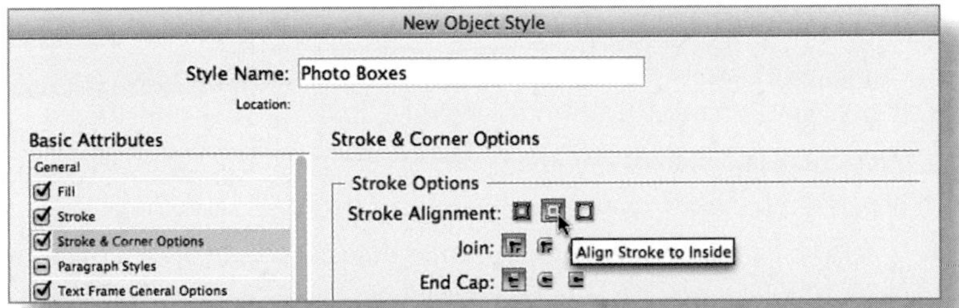

VISUAL | 9–22 |

The Stroke is aligned to inside under Stroke & Corner Options.

6. Now, let's make two more styles—a text frame with a green background and insets, and a rectangle with a light gold background. This time, we'll create the styles from existing elements. First, draw a rectangle text frame. Fill it with **C=61, M=38, Y=100, K=12**. Under *Text Frame Options*, specify *Left* and *Right insets* of **0.375"** and *Top* and *Bottom insets* of **0.25"**. With the text frame selected, **Opt+click** (Mac) or **Alt+click** (Windows) the *Create new style* icon. Name the style **Green Text Frame** and press **Return**. Now that the style is saved, you can delete the setup frame.

7. Press **F** to select the *Rectangle Frame* tool. Draw a rectangle and fill it with **C=0, M=5, Y=32, K=0**. With the box selected, **Alt** or **Opt+click** on the *Create New Style* icon and name the style, **Light Gold Background** and press **Return**. Your styles should look like Visual 9–23. Save and replace the original .indd file in the *Artwork* folder for completing the projects at the end of the chapter.

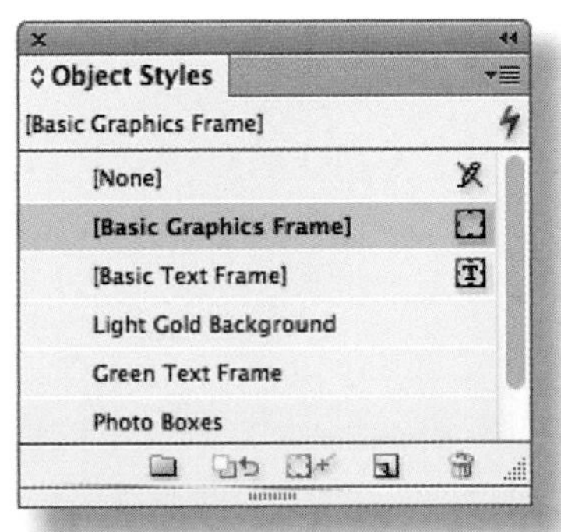

VISUAL | 9–23 |

Object styles for the Steve Miljat brochure are complete.

RESETTING OBJECT STYLE DEFAULTS

► *production tip*

Deselect All (Shift+Cmd+A or Shift+Ctrl+A) before resetting document, object, paragraph and character style defaults.

It's easy to change a document's default object styles—so easy, it's frustrating when done accidently. Whenever you select an object style, with no object selected, that style will become the default and will be applied to all new objects you create. (Similar behavior applies to other document defaults, such as paragraph or character styles.) The good news is that it's just as easy to change the defaults back to their normal settings. The key is to deselect everything and then reset the defaults. For instance, if you want to change the object style default back to *[Basic Graphics Frame]*, simply deselect everything (**Shift+Command+A** or **Shift+Control+A**) and choose *[Basic Graphics Frame]* in the *Object Styles* panel.

- *By default **[Basic Graphics Frame]** has a 1-pt. Black stroke. You can quickly remove this by applying the style **[None]** to the object.*
- *A rectangle drawn with the **Rectangle Frame** tool by default, has the **[None]** style applied.*

► *Override and redefine object styles*

You can modify any of the attributes of an object that has a style applied. Such a change is called an *override*. When an object has an override, a plus (+) sign appears next to the style name in the *Object Styles* panel. However, only modifications of defined attributes are considered overrides. For instance, if an object was assigned the *Photo Boxes* style you created earlier, changing the object's stroke to red would show as an override, because you defined the attributes of the stroke in the object style. If you changed the *Frame Fitting options*, no plus sign would appear because the attribute was not defined in the object style.

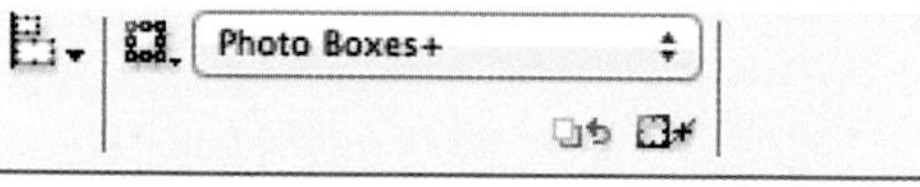

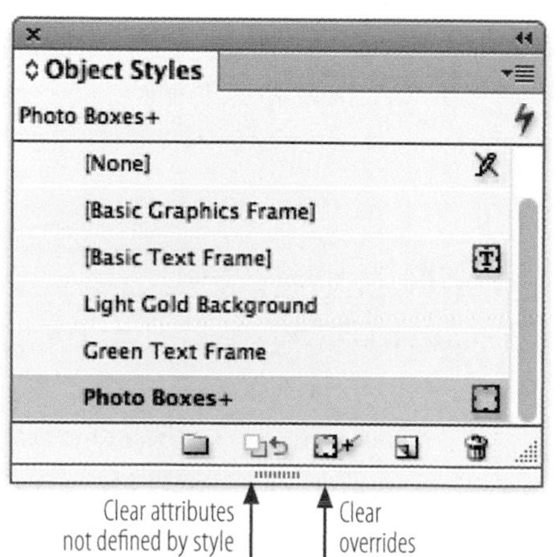

VISUAL |9–24|

Object styles can be found in the Control panel and in the Object Styles panel.

To clear overrides, first select the object, then press the **Clear overrides** button at the bottom of the *Object Styles* panel, or **Option+click** (Mac) or **Alt+click** (Windows) on the style name. If you want to clear modifications to the non-defined attributes of an object, select the object, and press the **Clear attributes not defined by style** button at the bottom of the panel (Visual 9–24).

If you decide to keep the overrides made to any object and to redefine the style to include those overrides, you can choose **Redefine Style** from the panel options. Only the categories you had originally included in the style definition will be updated. Redefining a style will not add attributes that were not part of the original definition. In those cases, it would be easier to create an object style from an existing object.

▸ *Duplicate, delete, and import object styles*

Duplicate, or delete an object style, by first selecting the style in the panel and then holding down **Control** (Mac) or **right-click** (Windows) to bring up the *Context* menu. If you delete a style that has been applied to objects, you will be asked to specify a replacement style. You can also delete a style by dragging its name to the *Delete selected style* icon in the lower right corner of the panel. To import styles from another document, select **Load Object Styles** from the panel options menu. As with importing paragraph and character styles, you must place a check next to the styles you wish to import.

▸ *Break the link to an object style*

You can break the link to an object style by selecting the object and choosing **Break Link to Style** from the panel options. When you break the link, the object style becomes *[None]+*. The object's appearance will remain the same, but it will not update when the original object style is modified.

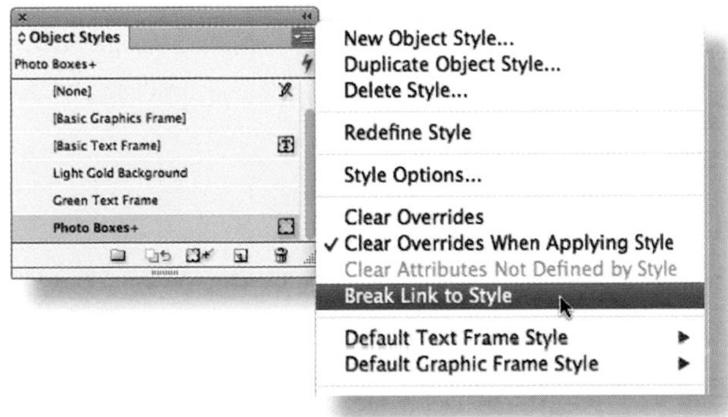

VISUAL |9–25|
When Break Link to Style is selected, future changes to the object style will not be applied.

Summary

In this chapter, you learned to bring consistency to a document by creating, duplicating, and modifying master pages. You learned how to release, override, and detach master page elements on document pages. Automated features including page numbering, jump lines, and continuation lines were introduced. You created an Object L,ibrary and used the Object Styles panel. Now, with Paragraph, Character, and Object Styles, as well as Master Pages "under your belt," you're ready to begin the projects for this chapter!

▸ IN REVIEW

1. In your own words, describe a master page and its purpose.
2. What is the keyboard shortcut for releasing an element from the master page, so that you can edit it on the document page?
3. If an element is detached from the master page and the master is changed, will those changes affect the detached element?
4. Where in InDesign will you find the Auto Page Number character?
5. If you create a jump line and it just isn't working, what might be the problem?
6. What is the process for creating an InDesign library?
7. What are the default object styles for any document?
8. What does a plus (+) sign mean when it follows the name of an object style?
9. How can you change the document default for a text or graphics frame?
10. What is the process for breaking the link to an object style?

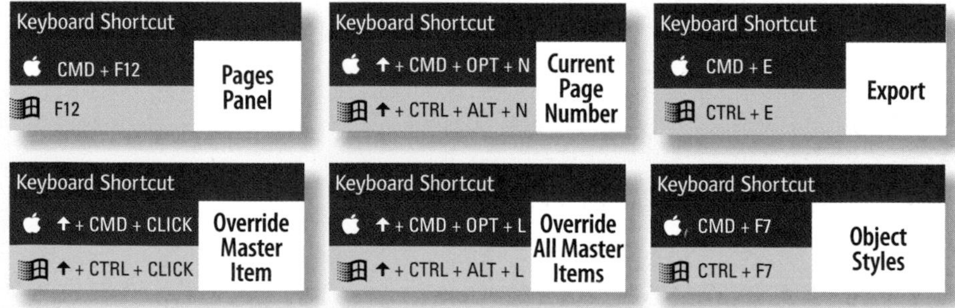

► CHAPTER 9 PROJECTS

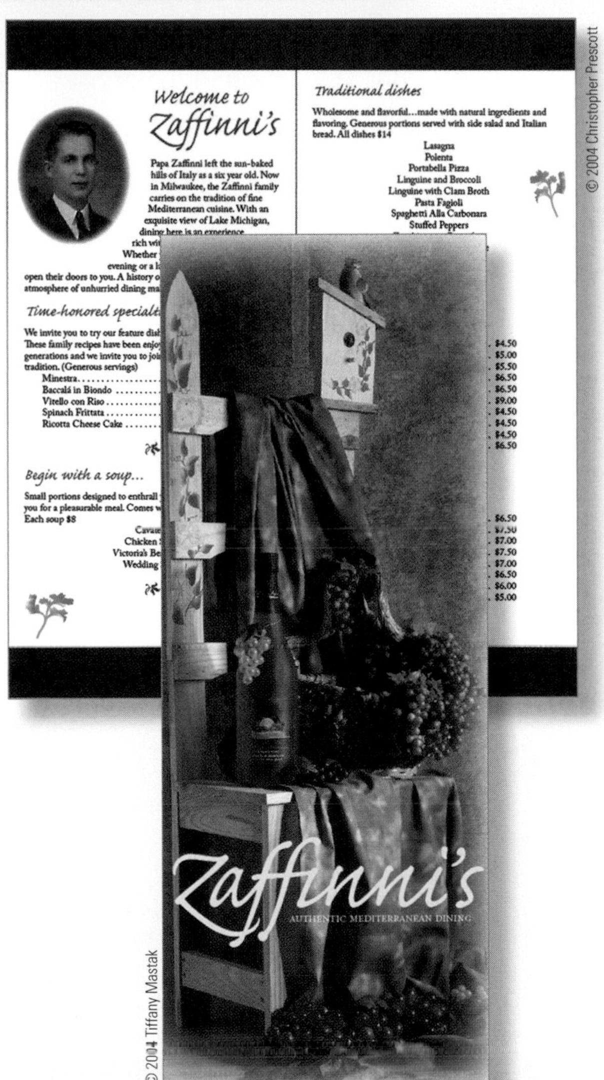

© 2004 Christopher Prescott

© 2004 Tiffany Mastak

© 2010 Steve Miljat, Waukesha County Technical College

EXPLORING INDESIGN CS6
Artwork & Resources

- Go to: http://www.cengagebrain.com
- Type: Rydberg
- Click Exploring InDesign CS6 in the list of search results.
- When the book's main page is displayed, click the Access button under Free Study Tools.
- To download files, select a chapter number and then click on the Artwork & Resources tab on the left navigation bar to download the files.

Two projects are included on the online companion resources, in the *09 Artwork and Resources* folder. The first, *09A Zaffinni's Mediterranean Dining*, uses the picture library created in this lesson. The second project, *09B Steve Miljat Brochure*, uses master pages, and a bonus feature not covered in the chapter: multiple page sizes. Be sure to fine-tune your résumé so that it's ready to go whenever a great opportunity presents itself!

Life in abundance comes **only** through great love.

Elbert Hubbard

| Identity Systems |

objectives

- *Create functional, well-designed, identity systems*
- *Consider printing, paper, and finishing processes when designing identity systems*
- *Learn when to use lining or old-style figures*
- *Typeset academic degrees, acronyms, and titles*
- *Design newspaper advertisements according to specifications*

introduction

How many times have you read, **Wanted: Graphic Designer. Two to five years' experience required.** Everyone wants someone with experience; but how will you get experience if you don't have a job? Graphic design is a highly competitive field. To be considered for an entry-level position, you not only need a fantastic portfolio, but you must also be able to demonstrate your ability to think quickly and creatively, work productively, and maintain exemplary interpersonal relationships. Even if you get hired, you must prove yourself before you are given more responsibility.

Sometimes your new boss will begin to try out your software skills (and your attitude) by assigning you lower-end production jobs. Before you begin to grumble, remind yourself that everyone has to start somewhere. First jobs aren't always the most glamorous. But remember that there are hundreds of unemployed graphic designers out there, and each of them would love to have your job! At first glance, producing business literature, forms, and identity systems seem to be on the bottom rung of the creativity ladder. But in reality, they require a high degree of precision, attention to detail, and layout skills. A skilled designer can turn a business materials into works of art; an unskilled designer can turn them into a nightmare!

essential project information

Knowing the details at the start of a project will save backtracking later on. Sometimes your art director will provide this information. Other times, you'll discuss the project with the client. In either case, it's important to ask the right questions about the project, because the answers will affect your document setup.

- *Is there an existing form? If so, what has worked or not worked with the current form? Or, is there a sample form the customer likes?*
- *Does the form have to match or blend with any existing forms? What kind of tone should the form convey?*
- *Who will be completing the form?*
- *How many colors will the form be printed in?*
- *Will the company logo be included on the form? Is a digital file of the logo available? What are the corporate colors?*
- *Is the form one- or two-sided?*
- *Does it have any requirements such as a perforation, a fold, or an address that shows through an envelope window?*
- *How will the form be printed? on separate sheets? in duplicate or triplicate? on a photocopier, in the office?*
- *How will the form be used? Will it be mailed out in a #10 envelope? Will it be returned in a #9 envelope? Will it be a self-mailer?*
- *Will it be drilled and held in a binder? Will it be padded as a tablet with tear-off sheets? Will it be held in a clipboard? Will it be filed in a file folder?*
- *Will individual completed forms be photocopied and distributed to team members? Will the data be collected and tabulated?*
- *What company information will be on the form? fax? e-mail? phone?*
- *How often is the form revised?*
- *Will it require sequential numbering?*
- *Is there any legally required wording that must be included on the form?*

GENERAL DESIGN CONSIDERATIONS

A form must be a positive representation of the business. If you were waiting for a surgical procedure and were given an old typewritten form to fill out, your confidence in the surgeon might begin to slip. A well-designed form is an asset to a business. A form should communicate professionalism, while incorporating the look and feel of the rest of the company's literature. A form should be easy to follow—the layout should create a visual hierarchy that organizes and sequences the reader's responses. The layout should clearly identify where each response should be placed. A form should be usable. The user should have enough vertical room to write below the previous line, and enough horizontal room to write a hyphenated last name, or a very long city name. Never consider a form complete unless you have "completed" the form yourself. Choose a paper stock that won't smudge when written on with a pencil, a felt tip pen, or a ballpoint pen.

DESIGNING IDENTITY PACKAGES

This chapter will focus on the development of an identity package for an environmental educator. The teacher, Dr. Rosemary Tollefson, needs a logo and identity pieces (letterhead, envelope, business card); a display advertisement for the phone book; and a ¾ page, vertical newspaper display ad and a letter fold brochure. Although each piece has its distinctive design and typographic challenges, all the pieces retain a visual unity that identifies them as members of the same family. When you have completed this identity package, you may want to print each piece on high-quality paper stock, for use in your portfolio.

▸ *Dragonfly Environmental Education*

Dr. Tollefson is a 30-something, tree-hugging intellectual. She dislikes the traditional look of the printed materials most schools use. She wants an upbeat, contemporary, energetic design for her school, Dragonfly Environmental Education. Here are some questions you should think about when designing logos:

- *Does the image convey the correct tone for the business?*
- *Can it be enlarged and reduced without losing legibility?*
- *Does it avoid any negative connotations?*
- *Is it copyright free?*
- *Can the image be used for ten years without being dated?*

▸ MOVING TOWARD MASTERY

typographic considerations

Some typefaces are designed specifically for reading, and some are designed more for display or decoration. When selecting a typeface for business communications, the overall concern is readability. Use a typeface that is highly legible, one that blends with the company logo or corporate identity system. If the company uses a trendy, cursive logotype, be careful how you use it in business forms. Find a legible face that blends with the company logotype and use that in the business form. Consider who will be completing the form. Baby boomers are now wearing reading glasses and require a more generous point size than high school students. Children mastering penmanship need more room for writing.

When choosing typefaces for display type and body copy, be sure to consider the contrast between the two faces. A page is interesting to look at, and easier to read, when continuous body copy is broken into blocks by darker, higher-contrast display type. A good layout will use type blocks as stepping-stones to move the reader through the piece.

Minion Pro Typeface.

Adobe Jenson Pro Typeface.

At first glance, you might not see the difference between these two faces. Check out the e-bar. Jenson has a slanted e-bar, and Minion does not. If your client uses Minion Pro for correspondence, you shouldn't choose Jenson for identity pieces.

VISUAL | 10–1 |

Each piece in the identity package has a distinct purpose and layout challenge, yet all remain part of the same visual family.

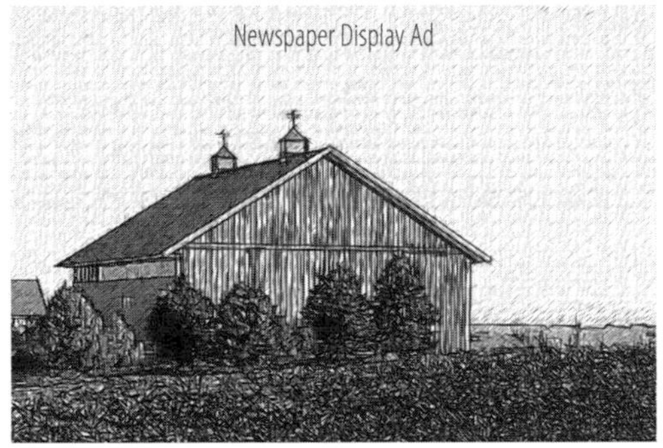

open house

Saturday, September 12, 2012

2:30–5:00 PM

Join us to celebrate the opening of our new facility at 300 Jacobs Avenue, ½ mile west of Woodley!

Meet staff, enjoy refreshments, and register for door prizes. Dr. Tollefson will be available to autograph her newly-released book, HANDS ON, FEET WET.

ing...the school Organic Growers!

ering an intensive three- l January 14–17, 2013 strate what it takes and run a successful arden or small farm.

Learn about:

- *soil fertility and crop rotations*
- *greenhouses*
- *pest management*
- *tools and equipment*
- *post-harvest handling*
- *USDA updates and regulations*

(507) 663-4457

dragon fly

ENVIRONMENTAL EDUCATION

- Grades 8–12 charter school
- Rosemary Tollefson, PH.D., Director
- Project-based, environmental focus
- High-achieving academic program

300 JACOBS AVENUE
(½ MILE WEST OF WOODLEY, NORTHFIELD)

(507) 663-4457

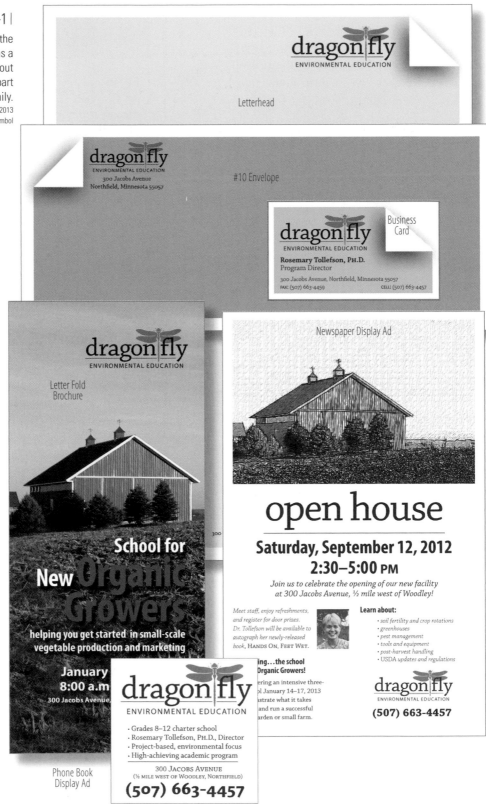

Phone Book Display Ad

LETTERHEAD DESIGN CONSIDERATIONS

Does anyone use a typewriter anymore? Hardly. So, make sure the paper you select for a letterhead will go through a laser or ink jet printer. Find out what typeface the client uses most often and try to coordinate that typeface with the one used in the letterhead. You may want to avoid gradients and screened background images if the letters will often be photocopied. Keep your client's budget in mind during the design phase—a nice effect can be created with colored ink on white or colored paper stock. Use the best paper stock your client can afford. Remember that some paper surfaces don't reproduce well on a photocopier. Include bleed images only if the client's budget can afford the extra cost of printing on an oversized sheet and cutting it down to letter size. If you have to choose between better paper and a bleed, choose better paper every time!

Use care when including names of personnel on the letterhead—if a person or position changes, all the old letterhead gets tossed. *Ouch!* Double-check all the information provided by the client. (Ask for a business card with the correct information.) Send a test fax just to confirm the fax number. Call your client and tell her the fax is coming—that way you can confirm the fax and phone number at the same time!

▸ *Use consistent formatting in all pieces*

Visual 10–2 shows the business card. The typefaces used in all pieces are Chaparral Pro and Myriad Pro. Minion Pro is used for the check box glyph. Typefaces followed by the word "Pro" have a wide selection of ornaments, ligatures, alternate letters, and symbols that can be viewed in the *Glyphs* panel. Use these faces consistently in all the identity pieces. Notice the academic degree, PH.D., listed after the name. When academic degrees follow the name, they look best set in small caps. Use either the degree (Rosemary Tollefson, PH.D.) or the title (Dr. Rosemary Tollefson) with the name, but not both.

VISUAL | 10–2 |

Academic titles are set in small caps. Use either the degree (PH.D.), or the title (Dr.), but not both.

VISUAL |10–3|

Old-style figures are used in this letterhead. The parentheses have been had a baseline shift of -1 pt. applied so that they would be more centered on the numbers they enclose.

► *Dragonfly identity package letterhead*

Visual 10–3 shows the lower portion of the letterhead, with the contact information positioned at the bottom of the page. This example uses numbers that extend below the baseline. These "lowercase" numbers are called *old-style figures* or *text figures*. Numbers that sit on the baseline are called *titling figures* or *lining figures*. Titling figures are ideal for use with display type and are sometimes used within body copy. Old-style figures are used within text and are rarely used in display type. Old-style figures have a graceful, elegant look. Notice that all the stationery pieces are two-colors, with the illusion of a folded corner. You'll create the logo and the folded corner later in this chapter. Be sure to save those elements for later use!

VISUAL |10–4|

Old-style figures are designed to be used in passages of body copy. Titling figures sit on top of the baseline.

ENVELOPE DESIGN CONSIDERATIONS

There are two things you should remember when designing envelopes: (1) allow at least an 18-pt. margin at the top and left edges; and (2) don't design an envelope with multiple colors that overlap or are close together (this is called *tight register*), unless your client has an ample budget. Printing a four-color envelope, with tight register and bleeds, is expensive because it has to be printed on a flat sheet, then die-cut, folded, and glued (a process called *converting*). Envelopes typically don't include the phone and fax number—but when elements are dragged in from a library to use on another piece, this can easily happen. You will want to watch for this. The image and type on an envelope will probably be smaller than that on the letterhead, but the size relationship should remain about the same. A standard commercial business-size envelope is called a *#10*, with dimensions of 4⅛ × 9½ inches. A *#9* business response envelope fits nicely inside a #10. Its dimensions are 3⅞ × 8⅞ inches.

If you don't have a chart of envelope styles and sizes, do a Google search for "envelope sizes." Several envelope sites will have information you can download and print. A nice reference site for envelope sizes is *www.designerstoolbox.com.*

▸ *Dragonfly identity package envelope*

Visual 10–5 shows the details of the upper left corner of the envelope. The logo was created, grouped, and saved as a Snippet. The logo can be resized by pressing **Shift+Command** (Mac) or **Shift+Control** (Windows) while dragging the lower right corner point. Notice that old-style figures are used for the zip code, and an ample margin has been maintained on the upper and left edges.

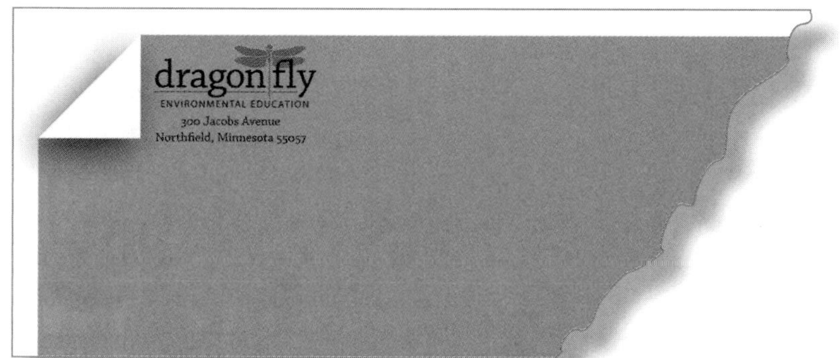

VISUAL | 10–5 |
The return address corner of the envelope. Telephone numbers aren't included with the return address.

BUSINESS CARD DESIGN CONSIDERATIONS

The client's budget determines whether or not you should design a card with a bleed. A standard business card size is 3½ × 2 inches. Allow at least a ⅛ inch margin inside the card. When designing landscape orientation cards, I try to keep the name prominent and important contact information in the lower right corner. That's where the eye usually stops last, and I don't want to waste a "hot" corner on a fax number! Discuss *imposition* with the printer. The imposition is how the card should be laid out for printing: 1-up, 2-up, 8-up, and so on. Sometimes the printer wants you to step and repeat your card many times on a single sheet of letter-size paper. Other times, a single card, centered on the sheet, will be requested.

Designers become very comfortable working in point size and leading with whole number increments of one or two points. With smaller type, one point is a much more significant unit of measure than it is for display type. When working at smaller type sizes, you will find yourself setting a leading value of 8.75 points, or a type size of 7.5 points, for example.

▸ *Change point size and leading keyboard shortcut defaults*

By now, using the shortcut keys to change point size and leading has become second nature. In the *Getting Started* section of Chapter 1, I recommended that you change the InDesign program preferences so that those keyboard shortcuts would enlarge or reduce in smaller increments. If you didn't change your preferences earlier in the *Getting Started* section in Chapter 1, you should do it now. When you want new preferences to apply to all future documents, the preferences should be changed when no document is open. When you change preferences with a document open, the changes apply only to the current document. If you are a Mac user, choose *InDesign> Preferences>Units & Increments.* In the Keyboard Increments section, change the *Size/Leading* to **1 pt.** and the *Baseline Shift* to **1 pt.** (Visual 10–6). Windows users, choose *Edit>Preferences>Units & Increments* and follow the same procedure.

VISUAL | 10–6 |

Change the Keyboard Increments in the Units & Increments page of the Preferences dialog box.

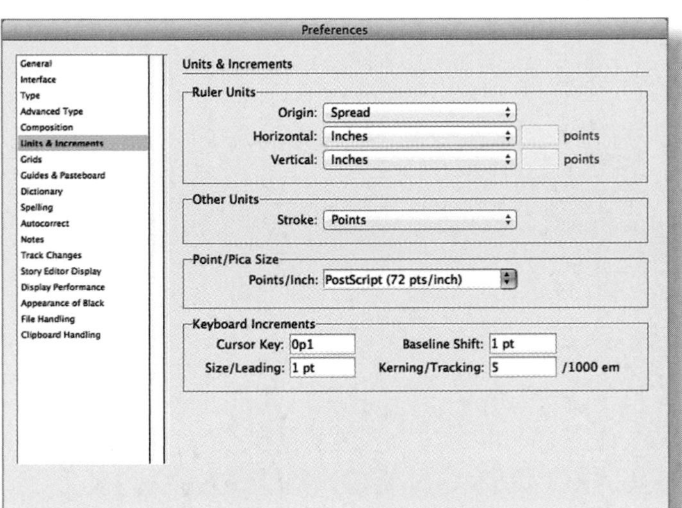

▸ *Dragonfly identity package business card*

Visual 10–7 shows Rosemary Tollefson's business card. Notice that the typefaces are the same here, as the other pieces. It's very important to maintain the size relationship of text to graphics on all the pieces. Readability always needs to be maintained—at all sizes and formats. Use the flush right tab (**Shift+Tab**) to align the cell phone text to the right margin.

VISUAL | 10–7 |

Rosemary Tollefson's business card shown at actual size.

NEWSPAPER DISPLAY AD DESIGN

Accurate measurement is essential when designing for newspapers. Each paper has standard dimensions to follow when preparing ads. Visual 10–8 shows a sample production worksheet for a Milwaukee, Wisconsin daily paper. When creating a newspaper ad, close enough is not good enough! Convert fractions into decimals, and enter those measurements in the *New Document* dialog box. As you can see in Visual 10–8, the advertisements butt right up to text or another ad, with no room for error.

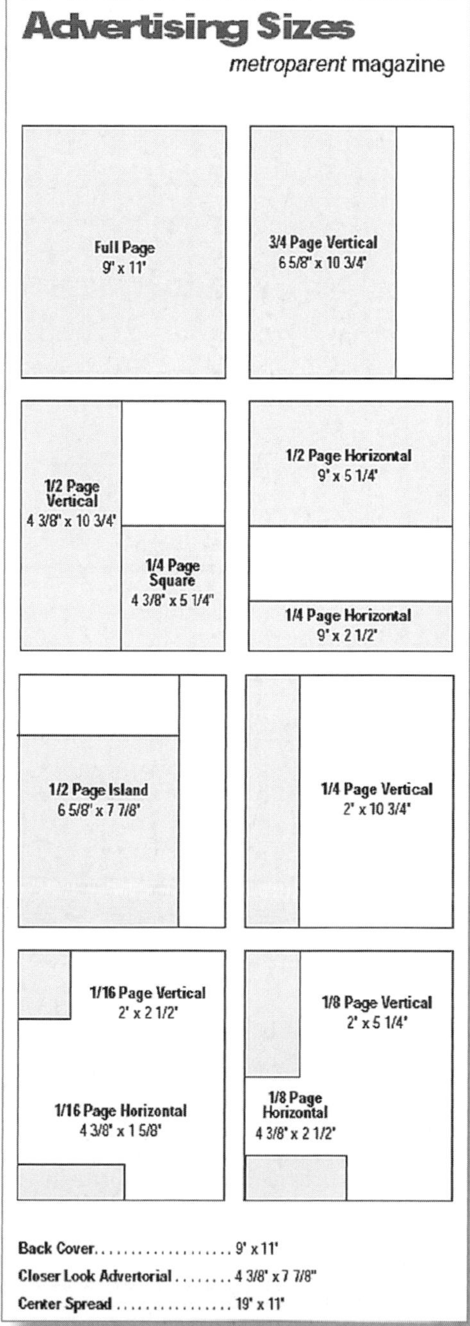

VISUAL | 10–8 |

Every newspaper and magazine publication has a different set of ad sizes. Always double check that your size specification is correct before submitting an ad for publication!

© Metroparent Magazine 2004

Many display ads are designed with an outer border. When adding a stroke to a text or graphics frame, you must specify that the stroke goes inside the frame. If the stroke is centered on the frame or placed on the outside of the frame, the dimension will change and the advertisement will not fit the newspaper specifications. If you frequently place newspaper ads, creating document presets for each size, and object styles with strokes aligned to the inside, would considerably reduce the margin of error.

When designing for newsprint, recognize that your final piece may not look like your laser print. Some newsprint is porous and the ink will spread. The counters of letters tend to fill in, so avoid using very small point sizes whenever possible. When your advertisement includes a photograph or a scan, work closely with the production department so that you provide the correct resolution and line screen. A piece that looks good printed on your laser printer, may look "muddy" in newsprint, because the halftone dots will fill in.

VISUAL | 10–9 |

This display ad demonstrates several typographic nuances: the use of roman type within italic text, showing initialisms without periods, and setting PM.

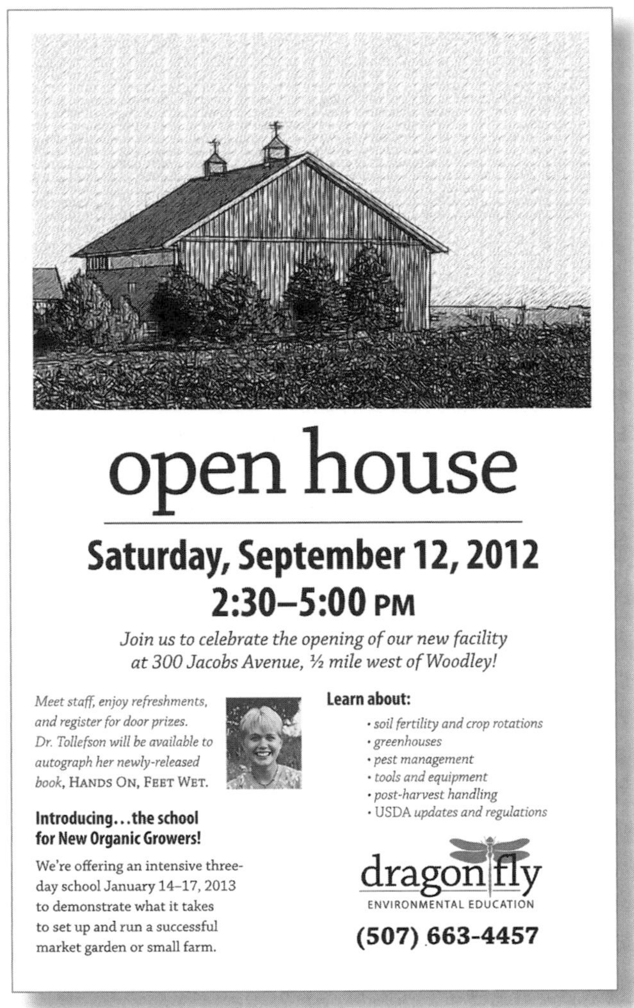

open house
Saturday, September 12, 2012
2:30–5:00 PM
Join us to celebrate the opening of our new facility
at 300 Jacobs Avenue, ½ mile west of Woodley!
Meet staff, enjoy refreshments, and register for door prizes. Dr. Tollefson will be available to autograph her newly-released book, HANDS ON, FEET WET.
Learn about:
• soil fertility and crop rotations
• greenhouses
• pest management
• tools and equipment
• post-harvest handling
• USDA updates and regulations
Introducing...the school for New Organic Growers!
We're offering an intensive three-day school January 14–17, 2013 to demonstrate what it takes to set up and run a successful market garden or small farm.
dragonfly
ENVIRONMENTAL EDUCATION
(507) 663-4457

▸ *Dragonfly newspaper display ad*

▸ production tip

When body copy is italic, names of books, plays, musical compositions—things which would normally be in italic, are set in Roman type.

Visual 10–9 shows a sample of the display ad. The words *open house* require manual kerning, which is common when working with display type. The phone number at the bottom of the ad, and the time at the top, are set in lining (uppercase) figures. It is appropriate to use lining figures in this instance because the numbers are being used in display type. The open house time, *2:30–5:00* PM, is separated by an en dash, used to indicate a range of time. The abbreviation "pm" is set in small caps, and including the periods is optional. If you don't have a typeface with small caps, it is permissible to set it in lowercase letters with periods *(p.m.)*. The body copy is set in italic type, with the OpenType fractions option turned on. Normally book titles are set in italic, but when the surrounding body copy is italic, the book title is set in Roman, as in the title of Dr. Tollefson's book, *Hands On, Feet Wet*. You'll also note that the bulleted copy contains a reference to the United States' Department of Agriculture, as USDA. When setting an initialism, no period is placed after each letter.

PHONE BOOK AD DESIGN

Scan through the yellow pages ads in a phone book and you will see that they've been designed by people with a wide range of design skills. Some ads include gradients and mushy photos, condensed or expanded type—that is almost impossible to read—and typographic blunders such as all-capital italics and incorrect quotation marks. You can also find some examples of excellent layout and readability. What makes the difference between a strong or a poor ad? The ability to use type, combined with an understanding of the printing process. A well-designed, 2½ inch square ad, packs more punch than a poorly designed ½ page ad! When you design an ad for the yellow pages, first look at samples to see what doesn't work. Then look specifically at what the competition is doing, and design an ad that will beat the best sample. It is a time-consuming process to fine-tune small display ads. Some people assume a small ad will require less production time. In reality, it takes more time to create an effective small ad than a larger display ad, because every incremental spacing decision you make in a small ad is critical!

▸ *Dragonfly yellow pages ad*

Visual 10–11 shows the completed yellow pages ad. The text portion is basically in a centered format—except the bulleted copy is flush left. Sometimes you see bulleted copy centered, leaving the left sides ragged (Visual 10–10). Setting bulleted copy in this manner is a poor design technique. When the bullets are not flush left, they blend in with the body copy and defeat the purpose of using them in the first place!

· Grades 8–12 charter school
· Rosemary Tollefson, PH.D., Director
· Project-based, environmental focus
· High-achieving academic program

300 JACOBS AVENUE
(½ MILE WEST OF WOODLEY, NORTHFIELD)
(507) 663-4457

VISUAL |10–10|
This is the incorrect way to set bulleted copy! Centering bulleted type defeats the purpose of using bullets, which is to lead the eye through the ad.

Here is the best way to align bulleted copy, while centering it in the text block:

- *Center all bulleted text. Position a vertical guideline flush to the bullet of the longest line.*
- *Then, change the alignment of the bulleted text to flush left.*
- *Finally, apply a left indent to push all the bulleted copy to the guideline you placed earlier. Now the text is flush left, but the longest line is still centered in the text column.*

· Grades 8–12 charter school
· Rosemary Tollefson, PH.D., Director
· Project-based, environmental focus
· High-achieving academic program

300 JACOBS AVENUE
(½ MILE WEST OF WOODLEY, NORTHFIELD)
(507) 663-4457

VISUAL |10–11|
When working on newspaper or yellow pages ads, remember that your laser copy will generally look better than the printed version. Therefore, err on the side of readability!

LETTER FOLD BROCHURE DESIGN

The letter fold brochure can be found in literature racks in county buildings, malls, rest stops, gas stations and beauty shops—just about everywhere! These ubiquitous publications make great additions to your stash of samples, and they showcase the differences between amateur and professional design skills. Remember…the printing costs for poorly- and skillfully-designed two-color brochures are basically the same. But differences in their ability to communicate the desired message are huge! There are numerous design considerations to remember when designing brochures:

- *Paper selection is critical! If your brochure will be in a literature rack, or a self-contained mailer, be sure to get durable paper. Your printer will help you make a good selection.*
- *Remember that the color of the paper stock affects how photos will look. The background color of the paper will be the highlight color of the photos. Coated paper is better for photos than is uncoated.*
- *Avoid* ***tombstoning*** *in your layout. Tombstoning occurs when all the headlines and/or images line up horizontally across all panels (like tombstones).*
- *When an image bleeds to the fold, extend the image 1/16 inch over the foldline to allow for inaccuracies in the folding process.*
- *A letter fold brochure should be designed with narrow and wide panels to accommodate the width of the paper when folding. Visual 10–12 shows the layout for a letter-size brochure. Remember that the front and back dimensions must mirror each other. This is accomplished by creating multiple page sizes which we'll cover in Chapter 11. For this project, you'll use a prepared template (that you should archive for future use).*
- *Page 1 is the front cover. Pages 2 and 3 describe features and benefits. Page 4 is a good place to ask for the sale. Page 5 is the narrow flap that folds in. This usually contains a mission statement or introductory information to draw the reader inside the brochure. Often unnoticed, Page 6 is the "dead panel," where the mailing address or nonessential information is placed.*

VISUAL |10–12|

You'll use a prepared template to create the brochure with offset panel widths. The measurements are shown below each panel. (This is not drawn to scale.)

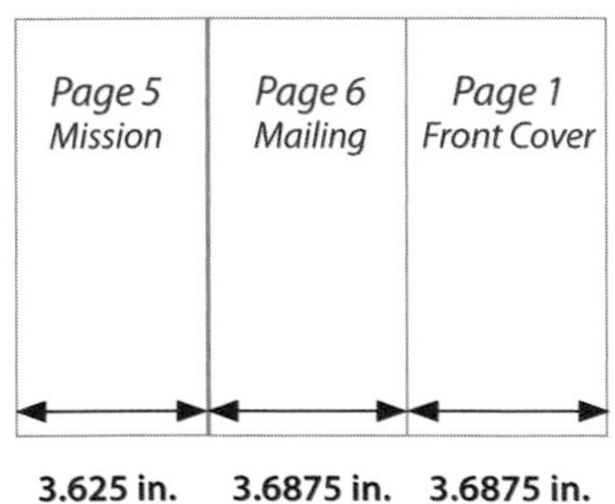

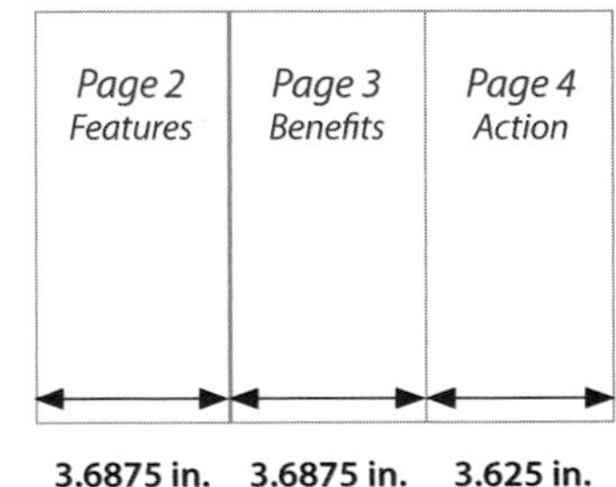

Emphasizing...
Organic production and Direct marketing

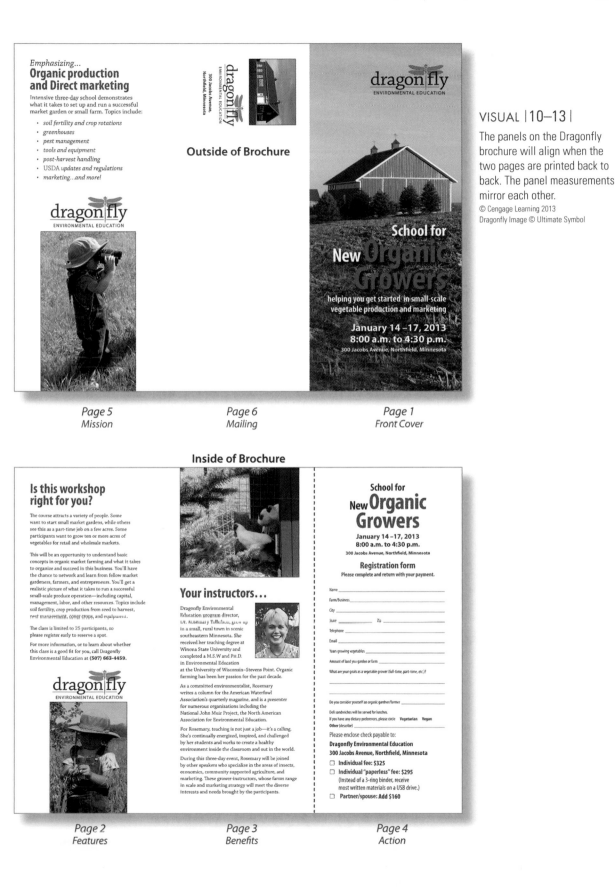

Intensive three-day school demonstrates what it takes to set up and run a successful market garden or small farm. Topics include:

- *soil fertility and crop rotations*
- *greenhouses*
- *pest management*
- *tools and equipment*
- *post-harvest handling*
- USDA *updates and regulations*
- *marketing...and more!*

Outside of Brochure

Page 5
Mission

Page 6
Mailing

Page 1
Front Cover

VISUAL | 10–13 |

The panels on the Dragonfly brochure will align when the two pages are printed back to back. The panel measurements mirror each other.

Inside of Brochure

Is this workshop right for you?

The course attracts a variety of people. Some want to start small market gardens, while others see this as a part-time job on a few acres. Some participants want to grow ten or more acres of vegetables for retail and wholesale markets.

This will be an opportunity to understand basic concepts in organic market farming and what it takes to organize and succeed in this business. You'll have the chance to network and learn from fellow market gardeners, farmers, and entrepreneurs. You'll get a realistic picture of what it takes to run a successful small-scale produce operation—including capital, management, labor, and other resources. Topics include soil fertility, crop production from seed to harvest, pest management, cover crops, and equipment.

The class is limited to 25 participants, so please register early to reserve a spot.

For more information, or to learn about whether this class is a good fit for you, call Dragonfly Environmental Education at **(507) 663-4459.**

Your instructors...

Dragonfly Environmental Education program director, Dr. Rosemary Tollefson, grew up in a small, rural town in scenic southeastern Minnesota. She received her teaching degree at Winona State University and completed a M.S.W and PH.D. in Environmental Education at the University of Wisconsin–Stevens Point. Organic farming has been her passion for the past decade.

As a committed environmentalist, Rosemary writes a column for the American Waterfowl Association's quarterly magazine, and is a presenter for numerous organizations including the National John Muir Project, the North American Association for Environmental Education.

For Rosemary, teaching is not just a job—it's a calling. She's continually energized, inspired, and challenged by her students and works to create a healthy environment inside the classroom and out in the world.

During this three-day event, Rosemary will be joined by other speakers who specialize in the areas of insects, economics, community supported agriculture, and marketing. These grower-instructors, whose farms range in scale and marketing strategy will meet the diverse interests and needs brought by the participants.

School for
New **Organic Growers**

January 14 –17, 2013
8:00 a.m. to 4:30 p.m.
300 Jacobs Avenue, Northfield, Minnesota

Registration form
Please complete and return with your payment.

Name ______________________
Farm/Business ______________________
City ______________________
State __________ Zip __________
Telephone ______________________
Email ______________________
Years growing vegetables ______________________
Amount of land you garden or farm ______________________
What are your goals as a vegetable grower (full-time, part-time, etc.)?
____
____
Do you consider yourself an organic gardner/farmer ______________________
Deli sandwiches will be served for lunches.
If you have any dietary preferences, please circle **Vegetarian** **Vegan**
Other (describe) ______________________

Please enclose check payable to:
Dragonfly Environmental Education
300 Jacobs Avenue, Northfield, Minnesota

- ☐ **Individual fee: $325**
- ☐ **Individual "paperless" fee: $295** (Instead of a 3-ring binder, receive most written materials on a USB drive.)
- ☐ **Partner/spouse: Add $160**

Page 2
Features

Page 3
Benefits

Page 4
Action

▸ *Create the Dragonfly logo*

We'll begin this project by making the logo. The Dragonfly logo looks simple enough—but it has been deliberately designed with unique production considerations that will introduce you to some new features of InDesign.

1. Create a new document and type ***dragonfly***. Change the font to **Chaparral Pro Regular**, **30/16**. Place the cursor between the ***n*** and ***f***. Open the ***Context*** menu and select ***Insert White Space>Thin Space***. A thin space is ⅛ the width of an em space.

VISUAL | 10–14 |

The Dragonfly logo uses a thin space. A thin space is 1/8 the width of an em space. © Cengage Learning 2013

VISUAL | 10–15 |

Change the opacity of the dragonfly image to 50%. © Cengage Learning 2013

> EXPLORING INDESIGN CS6
> **Artwork & Resources**
>
> - Go to: http://www.cengagebrain.com
> - Type: Rydberg
> - Click Exploring InDesign CS6 in the list of search results.
> - When the book's main page is displayed, click the Access button under Free Study Tools.
> - To download files, select a chapter number and then click on the Artwork & Resources tab on the left navigation bar to download the files.

2. Type ***Environmental Education*** underneath Dragonfly: **Myriad Pro Regular 8 pt**., **All Caps**, Tracking **88**. Place ***Dragonfly.psd*** from the ***10 Artwork and Resources*** folder on the online companion resources. Scale it to **30%**. Position the tail inside the space created by the thin space. Change the opacity to **50%** (Visual 10–15).

3. Use ***Underline*** button **T** on the ***Character formatting*** control panel to add an underline under all the letters except the ***g*** and ***y*** and ***thin space***. Notice the default line weight is much too heavy in relation to the type, and creates a clunky look (Visual 10–16). If the underline had been added to all the letters, it would have cut through the descenders of loop of the ***g*** and ***y's*** tail. That would be a typographic faux pas!

VISUAL | 10–16 |

The default underline style is usually too heavy and too close to the copy. © Cengage Learning 2013

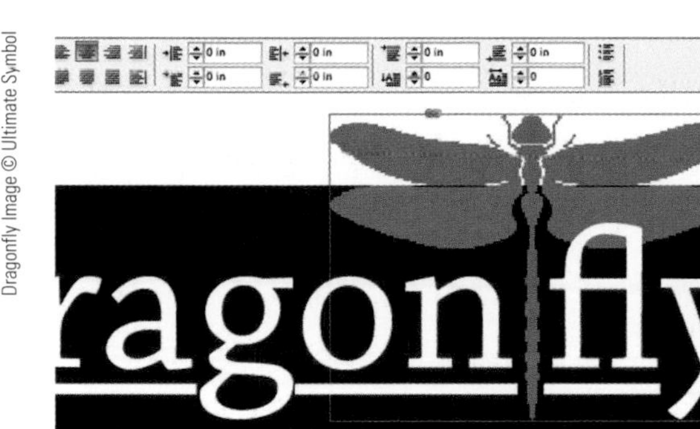

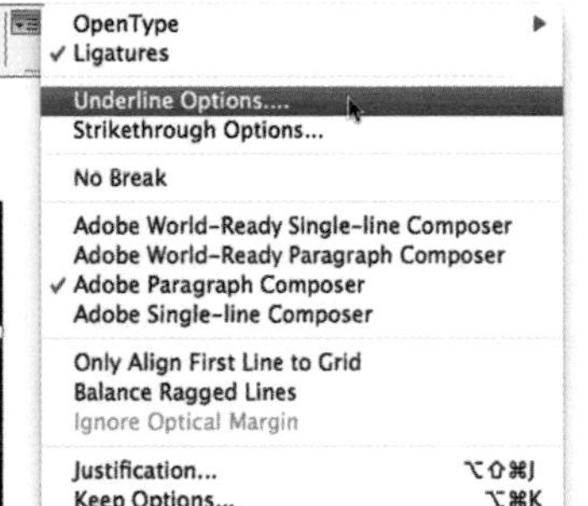

VISUAL | 10–17 |

Open Underline Options from the Control panel menu to change the weight and offset.

4. Highlight the copy. Open *Underline Options* from the *Control panel* menu (Visual 10–17). In the *Underline Options* window, enter **0.5 pt.** in the *Weight* field and the **3.5 pt**. in the *Offset* field (Visual 10–18). What an improvement!

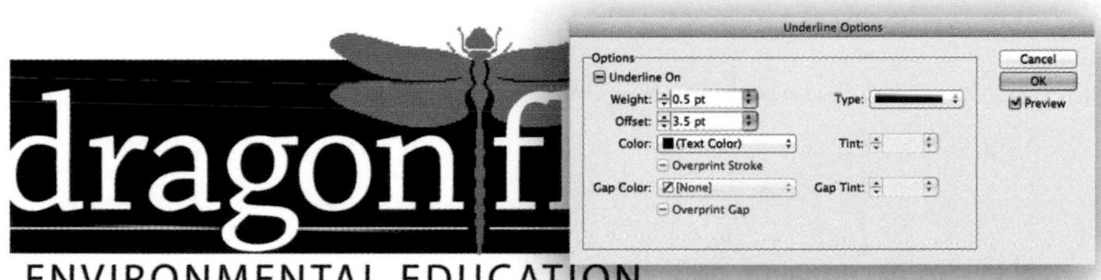

VISUAL | 10–18 |

In our logo, an underline is not applied to letters with a descender. However, in all cases, you should adjust Underline Options to prevent the line from cutting through any part of a letter!

5. Select the text box and dragonfly image. Group the elements. Press *Cmd+E* (Mac) or *Ctrl+E* (Windows) to open the *Export* window. Name the artwork *Dragonfly Logo* and choose *InDesign Snippet* from the drop down menu. Save to the desktop. The logo is now ready for use in the identity pieces.

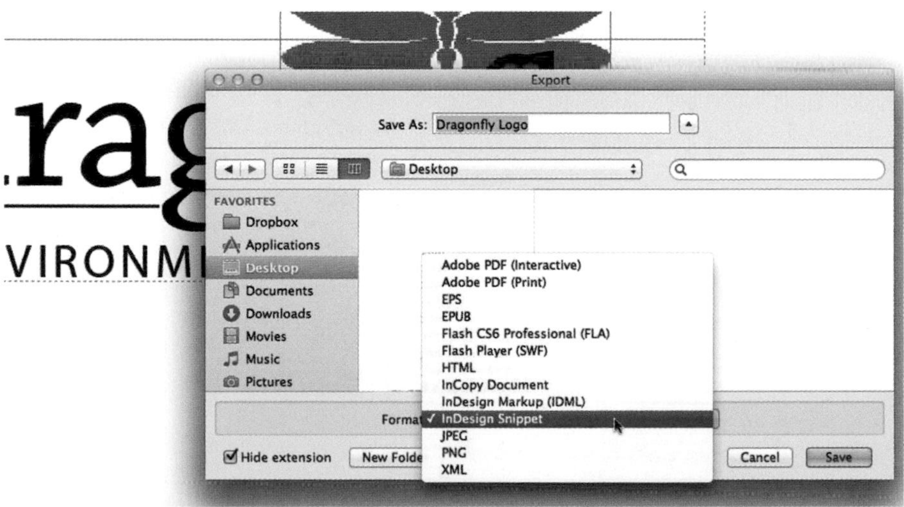

VISUAL | 10–19 |

The Dragonfly logo is now complete, and exported as a Snippet for use in future projects.

▸ *Create the folded corner*

All the stationery pieces have a repeating design element—a folded corner. In this exercise, you'll learn how to make the illusion of a bent corner. Then, you'll save the folded corner as a Snippet for later use.

VISUAL | 10–20 |

The stationery pieces are all 2-color designs, but each uses a unique color combination. The folded corner brings continuity to the stationery pieces.

1. Use the *Rectangle Frame* tool to create a **4"** square. Fill it with **Cyan**. **Option + Click** (Mac) or **Alt + Click** (Windows) on the *Corner Options* icon in the *Control* panel to open the *Corner Options* window. Enter **1.5** in the upper right corner field and choose **Bevel** in the drop down menu (Visual 10–21).

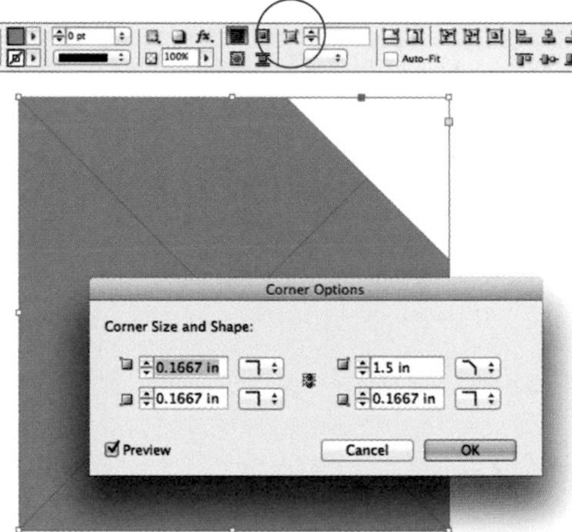

VISUAL | 10–21 |

Use Corner Options to specify which corners you would like to modify.

2. Use the *Rectangle Frame* tool to draw a **1.5"** square to match the missing corner. Zoom in, so that you can align it perfectly (Visual 10–22A). Delesect the square. Now, click the upper right corner point with the *Direct Selection* tool (Visual 10–22B). The point is selected when it is filled in. The other corner points should be hollow. Press *Delete*. A triangle should remain.

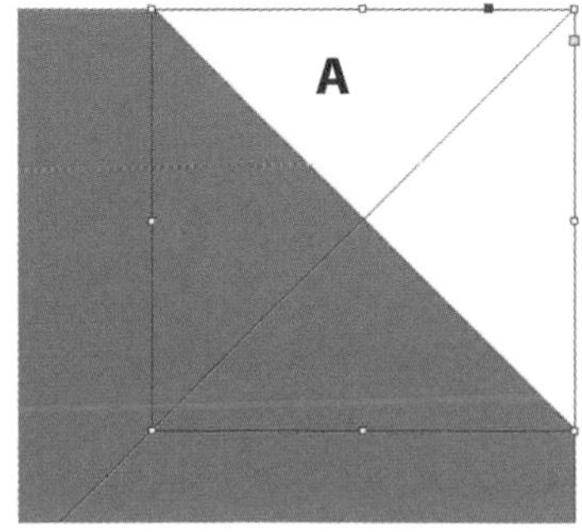

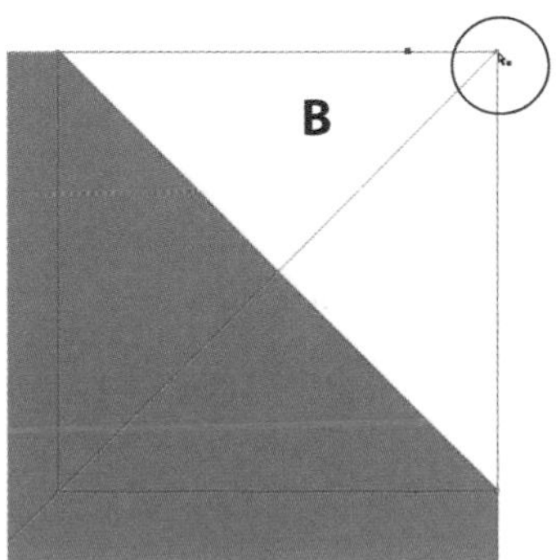

VISUAL | 10–22 |

The point in the upper right corner of the square is deleted to create a triangle on top of the cyan square.

3. Fill the triangle with **[Paper]**. Press **Cmd+Opt+M** (Mac) or **Ctrl+Alt+M** (Windows) to open the ***Effects*** dialog to the ***Drop Shadow*** pane. Enter the values shown in Visual 10–23.

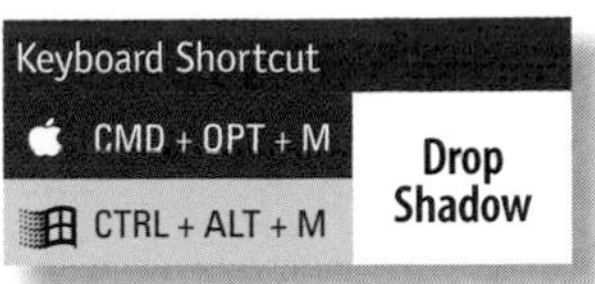

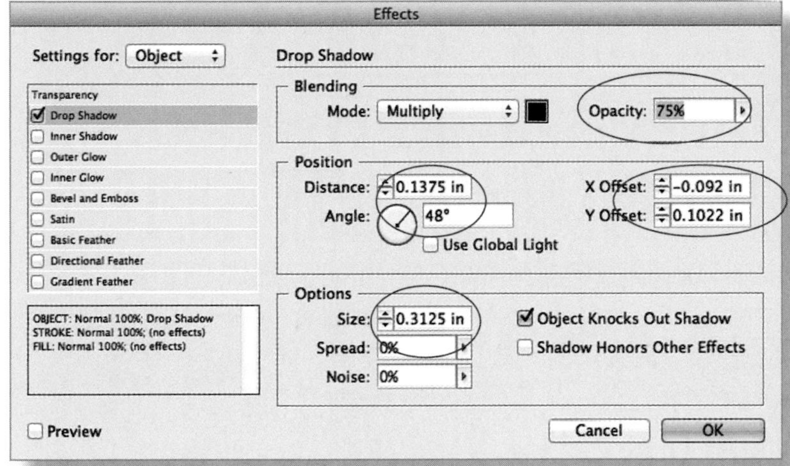

VISUAL | 10–23 |

Enter these values in the Drop Shadow panel window.

4. Your finished rectangle should look like Visual 10–24A. Select only the triangle with the drop shadow, and ***Export*** it as a ***Snippet***. Name it ***Folded Corner*** (Visual 1–24B).

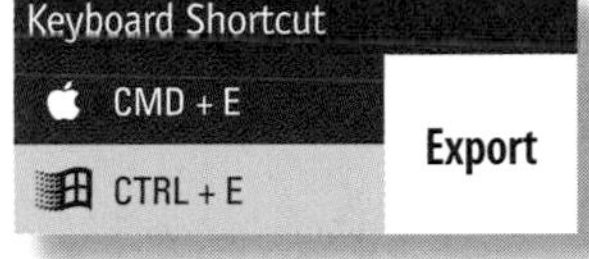

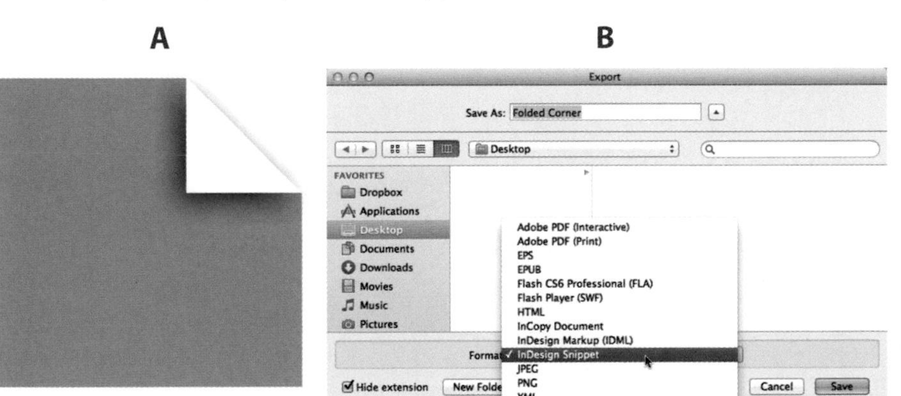

VISUAL | 10–24 |

Save the Folded Corner Snippet for later use in identity pieces.

Congratulations! Having these design elements completed and saved as Snippets will make the rest of this project go smoothly. Be sure to remember where you saved them! The student handout will give specifications for making the rest of the identity pieces. One last reminder—be sure to save the *10 Letter fold Template* to a permanent archive on your computer. It will save you time as you create brochures that are skillfully designed and technically correct.

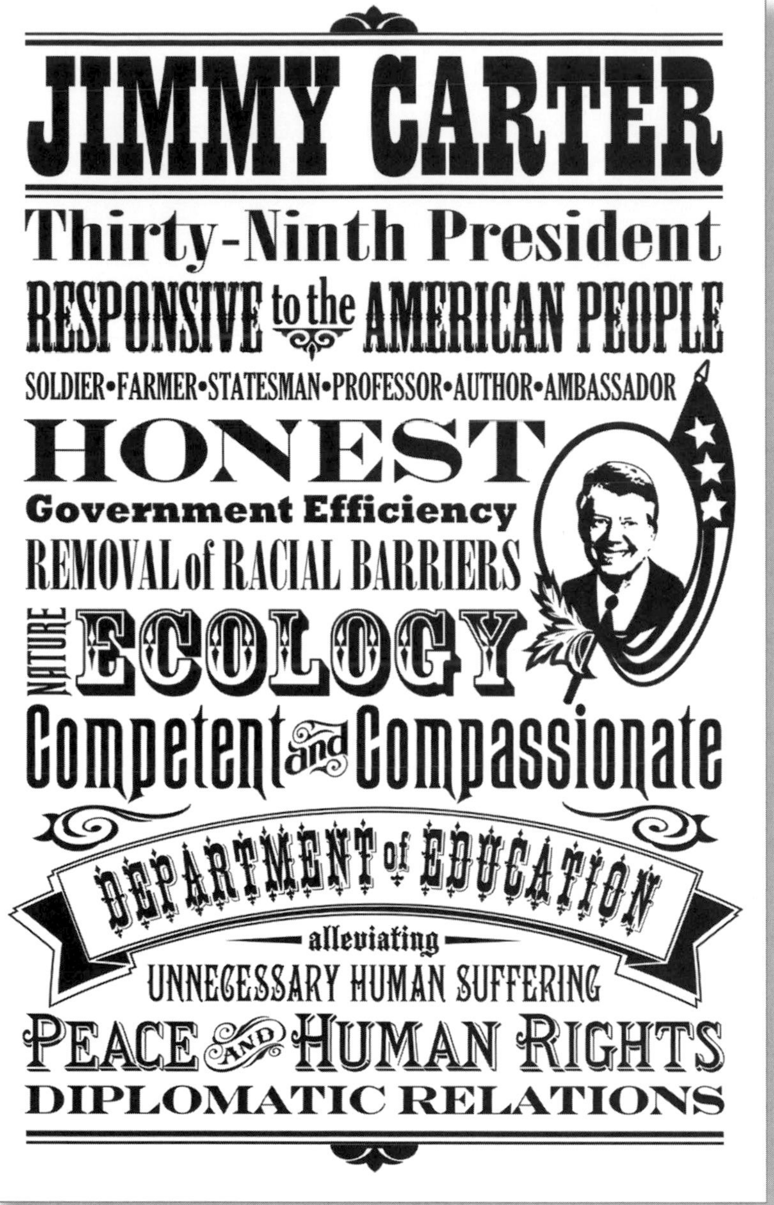

VISUAL |10–25|

This Victorian era style political poster demonstrates that type can be a powerful design element. Designers who are comfortable working with type and have strong InDesign production skills, are the best at creating type-heavy forms that are both functional and aesthetically pleasing.

Summary

Identity pieces, brochures and business forms are rigorous production tests for typesetters and designers. It is our responsibility to make sure that all pieces we design project the appropriate corporate image, are easy to read, and are easy to complete. When you are given the task of producing an order form, a sell sheet, or a catalog price grid, see it as a design opportunity. Flex your typesetting muscles. And remember, as a wise designer once said, "*There are no mediocre projects, just mediocre designers.*"

▸ IN REVIEW

1. The initial client meeting is a perfect opportunity to gather information about project specifications. What are four examples of information you should have before beginning the project?
a.
b.
c.
d.

2. Choosing the typeface is one of the most important decisions designers make. What are some considerations for choosing a typeface for an identity package?

3. What are two design considerations for letterhead?

4. How does paper quality affect design?

5. What is the difference between a lining figure and an old-style figure?

6. How should academic titles be typeset?

7. If you are designing a display ad for a newspaper, you must align the frame's stroke to the ________________.

8. A standard business-size envelope is called a ________ envelope.

9. What are the dimensions of a standard business card?

10. Normally, book titles are set in italic, but when the surrounding copy is italic, the title is set in ________________.

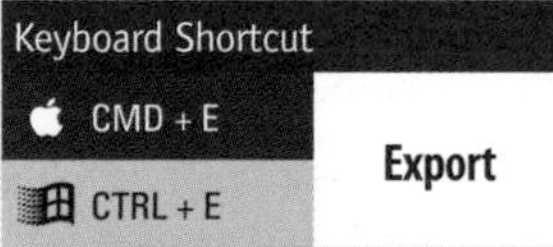

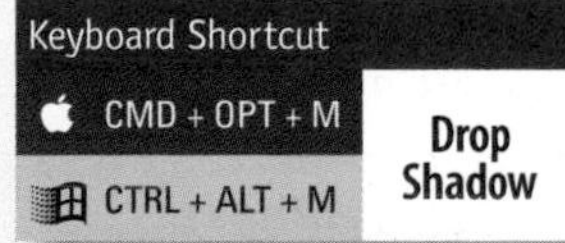

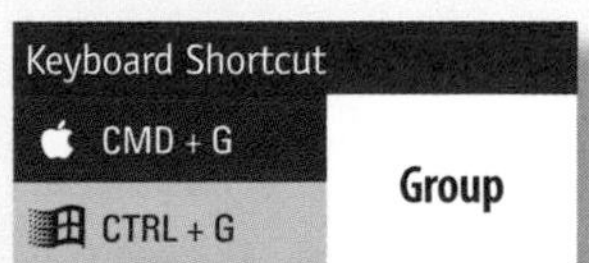

▸CHAPTER 10 PROJECTS

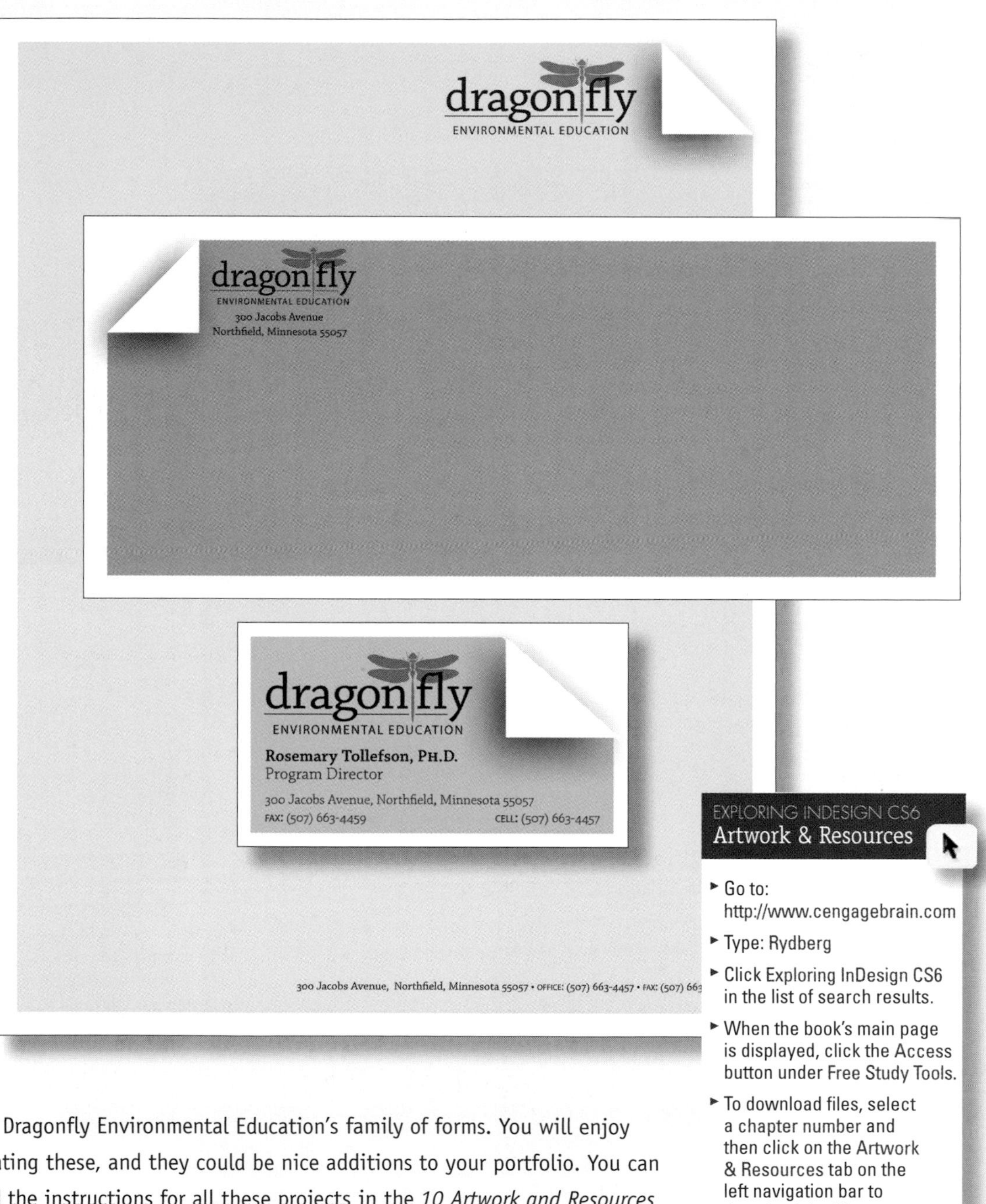

The Dragonfly Environmental Education's family of forms. You will enjoy creating these, and they could be nice additions to your portfolio. You can find the instructions for all these projects in the *10 Artwork and Resources* folder on the online companion resources accompanying this book.

EXPLORING INDESIGN CS6
Artwork & Resources

- Go to: http://www.cengagebrain.com
- Type: Rydberg
- Click Exploring InDesign CS6 in the list of search results.
- When the book's main page is displayed, click the Access button under Free Study Tools.
- To download files, select a chapter number and then click on the Artwork & Resources tab on the left navigation bar to download the files.

▸ CHAPTER 10 PROJECTS

- Grades 8–12 charter school
- Rosemary Tollefson, Ph.D., Director
- Project-based, environmental focus
- High-achieving academic program

300 Jacobs Avenue
(½ mile west of Woodley, Northfield)
(507) 663-4457

open house

Saturday, September 12, 2012
2:30–5:00 PM

Join us to celebrate the opening of our new facility at 300 Jacobs Avenue, ½ mile west of Woodley!

enjoy refreshments,
r for door prizes.
n will be available to
her newly-released
ds On, Feet Wet.

ng…the school
rganic Growers!

ring an intensive three-
l January 14–17, 2013
strate what it takes
nd run a successful
rden or small farm.

Learn about:

- *soil fertility and crop rotations*
- *greenhouses*
- *pest management*
- *tools and equipment*
- *post-harvest handling*
- USDA *updates and regulations*

(507) 663-4457

Courage
is not the
lack of fear.
It is acting
in spite of it.

~ Mark Twain

11

Designing with Type

objectives

- *Use the Type on a Path tool*
- *Use the Pen and Pencil tools*
- *Use the Pathfinder tool*
- *Convert type to outlines*
- *Create mulit-size master pages*
- *Create island spreads*
- *Use the Page tool*

introduction

You may wonder why software is always changing—it seems like as soon as you've mastered one version, another one is ready to be released. The graphics field is in a continual state of change, and the rate of change in recent years has been exponential! For over 500 years, type was set mechanically—a physical letter made of metal or wood was inked and pressed onto a sheet of paper. Phototypesetting emerged around 1950, the Mac (as we know it) was launched in 1984. Today, iPads and other tablets are everywhere. Type is now digital. Despite the changes in printing technology, one thing hasn't changed: letters—whether wood, metal, or digital—are carefully crafted by skilled typographers. There is an art to designing type. Working with type is the essence of our craft. This chapter focuses on type as a design element, and celebrates our proud print tradition.

It's impossible to cover all the features in InDesign in one textbook or one semester of class, and *Exploring InDesign CS6* definitely has a print perspective. Obviously, print is no longer the "only show in town." InDesign CS6 is leading the way with innovations that will usher designers into the digital publishing realm. This is an exciting time to be in this field.

But, whether it's digital or print, good design remains good design. Good typography is required in all good design. Design concepts discussed in this textbook will be incorporated into whichever part of the industry you find yourself. And by the way, if you'd be interested in another InDesign textbook that focuses on digital publishing, e-mail me at trydberg@mac.com. I'll pass along your thoughts to the folks at Cengage Publishing.

type: a versatile design element

When reviewing student portfolios, I look for two things: use of type and use of color. When a designer has control of these two critical design elements, everything else will fall into place. Even in black and white, type has "color" and text blocks can range in color from light gray to strong black. Typefaces also express a wide range of personalities inherent in their design. Visual 11–1 shows a collection of ampersands, each interesting and expressing a different personality.

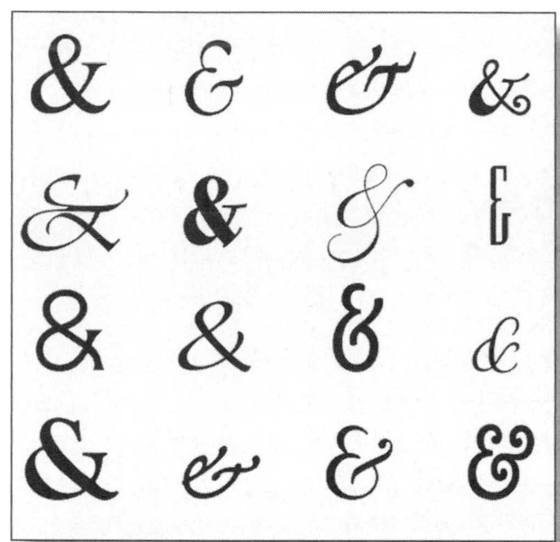

VISUAL |11–1|
This collection of ampersands shows the variation in personality of typefaces.
© Cengage Learning 2013

In this first exercise, we're going to add another ingredient to the type color and personality mixture: *shape*. The ability to create type that follows a path used to be the domain of illustration programs. Thanks to InDesign, these great special effects are right at your fingertips. So, launch InDesign and let's get started.

▸ *Place type on a closed shape*

In order to place text on a path, you first need a path. Then you need the *Type on a Path* tool, accessed by pressing **Shift+T** or by selecting it from the "hidden tool" menu, under the *Type* tool.

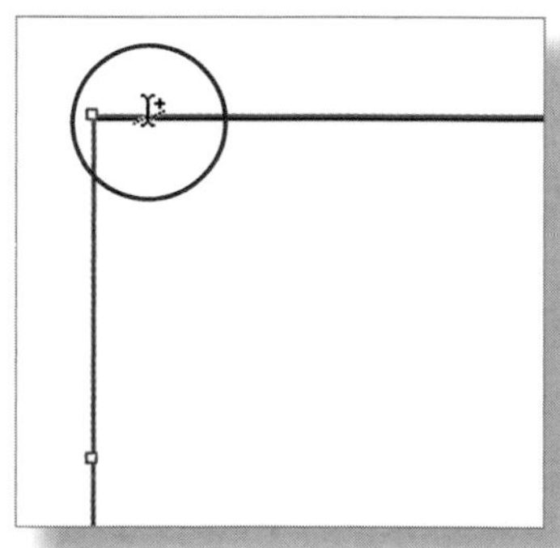

VISUAL |11–2|
The plus sign next to the cursor means that the Type on a Path tool has found a path.
© Cengage Learning 2013

1. Create a new document. Draw a rectangle and apply a **1 pt.** stroke.
2. Select the ***Type on a Path*** tool by pressing **Shift+T**. Position the tool cursor over the edge of the rectangle. A ***plus sign*** on the cursor indicates that the tool has recognized a path and is ready for action (Visual 11–2).

3. Click on the path to create a starting point. Type a line of text that extends around the rectangle. Highlight the text and change the point size and style. Change the alignment. The text considers the first point you clicked with the ***Type on a Path*** tool as the left margin. As you center and right-align the text, it will flow clockwise around the outside of the frame.

4. Visual 11–3 shows two vertical lines called the ***Start*** and ***End brackets***. (The path object must be selected and either selection tool must be active for you to see these.) By default, the brackets are butted up to each other, indicating that the text path extends around the entire rectangle. You can move the ***Start*** and ***End brackets*** to fine-tune the position of the text on your path. The ***Start*** and ***End brackets*** have in and out ports that work just like any other text frame.

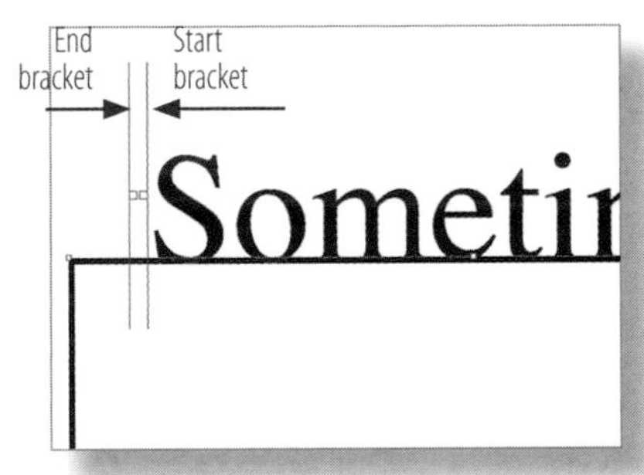

VISUAL |11–3|

The in and out ports are not handles you can use to adjust the Start and End brackets. Click on the vertical part of the Start and End brackets to adjust the location of the text.

5. Select the ***End bracket.*** Do not click on its out port; instead, click on the upper part of the line (the cursor arrow will show a sideways "t" when you are able to click on the bracket). Slowly ***drag*** the End bracket ***counter-clockwise***, closer to the end of the text (Visual 11–4). If you pull the bracket too far, the overset symbol will appear. Just bring the bracket to the end of the text.

6. If you look carefully in the center of the path, you will see a tiny vertical line (Visual 11–4). This line is the ***Center bracket*** (also called the ***Flip*** tool). Click and drag the ***Center bracket*** with either ***Selection*** tool, and the text will move back and forth around the edge of the rectangle.

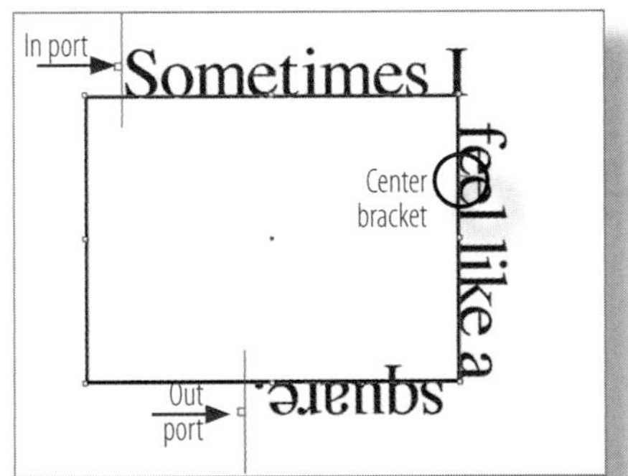

VISUAL |11–4|

There are three brackets on a text path. The tiny vertical line is the Center bracket, which indicates the center of the text.

7. Drag the ***Center bracket*** in toward the center of the rectangle, and the text will flow inside the box. Flip your text inside and outside a few times until it feels comfortable to you (Visual 11–5).

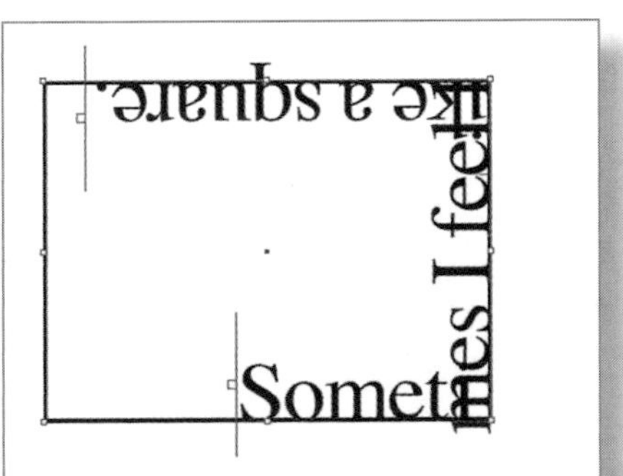

VISUAL |11–5|

Drag the Center bracket to flip text inside and outside of the path.

That was easy enough. Try the same technique with a circle as the path object. Be sure to flip the text inside and outside the circle, as in Visual 11–6. When the type is in place, you will want to set the stroke of the path object to **[None.]**

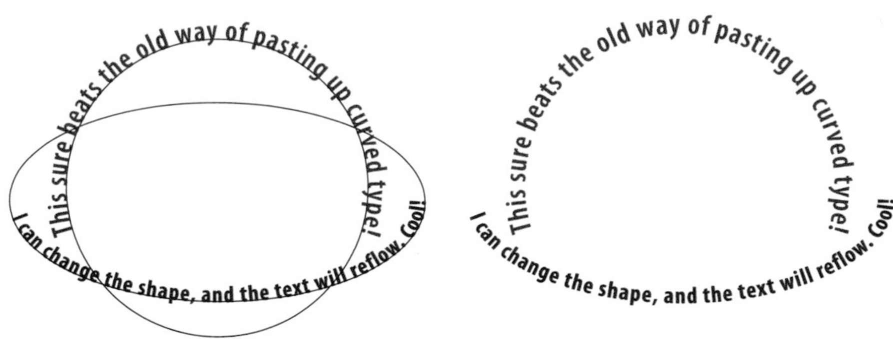

VISUAL |11–6|
A stroke is needed only to help you see the path while you are working on the text. Set the stroke to None once the text is in place.
© Cengage Learning 2013

▸ *Place type on an open path*

Most of the time, you will be creating your own path for type to follow. Type can be placed on paths of any shape. We'll create a few paths using the *Pencil* and *Pen* tools. You may not use the *Pencil* tool very often, but you should know it's there. If this is your first time using the *Pen* tool, note that Chapter 14 will go into detail on using it—you'll just get your toes wet in this chapter.

1. Select the *Pencil* tool by pressing **N** or by selecting it from the *Toolbox*. Draw some squiggles similar to those in Visual 11–7. The *Pencil* tool makes rough, random-looking paths. (The *Pen* tool makes smooth, curvy paths.)

VISUAL |11–7|
These paths were made with the Pencil tool.
© Cengage Learning 2013

2. Select the *Type on a Path* tool and click on one of your paths. (You don't need to select the path first.) Fill the line with text. You can use placeholder text if you prefer. Fill the remaining lines with text. Now experiment with the position, size, and color of your type. The results should look similar to Visual 11–8.

VISUAL |11–8|

Type has been placed on the paths created with the Pencil tool.

3. Use **Command+A** (Mac) or **Control+A** (Windows) to select and delete the text lines created with the *Pencil* tool. Drag down two horizontal guidelines about **1.5"** apart. Select the *Pen* tool by pressing **P**. Position the cursor by the left margin guide and click once on the bottom guidelines (do not drag). Position the cursor over the top guideline, but over to the right of the first point and click. This will create a diagonal line extending from the bottom to the top guidelines. Next, position the cursor on the bottom guideline, over to the right of the second point and click to create another diagonal line. Continue this pattern across the page to make a zigzag pattern, similar to what you see in Visual 11–9.

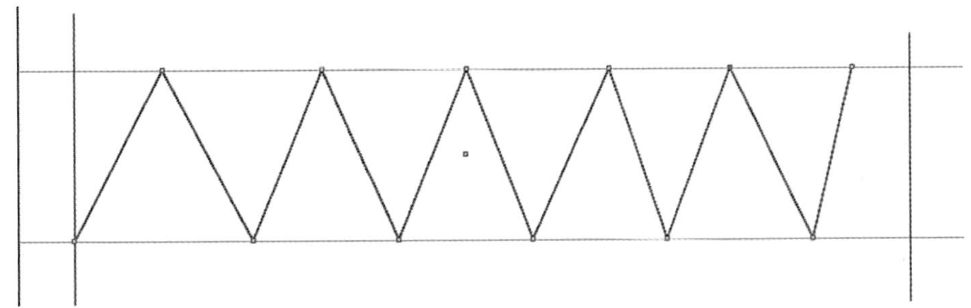

VISUAL |11–9|

Clicking with the Pen tool makes straight line segments.

4. Switch to the *Direct Selection* tool and move the guides out of the way or delete them. Click on an anchor point and drag it. Move it from side to side, then up and down. Continue moving all the points until your zigzag is a total mess (Visual 11–10). Now you know how to use the *Pen* tool to click from point to point, and to create paths made of straight line segments. Let's see what else the *Pen* tool can do. Press **Delete** to delete the path.

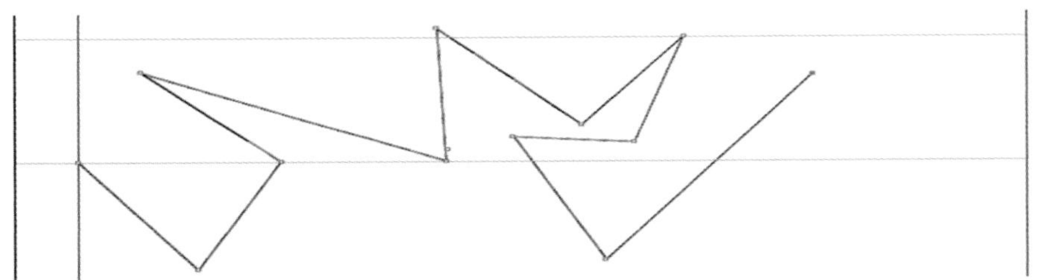

VISUAL |11–10|

Use the Direct Selection tool to move the anchor points of the path.

5. Pull down two horizontal guides about **2"** apart. You're going to make another path similar to the zigzag, except that you will make it with curved segments. With the ***Pen*** tool, click where the lower guideline meets the left margin guide to create the end point of your new path. Here's where the tricky part of creating curved segments comes in. Position the cursor over the top guideline, to the right of the end point, and click without releasing the mouse. This creates a "smooth" corner point. Without releasing the mouse, drag horizontally and you will see two handles extend from the corner point. These are called ***direction lines***. As you drag them out, a ***curved line segmen***t will develop. Move the cursor along the guideline to see how changing the length of the direction line affects the shape of the curve. Release the mouse when the curved segment looks similar to the one in Visual 11–11. Move to the lower guideline, click to make the next anchor point, and drag horizontally to create another curved line segment. Continue this process until you have waves, similar to those in Visual 11–11. Now you know how to use the ***Pen*** tool to make curved line segments by clicking and dragging.

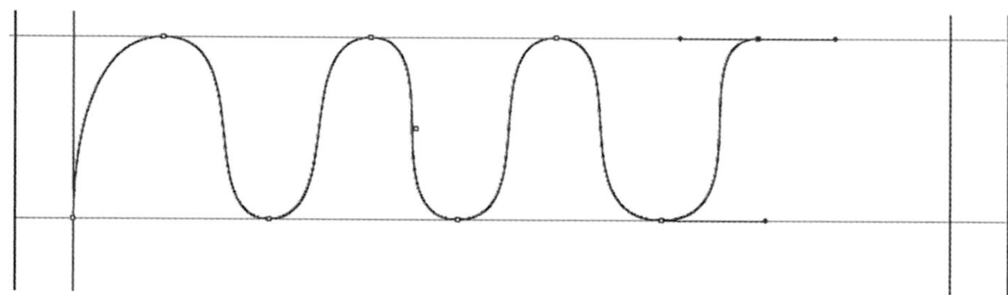

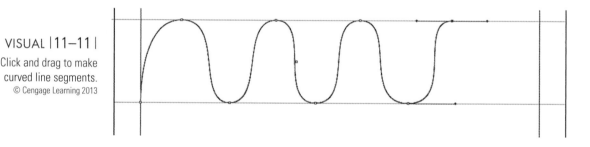

VISUAL | 11–11 |
Click and drag to make curved line segments.

VISUAL | 11–12 |
Within this mess is a combination of straight and curved line segments. Press the keyboard shortcut for any other tool and the Pen tool will be deselected.

6. Now, create a bizarre-looking path using a combination of clicks (straight line segments) and drags (curved line segments). Your mess should look just as bad as mine in Visual 11–12. To end the path, choose another tool or **Command+click** or **Control+click** anywhere on the page. When you're ready to move on, select your line with the *Selection* tool and press **Delete**.

7. Now we're going to make a path in the shape of an arch. If you deleted your two horizontal guidelines, drag down new ones, about **2"** apart. With the ***Pen*** tool, position the cursor over the lower guide, click and drag up. A directional line will extend from each side of the starting point. Keep dragging, trying to keep the upper directional line at a 45-degree angle. When the end of the directional line touches the upper guideline, release the mouse (Visual 11–13A).

8. Now position the *Pen* tool back on the lower guide, approximately **5"** to the right of the first point. Click to set an anchor point and drag the direction line down at approximately 45 degrees. Notice that the upper direction line angles back toward the upper direction line of the first point (Visual 11–13B). When you release the mouse, you should have a nice arch (Visual 11–13C). Use the *Text on a Path* tool to add text to the arch and experiment with the various options you have learned so far.

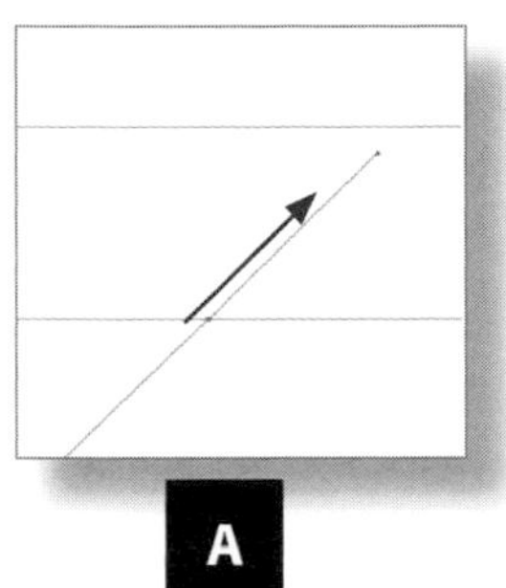

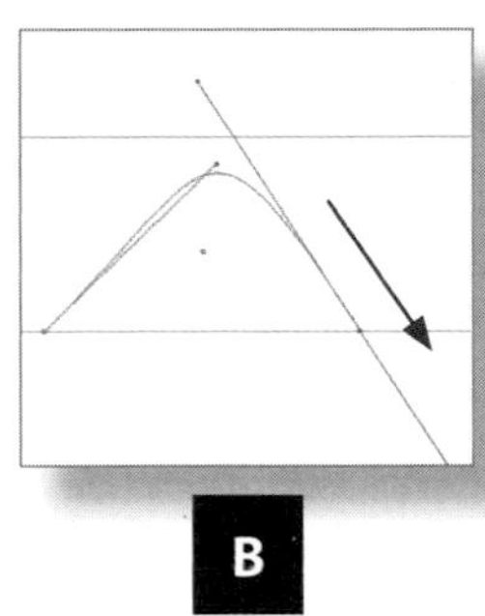

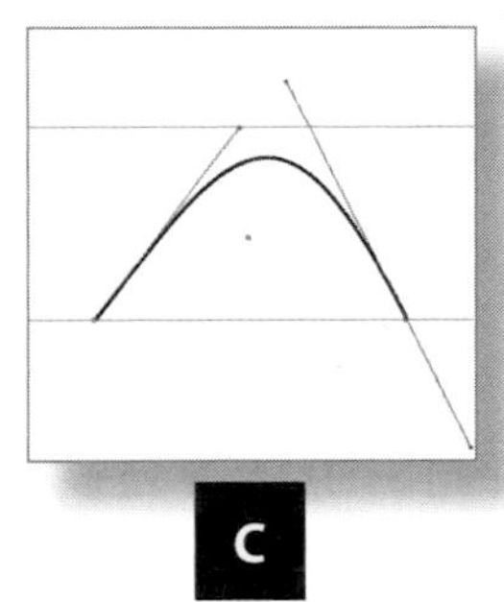

VISUAL |11–13|

Drag in the direction of the arrows to make this smooth arch.

© Cengage Learning 2013

You may realize it would be much easier just to draw an ellipse and place the text on its path, rather than using the *Pen* tool to create the arch shape. And you're right. But very often, you will want to use text paths that don't fit pre-made shapes—like the one you're going to create next.

▸ *Customize a type path*

1. Delete the arch-shaped path and drag down one horizontal guide. With the *Pen* tool, click on the guideline and drag up and to the right at a 45-degree angle. Release the mouse when the direction handle is about 1 inch long.

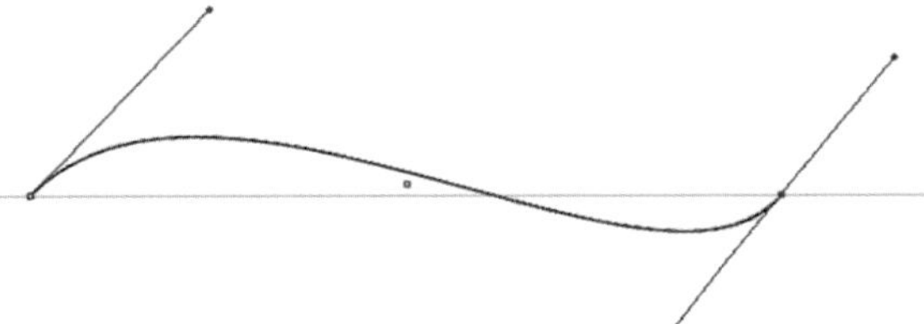

VISUAL |11–14|

You can create elegant, flowing curves using only two anchor points.

© Cengage Learning 2013

2. About **4"** away, click on the guideline to set another anchor point. Hold *Shift*, and drag the directional handle up and to the right to constrain to a 45-degree angle. Release the mouse button when your path looks like Visual 11–14.

3. Go ahead, use the *Type on a Path* tool and place some text on it. Then flip the type using the *Center bracket* line (Visual 11–15). If there is a stroke applied to the path, remove it to see only the text.

This is a path shape you'll often use.

And it flips, just like the other ones.

VISUAL |11–15|

Use the Center bracket to flip and reverse the direction of text placed on a path.

© Cengage Learning 2013

VISUAL |11–16|

The stroke width has been increased to a size larger than the point size of type. The center of the text has been aligned with the center of the stroke.

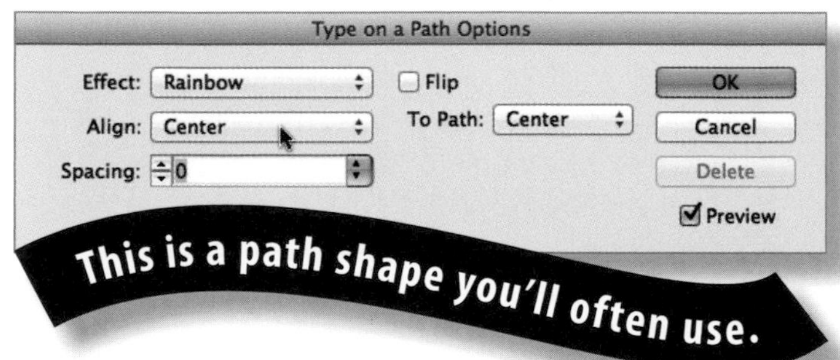

4. Highlight all the text on the path. Change the color to **Paper**. Select the path using either ***Selection*** tool. Change the stroke width of the path to be much wider than the point size of your text. Choose *Type>Type on a Path>Options.* When the *Type on a Path Options* dialog box opens, change the *Align* and *To Path* fields to *Center* to position the type vertically on the path (Visual 11–16). This is a technique you will often use.

▸ *Manage effects*

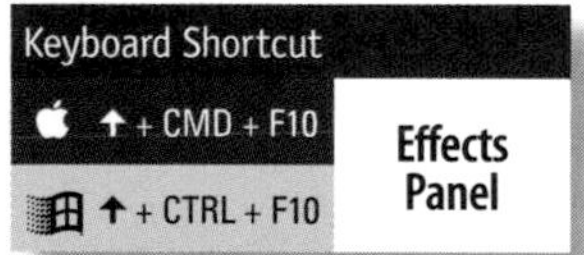

The *Effects* panel manages a variety of transparency effects, including drop shadows. The *Effects* panel can be opened by using the keyboard shortcut, **Shift+Command+F10** (Mac) or **Shift+Control+F10** (Windows.) The *Effects* panel allows you to choose which parts of the element you want to modify. When you select *Object,* the effect is applied to the entire object—its stroke, fill, and text. *Stroke* affects the object's stroke (and gap color). *Text* affects all the text inside the frame. (You can't apply an effect to individual words or letters in a frame.) *Graphic* affects only the graphic selected with the *Direct Selection* tool, and is visible only when a graphic is selected. You've used the *Effects* panel before—we'll go into a little more detail in the following steps.

VISUAL |11–17|

The Effects panel.

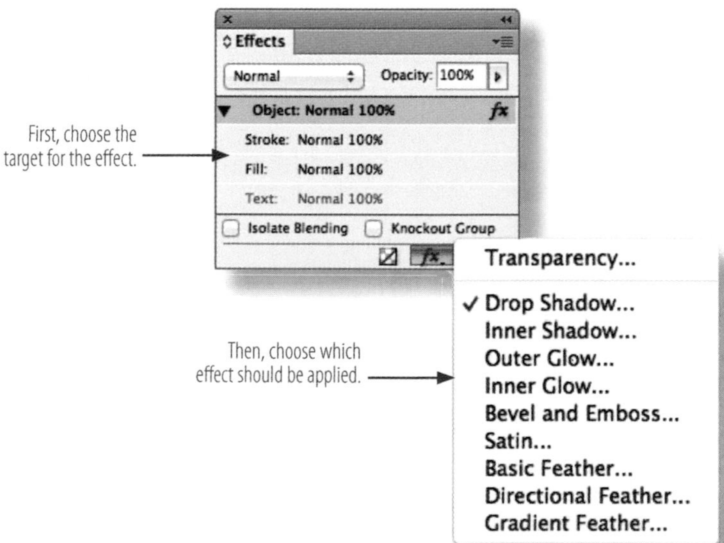

1. Create a small text frame. *Fill:* **None**. *Stroke:* **8-pt Japanese Dots.** Type your name, and center the copy horizontally and vertically. In the *Control* panel, hover the mouse over the *Apply Effect to Object* button and a tool tip will pop up, showing where the effect will be applied (Visual 11–18A). By default, the effect will be applied to *Object*.

▸ *production tip*

Before applying any effect, always check the Settings For field in the Effects window.

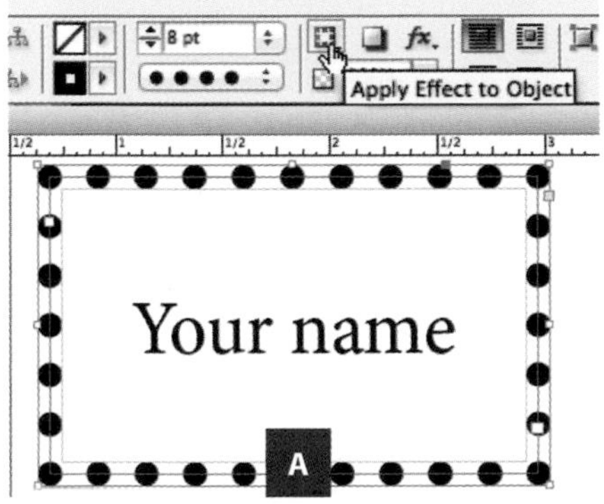

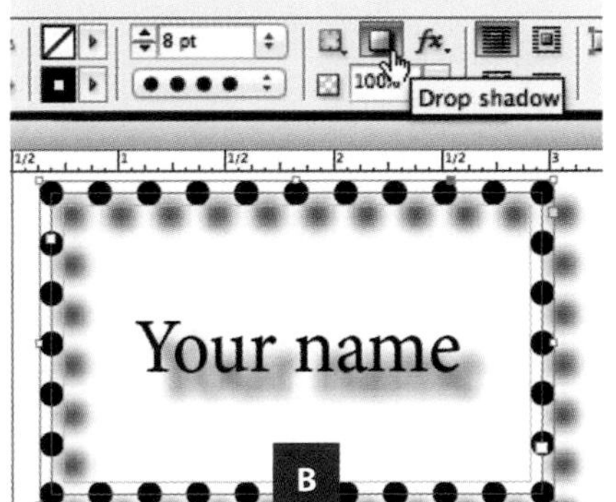

VISUAL |11–18|

Effects can easily be applied from the Control panel. Be sure to select the target from the Apply Effect to Object field before applying the effect.

2. The *Drop Shadow* button is directly to the right of the *Apply Affect to Object* button. Click the *Drop Shadow* button a few times to toggle the shadow on and off. There are three things you should notice (Visual 11–18B). First, because the effect is being applied to the *Object*, both the type and the border have a shadow. Second, the shadow is extremely dark! The default opacity is 75% Black, and this is too dark for most applications. Third, the offset is so far away that the shadow looks like a separate element all together! Because drop shadows usually need to be tweaked, it's faster to open the drop shadow controls in the *Effects* dialog box by using the keyboard shortcut **Command+Option+M** (Mac) or **Control+Alt+M** (Windows). *Deselect* the shadow effect if it is still applied, and use the keyboard shortcut to open the *Drop Shadow* dialog of the *Effects* dialog box.

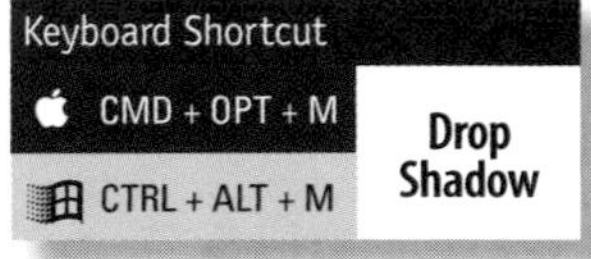

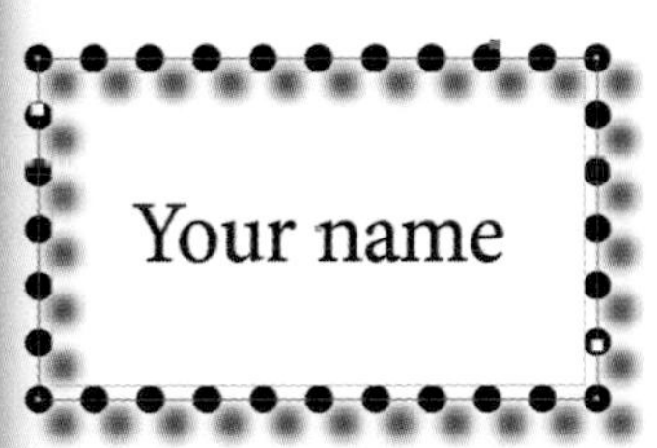

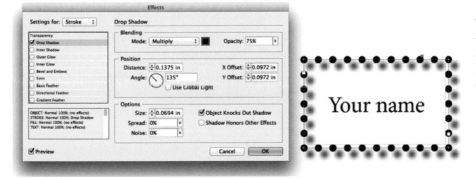

VISUAL |11–19|

The shadow is applied only to the Stroke, as shown in the Settings For window.

3. When you use the drop shadow keyboard shortcut, the window automatically opens and applies the default drop shadow settings. First, make sure that *Preview* is turned on. Then look at the *Settings For* field, in the upper left corner, notice that the drop shadow is being applied to *Object*. Turn this off by unchecking *Drop Shadow* in the left pane. Now, choose **Stroke** from the *Settings For* field and you will see the shadow is no longer applied to the type you used for your name (Visual 11–19).

VISUAL |11–20|

Each window in the Effects panel allows you to modify the appearance of the effect.

▸ *production tip*

A box in the lower left corner of the Effects window summarizes the effects applied to a selected object.

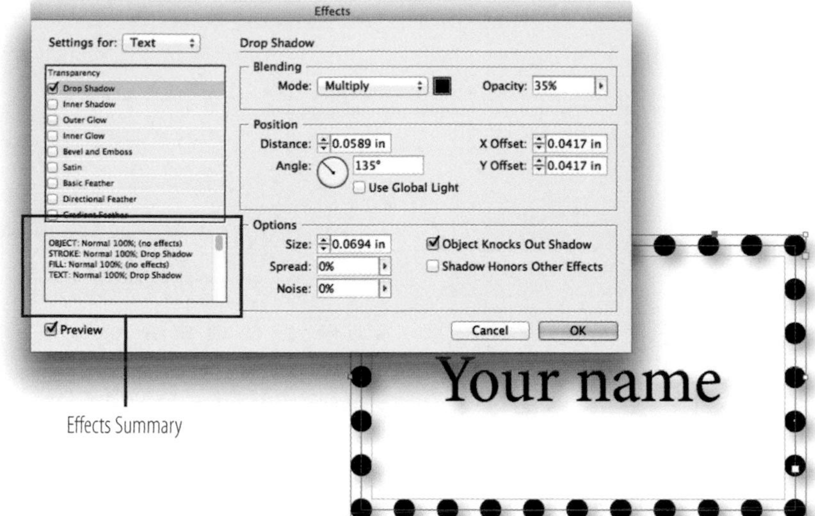

4. Now, let's adjust the *Opacity* and the *X* and *Y Offset* settings. Enter **35** in the *Opacity* field to create a more subtle drop shadow. The *X* and *Y Offset* fields adjust how far over and down the shadow falls. The *Offset* controls work in tandem with the circular *Angle* control, which sets the angle of the light source. The default angle is 135°. With *Preview* checked, rotate the *Angle* bar around the circle and watch the position of your shadow move. Usually, you're going to use the same light source angle for all items on a page. Enter **135** in the *Angle* field to set the light source back to the default. The shadow is still too far away from the stroke. Adjust this by entering **p3** in the *X Offset* and *Y Offset* fields. Now, the shadow looks much more professional. Before we move the next exercise, notice the box in the lower left corner that summarizes the effects applied to a selected object (Visual 11–20).

In the drop shadow exercise you just completed, you learned the basic operations of applying effects to type. When you want to apply an effect other than a drop shadow, you should use the *Effects* keyboard shortcut, **Shift+Command+F10** (Mac) or **Shift+Control+F10** (Windows). Practice using the *Effect Applies To* control, and experiment with applying the various effects.

Playing around with type effects is incredibly fun, but type effects are easily overused. It's like when my grandchildren "play" my piano. They sit on the bench and pound the keys to create the sounds of thunder, lightning, and rain. It's cute for the first 30 seconds. When the noise gets unbearable, I yell, "Please, don't pound on the piano keys!" They're not really playing music, they're just making noise. Similarly, designers are often tempted to add "noise" to type by pounding out one effect after another! Resist the temptation, and let type speak with its own beautiful voice. Effects are fine, when used with discretion.

Please, don't pound on the piano keys!

Inner Shadow effect

Please, don't pound on the piano keys!

Emboss effect

Pillow emboss with a stroke—starting to "cross the line."

VISUAL | 11–21 |

Effects can be easily overdone. Use them with discretion. Remove effects by choosing Clear Effects from the fx menu in the Control panel.

▸ *Create text outlines*

A convenient feature in InDesign is the ability to convert text to outlines. Once text is converted to outlines, it is no longer text, so you can't correct spelling or apply normal text attributes. Instead, each letter is a tiny piece of artwork, giving you the ability to modify the shape or place an image into it.

1. Type the phrase *Buttered Popcorn!* Apply a **Blue** fill. (Visual 11–22). Use the *Selection* tool to activate the frame, and press **Shift+Command+O** (Mac) or **Shift+Control+O** (Windows) to convert the text into *outlines*. You can also choose *Type>Create Outlines.* Now when you look closely at the type, you will see a series of anchor points. Even though each letter is now an individual shape, the letters are still linked together as one object—a *compound path*.

Keyboard Shortcut	
⌘ ⇧ + CMD + O	Create Outlines
⊞ ⇧ + CTRL + O	

Buttered Popcorn!

VISUAL | 11–22 |

When text is converted to outlines, each letter is converted to paths with editable points.

2. With the outline type selected, choose *Object>Paths>Release Compound Path* and the text unit will split apart. Now you can move and rotate each letter with the *Selection* tool. Notice, however, that all the counters are filled in. Select both the counter and the letter outline, and go to *Window>Object & Layout>Pathfinder* to open the *Pathfinder* panel. Then select *Subtract* from the *Pathfinder* section. The counter will be cut out (subtracted) from the underlying letter form. Repeat this process for all the letters with counters (Visual 11–23).

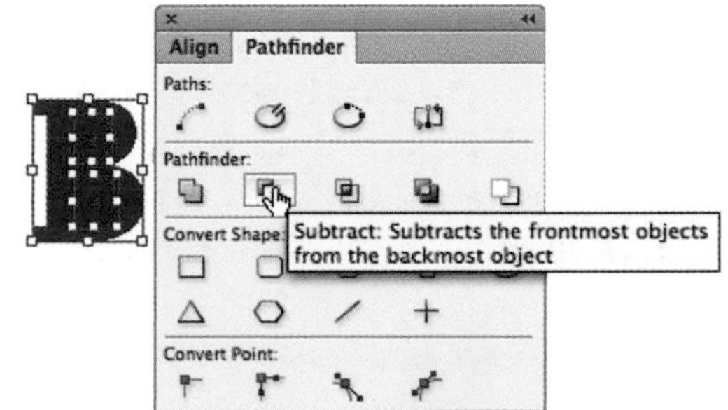

VISUAL | 11–23 |

When compound paths are released, the counters automatically fill in. Open the Pathfinder panel or go to Object>Pathfinder>Subtract to cut the counters out of the letter background.

VISUAL |11–24|

Individual letters can be moved and rotated. In this example, shadow and pillow emboss effects have been added.

3. Delete the dot from the exclamation point. Draw a small text frame in the dot's position and insert an ornament from the ***Glyphs*** panel. Apply ***Drop Shadow*** and ***Pillow Emboss*** from the ***Effects*** panel. ***Pillow Emboss*** is an option under the ***Bevel and Emboss*** page of the ***Effects*** panel.

▸ *Create shaped text frames*

By now, you're an old pro at putting text inside a frame. This exercise will teach you how to create a shaped frame using the *Pen* tool.

1. Delete the images in your document. Select the ***Pen*** tool. Click or click and drag to make an irregularly-shaped, closed object. When you are ready to close the shape, position the ***Pen*** tool cursor close to the path's starting point. You will see a tiny circle appear next to the pen tool icon. This circle indicates that your next click will join the two ends of the path, making a closed shape. Your shape should look very strange, similar to Visual 11–25A.

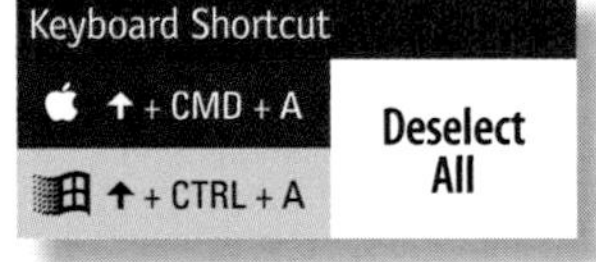

2. Click inside the new shape with the ***Type*** tool. You should see a blinking cursor. Fill with placeholder text. Select all the text and change to justified alignment. Adjust the point size and typeface until you have a fairly even fill (Visual 11–25B). Change the shape's stroke width to **0 pt**. Deselect all, and press **W** to preview your type.

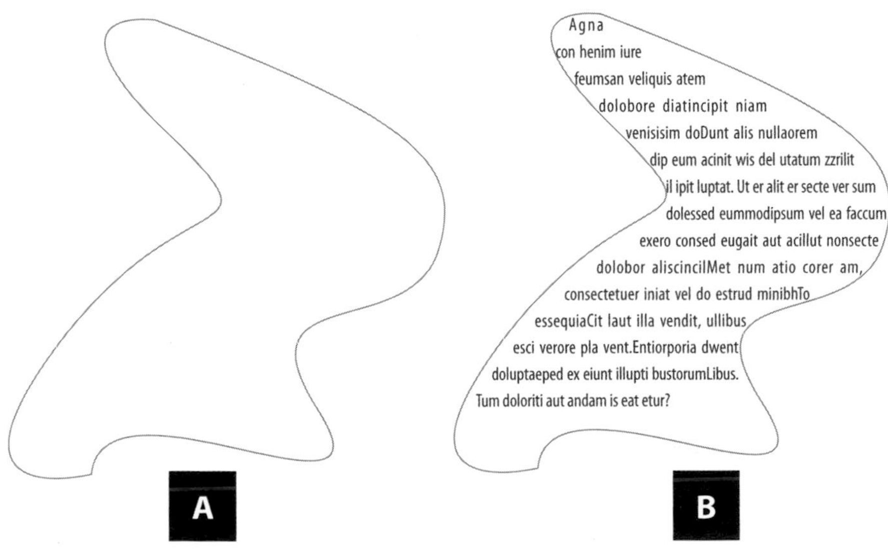

VISUAL |11–25|

First, an odd-shaped closed path was created with the Pen tool. The, text was added and alignment justified to create an irregularly-shaped text wblock with defined edges.

http://woodtype.org

VISUAL | 11–26 |

The Hamilton Wood Type & Printing Museum in Two Rivers, Wisconsin.

PASSIONATE ABOUT TYPE?

I want you to learn InDesign—but more than that, I want you to see type as the most important foundational design element in any project. InDesign is merely the tool for getting the mark on the paper or screen. The *designer* is the one who makes the important decisions about the aesthetic and mechanical use of type. In other words, knowing how to use software does not make one a designer!

For those of you already passionate about type, you probably fit into the category of *type nerd.* Type nerds live in their own, special world—and other people just don't get it. Symptoms of being a type nerd include:

- *Downloading type games on iPads, and font identification apps on smart phones*
- *Pointing out kerning and formatting errors on billboards and restaurant menus*
- *Buying a new typeface rather than a new pair of shoes*
- *Not purchasing a product because you hate the typography*
- *Visiting type museums and attending type conferences*
- *Having type designers as your role models and idols*

If any of those symptoms sound familiar to you, you're well on your way to being a type nerd. (Sometimes we're also called type *snobs.*) If you're a type nerd, you're in good company, and you'll love the next part of this chapter. You'll meet one of my idols—Ian Brignell, an incredible lettering and logo designer. Then, you'll learn about the coolest museum in the world—the Hamilton Wood Type & Printing Museum. You'll create a brochure to promote the museum's internship program.

If you're not yet a type nerd, you'll still learn a plethora of great InDesign techniques as you work through this second half of the chapter.

▸MOVING TOWARD MASTERY

MAN OF LETTERS
Ian Brignell

I love drawing letters. It started in Grade 4 when I used to copy the 16-point type from my reading books, just for the thrill of it. As I got older, I found the expressive power within letters intoxicating and wanted to create them myself, interpreting their moods, their texture and their geometry.

Type is the foundation of good graphic design. Sensitive choices regarding type styles, weights and sizes can amplify visual message and meaning. Art directors who want to go beyond available type solutions come to me. I am a lettering designer.

Letters convey feelings. Good lettering design can provoke a directed emotional response in the viewer: energy, stillness, vitality, reliability, youth, romance, power, purity. As human beings, we are so familiar with letters that we respond to even the subtlest detail or design cue. As a lettering designer, I work to harness this emotional connection in all of my logo work.

Generally, the most interesting design ideas emerge from a drawing done on paper because of the directness, speed and fluidity of expressing a thought or feeling by hand. Hands are quick and capable tools. I play around with pens, graphite, markers, liquid eyeliner, chalk—anything that makes marks on paper. Even if I'm designing a fairly tight corporate mark, I'll often start with a brush to sketch ideas, just to introduce energy into the structure. Then I distill this energy into the finished typography, scanning my designs into the computer and working from there.

 www.ianbrignell.com

Ian's amazing body of work includes the following logos, most of which are familiar to you. Go to his website to see a complete collection of his logos and typefaces.

- *Smirnoff*
- *Breyers Ice Cream*
- *Hormel*
- *Hunts*
- *Pantene*
- *Dove*
- *Burger King*
- *Scope*
- *Secret*
- *Hershey's*
- *Vaseline*
- *Schwan's*
- *Estee Lauder Pleasures*
- *Hellmann's*

▸ MOVING TOWARD MASTERY

- *Bauer*
- *Puffs*
- *Merck*
- *Wisk*
- *Jose Cuervo*
- *Playtex*
- *Schwan's*
- *Naturalizer*
- *Captain Morgan*
- *Varathane*
- *Wild Turkey*
- *Blue Corn*
- *Bell*
- *Stingrays*
- *Merillat*
- *Telefonica*
- *Harvard*
- *Chinet*

Lettering design is both a craft and an art. A non-specialist tends to approach letter spacing mathematically–they will place each letter exactly the same distance from the next letter. Their craft might be good but the resulting word will seem unbalanced and uneven. The art is in being able to gauge and adjust the optical space between the letters. The lettering designer also has to recognize that different letter combinations bring their own tension, and when this tension is resolved, balance is achieved.

Usually I work with creative/art directors of design and branding firms to develop specialized logos or wordmarks. What I create is based on the brief, i.e. the art director's understanding of the client's needs, who the target market is and how the logo should feel. I then transform this information into letterforms and logo designs. My clients hire me for the same reason that they hire a photographer or an illustrator: to enhance their design vision. My job is to bring typographic quality, clarity and integrity to their project, expressing some attribute or feature of a brand that type alone can't address.

I have worked as a lettering specialist for over twenty-five years and I still love drawing letters.

Ian Brignell is a Toronto-based logo and lettering designer. You may see more of his work at **www.ianbrignell. com**. When you visit his site, please thank him for contributing to *Exploring InDesign CS6*.

This article was co-written with Catherine A. O'Toole, Marketing Director, Brignell Lettering Design

the hamilton wood type & printing museum

VISUAL |11–27|
Nothing can match the texture inherent in printing with wood type.
© Mélanie Lévesque 2013

Most of you have learned the history of type—how our craft evolved from beautiful hand lettering done by scribes, to Gutenberg's printing press, to letter press, to phototypesetting, to desktop publishing, and most recently, to web and digital publishing. Letters have been made by human and machine, and the printing substrates have been derived from plants, animals, or electronics. Despite the changes in the method of making the mark, or the surface on which it is printed, the letter form itself, has retained the expressiveness inherent in its original design. Today's resurgence in letter press printing is evidence of the connection that designers have with the letter form, and the joy of experiencing the nuances of individual letters through the sense of touch.

There is no better place to experience the art of type than at The Hamilton Wood Type & Printing Museum, the only museum dedicated to the preservation, study, production and printing of wood type. Their collection of 1.5 million pieces of wood type in more than 1000 styles and patterns is one of the best in the world. The museum offers a variety of opportunities for interested individuals to learn about, and print from, wood type. The museum has an excellent internship program, and you will become quite familiar with it, as you create the corresponding promotional brochure. We'll begin by recreating a close facsimile of their logo, using type on a path. We're limited to using typefaces that were installed with InDesign, so our logo won't look exactly like the original. You'll use features of the *Pathfinder* tools, and make different size pages in a single document. Let's get started!

VISUAL |11–28|
The actual museum logo (A). Notice the perfect kerning and letter proportion in the logo. The facsimile (B) is not as good—we're limited to the typefaces and glyphs included in InDesign.
© Hamilton Wood Type & Printing Museum 2013

▸ *Create curved button text*

1. Create a new document. *Width:* **5 in**. *Height:* **5 in**. *All Margins:* **0**. Create 2 layers.

2. Move to *Layer 1*. Select the *Ellipse Frame* tool and click on the document. Enter **4 in** in the *Width* and *Height* fields (Visual 11–29A). Use the smart guides to center the circle horizontally and vertically on the document (Visual 11–29B).

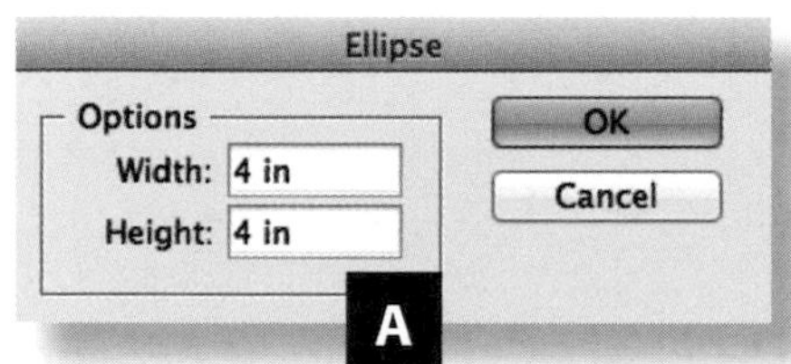

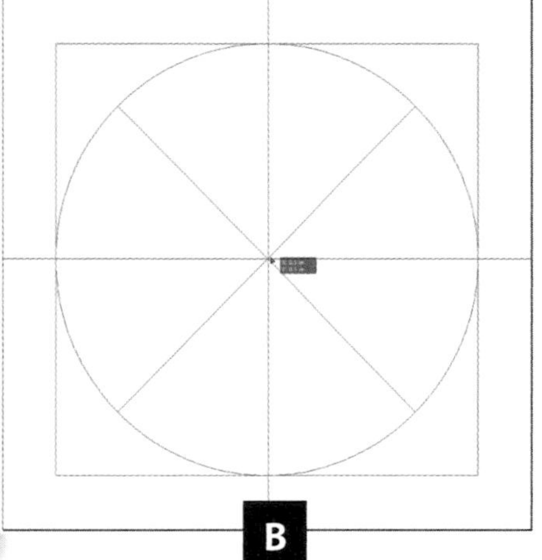

VISUAL |11–29|

Use smart guides to assist you in centering a 4-inch circle on Layer 1. © Cengage Learning 2013

3. Press **Shift + T** to select the *Type on a Path* tool. Click on the left side of the circle and type *Hamilton Wood Type*. As you type, notice that the baselines of the type are aligned to the center of the path. This is the default position for type on a path. With the *Selection* tool, adjust the start and end brackets so they are at the middle point on the text path (Visual 11–30). Format the type: **Chaparral Pro Bold, 33-pt. All Caps.** Use the keyboard shortcut to center the type on the path.

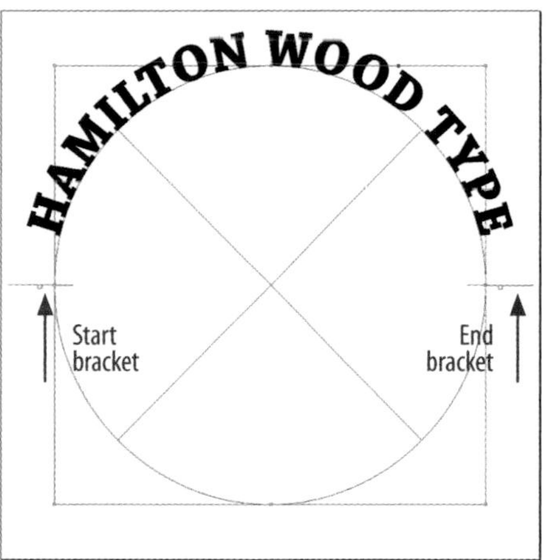

VISUAL |11–30|

Type is centered with the baselines aligned to the center of the path. © Cengage Learning 2013

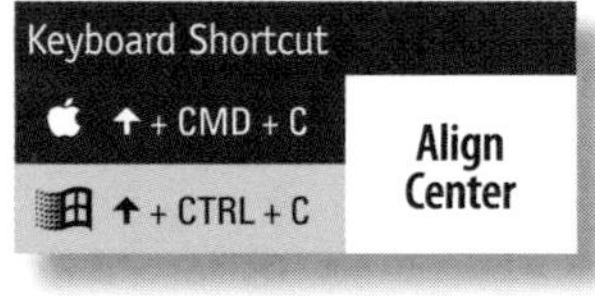

4. Select *Type>Type on a Path>Options* from the menu. In *Align:* choose **Center**. In *To Path:* choose **Center**. This makes the center of the type align to the center of the path. When you're creating buttons and logos using circular type on the upper and lower part of a circle, this is an essential step! (Visual 11–31)

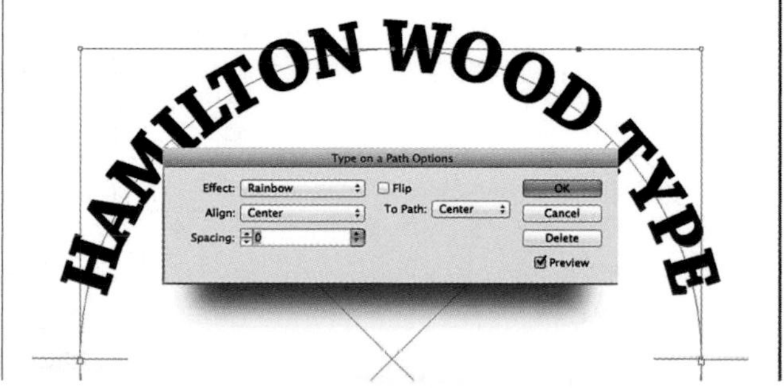

VISUAL |11–31|

Now, the center of the type is aligned to the center of the path. © Cengage Learning 2013

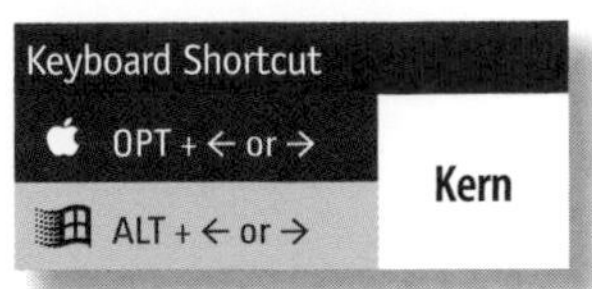

VISUAL | 11–32 |

Use the Context menu to add a thin space to separate the glyph from the type.

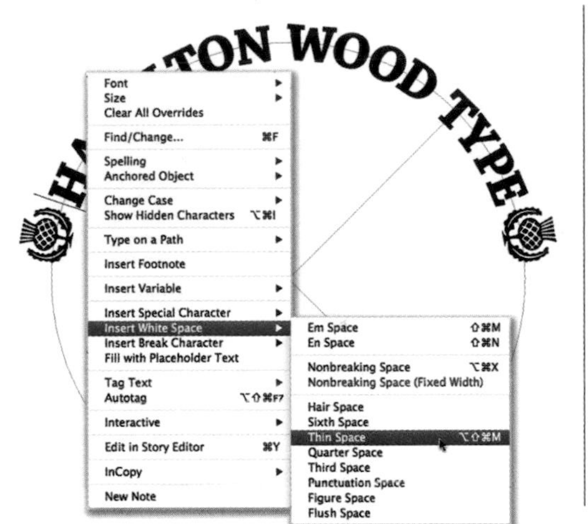

5. Use keyboard shortcuts to kern the letters so that the spacing looks even. Insert a glyph from ***Adobe Caslon Pro*** at the beginning and end of the line. Then, insert a ***thin space*** between the glyph and the type, using the ***Context menu>Insert White Space>Thin Space***. The upper half is now complete.

VISUAL | 11–33 |

Create a copy by pressing Option (Mac) or Alt (Windows) and dragging the selected content to a new layer.

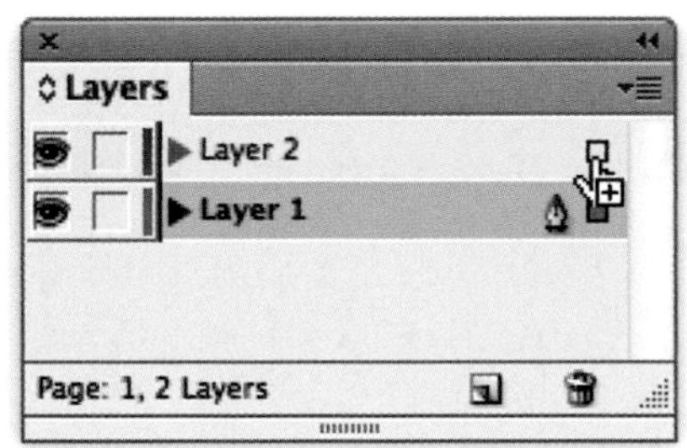

6. Select the type path with the ***Selection*** tool. Press **F7** to open the ***Layers*** panel. Click on the square selected item indicator on the far right end of ***Layer 1*** in the ***Layers*** panel. Press **Option** (Mac) or **Alt** (Windows) and **Click+drag** the indicator to ***Layer 2***. The plus sign (+) indicates that a copy of the item selected has been made on ***Layer 2***.

VISUAL | 11–34 |

Use the center bracket to rotate the type to the bottom and inside of the path.

7. Turn off the visibility and lock ***Layer 1***. The copy of the type should still be visible on ***Layer 2***. Click on the center bracket and rotate the type to the bottom of the circle, flipping it to the inside (Visual 11–34). Delete the pineapple glyphs and then retype the line: ***& Printing Museum.*** Format the type: **Chaparral Pro Bold**, **33-pt. All Caps.**

VISUAL |11–35|

Before (A), and after (B) fine tuning.

8. Unlock *Layer 1* and make it visible. Your logo should look similar to Visual 11–35A, shown above. As you can tell, it needs some revising. As you fine-tune the logo type, lock and hide each layer, as needed. In Visual 11–35B, the end brackets on the upper type on *Layer 1* have been extended, so that the center of the pineapple aligns with the horizontal center path point. The point size used on the museum name (not the glyph) has been increased to **36 pt**. Kerning and tracking have been applied as necessary. When you are satisfied with your final result, use the *Selection* tool to select the type path on *Layer 2*. In the *Layers* panel, move the *selection indicator* down to *Layer 1*. Now, both circles are on *Layer 1*. Lock *Layer 1*.

9. Move back to *Layer 2*. Draw a large text frame. Type **H**. Format: **Chaparral Pro Bold 270-pt.** Center the letter in the circle. Select the text frame with the *Selection* tool. Use the keyboard shortcut to convert the letter to outlines. Now, it's no longer text.

Keyboard Shortcut	
Mac: ↑ + CMD + O	**Create Outlines**
Windows: ↑ + CTRL + O	

10. Draw a rectangle the fills in the lower part of the "H". Fill the rectangle with: **Black** (Visual 11–36A). Select the "H" and the rectangle.

11. Go to *Window>Object & Layout>Pathfinder* to open the *Pathfinder* tools. Click **Add** (Visual 11–36B). Now, the rectangle and "H" are one element.

VISUAL |11–36|

Pathfinder>Add is used to add a black rectangle to the "H" graphic element.

VISUAL |11–37|

Pathfinder's Subtract button works like a cookie cutter as it cuts the "T" out of the "H."

© Cengage Learning 2013

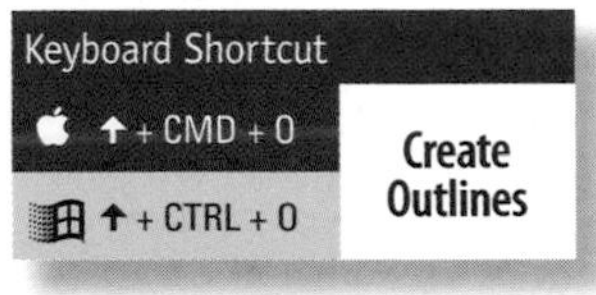

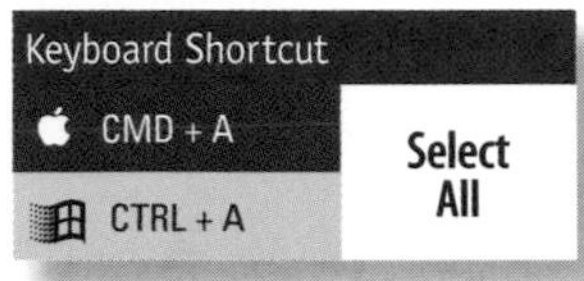

12. Draw a text frame on top of the "H". Type **T** in **Chaparral Pro Bold**, **120 pt**. **[Paper]** Align the bottom of the "T" to the bottom of the H. Use the ***Selection*** tool to select the text frame. Use the keyboard shortcut to convert the "T" to outlines. Center the "T" horizontally, select both letters and apply Pathfinder>Subtract.

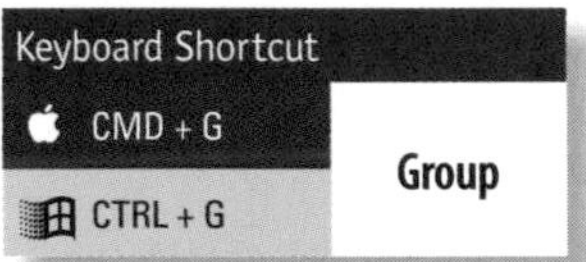

13. Congratulations! The logo is complete. Unlock Layer 1, use the keyboard shortcut to *Select All,* and then *Group* the elements. *Export>Format:* **InDesign Snippet**. Enter **Hamilton logo** in the *Save As* field (Visual 11–38).

VISUAL |11–38|

The finished logo is named, and exported as a Snippet.

© Cengage Learning 2013

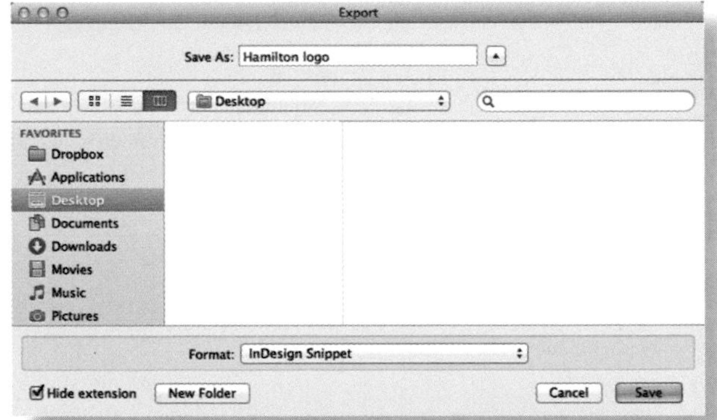

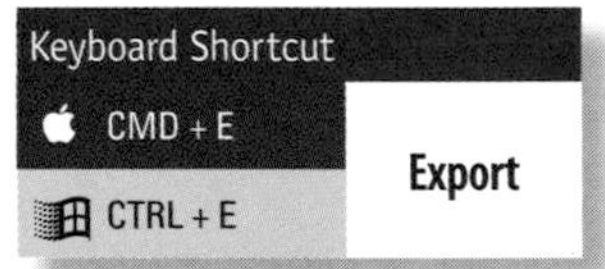

▸ *production tip*

InDesign is not the ideal software to use for creating logos—Adobe® Illustrator is. We're using InDesign for the purpose of showing various techniques, most of which are available in Illustrator.

Photography © Mélanie Lévesque 2012

MULTI-SIZE PAGES IN A SINGLE DOCUMENT

The logo is finished, now it's time to put together the letter fold brochure that describes Hamilton Wood Type & Printing Museum's internship program. The finished brochure is shown in Visual 11–39. You'll be using the *Pages* panel and the *Page* tool. Both allow you to create multiple page sizes in a single document. This feature is great for making letter fold brochures which require different panel widths to accommodate folding. In Chapter 10, you used this feature in the template used to create the Dragonfly Environmental Education brochure. Now, you'll create separate page sizes from scratch. These pages will be held together as multiple page spreads, also called *island spreads.* When the brochure is printed, each page's trim marks indicate the positions of folds.

► *production tip*

A great online resource is **http://designerstoolbox.com**. This site has resources ranging from folding styles to envelope sizes, to dielines for folders and CDs. You should bookmark it, because you will visit it often!

Multi-page sizes also make it easier to coordinate colors and design elements between related pieces. For instance, a single document could include a letterhead, envelope, business card, invoice, and a brochure—all with the same gradient blends, swatches, typefaces and graphic elements. Having all these pieces in one document is a great way to stay organized. You're already familiar with the *Pages* panel. You'll find the *Page* tool beneath the *Direct Selection* tool on the *Toolbox*.

► *production tip*

The page widths necessary for a standard letter fold brochure are $3\frac{5}{8}$" and $3\frac{11}{16}$".

VISUAL | 11–39 |

The finished Hamilton Wood Type & Printing Museum internship brochure.

Photography © Hamilton Wood Type & Printing Museum 2012

▸ *Make a brochure with different panel widths*

1. Make new document. *Number of pages*: **6**. *Width:* **3.6875 in.** (3¹¹⁄₁₆") *Height:* **8.5 in**. *All margins:* **1p6**.

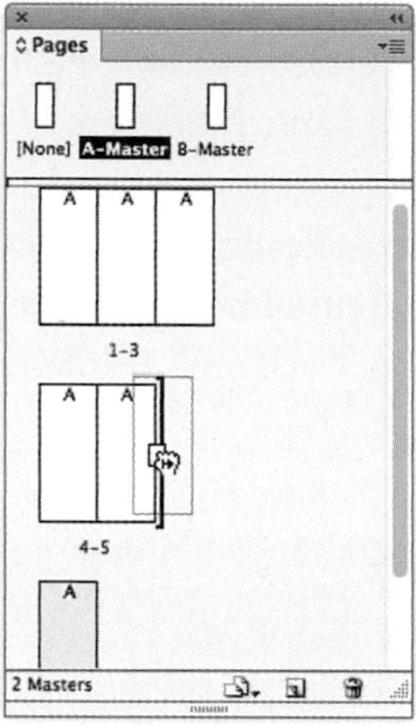

VISUAL | 11–40 |

Deselect Allow Document Pages to Shuffle and create two island spreads, composed of three pages each.

2. Open the *Pages* panel. In the panel options, deselect *Allow Document Pages to Shuffle*. Select *Page 2*, and drag it next to *Page 1*. Release the page when you see a bracket (Visual 11–40). Select *Page 3* and drag it next to *Page 2*. Release the page when the bracket is visible. The three pages are now side-by-side. You've just created a multiple-page spread, called an *island spread*.

3. Use the same technique to create an island spread from *Pages 4–6*. When complete, your document will have two spreads containing six pages.

4. At the top of the *Pages* menu, select *A-Master* page. From the *Pages* panel menu select *Master Options for "A-Master."* In the *Name* field, enter **3.6875 inches.**

5. Go to the *Pages* menu and select *New Master.* In the *Name* field, enter **3.625 inches**. Under *Page Size>Width:* enter **3.625 in.** (Visual 11–41A). The ability to change a page size when creating a new master is a new feature in CS6.

VISUAL | 11–41 |

InDesign CS6 allows you to create multiple page sizes when creating new master pages.

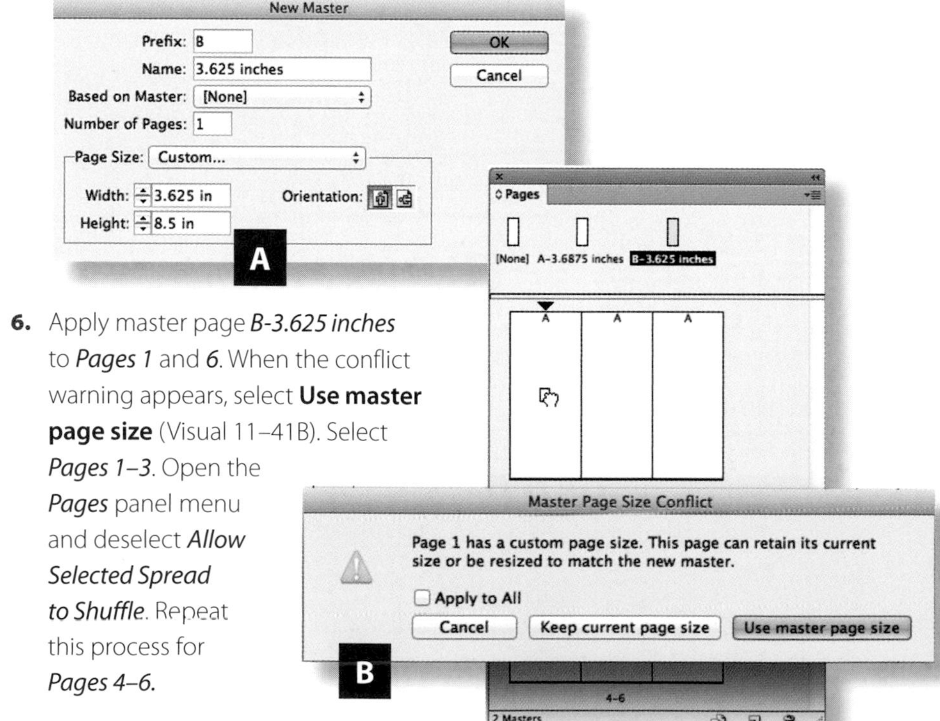

6. Apply master page *B-3.625 inches* to *Pages 1* and *6*. When the conflict warning appears, select **Use master page size** (Visual 11–41B). Select *Pages 1–3*. Open the *Pages* panel menu and deselect *Allow Selected Spread to Shuffle*. Repeat this process for *Pages 4–6*.

▸ *Format the brochure copy*

1. Create a new layer, named ***Backgrounds***. Move the ***Background*** layer below ***Layer 1***. You'll be working on the ***Background*** layer though Step 3. Go to ***Page 1***. Move the reference point in the proxy, on the ***Control*** panel, to the upper left corner. Drag a horizontal guide to ***Y:* 1.5 in.** Place the ***Hamilton Logo.idms*** you created earlier in the top, center of ***Page 1***. Activate the ***Selection*** tool and select the logo. Press **Shift+Command** (Mac) or **Shift+Control** (Windows) and drag the lower right corner up to reduce the size of the Snippet. The top of the curve should be at the top margin line on ***Page 1***. The bottom curve should be at the guideline.

▸ *production tip*

Use Shift+Command (Mac) or Shift+Control (Windows) as you drag to proportionately resize a combination of images and text.

2. On ***Page 1***, draw a rectangle ***H:* 5.25 in.** and position the bottom, left and right rectangle edges at the margin guides. Place ***11 Light Wood.psd*** into the frame. The image can be found in the ***11 Artwork and Resources folder*** on the student online companion (Visual 11–42A). Press **Shift+G** to select the ***Gradient Feather*** tool. This tool creates a transparent feather on the side you select. With the photo frame selected, drag the ***Gradient Feather*** tool from the bottom of the photo, to the top. The top of the photo should fade out, similar to Visual 11–42B.

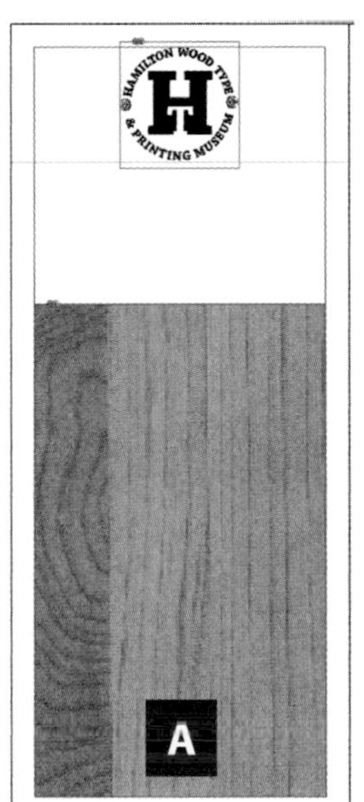

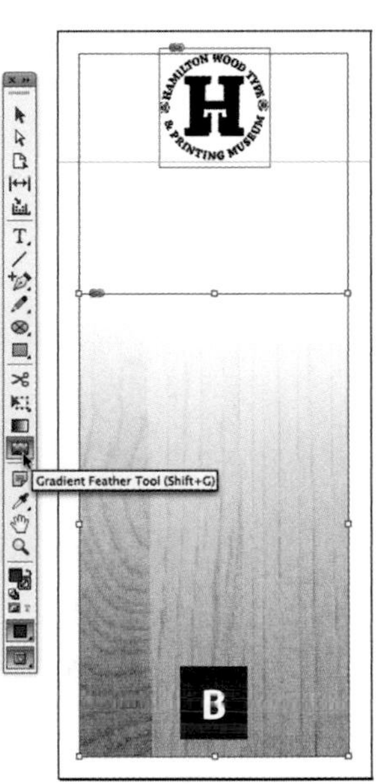

VISUAL | 11–42 |

The Gradient Feather tool creates transparency on individual edges.

- Go to: http://www.cengagebrain.com
- Type: Rydberg
- Click Exploring InDesign CS6 in the list of search results.
- When the book's main page is displayed, click the Access button under Free Study Tools.
- To download files, select a chapter number and then click on the Artwork & Resources tab on the left navigation bar to download the files.

3. Go to ***Spread 2***. Draw a rectangle ***H:* 5.25 in.** that spans ***Pages 4–6*** and is flush to the outer left and right and bottom margins. Place ***11 Light Wood.psd*** in the frame. Use the ***Gradient Feather*** tool from the bottom to the top of the image to create a same feathering effect used in Step 2. A single, feathered image should span across all three pages (Visual 11–39. Lock the ***Background*** layer.

4. Go to ***Page 1***. On ***Layer 1***, draw a text frame that begins at the upper guide ***Y:* 1.5 in.** and extends to the left, right, and bottom margins. Use ***Text Frame Options*** to add a **0.125 in.** inset on all four sides.

5. Create one text frame on *Page 4* and one on *Page 5*, that extend from the upper left, to the lower right margin guides. Use *Text Frame Options* to add a **0.125 in.** inset on sides of each frame. Go back to *Page 1*. Click on the text frame ***out port***, and thread it to the text frame on *Page 4*. Then, thread the text frame on *Page 4* to the one on *Page 5*.

6. Place ***Hamilton Internship Brochure.docx*** into the frame on *Page 1*. Place the text cursor before the line, ***"What will I work on?"*** and create a frame break by pressing **Enter** on the Number pad or from the ***Context menu>Insert Break Character>Frame Break.*** This makes the copy flow to the next linked text frame on ***Page 4.*** On *Page 4*, place the text cursor before the line, ***"When are internships offered?"*** and create a frame break by pressing **Enter** on the Number pad or from the ***Context menu>Insert Break Character>Frame Break.*** The copy should flow to *Page 5*.

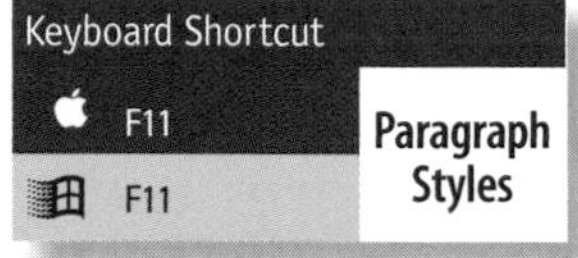

7. Select *Load All Text Styles* from the *Paragraph Styles* menu. Navigate to *11 Brochure Styles* from the *11 Artwork and Resources folder* on the student online companion. Load all styles. Open the *Paragraph Styles* panel. Put the cursor in the first line of copy on *Page 1* and *Select All*. With the text cursor still in the first line, press **Control** (Mac) or **right-click** (Windows) and click on the paragraph style, *Just our type*. Slide down to select *Apply "Just our type" then Next Style.* Since *Next Style* has been specified in the paragraph styles, all the copy automatically becomes formatted, just like a row of dominoes falling into place (Visual 11–43). You must admit, that's fun!

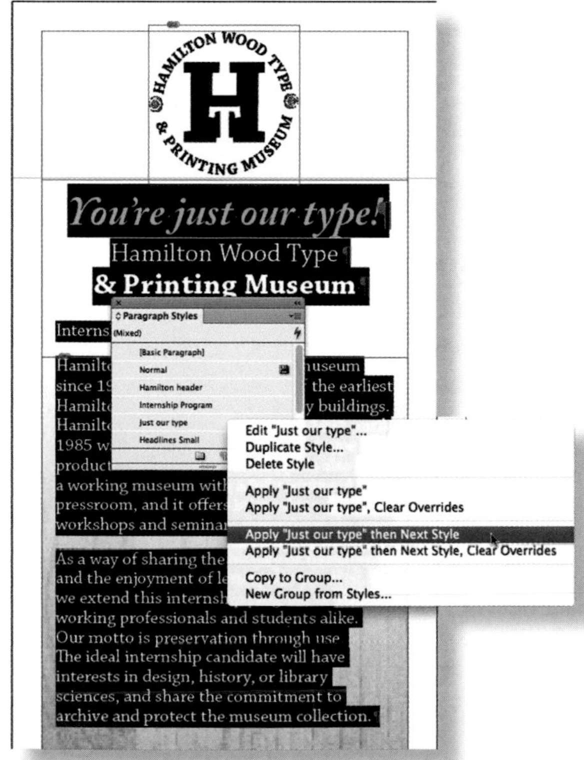

VISUAL | 11–43 |

You feel like the "master of the paragraph styles" when "Next Style" is specified with paragraph styles. You can format large amounts of copy with a single click!

8. Go to *Pages 4* and *5* and apply *Small Headline* to these three lines: *What will I work on?, When are internships offered?* and *How can I apply?*

9. Finally, apply the character style *Body Copy Italic* to the words, *preservation through use* on *Page 1*, and and *Body Copy Blue* to the museum's address and *info@ woodtype.org* on *Page 5*.

▸ *Place Snippets*

10. Go to the *Preferences* dialog box and choose *File Handling>Snippet Import*. Select **Original Location** in the *Position At* field. We're going to speed up the production process by using photos saved as Snippets. The Snippets are found in *Snippets* folder inside *11 Artwork and Resources*. Follow this sequence when placing the Snippets:
    Page 1: *11 Photo You're just our type.idms*
    Page 2:*11 Mailing Address.idms*
    Page 4: *11 Photo What will I work on.idms* (Open the *Text Wrap* panel, and then specify *Jump Column* to this photo after it is placed.)
    Page 5: *11 How can I apply.idms*
    Page 6: *11 Photo Internship Application.idms*

11. And now…a special treat which will only happen in textbooks…the application form has been created as a Snippet. Go to *Page 6*, and place *11 Internship Application.idms*. (You can thank me, later!) Except for Page 3 (the front cover), the brochure should be finished.

▸ *Create type effects*

Because I'm trying to introduce you to as many effects as possible, the cover incorporates more effects than you will probably ever use again in a single document! This might also be one of the few times you use these typefaces which come standard with InDesign: *Rosewood, Birch, Poplar,* and *Blackoak*. As you're working with effects, feel free to experiment—you might come up with an effect that is unique and perfect for what you're wanting to say!

VISUAL |11–44|
The cover uses effects and typefaces that you may never again use in a single document!

1. Unlock, and move to the layer, *Background*. On *Page 3*, draw a rectangle on the *Background* layer: *X*: **.25 in.**, *Y:* **1.25 in.**, *H:* **7 in.** (reference point in upper left corner). Apply a **6-pt. Thin-Thin**, **Black** stroke. Open the *Stroke* panel and align the stroke to the inside.

2. Place ***11 Light Wood 2.psd*** from the ***11 Artwork and Resources*** folder inside the rectangle. Place ***11 Front Cover Logo.idms***. Use Smart Guides to make sure the logo is centered horizontally on the page. Move the logo to ***Layer 1***, and **lock** the layer. Do not lock the ***Background*** layer. The front of the brochure should look like Visual 11–45A.

3. Now, you'll use ***Pathfinder>Subtract*** to cut a curve under the logo. Move to the ***Background*** layer. Choose the ***Ellipse*** tool. Hold **Shift+Option** (Mac) or **Shift+Alt** (Windows) and draw a circle out from the center of the logo, slightly bigger than the logo (Visual 11–45B). Open the ***Pathfinder*** panel from ***Window>Object & Layout>Pathfinder***. Select the rectangle and the circle. Choose ***Subtract*** from the ***Pathfinder*** options (Visual 11–45C).

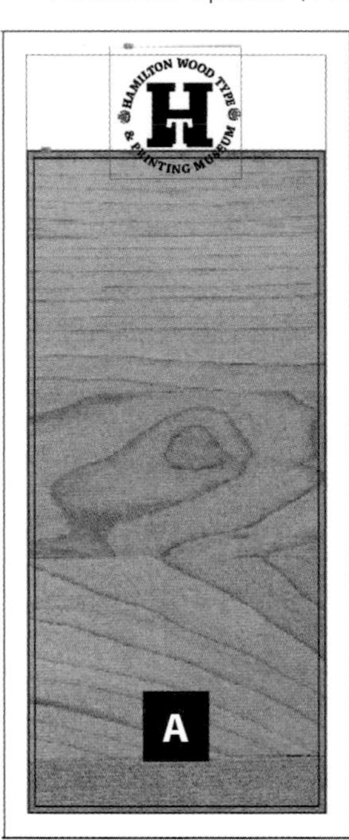

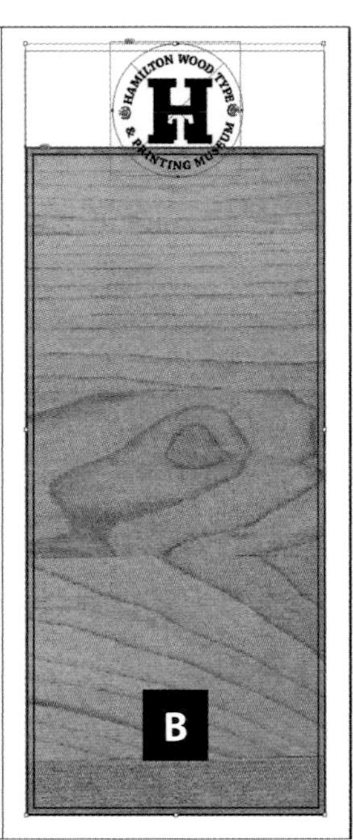

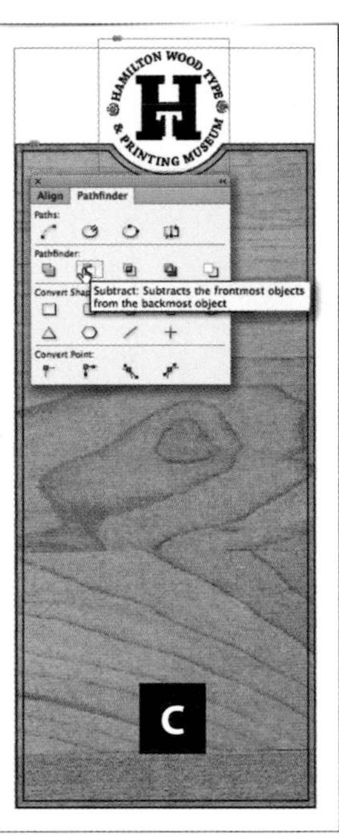

VISUAL |11–45|

The Subtract option in Pathfinder cuts a curve to fit around the logo.

© Cengage Learning 2013

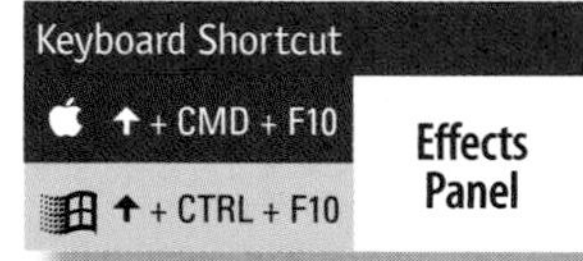

4. Select the stroked frame filled with wood grain. Open the ***Effects*** panel. Select **Stroke** as the target. Under ***Bevel and Emboss***, choose ***Pillow Emboss***, and enter the values shown in Visual 11–46. Lock the ***Background*** layer.

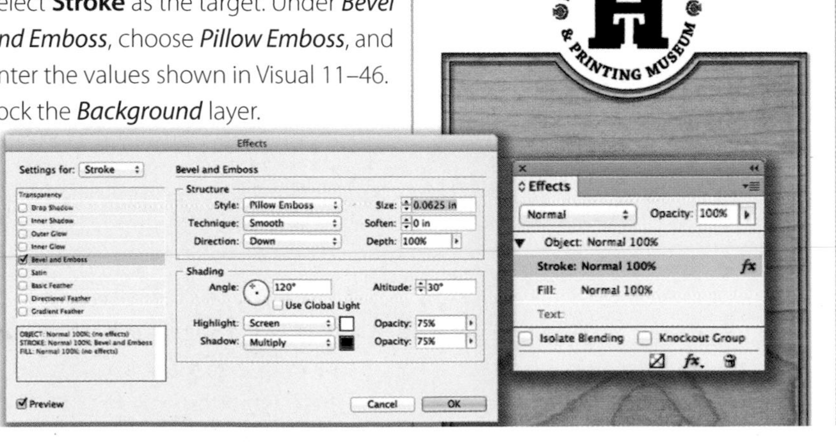

VISUAL |11–46|

The Subtract option in Pathfinder cuts a curve to fit around the logo.

© Cengage Learning 2013

5. Move to ***Layer 1*** and unlock it. Place ***11 Front Cover type.idms*** and ungroup. The sizes and styles are done—you need to select each individual block of type. and then apply the effect. In the steps below, each block of type will be shown with its corresponding effect, and you will need to duplicate the effect on your document. Make sure to monitor the ***Settings For*** field so that you choose the correct target for each effect. Begin with the word, "one," and the pointing finger, shown below.

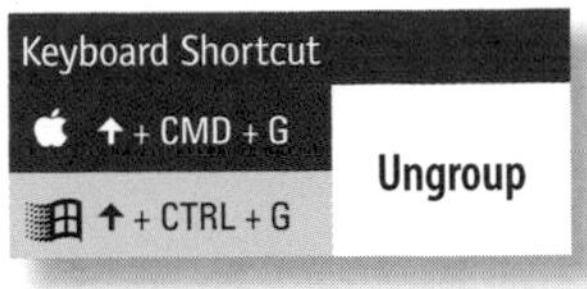

VISUAL |11–47|

The Effects settings for the word, "one" and the pointing finger.

Effects

Settings for: Text

Outer Glow

Blending
Mode: Screen Opacity: 75%

Options
Technique: Softer Noise: 3%
Size: 0.25 in Spread: 0%

Transparency
Drop Shadow
Inner Shadow
Outer Glow
Inner Glow
Bevel and Emboss
Satin
Basic Feather
Directional Feather
Gradient Feather

OBJECT: Normal 100%; (no effects)
STROKE: Normal 100%; (no effects)
FILL: Normal 100%; (no effects)
TEXT: Normal 100%; Outer Glow

Preview Cancel OK

ONE

Effects

Settings for: Object

Bevel and Emboss

Structure
Style: Pillow Emboss Size: 0.0625 in
Technique: Chisel Hard Soften: 0 in
Direction: Down Depth: 57%

Shading
Angle: 120° Altitude: 30°
Use Global Light
Highlight: Overlay Opacity: 75%
Shadow: Multiply Opacity: 89%

Transparency
Drop Shadow
Inner Shadow
Outer Glow
Inner Glow
Bevel and Emboss
Satin
Basic Feather
Directional Feather
Gradient Feather

OBJECT: Hard Light 100%; Bevel and Emboss
STROKE: Normal 100%; (no effects)
FILL: Normal 100%; (no effects)
TEXT: Normal 100%; (no effects)

Preview Cancel OK

Effects
Hard Light Opacity: 100%
Object: Hard Light 100%
Stroke: Normal 100%
Fill: Normal 100%
Text: Normal 100%
Isolate Blending Knockout Group

POINTING FINGER

VISUAL |11–48|

The Effects settings for the word, "Big".

Effects

Settings for: Object

Transparency
Drop Shadow
Inner Shadow
Outer Glow
Inner Glow
Bevel and Emboss
Satin
Basic Feather
Directional Feather
Gradient Feather

OBJECT: Multiply 100%; Drop Shadow, Bevel and Emboss
STROKE: Normal 100%; (no effects)
FILL: Normal 100%; (no effects)
TEXT: Normal 100%; (no effects)

Drop Shadow

Blending
Mode: Multiply Opacity: 50%

Position
Distance: 0.0884 in X Offset: 0.0625 in
Angle: 135° Y Offset: 0.0625 in
Use Global Light

Options
Size: 0.0694 in Object Knocks Out Shadow
Spread: 0% Shadow Honors Other Effects
Noise: 7%

Preview BIG Cancel OK

Effects

Settings for: Object

Transparency
Drop Shadow
Inner Shadow
Outer Glow
Inner Glow
Bevel and Emboss
Satin
Basic Feather
Directional Feather
Gradient Feather

OBJECT: Multiply 100%; Drop Shadow, Bevel and Emboss
STROKE: Normal 100%; (no effects)
FILL: Normal 100%; (no effects)
TEXT: Normal 100%; (no effects)

Bevel and Emboss

Structure
Style: Inner Bevel Size: 0.0625 in
Technique: Smooth Soften: 0 in
Direction: Up Depth: 100%

Shading
Angle: 120° Altitude: 30°
Use Global Light
Highlight: Screen Opacity: 75%
Shadow: Multiply Opacity: 75%

Preview BIG Cancel OK

VISUAL | 11–49 |

The Effects settings for the words, "Happy" and "Type."

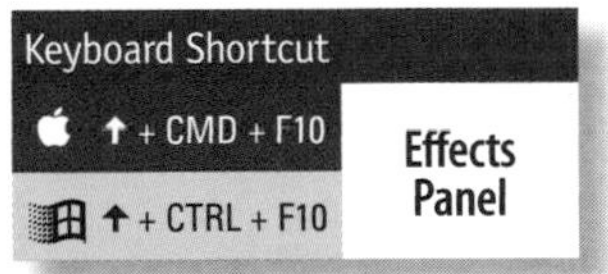

Effects

Settings for: Object

Drop Shadow

Transparency
Drop Shadow
Inner Shadow
Outer Glow
Inner Glow
Bevel and Emboss
Satin
Basic Feather
Directional Feather
Gradient Feather

Blending
Mode: Multiply Opacity: 75%

Position
Distance: 0.0393 in X Offset: 0.0333 in
Angle: 148° Y Offset: 0.0208 in
Use Global Light

Options
Size: 0.0694 in Object Knocks Out Shadow
Spread: 8% Shadow Honors Other Effects
Noise: 19%

OBJECT: Normal 100%; Drop Shadow
STROKE: Normal 100%; (no effects)
FILL: Normal 100%; (no effects)
TEXT: Normal 100%; (no effects)

Preview

HAPPY

Cancel OK

Effects

Settings for: Object

Drop Shadow

Transparency
Drop Shadow
Inner Shadow
Outer Glow
Inner Glow
Bevel and Emboss
Satin
Basic Feather
Directional Feather
Gradient Feather

Blending
Mode: Multiply Opacity: 75%

Position
Distance: 0.0393 in X Offset: 0.0278 in
Angle: 135° Y Offset: 0.0278 in
Use Global Light

Options
Size: 0.0694 in Object Knocks Out Shadow
Spread: 0% Shadow Honors Other Effects
Noise: 3%

OBJECT: Normal 100%; Drop Shadow
STROKE: Normal 100%; (no effects)
FILL: Normal 100%; (no effects)
TEXT: Normal 100%; (no effects)

Preview

TYPE

Cancel OK

VISUAL | 11–50 |
The Effects settings for the word, "Family."
© Cengage Learning 2013

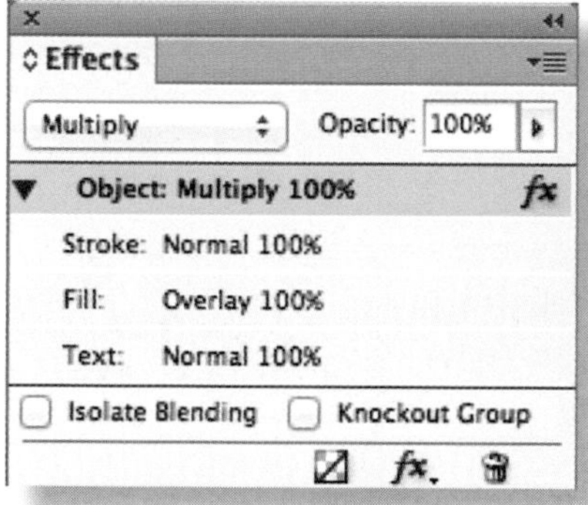

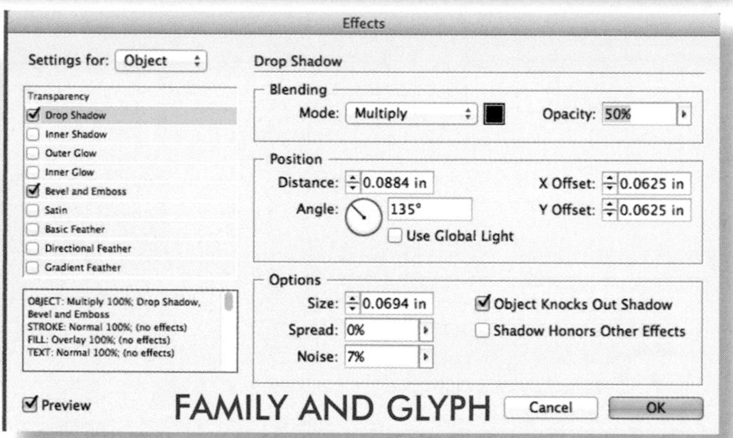

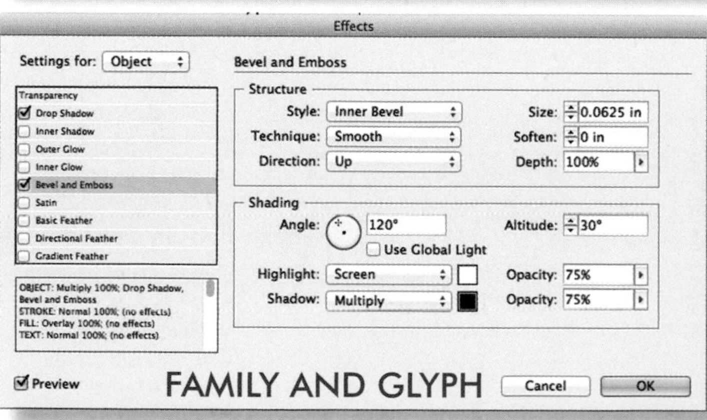

▸ *Create text on a ghosted background*

The final touch on the front cover is the information block on the lower half. This block has a transparency effect known as *ghosting*. It's important to note that this copy block is created in a single frame. A common mistake is to create the text portion in a separate frame and then position it on top of a transparent box. Remember…when building documents, you want to use the fewest frames as possible. Keep your documents "mean and clean."

VISUAL | 11–51 |

The opacity of the Paper fill has been reduced to 50%. This effect is called "ghosting."

1. Place *11 Bottom Copy.idms* on the lower half of the cover.

2. Select the frame, and use the keyboard shortcut to open the *Effects* panel. Select **Fill** in the *Effects* panel. Enter **50** in the *Opacity* field (Visual 11–52A)

3. Choose **Basic Feather** from the *FX* drop down menu. Select **Fill** in the *Settings For* field. Enter **0.25 in** in the *Feather Width* field to create a edge with a nice vignette (Visual 11–52B). Congratulations! The internship promotional brochure is finished!

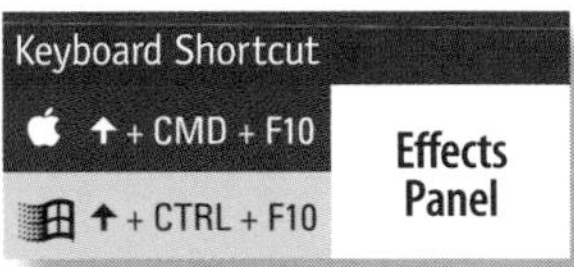

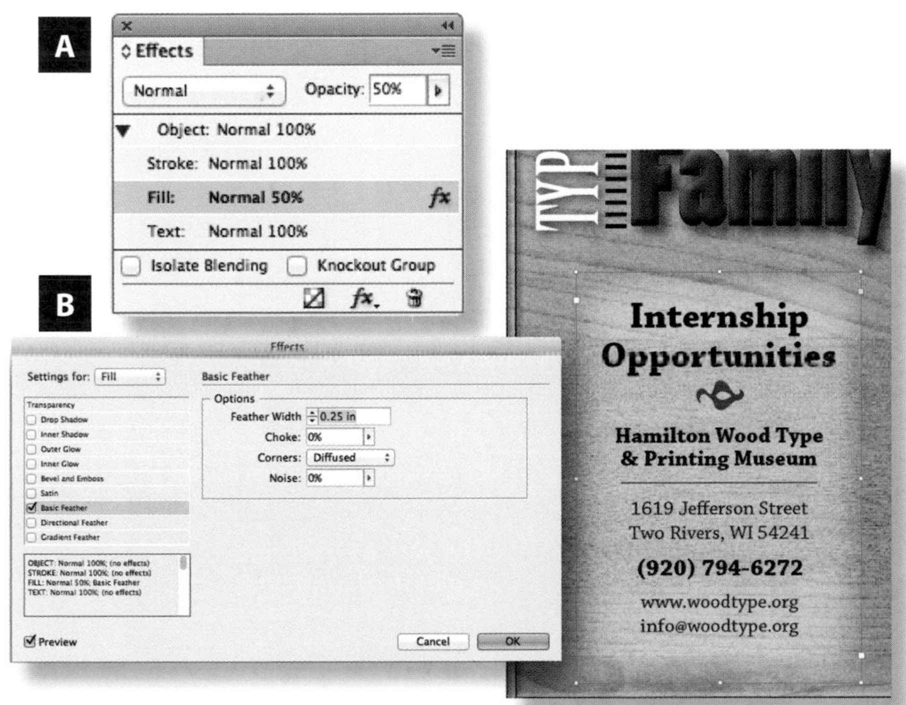

VISUAL | 11–52 |

The ghosted background is enhanced with a vignette.

You should be impressed with the brochure you've just made. It was complex, and if this is your first introduction to InDesign, you should really pat yourself on the back! We have one more little exercise and then we'll close this chapter. You're going to add one more page to the brochure document so that you can practice using the *Page* tool to change page sizes. This will be an easy one, so hang in there!

▸ *Use the Page tool for multi-page documents*

The *Page* tool, located beneath the *Direct Selection* tool on the *Toolbox*, is used to create multi-size master pages or document pages. We're going to add a business card to the end of our document.

1. Use the ***Pages*** panel to add master page ***B-3.625*** to the end of the document (Visual 11-53A).
2. Select the ***Page*** tool from the ***Toolbox*** and click on ***Page 7***. When the page is highlighted on the ***Control*** panel, select **US Business Card** from the pull down menu to change the page size (Visual 11–53B). Choose ***Portrait*** orientation.

VISUAL | 11–53 |

The Page tool changes page sizes on the document or master page level.

© Cengage Learning 2013

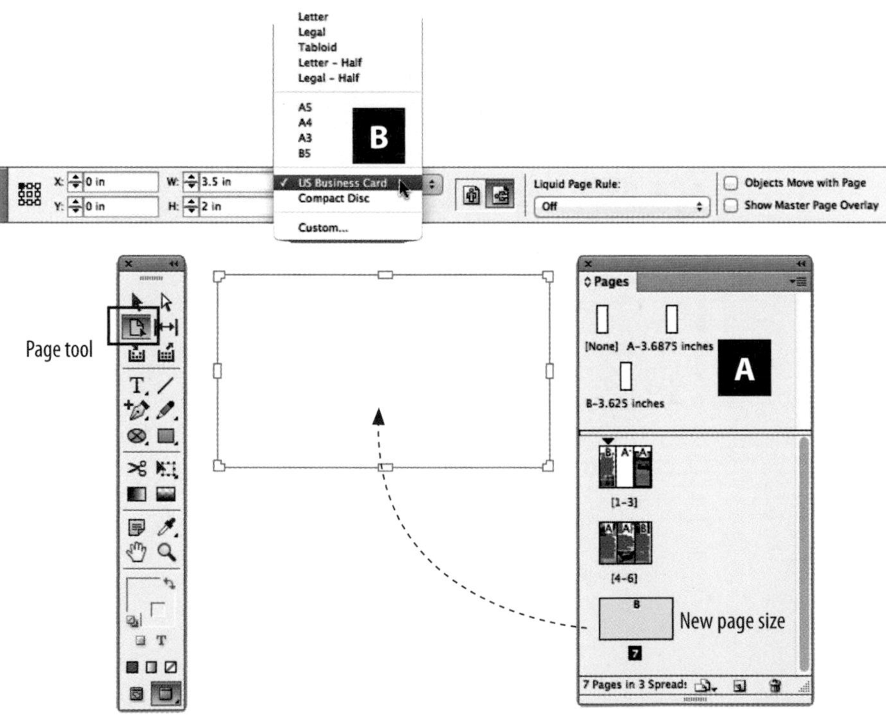

3. Go to *Preferences>File Handling>Snippet Import* and select *Cursor Location* in the *Position At* field. Place *11 Mailing Address.idms*, rotate it 90 degrees and then position it in the center of the business card. Your project is now complete (Visual 11–54).

VISUAL |11–54|

The completed business card.

© Cengage Learning 2013

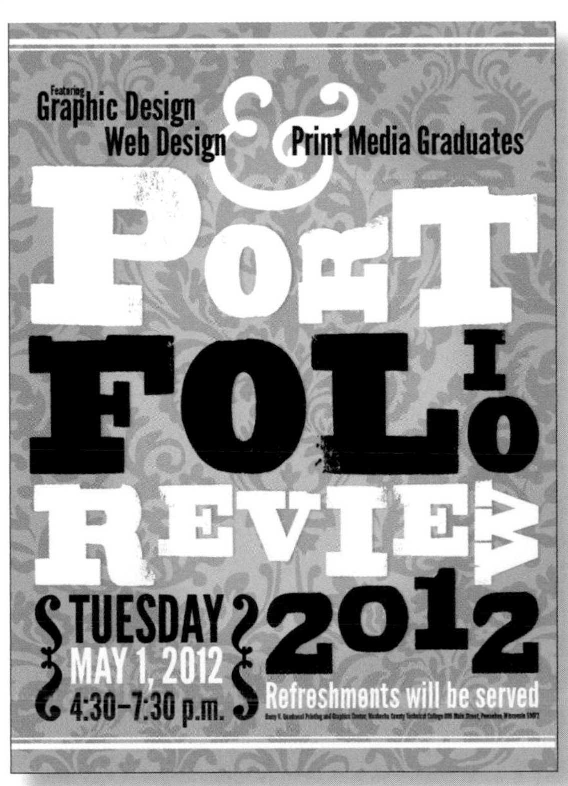

VISUAL |11–55|

A poster inspired by wood type printing, featuring excellent use of color, texture and type.

© Mélanie Lévesque 2012

Summary

This chapter introduced design techniques that can add interest to type. Just as using too many typefaces can overpower a document, so can using too many text effects. Knowing how to use these techniques is the first step. Knowing *when* to use them is the second. My thanks to designer Ian Brignell, and Jim Moran and Stephanie Carpenter from the Hamilton Wood Type & Printing Museum for sharing their inspiration and commitment to our craft in *Exploring InDesign CS6*.

1. How do you know when the Type on a Path tool is ready to place text on a path?
2. How does the center bracket work?
3. How does the Page tool work?
4. What does the Gradient tool do?
5. What is the keyboard shortcut for creating a true ellipsis?
6. How can you draw a shape from the center, outward?
7. What are five options found under the Pathfinder tool?
8. Your coworker is struggling with adding a drop shadow to a text frame. When the drop shadow option is selected, the shadow appears on the type, but not behind the text frame. What advice would you give her?
9. How does type handling change when the type has been converted to outlines?
10. What is the process for proportionately scaling elements that contain text?

Keyboard Shortcut
CMD + OPT + M
CTRL + ALT + M
Drop Shadow
Keyboard Shortcut
↑ + CMD + F10
↑ + CTRL + F10
Effects Panel
Keyboard Shortcut
CMD + E
CTRL + E
Export
Keyboard Shortcut
↑ + CMD + O
↑ + CTRL + O
Create Outlines

▸ CHAPTER 11 PROJECTS

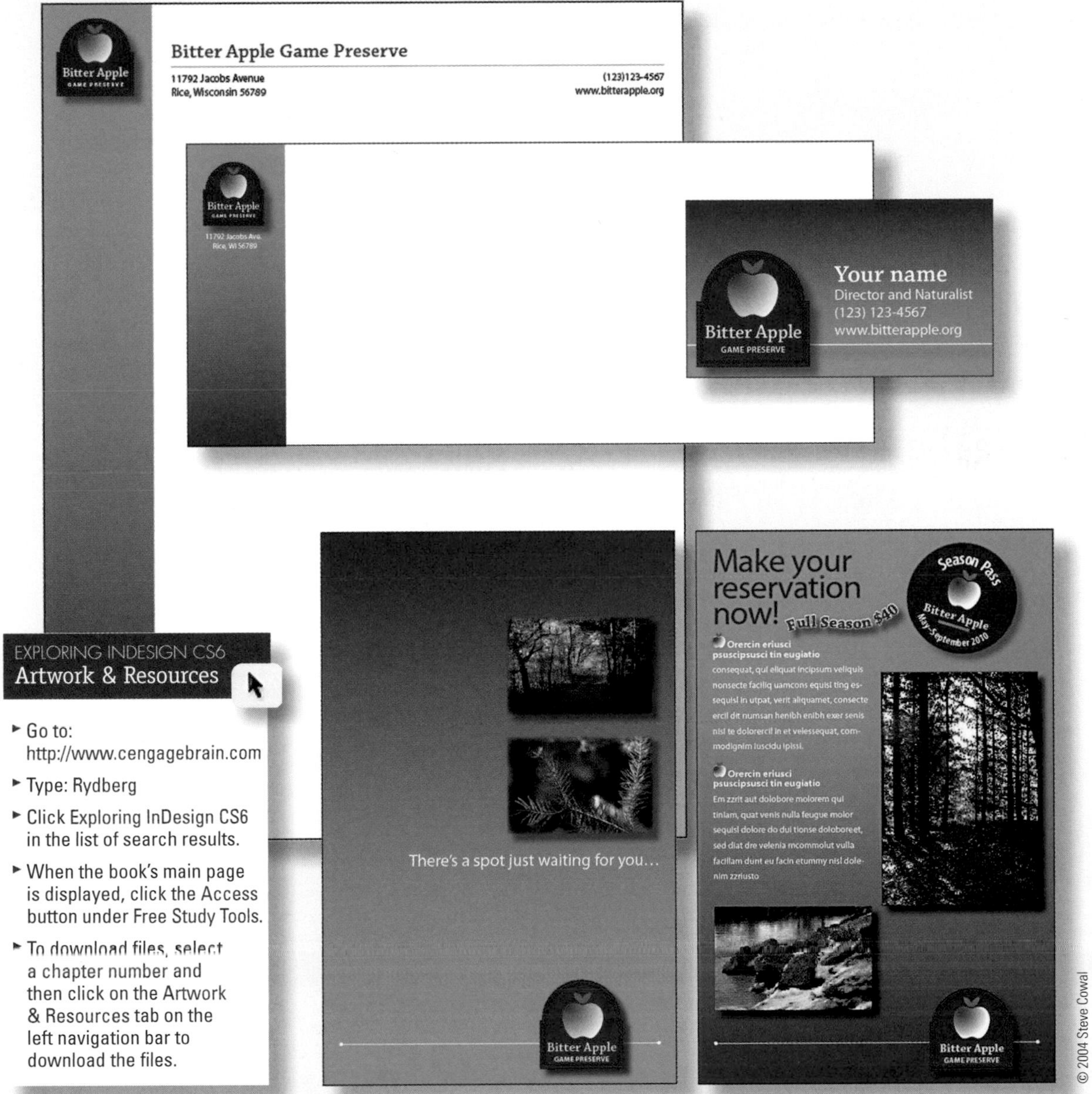

EXPLORING INDESIGN CS6
Artwork & Resources

- Go to: http://www.cengagebrain.com
- Type: Rydberg
- Click Exploring InDesign CS6 in the list of search results.
- When the book's main page is displayed, click the Access button under Free Study Tools.
- To download files, select a chapter number and then click on the Artwork & Resources tab on the left navigation bar to download the files.

Chapter 11 projects for the Bitter Apple Game Preserve are all created in a single InDesign document, using multiple page sizes. You'll use Pathfinder features, gradient fills, and effects. Inline graphics will be introduced and used in the flier. You'll find project assets in the ***11 Artwork and Resources*** folder on the student online companion.

| Color Essentials |

objectives

- *Understand the difference between spot and process colors*
- *Use the Swatches panel to define color, tint, gradient, and mixed ink swatches*
- *Choose document print specifications*

introduction

Henry Ford's legendary adage, "You can paint it any color, so long as it's black," could well have been the motto for many printers during the last century. Printers might advertise that they "print red on Wednesdays and blue on Thursdays," but black was the "bread and butter" color used everyday for almost all projects. There were some two- and three-color print jobs, but full-color printing, in catalogs for instance, was too expensive and out of reach for the average print consumer. How things have changed! Advances in printing have created a kaleidoscope of color options for jobs that in years past, would have been printed in basic black. Full-color printing is now affordable on the leanest budget.

With each technological change comes a new set of challenges. Today, designers need to understand the physical properties of color and production processes. They need to define and use color correctly in their documents, and focus on principles of design, while creating a layout alive with color. For those of us who began our careers using X-acto knives, rubylith, and acetate overlays to manually separate color on pasteup boards, any effort required to expand our knowledge base is a small price to pay for the ease of incorporating color in our layouts.

A great way to continue learning is to join an InDesign User Group. Membership is free, and you will learn something new at every meeting you attend (plus, you might win new software!) The map to the right shows the Milwaukee, Wisconsin chapter—and new chapters are continually forming all over the world. For more information, or to find your local chapter, go to www.indesignusergroup.com.

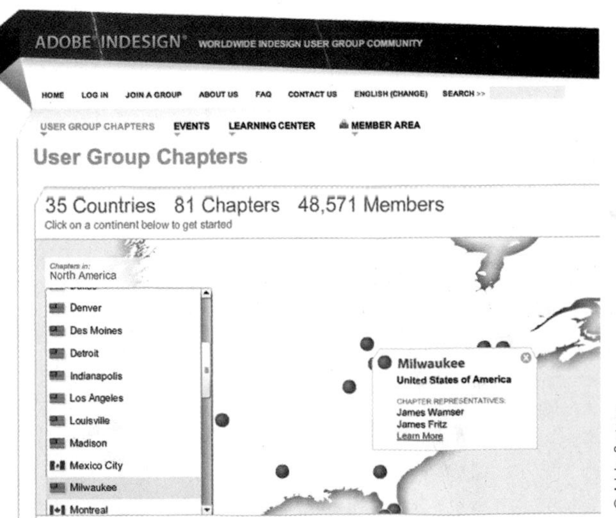

color essentials

One of the best decisions I made in my college career was to double major in graphic design, and printing and publishing. Understanding how document design and construction affects production, has been invaluable. The same project that is greeted with cheers when presented to a client, may elicit groans, after it is opened by the prepress technician. File construction tells a lot about the designer's training and skill. A poorly constructed file will do more damage to a designer's reputation than almost anything else. If that designer also misses production deadlines, vendors will shudder every time he walks through the door, because they know they will be working on a file that is not only late, but also technically incorrect! This chapter will focus on one file preparation area that can be challenging: specifying color. Then, Chapter 13 will discuss managing graphics files and images, and organizing fonts.

Color is an important component in any project. If you don't understand how color is created and how a piece will be printed, you will not be able to create a document that uses color correctly. Errors in using color are costly. Of course, color mistakes on garage sale posters, printed on your own color inkjet printer, aren't going to ruin your life. But making a mistake on a catalog project, where accurate color is critical, will negatively impact your career. We will begin with some basic theory about the physical characteristics of color. For more information on the complex world of color, I recommend *Graphic Communications Today, Fourth Edition*, by William Ryan and Theodore Conover, published by Thomson Delmar Learning.

COLOR: TRANSMITTED OR REFLECTED LIGHT WAVES

Color is created by light waves that are either *transmitted* or *reflected*. Your computer monitor transmits light waves to create color. Three primary colors of light—red, green, and blue (RGB)—are combined in different proportions to create the millions of colors on your screen. Colors displayed on a monitor are described by a formula that specifies the level of each component color. The range of levels goes from 0 to 255. For example, the formula R=255, G=55, B=45 would describe a bright red. RGB is *additive* color. This means that when the levels of RGB are at the maximum, 255, the color you see is white. When all RGB values are at 0, the color is black. When creating documents that will be viewed on a monitor, such as web pages, using colors defined by the RGB system are natural choices.

Ink and toner, on paper, work differently. They absorb some light waves and reflect the rest. The light waves that are reflected back to our eyes create the illusion of color. Color created by reflected light waves is called *subtractive*. That means that if all the light is absorbed (subtracted), we see black. The primary colors in subtractive color are cyan, magenta, and yellow (CMY). Formulas that specify the amounts of each component color are used to describe subtractive color. The bright red color described in the preceding paragraph would be expressed as C=0, M=91, Y=87. An important difference is that the range of levels is different, from 0 to 100. It's also appropriate to refer to the levels of component colors as percentages. In theory, when you combine pigments of pure cyan, magenta, and yellow, all the light waves will be absorbed and the color will look black. In reality, pure pigments are impossible to obtain, so 100% cyan, 100% magenta, and 100% yellow blend to create a washed-out black. That's why black ink (referred to as K) is added in the printing process, to compensate for the weak black, created by the CMY combination. Now we've arrived at what is known as the CMYK *color space.* RGB (additive color) images are perfect for monitor or web display, but must be redefined as CMYK (subtractive) colors, before being commercially printed.

SPOT AND PROCESS COLOR

Commercial printers always work with subtractive color. Defining colors to print correctly on a press is one of the challenges designers face on a daily basis. In commercial printing, color is created by reflected light waves. That's why it's not a good idea to put colors in your InDesign file that are defined as RGB (transmitted light waves).

Commercial printers use ink, and they talk in terms of *process color* or *spot color.* Spot color ink is like a can of premixed paint. There are about a dozen basic ink colors that can be combined, in different proportions, to make thousands of spot color inks. Each spot color is described by a standardized number and a mixing ratio (another formula!). This enables printers anywhere in the world to mix up and match a specific color, as long as they are using the same color/ink system. For instance, one popular color matching system is the Pantone Matching System®. When a printer in

▸ MOVING TOWARD MASTERY

When working with spot or process color, remember that what you see on your screen, is probably not what you will get from your commercial printer!

Unless a color calibration system is in place, every computer monitor will display color a little differently. Always use an ink swatch book to select colors for your printed document. Even if the colors don't look just right on the screen, they will print correctly on a printing press.

*A color at 100% is the actual hue. The hue can be tinted in increments, from very dark (90%) to very light (10%). The **C** at the end indicates that this is what the color will look like when printed on coated paper (as opposed to uncoated paper)*

PANTONE Colors displayed herein may not match PANTONE-identified standards. Consult current PANTONE Color Publications for accurate color. PANTONE® and other Pantone, Inc. trademarks are the property of Pantone, Inc. PANTONE Trademarks and Copyrights used with the written permission of Pantone, Inc.

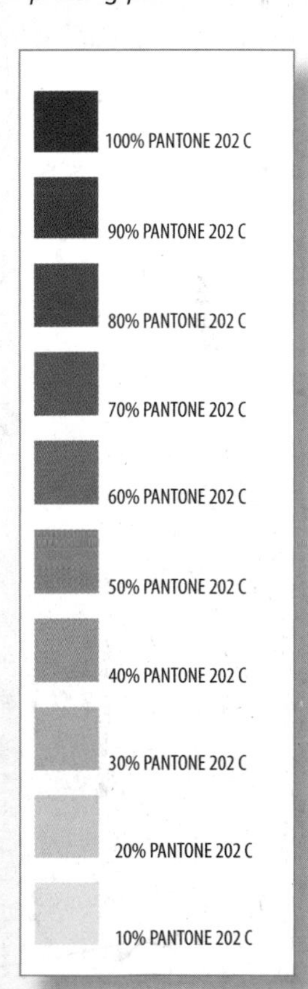

© Cengage Learning 2013

Philadelphia puts PANTONE® 541 on his press, it will be exactly the same color as the PANTONE 541, printed across the ocean in Calcutta. Tints of spot colors can also be used and are described in percentages: 0% to 100%. This allows you to use the full-strength spot color (100%) or lighter tints, to create a variety of color.

▸ *production tip*
Find out more about the Pantone® system at *http://www.pantone.com*

Many of your projects will be one-color documents—and yes, black counts as a color. Business forms, reports, books—many of the materials we read every day are single-color documents, usually black and white. However, don't underestimate the power of a well-designed single-color document! A blue, for example, can range from a pale 10% shade, to a strong 100% navy. And when it is printed on a sheet of cream paper, it can give the impression of a two-color job. For just slightly more than the cost of black ink, you can create an attractive document with just one spot color, incorporating tints and solids and good design skills. If your client wants a full-color brochure, but doesn't have a full-color budget, suggest going with a two-color brochure using spot colors. Two spot colors, combined with careful paper selection, can give a project an upscale look without the upscale cost.

Process color (also referred to as *full-color*) is much different from spot color. Full-color posters, magazines, catalogs, artist prints—anything that has the full range of the color spectrum—will be printed using process colors. In process color printing, four basic transparent inks, in different tints, are printed on top of each other to create the illusion of many colors. As discussed earlier, these transparent colors are cyan, magenta, yellow, and black (CMYK). Cyan is greenish-blue and magenta is a violet-red. When you look at a full-color job under a magnifying glass, you will see that the "color" is actually made from a series of tiny dots, printed close together. When each of the four inks is printed in the correct location, the dots merge together to give the impression of color. The color could be one hue (like a spot-color ink) or the millions of color variations that create a photograph. However, when one ink color is printed slightly off from the others, it makes the finished image look distorted. This is called *out of register*. We have all seen examples of this when Sunday comics aren't printed quite right and have a blurred image.

▸ *production tip*
Digital color printers (used for smaller full-color runs) often use cartridges of cyan, magenta, yellow, and black ink or toner.

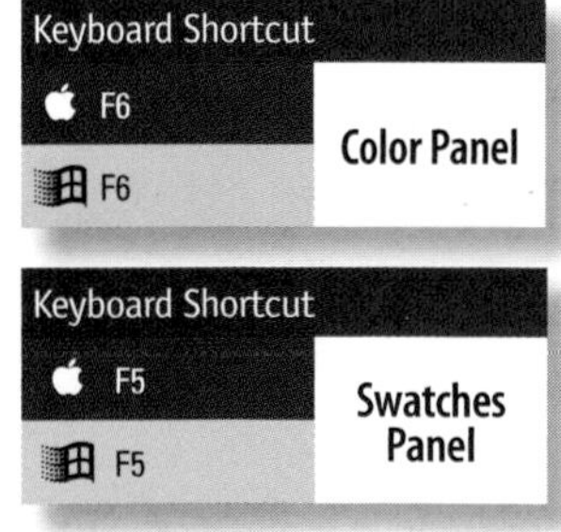

TOOLS FOR CREATING COLOR

InDesign has two panels for assigning color to objects: the *Color* panel and the *Swatches* panel. Although they have some overlapping features, each offers unique ways to create and apply color. The keyboard shortcuts are right next to each other on the keyboard—**F5** and **F6**. You can also open the panels from the dock. Let's start with the *Color* panel.

▸ *Use the Color panel*

1. Make a new document, **8.5" × 11"**. Press **F6** to open the *Color* panel. At the bottom of the panel you will see a bar called the *color spectrum*. It will contain either a gradient of one single color or a rainbow of colors. If the spectrum contains a single color, click on the *Color* panel menu and choose **CMYK** (Visual 12–1).

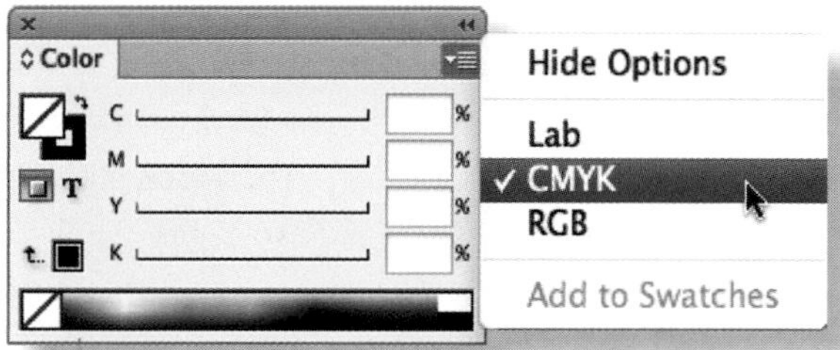

VISUAL | 12–1 |

If the color spectrum shows shades of one color only, choose CMYK from the panel menu.

© Cengage Learning 2013

2. Draw a rectangle and activate the *Fill* icon on the *Toolbox*. Move your mouse over the color spectrum on the *Color* panel and notice that your cursor turns into the *Eyedropper* tool. Click the *Eyedropper* tool on a color that looks good to to you. The rectangle instantly fills with the color you have selected. Notice that the *Fill* icon in the *Toolbox* has been updated with the same color. Click back and forth along the *CMYK spectrum* bar and fill your rectangle with different colors (Visual 12–2).

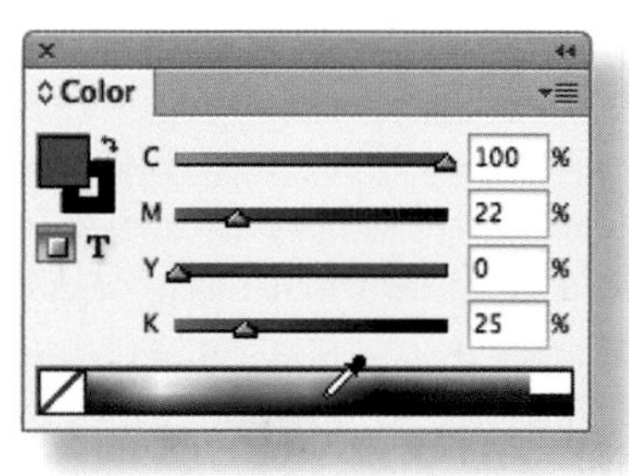

VISUAL | 12–2 |

Each time you select a new color from the CMYK spectrum bar, the Fill icon in the Toolbox displays the same color.

© Cengage Learning 2013

3. There are four sliders above the *CMYK spectrum*. These show the percentages of each of the four process colors. Slide the triangles along each of the individual color bars, noticing how the color changes and how the percentage values in the boxes to the right also change. Fine-tune your chosen color by making it a lighter shade.

4. Click on the **[None]** box (the square with the red diagonal line), at at the left of the *CMYK spectrum*. The rectangle now has no fill and the *Fill* icon on the *Toolbox* also indicates no fill. But you have not lost your color because a new box has appeared in the *Color* panel: *Last Color* (Visual 12–3). Click on it and your last color returns. The smaller boxes, at the right of the *CMYK spectrum*, are for white or black fills. Remember that assigning *White* (a color), to the fill or stroke of an object, is not the same as applying *[None]* (no color at all).

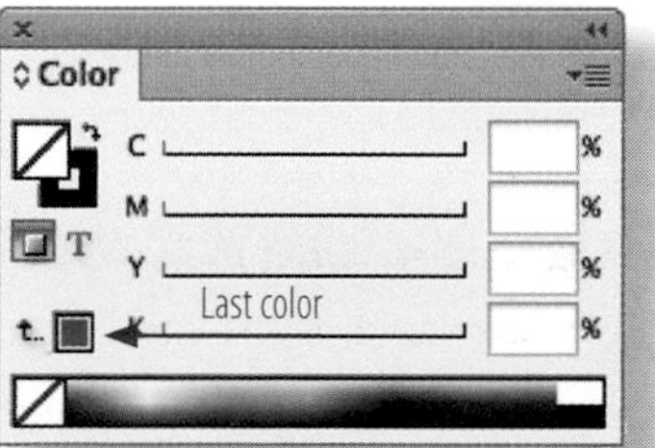

VISUAL | 12–3 |

The Color panel displays the last color used in a box above the color spectrum.

© Cengage Learning 2013

▸ *production tip*

Assigning White (a color) is not the same as applying None (no color at all).

5. Click on your rectangle with the ***Type*** tool and convert it to a text frame. The ***Color*** panel now indicates the color of the text. Type a short sentence and bump up the point size to fill the text frame. Select all the text and change the color of the text in the same way you changed the color of the rectangle. Remember to choose CMYK, if your color bar shows a spectrum of only one color.

6. Click on the text frame with one of the selection tools. The two small buttons below the ***Fill*** and ***Stroke*** icons in the ***Color*** panel (or the ***Toolbox***) will now allow you to choose which color you change, either the text or the frame (Visual 12–4).

VISUAL | 12–4 |

The arrows show the controls you use to toggle between applying color to the container or to the text.
© Cengage Learning 2013

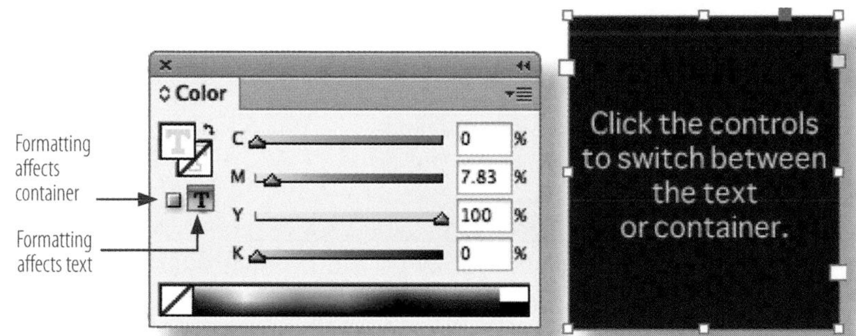

7. Open the ***Color*** panel options menu again and change the mode from ***CMYK*** to ***RGB*** (Visual 12–5). The shades of color do not change; but you are now working in additive color rather than subtractive color. The yellow triangle that sometimes appears above the color spectrum is the ***out of gamut*** warning. This is a warning that the RGB color you have selected will not reproduce satisfactorily in a CMYK printed document. If you click on the warning icon, the color will be modified to the closest CMYK equivalent.

VISUAL | 12–5 |

It is easy to change between single color, CMYK, and RGB color models. Always be aware of what color mode you are working in. CMYK is for commercial printing. RGB is basically for documents that will be viewed on a computer monitor, like web pages.
© Cengage Learning 2013

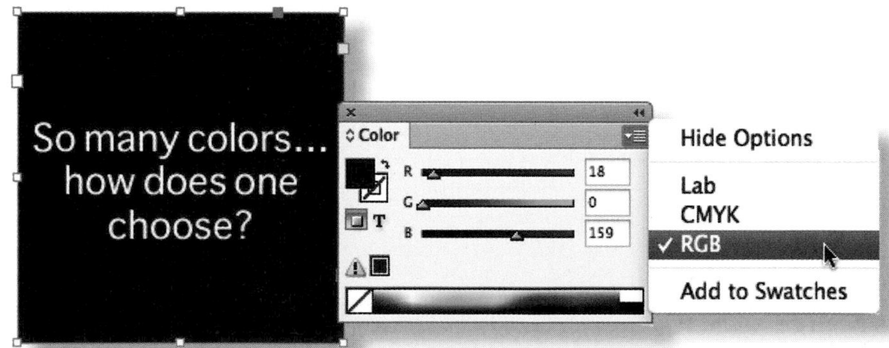

Now that you have been introduced to the *Color* panel, a word of caution: The *Color* panel is handy for applying color in "quick and dirty" documents that you will output yourself, on your home color printer. But if you're working in a production setting—and especially if your file is going out to a service bureau or a commercial printer—be sure to select *Add to Swatches* from the *Color* panel menu, or just use the *Swatches* panel when adding colors to your document.

THE SWATCHES PANEL

The *Swatches* panel can do everything the *Color* panel does, but with one important difference: You can *define* each color in your document and assign it a meaningful name. Colors from the *Color* panel, like the ones you had so much fun clicking on in the preceding pages, are unnamed, and *undefined,* unless you add them to the *Swatches* panel. It's difficult to track and manage undefined colors throughout your document. Colors created and stored in the *Swatches* panel are much easier to manage.

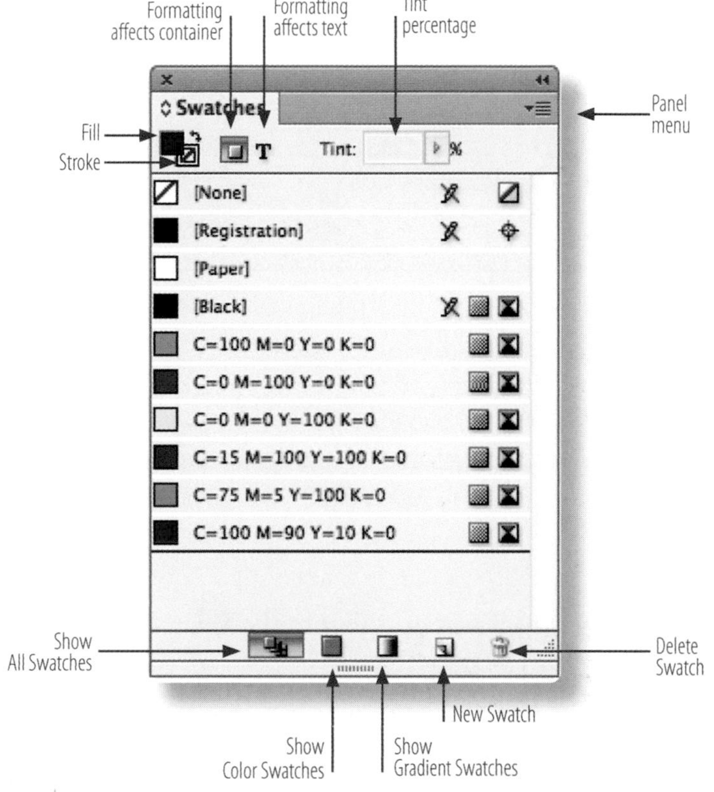

VISUAL | 12–6 |

Press F5 to open the Swatches panel. The panel is set up like many other InDesign panels.

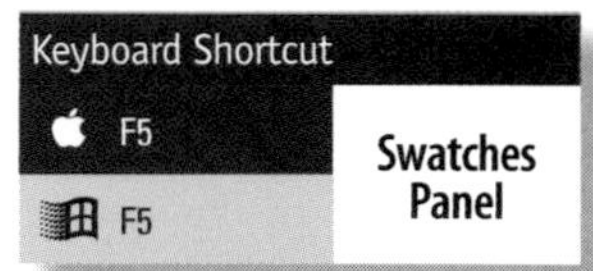

▸ *Transfer an undefined color to the Swatches panel*

In the following exercise, you will learn how to convert an undefined color, created in the *Color* panel, into a color swatch.

1. Make sure the *Color* panel is open and the rectangle is active.
2. Press **F5** to open the *Swatches* panel (Visual 12–6). To make room for additional swatches, lengthen the panel by dragging the lower right corner until the scroll bar disappears. Go back to the *Color* panel and make sure the *Fill* color icon for your active rectangle is active.

3. Open the ***Color*** panel options menu and choose ***Add to Swatches*** (Visual 12–7). The color of your frame is now a swatch in the ***Swatches*** panel and has changed from an undefined color, to a defined color. Do the same for the color you chose for your text.

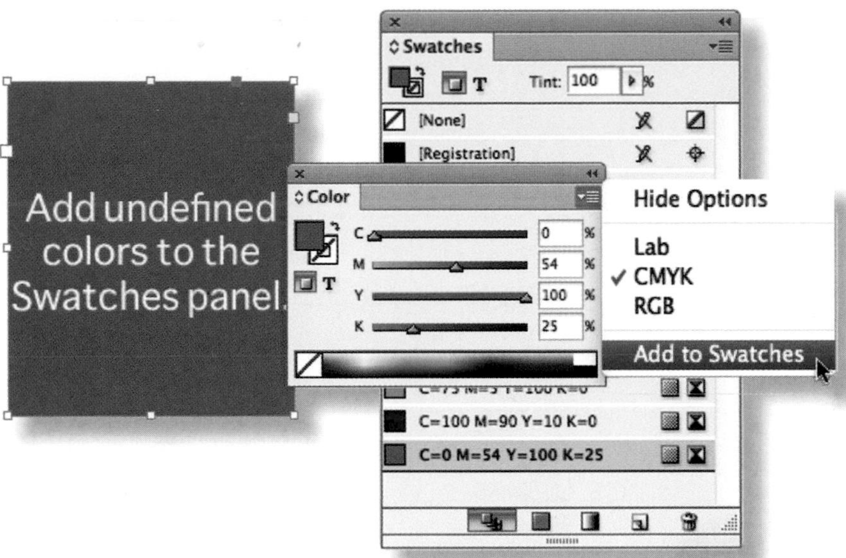

VISUAL | 12–7 |

An undefined color can easily be added to the Swatches panel by selecting Add to Swatches in the Color panel menu. The new swatch is now defined and is at the bottom of the Swatches panel list.

4. There are other methods of transferring an undefined color to the ***Swatches*** panel. You can select your rectangle and click the ***New Swatch*** button at the bottom of the ***Swatches*** panel (shown in Visual 12–6). Or you can drag the ***Fill*** or ***Stroke*** color icon right from the ***Color*** panel and drop it into the ***Swatches*** panel.

▸ *Transfer an undefined gradient to the Swatches panel*

Generally, it is best to convert undefined colors to defined swatches. The same holds true for undefined gradients. Converting an undefined gradient to a gradient swatch is a process similar to the one you just completed for undefined color.

1. Open the ***Gradient*** panel (***Window>Color>Gradient***) and choose ***Show Options*** under the ***Swatches*** panel menu. In the ***Type*** field, choose ***Linear*** or ***Radial.*** A ***linear gradient*** changes color along a line, a ***radial gradient*** radiates from one color to the next in a circular pattern. You should see a horizontal bar called a ***ramp***, extending across the bottom of the ***Gradient*** panel. At the top and center of the ramp is a diamond. This diamond is a stop that defines the midpoint of the gradient. As you slide the stop toward either end of the ramp, you will see the gradient swatch in the upper left corner change.

2. Open the ***Color*** panel and arrange it so that it's next to the ***Gradient*** panel. You're going to apply some colors to the gradient.

3. In the ***Gradient*** panel you should see two house-shaped icons below the ramp. If you don't see them, click on the ramp and they will appear. These are the ***color stops***. Click on the left color stop and then adjust the color sliders in the ***Color*** panel. Notice that the color stop in the ***Gradient*** panel changes accordingly (Visual 12–8).

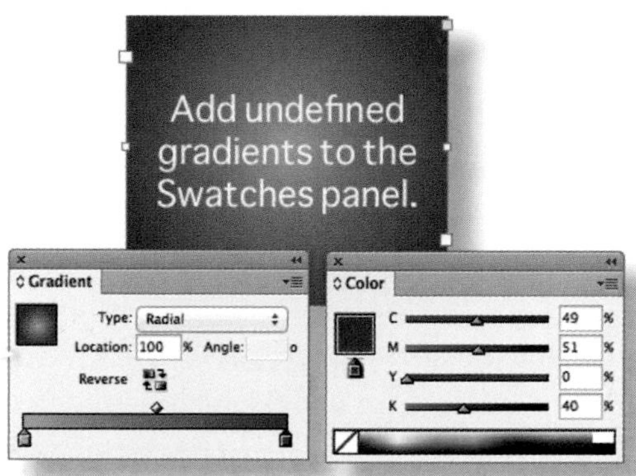

VISUAL | 12–8 |

Color stops define the beginning and ending colors in the gradient.

4. Now, click on the ***right*** color stop. Apply a color using the ***Color*** panel. Experiment with adjusting the look of your gradient by sliding the midpoint and color stops to the left or the right. Watch as the gradient swatch in the upper left corner changes to reflect your color adjustments.

5. You can also apply color to a gradient from the ***Swatches*** panel. The process is similar to the one described above, but instead of choosing a color from the ***Color*** panel, you press **Option** (Mac) or **Alt** (Windows) as you click on a color swatch from the ***Swatches*** panel.

6. Now we will define the gradient you have just created. Open the ***Swatches*** panel menu and choose ***New Gradient Swatch***. When the ***New Gradient Swatch*** dialog box appears, you can name your new gradient swatch in the ***Swatch Name*** field.

7. An alternate method is to drag the color preview from the ***Gradient*** panel into the ***Swatches*** panel. Double-click the new swatch to open the ***Gradient Options*** dialog box and rename it (Visual 12–9). If you don't see your gradient, select either the ***Show Gradient Swatches*** or ***Show All Swatches*** button at the bottom of the ***Swatches*** panel (shown in Visual 12–6).

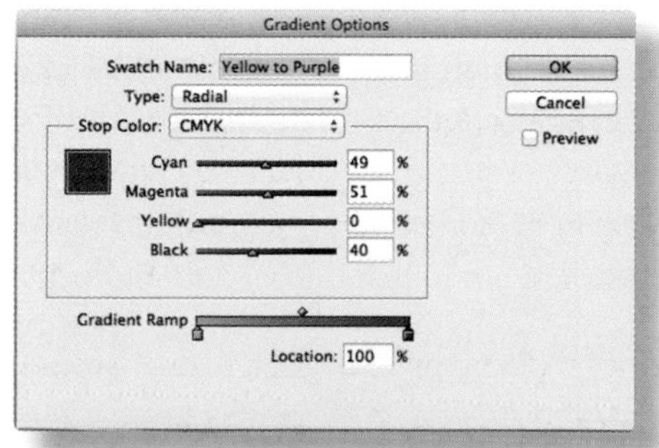

VISUAL | 12–9 |

Gradient swatches are defined in the Swatches panel menu.

The icons at the top of the *Swatches* panel should be familiar to you by now—*Fill, Stroke, Formatting affects container,* and *Formatting affects text.* There is also a field where you can set the tint of a selected color. The various colors in the list are those available to your document and are labeled with their CMYK values (Visual 12–7).

USE A SWATCH BOOK TO SELECT COLORS

You can define colors directly from the *Swatches* panel. But before you can define a color for your document, you must know whether you need to create spot or process colors. When you define a color in your document as spot, it means that the printer will premix the color according to the formula specified by the ink manufacturer's swatch book and use that colored ink on the press. A plate on the press picks up the ink and transfers it to the paper. After the color is printed, the press is cleaned, a new plate is put on, and the ink is replaced with the next color needed. A job that uses yellow, blue, green, orange, red, and black will require six premixed colors and six plates—and a significant amount of time for mixing ink and cleaning the press.

Process color works differently. Instead of premixing each individual ink color, only four inks—cyan, magenta, yellow, and black—and four plates are used to create all the other colors that will be printed. The four colors are overlaid in various tints, to create the illusion of many colors. The six-color job we just discussed, could be printed by using only four inks and plates, and would require much less production time. Orange would be created by percentages of yellow and magenta. Green would be created by percentages of cyan and yellow, and so on. Of course, if your job only has two colors—two inks and two plates—then using spot colors would be the way to go.

A swatch book should be used at the design stage for selecting and defining either spot or process colors. The swatch book provides the exact color formula needed and shows an accurate sample of how the printed color will look. Basing a color selection on what you see on your computer screen is risky, because most monitors do not display color accurately. There are many variables that go into choosing color. Until you have a clear understanding of the printing process, it is a good idea to have an experienced designer check your document files, before you send them to the printer. We will now create a new process color swatch.

VISUAL | 12–10 |
The Swatches panel has many options for displaying swatches. When Name is selected (the default), the colors in the list are displayed with their names next to them. If you select Small Swatch, the colors will be displayed as tiny swatches and no names. In this example, Large Swatch has been selected.

▸ *Make a new color swatch*

1. Choose *New Color Swatch* from the ***Swatches*** panel menu (Visual 12–10). A dialog box displaying the four CMYK sliders will open. The color settings in the dialog box will be for the last color selected in the ***Swatches*** panel.

2. If you know them, type in the percentages of cyan, magenta, yellow, and black that define your color. Or, slide the color bars until you get the color you want. InDesign will define and name the color for you, using the CMYK values. Or, you can deselect the ***Name with Color Value*** option box and assign it a name of your own choosing. It's better to name a color by its CMYK values because that's a language everyone understands. Even though a color may look exactly like what you saw when your cat was car sick, naming a color: *Sick Kitty,* conjures up a very different color in each person's mind.

▸ *Make a new gradient swatch from "scratch"*

When you select **New Gradient Swatch** from the *Swatches* panel menu, you are making a defined gradient.

1. Choose *New Gradient Swatch* from the panel menu. Click on the ***starting color*** stop icon, at the left end of the gradient ramp. The ***Stop Color*** field becomes active, allowing you to select **CMYK** from the list and then adjust the sliders in the CMYK mode. You can also select ***Swatches*** from the ***Stop Color*** field list and then choose a color from your already defined swatches.

2. Click the ***ending color*** stop icon, at the right side of the gradient ramp and assign it a different color (Visual 12–11).

3. Drag one of the stop icons to the middle of the gradient ramp. Click below the ramp where the original color stop was, and a new stop will appear. Give this new stop a third color.

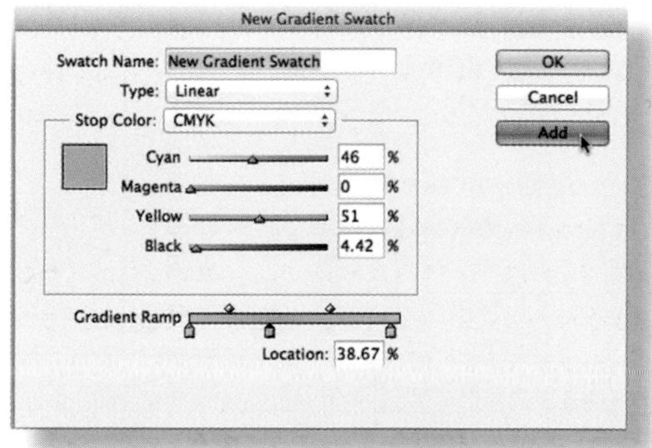

VISUAL | 12–11 |

Use the Gradient Ramp to add color stops and to control the span of each color.

4. Slide the diamond-shaped midpoint stops at the top of the gradient ramp to adjust the span of each color between color stops. Press **Return** to add this swatch to the *Swatches* panel.

The *Show Gradient Swatches* button at the bottom of the panel, limits the display to only the defined gradients in the document. If you have a gradient swatch selected and click the *New Swatch* button, the gradient swatch will be duplicated. If you select the *Trashcan* icon, the gradient swatch will be deleted.

▸ Make a color tint swatch

If you were designing a single-color document using many shades of the same blue, first you would want to create the solid blue swatch and then make tint variations from it.

▸ *production tip*

When making tint swatches. you have to press the Tab key before the Add button becomes active again.

1. Create a new swatch—*Color Type*: *Spot*, *Color Mode: Pantone + Solid Coated.* Scroll down the list and select a Pantone blue that you like. Press **Return**.
2. With the new blue swatch selected, open the *Swatches* panel menu and choose *New Tint Swatch.* In the *New Tint Swatch* dialog box, drag the tint slider to **10%** and click **Add.** You can type numerical values into the *Tint* field, but you have to press the *Tab* key before the *Add* button becomes active again.

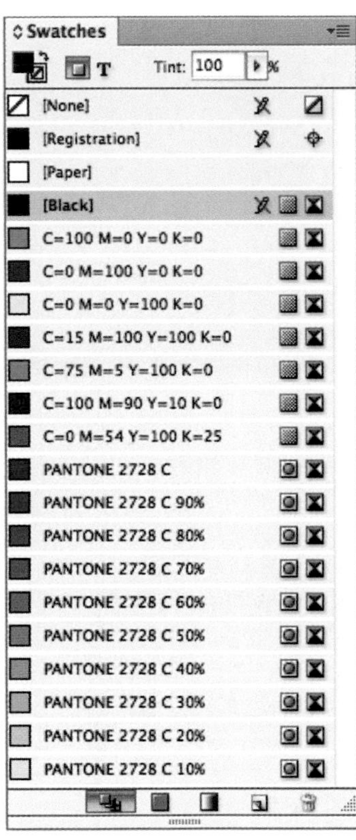

VISUAL |12–12|

Tint swatches display the percentage to the right of the color name.
© Cengage Learning 2013

3. Repeat this process, creating tint swatches from **10%** to **90%**, in 10% increments, using a green color. Click **Done.** Your *Swatches* panel should look like Visual 12–12. Notice that the percentage of each tint is displayed at the end of the name.
4. If the tint isn't exactly what you want, you can double-click on the tint swatch in the panel list, and when the *Swatch Options* dialog box opens, adjust the sliders.

Changing the color values of a tint swatch also changes the values of the original color the swatch is based on. Be sure that when you are in the *Swatch Options* dialog box, you don't change color values—unless you want the original color swatch to change, too.

▸ Add swatches from other documents

You can pull color swatches from other InDesign documents into a document you are working on. The following method allows you to choose which colors you bring into your document.

1. Open the *Swatches* panel menu and choose *New Color Swatch.* In the *New Color Swatch* dialog box, pick *Other Library* at the bottom of the *Color Mode* list (Visual 12–14).

2. Navigate to the document you want to import color from, and click *Open*. Select a color you want, from the list of available colors in the document, and click *Add* to transfer them to your *Swatches* panel. When you are done adding colors, press **Return**.

▸ *Load swatches*

You can also add swatches from another document by using the *Load Swatches* option and then selecting the file. This method will load all the colors from the second document rather than letting you choose the ones you want (Visual 12–13).

VISUAL | 12–13 |

You will want to use the Load Swatches command when you want all the colors from an existing document to come into the document you are working on.

▸ *Standard swatch libraries*

Although it stimulates your creative juices to create your own colors from the color spectrum bar and those cool little CMYK sliders, the safest thing to do is choose colors from standard swatch libraries—like Pantone or Trumatch. You find the standard swatch libraries in the *Swatch Options* dialog box. First, open the *Swatches* panel menu and choose **New Color Swatch** (or **Swatch Options** if you have a swatch selected). When the dialog box opens, choose **Color Mode.** Each of the names in the center section of the list corresponds to a specific color swatch system (Visual 12–14).

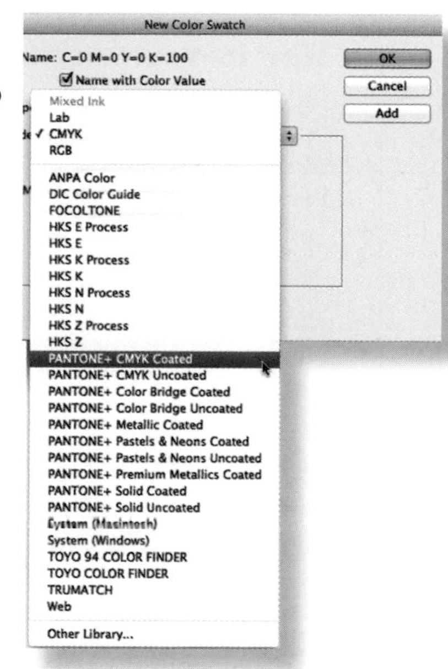

VISUAL | 12–14 |

Each of the names in the center section (DIC Color, PANTONE, TRUMATCH, and so on) corresponds to a specific manufacturer's color swatch system. Be sure to choose a system your printer uses.

Using a swatch book to choose colors assures that you are speaking the same language as your printer—as long as you're both using the same swatch book.

A TWO-COLOR BILL STUFFER

Let's say you're designing a small flyer for a large bank. The bank wants the piece to look good, but doesn't want to spend the money on four colors. You suggest going with two colors on coated ivory paper. The finished product will look like Visual 12–15.

VISUAL |12–15|

This is a two-color project called a "bill stuffer," similar to the ones that come in your credit card statements.

Gibraltar Metropolitan Bank

How We Protect Your Information

psuscipit ex er iustrud magnis elis aliquisit vendrem augueřci blam dolore dolum dunt il erostissed min eui eum auguer sum nos nis eugait vullaore consent ipsum nostio do dunt nim iriustrud dui exer sequisi bla feugue minciliquat nullam veriure min ulla faci et am zzrit prat, veraesto ercipis ea feum do odiamconsed eum ipsustrud tat. Ut lutpat.

Our Security Procedures

Bore molor sim ipis dolent wisit accumsan ut veril et dolor ad modo diatuer susto diamcon sequat ullut am eugiametue ting etum del dionsecte duipis nostrud eros ex estio consequamet in velessendre facipis adit iriusto dipsum ing exerit eummy nulla feu feuisci tie magnibh eu facillaore dolorem del exerci eu facing ea aliquat dio ex eugiam nim acidui tinim ing ent acidunt lore dolore vel eu facing euisi.

What Information We Disclose

tet ea commodolore feuismolore commodiat ad eugait velit lamet, quisit adipit iuscil ero od dolortincin henibh et praesse quipsumsan hent dui blaore feum ilis nulla ad tionsed exero consequisi.

- Re tionsed dolorperos am inibh eugiam nos at, quis euguerit nummy nos ex estin hendipis acidunt am
- Volorero od et, quis amet la feugiate magnibh enisse consequat.
- Duisl irit at aute diamconse venisi tionullam erillan hent wis amet nulla acidunt adionsequam, voluptat utatums andreet nos nonsequis augueroštrud

endiam zzriustin velesequisl irilisim ex elisLiquis autet prat. Velit esed mincidunt laore venibh eratet quisisisis autate mod eu facillaor ad eugueros et prate vullaor sit quisl il dolortion el eugiat, volenim vel ute tinibh eugait velendrer sit vero consequat lorper sed tie con ulputet velis eugait ipit ipit vulpute diate tatum dolore con ullut

Gibraltar Metropolitan Bank
123 Center City Suites
Yorkton, Virginia 09876
121-233-4567 www.gibraltarmetro.com

▸ *Create a solid and a metallic color*

1. Make a new document **22p × 8.5"**, **0.25"** margins, and **0.125"** full bleed. Delete all swatches that may be in the *Swatches* panel. You will not be able to delete *[None], [Paper], [Black]*, or *[Registration]*.

2. Choose *New Color Swatch* in the panel menu. In the *New Color Swatch* dialog box, choose **PANTONE + Solid Coated** in the *Color Mode* list. Scroll down the list of available colors, select **202 C,** and click *Add*. Now, choose **Pantone + Metallic Coated** from the *Color Mode* list. Scroll down to **876 C** (or type **876** in the PANTONE field), select this color, click *Add*, and then click *Done* (Visual 12–16). You have selected two standard Pantone colors to use in your document (if you had a Pantone Color Swatch book, you'd see that 876 C is an eye-catching metallic gold).

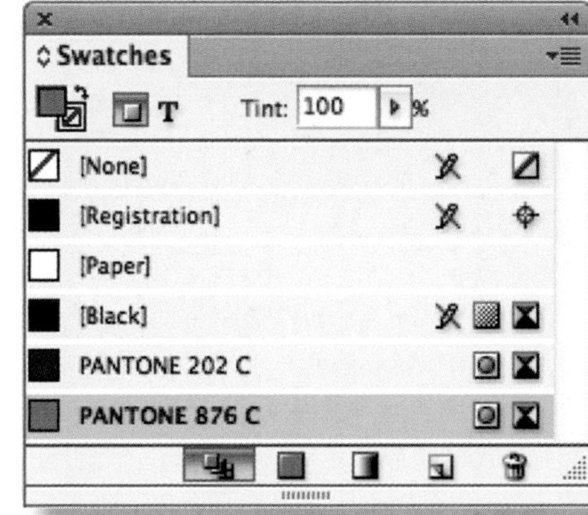

VISUAL | 12–16 |

The new swatches have been added.

EXPLORING INDESIGN CS6
Artwork & Resources

- Go to: http://www.cengagebrain.com
- Type: Rydberg
- Click Exploring InDesign CS6 in the list of search results.
- When the book's main page is displayed, click the Access button under Free Study Tools.
- To download files, select a chapter number and then click on the Artwork & Resources tab on the left navigation bar to download the files.

3. Draw a text frame from margin to margin and place the *12 Gibraltar Bank. docx* text file. You will find the file in the *12 Artwork and Resources* folder, on the online companion resources.

4. Open the *Paragraph Styles* panel and choose *Load All Text Styles.* Find the *12 Gibraltar Style Sheets.indd* file, in the same folder as the text file. Click *OK* in the **Load Style** dialog box. Select all the text and assign the *Body Copy* paragraph style. Apply the *Headline* style to the first line of type. Apply the *Sub Head* style to the lines *"How We Protect…," "Our Security…,"* and *"What Information…."*

5. Apply the *Body Copy-Bulleted* style to the three bulleted paragraphs. If the bullets don't display correctly, replace them, using **Option+8** (Mac) or **Alt+8** (Windows). Remember to use the *Indent to Here* character to hang the bullet.

6. Apply the *Footer* style to the bottom four lines, making sure there is a soft return at the end of each line. Place a flush right tab (**Shift+Tab**) between the phone number and website. The text in your document should look like Visual 12–17.

Gibraltar Metropolitan Bank

How We Protect Your Information

Our Security Procedures

What Information We Disclose

Gibraltar Metropolitan Bank
123 Center City Suites
Yorkton, Virginia 09876
121-233-4567 www.gibraltarmetro.com

VISUAL | 12–17 |

The paragraph styles have been applied.

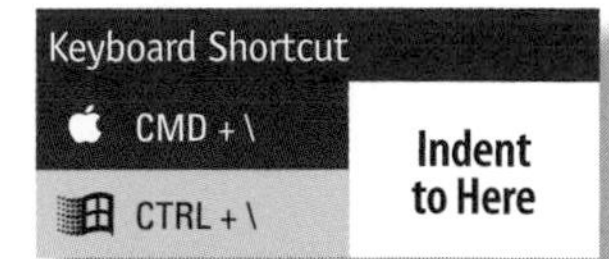

7. Draw a rectangle that bleeds from the top, left, and right sides. Include just the first section of placeholder text in the rectangle (refer to Visual 12–15). Fill the rectangle with **876 C** and send it to the back.

8. Make a similar rectangle at the bottom of the document, bleeding it off the right, left, and bottom edges. The rectangular shape should enclose the name, address, and web information. Fill it with **876 C** and send it to the back. Deselect everything. We've now used our two colors: 876 C for the background rectangles and 202 C for the type.

9. Since the document will be printed on ivory paper, let's add a color to our paper and see what it will look like when it is printed. Double-click the *[Paper]* color in the *Swatches* panel. In the *Swatch Options* dialog box, give the paper a light ivory color: **5% Cyan**, **10% Magenta**, **36% Yellow**, **0.39% Black**. Press **Return**. Save your document, and let's try printing color separations.

COLOR SEPARATIONS

One of the most common problems printers have, when designers bring in "finished" documents, is in creating color separations. Every color in your document needs its own plate and printing unit on the press. A two-color document will need two plates and two printing units; a four-color document will need four plates and four printing units, and so on. (Tints based on an original spot color do not require an additional plate.)

You may think you are bringing a two-color document to your printer, but when he goes to create separations, he finds four, five, six, or more colors. Why? It could be that what looks like a single color on your monitor is actually a blend of CMYK or RGB values. It could be that you didn't notice a hairline stroke on a text frame. It could be that a hidden character is assigned a color you can't even see on your monitor. There can be any number of reasons why there are more colors in your document than it appears. The following exercise uses features in the *Print* dialog box to identify how many colors are really in your document.

▸ *Print color separations*

1. Before you print separations, change the *[Paper]* color in the *Swatches* panel back to **0%** of **CMYK.** Now, go to the *Print* dialog box. On the *Setup* page, in the *Page Position* field, choose *Centered*.

2. On the *Marks and Bleed* page, select *All Printer's Marks.* Be sure that *Use Document Bleed Settings* is selected. On the *Output* page, select *Separations* in the *Color* field (Visual 12–18).

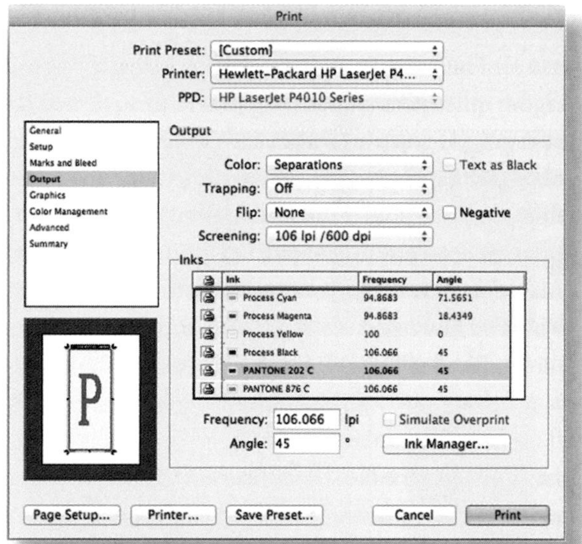

VISUAL | 12–18 |

The Output page offers choices for color separations.

▸ *production tip*

You must have a postscript printer in order to print separations. Color separations always print out black—even if you're using a postscript color printer.

3. Click **Print.** You should get two sheets from the printer, one labeled PANTONE 202 C and the other labeled 876 C. Each color is "separated" onto an individual page, and the black areas show where the color will be printed. A color identification label appears outside the image area near the crop marks.

4. Go back to your document and deliberately confuse things. Make hidden characters visible and select a single hard return character. Color it ***black*** and run separations again. You will get a third sheet labeled Process Black, although you won't see any text or element. InDesign "saw" a hidden character with a third color (black), that nobody else saw. Since we're printing separations, it printed a black plate—just for that one invisible character!

5. Make a new process swatch: **C=0, M=100, Y=61, K=43** (the equivalent values of PANTONE 202 C). Name it **Process Red.** Select all your text and change it to *Process Red*. The color of your text looks exactly the same, but now when you print, you get four separations: Magenta, Yellow, Black, and 876C. (Cyan didn't print because its value was 0. Also notice how the Black plate is screened back to 43%.)

▸ *production tip*

A color assigned to [Paper] is for your eyes only, to give you an approximate feel for how your final document will look.The color will not print with your color separations

Modify the paper color in your Swatches panel as close as possible to the actual paper color, but remember that your monitor will not give you a 100% match. Also keep in mind that a single PANTONE color may look different when printed on different color papers.

If you have a postscript printer, it's a good idea to print out a sample set of separations, before sending the project to the commercial printer. Printing sample separations is an effective way of catching color mistakes before they end up costing you money. If you can't print separations, you can still check colors using the *Separations Preview* panel. Go to *Window>Output>Separations Preview*. Select **Separations** in the *View* menu, and turn on the visibility of each color to see how it is used. Knowing a few color basics and always paying attention to how color is defined and used in your document will help avoid production pitfalls and increase your chances of being the next one in line for that promotion. Your documents need to be aesthetically pleasing, *and* technically correct.

PRINTER'S MARKS AND PRINTING OPTIONS

You will want to be familiar with the marks your printer uses for printing and finishing your document. Since all printer's marks are outside the copy area of the document, the paper size will always have to be larger than your finished document size, in order to use them.

Color Bar
Registration mark
Trim size
Bleed size
Page information
Plate information
Gibraltar Metropolitan Bank
How We Protect Your Information
psuscipit ex er iustrud magnis elis aliquisit vendrem auguerci blam dolore dolum dunt il erostissed min eui eum auguer sum nos nis eugait vullaore consent ipsum nostio do dunt nim iriustrud dui exer sequisi bla feugue minciliquat nullam veriure min ulla faci et am zzrit prat, veraesto ercipis ea feum do odiamconsed eum ipsustrud tat. Ut lutpat.
Our Security Procedures
Bore molor sim ipis dolent wisit accumsan ut veril et dolor ad modo diatuer susto diamcon sequat ullut am eugiametue ting etum del dionsecte duipis nostrud eros ex estio consequamet in velessendre facipis adit iriusto dipsum ing exerit eummy nulla feu feuisci tie magnibh eu facillaore dolorem del exerci eu facing ea aliquat dio ex eugiam nim acidui tinim ing ent acidunt lore dolore vel eu facing euisi.
What Information We Disclose
tet ea commodolore feuismolore commodiat ad eugait velit lamet, quisit adipit iuscil ero od dolortincin henibh et praesse quipsumsan hent dui blaore feum ilis nulla ad tionsed exero consequisi.
• Re tionsed dolorperos am inibh eugiam nos at, quis euguerit nummy nos ex estin hendipis acidunt am
• volorero od et, quis amet la feugiate magnibh enisse consequat.
• Duisl irit at aute diamconse venisi tionullam erillan hent wis amet nulla acidunt adionsequam, voluptat utatums andreet nos nonsequis auguerostrud
endiam zzriustin velesequisl irilisim ex elisLiquis autet prat. Velit esed mincidunt laore venibh eratet quisisisis autate mod eu facillaor ad eugueros et prate vullaor sit quisl il dolortion el eugiat, volenim vel ute tinibh eugait velendrer sit vero consequat lorper sed tie con ulputet velis eugait ipit ipit vulpute diate tatum dolore con ullut
Gibraltar Metropolitan Bank
123 Center City Suites
Yorkton, Virginia 09876
121-233-4567 www.gibraltarmetro.com
Bank flyer.indd 1
4/15/12 9:26:30 AM
PANTONE 202 C

VISUAL | 12–19 |

Each of these printer's marks means something different. The Page Information gives the file name on the lower left side, with the plate color and day and time the file was printed, on the right. Color Bars are located at the top of the page. The trim size is always smaller than the bleed size.

- ***Crop Marks*** (sometimes called *trim marks*) are placed just outside the four corners of your document and indicate where to cut the paper to its finished size. If a document is printed on oversized paper, the cutter will trim away the excess according to the crop marks. You can adjust the weight and placement of crop marks using the *Weight* and *Offset* fields on the right side of the *Marks* area, on the *Marks and Bleed* page of the *Print* dialog box.

- ***Manual Crop Marks*** are created when more than one copy of your document will be printed on a single sheet (two up, three up, and so on), or if the front and back of your document will be printed in a single pass (work and turn, work and tumble—types of imposition), you may want to draw your own crop marks manually. Make your manual crop marks short and thin—about a quarter of an inch long and hairline width—and an eighth of an inch away from the edge of the finished piece. Make sure the corners don't touch. Before you take your document to final production, it's a good idea to print it from your laser printer, and with a pencil, connect the crop marks, you created. This is a way to double-check the accuracy of your marks, to make sure that you're not cutting off something you want to keep.

- ***Bleed Marks*** sit in the corners of your document, just outside the crop marks, and set the limits of your printed bleed. You will usually use the settings you entered when your document was first set up, but you can deselect the *Use Document Bleed Settings* option and enter new settings, in the *Bleed and Slug* area of the *Print* dialog box. Even if the bleed in your electronic file extends beyond the settings in the *Bleed and Slug* area, it will print only out to the bleed marks.

- ***Registration Marks*** are the targets along the sides of your document. Your printer uses these marks to straighten and center your document, and to align multiple colors. All your hard work and great design ideas will go down the drain, if your job is printed out of register.

- ***Color Bars*** are used in production to be sure that ink coverage is running right—not too light and not too heavy. They appear at the top of a document.

- ***Page Information*** will give you the title of the document, the date and time printed, and separation color. Very handy stuff.

▸MOVING TOWARD MASTERY

By now you should understand these color basics:

- *In offset printing, jobs are either process or spot color jobs. In general, the more colors used, the more expensive the job.*
- *The color swatch should be created according to its final use. If its intent is for the web, use RGB, if for print, use CMYK or Spot.*
- *Since most monitors don't accurately display color, you should select color from a color swatch book, such as a Pantone® Color Selector.*
- *In traditional printing, each color uses a separate printing plate. If the job has three colors, there will be three printing plates. When you print separations, the number of separations should equal the number of colors used in the document.*
- *Although Black is counted as a color, tints created from a solid color aren't considered additional colors. For instance, if you had a newsletter that used black and a 10%, 20%, and 50% tint of blue, it would still be a two-color newsletter.*
- *If you print and overlay two tints—process or spot color—a new color will result. A tint of yellow, printed over a tint of blue, will result in a shade of green. A tint of black printed over a tint of red will result in a much darker red. This concept is important for you to keep in mind, as we move on to mixed inks.*

OTHER PRINT DIALOG BOX OPTIONS

- *All pages in a document are printed, by default. You can also specify a page range, or choose to print odd or even pages. To print a single page, enter the page number in the* ***Range*** *field. Entering* ***1, 4-7*** *in the* ***Range*** *field would result in printing pages 1, 4, 5, 6, and 7. If you entered* ***5-****, you would print page 5 through the end of the document. Entering* ***-5*** *would result in printing all pages from 1 through page 5.*

- *Under the* ***Setup*** *category you can scale the document by entering a percent in the* ***Width*** *or* ***Height*** *field. If* ***Constrain Proportions*** *is checked, your document will be scaled proportionately. Checking* ***Scale to Fit*** *will automatically resize your document to fit the paper size you have chosen.*

- *You may want documents created with facing pages to print two pages, side by side, on one sheet of paper. This is called printing a "spread," and you can print one spread per sheet. Select* ***Spreads*** *under the* ***General*** *category and then check the preview icon to determine if you need to change the orientation of your pages. If the spread size is too large and won't fit on your paper size, you can reduce the spread to fit by selecting* ***Scale to Fit*** *under the* ***Setup*** *category.*

- *Any object on a document page can be specified as non-printing. First, select the object. Then go to* ***Window>Output>Attributes*** *and check* ***Nonprinting****. If desired, you can override this setting in the* ***Print*** *dialog box; in the* ***General*** *options, select* ***Print Non-printing Objects****.*

- *You can save a print summary for a specific job that records all the print settings. Go to the* ***Summary*** *category, select* ***Save Summary****, and name the file. A text file containing all the specifications for this job will be created. This is a helpful checklist for the next time you need to print a complex job.*

USING MIXED INKS

When you are planning on using mixed inks, it's a good idea to check with your printer to identify any potential printing issues. With that said, let's begin using mixed inks. First, you will create a mixed ink swatch. Then, you will generate a mixed ink swatch group. Finally, you will use a mixed ink swatch group in creating a poster for the Midwest Quilters Convention. This project will utilize many of the effects introduced in Chapter 11, and will incorporate a two-color palette.

VISUAL |12–20|

This two-color project uses a mixed ink swatch group to create the illusion of many colors.

▸ *Create a mixed ink swatch*

1. Create a new InDesign document using the default settings. Open the *Swatches* panel and create two spot color swatches: **PANTONE+ Solid Coated 127 C** (yellow) and **PANTONE+ Solid Coated 302 C** (blue).

2. From the *Swatches* panel menu, choose *New Mixed Ink Swatch*.

3. **Click** the empty boxes to the left of the PANTONE 127 C and PANTONE 302 C swatch names. A *mixed ink* icon will appear. Enter the percentages of each color by typing in the percentage field, or by dragging the sliders. The new color appears in the upper left swatch box. Press **Return**. The mixed ink swatch now appears in the *Swatches* panel.

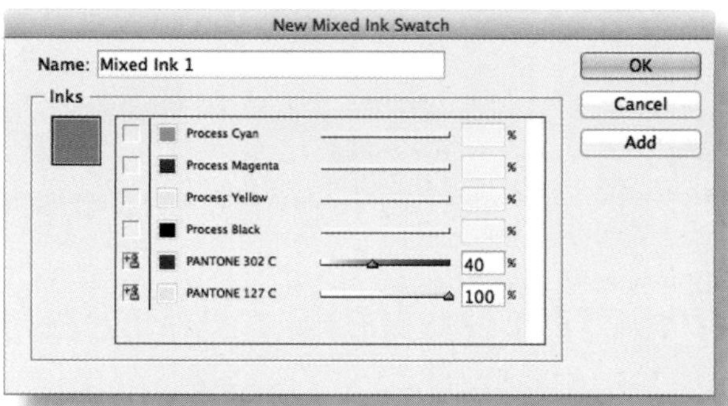

VISUAL | 12–21 |
The mixed ink icon appears to the left of the swatch name.

You can see how using mixed ink swatches can create the illusion of a third color—without the additional cost. In this case, we now have blue, yellow, and khaki colors to use in our two-color document. Think of the possibilities…you could spend a considerable amount of time creating mixed ink swatches—or you could let InDesign automate the system for you.

▸ *Create a mixed ink group*

1. Choose *New Mixed Ink Group* from the *Swatches* panel menu.

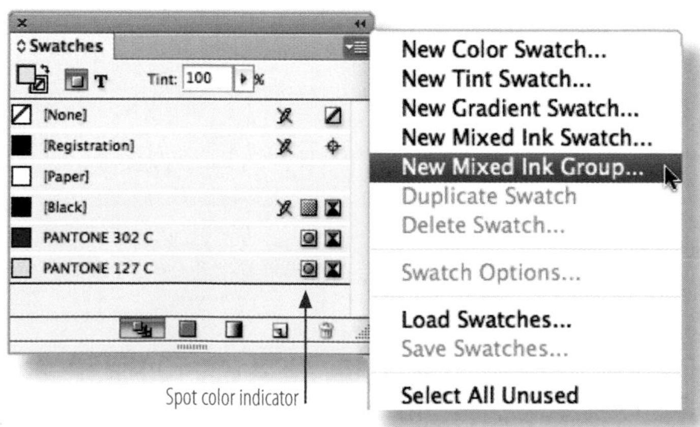

VISUAL | 12–22 |
A swatch that has been created as a spot color will be displayed with a circle inside a square.

2. **Click** the empty boxes to the left of PANTONE 127 C and PANTONE 302 C. The mixed ink icon will appear. Carefully refer to Visual 12–23 as we move on with the steps. InDesign is going to automatically generate mixed ink group swatches from the yellow and blue spot colors in our document. In the *Initial* column, enter a percentage of each color. In Visual 12–23, a **20%** tint of **PANTONE 302 C** and a **20%** tint of **PANTONE 127 C** would be our first and second swatches. The *Repeat* column indicates how many separate swatches should be created. In this example, there would be the initial swatch, plus four more—for a total of five swatches of yellow, and five swatches of blue in increments of 20%. Click *Preview Swatches* to see how many swatches InDesign will create when you press Return. In this example, five tints of each color will be mixed, for a total of 25 swatches. Be realistic with the number of swatches you create—you probably don't need to generate 100 mixed ink swatches!

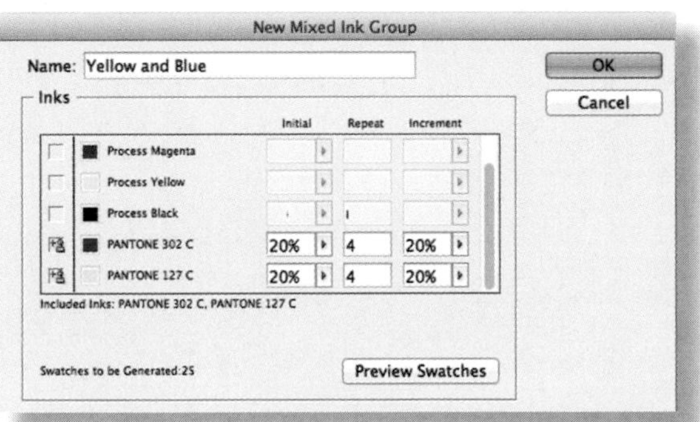

VISUAL | 12–23 |

Using colors from a mixed ink group creates the illusion of many colors in a document.

Examine Visual 12–24. First, find the single mixed ink swatch, named "Mixed Ink 1." Then, locate the 25 new mixed ink swatches. Notice that all mixed ink swatches are indicated with a light yellow and blue teardrop shape. When you create a document using PANTONE 127 C and PANTONE 302 C and use all the mixed ink swatches, you will only get two separations, because all the colors are tint mixes of the yellow and blue main colors.

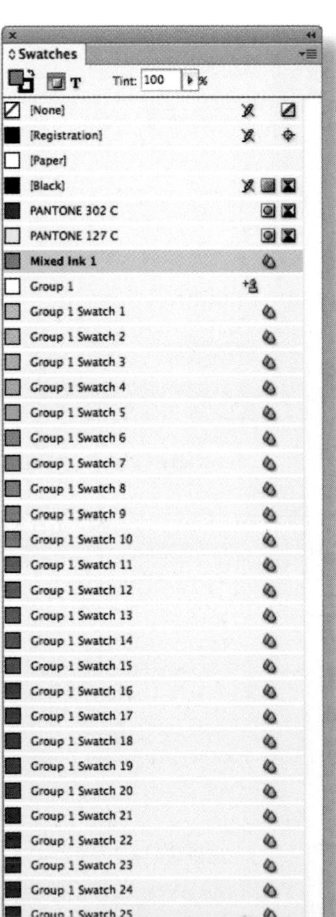

VISUAL | 12–24 |

Mixed ink group swatches are identified in the Swatches panel by a teardrop displayed in the column to the right of the swatch name.

THE MIDWEST QUILTERS CONVENTION

In the next series of steps, you'll create your own mixed ink group from two spot colors and use your swatches to create the illustrations for the *Midwest Quilters Convention*. Be creative and experiment with different spot colors for your project, but remember that you should have one color dark enough for readable body copy.

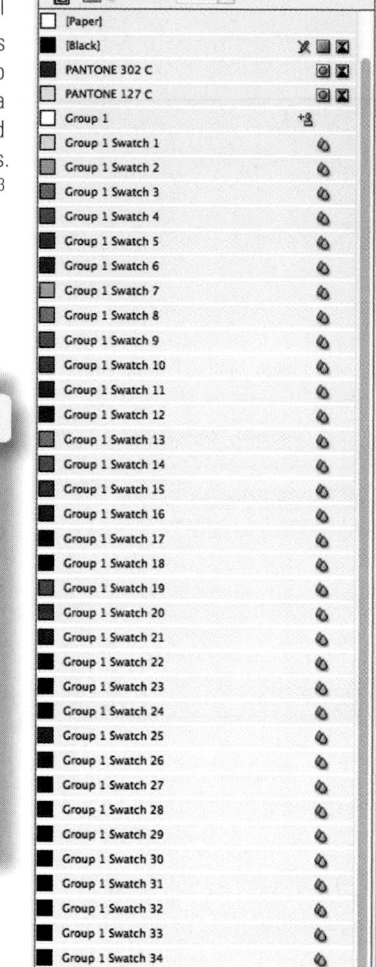

VISUAL | 12–25 |

This mixed ink group has too many swatches that are too close in color. Try to achieve a full range of distinctly-colored mixed ink swatches.

EXPLORING INDESIGN CS6
Artwork & Resources

- Go to: http://www.cengagebrain.com
- Type: Rydberg
- Click Exploring InDesign CS6 in the list of search results.
- When the book's main page is displayed, click the Access button under Free Study Tools.
- To download files, select a chapter number and then click on the Artwork & Resources tab on the left navigation bar to download the files.

► *Create a mixed ink group and design four quilt blocks*

1. Open *12 Quilt Block Template* from the *12 Artwork and Resources* folder, on the online companion resources. Open the *Swatches* panel and create two spot colors for use on coated paper. One color should be dark enough for displaying copy. Delete all other colors from the *Swatches* panel, except for your spot colors.

2. Create a mixed ink group, keeping the final number of swatches to 36 or less. Visual 12–25 shows the importance of using the *Preview Swatches* button while creating mixed ink groups. Swatches 26–36 are so close in color that it would be easy to select the wrong color during production. Try to create a palette with a full-range of distinct color blends.

3. Fill the center square with the color of your choice. Then, fill all the other triangles in a symmetrical manner. A good technique is to add one fill and then use the *Eyedropper* tool to transfer the fill to other shapes (Visual 12–26). As you are working on your block, you can easily revise your color scheme if you find a combination that would be more effective. When you are satisfied with your quilt block, save it as **Quilt Block 1** someplace you will easily remember, because you will need it for the end of chapter project.

4. With Quilt Block 1 still open, do a *Save As* and name the file **Quilt Block 2**. Revise the color scheme to make a block with a totally different color balance or pattern. When you are finished, save the block.

5. Do a *Save As* and name the new file **Quilt Block 3**. Again, revise the color scheme and save the finished block. Finally, save Quilt Block 3 as **Quilt Block 4** and revise the colors. Save the finished result.

You now have four different quilt squares that will be the "building blocks" (my apologies) for the *Midwest Quilters Convention* project at the end of this chapter.

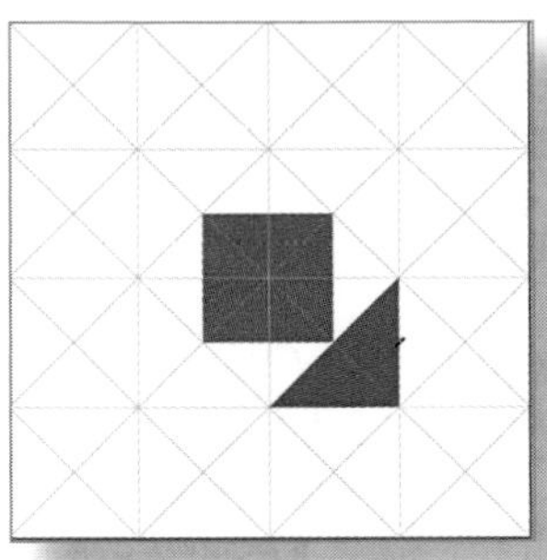
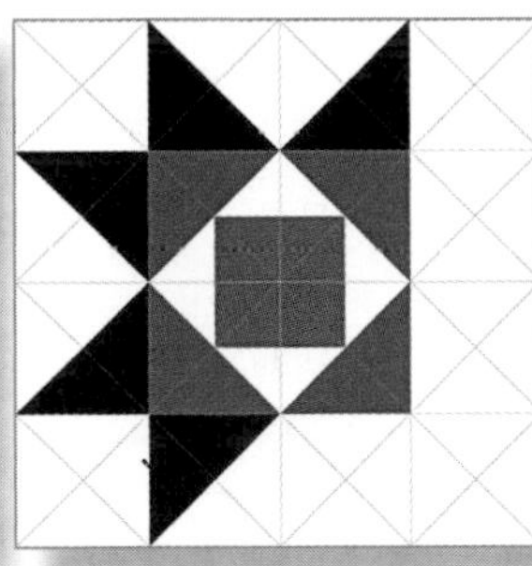
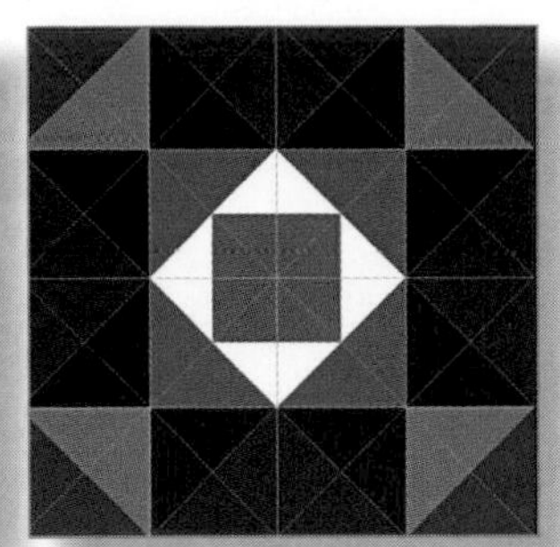

VISUAL | 12–26 |
Use the Eyedropper tool to transfer your mixed ink swatch colors from triangle to triangle in the quilt block template.

Summary

As this chapter has demonstrated, getting images and type on your document is just the tip of the iceberg, in terms of production. There are many ways designers can innocently flub up a document—and defining color incorrectly, is one of them. Spend some extra time experimenting with the *Swatches* panel, until you are comfortable with all of its functions.

Before you send a document out to the printer, ask someone with more experience to look it over. Finding and fixing errors before they go to prepress is a good way to establish and maintain a good reputation, as a designer.

In the next chapter, you will learn about InDesign's powerful *Links* and *Preflight* operations, the difference between vector and bitmap artwork, dealing with resolution issues, and the *Separations* and *Overprint Preview* features. This is all important information, critical for you to understand. Take your time and carefully read the chapter.

▸ IN REVIEW

1. Explain the difference between RGB and CMYK color. What does it mean that one of them is additive and one is subtractive?

2. When would you use spot color? When would you use process color? When might you use both?

3. What is the difference between the Color panel and the Swatches panel and why should you prefer to use one instead of the other?

4. Why is it best to select standard Pantone or Trumatch colors from a swatch book rather than create your own?

5. True or false: When you're finished with a project, a good way to check how many colors you actually have in your document is to print color separations or use the Separations Preview panel.

6. You've designed an 11 x 17 inch poster, but your printer only handles letter-size paper. Describe how to scale to fit the poster on a smaller paper size.

7. What is the process for suppressing the printing of an individual object on a page?

8. If "-19" was typed in the Range field of the Print dialog box, what would happen during printing?

9. What is a "spread" and how is a spread printed?

10. How is a spot color identified in the Swatches panel? A mixed ink?

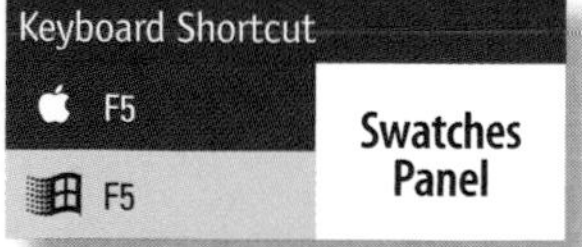

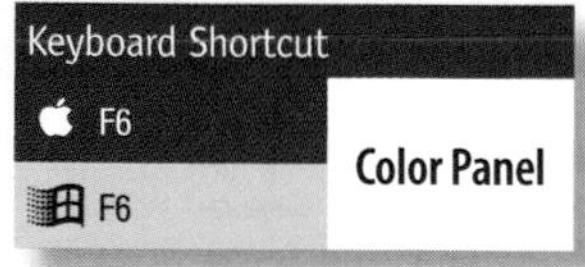

▸ CHAPTER 12 PROJECTS

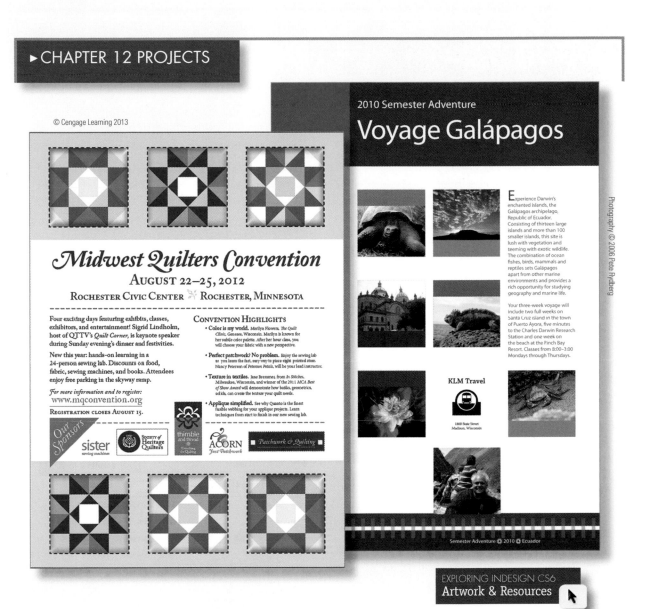

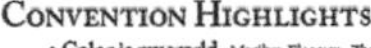

Midwest Quilters Convention

AUGUST 22–25, 2012

ROCHESTER CIVIC CENTER ROCHESTER, MINNESOTA

Four exciting days featuring exhibits, classes, exhibitors, and entertainment! Sigrid Lindholm, host of QTTV's *Quilt Corner*, is keynote speaker during Sunday evening's dinner and festivities.

New this year: hands-on learning in a 24-person sewing lab. Discounts on food, fabric, sewing machines, and books. Attendees enjoy free parking in the skyway ramp.

For more information and to register:
www.mqconvention.org

REGISTRATION CLOSES AUGUST 15.

CONVENTION HIGHLIGHTS

- **Color is my world.** Marilyn Flowers, *The Quilt Clinic*, Genesee, Wisconsin. Marilyn is known for her subtle color palette. After her hour class, you will choose your fabric with a new perspective.
- **Perfect patchwork? No problem.** Enjoy the sewing lab as you learn the fast, easy way to piece eight pointed stars. Nancy Peterson of *Peterson Petals*, will be your lead instructor.
- **Texture in textiles.** Jane Bremmer, from *In Stitches*, Milwaukee, Wisconsin, and winner of the 2011 *MCA Best of Show Award* will demonstrate how batiks, geometrics, solids, can create the texture your quilt needs.
- **Applique simplified.** See why Quanto is the finest fusible webbing for your applique projects. Learn techniques from start to finish in our new sewing lab.

Our Sponsors

2010 Semester Adventure

Voyage Galápagos

Experience Darwin's enchanted islands, the Galápagos archipelago, Republic of Ecuador. Consisting of thirteen large islands and more than 100 smaller islands, this site is lush with vegetation and teeming with exotic wildlife. The combination of ocean fishes, birds, mammals and reptiles sets Galápagos apart from other marine environments and provides a rich opportunity for studying geography and marine life.

Your three-week voyage will include two full weeks on Santa Cruz island in the town of Puerto Ayora, five minutes to the Charles Darwin Research Station and one week on the beach at the Finch Bay Resort. Classes from 8:00–3:00 Mondays through Thursdays.

KLM Travel

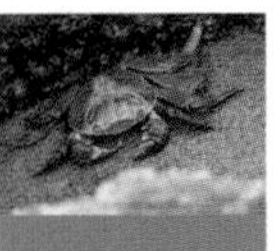

Semester Adventure 2010 Ecuador

You have already created components for the Midwest Quilters Convention. It looks simple on the surface, but this project will exercise your problem-solving skills by using many techniques introduced in the past few chapters. The second project, Voyage Galápagos is an 8-page booklet that uses multiple master pages, nested styles, and many InDesign features found in the *Effects* panel, including transparency, drop shadow, and blending modes. This is a two-stage project that you will finish after Chapter 13.

EXPLORING INDESIGN CS6
Artwork & Resources

- Go to: http://www.cengagebrain.com
- Type: Rydberg
- Click Exploring InDesign CS6 in the list of search results.
- When the book's main page is displayed, click the Access button under Free Study Tools.
- To download files, select a chapter number and then click on the Artwork & Resources tab on the left navigation bar to download the files.

Never discourage anyone who continually **makes progress**, no matter how slow.

— Plato

Production Essentials

objectives

- *Differentiate between continuous tone (bitmap) and vector artwork*
- *Use the Links panel*
- *Adjust image resolution for printing*
- *Find and replace fonts*
- *Use Separations and Overprint Preview operations*
- *Perform document preflight and package operations*

introduction

Some ideas sound good in theory—self-generating electricity, cars that run without an external fuel source, gears that keep turning on their own momentum. But not every great idea works out in reality.

That's what can happen to a great design idea, too. You spend a lot of time and creative energy on a document—it looks beautiful on your monitor and when printed on your desktop color printer. So, you take it to your commercial printing company and order 5,000 printed pieces. But when you pick up your job, you get a bill for hundreds of dollars more than you were quoted. You're told that the additional charges are for something called "prepress." They explain that it was necessary to take your electronic file—the one you thought was finished—and spend additional time getting it ready to print properly. This chapter will explain the basic production concepts you need to create documents that run smoothly, and avoid unexpected budget overruns.

an introduction to image management

A typical InDesign document includes text and images. The previous chapters have focused primarily on text: how to choose appropriate typefaces, format paragraphs, use hyphens and dashes, create styles, and so on. This chapter will focus on working with images. This chapter covers only the basic information required for documents destined for commercial print shops. For more detailed information on each topic, consult InDesign's Help menu.

INPUT: PREPARING IMAGE FILES FOR USE IN INDESIGN

Let's say you're creating a fund-raising brochure for a museum's building project. The copy has been written, and you have gathered the artwork that will be featured in the piece, including:

- *An old, glossy color photograph of the museum's founder;*
- *An architect's full-color marker rendering of the proposed addition to the museum;*
- *A black and white printout of the new floor plan;*
- *A file containing a digital photograph of the current board of directors; and*
- *The museum logo, created in Adobe Illustrator®.*

Each of these images have different production considerations. But they also have two things in common: input and output. You need to prepare them correctly during the input stage, and use appropriate production techniques, so that they output correctly and produce a quality printed piece.

DOTS, PIXELS AND LINES PER INCH

Before we begin, you need to know how commercial printing presses reproduce full-color paintings, charcoal drawings, photographs, or other pieces of artwork that artists and photographers create. A printing press can't blend a myriad of colors; it has only two options—either it puts a particular color ink, at a specific location on the paper, or it doesn't. What's the secret? With a magnifying glass, take a look at any color or black and white picture, in a newspaper or magazine, and you will see that it is composed of millions of tiny dots. Whether the dots are all black or various colors, the varying sizes and arrangement visually blend together and create the illusion of color and shading. The graphics industry uses many acronyms when talking about dots (in some cases, they are squares). The most important to know are: *dots per inch (dpi)*, *pixels per inch (ppi)*, and *lines per inch (lpi)*. These terms define the *resolution* of desktop printers or scanners, digital image files and commercial printing presses. Resolution has a direct bearing on the capabilities of a device, or the quality of an image. Generally, the higher the resolution, the crisper the image.

► *production tip*

dpi: Dots per inch
ppi: Pixels per inch
lpi: Lines per inch

CONTINUOUS TONE ARTWORK

Let's begin with the color photo of the museum's founder. Traditional photographs, taken with a film camera and printed on photographic paper, fall into the artwork classification known as *continuous tone*. Any artwork that contains a full-range of color or tonal values—such as paintings, black and white photographs, or pastel drawings—falls into this category. A scanner is used to digitize continuous tone artwork, so that it can be placed into an InDesign document. This process converts the colors and tones of the artwork into a specified number of *dots per inch* (*dpi*) that you determine when you set up the scan. However, the resolution of the resulting image file is described in *pixels per inch* (*ppi*). (When talking about scanners and scanned images, dpi and ppi are often used interchangeably.) Understanding how resolution affects the quality of the digital image and its file size, is critical to creating efficient and problem-free InDesign documents.

► *production tip*

Continuous tone artwork needs to be converted to dots by scanning, before it can be printed.

If the photo is scanned at a *low resolution*, there will be fewer pixels per square inch, and some of the detail in the photo will be lost. A photo scanned at *high resolution* will retain much more detail, because there will be more pixels to record more information per square inch. You will need to refer to your scanner's manual to find out how to adjust the scanning resolution. Generally, a photograph scanned at 300 dpi is sufficient for most print production needs. Once the scan of the old photograph is placed into the InDesign document, it can be scaled and cropped.

Next, let's take a look at the architect's marker rendering of the proposed addition. This illustration is also considered continuous tone artwork. And just like the color photograph, this illustration will be converted to pixels in the scanning process. Again, a scanning resolution of 300 is sufficient.

VISUAL | 13–1 |

Continuous tone artwork (left) includes a full-range of tonal values. Line art (right) consists of straight and curved lines without variations in shade.

LINE ART

The black and white printout of the floor plan falls into a different artwork classification called *line art*. Line art does not contain any tonal values—the image is comprised of pure black or white elements. A pen and ink or scratch board drawing is line art, so is pure black type printed on a laser printer. When this type of artwork is scanned, you will select "line art" in the scanner setup controls. Your

► *production tip*

Line art doesn't contain any tonal values. It needs to be scanned as line art before it is printed.

scanner's manual will be able to walk you through the process. Since there are no tonal variations in the floor plan art, each pixel will be either a solid black or solid white square. If we choose a scanner resolution of 600 pixels per square inch, the pixels will be very small, and will capture fine details in the floor plan. This may seem fine, but the general rule of thumb is to capture line art at the resolution of the final print device. While 600 dpi is customary for today's laser or inkjet printers, the digital presses and imagesetters found in many commercial printers can print at 1200, 2400 and higher dpi. If possible, always consult with your printer for the best scanning recommendations.

Finally, we have the digital photo of the board of directors. A digital photograph has already been converted to pixels. This is where the resolution of the digital camera comes into play. The higher the resolution setting of the camera, the more pixels—which then capture more detail in the photo. There is little you can do to improve the overall quality of a digital image taken with a low resolution camera, because the camera did not capture enough pixels to record the nuances of the photo in the first place.

ART: RESOLUTION INDEPENDENT OR DEPENDENT

We have one more piece of artwork to discuss before we begin our museum fund-raising piece—the museum logo. This logo was created in Adobe Illustrator®, one of the members in the Creative Suite. Adobe Illustrator is a drawing program that uses mathematical equations to create precise, curved and straight paths that extend from point to point. This type of digital artwork is vector-based artwork. The paths can be edited by repositioning the points. As the points are rearranged, the mathematical data is recalculated, and the path is updated. This type of digital artwork is resolution independent, which means that the image quality is not adversely affected, regardless of how the artwork is scaled. Native Illustrator files (with the file extension .ai) can be placed directly into InDesign.

VISUAL | 13–2 |

The "dots" that make up digital photos, are picture elements, or pixels. These give the impression of continuous tones. The photo on the right has been enlarged to show the pixels.

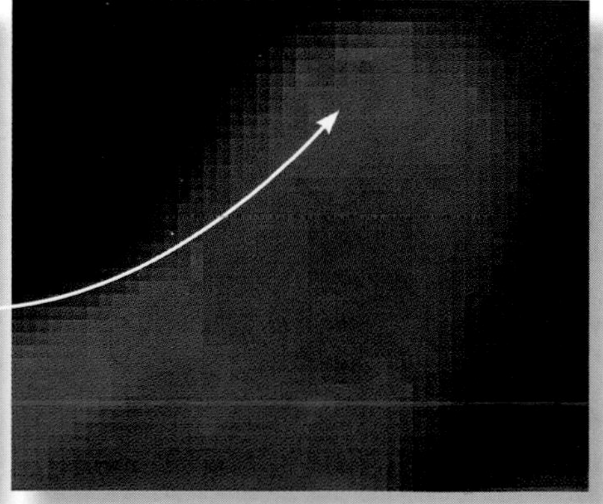

BITMAP (RASTER) IMAGES

The other images in our museum piece were not created by mathematical formulas, so instead of being vector-based artwork, they are called *bitmap* or *raster* images. During the scanning or digital photography process, the images were converted to *pixels*, which are bits of data that are mapped to a grid of rows and columns. When these pixels are small enough, they create the illusion of a continuous tone image. In contrast to vector images (which are resolution independent), images composed of pixels are said to be *resolution dependent*. What this means is the size of the individual pixels will get larger or smaller as the image is scaled in InDesign. Unfortunately, the quality of bitmap images may deteriorate. As shown in Visual 13–2, greatly enlarging a bitmap image will make its individual pixels visible to the human eye.

► *production tip*

Bitmap images are resolution dependent, which means the quality of the image may change as the image is scaled.

The term *resolution* is used to describe the number of pixels in each square inch of the image. The images for the museum project, scanned at a resolution of 300 pixels per inch (ppi), resulted in a resolution of 90,000 incredibly tiny pixels, per square inch (300 pixels wide by 300 pixels high). The architectural floor plan was scanned at 600 ppi, resulting in 360,000 data-filled pixels, in each square inch! Let's compare that to a piece of line art with a resolution of 72 ppi. With only 5,184 total pixels per square inch (72 × 72 = 5184), the physical size of each individual pixel would be much larger than the 360,000 microscopic pixels, per square inch, in the floor plan scan. The larger pixel size would result in a coarser, less-detailed image when printed. So when it comes to bitmap images, fewer or larger pixels, per inch = less data = less detail. More tiny pixels, per square inch = more data = more detail. So, why not input everything at 1200 ppi? Because the file sizes would be enormous and your files would be difficult to output—which brings us to the next topic.

► *production tip*

Resolution describes the number of pixels in each square inch of an image.

FROM INPUT TO OUTPUT: IMAGES IN INDESIGN

Quality designs, like the museum brochure, start with careful planning. Usually a detailed layout is worked out that determines how an image will be used, such as where, how large, and what portion of it will be used in the piece. If all these details are known before the artwork is converted to bitmap images, it will be easy to create optimal scans. For example, the entire 8 × 10 photo of the founder need not be scanned, if only his head and shoulders will be used. Perhaps a portion of the architect's marker rendering will need to be enlarged considerably. Producing the most efficient bitmap image files means setting up the scanner to:

- *the correct dpi setting for the final printing device,*
- *capture only the portions needed and*
- *scale them to final size needed in the document.*

But during the production process, when layouts and copy changes often occur, the size and cropping of images may need to be changed—sometimes drastically. What affect will this have on your various images?

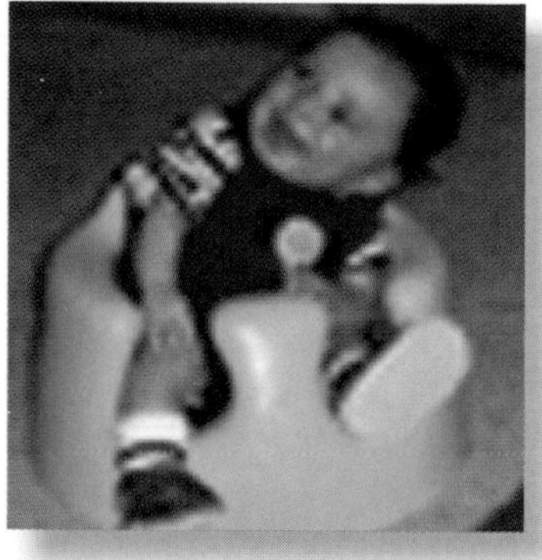

VISUAL | 13–3 |
This photo has a resolution of 72 ppi and has been greatly enlarged in InDesign, resulting in a blurred image.

VISUAL | 13–4 |
This photo has 300 ppi resolution and is used at its actual size, 100%.

For resolution independent, vector artwork—like the museum's logo—you don't need to worry about scaling and its effects on image quality. These types of images will print beautifully at almost any size. However, scaling is a major concern when using pixel-based, resolution dependent images. In Visual 13–3, the photo is a low-resolution, 72 ppi image, which has also been scaled larger in InDesign. Not only does this low-resolution image start out with larger pixels and less data, as the image size increased, the size of each pixel has also increased. The result is a blurry photo with huge pixels, and very little detail.

In contrast, Visual 13–4 shows a high-resolution, 300 ppi photo, used at its actual size in the InDesign document. The pixels remain imperceptible, and the detail in the image is crisp, right down to the drool on the knuckles.

The keys to having bitmap images print correctly are:

- *Begin with the correct resolution; and*
- *Use images at 100% in the InDesign document.*

Next, you'll learn how the *Links* panel, in partnership with Adobe Photoshop®, can optimize bitmap images to the ideal size and resolution for your document.

THE LINKS PANEL

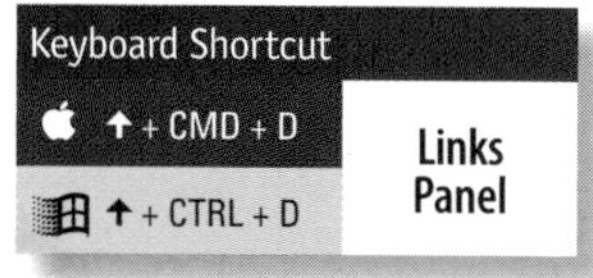

When you place an image in InDesign, it creates and then maintains a *link* to the original source file. The *Links* panel displays information about all the files linked to your document. The *Links* panel is accessed by pressing **Shift+Command+D** (Mac) or **Shift+Control+D** (Windows). You can also access the *Links* panel by going to *Window>Links*. When you choose *Panel Options* from the *Links* panel menu, you can customize the information that will be displayed in the *Links* panel. The numbers in Visual 13–5, identify important information that can be displayed in the *Links* panel. Each numbered item is explained on the next few pages. If your *Links* panel does not look the same, follow the instructions at the end of the section to customize it.

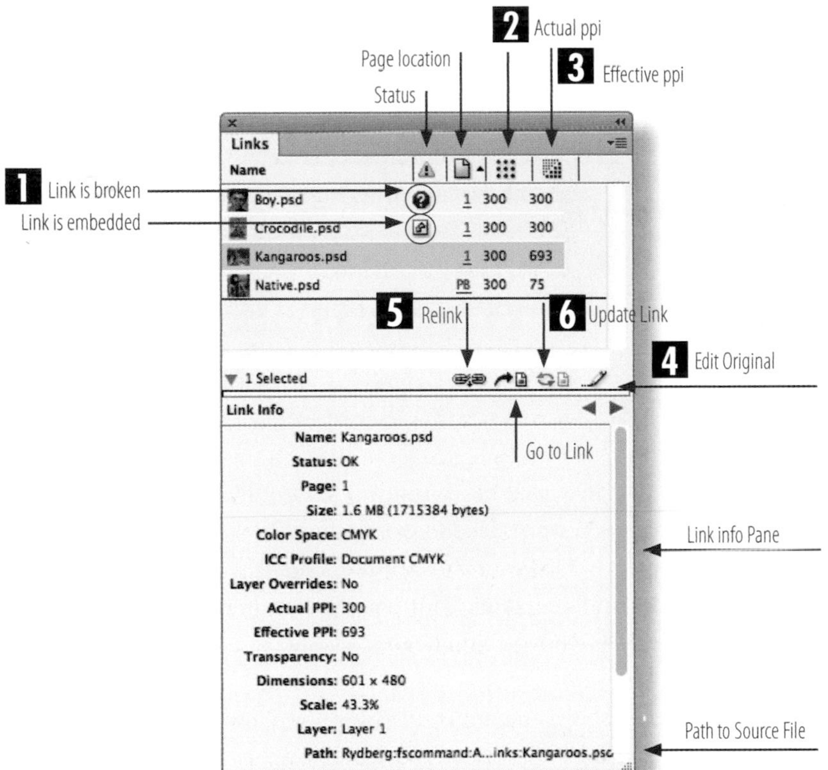

VISUAL | 13–5 |

The Links panel shows information that is critical for successfully using images in your project. It is important to spend some time learning the features of this powerful panel.

1 Embedded and Linked images. When an image is placed into InDesign, the graphic can either be *linked* or *embedded.* By default, InDesign creates linked graphics. This means that data from the graphic file is not brought into the document—instead, InDesign simply creates a link to the image's original source file. Later, during printing, it retrieves the data needed to generate the image. InDesign continually monitors all linked source files to determine if they have been modified or moved. If you place an image from a CD and then remove the CD, the link is broken because InDesign can't follow the path to the original image file. Similarly, if you place images that were located in a specific folder and later change the location or name of the folder, the links to all those source files are broken. If the link to an image is broken, at print time, InDesign warns you. If you cannot fix the link, it will print the low-res image displayed on your monitor. This poor quality image is not what you want when printed on a high quality commercial press. For this reason, all links must be in place before printing your project. When you take a project to the printer, you must include all graphics and font files. (Fortunately, InDesign has a feature that will "package" your project correctly, notifying you of any problems. This process will be covered later in this chapter.)

When you embed an image, the data from the image file becomes part of the InDesign file and is displayed with a special icon in the *Status* column of the *Links*

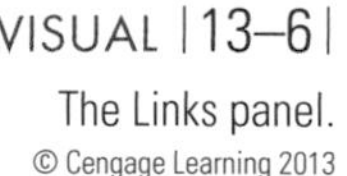
VISUAL | 13–6 |

The Links panel.

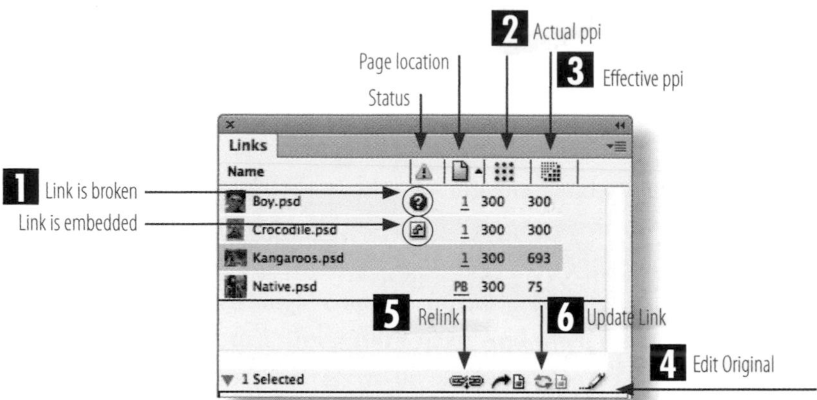

panel, as shown in callout #1 in Visual 13–6. Your InDesign file will be much larger with embedded images, but you won't need to worry about broken links when you take your project to the printer. However, most printers prefer that graphics files not be embedded in InDesign documents. This is a production issue you should discuss with your printer before production begins!

2 Actual ppi. Visual 13–6 shows the *Actual ppi* column turned on to display in the upper portion of the *Links* panel. When you scan down the far right column, you can quickly see the resolution at which each image was scanned. Each image has an *Actual ppi* resolution of 300. If scaled to 100%, these images would be ideal for printing in full-color on printing press.

3 Effective ppi. As you click on each link in the upper portion of the *Links* panel, the *Link Info* pane at the bottom, will display image-specific data, including the image's scale percentage and the *Effective ppi*. Visual 13–6 also shows the *Effective ppi* column turned on to display in the upper part of the *Links* panel.

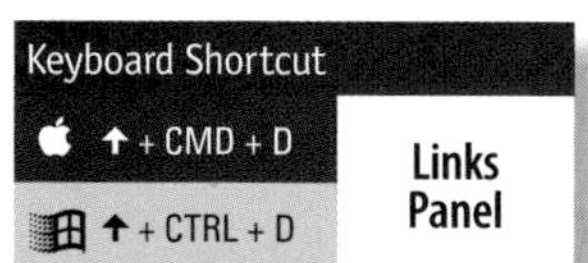

Unlike the numbers in the *Actual ppi* column, the numbers in the *Effective ppi* column are not all the same. Look at the first two links, *Boy.psd* and *Crocodile. psd.* The *Effective* and *Actual ppi* for both these links are 300, because both images are used at 100% in the InDesign document. This is the ideal scenario. Now, look at the *Link Info* pane area for *Kangaroos.psd* shown in Visual 13–5 on the previous page. Notice that the *Scale* category shows 43.3%. Because the image has been reduced, the pixels were squeezed together to fit into a much smaller space. Although we began with an *Actual resolution* of 300 ppi, the *Effective resolution* has now increased to 693 ppi, more than twice the ideal of 300 ppi. Now, look at the link for the *Native.psd* image. Even though the *Actual ppi* is 300, the *Effective ppi* is 75—much less than the ideal resolution. Why? Because the image was scaled to 400% in the document. So, the *Effective ppi* was reduced by scaling the image larger. Remember, when the *Effective ppi* is lower than the ideal resolution, you will begin to have problems with image quality. When working on documents intended for high quality, commercial printing, you want to keep the *Effective ppi* at the ideal, 300 ppi resolution. You'll learn how to do that next, using *Edit Original.*

▸ *Edit Original*

Often, after placing and scaling images in InDesign, the *Effective ppi* is too high, or too low. In the following exercise, you will learn how to use Adobe Photoshop® in conjunction with InDesign to remedy this situation. (If you don't have Photoshop, study the visuals in the following steps.)

This document contains links to sources that have been modified. You can update the modified links now, or update them later using the Links panel.
1 - Missing Link(s)
3 - Modified Link(s)
Don't Update Links | Update Links

VISUAL | 13–7 |

This message appears when opening a document. It lets you know if there are Link issues that you need to resolve.
© Cengage Learning 2013

1. From the *13 Artwork and Resources* folder on the student online companion, open the file *13 Resolution. indd.* found inside the *13 Resolution* folder. As the file opens, you will see this warning message. You'll use the ***Links*** panel to manage missing and modified links, you can choose ***Don't Update Links*** (Visual 13–7).

2. Open the ***Links*** panel. Click on *Kangaroos.psd*, and read the ***Link Info*** underneath. Notice that the *Kangaroos. psd* link has been scaled down to 43.3%, creating an *Effective ppi* of 693, which is unnecessarily too high. In the lower right corner of the ***Links*** panel, click the ***Edit Original*** icon (Visual 13–8).

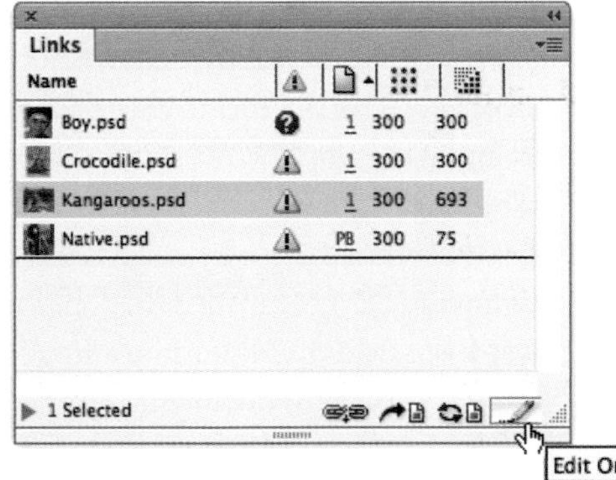

VISUAL | 13–8 |

Click the pencil icon in the lower right corner to edit an image.
© Cengage Learning 2013

3. Adobe Photoshop should launch, opening the *Kangaroos.psd* source file. When it opens, go to the menu and select *Image>Image Size.* At the bottom of the window, check ***Resample Image***. In the ***Document Size*** section, choose ***Percent,*** next to the ***Width*** and ***Height*** fields. Enter **43.3** in the ***Width*** field, and the same value should automatically transfer to the ***Height*** field (Visual 13–9). Press **Return**. When you ***resample*** an image, you actually change the number of pixels in it. In this case, there were too many pixels per inch, so we had Photoshop eliminate the extra data.

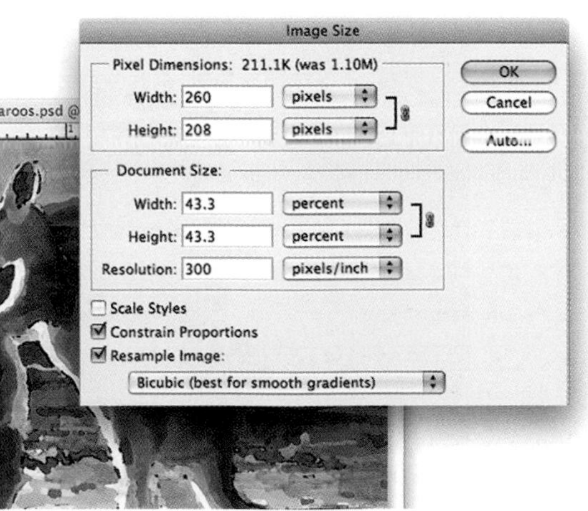

VISUAL | 13–9 |

Use Photoshop to scale and resample images.
© Cengage Learning 2013

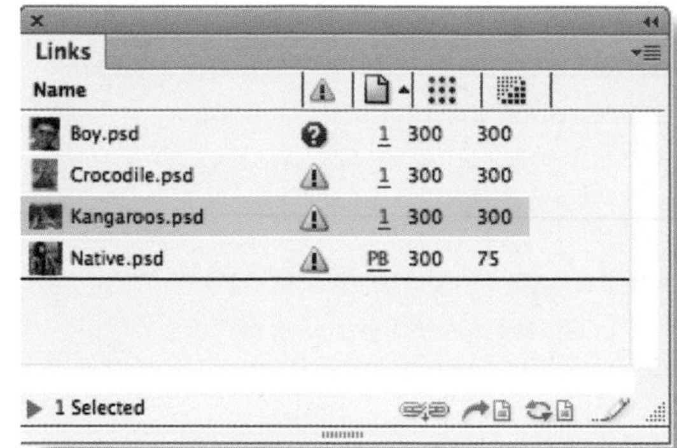

VISUAL | 13–10 |
The Actual and Effective ppi are 300 because the image is used at its actual size.
© Cengage Learning 2013

4. Save the Photoshop file. Now look at the ***Links*** panel, and you will notice that the ***Effective*** and ***Actual ppi*** are both 300. InDesign automatically updated the link with the revisions you made in Photoshop. (Visual 13–10).

5. Select the ***Native.psd*** file in the ***Links*** panel. Notice that a "PB" appears in the ***Page*** column of the ***Links*** panel. "PB" means that the image is on the pasteboard, not on the document (Visual 13–10). If the document had many pages, it might be hard to find exactly where the image was located; but if you look in the ***Link Info*** section, the ***Page*** category shows PB:1. This means the image is on the pasteboard of page 1.

The *Native.psd* link has a problem—an *Effective ppi* of 75. If you look at the *Link Info* you will see that the image has been scaled to 400%. Each pixel has increased in size to fill the space. Choose *Edit Original* and the Photoshop file will open. Go to the menu and select *Image>Image Size*. In the *Pixel Dimension* section of the window, notice that there are 557 pixels in the width, and 565 in the height. Now, with *Resample Image* checked, change the *Document Size: Width* and *Height* fields to **400%**. Before you press **Return**, notice how resampling has greatly increased the values in the *Pixel Dimensions: Width and Height* fields of Photoshop's *Image Size* window. Save the Photoshop file, but don't close your document—we need it for the next few techniques!

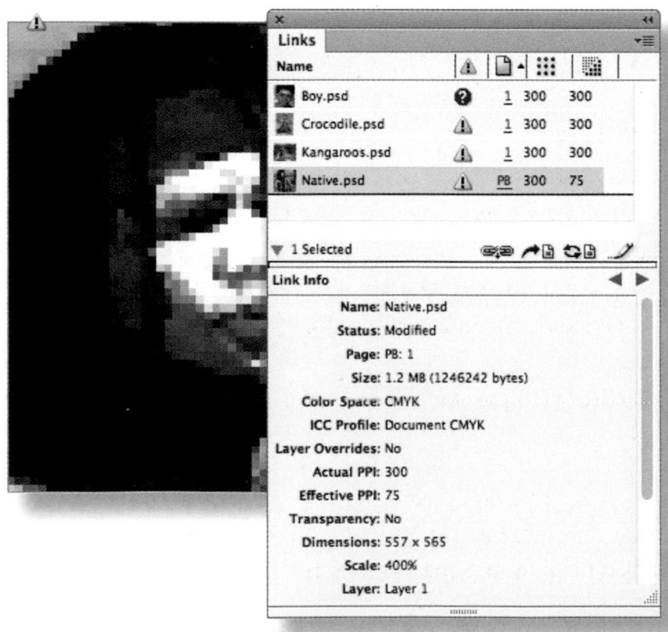

VISUAL | 13–11 |
Pixels are visible in this image. Enlarging the image has created an Effective ppi of only 75, significantly below the ideal 300 ppi. We will use Photoshop to resample and remedy the situation.
© Cengage Learning 2013

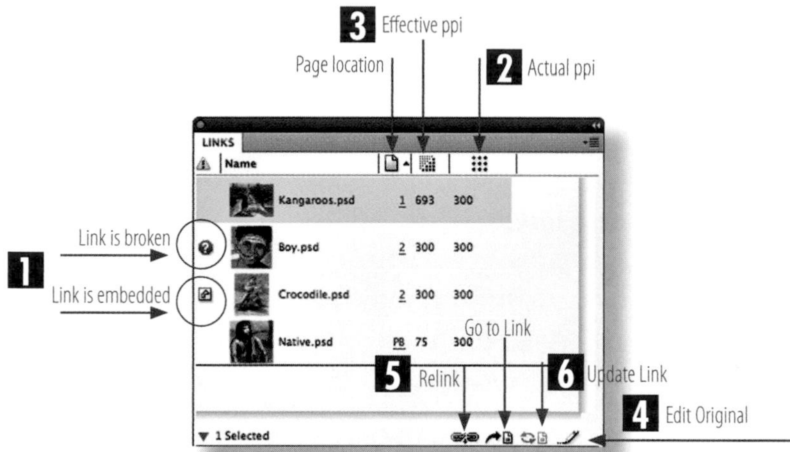

VISUAL | 13–12 |

The Links panel.

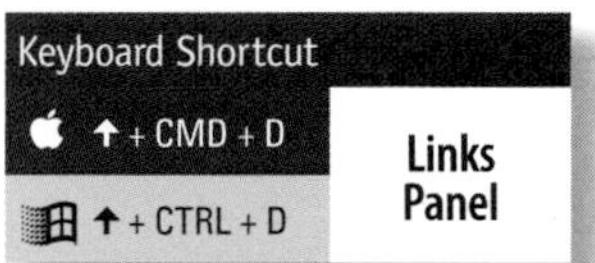

5 Relink. A question mark inside a red hexagon on the *Links* panel means that the link pathway is broken. This scenario happens frequently—somehow, the original file for an image is not where it is supposed to be. (Later in this chapter, you will learn about the *Package* function that takes care of this issue.) Broken links happen anytime the pathway to the original graphic file has been changed, after the link was initially established in InDesign. If you are placing images from your laptop, and then open the document on another computer, you will receive a missing link message when you attempt to print the document. Or, suppose you had several images on your desktop that you placed into an InDesign document. After saving the document, you decide to organize things by moving all the image files into a folder labeled with the job name. The next time you open the document, every link will be displayed with a broken link icon because the files are not in their original location and InDesign can't reestablish the link. Fortunately, the *Links* panel makes it easy to relink the image to the new location.

▸ *Relink an image*

To reestablish a single link, simply select the filename with the missing link icon and click the *Relink* icon on the bottom of the *Links* panel. When the dialog box opens, locate the graphics file and select it. When you have many missing links, you can **Option** (Mac) or **Alt** (Windows) and click the **Relink** icon to relink multiple image files.

1. Click on the ***Boy.psd*** file name in the ***Links*** panel. Click the ***Relink*** icon below the ***Links*** panel.

2. Navigate to the ***13 Artwork and Resources*** folder on the student online companion. Select the ***Boy2.psd,*** located inside the folder. Look in the ***Links*** panel and you will see that the link is now intact. Save the document.

6 Update Link. A yellow triangle ⚠ means that the original image file has been changed since it was placed in the document. When a job is sent out to the printer, the *Status* column shouldn't display any links that need updating, or that are missing.

▸ *Update document links*

1. Place *13 InDesign Sample File.indd* into your open document. The file is found in the *13 Resolution>Links* folder. Save the exercise. Now, use InDesign to open and modify the *13 InDesign Sample File .indd*. Change the color of the type to Magenta and save and close the document.

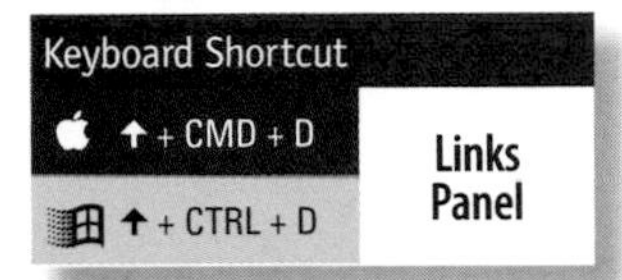

2. Since an attribute of the link has been changed since it was placed in the document, a yellow triangle appears in the status column. Click the *Update Link* icon at the bottom of the *Links* panel to update to the most current file. Repeat the process for each of the modified links. All the triangles will disappear. (Visual 13–13).

VISUAL | 13–13 |

A yellow triangle means the original file has changed since it has been placed in the document.

VISUAL | 13–14 |

The Links panel menu allows you to embed and unembed graphics files.

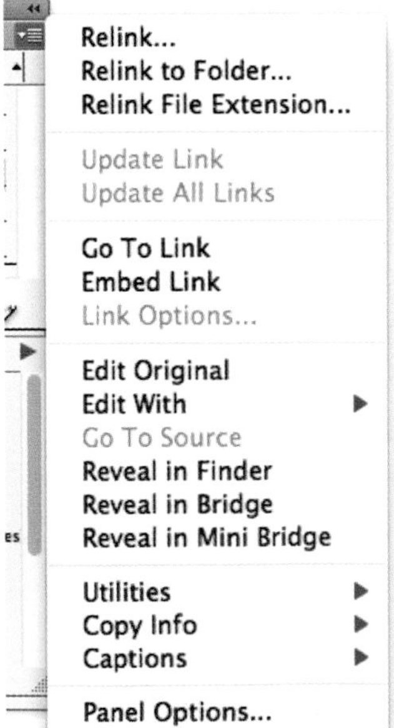

The *Links* panel menu offers many options. In those rare instances when you want to embed an image file, you choose **Embed Link** from the panel menu. When a link is embedded, the link data becomes part of your InDesign document.

To customize the information you would like to have displayed in the upper and lower halves of the *Links* panel, open the panel menu and choose *Panel Options*. Visual 13–15A shows the *Panel Options* modified to display *Color Space* and *Scale*. In Visual 13–15B, *Color Space* and *Scale* are now displayed in the upper half of the *Links* panel. This is a convenient, timesaving feature, because you can view important production information for all your links, instead of selecting each link and reading its link information in the lower half of the *Links* panel.

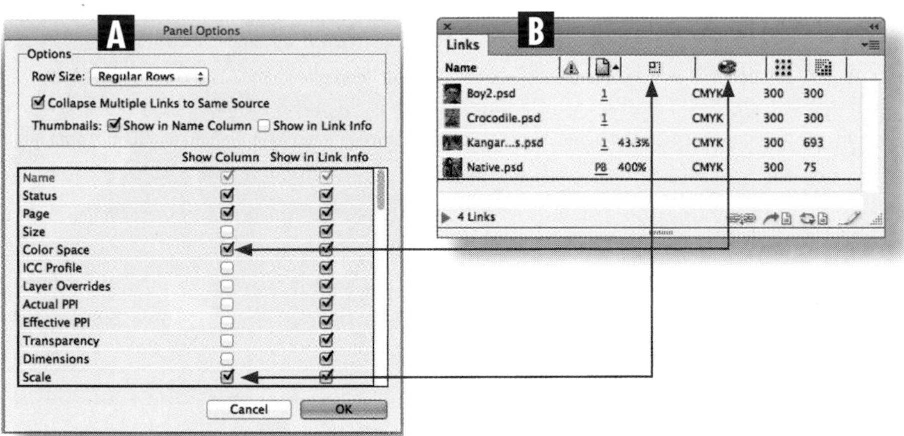

VISUAL |13–15|

The Panel Options dialog box allows you to choose the information that is displayed in the upper and lower halves of the panel. In this example, panel options have been modified to display the color space and scale in the upper half.

PACKAGE THE DOCUMENT FOR PRINTING OUTPUT

When your document is ready to go to press, you need to collect all the electronic elements of your file—all fonts and graphics—and bundle them up for transporting to your service bureau or printer. Fortunately, InDesign makes this process quick and painless with the *Package* function. Choose *File>Package* to access the *Package* dialog box. The *Summary* page appears first, telling you how many fonts, colors, and graphics are included, and other document information. If an element is missing or needs your attention, there will be a yellow caution icon in front of it.

Visual 13–16 shows a problem with *Links and Images*. Seven images in the document use RGB color space. Images composed of Red, Blue and Green need to be converted to CMYK in Photoshop, before going to press.

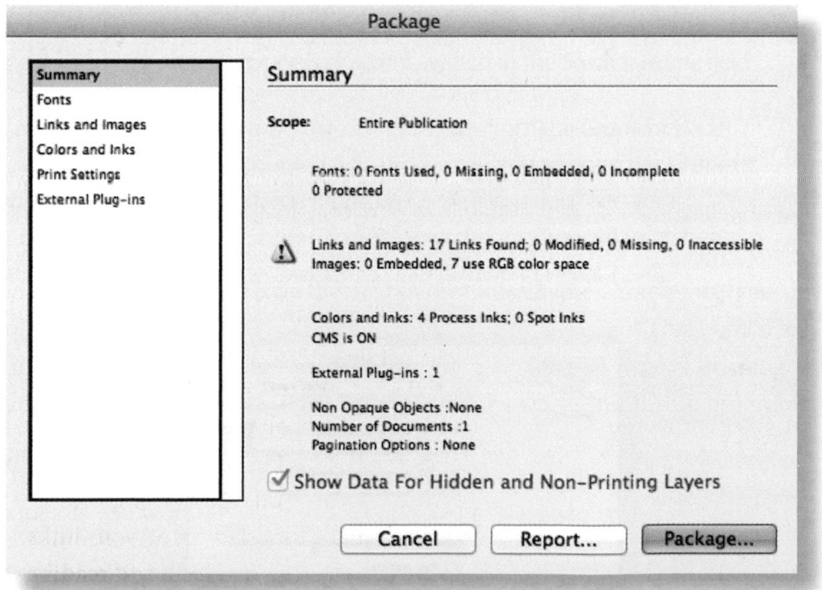

VISUAL |13–16|

The yellow warning triangle shows that there are problems in the Links and Images portion of the document.

If there is a caution icon next to the *Fonts* summary paragraph, click on the *Fonts* category in the list on the left. The *Fonts* page lists the names of all fonts used in the document and their status will be displayed. If a font is marked as *Incomplete*, it means that although the font shows on the screen, the font file required for printing is missing. You will need to reinstall the font. If a font is listed as *Missing*, it means the font used in the document is not installed on your computer, and you will need to purchase it. These types of font problems can occur when opening files created on other computers. Don't simply replace the font with another font of the same name, because fonts purchased from different vendors will have differences in font design, letter shape, and spacing. Visual 13–17 shows a sample of Garamond from two different digital type manufacturers. The point sizes and weights of each sample are identical. But, look at the differences in the overall color, letter width, the design of the capital G's and the shape of the bowls. Substituting a typeface with the same name, but from different manufacturers is generally not a perfect match, and will usually result in the copy reflowing, which can be disastrous!

VISUAL | 13–17 |

Although typefaces from different manufacturers share the same name, their characteristics may be quite different.

Garamond Sample from Adobe

Garamond Sample from Bitstream

If you are unable to locate the correct typeface, you may need to replace it throughout the document. You can replace fonts in the *Package* dialog box by selecting the **Find Font** button. In the upper half of the *Find Font* dialog, select the font you want to replace. Then choose the replacement font in the lower half. You can then choose to replace the fonts one occurrence at a time, or all at once. (Font replacement can also be performed by selecting *Type>Find Font.*) Whenever you replace fonts, you need to proof your document again, to make sure none of the text has shifted position.

VISUAL | 13–18 |

Use the Find Font operation to replace fonts in a document. Resolve any font issues in a document so that the Package will be complete and correct.

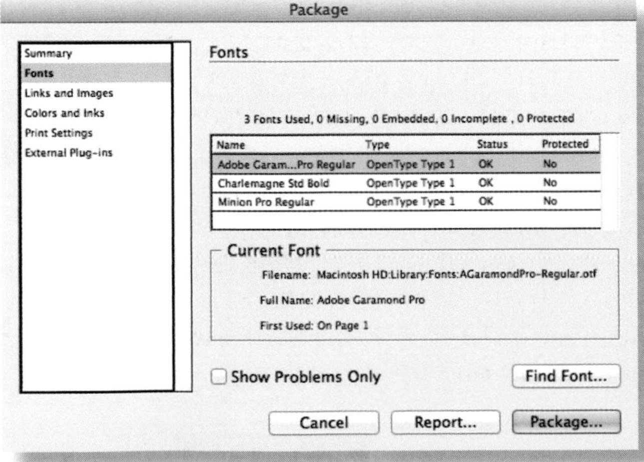

Like the *Links* panel, the *Package* feature also provides the status of *Links and Images*. If the original file has been moved since the file was created, InDesign needs help finding the new path to the image. Click on the missing image and click **Relink**. InDesign will lead you through the navigation necessary to find the source file. The *Package* feature summary won't alert you of any RGB files that are contained in Illustrator or PDF files. Those files will need to be opened in the original application and changed accordingly.

When you have remedied any problems, select **Package**, and InDesign will collect all the fonts and images used to build the document. You will be asked to save the document and will have the opportunity to provide printing instructions (Visual 13–19). Next, all the elements required to print your job are saved in one, organized folder, that you can send to your printer.

Printing Instructions

Filename: Metro Annual Report
Contact: Terry Rydberg
Company: Bluebird Ridge Design
Address: 11792 Jacobs Avenue
Northfield
Phone: 262 566 5454 Fax:
Email: trydberg@mac.com
Instructions: Print 5000, shrink wrap in groups of 25, package 50 to carton.
Ship to warehouse at 800 Capitol
Send invoice to Bluebird Ridge
Continue
Cancel

VISUAL | 13–19 |

Completing the Printing Instructions form during the Package operation provides easy access to project information your printer may need.

The project's done, you've packaged it, and it is all ready to go to the printer. But wait—you just realized that you forgot to check spelling one final time. Since your document is still open, you run spell check and find three spelling errors that would have appeared in the final version. Whew! That was close. You save your document, feeling relieved that you remembered this crucial production step. But guess what—you haven't fixed the spelling on the InDesign document that's packaged and ready to go to the printer! When you package a project, the components that go into the folder—the InDesign file, links, and fonts—are actually duplicates. Once the packaging operation has been completed, any changes you make to the original working document requires you to either repackage the entire job, or replace the InDesign document in the packaged folder with your revised version. This scenario is usually what has happened when my students say, *"I can't believe there are still spelling errors! I know I ran spell check and caught those mistakes before I turned in that project!"*

▸ *production tip*

Always check spelling before packaging a document!

▸ MOVING TOWARD MASTERY

James Wamser, Ripon Printers, is an Adobe Certified Instructor with over 20 years of experience in the graphic arts industry. James provides training and technical support for Ripon's customers, as well as its prepress department. James has been working with Adobe InDesign prior to the release of version 1.0, and is an InDesign instructor at Waukesha County Technical College. He co-chairs the Milwaukee InDesign User Group, is an author at Lynda.com and has spoken at numerous industry events over the years.

WAMSER'S ESSENTIAL PREPRESS TIPS

InDesign CS6 offers powerful tools for the creative professional as well as the prepress specialist. The following tips will help you identify and prevent potential problems when preparing your files for commercial printing.

- ***Preflighting** is a process that examines a file for potential printing problems. This process will look at many issues including: color use, resolution, and font issues. Every printer has unique printing specifications. These requirements are called **preflight profiles**. You can create preflight profiles yourself, or better yet, ask your commercial printer to provide them for you. The image below shows the **Preflight** profile that Ripon Printers in Wisconsin, provides to customers.*

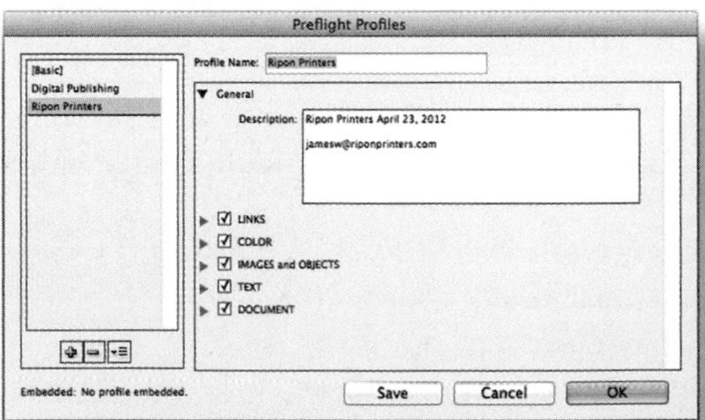

When enabled, CS6 provides a continual preflight status update in the bottom left corner of the document window.

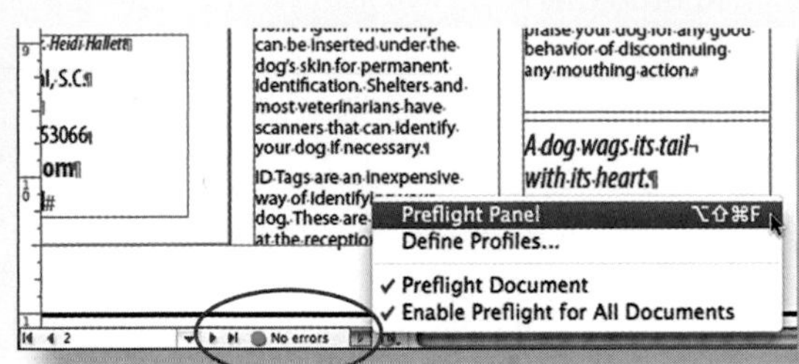

The preflight function checks for numerous production issues, and notifies you of problems including any low resolution images, bleed issues and live area concerns (meaning the images or type are too close to the trim edge). If an error appears, open the Preflight panel to identify and remedy the situation. Sending out errorless files saves time and money, and keeps production on schedule.

- ***Rich Black** is a defined color used in full-color printing and is composed of 60% Cyan, 40% Magenta, 20% Yellow, and 100% Black. The advantage of creating and using a rich black swatch is that the final print will show a black that is more **opaque.** However, rich black is a different color than Process Black. When you are using InDesign, the application preference is set to display all blacks as rich black. You should change this application preference so that you can see where Process Black and rich black are used in your document. Choose **Display All Blacks Accurately** in Preferences.*

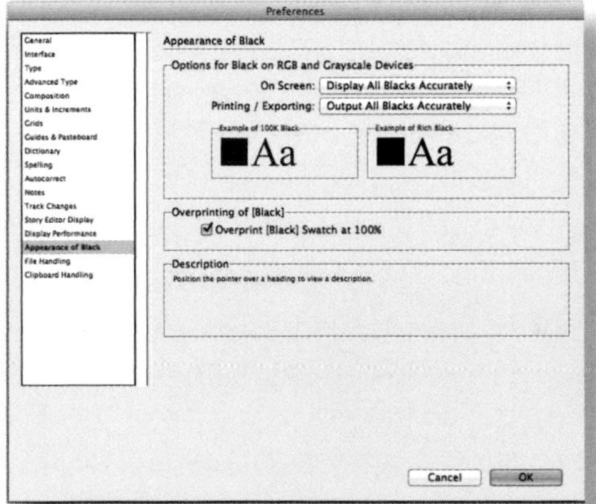

▸MOVING TOWARD MASTERY

- *The **Separations Preview Panel** is one I use all the time. (**Window>Output>Separations Preview**). This panel serves several purposes: It allows you to see all the inks used in a document (CMYK + spot inks). It also shows you the percentages of inks used in images and type. This is useful when verifying that a large solid black area contains rich black (CMYK).*

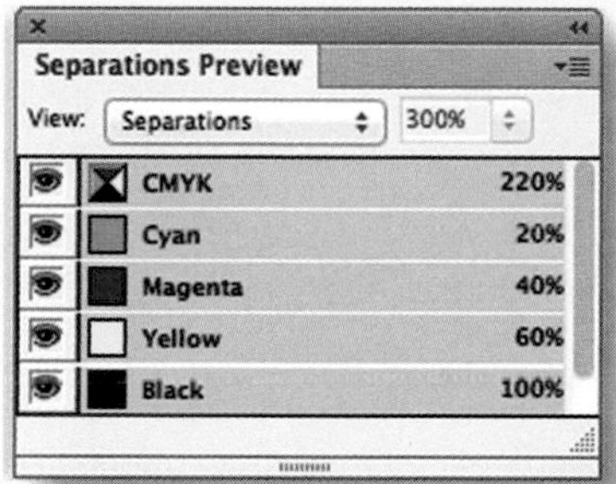

- *In Chapter 12, you learned how to print separations to verify the number of colors in your document. Using **Separations Preview**, verify the individual colors used in your document by clicking the eye next to each color swatch.*
- ***Find Font.** Fonts have a history of causing reflow and output issues. (That's one of the reasons why so many people have embraced the PDF workflow.) Anytime you see text highlighted with pink in your document, it means the required font is missing on your computer. The **Find Font** dialog box automatically pops up before printing to alert you of any problems. This dialog box will tell you how many fonts are used, notify you of any missing fonts, and give you the opportunity to replace fonts as necessary. Please be aware that you can access **Find Font** at any time by going to **Type>Find Font**.*

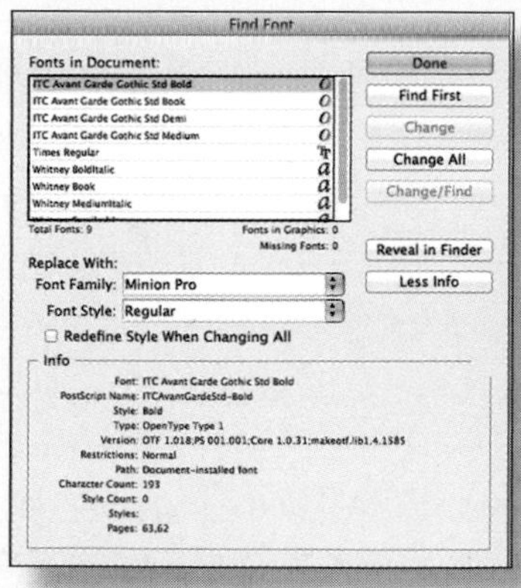

- ***Exporting PDFs.** PDF is an acronym for **Portable Document Format**, and was developed by Adobe Systems in 1993. PDF files can be opened and printed by Adobe Acrobat. In InDesign, you can export a file to a PDF, and it will retain its overall layout, fonts, and hyperlinks.*
- *PDF files, when prepared correctly, streamline the printing process while providing more consistent and reliable results. They eliminate delays due to missing components such as fonts, images and graphics. Using PDF files in printing is referred to as PDF workflow. Printers who use the PDF workflow have individual specifications for how a PDF file should be prepared. It is important to communicate with your printer to create a **PDF Preset** that will contain the specifications required for the job. Once you create the settings, they are saved for future use, and you can export them, eliminating the need to recreate them on each computer. Our Ripon Printers preset is shown below.*

- *To create a **PDF Preset**, choose **Adobe PDF Presets> Define** from the **File** menu. Or, you can use one of the default **PDF Presets**. For instance, if you are e-mailing a PDF of an InDesign document to show a concept to a client, you should select **Smallest File Size**. Notice the three PDF/X presets in the list. The PDF/X presets are standards created to eliminate many common output issues. PDF/X-4 is*

▸ MOVING TOWARD MASTERY

the newest standard. As shown below, you can begin with the basic settings in any of these standards and then customize it for your printer's specific needs. You can see why it is so important to work closely with your printer when selecting or creating PDF presets.

Define...
[High Quality Print]...
[PDF/X-1a:2001]...
[PDF/X-3:2002]...
[PDF/X-4:2008]...
[Press Quality]...
[Smallest File Size]...

When I create PDF presets, I don't rely on the document bleed settings in the InDesign document; I create a bleed in the preset just in case the person who set up the InDesign document did not include them. This leads to the next prepress tip...

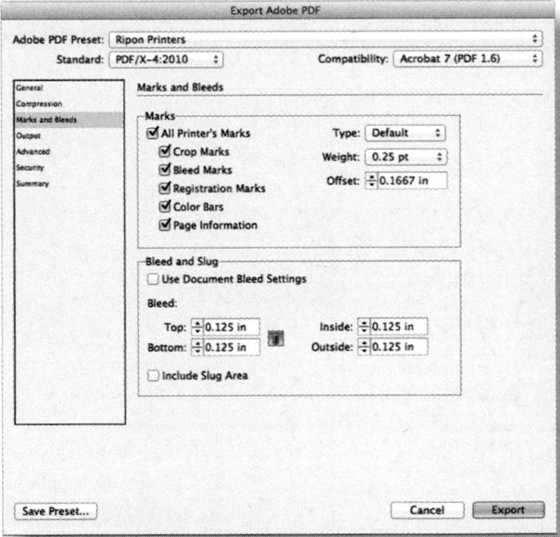

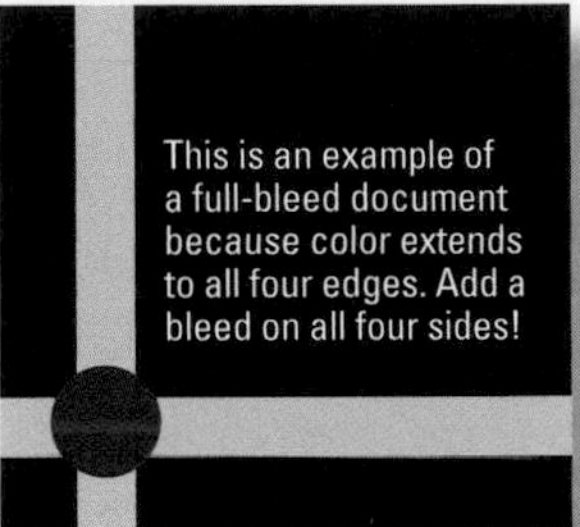

This is an example of a full-bleed document because color extends to all four edges. Add a bleed on all four sides!

- ***Build Bleeds.*** *As you know, a bleed is any image or object that extends to the edge of a page. During the printing process, the document is printed on oversized paper, with the bleed images extending beyond the trim size. After the ink has dried, the project is cut down to size, leaving crisp images that run out to the edge. When creating a new document or document preset, you need to enter a bleed amount of 0.125" (1/8") on each side with a bleed. This will create guides indicating where the bleed should extend. This area is outside the final size of the document. Each page element that bleeds must extend out to the bleed guide. Without bleed guides, InDesign won't recognize any part of an image that extends beyond the document's trim edge.*

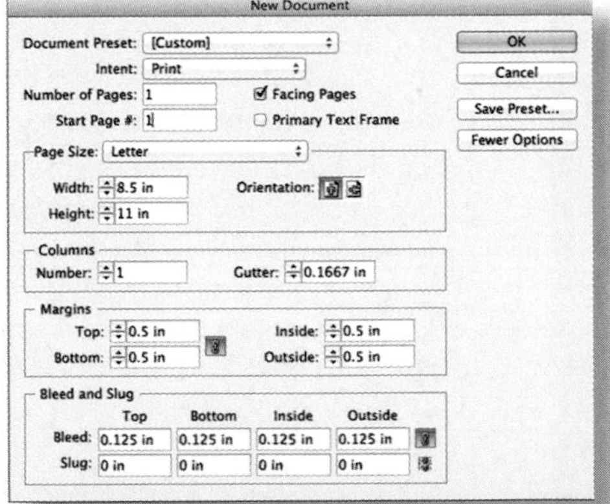

You can add a bleed to your document at any time during production. Go to ***File>Document Setup*** *and enter* ***0.125"*** *on each edge with a bleed.*

► MOVING TOWARD MASTERY

- ***Use Overprint Preview.*** *There are many ways colors interact with each other in a document. First, they can be printed next to each other. When colors are printed right next to each other, the press operator is going to make sure the colors are exactly aligned. When they are, the job is in register. When the colors are a hairline distance apart, the job is said to have tight register. Four-color process printing, with each separate plate composed of a series of dots, has extremely tight register.*
- *Another way colors interact is to have one color* ***knock out*** *the other. This means that the top object cuts away any color beneath it. In Example "A", below, the yellow circle has been placed on top of the blue box. Example "B" shows how the images would actually be printed. The yellow circle has been pulled aside to show that the blue area underneath is gone. This is a simulation of how a knock out works. By default, all colors except black knock out the colors underneath.*

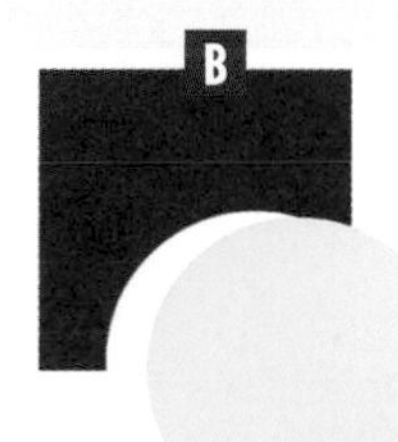

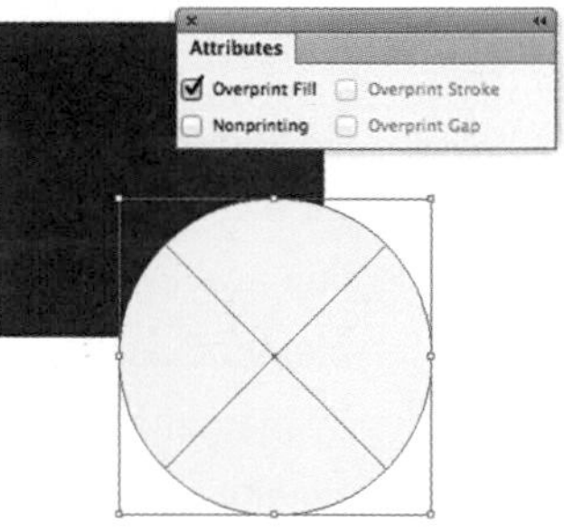

- *The picture above shows that the circle has now been assigned* ***Overprint Fill*** *on the* ***Attributes*** *panel.*
- *You know that the area where the colors intersect should look be a different color. But you can't really tell how it will look…or can you?* ***Overprint Preview*** *is a great feature found under the View menu. As shown below, you will see just how the colors will look when printed.*

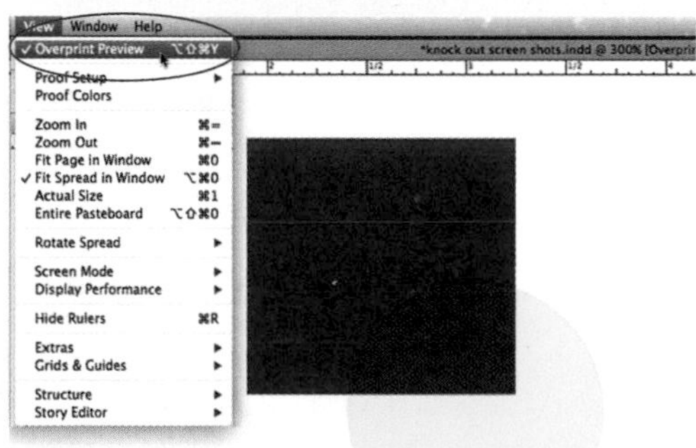

- *Colors can also* ***overprint*** *each other. When colors overprint, the ink goes on top of the color below, but does not knock it out. By default, black always overprints other colors. Then, how do you create an area of overlapping colors? The Attributes panel.*
- *You were introduced to the* ***Attributes*** *panel in Chapter 12, and its capability to apply* ***Nonprinting*** *to image or text, preventing the object from being printed. In the* ***Attributes*** *panel you can set an object's fill or stroke color to overprint, rather than using the default knockout setting.*

The ability to see how an image or object will overprint right on screen is a huge time saver and can help you identify any problems before a single proof is made. By the way, when you open the ***Separations Preview*** *panel and select* ***Separations*** *in the* ***View*** *menu,* ***Overprint Preview*** *is automatically enabled.*

One last word—each print shop has its own set of technical specifications. Prepress managers are available to answer your questions. Make use of their expertise during your production process!

Summary

The biggest thing you have probably learned from this chapter is that there is much more to document preparation than simply dropping in text and images!

The chapter began with input issues, describing the production considerations for a variety of artwork. You know the difference between continuous tone, and line artwork. You know that raster or bitmap images are composed of picture elements, called pixels, and are resolution dependent. Vector images are created by mathematical formulas, and are resolution independent. You know that image resolution describes how many pixels are contained in an image. And you know that the more pixels in the image, the more detail will be recorded. Finally, since printing presses cannot do shading, continuous tone artwork must be converted to a series of dots that will create the illusion of shading.

On the output side, we discussed the difference between *Actual* and *Effective ppi.* Although you may have started with a bitmap image with appropriate *Actual* resolution, the *Effective* output resolution is changed by scaling, during the production process. You used Photoshop to resample and resize raster images to achieve ideal *Effective ppi.*

InDesign's powerful *Package* operation was discussed, and you saw first-hand, that it can be disastrous to make last-minute font substitutions—even if the replacement font has the same name as the original!

There's a lot to know about production and we've just scratched the surface. As a new designer, you will have fewer errors if you follow these production steps:

1. *Format document size, margins, and columns.*
2. *Add text insets and align strokes if necessary.*
3. *Place and size graphics. Specify spot or CMYK color.*
4. *Do the typing or place all the text.*
5. *Add paragraph formatting.*
6. *Add character formatting and glyphs.*
7. *Proof carefully and print. Proof again.*
8. *Make a folded or trimmed mock-up, if necessary.*
9. *Check the images in the Links panel.*
10. *Package the document.*

Bottom line: when in doubt, ask someone with more experience!

▸ IN REVIEW

1. What is the difference between continuous tone art and line art?
2. What is a bitmap image?
3. What is a vector image?
4. What does image resolution refer to?
5. What is a pixel?
6. Why is it dangerous to substitute fonts in a document—even if their names are identical?
7. How does scaling affect a resolution dependent image?
8. You have pulled a logo from the web to use as a placeholder image. The image has been scaled to 450%. Explain why the image quality is poor at this scale.
9. What does a yellow triangle in the Links panel mean?
10. What does a red circle with a question mark in the Links panel indicate?
11. What is the difference between actual and effective ppi?
12. An 300 ppi image is being used at 227% in your InDesign document. Describe the steps you would take, when editing the image to keep the resolution at 300 ppi, while changing the scale to 227%.

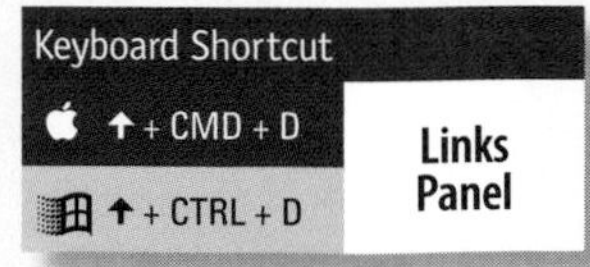

▸ CHAPTER 13 PROJECTS

The voyage continues! You will create and apply table styles and place an InDesign document. Take the time to create a booklet and trim the assembled project for a nice addition to your portfolio.

- Go to: http://www.cengagebrain.com
- Type: Rydberg
- Click Exploring InDesign CS6 in the list of search results.
- When the book's main page is displayed, click the Access button under Free Study Tools.
- To download files, select a chapter number and then click on the Artwork & Resources tab on the left navigation bar to download the files.

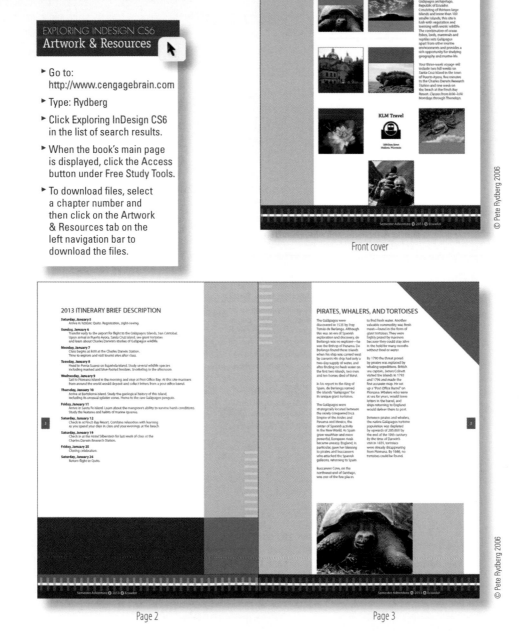

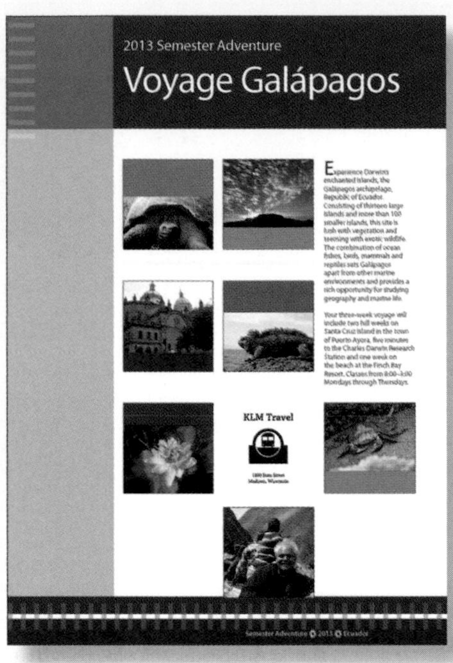

Front cover

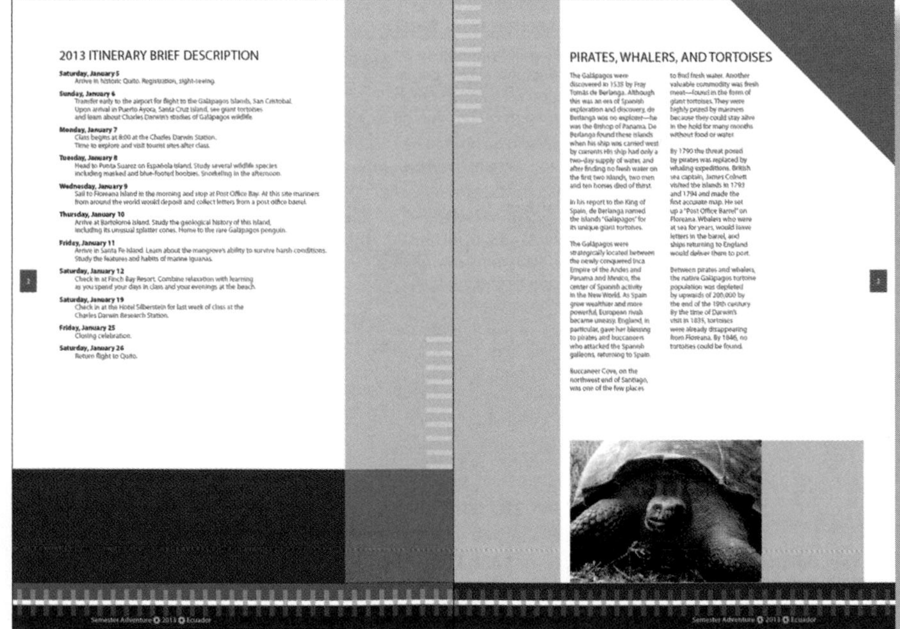

Page 2

Page 3

▸CHAPTER 13 PROJECTS

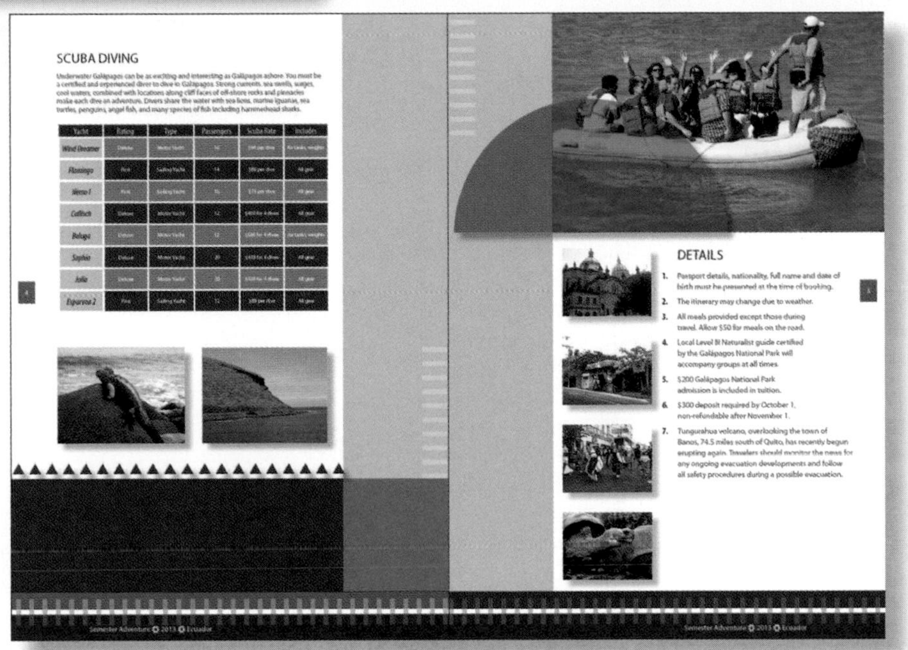

Page 4

Page 5

© Pete Rydberg 2006

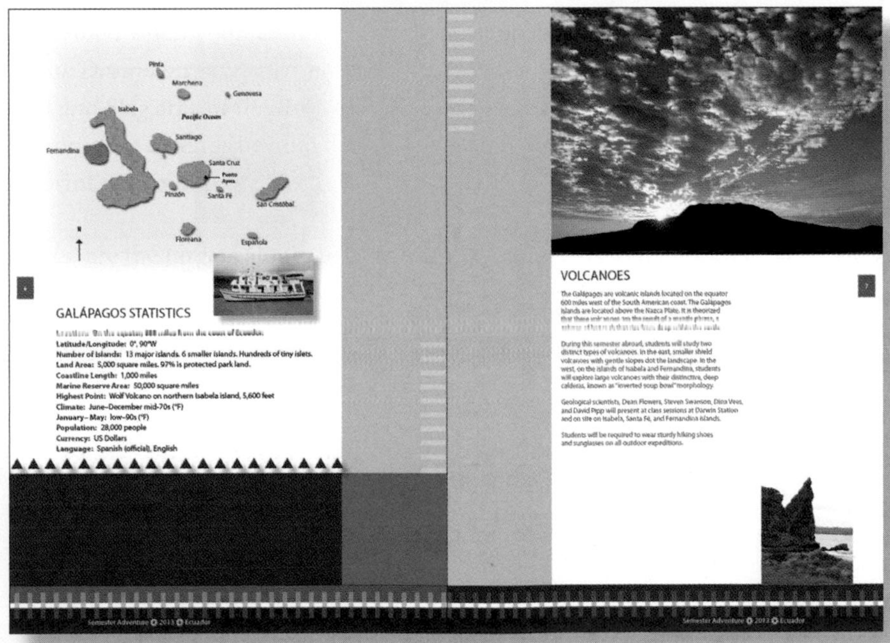

Page 6

Page 7

© Pete Rydberg 2006

| Basic Graphic Elements |

objectives

- *Review basic drawing tools*
- *Master the mighty Pen tool*
- *Create and modify open, closed, and compound paths*
- *Integrate drawn elements with text*

introduction

Twenty years ago if you wanted to buy a comfortable family car, you more than likely bought a four-door sedan. If you wanted to haul cargo, you bought a pickup truck or full-size van. Both did a good job for their particular purposes.

Then someone asked the perfect question: Why not combine the two? And the minivan was born! It was the perfect way for the whole family to go to Grandma's, and just the right vehicle for picking up a few sheets of 4' × 8' drywall for that weekend project in the utility room. The minivan changed the course of the U.S. auto industry and has proven to be one of the most successful innovations in American transportation.

InDesign has combined the digital page capability of an electronic publishing program and the creative artistry of a drawing program into the most successful innovation in graphics software today. The extraordinary page layout features of InDesign are the reason this program is taking the world by storm. But with the addition of many drawing features, similar to those you'll find in Adobe Illustrator, you now have a tool that—like the minivan—is changing the face of an entire industry.

If you have already worked with Adobe Illustrator, much of this chapter will be a review of what you already know. Have fun combining your drawing skills with the good typography and digital page layout principles you have been learning in *Exploring Adobe InDesign CS6*.

graphics tools

You already know how to use the *Rectangle*, *Ellipse*, and *Polygon* tools to create two-dimensional shapes, and the *Line* tool for—well—lines. You know that the **Shift** key will constrain shapes to perfect squares or circles, and lines to increments of 45 degrees. You know that if you hold down the **Option** or **Alt** key while you drag, you will draw a shape from its center instead of from a corner.

▸ *Create a shape with specific dimensions*

In the following exercise, you will learn to make a shape by specifying dimensions numerically in a dialog box.

1. Make an **8.5" × 11"** document (with the ruler set to inches) and select either the *Rectangle* or *Ellipse* tool (not the *Polygon* tool). Put the cursor where you want the upper left corner of the shape positioned and click (do not drag).

2. The dialog box for creating the Rectangle or Ellipse will appear. Enter *Width* and *Height* dimensions in the fields and press **Return**.

3. Do this a few times to make several different-sized shapes. If you hold down the **Option** key (Mac) or **Alt** key (Windows) when you click on your document, the shape will be centered on that point.

4. Use the *Direct Selection* tool and drag one of the points of a shape. You can distort the shape any way you want it. **Click+drag** on a line segment and move it around without moving the rest of the shape. Select different combinations of points and line segments by dragging a marquee, or **Shift+clicking**. See what kinds of weird shapes you can make.

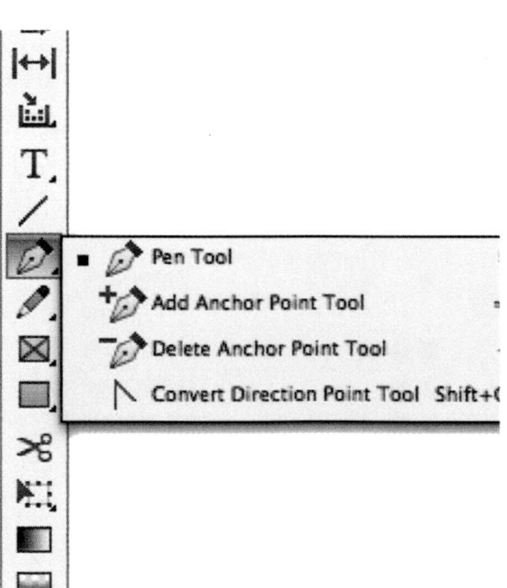

VISUAL |14–1|

Pen tool options in the Tools panel. Notice how to access them with keyboard shortcuts

THE MIGHTY PEN TOOL

One of the most versatile tools in the InDesign arsenal is the *Pen* tool. For some, it can also be a difficult one to master. I sat in my first Illustrator class for hours, trying to figure out why my shapes never ended up the way I intended them to look. But once I mastered the *Pen* tool, it became one of my favorite tools.

▸ *Make a closed path*

InDesign creates shapes using *paths*. Paths are made up of a series of line segments, which can be either curved or straight. These line segments are connected by anchor points, which can be either corners or smooth. The *Rectangle*, *Ellipse*, and *Polygon* tools make closed paths—their paths are unbroken. If you were to break a line segment or anchor point on the path, it becomes an open shape. The *Pen* tool allows you to create both open and closed paths.

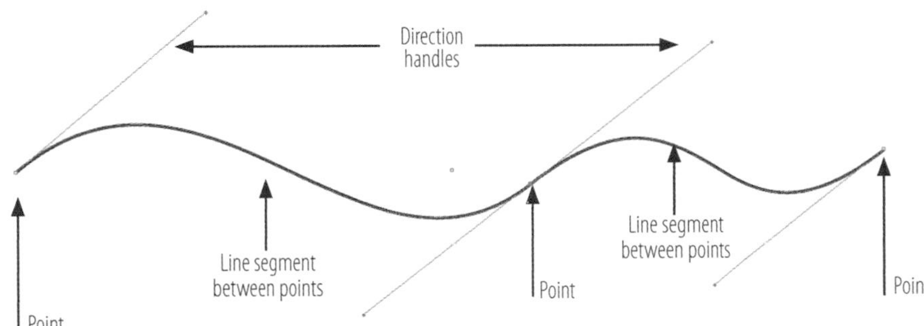

VISUAL | 14–2 |

Parts of a path.

1. Delete the shapes you made in your document and select the *Pen* tool. (As with every tool, always use the keyboard shortcut—in this case press **P**.) Set the ***Stroke*** color to **Black**, the *Width* to **1 pt.**, *Fill* to **[None]**. Place your cursor about two inches, in and two inches down, in your document (**X: 2** and **Y: 2**). Notice that the *Pen* cursor has a little "x" by it. This means that the path you are about to draw begins a new shape. Hold down **Shift, click+drag** horizontally to the right, about an inch. Release the ***mouse***, then the *Shift* key. As you were dragging, two direction handles appeared: one following the cursor and the other extending 180 degrees in the opposite direction (Visual 14–3). These direction handles are like a teeter-totter, pivoting on your anchor point. The direction handles are not part of the actual line segment you are drawing; they only point you in the direction the path will be going when you begin your next stroke. So far, you have only established an initial anchor point for the first segment of your shape.

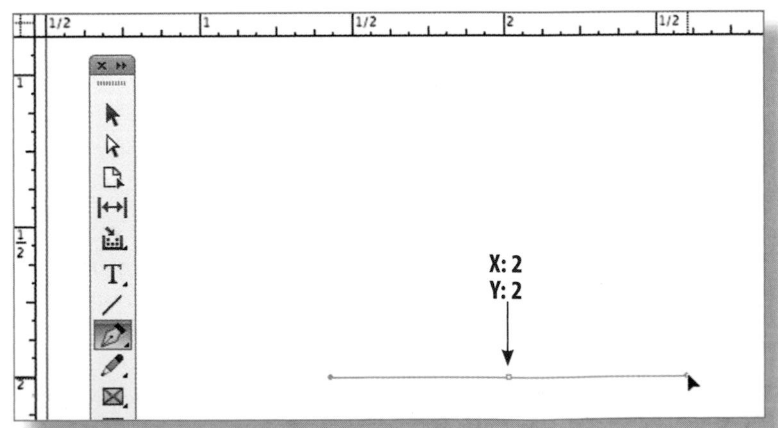

VISUAL | 14–3 |

Direction handles appear when you drag with the Pen tool.

▸MOVING TOWARD MASTERY

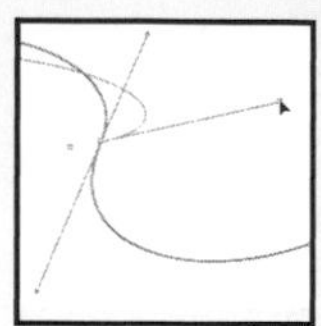

Direction handles for drawing tools are like hidden characters when you are working with text. They are not part of your shape and do not print, but they determine much of what your path will look like. Direction handles and anchor points—like hidden characters—give you a critical advantage: They allow you to see your document as the computer sees it.

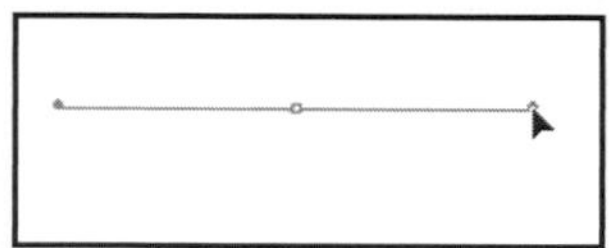

*Holding the **Shift** key while you drag with the **Pen** tool will constrain your direction handles to increments of 45 degrees, just as it does with the Line tool. Press **Shift** after you begin to drag. Holding **Shift** continuously may send your path in unexpected directions.*

2. When you release the mouse and the *Shift* key, the little "x" next to the *Pen* tool cursor disappears. This means that the next stroke of your pen will be "step two" in creating your path. Place the cursor at coordinate **X: 4** and **Y: 1**. Again, **click, Shift+drag** horizontally to the right, for about an inch. *Release* the mouse and the Shift key, and your path should look like Visual 14–4. You now have two anchor points and the first curved line segment of your shape.

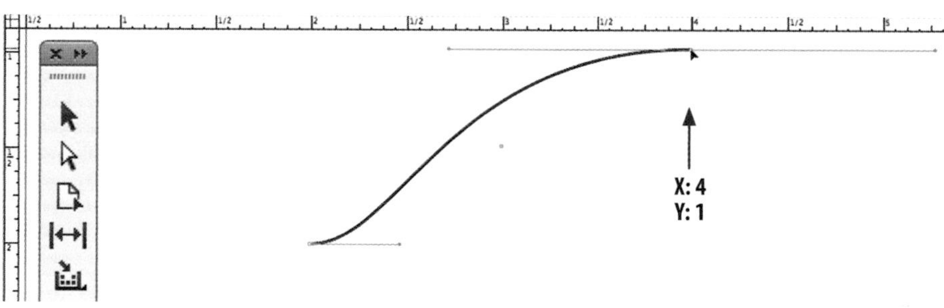

VISUAL | 14–4 |
Two anchor points have been established.

3. Place your cursor at these coordinates: **X: 6**; **Y: 2**. **Click, Shift + drag** horizontally to the right, for about an inch. Then, ***release*** the mouse and the *Shift* key. You now have a path that looks like a bell curve (Visual 14–5).

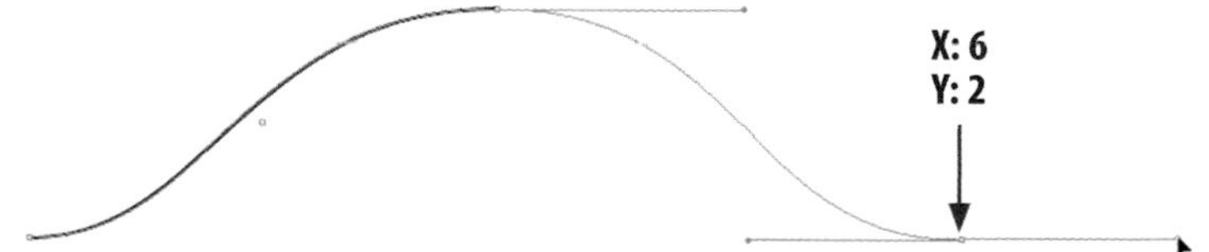

VISUAL | 14–5 |
The path takes the shape of a bell curve.

If you get interrupted in the middle of drawing a shape, you may return to your path and find the little "×" has reappeared next to your *Pen* tool cursor. This means you will begin a new path instead of continuing the same one you were working on. To get rid of the little "×" and continue with the original path, place your cursor over the last anchor point, when the "×" changes to a slash, **click** the mouse. You are now ready to continue with the next line segment of your path.

4. Apply a fill color to the path. Notice that you can fill a path that is not closed. An imaginary straight line, from the starting anchor point to the ending anchor point, is used as the boundary for the fill. Remove the fill, before you continue, by applying *[None]*.

5. Place your cursor at **X: 4** and **Y: 3**. This time, instead of dragging, simply **click**. You have established a new anchor point, but notice that the path is sharply curved at the previous point (Visual 14–6). The direction handle—extending further to the right—told this new line segment to continue on to the right, but your new anchor point told it to go the opposite direction: down and to the left. Choose *Undo*.

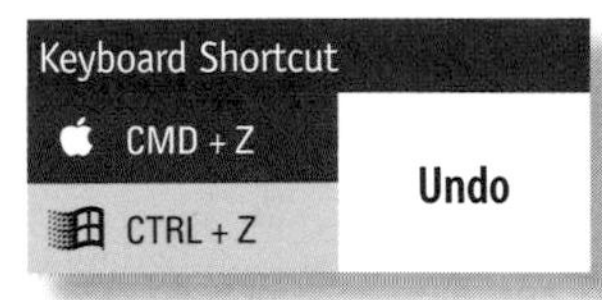

6. This time hold down the **Option** (Mac) or **Alt** (Windows) key and your *Pen* tool will turn into the *Convert Direction Point* tool (Visual 14–7).

X: 4
Y: 3

VISUAL | 14–6 |

A new anchor point changes the direction of the path.

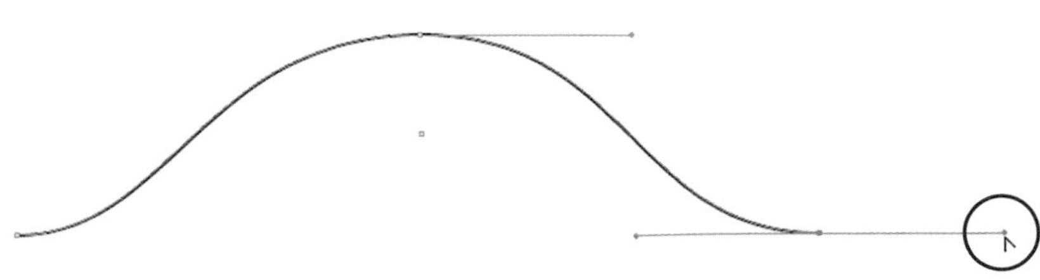

VISUAL | 14–7 |

Holding the Option or Alt key will change the Pen tool to the Convert Direction Point tool. Use the Convert Direction Point tool to move just one of the direction handles that extend from a selected point.

7. *Click* on the right end of the last direction handle you made and drag it down so that **X: 5** and **Y: 2.5** and ***release*** the mouse button (Visual 14–8).

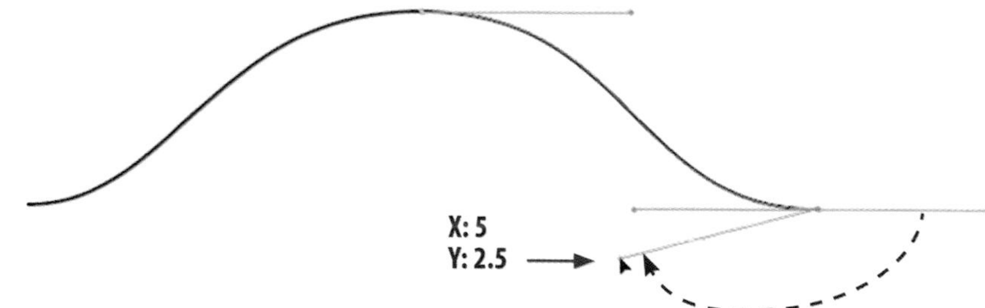

VISUAL | 14–8

Drag the direction handle dowı and to the left, as shown

© Cengage Learning 201:

8. *Release* the **Option** or **Alt** key and the *Pen* tool is active again. Place your cursor at approximately **X: 4**, **Y: 3**, *click* and *release*. Your new path now has a crisp corner at the previous anchor point (Visual 14–9). Your converted direction handle told the path to go down and to the left, and your new point also told the path to go down and to the left.

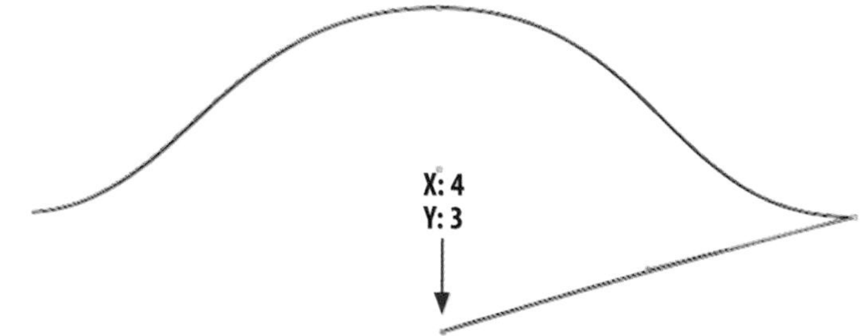

VISUAL | 14–9 |

A corner has been created at the previous anchor point.

© Cengage Learning 2013

9. Move the *Pen* tool to the first anchor point you made for your path. (Always check to see that there is no little "x" or slash next to your *Pen* tool cursor.) When you get close to the starting anchor point, a small circle should appear next to the *Pen* tool cursor. This means that your path will be closed with your next click. **Click** to close your path. It should look something like Visual 14–10. Now, apply a fill to your path. Practice applying different colors to the fill, as well as applying *[None]*.

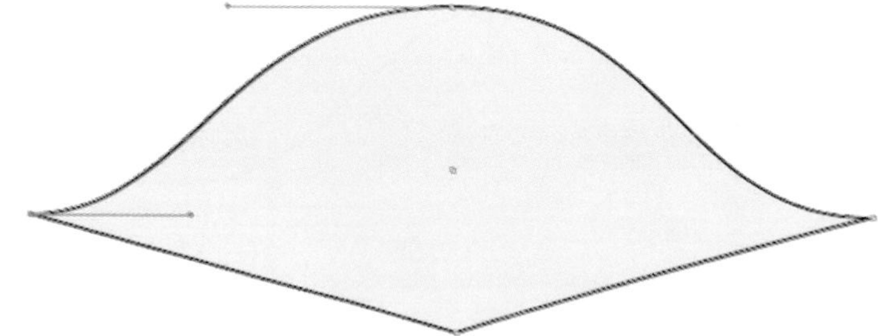

VISUAL | 14–10 |

Closing the path completes your shape.

© Cengage Learning 2013

▸ *Make an open path*

You made your first open path in Chapter 11, working with text on a path. Let's review and practice another open path.

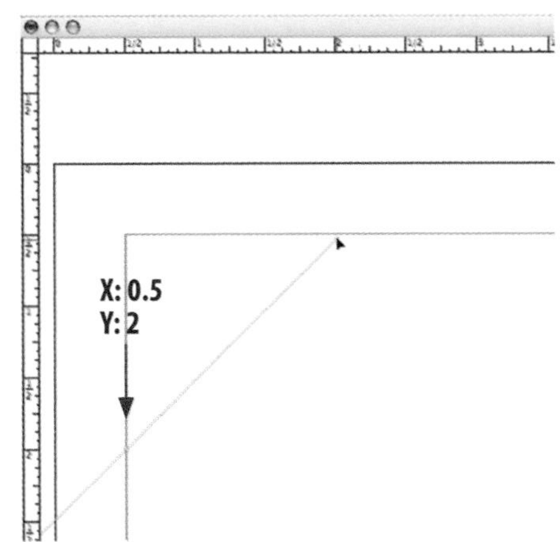

VISUAL |14–11|

Drag up and to the right.

1. Delete your bell curve. Place the *Pen* tool (now with the little "x" next to it) at **X: 0.5**, **Y: 2**. **Click+drag** up and to the right, until **X: 2** and **Y: 0.5** (Visual 14–1). *Release* the mouse button.

2. Now place your *Pen* tool cursor at **X: 4** and **Y: 2**, **click+drag** a new line segment down and to the right, until **X: 5** and **Y: 3** (Visual 14–12). *Release* the mouse button.

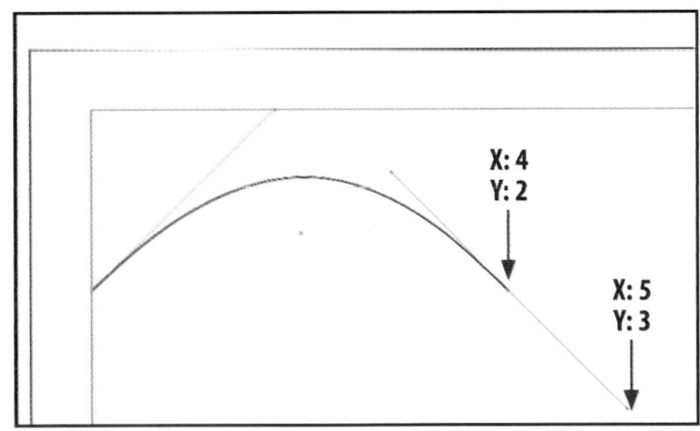

VISUAL |14–12|

Drag a new line down and to the right.

3. Finally, place your tool cursor at **X: 7**, **Y: 1.5**. **Click+drag** up to **X: 8**, **Y: 0.5** and *release* the mouse button (Visual 14–13).

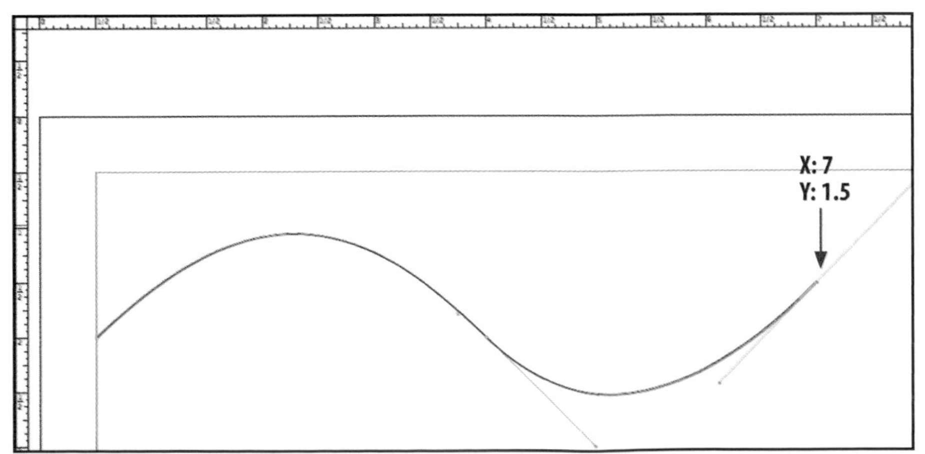

VISUAL |14–13|

Drag the tool up and to the right.

4. Your path looks like a wave of the ocean, similar to the wave in Visual 14–14. This line is an open path because the last anchor point is not connected to the point of origin. Select a fill color. Again, the open path is filled along an imaginary line that connects the starting and ending anchor points. The effect is not exactly what you might have expected. Change the fill back to ***[None]***.

VISUAL | 14–14 |

The open path is filled along an imaginary line between the starting and ending anchor points.

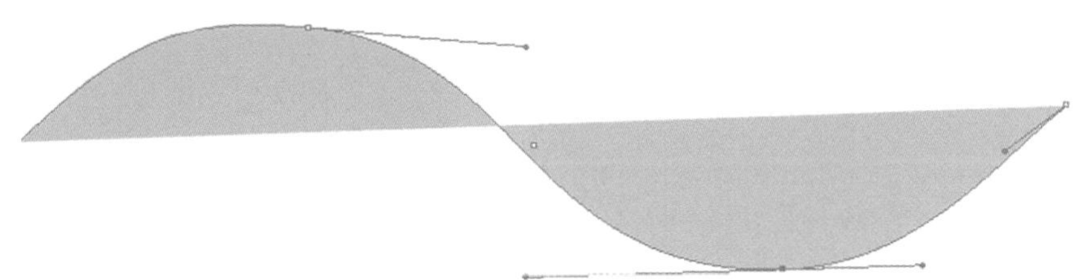

5. Switch to the ***Direct Selection*** tool, while still using the ***Pen*** tool, by holding down **Command** (Mac) or **Control** (Windows) and **click** anywhere on the top curve. You have selected the first of the two line segments in your "wave" and you can see the direction handles indicating the direction each segment is going (Visual 14–15).

VISUAL | 14–15 |

New direction handles appear.

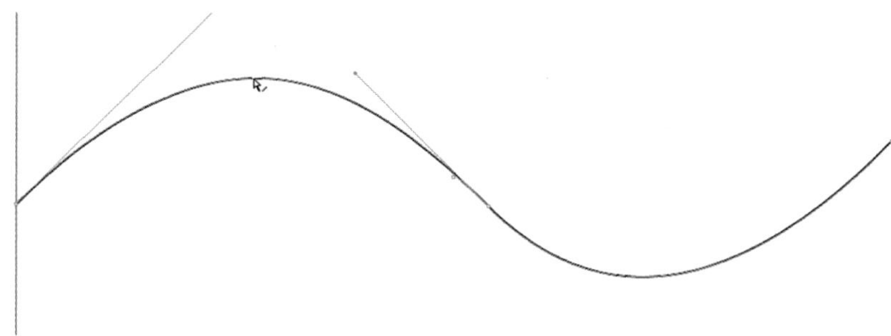

6. While continuing to hold the modifier key, **click** on on the direction handle extending up from the middle anchor point and move it back and forth. Your wave changes pitch. Notice that both direction handles move simultaneously (Visual 14–16).

VISUAL | 14–16 |

Moving both direction handles with the Direct Selection tool.

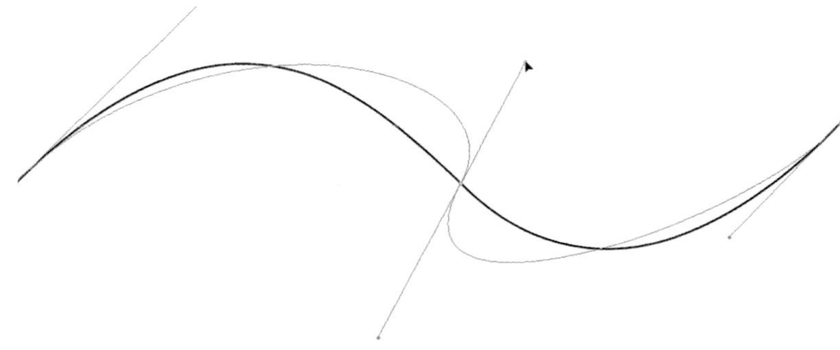

7. Select the *Convert Direction Point* tool by pressing **Shift+C**. Again, when you move the end of the top direction handle, it changes the shape of the wave, but only the selected direction handle moves (Visual 14–17). You have just changed a smooth anchor point into a corner anchor point.

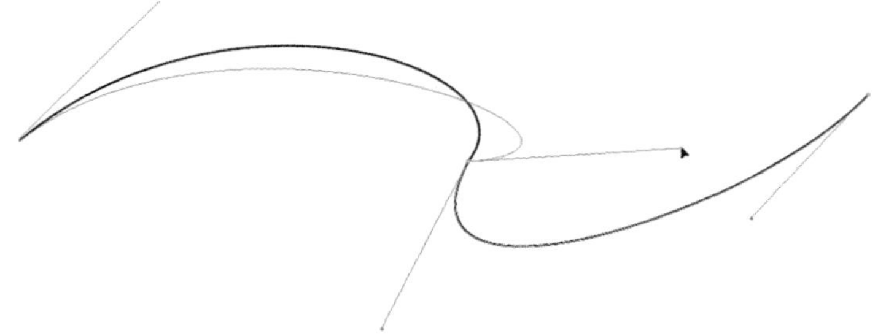

VISUAL | 14–17 |
Moving one direction handle with the Convert Direction tool.

8. Go back to the *Direct Selection* tool by pressing **A**. **Click** on the middle anchor point to select it. This time, instead of moving the direction handles, move the point itself to the left (Visual 14–18). The curve of your wave changes dramatically as you move the middle anchor point between the start and end anchor points. Move the center anchor point of your wave to the left, right, up and down. If you want to make your wave longer or shorter, select one of the end anchor points and move it in or out.

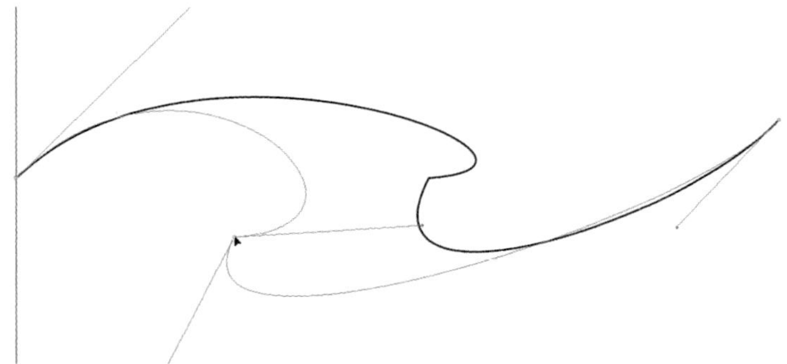

VISUAL | 14–18 |
Moving the middle anchor point with the Direct Selection tool.

If an anchor point is hollow, it is not selected; an anchor point that is filled in is selected. In Visual 14–19, you will see one more small box to the left of the path. This point is not an anchor point, and you do not draw it. This box indicates the center of your path's bounding box. It functions just like the center point of a frame or circle: You can click and drag it with a selection tool to move the entire path.

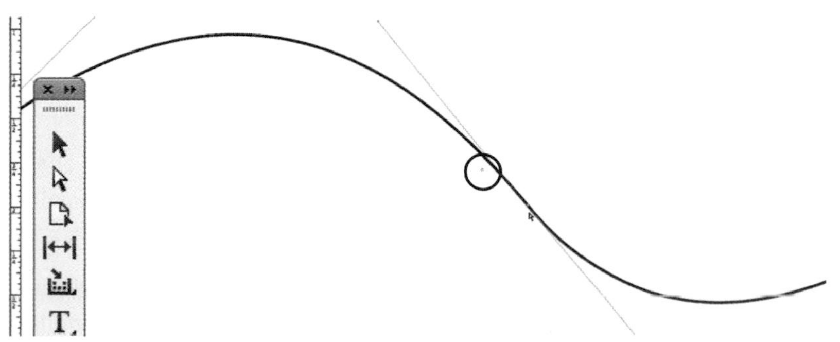

VISUAL | 14–19 |
Use a selection tool and click+drag the center point of the bounding box to move the entire path.

▸ *Add and delete anchor points*

You will sometimes finish a path you thought was perfect, only to discover that you need an extra anchor point here or there, or maybe there are too many points in one area. No problem! Adding and deleting points in InDesign is just a click away.

1. Get your wave back to its original shape or (if it's beyond repair) delete it and make a new one, repeating Steps 1 through 3 in the previous exercise.

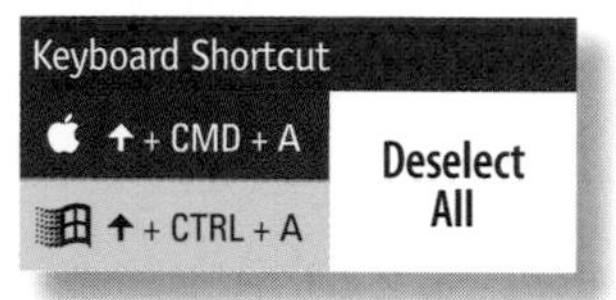

2. Let's say your wave is not wavy enough. Press the **equals** sign (=) to activate the *Add Anchor Point* tool. The *Add Anchor Point* tool has a small plus sign (+) by the *Pen* tool cursor (Visual 14–20). Click in two or three places on each segment of your wave. (Notice that direction handles extend from each new point, and the new points all remain selected.) *Deselect all* and press **A** to switch to the *Direct Selection* tool.

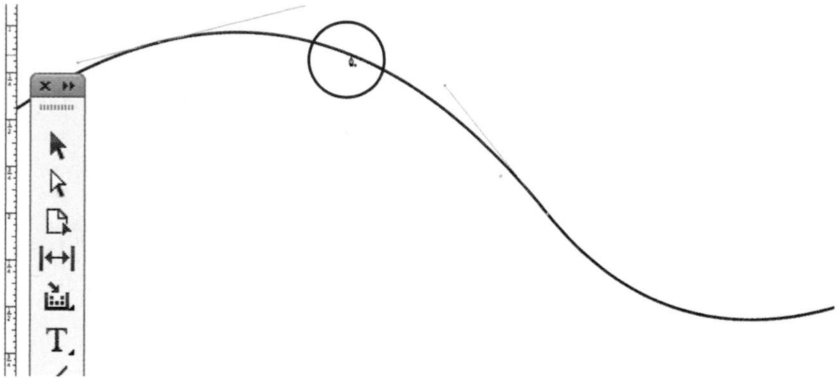

VISUAL | 14–20 |
The Add Anchor Point tool about to add a point to a path.

3. Click on the line and you will see all the anchor points are hollow (deselected). Drag each of the new anchor points up or down to make a series of smaller, irregular waves, similar to Visual 14–21. Practice adjusting the length and angles of the direction handles until you are comfortable with the process.

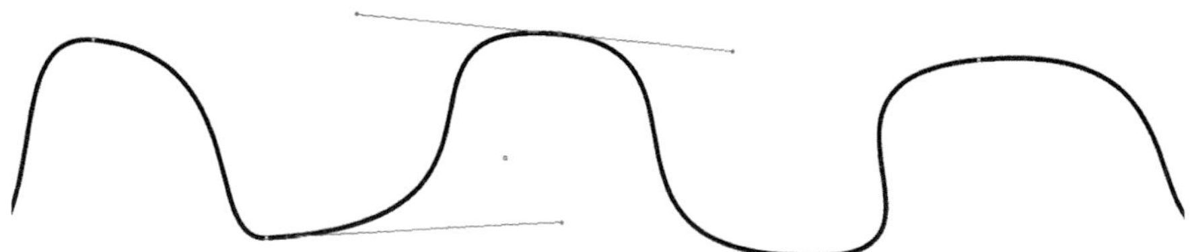

VISUAL | 14–21 |
Drag the new anchor points up or down to make shorter waves.

4. To delete one or more points from a path, press the *hyphen* key (-) to activate the *Delete Anchor Point* tool. As you click on the anchor points you want to delete, they will disappear.

▸ *Manage smooth points and corner points*

Smooth points are made by dragging after you place an anchor point. Smooth points have direction handles. *Corner points* are made by one click of your mouse. Corner points do not have direction handles.

1. Delete everything in your document and press **P** for the *Pen* tool. You will use the directions in Visuals 14–22 to 14–26 to make a circle by dragging four successive curve points: one at the top, the right side, the bottom, and the left side. **Click** on the starting anchor point to close the circle. (This last point is a little tricky. You will need to drag the *Pen* tool to the left to create a reasonable looking curve. Don't worry if your circle is a little lopsided.)

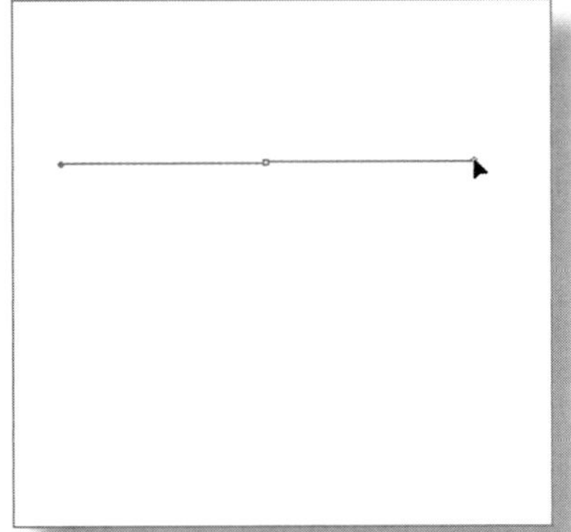

VISUAL | 14–22 |

Click with the Pen tool, and Shift+drag to make the starting point of the circle.

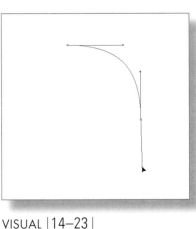

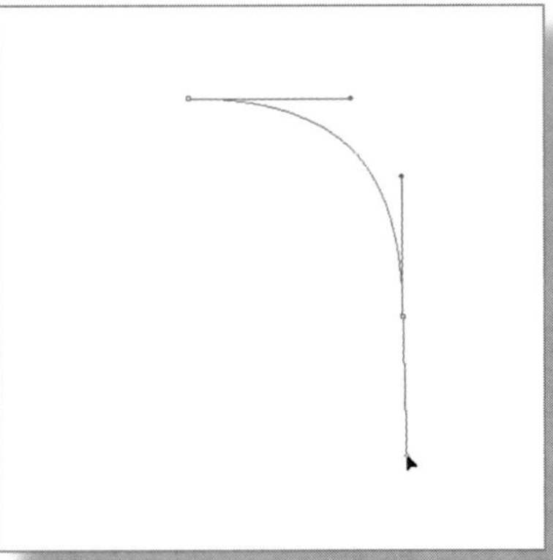

VISUAL | 14–23 |

Click with the Pen tool, and Shift+drag to make the first segment of the circle.

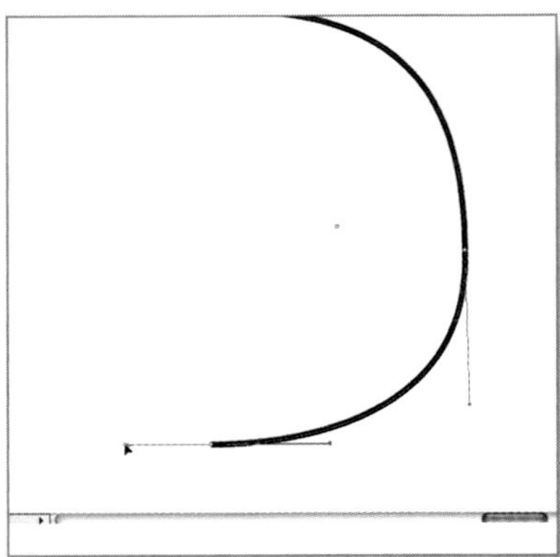

VISUAL | 14–24 |

Click with the Pen tool, and Shift+drag to make the second segment of the circle.

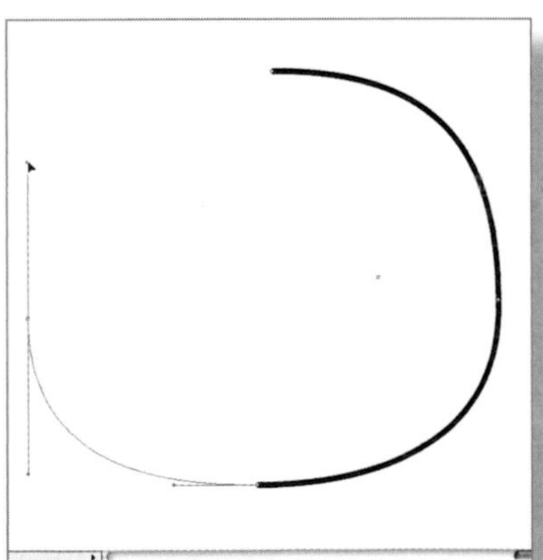

VISUAL | 14–25 |

Click and Shift+drag to make the third segment of the circle.

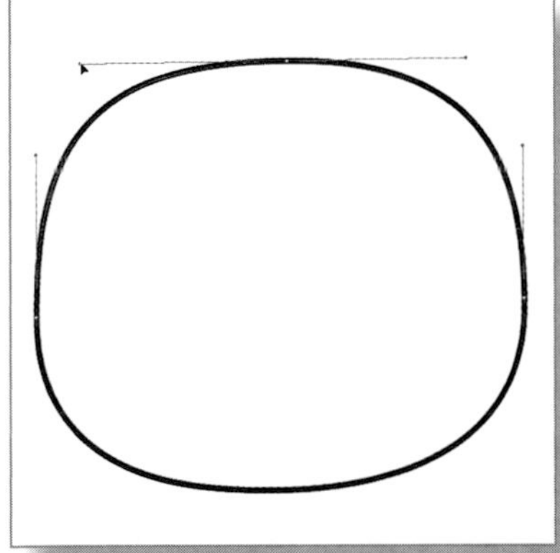

VISUAL | 14–26 |

Click the starting point and Shift+drag to the left to complete the shape.

When using the *Pen* tool, use as few anchor points as possible. The fewer the points, the smoother your path will be. Too many anchor points will make what should be a graciously curved line look jagged and choppy. Practice making circles with only four anchor points.

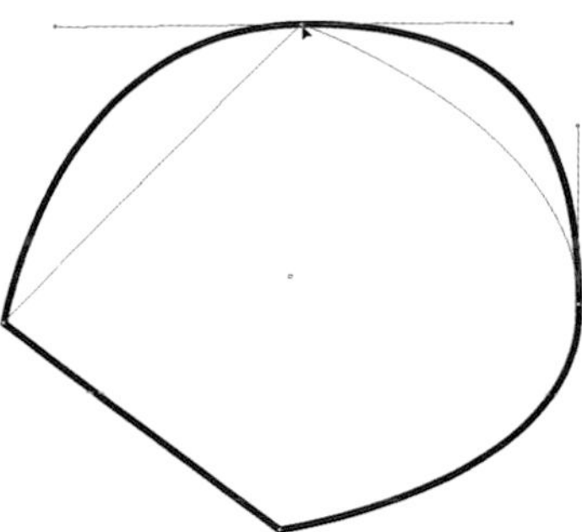

VISUAL | 14–27 |
The Convert Direction Point tool changes smooth points to corner points.
© Cengage Learning 2013

2. Hold down the **Option** or **Alt** key to switch to the *Convert Direction Point* tool and click on one of your smooth anchor points. It becomes a corner point (Visual 14–27). Click the *Convert Direction Point* tool on the other three points. Your circle has become a rectangle.

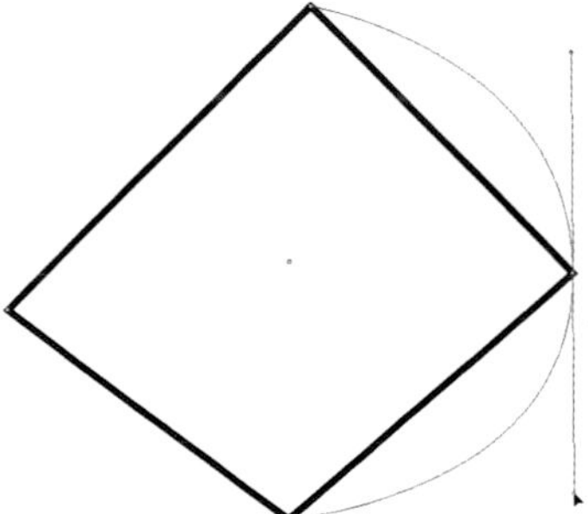

VISUAL | 14–28 |
Now you have a corner point with direction handles.
© Cengage Learning 2013

3. With the **Option** or **Alt** key still held down, drag with the *Convert Direction Point* tool on one of the corner points of your newly created rectangle. The corner point will change into a curved point with direction handles (Visual 14–28). Be careful! Dragging in the same direction as the original point will restore the curve of the circle, but dragging the opposite way will twist your curved line segment into a pretzel. Don't worry, though. If your line segment is twisting in the wrong direction, just do a 180-degree turn and drag the handle in the opposite direction.

▸ *Cut paths with the Scissors tool*

The *Scissors* tool does just what you might expect—it will cut a line segment into two parts. Do you still have the circle from the last exercise? Use it for the following exercise.

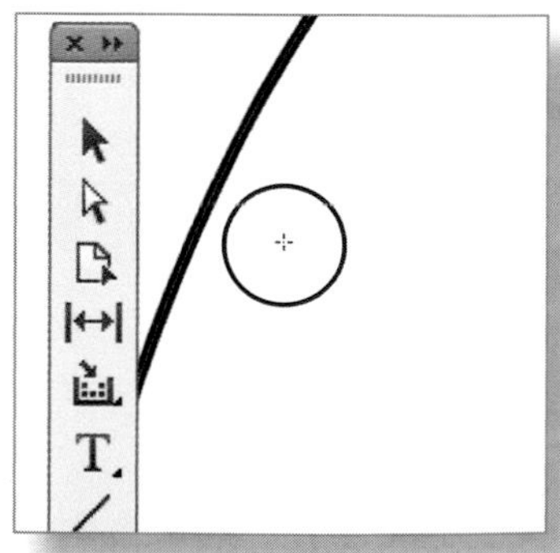

VISUAL | 14–29 |
With just a click of the mouse, the Scissors tool will take a snip where it is placed on the path.
© Cengage Learning 2013

1. Press **C** to get the *Scissors* tool (or select it from the *Tools* panel). The cursor will look like a set of cross hairs and when it moves over your path, the point in the middle of the cross hairs becomes a small circle (Visual 14–29). With the cross hairs directly over the path, click the mouse. A new point appears on the line segment. Although it looks like one point, there are actually two new points—one on top of the other.

2. Press **A** for the *Direct Selection* tool and drag the new point away from the center of the circle. You have just cut one of the line segments, and the closed path is now an open path (Visual 14–30).

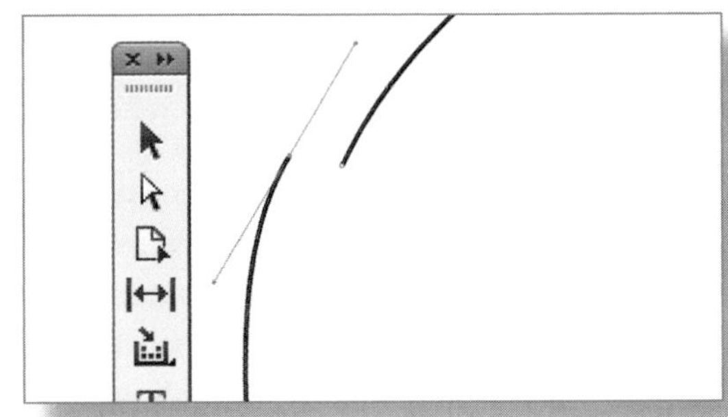

VISUAL | 14–30 |
Your closed path is now an open path.

▸ *Join paths*

Sometimes you will have two paths and need to combine them into one. Here's how to do it.

1. First delete everything, then select the *Pen* tool and begin a new path at **X: 0.5** and **Y: 2**. **Shift+drag** the direction handle horizontally to the right until **X: 2**. Next, place your cursor at **X: 3.5** and **Y: 0.5**, **click** and **Shift+drag** horizontally until **X: 5.5**. After you ***release*** the mouse button, press the **Option** or **Alt** key to switch to the *Convert Direction Point* tool. **Click + drag** the end of the direction handle that extends to the right of the last anchor point. ***Release*** the mouse button at **X: 3** and **Y: 0.875**. *Release* the **Option** or **Alt** key and click the *Pen* tool at **X: 4** and **Y: 2**, hold down **Shift+drag** horizontally until **X: 6.** When you release the mouse button, your path should look like Visual 14–31.

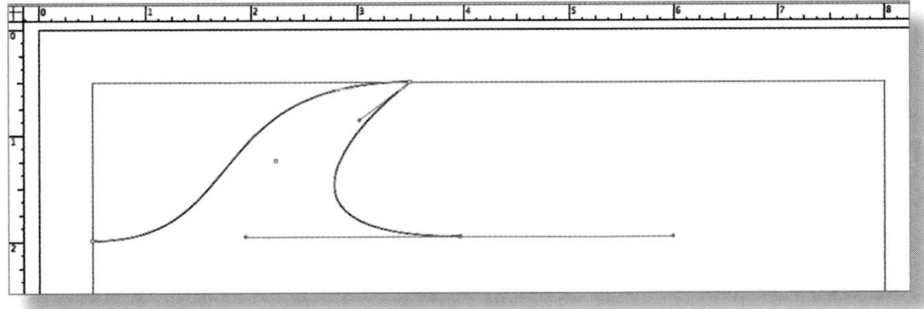

VISUAL | 14–31 |
Drawing a wave is as easy as placing three anchor points.

2. Let's say this is the perfect shape for a cresting wave you need for a project, but you need two of them exactly the same. Switch to the *Selection* tool and use **Option+drag** or **Alt+drag** to make a duplicate wave. Place the new wave to the right of the original, as shown in Visual 14–32.

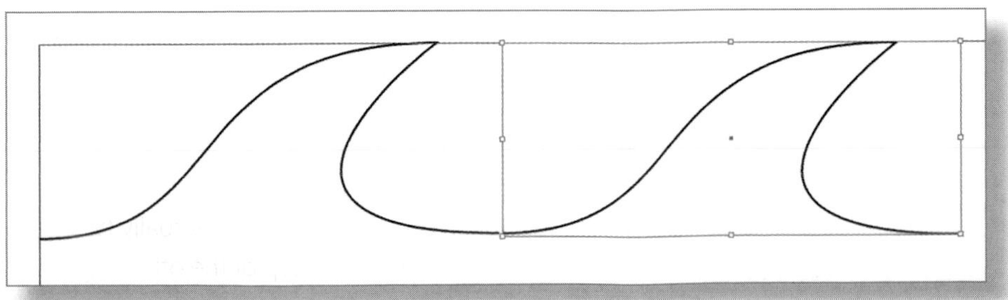

VISUAL | 14–32 |
The new wave, next to the original.

3. To join these two waves into one, switch to the ***Pen*** tool and select the last anchor point of the first path. The little "x" by the ***Pen*** tool cursor will turn into a slash when you get near the point. (It's often a good idea to zoom in closely when editing anchor points.)

4. Place the ***Pen*** tool cursor over the first point of the second wave and a small square with two little line segments will appear next to the ***Pen*** tool cursor (Visual 14–33). **Click**, and your two paths will be joined into one. However, you now have an unwanted line segment connecting the two points.

VISUAL |14–33|

The Pen tool is about to join two separate paths into one.

5. Undo to get two separate paths again. Before you connect them a second time, use the ***Direct Selection*** tool to select the last anchor point of the first wave. This will make the point's two direction handles visible. Switch to the ***Convert Direction Point*** tool and retract the right direction handle, by dragging the handle all the way back to the left, until it nearly touches the anchor point. Now join the two paths into one.

VISUAL |14–34|

The Pen tool is about to join two paths with the direction handle retracted on the first path.

▸ *Create compound paths*

You will love compound paths when it comes to making logos, transparent areas inside of shapes, and creative picture and text frames. Begin the next exercise with a new document.

VISUAL |14–35|

Both circles are selected.

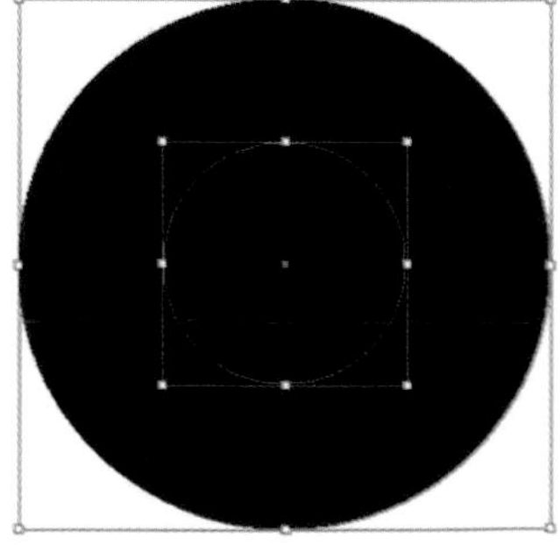

1. Draw two circles, one larger than the other, using the ***Ellipse*** tool. ***Select all*** and use the ***Align*** buttons on the ***Control*** panel to center them horizontally and vertically. Fill them both with **Black**. Your document should look similar to Visual 14–35.

2. Press **Command+8** (Mac) or **Control+8** (Windows), or choose *Object>Paths>Make Compound Path.* Now you have a donut!

3. Make a larger circle with a fill and send it to the back. Move your donut around and you will see that your donut has a real donut hole! (Visual 14–36.)

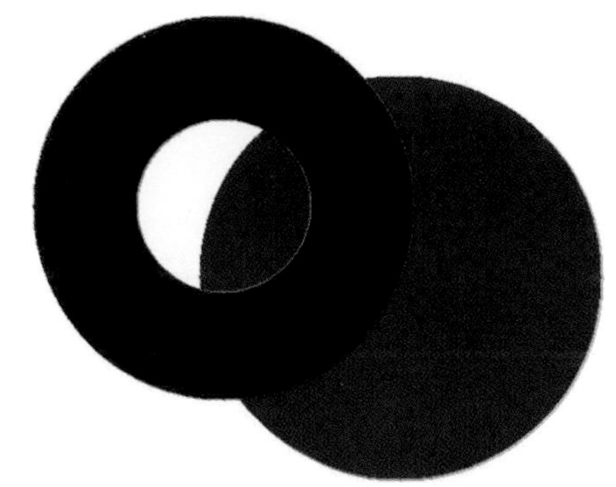

VISUAL | 14–36 |

Move your donut around to see the donut hole.

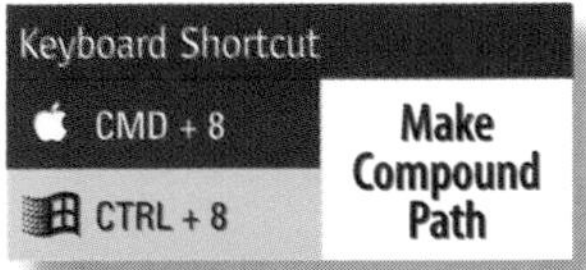

Keyboard Shortcut
CMD + 8
CTRL + 8
Make Compound Path

4. If you change your mind and don't want the compound path, select your donut and choose *Object>Paths>Release Compound Path.*

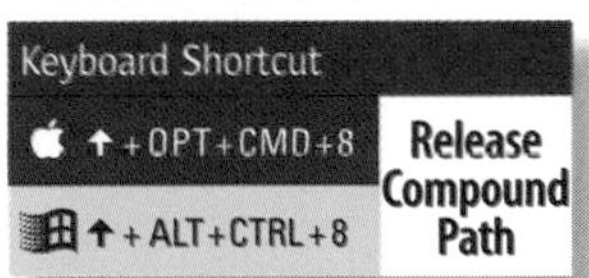

5. Delete everything and start over. This time draw two rectangles, one above the other with the smaller one on top. Put them close together, but do not have them touch or overlap. Select them both and choose *Object>Paths>Make Compound Path.* Although it may appear that nothing has occurred, notice that a bounding box now surrounds both rectangles. This means that the two are now part of one path (Visual 14–37).

VISUAL | 14–37 |

Two rectangles independent of each other, but part of the same path.

VISUAL |14–38|
Use the Direct Selection tool and Shift+drag out each corner point to create a trapezoid.
© Nancy Wolck 2004

6. Press **Command+D** (Mac) or **Control+D** (Windows) and place an image large enough to fill both rectangles. Drag the image around inside the rectangles using the ***Direct Selection*** tool.

7. Next you will change the shape of your small rectangle to a trapezoid. ***Deselect*** everything, and click on a bottom corner point of the top rectangle with the ***Direct Selection*** tool. Hold down **Shift** and drag it out, so that it's above the corresponding upper corner of the large rectangle. Do the same for the other bottom corner (Visual 14–38).

8. Delete the picture from the compound path and click in the path with the ***Type*** tool. Fill with placeholder text. Your compound path now works like linked text frames.

In the exercises you've just completed, you used the *Pen* tool to create and modify closed and open paths. Then, you used some path options to create compound paths. Great job!

Summary

Having completed the exercises in this chapter, you can see why there's no way any other page layout program can compete with InDesign. By combining advanced page layout and drawing capabilities, InDesign gives you the best of both worlds. Once you master the versatile *Pen* tool, your creative energy knows no bounds. Use compound paths to make your readers sit up and take notice of your message and images. And when you are done with this book, there's much, MUCH more to explore!

▸ IN REVIEW

1. What effect does holding down the Shift key have when drawing shapes and lines?
2. When working with a shape or path, how do you tell the difference between a point that is selected and a point that is not selected?
3. What is the keyboard shortcut for accessing the Convert Direction Point tool when you are using the Pen tool?
4. What is the difference between a smooth point and a corner point?
5. You have made a path with the Pen tool, but it looks jagged and you think you might have too many points on it. How do you smooth it out?
6. What is the difference between an open path and a closed path?
7. Describe the process for joining two open paths.
8. Describe the process for making compound paths.
9. What are direction handles?
10. How does the Scissors tool work?

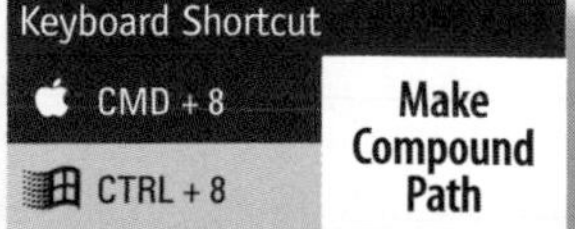

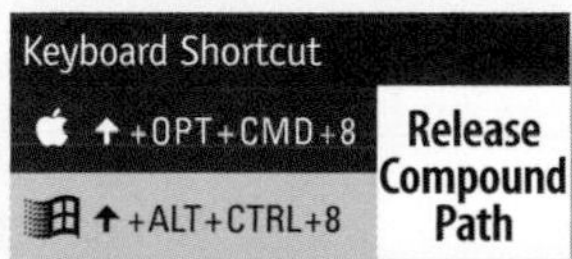

The following fonts are installed with Adobe InDesign CS6:

Birch Std Regular
Blackoak Std Regular
Brush Script Std Medium
Adobe Caslon Pro Bold
Adobe Caslon Pro Bd It
Adobe Caslon Pro Italic
Adobe Caslon Pro Regular
Adobe Caslon Pro Smbd
Adobe Caslon Pro Smbd It
Cooper Black Std Black
Cooper Black Std Black It
Charlemagne Std Bold
Chaparral Pro Regular
Chaparral Pro Light Italic
Chaparral Pro Italic
Chaparral Pro Bold Italic
Chaparral Pro Bold
Adobe Garamond Pro Bold
Adobe Garamond Pro Bd It
Adobe Garamond Pro Italic
Adobe Garamond Pro Regular
Giddyup Std Regular
Hobo Std Medium
Letter Gothic Std Bold
Letter Gothic Std Bd Slant
Letter Gothic Std Medium
Letter Gothic Std Slanted
Lithos Pro Black
Lithos Pro Regular
Mesquite Std Medium
Minion Pro Bold
Minion Pro Bold Cond
Minion Pro Bold Cond Italic
Minion Pro Bold Italic
Minion Pro Italic
Minion Pro Medium
Minion Pro Medium Italic
Minion Pro Regular
Minion Pro Smbd
Minion Pro Smbd Italic
Myriad Pro Bold
Myriad Pro Bold Cond
Myriad Pro Bold Cond Italic
Myriad Pro Bold Italic
Myriad Pro Cond
Myriad Pro Cond Italic
Myriad Pro Italic
Myriad Pro Regular
Myriad Pro Semibold
Myriad Pro Semibold Italic
Nueva Std Bold
Nueva Std Bold Cond
Nueva Std Bold Cond Italic
Nueva Std Cond
Nueva Std Cond Italic
Nueva Std Italic
OCR A Std Regular
Orator Std Medium
Orator Std Slanted
Poplar Std
Prestige Elite Std Bd
Rosewood Std Regular
Stencil Std Bold
Tekton Pro Bold
Tekton Pro Bold Cond
Tekton Pro Bold Extended
Tekton Pro Bold Oblique
Trajan Pro Bold
Trajan Pro Regular

Arabic Fonts

Adobe Arabic Bold
Adobe Arabic Bold Italic
Adobe Arabic Italic
Adobe Arabic Regular
Adobe Naskh Regular
Myriad Arabic Bold
Myriad Arabic Bold Italic
Myriad Arabic Italic
Myriad Arabic Regular

Devanagari Fonts

Adobe Devanagari Bold
Adobe Devanagari Bold It
Adobe Devanagari Italic
Adobe Devanagari Regular

Korean Fonts

Adobe Gothic Std Bold
Adobe Myungjo Std Medium

Hebrew Fonts

Adobe Hebrew Bold
Adobe Hebrew Bold Italic
Adobe Hebrew Italic
Adobe Hebrew Regular
Myriad Hebrew Bold
Myriad Hebrew Bold Italic
Myriad Hebrew Italic
Myriad Hebrew Regular

Japanese Fonts

Kozuka Gothic Pr6N Bold
Kozuka Gothic Pr6N Extra Lt
Kozuka Gothic Pr6N Heavy
Kozuka Gothic Pr6N Light
Kozuka Gothic Pr6N Medium
Kozuka Gothic Pr6N Regular
Kozuka Gothic Pro B
Kozuka Gothic Pro EL
Kozuka Gothic Pro H
Kozuka Gothic Pro L
Kozuka Gothic Pro M
Kozuka Gothic Pro R
Kozuka Mincho Pr6N Bold
Kozuka Mincho Pr6N Extra Lt
Kozuka Mincho Pr6N Heavy
Kozuka Mincho Pr6N Light
Kozuka Mincho Pr6N Medium
Kozuka Mincho Pr6N Regular
Kozuka Mincho Pro B
Kozuka Mincho Pro EL
Kozuka Mincho Pro H
Kozuka Mincho Pro L
Kozuka Mincho Pro M
Kozuka Mincho Pro R

Simplified Chinese Fonts

Adobe Fangsong Std Regular
Adobe Heiti Std Regular
Adobe Kaiti Std Regular
Adobe Song Std Light

Traditional Chinese Fonts

Adobe Fan Heiti Std Bold
Adobe Ming Std Light

Symbols

A

B

C

D

E

F

G

H

I

J

K

L

M

N

O

P

Q

R

S

T